The Globalization of Financial Services

The Globalization of the World Economy

Series Editor: Mark Casson
Professor of Economics
University of Reading, UK

Future titles will include:

The Globalization of Business Firms from Emerging Economies
Henry Wai-Chung Yeung

Privatization, Deregulation and the Transfer to Markets
David Teece, Leonard Waverman and Pablo T. Spiller

Financial Market Integration and International Capital Flows
David Vines

Globalization and Labour Markets
David Greenaway and Robert C. Hine

Wherever possible, the articles in these volumes have been reproduced as originally published using facsimile reproduction, inclusive of footnotes and pagination to facilitate ease of reference.

For a list of all Edward Elgar published titles visit our site on the World Wide Web at
http://www.e-elgar.co.uk

Contents

PART III   EUROCURRENCY BANKING

PART IV   OFFSHORE SERVICES

Acknowledgements

The editor and publishers wish to thank the authors and the following who have kindly given permission for the use of copyright material.

Association for Investment Management and Research for article: Richard Roll (1988), 'The International Crash of October 1987', *Financial Analysts Journal*, September–October, 19–35.

Banca Nazionale del Lavoro for articles: Herbert G. Grubel (1977), 'A Theory of Multinational Banking', *Banca Nazionale del Lavoro Quarterly Review*, **123**, December, 349–63; H.W. Arndt (1984), 'Measuring Trade in Financial Services', *Banca Nazionale del Lavoro Quarterly Review*, **XXXVII** (149), June, 197–213; H.W. Arndt (1988), 'Comparative Advantage in Trade in Financial Services', *Banca Nazionale del Lavoro Quarterly Review*, **164**, March, 61–78.

Bank of England for articles: R.B. Johnston (1979), 'Some Aspects of the Determination of Euro-currency Interest Rates', *Bank of England Quarterly Bulletin*, **19** (1), March, 35–46; T.J. Allen (1990), 'Developments in the International Syndicated Loan Market in the 1980s', *Bank of England Quarterly Bulletin*, **30** (1), February, 71–7; Alan Kirman (1995), 'The Behaviour of the Foreign Exchange Market', *Bank of England Quarterly Bulletin*, **35** (3), August, 286–93.

Blackwell Publishers Ltd for articles: Fariborz Moshirian (1994), 'Trade in Financial Services', *World Economy*, **17** (3), May, 347–63; Barry Williams (1997), 'Positive Theories of Multinational Banking: Eclectic Theory versus Internalisation Theory', *Journal of Economic Surveys*, **11** (1), March, 71–100.

Richard Dale for his own article: (1991), 'Regulating Banks' Securities Activities: A Global Assessment', *Journal of International Securities Markets*, **5**, Winter, 277–90.

De Pecunia, Commission Européenne for article: Gavin Bingham (1991), 'Foreign Exchange Market: Structure, Intervention and Liquidity', *De Pecunia*, **III** (2), October, 85–121.

Elsevier Science Publishers BV for articles: Jean M. Gray and H. Peter Gray (1981), 'The Multinational Bank: A Financial MNC?', *Journal of Banking and Finance*, **5** (1), March, 33–63; Ingo Walter and H. Peter Gray (1983), 'Protectionism and International Banking: Sectorial Efficiency, Competitive Structure and National Policy', *Journal of Banking and Finance*, **7** (4), December, 597–609; Charles P. Kindleberger (1983), 'International Banks as Leaders or Followers of International Business: An Historical Perspective', *Journal of Banking and Finance*, **7**, 583–95.

the Barings Experience', *Proceedings of the 31st Annual Conference on Bank Structure and Competition*, 91–6.

Routledge for excerpt: Brian Scott-Quinn (1990), 'US Investment Banks as Multinationals', in Geoffrey Jones (ed.), *Banks as Multinationals*, Chapter 14, 268–93.

Sweet & Maxwell Ltd for article: Sydney J. Key (1990), 'Is National Treatment Still Viable? US Policy in Theory and Practice', *Journal of International Banking Law*, **5** (9), Winter, 365–81.

University of Chicago Press for article: Harry G. Johnson (1976), 'Panama as a Regional Financial Center: A Preliminary Analysis of Development Contribution', *Economic Development and Cultural Change*, **24** (2), January, 261–86.

John Wiley & Sons Ltd for excerpt: Richard Dale (1994), 'International Banking Regulation', in Benn Steil (ed.), *International Financial Market Regulation*, Chapter 7, 167–96.

Every effort has been made to trace all the copyright holders but if any have been inadvertently overlooked the publishers will be pleased to make the necessary arrangement at the first opportunity.

In addition the publishers wish to thank the Library of the London School of Economics and Political Science, the Marshall Library of Economics, Cambridge University and B&N Microfilm, London, for their assistance in obtaining these articles.

The Globalization of Financial Services: An Overview

Mervyn K. Lewis

Globalization

Globalization is one of those terms which everyone uses but is difficult to define precisely. Broadly speaking, it refers to the growing integration of markets for goods, services and capital. But globalization does not mean that the whole world is one market, free of borders and frontiers. Nation states and regions still exist; they have borders and frontiers, they impose constraints upon cross-border trade, and they restrict the mobility of labour, capital and technology. Not all products are like crude oil and jet aircraft, sold and produced on a worldwide basis. In the case of some products, there is global production and sourcing of components and materials, co-existing with a collection of distinct national markets for distribution (e.g. automobiles). For others, branding and marketing are global but most production is left to local franchises (e.g. car rentals, food and beverages, accountancy services). Obviously, the degree and type of globalization are governed by the commodity concerned, and this volume explores the nature of globalization of financial services.

In financial services, as in other fields, globalization can be seen as a process opening up national economies and markets. It relates to the ease and speed with which knowledge, technology, people, ideas, goods and services, and capital move from country to country, thus widening the extent and form of cross-border transactions and deepening the international character of economic activity. Sometimes a distinction is made between globalization and internationalization, with globalization as the catalyst for change, to which firms respond by becoming more international. As such, globalization is propelled by liberalization of trade and deregulation of capital markets, underpinned by technological change which lowers communication and transport costs and enhances the international tradeability of goods and services.

One manifestation of globalization is an intensification of international trade and an increase in the scope and significance of all kinds of cross-border transaction. A second feature is an expansion of foreign production via foreign direct investment and the development by corporations of international production and distribution strategies. Accordingly, the volume begins with the topic of international trade in financial services and then looks at the overseas expansion and organization of financial services in the form of multinational banking. It then focuses on globalization in three areas – banking, offshore financial services and securities – before examining some of the regulatory issues posed by the globalization of financial services.

Trade in Financial Services

The internationalization of services has been central to the process of economic globalization, and the growth which has taken place in financial services internationally has had significance not only for the operation of the financial sector but also for resource allocation in other sectors. Financial services for the most part fall into the category of services treated by the General Agreement on Tariffs and Trade (GATT) as being complementary to international trade in goods. Financial services can also be seen as an intermediate input in the production process for non-financial enterprises. On both accounts there must be the presumption that cross-border financial flows need to be liberalized in order to realize fully the benefits of freer trade in goods (and non-financial services).

In the past, specialized knowledge and the need for services to be fashioned to the requirements of the customer effectively rendered many services non-tradeable. The essence of a service is that it is performed on a particular person's or organization's behalf and it brings about a change in the condition of an individual or organization or in that of a good belonging to an individual or organization (Hill, 1977). Given the fundamental nature of a service, it cannot be regarded as existing until it is exchanged and, consequently, it cannot be produced in advance and stored on the shelf awaiting sale. Nor can services be ordered from stocks kept elsewhere. Hence a service is intangible and non-storable, whereas physical products have tangibility and can be stored and inventoried. Since a service does not exist until it is consumed, there is, by definition, an inherently close communication between the supplier of service and the potential customer.

These inherent characteristics have been seen to have important implications for the way financial services are produced and for the location of financial services operations, in two respects. First, the popular conception that services are non-traded is derived from the idea that services must necessarily be used as they are produced. Second, if services cannot be stored in advance of subsequent interactions with the users, the geographic and temporal separation made in goods markets between manufacturing, assembly, marketing, distribution and servicing of products may not apply in the case of financial services.

However, in terms of their inherent tradeability the differences between goods and services can be overstated. Services can be distinguished in terms of those that necessarily require the physical proximity of user and provider, and those that do not. Since for those of the first type the user can travel to the provider or the provider can go to the user, either temporarily or by means of establishing a local commercial presence, we can identify four modes of supply:

- movement of the service consumer to the territory of the supplier;
- temporary movement of the supplier to the location of the consumer;
- through the local commercial presence of service-providing entities in the territory of the consumer;
- cross-border supply of the service not requiring the physical movement of consumer or supplier.

For those in the first three categories, the need for proximity is met by the provider going to the user or the user travelling to the provider, although there is a range of services (e.g. bespoke tailoring, lectures) for which transmission can occur either way. For services supplied across borders, the transactions do not require the immediacy of geographical contiguity, even though that may be useful and desirable. Many financial transactions are of this nature: loans can be arranged by telephone, deposits made by mail, and so on. By contrast, non-tradeables comprise those activities for which demand and supply are physically contiguous; haircuts are the usual example.

Nevertheless, the boundaries between these categories are not immutable, and technical change, especially in communications and information technology, has tended to bring more services into the tradeable category because they can be carried out 'over the wire' and thus over long distances. As examples of some long-distance services (Bhagwati, 1986), we have electronic banking, screen-based dealing systems, transmission of engineering computations by satellite, design services by fax, and communication of medical diagnoses by video. They remain services, in that they are non-storable and intangible, but resemble goods in so far as they can be transmitted geographically without the necessity of factor mobility. In banking, information technology has made it possible for institutions to centralize information resources in areas such as derivatives trading and market forecasting on a global basis. These same facilities can be used to offer services to clients, as when a bank sells access to its global information system, enabling corporate treasurers to monitor balances and financial data around the world. Internal managerial and support services can be exported and imported from parent to subsidiary, or from one subsidiary to another. Back-office operations can be shifted overseas to lower-cost environs.

Long-distance services are now an established feature of international banking and securities markets, with the rise of the 'offshore' markets for finance – examined in later sections of this book. Yet not all financial services lend themselves to offshore provision – examples are personal banking, small-business finance and payments services. And even in circumstances where long-distance transacting is possible, efficient cross-border trade relies upon some form of local commercial presence. In banking and other financial services, foreign direct investment may range from some low-level presence – such as a representative office – through agencies, subsidiaries or joint ventures to a full branch operation. When credit is provided, borrowers have to be sought out, and contact made, borrowing proposals evaluated, the performance of loans monitored, and (possibly) work-out arrangements and repayment holidays negotiated. All of these are aided by some form of physical interaction, if only because people are social animals who rely on body language and face-to-face contact. Increasingly also, financial services are sold rather than bought, and the marketing of loans and other products such as derivatives is facilitated by close proximity in order to establish and sustain business custom. In the absence of foreign direct investment and the establishment abroad of branches or other types of affiliate, the scope for international trade in financial services would be greatly reduced.

Thus an examination of trade in financial services involves access and establishment: access to markets from abroad on a trade basis and the establishment of commercial operations in the importing countries. The essays in Part I have this twin focus, because, as Arndt (1988) argues in Chapter 2, in banking international trade and foreign direct investment tend to be complementary, rather than alternatives as is the case in manufacturing (although there is some change on this score as marketing and after-sales service assume greater significance in the total product offering for manufactured goods – see Walter, 1988, Chapter 5).

The first three chapters of the book are concerned with the concept of trade in financial services and its measurement. Trade in financial services refers to the sale of services from a domestic financial firm to non-residents, with exports comprising that part of the output of the financial sector that is sold to non-residents. A starting point to measuring trade in financial services is to consider how we measure the output of the financial services industry in the national accounts. In Chapter 1, Arndt (1984) reviews the three methods which have been used by the official statisticians – based around wages and salaries, imputed income (old System of National Accounts approach) and imputed service charge (new SNA method). All are found to have deficiencies, even in the context of a closed economy, and are unsuited for measuring financial services which are exported. Moshirian (1994; Chapter 3) analyses the OECD data on trade in financial services. While the data cover some of the omissions noted by Arndt in terms of fee income for trading activities, they in turn suffer from the inclusion of factor services as part of trade in financial services.

As the authors make clear, these difficulties in quantifying trade in financial services are to a large degree conceptual. It is necessary to distinguish the concept of financial trade in services from that of trade in financial assets, while flows of services may need to be separated from factor income flows, and financial services proper differentiated from ancillary services. At the same time, there are practical problems in de-segregating accounts according to the residency of the account-holders, and recording inter-office and inter-bank transactions as well as from those with customers. For example, financial services which are transmitted electronically or which occur between the affiliate and the parent of a multinational enterprise frequently go unrecorded (GATT, 1989). For these reasons, as Grilli (1992) notes, those seeking to measure international trade in financial services frequently supplement available data with various proxies, such as flows of bank loans and financial assets, to quantify cross-border financial services.

On such measures, trade in financial services is substantial; for example, it has been estimated that one in seven equity trades involves a foreigner as a counter-party (Qureshi, 1996). Yet it was not until December 1997 that a World Trade Organization-sponsored agreement covering banking, insurance and other financial services was concluded among the 130 member countries. Obstacles to trade in financial services can take a variety of forms, analysed by Walter and Gray (1983) in Chapter 4. In particular, the authors recognize that controls over the establishment and local operations of foreign banking offices substitute for conventional trade barriers and may especially disadvantage the foreign supplier.

If rights of establishment are important in financial services, what principles would allow market access on reasonable terms? A few key concepts have dominated most negotiations: most-favoured-nation treatment, reciprocity, national treatment, *de facto* national treatment or equality of competitive opportunities, mutual recognition, minimum harmonization and regulatory convergence, and effective market access. National treatment is the cornerstone of US policy, as enacted into the International Banking Act of 1978, and it has proven to be both workable and durable in a large number of applications (OECD, 1993). However, it may not go far enough, and some newer principles that go beyond national treatment, including those adopted by the European Union, are reviewed by Sydney Key (1990) in Chapter 5. It may be noted that the same issues arise in regional trade agreements such as Canada – USA Free Trade Agreement and North American Free Trade Agreement – see Lewis (1996).

To this point, the articles in Part I revolve around trade in banking services and, to a lesser extent, securities. Trade in insurance is a notable omission, and this absence is corrected by Robert Carter, Professor Emeritus of Insurance Studies at the University of Nottingham, in Chapter 6. In his comprehensive chapter, Professor Carter examines the nature of international trade in the different types of insurance, the extensive – and often subtle – restrictions upon trade, and the substantial benefits which would flow from opening up insurance markets.

Multinational Banking

In Chapter 2, Professor Heinz Arndt of the Australian National University explored to what extent the theory of international trade could explain comparative advantages in the provision of financial services. Because of the complementarity between trade and establishment noted above, he observes that in banking it is also desirable in this context to employ the theory of foreign direct investment to examine the motives for 'going multinational', however useful it is to distinguish between trade and foreign investment in other activities. Why banks go multinational, and their competitive advantages when doing so, is the subject matter of Part II. Five papers are included, comprising three early contributions by Grubel, Gray and Gray, and Kindleberger, followed by two surveys of the substantial literature which has since developed, one by Aliber in 1984 and the other by Barry Williams in 1997.

Grubel's 'A Theory of Multinational Banking' (Chapter 7) was not the first paper published on the topic, but it was one of a number written in the mid-1970s (see note 1 of his paper) and provides a comprehensive treatment of many of the issues. Multinational banking is defined by Grubel as 'the ownership of banking facilities in one country by citizens of another'. Many contemporary studies instead used the term 'foreign banking'. Use of the description 'multinational' seems more appropriate in signifying that banks today operate in a large number of countries and geographic regions. Evidence on this point is provided by Lewis and Davis (1987, Chapter 8) and City Research Project (1995).

While on definitional issues, we may note that Grubel's definition of multinational follows that invariably adopted for multinational enterprises generally, in centring on the operation of productive assets in different countries. Yet there are other possibilities which ought to be noted (Aharoni, 1971). Multinationality might be defined in terms of share ownership (e.g. a company owned by citizens of many countries) or management control (e.g. a company managed by nationals of many countries), with the emphasis more upon corporate governance than the pattern of production and distribution. These aspects are generally neglected in the literature.

It is also important that we clarify what sorts of banking activity are being discussed. As emphasized by Gray and Gray in Chapter 8 (and also by Grubel), banks go multinational for two distinct reasons. One is to provide banking services in foreign national markets; the other is to participate in the offshore or 'supranational' financial markets. Aliber (Chapter 10) argues that the former was the sole activity of US banks' foreign branches prior to 1960 and is still the principal activity of most branches. In terms of assets, however, it is the offshore business which predominates. If it is to be comprehensive, an analysis of multinational banking must seek to explain both. For example, in terms of Euro activities, Grubel examines 'multinational wholesale banking', while Gray and Gray write of 'the escape motive'. In this volume, however, we will consider such topics further in Parts III and IV.

Charles Kindleberger (Chapter 9) reminds us that multinational banking is not new. While banks' international operations have grown rapidly over the past three decades (admittedly from a low base), multinational banking has waxed and waned at various times in the past. In the 14th and 15th centuries the Florentine banking houses – the Bardi, Peruzzi, Acciaiuoli and Medici – rose on the back of the growth of international trade in wool, cloth and silks, and declined just as rapidly under the weight of bad loans, mostly emanating from London operations. What clearly differs today is the scale of activities. In 1470, the entire European network of branches and subsidiaries of the Medici empire employed in total 57 individuals spread over offices in Florence, Avignon, Bruges, Geneva, London, Rome and Venice. This operation contrasts with that of, for example, Hong Kong Bank, covering 68 countries, or that of Barclays Bank with 2900 domestic branches, 1200 overseas branches and 118,000 employees worldwide. Another difference today is the offshore dimension, although the 'escape motive' was not entirely absent before, since the business of foreign money-changing enabled medieval banks to avoid the Church's ban on usury!

All the chapters in this section utilize the body of theory developed to explain foreign direct investment by non-financial corporations and attempt to adapt it to the case of multinational banking. However, the reader will notice that the explanations offered to account for the phenomenon of multinational banking change over time, reflecting the fact that the theory of foreign direct investment has not stood still since the original contributions. Thus the first three chapters essentially employ the framework of industrial organization theory, on a cross-border basis. The emphasis is on market imperfections, horizontal integration and vertical integration. To these can be added what Aliber in Chapter 10 calls the 'currency clientele' effect, whereby banks benefit because their home currency is used in international trade and finance. Since then the literature has been framed almost entirely around the internalization framework of Buckley and Casson (1976) and the 'eclectic' ownership– locational– internalization paradigm developed by Dunning (1981). Williams (1997) reviews these approaches in Chapter 11, along with other explanations of multinational banking.

One merit of internalization theory is in addressing an issue neglected by the original foreign direct investment theories, namely the alternatives to international banking and thus the rationale for the multinational banking firm. International financing may take place in the internal capital market of a non-financial multinational enterprise. A number of multinationals (e.g. BP, Volvo, Swedish Match, Scania, GEC) have established what amount to 'in-house banks', coordinating Treasury operations and managing risks in a variety of currencies on a global basis. Also, a major trend in international financing since the mid 1980s has been the securitization of bank lending and the concomitant rise of securities issues. An alternative to the production of financial services by banking firms is for the financial exchanges to occur through markets.

Thus the choice between hierarchical structures and markets, as means of organizing financial exchanges internationally, needs to be considered. Since a multinational bank is merely a particular class of firm, the issue of why multinational banks exist is another way of asking why banks exist as firms (Lewis, 1991). This echoes the question, originally posed by Coase (1937) in a different context, of whether transactions can be internalized more cheaply than they can be marketized. Some aspects of securities markets and activities are examined in Part V (see below).

Eurocurrency Banking

The architects of the Bretton Woods system envisaged that cross-border financial flows, particularly of short-term capital, would be restricted in the interests of maintaining fixed exchange rate parities (Artis and Lewis, 1991, Chapter 2 give a brief account). Many countries applied rigid exchange controls, and most banking systems were subject to interest rate ceilings, reserve ratios, lending restrictions and other controls which cocooned them from foreign competition. By the 1960s, a way had been found around some of the controls through the growth of Eurocurrency banking.

In the Euromarkets, banks located in one country took deposits and made loans in the currencies of other countries, initially almost entirely in US dollars. Being offshore, the business lay outside the jurisdiction of the Federal Reserve Bank and US authorities. Being in dollars, the transactions were not subject to monetary controls applied by the host European country to local currency business. A Eurocurrency transaction's 'essential feature' (Niehans, 1984) was to combine the exchange risk of one currency (e.g. the US dollar) with the regulatory, political and economic climate of another country (e.g. the United Kingdom). The banks in Europe which provided this financial service did so in order to circumvent restrictions on the use of their domestic currency (e.g. sterling) for external purposes, and since the activity was unregulated, they could set competitive spreads on intermediation undertaken in dollars. Quite unintentionally, their private self-interest set the stage for the creation of a worldwide market which would rival the largest national financial systems.

Henry Wallich (1979) in Chapter 12 provides a succinct account of the features of the Eurocurrency market. Obviously, some aspects have changed since he wrote. Wallich noted that the market is no longer exclusively in dollars. By 1997, the share of US dollars had fallen to 45 per cent, although the dollar remains the largest single currency in use (Lewis, 1999). Wallich reports a gross size of around $800 billion. Table 1 shows that the market had grown to over $8000 billion by 1997. (The gross Eurocurrency market is the sum of columns 2 and 3, and comprises cross-border and cross-currency lending from the centres.)

Table 1 also reveals a remarkable statistic. Today about 83 per cent of international banking takes place in the Eurocurrency banking market. Prior to the 1960s, virtually all international banking was traditional foreign banking (column 1), such as US banks lending to foreigners in dollars from New York. Two other features of Table 1 are noteworthy. One is the extent of lending from the so-called 'offshore centres' – the Asian and Caribbean locations. The other is that the traditional definition of Eurocurrency as 'deposits and loans that are denominated in currencies other than the currency of the country where the bank is located' is invalidated by International Banking Facilities (IBFs), in which the external business in dollars is undertaken onshore. Offshore centres and IBFs are covered in the next section.

The large size of the Eurocurrency market (and Eurodollar market in excess of $3,500 billion) begs the question: where do all the dollars come from? Until Milton Friedman's 1969 paper, reproduced in Chapter 13, analysis of the growth of the Eurodollar market had tended to focus on the US balance of payments position and especially on the contribution of the US balance of payments deficit in pumping out a flow of dollars to overseas holders. Friedman's article made clear that the Eurodollar market was a monetary and banking phenomenon. He showed that Eurodollars could be 'created' with an unchanged balance of payments position.

Table 1. Measures of International banking and Eurocurrency operations, June 1997 (US$ billion)

Reporting location	Traditional foreign lending	Eurocurrency market activities		Total international lending	Per cent
		Cross-border Euro-lending	Foreign currency lending to residents		
	1	2	3	4	5
All European countries	1040.1	3673.1	993.9	5707.1	57.4
(of which UK)	(167.5)	(1367.3)	(451.8)	(1986.6)	(20.0)
Japan (Japan Offshore Market)	162.4	1010.6 (593.4)	213.2 (34.6)	1386.2	13.9
Asian centres[1]	33.2	1097.7	75.7	1206.6	12.1
United States (International Banking Facilities)	418.8	317.4 (275.8)	– –	736.2	7.4
Caribbean centres[2]	–	680.9	33.9	714.8	7.2
Others[3]	16.0	150.9	31.3	198.2	1.9
All reporting centres	1670.5	6930.7	1348.0	9949.2	100
Per cent	16.8	69.7	13.5	100	

Notes:
1. Hong Kong and Singapore.
2. Bahamas and Cayman Islands.
3. Canada, Bahrain and others.

Source: Bank for International Settlements, *International Banking and Financial Market Developments,* November 1997.

Friedman's hypothesis was that the Eurodollar market should be seen as part of the US banking system and that Eurodollars are created, like domestic deposits, by the portfolio decisions of banks and depositors. Because banks operating externally are not subject to reserve ratios and other regulatory constraints, they are able to offer depositors a higher return than is obtainable from deposits held with US banks operating domestically. At the same time, they are able to lend to borrowers at rates lower than those charged domestically. That is, they are able to operate with a lower spread than domestic US banks, encouraging production of banking services to be shifted offshore to the Euromarkets which constitute, in effect, a vast duty-free banking system.

Friedman's treatment of Eurodollar credit creation invited a direct comparison of the Eurodollar market and domestic banking systems. Indeed, at one juncture Friedman likened the Eurodollar institutions to 'Chicago banks'. Since Eurobanks were seen as maintaining very low working balances, this comparison conjured up the image of an almost limitless expansion, deriving from an initial primary deposit, based on the reciprocal of the market's low reserve ratio. Friedman is often attributed with the view that the Euromultiplier must be 'extremely high' (see Niehans, 1984, p.186). In fact, Friedman's original piece contained almost all the points raised by later critics and clearly stated that the actual multiplier would be low. The reason is simple. Any bank or group of banks forming part of a wider whole has little independent capacity to create credit. Loans made by Chicago banks leak to other parts of the US monetary system, with little in the way of re-deposits at Chicago banks. By the same token, however, loans made by other banks flow to Chicago banks, enabling them to participate in the multiple expansion of credit and deposits which follows an increase in reserves. Similarly, Eurobanks are part of a system – the dollar banking system – so that they may share in a generalized process of multiple credit and deposit creation, but correspondingly have little independent credit-creating ability. A careful reading of Friedman's article would have saved a lot of academic ink.

Niehans and Hewson (1976), building on earlier work by Hewson and Sakakibara (1974) and Hewson (1975), was also a path-breaking study which had a significant influence on the subsequent literature. It is reprinted here as Chapter 14. For the sake of our analysis of the paper, we shall regard it as comprising two parts – one dealing with multiplier analysis and the other with liquidity creation and maturity transformation.

Niehans and Hewson's analysis of Eurocurrency deposit multipliers was much influenced by the 'new view' of James Tobin (1963). The new view argued that fixed coefficient multipliers commonly employed in monetary analysis – of which those developed for the Eurocurrency market were one special class – ignored the role of interest rates in response to changes in Eurocurrency *vis-à-vis* domestic banking services. Analysis of the Eurocurrency market in terms of demand and supply – the preferred 'portfolio approach' – makes this clear. A positive demand shift will expand the size of the market and, given the required spread, can be expected to raise interest rates on both deposits and loans relative to the domestic market. A positive supply shift, on the other hand, will also increase the size of the market while lowering deposit and loan rates *vis-à-vis* domestic banking. These adjustments in Eurocurrency interest rates can, in turn, be expected to modify the size of the Eurocurrency multipliers derived in earlier models.

Consider, to illustrate, a shift in the supply curve for Eurodollar deposits of the type used by Friedman in his analysis. This will have the effect of slightly depressing rates in the Eurodollar segment of the dollar banking system, or slightly raising rates in the domestic money market, or both. Some depositors will be induced at the margin to shift funds back to the US domestic market. However, lower deposit rates in the Eurodollar market, with an unchanged spread, will induce lower loan rates, thus attracting some borrowers of dollars from the domestic to the external market. Overall, there is an expansion of the Eurocurrency market, but it is less than the initial shift. The Eurodollar multiplier is necessarily less than unity.

By contrast, in the Friedman-type analysis, the multiplier is expected to be unity or more, as the initial shift (unity) is augmented by some re-depositing. Niehans and Hewson draw a parallel between the relationship of the Eurodollar system and US domestic markets and any other two substitute products, such as butter and margarine. 'If there is a spontaneous shift in preferences from butter to margarine, the ultimate increase in the quantity of margarine will be less than the spontaneous shift, because the relative increase in the price of margarine will induce some former users to shift to butter. The "margarine multiplier" would thus be less than unity.' (p. 5)

This result raises the question of how the portfolio analysis can be reconciled with the multiplier analysis, and with empirical estimates of multipliers slightly in excess of unity – findings which seem to support the Friedman-style approach. A reconciliation is provided in Chapter 15, drawn from an appendix to the book *Domestic and International Banking*. While the exposition shows the relationship between the two, the real implication is that, because it is necessary to examine the cause and extent of interest rate variations, the multiplier approach loses much of its appeal. Instead, the focus should be on what determines Eurocurrency interest rates, and this is what is done in Chapters 16 and 17.

Johnston (1979) in Chapter 16 first models the relationship between Eurocurrency and domestic interest rates, and then extends the analysis to those between the different Eurocurrencies. One surprising upshot of his article, and later additions to it in his book (Johnston, 1983), is that all is not lost in terms of the old multiplier approach, at least at a practical level. Its use rests on factors which render Eurocurrency interest rates insensitive, in the short run, to portfolio shifts of the Friedman-type. As Johnston (1983) notes: 'it is very difficult to find evidence that short-term Eurocurrency interest rates adjust to non-bank deposit flows' (p.239). A number of reasons can be offered, but his own explanation for the apparent insensitivity of Eurocurrency interest rates to customers' deposit flows comes from the arbitrage activities of US domestic banks (in many cases head offices of the Euro-banks). If arbitrage is effective, the Eurodollar deposit rate (and with competition, the loan rate also) will vary within, or solely around, what is called the 'arbitrage tunnel'. Kreicher (1982) and Johnston (1979, 1983) present evidence which shows that such was the case.

A number of implications follow from the existence of arbitrage between the domestic and the Eurocurrency interest rates. First, arbitraging by both banks and non-banks means that Eurodollar interest rates closely follow movements in interest rates in the US. Second, when the Eurocurrency markets were small relative to the domestic market, it made some sense to think of Eurocurrency interest rates as primarily determined by domestic interest rates. As the external markets have grown relative to domestic rates, it now makes more sense to think of the two sets of interest rates as being jointly determined by the overall demands and supplies for dollar funds, including policy changes by the Fed. To the extent that the latter has the decisive influence, then monetary restraint in the US remains effective (as Henry Wallich argued in Chapter 12). Third, Johnston argues that, in the short term, inter-bank arbitrage between the two segments of the dollar banking system dominates the non-bank arbitrage. Consequently, inflows and outflows of funds by non-banks can occur without the alterations to Eurocurrency interest rates implied by the portfolio analysis. To this extent, the prediction of that analysis – that the Eurocurrency multiplier must necessarily be less than unity – is invalidated. But the corollary is that a multiplier for non-bank deposits makes less sense in an environment in which inter-bank transactions are of such importance.

Inter-bank transactions form the basis of loan pricing on Eurocurrency transactions, most notably on the largest and most visible component – the syndicated Eurocurrency credit.

Interest costs to the borrower consist of two parts, base plus margin, most often calculated as:

$$\text{Interest cost} = \text{LIBOR} + \text{spread}$$

where LIBOR (London inter-bank offer rate) is the rate at which banks offer to place deposits inter-bank with other prime banks. This pricing arrangement, along with the syndication process, is outlined by Goodman (1980) in Chapter 17.

LIBOR is a market-determined funding cost. What governs the spread? From the viewpoint of a participating bank, the spread, along with any funding profit, constitutes the (or one part of the) anticipated return from the loan, available to pay wages and 'overheads' and to earn profits for shareholders. These costs plus the extent of competition among banks (i.e. whether it is a lenders' or borrowers' market) will govern the margin which banks seek. But part of the margin must also be seen as the 'insurance premium' which banks levy to cover the risk of default and the funding risk, and in assessing the 'insurance premium' levied to cover these risks, banks can be expected to look at the totality of their operations. In the theory of finance, it has long been appreciated that the appropriate measure of an asset's riskiness is its perceived contribution to the risk of the investor's portfolio rather than its objective risk considered in isolation. Since Eurobanks are almost all domestic banks as well, the risk premium demanded will depend on the extent to which banks already have an internationally diversified portfolio, and whether international risks have characteristics which offset or magnify domestic banking risks. Empirical evidence gathered by Goodman finds support for most of these factors (see also Fleming and Howson, 1980 and Johnston, 1980).

Maturity is one element which appears to govern the 'spread', and on this point we are drawn back to Niehans and Hewson (1976) and the second – and more radical – part of their article. They ask whether the financial services associated with intermediation in the Eurocurrency markets are different from those in domestic banking systems. Of course, in two respects the intermediation obviously is different. Eurobanks collect deposits in one country and make loans in another – country transformation. They also take deposits in one currency and make loans in others – currency transformation. What is at issue is maturity transformation. In domestic banking markets, banks accept deposits, say, at call and transform them into, in the extreme case, 25-year mortgage loans, creating liquidity in the process. Niehans and Hewson argue that the Eurobanks do not create liquidity by means of maturity transformation, but rather spread or distribute liquidity by collecting idle funds from one region of the world and channelling them via inter-bank and intra-bank networks to other regions of the world.

Lewis and Davis (1987) question this argument, and the article by Lewis (1986), reprinted here as Chapter 18, provides a summary. Liquidity distribution is accepted by these authors as an important function of Eurobanking, but it is not seen to be the whole story. The basic point of contention is the view expressed by Niehans and Hewson (and also McKinnon, 1977) that little maturity transformation occurs and that the liabilities of Eurobanks are as liquid as their claims – in other words, that there is a substantial extent of maturity matching in the market as a whole. From this, Niehans and Hewson argue that in Eurocurrency operations the 'brokerage' function dominates that of 'liquidity production', so that Eurobanks distribute liquidity but do not create it.

One immediate observation would be that, if Niehans and Hewson's position were the whole story, then it is difficult to reconcile the absence of maturity transformation with the known role of the Eurocurrency markets during the 'recycling' episode of the 1970s of matching OPEC preferences for short-term deposits, on one side of the balance sheet, with the developing countries' demand for long-term loans, on the other. This particular episode is discussed by Goodman in her analysis of the syndicated Eurocurrency credit market in Chapter 17.

As it turns out, this financing instrument is central to the debate. What is the maturity of a syndicated loan or rollover credit? About one half of the lending by Eurobanks is nominally for terms in excess of one year, and some is well in excess of five years, renegotiated ('rolled over') on a three- or six-monthly basis at variable interest rates. In Table 1 of Chapter 18 these assets are classified according to the period remaining to the ultimate maturity date of the loan and not to the next rollover date, and on this basis it is apparent that there is a vast difference in the maturity structure of deposits and assets. However, Niehans and Hewson, and Niehans (1984), contend that use of the final date of maturity grossly overstates the extent of maturity transformation undertaken in wholesale banking, and especially Eurocurrency banking. Legally, the bank is not compelled to renew the credit (there is normally an escape clause) or, if it does renew, it may be completely confident of obtaining the deposits, and so it is argued that 'the rollover period is more relevant than the commitment period. A five-year loan with a three-month rollover is more like a succession of three-month loans than a five-year loan (Niehans, 1984, p.190). Lewis and Davis query this interpretation. Certainly, from the viewpoint of interest rate risk, a rollover credit does reprice every three or six months and should be classified by the repricing term (Lewis and Morton, 1996). But loans also have a default risk which is built into the spread (see Goodman, 1980). Consequently, the question which must be asked of each banker is whether he or she is carrying the default risk on a rollover loan for six months (i.e., to the next renewal date) or for five years. Lewis and Davis suggest the latter.

The other area of contention concerns the inter-bank market and the nature of wholesale banking operations. Conventional banking theory is informed by the retail banking model, in which individual banks take in short-term deposits and transform them into longer-term loans across their own balance sheets. Inter-bank transactions, if they occur, are largely incidental to the story. But this is not so in wholesale business, and the difference in maturity between a customer's deposit at one end of the chain and a loan of several years at the other end can be broken up into several steps carried out by different banks. In retail banking, one bank will have, say, a demand deposit and a three-year loan. In wholesale banking, funds may be channelled from ultimate lenders to ultimate borrowers through several banks. In the process, what begins as a short-term deposit may be transformed into a loan of several years' maturity. Each bank is mismatched, but not to a great extent, and no one bank is left with a large share of the transformation process.

On this interpretation, the difference of views revolves around the distinction between 'intra-bank' and 'inter-bank'. In retail banking, the maturity transformation is undertaken fully within the bank which accepts the deposit. In wholesale markets, the transformation can occur in the system as a whole. Just as loan syndication procedures enable banks to divide up credit risks among the group, in much the same way the inter-bank markets allow banks to share the liquidity and funding risks of maturity transformation. Consequently, the contrast

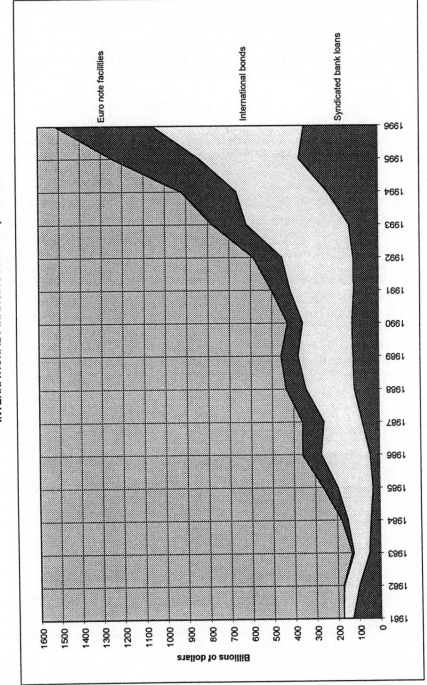

FIGURE 1

INTERNATIONAL FINANCING ACTIVITY, 1981-1996

Source: OECD Financial Markets (various)

between international wholesale and retail banking may come not so much in terms of the extent of liquidity creation but rather from the manner in which it occurs.

In the final chapter in this section, Allen (1990), the focus is again on the syndicated loan market. In Chapter 17 Goodman examined the market in 1980 when it was in full swing. In 1986, when Chapter 18 was written, the market was in full retreat as banks were struggling with the aftermath of the Third World debt crisis of 1982. By 1990, Allen was surveying a market which had risen phoenix-like from the ashes. Figure 1 shows international financing activity from 1981 to 1996 in terms of three instruments: new syndicated lending, issues of international bonds and Euro-note facilities established. The strong resurgence in syndicated lending since the mid 1980s, despite the sustained growth of securities issues, can readily be seen.

Three factors appear to have been instrumental in the revival of the syndicated loan market. First, banks have restructured the product. The syndicated credit is now a much more flexible instrument; borrowings can be made in a variety of currencies, and borrowers have a large number of options with respect to drawdowns and repayments. Second, as in domestic markets, banks have responded to the securitization trend among large corporates by shifting their focus to the 'middle market' – those second-tier corporate borrowers which do not possess a sufficiently high credit rating to have stand-alone access to the international bond market and which are unable to obtain swap financing at favourable margins. The third factor is the growth in debt-financed acquisitions and management buyouts; these sources of financing have been supplemented in the 1990s by borrowings associated with privatizations and economic restructuring in industrial countries. Notably, also, there has been a renewal of lending to emerging market borrowers – particularly in Asia (Korea, Thailand, Indonesia) – although hopefully not on a scale likely to lead to a repetition of the debt crisis of the 1980s.

Offshore Services

In a survey of globalization, Dunning (1994) observes how trends to globalization today are underlaid by a quite different international division of labour than that which existed in earlier years. This new division of labour is based around what he terms 'created assets'. In the past, international trade and the international division of labour were largely a consequence of the distribution of natural resources. For example, the UK and Germany developed as producers and exporters of manufactured goods because they had an abundance of coal, raw materials and human capital. Similarly, London and New York were the pre-eminent financial centres and suppliers of financial services because the UK and US had the largest amount of capital to export (Kindleberger, 1974).

Nowadays, it is possible for trade, finance and wealth creation to stem from man-made or created resources based on technology, education, information, managerial techniques, organizational skills and entrepreneurial talents. The example of Singapore comes to mind, where created assets have taken the form of an airport, communications, education of the workforce, shipping facilities, and so on.

In the case of financial services, the Eurocurrency markets are an example of created assets. Their establishment enabled centres such as London and Paris, which had lost their comparative advantage in terms of national savings and capital exports, to survive the dollar, yen and mark hegemony in world trade and finance and flourish as suppliers of international financial services.

However, the clearest example of created assets in financial services is provided by the various islands and small states which have deliberately structured their taxation and business regimes to become suppliers of offshore financial services. British dependencies in Europe and the Caribbean, such as the Channel Islands, Isle of Man, Bahamas and Cayman Islands, are particularly prominent. The small states in Europe are Andorra, Cyprus, Iceland, Liechtenstein, Luxembourg, Malta, Monaco and San Marino. Singapore, Hong Kong, Vanuatu, the Cook Islands and Labuan are in the Asia-Pacific.

With the rise of global financing in the Eurocurrency markets came an associated demand for centres in low-tax, stable economies where fund raisings could be deposited and intra-firm financings made, facilitating cash management and tax planning at an international level. Individuals can use the offshore facilities offered to form companies and trusts to hold and manage assets, or avoid inheritance or capital gains tax. Some with high incomes choose to take up residence offshore. Companies can greatly reduce costs by using offshore centres to set up captive insurance companies, treasury centres and subsidiaries, or to register ships. The result has been a worldwide proliferation of offshore financial centres.

Part IV of the book examines the phenomenon. It begins, like the previous section, with a remarkably succinct, yet at the same time comprehensive, account by Henry Wallich. In the space of a few pages (Chapter 20) he outlines the essential characteristics of the offshore financial centres, the role of the US banks in them, and the Federal Reserve System's attitude towards the 'shell' offices in the Caribbean and their supervision.

The next two chapters continue this general perspective. Taxation, and its avoidance, is a major driving force in many offshore financial services. Milka Casanegra de Jantscher considers the role of the tax havens (some call them 'heavens') in Chapter 21. Some tax havens are also offshore banking centres, which is the topic of Chapter 22 by Ian McCarthy. As 'created assets', an obvious question to ask is whether there are net benefits from their establishment. In general, the benefit–cost equation appears favourable on his estimates, but a distinction has to be made between paper centres and functional ones, particularly in terms of the prospects for new entrants.

This brings us to Chapter 23 by K. Alec Chrystal (1984) on the IBFs which operate in the United States. On first sight, the inclusion of these onshore facilities in a section dealing with offshore services may seem to need some explanation. In Chapter 20, Henry Wallich makes clear that when granting approval for member banks to establish 'shell' branches in booking centres, the Federal Reserve Board makes its approval conditional upon full records being kept at head office. These are available for inspection by US bank supervisors. Another condition has been that the branches may not be used to shift deposits and other banking business from the United States. That is, they can be used for business that has already shifted offshore, but not for the shifting offshore of new business. It was a short step from these 'shell' branches of US banks in the Caribbean to the establishment in 1981 of 'duty-free zones' for banking, the IBFs, at the head offices themselves. Since they operate in an environment which is broadly similar to that in offshore centres, in that they are exempt from reserve requirements and some other controls, they can be thought of as offshore. But they are located onshore – hence Chrystal's description of IBFs as 'onshore offshore banks'. The idea was copied in Tokyo in 1986 with the Japan Offshore Market. Dublin has also introduced the International Financial Services Centre along similar lines.

Usually the motive for establishing an offshore financial centre is to generate income and employment for the local economy, and in general to act as a platform for economic development. Harry Johnson (1976; Chapter 24) provided the first systematic analysis of this strategy, using Panama as an illustration. He argued that although financial services may be thought to have some important advantages in this respect, in terms of the skill mix and improvements in financial technology, the available data provided scant evidence of this interconnection.

Hodjera (1978; Chapter 25) examines the rise of Singapore as a financial centre. As noted earlier, Singapore is a classic example of using created assets – in this case the Asian Currency Unit (ACU) – as a vehicle for engineering changes in national comparative advantage. The ACU is essentially an operational entity within a financial institution which has been granted a licence by the Monetary Authority of Singapore to deal in the Asian Dollar Market (or Asian equivalent of the Eurodollar market). Although the unit remains an integral part of the bank or institution, it must maintain separate accounting records for its transactions. This is to ensure that freedom in the flow of funds to and from the ACU will not disrupt domestic monetary management. ACU transactions began in 1968 and by 1976 it was estimated by Hodjera that the contribution of the Asian currency market to GDP was around 3 per cent. Now Singapore hosts about 130 foreign banks and is the seventh largest centre for international banking.

Hodjera was rather more fortunate than Johnson in his choice of case study, for Panama was later badly tainted by involvement in drugs and money-laundering operations. The emphasis that Hodjera placed on the regulatory climate in Singapore was completely justified. To be successful as an offshore location, an appropriate mix of company laws, taxation, accounting requirements, financial secrecy, reporting requirements, entry requirements, licensing and regulations is required. The aim is to achieve a long-run reputation for business stability and security of investment. Solvency and prudential oversight are needed for depositor and investor protection. Regulation must be flexible but not too lax, as under-regulation encourages practices which may lead to adverse publicity for the centre and tarnish those using it. In short, the commercial environment must be responsive to the requirements of genuine business, while deterring those seeking to abuse accepted international standards.

The final two chapters of this section pull some of the elements together. In his second appearance in this volume, Grubel (1982; Chapter 26) examines offshore financial services in a broader context as one of a number of possible free economic zones. As well as banking, there are free trade zones, free ports, export-processing zones, duty-free shops, free insurance zones, free enterprise zones and free gambling zones. These can all be broadly seen as deregulatory moves which lower protection in the country hosting the zones and are thus amenable to analysis by theories of trade creation and diversion. But the partial deregulation involved and piecemeal character of the changes raise questions about the overall impact and welfare implications. These are the matters addressed by Grubel.

In Chapter 27, Hampton (1996) examines some of the broader economic and social issues associated with offshore financial services. One of the dark sides of offshore financing is the association with tax evasion and a variety of other criminal activities, which can have a corrupting influence on the social fabric of the countries involved, and the global financial system generally. Hampton provides a framework for examining the various offshore centres before exploring what he calls the 'offshore interface', using as illustrations Jersey and other offshore locations. This topic reappears in Part VI of the volume when the offshore centres are shown to have played a crucial role in BCCI's fraud.

Exchange and Securities

Whenever the term 'global' is used in the context of financial services, the example invariably cited is the foreign exchange market. It is one of the four 'cornerstones' of global financing identified by Smith and Walter (1992), the others being the Eurocurrency market, the Eurobond market and the equity market. We examined the Eurocurrency market in Part III. The remaining three cornerstones feature in this section.

Chapters 28 and 29 focus on the foreign exchange market, a 24-hour worldwide operation sourced from the dealing rooms of banks. In Chapter 28 Bingham examines the workings of the market. Much of his information is based on the Bank for International Settlements – sponsored survey of the market in April 1989. Since then there have been two further surveys, and Table 2 shows the overall turnover figures revealed. By any standards, daily turnover in excess of $1.5 *trillion* is remarkable. London remains the hub of the market, and the table shows that its market share has increased to 30 per cent of total turnover. The 1995 survey also confirms that trading in Hong Kong and Singapore combined exceeds that in Japan. This

Table 2. Foreign exchange market activity by country, 1986-95 (average daily net turnover in US$ billion)

Country	March 1986	April 1989	April 1992	April 1995
United Kingdom	90	187	291	464
United States	58	129	167	244
Japan	48	115	120	161
Singapore		55	74	105
Hong Kong		49	60	90
Switzerland		56	66	87
Germany			55	76
France		23	33	58
Australia		29	29	40
Denmark		13	27	31
Others	–	*62*	*154*	*215*
Total turnover	n.a.	718	1076	1572
Memo:				
Share of largest centre in total	n.a.	26	27	30

Source: Bank of England, Bank for International Settlements.
n.a. = not applicable.

feature, and the City's dominance over New York in dollar trading in particular, suggests a close connection between foreign exchange trading and Eurocurrency banking, despite the formal differences between the two (one buying and selling currencies, the other borrowing and lending them).

Those using the services of the foreign exchange market must, of course, do so on terms set in the marketplace, and are thus subject to the well-documented vagaries of exchange movements. That volatility is studied in a later Volume of this series, *Financial Market Integration and International Capital Flows*. The chapter here by Alan Kirman concentrates on the market structure (Chapter 29). If we start with the premise that the way in which a market is organized can have important consequences for the way in which prices evolve, then it is apparent that the foreign exchange market is a very special market indeed. Users and suppliers of the financial services come from a large number of countries and, without a central trading venue, have no way of observing price-setting behaviour in aggregate. While they are observing outcomes and quotations from a large number of other locations, they interact directly with only a small subset of possible partners. The market can be viewed as a complex network, and the way in which information is transmitted through the system seems likely to influence the evolution of prices. One exemplification may be in terms of imitative behaviour and 'following the leader' (herd behaviour); another may be information cascades (or the blind leading the blind). The market may also be subject to mood changes, as the weight of market opinion swings from one position or model to another.

Volatility is also a feature of stock market prices, and those buying and selling stocks must do so at prices which cannot be predicted in advance. This characteristic of equity prices was brought home to investors by the stock market crash of October 1987. Stock market prices had fallen at other times, but not as much on one day as on 19 October 1987 and, unlike other crashes such as October 1929, this was a global occurrence. Prices of common stocks fell by about 20 per cent on most of the stock markets around the world. Was such a global pattern an exceptional occurrence or are investors now exposed to the risk of global contagion? Chapter 30 by Richard Roll searches for answers.

Ever since 1963, when the British merchant banking house Warburgs issued the first Eurobond for the Italian Autostrade, the Eurocurrency market has been flanked by the international bond market. That market too, is centred on London (which accounts for about 90 per cent of issue volume and 75 per cent of secondary trading), although there are substantial 'onshore' foreign bond segments in New York, Frankfurt and Tokyo, the more domestic currency-oriented financial centres. Figure 1 shows that issues of international bonds have grown strongly since the early 1980s, when the syndicated loan market went into decline and lost its pre-eminent position in international financing. Another feature of financing activity in the international markets has been the creation of Euro-note facilities which blur the borders between traditional banking and securities operations (Lewis, 1990). These facilities have also expanded at a rapid rate.

Financial institutions have responded to these developments by initiating global strategies, paralleling earlier moves to multinational status among commercial banks. However, the routes to globalization and integration in investment banking have differed for the three main classes of institution in the marketplace: US investment banks, European universal banks and commercial banks. The US investment banks have the dominant market position and their moves to globalization are the subject of Chapter 31 by Professor Brian Scott-Quinn of

Reading University. (The paths to internationalization among European universal banks are examined by Lewis, 1997.)

Innovation has been a hallmark of the offshore markets. The origins of the Eurocurrency markets for both banking and bonds were innovative in that, for the first time on a vast scale, the currency risk of one country was combined with the regulatory environment and political risk of another country – an early illustration of the fungibility of finance. Afterwards, Eurobanking gave banks the freedom to create new instruments and try out new ideas. Rollover credits, flexi-rate lending, wholesale funds markets, floating rate notes and multiple currency loans are examples of innovations which are now part of the nuts and bolts of modern banking. The recycling crisis of the 1970s was resolved by a new financial instrument – the syndicated credit – enabling long-term financing to be made on the back of short-term deposits of dollars from OPEC countries. When in the 1980s the wealth transfer process internationally reverted to capital market channels, new financing facilities were fashioned which combined banking and securities instruments, and provided tailor-made financial structures which blurred long-standing distinctions between banking and securities. This record has continued with the growth of derivative instruments. Charles Lucas, formerly of the Federal Reserve Bank of New York and now with the Republic National Bank of New York, surveys these innovations in Chapter 32.

What of the future? Will the trend to globalization in financial services continue or will financial markets turn inward, as they did in the middle of the twentieth century? Charles Sanford, Chairman of Bankers Trust, New York, polishes his crystal ball in Chapter 33 and envisages a world in 2020 in which many transactions presently passing through banks and other financial intermediaries will be 'disintermediated'. As more financial information is disseminated electronically, individuals will themselves access information before they make decisions about their investments, as they are beginning to do already via the Internet. They will trade on electronic markets in which the prices of a vast array of assets are constantly displayed and updated. Advertisements on electronic bulletin boards will match buyers with sellers, borrowers with lenders. Transactions will be instantly verified and settled through a global, real-time payments system.

As for the financial institutions of the future, a feature of Sanford's article is a division of financial activities into five basic functions: (1) financing; (2) risk management; (3) trading and positioning; (4) advising; and (5) transactions processing. All of these functions will continue, but the way in which they are performed will change, and many will be undertaken either by individuals or by specialists. Instruments such as futures, options and other types of derivative, and new financial theories, enable firms to 'un-pick' risks in much the same way that physicists split the atom. In what he calls 'particle finance', financial intermediaries will survive on their ability to bundle and unbundle different risks, keeping some, selling others and charging fees for doing so, as they evolve into specialist managers of financial risks.

Regulatory Issues

This section assesses the regulatory implications of some of the developments outlined in the earlier parts of this volume. One such area, noted by Sanford, is the growth of electronic money – the utilization of computer and electronic components in order to transfer money or financial instruments. Of particular concern are the counter-party and settlement risks of large-value electronic fund transfer systems which a number of defining events (the Bankhaus Herstatt failure of 1974 and Bank of New York computer malfunction in 1985) have shown to be of considerable significance. In Chapter 34 Yoshiharu Oritani examines the evolving forms of global payment network. He then identifies the risks and asks how they might be ameliorated. His recommendation is for participating institutions to opt for joining the payments network with each country's central bank at the core, ensuring finality to each transaction. This, by and large, is what has emerged from the deliberations of the world's central banks, with countries moving to establish real-time gross settlement systems based around each individual bank's settlement account at the country's central bank.

The last decade has seen a merging of banking and securities, both within many national financial systems and globally in the Eurocurrency markets. As commercial banks have sought to gain a foothold in the securities business, they have bought out merchant banks and securities dealers, forming new financial conglomerations to provide a wider range of financial services. Professor Richard Dale of Southampton University in Chapter 35 outlines the regulatory principles involved in these financial combinations, and shows that national authorities have followed divergent approaches. He then considers the consequences of these different policies for the competition and safety of the global financial system.

In his second contribution to the volume, Professor Dale in Chapter 36 reviews developments in international bank regulation. As might be expected, regulatory moves have lagged behind market developments and have been driven by events. Thus it was not until the mid 1970s that a formal machinery was established for coordinating national regulation of international banks. The disturbances that followed in the wake of Bankhaus Herstatt's closure in the summer of 1974 drew attention to the interdependence of national banking systems and led to the creation in the following year of a standing committee of bank supervisors, under the auspices of the Bank for International Settlements. This Committee on Banking Regulation and Supervisory Practices, chaired by Peter Cooke of the Bank of England, did not seek to harmonize national laws and practices, but rather to interlink disparate regulatory regimes with a view to ensuring that all banks are supervised according to certain broad principles. These principles were enunciated in a number of concordat. Professor Dale assesses these principles in the wake of subsequent events and developments, and notes that, despite the Committee's avowed intentions, there has been a shift in focus internationally from regulatory cooperation to regulatory harmonization.

Two defining episodes in the course of international bank regulation are the topics of the two final chapters. Chapter 37 deals with the astonishing case of how one trader brought down Barings Bank in 1995. The assessment is provided by the man responsible for deciding to close the bank rather than mount a rescue operation – Brian Quinn, Executive Director of the Bank of England. It would seem that the globalization of the financial services industry had an important influence on the outcome. Barings' operations straddled three locations, namely Singapore, Osaka and London, and there was an apparent failure of the three regulatory bodies involved to communicate with each other. This dispersion also hindered any rescue operation. The case also illustrates the operational risks facing financial firms undertaking financial services provision on a global basis.

Chapter 38 reassesses the case of the Bank of Credit and Commerce International in the light of later financial scandals. Globalization was at the heart of this fraud since the bank virtually pioneered the art of spinning funds from one location to another in a complex paper trail to exploit gaps in regulations. While bank supervisory practices have been amended in the wake of the collapse, the single most important factor which allowed the fraud to remain undetected for so long – bank secrecy laws in offshore centres – remains. The article echoes the view of John Moscow, Assistant District Attorney of New York County, that in frauds of this nature where the institution is supplying in effect, global *criminal* services, bank supervision and law enforcement agencies may not be so very different.

References

Aharoni, Y. (1971), 'On the definition of a multinational corporation', *Quarterly Review of Economics and Business*, **11** (3), 27–37.

Artis, M.J. and Lewis, M.K. (1991), *Money in Britain. Monetary Policy, Innovation and Europe*, Oxford: Philip Allan.

Bhagwati, J. (1986), *Trade in Services and Developing Countries*, Columbia University, Department of Economics, Discussion Paper No. 307.

Buckley, P.J. and Casson, M.C. (1976), *The Future of the Multinational Enterprise*, London: Macmillan.

City Research Project (1995), *The Competitive Position of London's Financial Services. Final Report*, London: Corporation of London.

Coase, R.H. (1937), 'The nature of the firm', *Economica*, New Series 4, 386–405.

Dunning, J.H. (1981), *International Production and the Multinational Enterprise*, London: Allen and Unwin.

Dunning, J.H. (1994), *Globalisation: The Challenge for National Economic Regions*, Discussion Papers in International Investment and Business Studies 186, University of Reading.

Fleming, A.S. and Howson, S.K. (1980), 'Conditions in the syndicated medium-term Euro-credit market', *Bank of England Quarterly Bulletin*, September **20** (3), 311–18.

GATT (1989), 'Services in the domestic and global economy', *International Trade 1988–89*, Vol. 1, Geneva.

Grilli, V. (1992), 'Trade in financial services', in P. Newman, M. Milgate and J. Eatwell (eds), *The New Palgrave Dictionary of Money and Finance*, Vol. 3, London: Macmillan.

Hewson, J. and Sakakibara, E. (1974), 'The Euro-dollar deposit multiplier: a portfolio approach', *IMF Staff Papers*, 21 (2), July, 307–28.

Hewson, J. (1975), *Legendary Creation and Distribution in Eurocurrency Markets*, Lexington, Mass: Heath.

Hill, T.P. (1977), 'On goods and services', *Review of Income and Wealth*, **23** (4), 315–38.

Johnston, R.B. (1980), *Banks' International Lending Decisions and the Determination of Spreads on Syndicated Medium-Term Eurocredits*, Bank of England Discussion Paper No. 12, September.

Johnston, R.B. (1983), *The Economics of the Euromarket: History, Theory and Policy*, London: Macmillan.

Kindleberger, C.P. (1974), 'The formation of financial centres: a study in comparative economic history', *Princeton Studies in International Finance*, **36**, November.

Kreicher, L.R. (1982), 'Eurodollar arbitrage', *Federal Reserve Bank of New York Review*, **7**, Summer, 10–22.

Lewis, M.K. (1990), 'Banking, securities and commerce: a European perspective', *Cato Journal*, **10** (2), Fall, 347–56.

Lewis, M.K. (1991), 'Theory and practice of the banking firm', in C.J. Green and D.T. Llewellyn (eds), *Surveys in Monetary Economics*, Vol. 2, Oxford: Basil Blackwell.

Lewis, M.K. (1996), 'Financial Services', in B. Bora and C. Findlay (eds), *Regional Integration and the Asia-Pacific*, Melbourne: Oxford University Press.

Lewis, M.K. (1997), 'Universal banking', *Journal of Applied Finance and Investment*, Special Supplement, 47–56.

Lewis, M.K. (1999), 'International banking and offshore finance: London and the major centres', in M. Hampton and J. Abbott (eds), *Offshore Finance Centres and Tax Havens*, London: Macmillan (forthcoming).

Lewis, M.K. and Davis, K.T. (1987), *Domestic and International Banking*, Deddington, Oxford: Philip Allan and Cambridge, Mass: MIT Press.

Lewis, M.K. and Morton, P. (1996), 'Asset and liability management in retail banking', in F. Bruni, D.E. Fair and R. O'Brien (eds), *Risk Management in Volatile Financial Markets* for SUERF, Dordrecht: Kluwer Academic Publishers.

McKinnon, R.I. (1977), 'The Euro-currency market', *Essays in International Finance*, No. 125, Princeton University.

Niehans, J. (1984) *International Monetary Economics*, Baltimore: The John Hopkins University Press.

OECD (1993), *National Treatment for Foreign-Controlled Enterprises*, Paris: OECD.

Qureshi, Z. (1996), 'Globalisation: new opportunities, tough challenges', *Finance and Development*, **33** (1), March, 30–33.

Smith, R.C. and Walter, I. (1992), 'Global financial markets', in P. Newman, M. Milgate and J. Eatwell (eds), *The New Palgrave Dictionary of Money and Finance*, Vol. 2, London: Macmillan.

Tobin, J. (1963), 'Commercial banks as creators of money', in Carson (ed.), *Banking and Monetary Studies*, Homewood Illinois: R.D. Irwin, 408–19. Reprinted in Lewis, M.K. (ed.), *Financial Intermediaries*, International Library of Critial Writings in Economics 43, Cheltenham: Edward Elgar, 1995.

Walter, I. (1988), *Global Competition in Financial Services*, Washington: American Enterprise Institute.

Part I
Trade in Financial Services

[1]

Measuring Trade in Financial Services

There has always been trade in financial services.[1] Bankers have provided financial intermediation, foreign exchange market and other financial services across national boundaries. But the importance of such trade has increased greatly in the past two decades with the internationalisation of banking and the growth of international financial centres as the bases for offshore currency markets and other activities linking national capital markets. The question naturally arises how to measure the value and growth of this trade in financial services. The issues involved in this question are closely related to the difficulties that have been encountered in the treatment of financial enterprises in social accounts for national economies. It is best approached by going back to these issues.

Financial Services in Closed Economies

The crux of the problem was clearly explained in the 1947 memorandum by Richard Stone which laid the foundations for the original United Nations system of national accounts. "If we treated banks (and other financial intermediaries) like ordinary businesses, we should show as their sales proceeds simply their charges to customers and, as a consequence, a deficit rather than a surplus would appear on the other side of the operating account. In practice, this deficit would be so large that the property income generated in banking and even perhaps the whole income generated in banking would appear to be negative. This is clearly unsatisfactory".[2]

---

[1] This paper deals with financial services other than insurance.
[2] *Measurement of National Income and the Construction of Social Accounts*, "Appendix: Definition and Measurement of the National Income and Related Totals" by RICHARD STONE, United Nations, Geneva, 1947 (hereafter cited as "Stone Memorandum"), p. 40.

The solutions to this conundrum which have been adopted by social accountants fall into three classes corresponding to the three main functions of banks, the creation of money, the provision of a payments mechanism and related services, and financial intermediation; or, in the words of an early contributor to the debate, "loan services, clearance or transfer of circulating medium services, and the creation and maintenance of circulating medium".[3] Those who have put the emphasis on the creation of money function have regarded the services of banks as being provided to the community at large and have treated them, by analogy with government services, as final products and thus as contributing to gross domestic product (GDP). Those who have emphasised the payments mechanism function have regarded the services of banks as being rendered primarily to depositors and have divided them into those rendered to households, considered as final products and therefore included in GDP, and those rendered to enterprises, considered as intermediate products and therefore excluded from GDP. Those, finally, who have focused on the intermediation function have viewed bank services as being rendered mainly to borrowers and have therefore treated them wholly as intermediate products used as inputs by enterprises (except sometimes for those associated with consumer loans, considered as a service to households).[4]

Services to the Community. The first approach has not been widely used. But it was proposed in Australia by H.P. Brown and was employed in the Australian national accounts from 1947 until 1972.[5]

---

[3] CLARK WARBURTON, "Financial Intermediaries" in National Bureau of Economic Research, *Studies in Income and Wealth*, vol. 22, Princeton University Press, 1958, p. 511.

[4] There have also been suggestions for dealing with the problem by doing away with the distinction between factor and non-factor services. Industrial economists using an input-output approach to the study of the service sector tend to treat all non-factor service incomes as though they were factor incomes (e.g. Bureau of Industry Economics, *Features of the Australian Service Sector*, AGPS, Canberra, 1980), while there has also been a proposal, on the contrary, to treat all interest as a non-factor service income (P.T. SUNGA, "An Alternative to the Current Treatment of Interest as Transfer in the United States and Canadian System of National Accounts", IARIW 18th General Conference, Luxembourg, August 1983). This would seem to be a case of throwing out the baby with the bath water. The distinction between output of enterprises (consisting of goods or services) and the services of factors of production which constitute the ultimate inputs of such enterprises, even though it breaks down in marginal cases, seems of sufficient importance not to be lightly jettisoned.

[5] See H.P. BROWN, "Some Aspects of Social Accounting - Interest and Banks", *Economic Record*, August 1949; also B.D. HAIG, "The Treatment of Banks in the Social Accounts", *Economic Record*, December 1973 and comment by A.W. ROCHE and reply by B.D. HAIG, *Economic Record*, March 1975.

Brown argued that the function of banks was essentially similar to a major function of government, "oiling the wheels of industry and the community generally".[6] He therefore proposed that "as for governments, the contribution of banks to the national income is equal to the wages and salaries paid by banks".[7] In effect, though not in rationale, Brown's approach was similar to the "aggregation of individuals" approach originally proposed by Kuznets and used by the US Department of Commerce until 1947, except that Brown excluded bank profits on the ground that they were merely a channel through which surplus of trading enterprises was passed on to shareholder-depositors, so that their inclusion would have involved double counting.[8] The crucial feature of both versions was that the output of banks, valued at factor incomes (including or excluding profits) in banking, was included in national income without any deductions in other parts of the economy. In treating the whole output of financial enterprises as final products, this approach certainly involved double counting (though not more so than in the case of government services) and has therefore been generally discarded.

Services to Depositors. The second approach was first worked out in the US Department of Commerce and then adopted in the first United Nations system of national accounts on the recommendation of a committee chaired by Richard Stone. Its rationale was explained by Stone as follows: "Financial enterprises require special treatment in view of the different functions they perform and the method they adopt in charging for services. Consider commercial banks as a typical example. On the one hand, they provide services to their customers in the form of keeping their accounts for them and providing advice on various financial matters. For this they make a charge which, in many cases, is inadequate. On the other hand, they lend the money deposited with them, whether as a result of their own activities or not, and from this receive a net return large enough to enable them to subsidise the other aspect of their business".[9]

To overcome this difficulty, he proposed the following procedure: "An income is imputed to bank depositors for the use of their money

---

6 H. P. Brown, cited B. D. HAIG, *Economic Record*, December 1973, p. 625.
7 *Ibid.*
8 *Ibid.*, p. 626. For references to earlier literature on the subject, see R. E. SPEAGLE & L. SIL-VERMAN, "The Banking Income Dilemma", *Review of Economics & Statistics*, vol. 35, 1953, pp. 139.
9 "Stone Memorandum", p. 40.

equal to the excess of interest and dividends received by banks over interest paid out and this income is assumed to be used in 'paying' for uncharged banking services. In the case of persons, this imputed income and outlay appears on either side of the revenue account of persons, but, in the case of enterprises of all kinds, the imputed outlay is charged to operating account, thus diminishing the surplus of the enterprise, while the imputed income is credited to the appropriation account, thus restricting the effects of the adjustment to the operating surplus alone... The allocation of the total amount imputed between persons and businesses can only be based on knowledge of the bank expenses incurred in respect of, but not charged to, these two types of depositor".[10] In effect, depositors were regarded as receiving, in return for depositing their money with banks, an income in kind in the form of payments mechanism and other services, in much the same way as factory workers may receive, in addition to their cash wages, free canteen meals.

When this approach was adopted by the US Department of Commerce the allocation of the imputed bank service charge between households and enterprises, and thus between final and intermediate products, was based on deposit ownership.[11] When the same approach was adopted in the first UN system of national accounts (SNA), the same procedure was recommended, though the difficulty of inadequate statistics of deposit ownership in many countries was acknowledged. "The contribution of banks, etc. to gross domestic product is here evaluated by imputing to depositors a service charge equal to the excess of investment income accruing to these institutions and by imputing at the same time a corresponding amount of income to depositors. Thus these imputations do not change the income of banks or of other enterprises, but they result in a change in the industrial classification of domestic product (from other enterprises to banks) in so far as the imputation is made in respect of business deposits, and in an increase in the domestic product to the extent that the imputation is made in respect of the deposits of households, etc. The main problem in applying this rule is of a statistical character, but the total amount involved in most countries is small" and inaccuracies hardly serious.[12]

---

[10] *Ibid.*, p. 41.
[11] U.S. DEPARTMENT OF COMMERCE, *National Income 1951 Edition*, cited R.E. SPEAGLE & L. SILVERMAN, *op. cit.*, p. 130.
[12] *A System of National Accounts and Supporting Tables*, UNITED NATIONS, New York, 1953, [ST/STAT/SER F./No. 2], p. 32.

In the following years, the second approach came under heavy criticism, chiefly on the ground that it misconceived the functions of banks. One exposition of this view criticised the Department of Commerce interpretation of the banking function as "primarily a matter of keeping accounts for depositors, including the mechanical operation of monetary transfers... As far as these lending institutions are concerned, lending and investing functions are performed free of charge to borrowers. The creation of purchasing power through the lending process is passed over."[13] In the view of these critics, "the chief business of commercial banks... consists of two things: the expert management and investment of funds belonging to the banks' owners and creditors and, of equal importance under a fractional reserve system, the simultaneous creation of money." Since the capacity of banks to provide credit depends on their ability to maintain the convertibility of deposits, even "the expense of an elaborate clearing machinery set up expressly to keep deposit money freely convertible" should be regarded as part, indeed "a major part of lending costs".[14]

Apart from its complexity and its neglect of bank services to borrowers, the Department of Commerce (and old SNA) approach was criticised also on the ground that ownership of deposits was a very inadequate guide to the relative costs of services provided by banks to household and business depositors, if only because of economies of scale.[15]

Services to Borrowers. The third view, that bank services should be regarded as rendered primarily to borrowers rather than to depositors, because the primary function of banks is financial intermediation, prevailed in the 1960s. In 1968 it was incorporated in a revised UN system of national accounts. "The imputed service charge is to be treated as intermediate consumption of industries for a number of reasons" of which the first was that "a key service performed by banks and similar institutions is to channel the savings of other economic agents into loans to industries".[16] Or, as it was put by the Australian government stati-

---

[13] R.E. SPEAGLE & L. SILVERMAN, *op. cit.*, pp. 131f.
[14] *Ibid.*, p. 131.
[15] G. JASZI, "The Conceptual Basis of the Accounts: A Re-Examination" in NBER, *op. cit.*, p. 63.
[16] *A System of National Accounts (Rev. 3)*, UNITED NATIONS, New York, 1968. Other reasons given for the change were the statistical difficulty of allocating the imputed service charge among industries and the advantage that under the new system, unlike the old, "the value of gross domestic product... is not inflated by assigning part of the service charge to final consumption expenditure" (*ibid.* p. 97). For reasons which are not clear, it was also argued that, in principle, the imputed bank service charge should be equated to net investment income of banks arising from loans and other investments "made from the deposits they hold" but not "from their own funds" (*ibid.*).

stician who changed over to the new SNA procedure in 1973, the imputed bank service charge "measures the expenses associated with organising borrowing and lending".[17]

The Australian explanation gives a clear account of the mechanics of this approach. "Interest received is viewed as consisting of a pure interest component and a service charge for organising the funds. It is not practicable to allocate all the service charge to customers [i.e. among borrowers by industry]. The part relating to consumer loans (including hire-purchase) is treated as being paid by the customer and included in private consumption expenditure. The remainder, termed the imputed bank service charge, is not allocated to customers but treated as being paid by a 'nominal industry' which accordingly has a negative operating surplus of this amount".[18]

Thus, whereas on the second approach the output of banks (other than services explicitly charged for) is divided between final products (included in GDP) and intermediate products (excluded from GDP) in proportion to household and business ownership of deposits, on this third approach, most of the output of banks (and other financial intermediaries) is treated as consisting of intermediate products which enter into the costs of enterprises and are therefore excluded from GDP, the only exceptions being services to household depositors for which banks make explicit charges and services to household borrowers for which banks receive interest on consumer loans.

The Primacy of the Financial Intermediation Function. Two surprising facts stand out from this summary history of the treatment of financial enterprises in national accounts. One is that each school of thought focused on only one of the three major functions of banks, *either* services rendered to the community at large, such as the creation of money, *or* services to depositors, such as keeping accounts and providing payments facilities, *or* services to borrowers, such as financial intermediation. It would seem obvious that banks perform all three functions and, more particularly, provide services to both depositors and borrowers. Ideally, therefore, one would look for an allocation of the imputed bank service charge between these two main categories of bank customers and then, within each category, between services which

---

[17] *Australian National Accounts: Concepts, Sources and Methods*, AUSTRALIAN BUREAU OF STATISTICS, Canberra, p. 108.
[18] *Ibid.*, p. 109.

meet final demand and thus contribute to GDP, such as those rendered to households, and those which enter into the costs of production of enterprises (and government) and should therefore be excluded from GDP as intermediate products. If this makes unmanageable demands on statistical services, it becomes a question of which simplification is conceptually to be preferred.

The old SNA approach of treating bank services as being rendered to depositors, although usually explained by reference to the payments mechanism functions of banks (keeping accounts, cheque facilities, clearing machinery, etc.) had its original rationale in the old-fashioned notion that banks merely lend out money they have borrowed from depositors. The services rendered by banks to depositors were therefore viewed as "financed from interest received to the account of depositors but retained by the banks rather than actually credited or remitted to their customers",[19] and when an income equal to the banks' net investment income was imputed to depositors to enable them to pay the imputed bank service charge it was "for the use of *their* money".[20]

The most obvious reason why this rationale of the net investment income of banks is difficult to accept is that it is applied in the national accounts equally to banks *and other financial enterprises*, yet non-bank financial intermediaries have a net investment income without rendering any payments mechanism services to demand depositors. Clearly, at the very least, not *all* net investment of income of banks represents payment for services rendered to depositors. The rationale of the old SNA derived what plausibility it had from too exclusive concentration on deposit banks.

There is of course a difference between deposit banks and non-bank financial intermediaries (NFI) in that the former secure a large part of their deposits interest free, and thus pay a lower average rate of interest on their deposits, and instead attract demand deposits by the provision of cheque and other facilities. To this extent, deposit banks must, *cet. par.*, be assumed to have a larger net investment income per dollar of funds employed, balanced by larger administrative costs, than NFI. It is reasonable to assume that deposit banks, as profit-maximising firms, have provided services to demand depositors to the extent they have judged necessary to attract demand deposits, not least in competition with one another. Thus, there is a case for treating

---

[19] R.E. SPEAGLE & L. SILVERMAN, *op. cit.*, p. 130.
[20] "Stone Memorandum", p. 41; italics supplied.

some part of the cost of bank administration as a payment to demand depositors in lieu of interest.

However, there has been a marked tendency in recent years for deposit banks to charge explicitly for an increasing proportion of the services rendered to depositors, such as keeping accounts, providing cheque facilities, making transfers, etc., without any evident shift of depositors' funds to time deposits or currency holdings or any decline in the banks' net investment income. It is not unlikely that the payments mechanism facilities provided by banks are so valuable to demand depositors that they would be willing to pay for them in full in explicit charges. While there might be some drift of funds from demand deposits to time deposits or currency, it would probably be slight and temporary, at least in countries in which the cheque habit is well established. In that case, the rationale for an imputed bank service charge *to depositors* would disappear, yet the banks' net investment income would not diminish significantly.

The conclusion to which this argument points is that all of the net investment income of NFI and a large and increasing proportion of the net investment income of deposit banks is appropriately regarded as payment for financial intermediation rather than for payments mechanism services, in other words, for services to borrowers rather than to depositors. Since the bulk of bank credit is to enterprises rather than to households, the argument supports the new rather than the old SNA treatment of financial enterprises. There remains, however, the second surprising feature of the traditional social accounting treatment of financial enterprises. This is the assumption of a closed economy.

The Closed Economy Assumption. The assumption was made quite explicitly by Stone in his 1947 memorandum. "This example relates to a closed economy with no public authorities".[21] Others as best mentioned in passing "deposits held by governmental bodies, foreigners and individuals".[22] Generally, in all the discussions of the treatment of financial enterprises in national accounts, the assumption was implicit – international aspects of the problem were simply ignored. Yet, there is here a major difference between a closed and an open economy. For the conclusion of the preceding argument, that most services of banks and other financial intermediaries are rendered to business enterprises and

---

[21] *Ibid.*, p. 89. Public authorities which have also been neglected should, of course, be treated like enterprises; banking services rended to them are intermediate products.

[22] R. E. SPEAGLE & L. SILVERMAN, *op. cit.*, p. 130.

must *therefore* be treated as intermediate products, while valid for the closed economy, is clearly invalid for an open one. Services rendered to non-residents represent final products, whether the customers are business enterprises or not. They are in this respect on a par with services rendered to domestic households. The consequence is that the new SNA treatment understates GNP to the extent that financial services are exported.

This defect has not mattered very much for countries with very large finance sectors only a small proportion of whose business has been with the rest of the world, and the same still applies to the majority of countries in varying degree. But with increasing internationalisation of banking the error has become significant for a good many countries, and for some it has become very large indeed. And it is of course central to the measurement of trade in financial services, the subject of this paper.

Before examining possible ways of handling this problem, it is worth noting that the assumption of a closed economy has also led to complete neglect of another function of banks which, in countries like Australia, has provided a considerable part of bank profits. This is their role as dealers in foreign exchange. The income which banks derive from the provision of spot (and in some countries forward) exchange market services is distinct both from explicit charges and from the net investment income which finances the imputed bank service charge. It consists of trading margins (spreads between buying and selling rates) analogous to the income of shopkeepers and other traders. But, partly because much foreign exchange business takes the form of discounting usance bills where the foreign exchange trading margin enters into the discount rate, the banks' receipts from foreign exchange trading margins are not usually itemised separately in statistics for financial enterprises but included in their net investment income.

Trade in Financial Services

Table 1 shows, for all countries for which the data are available in the UN *Yearbook of National Accounts Statistics*, the imputed bank service charge as a percentage of GDP in 1970 and 1979. In 1970 the (unweighted) average percentage for the developed countries was 2.5

TABLE 1

IMPUTED BANK SERVICE CHARGE AS PERCENT OF GDP, 1970, 1979

%

	1970	1979
I.		
Australia	2.2	2.5
Austria	3.1	4.6
Belgium	0.9	1.5
Canada	0.7	0.7
Finland	1.5	2.2
France	2.8	3.5
Germany, F.R.	2.3	3.3
Italy	2.8	4.1
Japan	4.4	4.3
Luxembourg	4.6	26.7 [af]
Netherlands	2.1	3.5
UK	2.8	4.1
USA	2.2	2.5
average (unweighted)	*2.5*	*4.8*
		3.1 [d]
II.		
Ghana	1.2	1.7 [a]
Ivory Coast	1.2	2.0 [b]
Kenya	1.8	1.9
Malaysia	1.1 [c]	1.2 [a]
Mexico	1.1	1.1
Saudi Arabia	0.2	1.0 [b]
Singapore	1.9	4.3
Sri Lanka	0.3	0.3
Venezuela	2.1	6.8
average (unweighted)	*1.2*	*2.3*
		1.7 [e]

a 1977.
b 1978.
c 1972.
d Excluding Luxembourg.
e Excluding Venezuela.
f Since 1977, on revised definition, excluding exports of financial services (see text), 1977: 12.4; 1979: 8.0 (*Comptes Nationaux 1960-1980*, Luxembourg, September 1982).
Source: UN Yearbook of National Accounts Statistics 1980.

and for less developed countries 1.2. By 1979 it had risen to 3.1 for developed countries (excluding Luxembourg) and to 1.7 per cent for less developed countries (excluding Venezuela). Most striking, however, are the figures for Luxembourg and, to a less extent, for Venezuela and Singapore. For Luxembourg, the percentage, already 4.6 in 1970, had by 1977 risen to 26.7 per cent. In other words, close to a quarter of the country's GDP was omitted because of the treatment of financial services as intermediate products. In the case of Singapore, the rise was from 1.9 to 4.3 per cent in 1977; by 1981, it had reached 6.8 per cent.[23] Unfortunately, no such data are available for the pre-eminent international financial centres, Switzerland and Hong Kong. But it is worth noting that Austria, the United Kingdom and (rather surprisingly) Italy and Japan have relatively high percentages. It would be interesting to know how far these are accounted for by international financial business.

The inappropriateness of the SNA treatment of financial enterprises for countries with large international financial business has been raised for discussion in OECD and other fora by the government statistical service of Luxembourg.

Luxembourg. In a memorandum presented to an OECD conference in May 1982, the government statistical service of Luxembourg argued that the SNA treatment of financial services "is not well suited for analysing the activities of an international financial sector, whose banks export their services and so produce a 'final' output".[24] "The growing contribution of the banking sector to the economy of Luxembourg, and to economic progress in general, could not be brought out by GDP statistics compiled according to the rules of the ESA [the European version of the SNA], since the effect of these rules was to conceal the contribution from the banking sector. We were in the paradoxical position that the most prosperous branch of the economy appeared to have no effect on the structure of production".[25]

The solution adopted in Luxembourg "consisted in making a distinction between those banking services provided to residents and

---

[23] *Economic Survey of Singapore 1981*, Singapore, 1982, Table 1.2.

[24] "Imputed Bank Services", Note prepared by the Central Office of Statistics and Economic Studies of the Grand Duchy of Luxembourg (mimeo), OECD, Paris, May 1982, p. 7; French version printed in *Comptes Nationaux 1960-1980*, MINISTÈRE DE L'ECONOMIE, STATEC, Luxembourg, September 1982.

[25] *Ibid.*, p. 8.

those provided to foreigners, these latter being estimated on the basis of the percentage of [banks'] liabilities towards non-residents to total liabilities".[26] The memorandum added that "recently, other countries which find themselves in a similar situation (Singapore, Bahrein, Kuwait) have proposed that the accounting system of the United Nations... should be revised regarding the treatment of banks".[27]

The memorandum does not give reasons for the decision to allocate bank services between those rendered to residents and non-residents, or in effect between exports and production for the home market, on the basis of deposit ownership. Ideally, the allocation, as Stone pointed out in his 1947 memorandum, "can only be based on knowledge of the bank expenses incurred in respect of... these two types of" customers.[28] It seems most unlikely that the share of non-residents in the business of Luxembourg financial enterprises is correctly measured by their share in the deposits (or even total liabilities) of Luxembourg banks. If the procedure has been adopted simply on the precedent of the US Department of Commerce practice, it is even less appropriate in relation to exports of banking services than we have shown it to be in a closed economy. For in international banking business, the financial intermediation function clearly predominates over the payments mechanism function even more than in domestic banking, if only because so much of it is inter-bank business. The real explanation for the Luxembourg procedure is probably the pragmatic one that no better statistical data for distinguishing between export and home-market business of Luxembourg banks are available.

The Luxembourg memorandum also points out that the decision to include a part of the imputed bank service charge in GDP as exports of bank services requires consequential adjustments in the social accounts.[29] Three adjustments are necessary. First, in the balance of payments accounts, there has to be a transfer from factor service to non-factor service receipts (which, of course, leaves the balance on current account unaffected). Secondly, in the sector accounts for financial enterprises, there has to be a transfer from interest received to operating surplus (the increase in the latter taking the form of a reduction in the imputed bank service charge by the amount treated as

---

[26] *Ibid.*; the English version refers to "assets", the French to "*engagements*".
[27] *Ibid.*
[28] "Stone Memorandum", p. 41.
[29] *Op. cit.*, p. 11.

receipts from exports of bank services). Thirdly, net property income received from abroad (which is added to GDP to give GNP) includes the banks' net investment income from abroad, part of which is now to be treated as receipts from export of non-factor services; if it is thought desirable to retain the whole of the banks' investment income from abroad in the total of the country's net property income received from abroad, a negative adjustment is necessary. All these adjustments are required in order to avoid an apparent increase in domestic savings as a result of the inclusion of exports of banking services in GDP. Corresponding adjustments would be needed if bank services rendered to domestic households were also treated as meeting final, not intermediate, demand.

Singapore. In international financial centres, such as Singapore, where banks and merchant banks operating in the offshore currency market as Asian Currency Units (ACUs) are required to keep separate accounts, the measurement of exports of financial services may be easier. Although ACUs provide some financial intermediation services to resident Singapore borrowers, the great bulk of their business is with non-residents. Conversely, the bulk of the business of Singapore banks, whether locally or foreign owned, is with residents. As a first approximation, therefore, it may be legitimate to equate Singapore's exports of financial services with explicit charges by Singapore financial enterprises to non-resident *plus* the net investment income of its ACUs. The latter amount (including profit from foreign exchange trading) has been estimated at about $ US 196-233 million (or 1.1-1.3 per cent of GDP) in 1979.[30] This may be compared with the imputed bank service charge for Singapore of $ US 881 million in the same year[31] and an estimated contribution of financial institutions to GDP of about $ US 1,115 million.[32] This would suggest that the services measured by the imputed bank service charge accounted for about four-fifths of the contribution of financial institutions to Singapore's GDP (the balance being due presumably to services charged for explicitly); and that about one-quarter of the imputed bank service charge was accounted for by

---

[30] J.R. HEWSON, "Offshore Banking in Australia" in Australian Financial System Inquiry, *Commissioned Studies and Selected Papers*, Part 2, Macroeconomic Policy: External Policy, AGPS, Canberra, 1982, p. 529.
[31] *Economic Survey of Singapore, loc. cit.*
[32] J.R. HEWSON, *op. cit.*, p. 528.

exports of financial services (i.e. the contribution of the offshore currency market).[33]

These, of course, are very rough figures. But they may serve to indicate how trade in financial services might be measured in the relatively straightforward case of offshore currency markets with separate accounts.

Australia. What of the majority of countries, such as Australia, which are not major international financial centres and not, as such, clearly net exporters of financial services?

Two of the main categories of what Australian banks would regard as their foreign business do not give rise to Australian exports of financial services. One of these is most income from foreign exchange trading margins. For the bulk of foreign exchange bought by Australian banks is bought from Australian residents (exporters) and most foreign exchange sold is sold to Australian residents (importers). None of this is business with non-residents. It is true that there were, even before the recent abolition of exchange control, certain exceptions to the general prohibition on non-resident holdings of $A balances.[34] Among them were working balances held by foreign banks and $A balances held temporarily in connection with capital (portfolio and direct investment) transactions which had received exchange control approval. Australian banks, therefore, derive some income from foreign exchange dealings with non-residents in connection with capital account transactions. But this probably accounts for only a small part of their foreign exchange business. Statistically, all bank income from foreign exchange trading, whether with residents or non-residents, appears to be included in the banks' investment income. Special returns by banks would be needed to separate it out, and even the banks themselves would have difficulty in distinguishing business with non-residents.

The second category of foreign business which does not statistically give rise to exports of financial services by Australian banks is the large proportion of such business which is handled by the Australian banks' overseas branches, whether operating as Singapore ACUs or as bran-

---

[33] It is worth mentioning that Singapore has not yet followed the example of Luxembourg in adapting its social accounts to its new role as a major international financial centre. One reason may be that Singapore is not anxious to see an upward adjustment in its per capita income which would hasten the day of its "graduation" out of the category of developing countries.

[34] Since 12 December 1983, this prohibition has been confined to foreign governments and banks.

ches in Hong Kong, London, New York and other financial centres. Such business includes net investment income of overseas branches, income from their foreign exchange trading, commissions on loan syndications, bank charges, fees, etc. Since these branches operate as financial enterprises of the countries in which they are domiciled, their output and exports of financial services enter into the national accounts of these countries. Only their net profits which accrue to the parent banks enter the Australian balance of payments and national accounts. In effect, a large part of the business of Australian banks is analogous to that of Australian manufacturing companies which, instead of exporting their products from Australia, set up subsidiaries to produce offshore. The implication is that part of the net investment income of the overseas branches would, on the SNA treatment of financial enterprises, be included in the imputed bank service charge (i.e. as income from the sale of non-factor services) of the countries in which they are located. But by the time the net profits enter the Australian statistics they have become pure factor income.

This is not to say that none of the business of Australian banks and other financial enterprises is of a character that its output would properly be regarded as exports of financial services. Such exports are of three kinds.

The first is income from explicit charges, such as bank and brokerage charges, fees and commissions, for services rendered by Australian financial enterprises (as contrasted with their overseas branches) to non-resident customers. Such income is recognised in the national accounts as explicit bank charges and in the balance of payments accounts as receipt from non-factor services among current transactions. There is, secondly, such income from foreign exchange trading margins as arises from business of Australian banks with non-residents; as we noted above, this probably constitutes a small part of the banks' foreign exchange trading income and is in the statistics lumped in with investment income. There is, thirdly, net foreign investment income of Australian banks, i.e. income received on foreign assets less interest paid out on foreign-owned deposits, which in the national accounts is at present included in the imputed bank service charge and mostly excluded from GDP. By far the largest component of this is probably the interest earned by the Reserve Bank on its foreign exchange reserves. But Australian banks also hold working balances in foreign exchange and there may be other foreign investment income by Australian financial enterprises, on some of which they earn some interest. All such deposit interest income of banks, as contrasted with loan interest, doubtfully qualifies for treatment as a return on bank (non-factor) services. A central bank, for example, hardly renders services of financial intermediation to foreign banks with which it holds its foreign exchange reserves. But since such receipts are included in the net investment income which is treated as the imputed bank service charge, they should logically be regarded, like interest on consumer loans, as payment for final (not intermediate) products.

Australia is also a large importer of capital. Some of this capital is obtained from foreign banks, and the interest paid on this external debt, by enterprises, governments or households, enters into the net investment income of these foreign banks and, under SNA procedure, into the imputed bank service charge in the national accounts of the home countries of these banks. Such interest income, which at present is included in the Australian national and balance of payments accounts as "property income to overseas", i.e. as factor income, should be regarded as imports of financial services, i.e. as payment for non-factor services of financial intermediation.

Obviously, for none of these components of Australian exports and imports of financial services are adequate statistical data available, and it is doubtful whether in Australia's case the amounts are large and significant enough to warrant the cost of collection and processing. But there may be such trade in financial services in countries which, without being major international financial centres, export or import financial services on a scale significant relative to their GDP or their current account balance of payments.

Conclusions

The conclusions of the preceding discussion of the conceptual problems of measuring trade in financial services may be summarised as follows.

First, the new SNA treatment of financial services which regards the imputed bank service charge as a charge for services of financial intermediation to borrowers is conceptually superior for a closed economy to the old SNA treatment which regarded it as a charge for payments mechanism and related services to depositors. But even on this interpretation, services to household borrowers (personal loans) should be treated as final, not as intermediate, output and therefore included in GDP.

Secondly, in an open economy, even bank services to enterprises must be regarded as final output if the enterprises are non-residents. For countries, such as Luxembourg, where exports of financial services represent a large sector of the economy, it is essential to include the value of exports of financial services in GDP. Conceptually, ownership of deposits is not a suitable criterion for allocation of this output between residents (strictly, enterprises and public authorities) and non-residents, unless there are reasons to believe that the value of financial intermediation services rendered to borrowers is roughly proportionate to their ownership of deposits. In practice, no better statistical measure may be available.

Thirdly, for countries, such as Singapore, where most exports of financial services are provided by statistically distinct units of an offshore currency market, the net investment income of these units, together with their receipts from explicit charges, may be an adequate measure of exports of financial services.

Fourthly, for all other countries, where trade in financial services is not large relative to the economy as a whole, it may not be worth going to the trouble of collecting and extracting the statistics that would be needed to measure exports and imports of financial services. But it is desirable to secure agreement, for such purposes as internationally comparable national and balance of payments accounts, on what, ideally, should be measured. Exports of financial services should be taken to include that part of the net investment income of financial enterprises which is received from abroad, together with explicit charges to non-residents by financial enterprises. Where local banks provide a significant volume of foreign exchange market services to non-residents, it would be desirable to include an appropriate part of bank receipts from foreign exchange trading margins. Imports of financial services, conversely, should consist of that part of (net) interest on external debt that is paid to foreign financial enterprises, together with payments to such enterprises in the form of explicit charges. It is unlikely that the contribution of nationals to the income of foreign banks from foreign exchange trading margins could ever be identified.

Canberra

H.W. ARNDT

[2]

Comparative Advantage in Trade in Financial Services

In the past decade there has been a great increase in interest in trade in services, both in academic and official circles, largely because the comparative advantage of the United States is believed to be shifting towards service trade. But what is almost certainly the fastest growing and possibly the largest component of international trade in services, trade in financial services, has received little attention in this connection. A major reason is that the volume of trade in financial services is difficult to measure. But the very concept of international trade in financial services is elusive and subject to a good deal of confusion. An earlier article has dealt with the problem of measurement (Arndt, 1984). The object of this article is to clarify the concept and to show that the pattern of trade in financial services is as amenable to explanation, in terms of comparative advantage and distortions, as trade in manufactures.*

The concept of trade in financial Services

A country's exports of manufactures consist of that part of its manufacturing industries' output that is sold to non-residents. By analogy, a country's exports of financial services consist of that part of the output of its finance industry, in the form of financial services of all kinds, that is sold to non-residents. Among them are the payment and transfer facilities provided to depositors, including spot and forward facilities in the foreign exchange market, all the services in the long

* The author is indebted to P.J. Drake, R.E. Falvey, H.G. Grubel and C.P. Kindleberger for helpful comments on an earlier draft. The usual *caveat* applies.

chain of intermediation between ultimate lenders and final borrowers rendered by banks and non-bank financial intermediaries, as well as brokerage and advisory services and life and other insurance. These are all non-factor services, as distinct from the factor services provided by capital which generate interest or dividends. Before examining the list more closely, it will help clarify the concept if, to start with, trade in financial services is distinguished from a) international capital movements and property income, b) direct foreign investment in banks and other financial institutions and c) growth of international financial centres.

a) *International capital movements and property income.* The object of trade theory is to explain the location of industries and the pattern of trade as determined by comparative advantage, not the initial factor endowment of different countries and the way in which this may be modified by international factor movements. The theory of international trade, therefore, is concerned with trade in outputs, not inputs, in other words with trade in goods and non-factor services, not with international movements, or with earnings, of factors of production, labour and capital. It is true that, in a general equilibrium model of economic activity, the distinction between factor and non-factor services loses importance because there is little reason for distinguishing between the labour component of value added (a factor service) and labour services purchased as intermediate products from other firms (non-factor services). One can easily think of borderline cases in trade in services, such as the architect from country A who renders a factor service if he goes to country B as a consultant, but contributes to a non-factor service if he does the same work as employee of a firm in A which sells its consultancy services under a contract with its customer in B. But in the context of international trade theory the distinction is crucial. Thus, in terms of the balance of payments accounts, the theory of international trade concerns itself with activity reflected in receipts and payments on account of exports and imports of goods and non-factor services, not with the capital account or with factor income, such as interest and dividends or migrant labour remittances.

The difficulty in the case of trade in financial services is that for a considerable part of their output of non-factor services banks do not charge customers directly but recoup themselves in the form of factor income, *i.e.* net interest earned (interest received on loans less interest paid out on deposits); even their receipts from trading margins in foreign exchange business tend, in banking statistics, to be lumped in with their (gross) interest receipts. This difficulty greatly complicates measurement but does not invalidate the commonsense definition of trade in financial services.

   b) Direct foreign investment in financial enterprises. What is often referred to as the "internationalisation of banking" covers two distinct though interrelated developments. One is the expansion of international business by a country's banks, that is sale of their services to non-residents. The other is the establishment by a country's banks of branches or subsidiaries abroad, for business with residents or non-residents of the host country. In relation to goods, such as manufactures, the distinction between trade and direct foreign investment (DFI) is familiar and fairly clearcut (though even here there are problems in defining "residents"). The theory of international trade seeks to explain the pattern of trade in terms of the natural comparative advantage of a country's manufacturing industries and in terms of barriers and inducements through government intervention. The theory of DFI seeks to explain why manufacturing companies establish subsidiaries to produce their products in foreign countries rather than export them to these countries.

   Conceptually, the distinction is just as relevant to banking as to manufacturing, and it seems desirable to distinguish between a country's comparative advantage in trade in financial services and a bank's motives for going "multinational". In relation to banking, however, the distinction is less familiar and often blurred in the literature, and there are at least two reasons for this.

   One is that in banking international trade and investment tend to be complementary rather than, as in the case of manufacturing, alternatives. In principle, given modern telecommunications technology, one could imagine all international banking services being supplied by one or more banks in a single international financial centre, dealing with customers in other countries directly or through purely domestic banks. In practice, quite apart from the diseconomies of such extreme concentration, banks have always felt the need for a more substantial presence than through "corresponding banks" in major foreign markets for their services. Even nineteenth century imperial banks, engaged in trade finance and other traditional international banking from their home bases in London, Amsterdam or Paris, set up overseas branches, whether to conduct domestic business in the absence of (or in competition with) local banks or for international business, because they felt the need for local contacts and knowledge. In the twentieth century, multinational banking has spread partly for the same reasons as multinational manufacturing, to defend markets against host or third country competition (Grubel, 1983). But in banking, distortions such as those which have given rise to the Eurodollar market and other offshore banking have probably had even more influence on the pattern of trade and DFI than in manufacturing.

The other reason relates back to the problem of measurement. The receipts from exports of financial services and the returns on international investment in financial enterprises are inextricably mixed up in the banks' own accounts and in any national statistics. If it is difficult to estimate the contributions made to British earnings of foreign exchange by exports of financial services by purely British banks trading from London, it is even more awkward for those made by a British bank operating in the Singapore offshore currency market. In principle, the situation in the latter case is exactly analogous to that of a British manufacturing subsidiary in Singapore which contributes to Singapore's export earnings but whose profits constitute an offsetting debit item in Singapore's, and credit item in the British, current account. But since the export earnings, in the case of banking services, themselves largely accrue as interest income, the distinction is harder to maintain.

c) International financial centres. There is a large literature on the growth of international financial centres (*e.g.* Kindleberger, 1974; Reid, 1981). But trade in financial services rarely receives any explicit mention in this literature, even though much of the business of international financial centres consists of such trade and the explanation of the growth of international financial centres is largely to be found in international trade theory. There are a number of reasons for this, apart from the general elusiveness and neglect of the subject.

Some of the interest in international financial centres is in the role of the single world centre, London or New York, as the key or reserve currency centre and lender of last resort of the international monetary system, analogous to the domestic role of the central bank (*e.g.* Kindleberger, 1974, pp. 61ff.). This role clearly has more to do with monetary than with trade theory.

Even when the focus is on the role of international financial centres as providers of financial services, there are differences. Centres are by definition cities, not — with obvious exceptions of city states, such as Hong Kong and Singapore — countries; their external transactions therefore are not necessarily international. In any case, much of the business of the major international financial centres, such as London, New York or Zurich, or even Singapore, is domestic business within the city which does not involve international, or even interregional, trade. More important, all countries have some international trade in financial services, but only a handful have international financial centres.

For all these reasons, the literature on international financial centres cannot be expected to give an adequate account of the nature and determinants of international trade in financial services. But there is enough overlap to make this literature a useful source.

Having decided what international trade in financial services is not, it is time to look more closely at its nature and composition.

Definitions

Our earlier preliminary definition — that a country's exports of financial services consist of that part of the output of its finance industry, in the form of financial services of all kinds, that is sold to non-residents — has several loose ends.

The bulk of financial services consists of services of financial intermediation, lending and borrowing (other than lending by ultimate savers and borrowing by ultimate investors). But international finance also involves the provision of payments and transfer facilities, in the form of drafts, travellers cheques, credit cards, etc., and the sale and purchase of foreign exchange, spot and forward, swap and hedge transactions. A broader definition, therefore, would be trade in paper assets, if this can be taken to include both currency and book entries in bank ledgers (or computers).

This definition clearly includes the international business of security brokers and money market dealers, and of leasing, factoring and other such finance companies. It is more debatable whether one should also include trade in commodity futures or the sale of life and other insurance policies which both combine financial intermediation with distinct risk-cover services. Certainly, many ancillary services provided by banks and other financial enterprises, such as safe deposit, account-keeping, travel, investment-advisory and other consultancy services, are not financial services in this sense, and such services rendered to non-residents would not properly be part of a country's trade in financial services.

For similar reasons, it is not easy to give a precise definition of financial enterprises, and familar problems attach to the precise definition of "non-residents". Do the international transactions of a country's central bank constitute part of its trade in financial services? What about a bank's transactions with its own representative offices or branches abroad, or with an overseas bank in which it has a 26 or 49 or 51 per cent equity interest? But, except for statistical purposes where these fine points have to be settled somehow, there is no need to split hairs. It seems reasonable to assume that the largest part of international trade in financial services is conducted by banks and consists of financial intermediation business. It is the pattern of this dominant component that one wants to explain. It is also for this dominant component that we can put some figures to the pattern of international trade in financial services.

Statistics

The IMF in its *International Financial Statistics* regularly publishes data on international bank lending under the headings of "cross-border interbank claims" and "cross-border bank credit to nonbanks", both by country of residence of lending bank. Table 1 shows totals outstanding at the end of 1978, 1984 and (where available) 1986 for the major lending countries. Between them, these accounted in 1984 for over 90 per cent of the world total.

At first sight, the twenty countries seem to fall readily into two categories, industrial countries with highly developed financial systems and less developed countries with offshore currency markets or surplus petro-dollars. Closer inspection, however, shows this to be an oversimplification. Table 2, which ranks the twenty countries according to the ratio of total (interbank and nonbank) cross-border bank credit (CBBC) outstandings to domestic money supply (M_1) at the end of 1984, shows that there were five distinguishable categories:

1) Industrial countries with relatively small CBBC (USA, Japan, Germany, Italy, Spain).

Comparative Advantage in Trade in Financial Services   67

TABLE 1

CROSS-BORDER CREDIT BY RESIDENCE OF LENDING BANK

$US billion

End of period	1978			1984			1986		
	Interbank	To Non-Bank Borrowers	Total	Interbank	To Non-Bank Borrowers	Total	Interbank	To Non-Bank Borrowers	Total
United Kingdom	150	68	218	345	145	490	527	188	715
United States	97	33	130	324	119	443	397	110	507
Japan	23	11	34	90	37	127	260	85	345
Belgium-Luxembourg	61	48	109	99	74	173	177	114	291
Switzerland	68	24	92	133	28	161	205	49	254
Cayman Islands	13	6	19	83	60	143	102[a]	72[a]	174[a]
Germany	40	34	74	43	32	75	117	61	178
Singapore	22	7	29	69	36	105	131	41	172
France	69	29	98	94	56	150	n.a.	n.a.	n.a.
Bahamas	70	36	106	108	39	147	114	42	156
Hong Kong	12	8	20	60	19	79	133	23	156
Netherlands	36	11	47	43	15	58	63	28	91
Bahrain	15	6	21	38	18	56	38	14	52
Canada	17	4	21	34	8	42	42	8	50
Saudi Arabia	29	1	30	49	:	49	n.a.	n.a.	n.a.
Italy	n.a.	n.a.	n.a.	34[b]	:	34[b]	n.a.	n.a.	n.a.
Austria	7	7	14	15	15	30	24	25	49
Spain	17	2	19	23	6	29	29	8	37
Panama	7	12	19	9	23	32	10[c]	23[c]	33[c]
United Arab Emirates	3	1	4	12	2	14	14	3	17
Netherlands Antilles	1	2	3	4	4	8	3[c]	3[c]	6[c]
Venezuela	n.a.	n.a.	n.a.	6	:	6	4	:	4
Total (excl. Comecon)	842	356	1,298	1,924	761	2,680	2,895	1,001	3,896

Notes: [a] 1985; [b] 1983; [c] 1986 (II).
    Countries with total outstandings of less than $US 5 billion at end of 1984 have been omitted.
Source: IMF, *International Financial Statistics.*

TABLE 2

RATIO OF CROSS BORDER BANK CREDIT TO MONEY SUPPLY, END OF 1984

< 1		1-5	
Italy	0.23	Canada	1.06
Japan	0.37	France	1.36
USA	0.78	Saudi Arabia	2.11
Germany	0.80	Netherlands	2.42
Spain	0.88	Austria	3.75
5-100		> 100	
UAE	5.78	Bahamas	773.4
UK	8.12	Panama	839.9
Belgium-Luxembourg	10.88	Bahrain	875.0
Hong Kong	17.40	Cayman Islands	
Singapore	25.80		
Switzerland	54.89		

Source: IMF, *International Financial Statistics.*

2) Industrial countries with more substantial but moderate CBBC (Canada, France, Netherlands, Austria).

3. Industrial countries (and NICs) with very large CBBC (UK, Belgium-Luxembourg, Switzerland, Singapore, Hong Kong).

4. Booking or reporting centres (Bahamas, Bahrain, Cayman Islands, Panama).

5) Oil exporters with surplus petro-dollars (Saudi Arabia, UAE).

This suggests that, while the countries in the first two categories have been responsible for bank lending abroad more or less in proportion to the relative size of their financial systems, those in the three latter categories have, in one way or another, specialised in international bank lending.

One might suppose that CBBC by countries in the first two categories would be preponderantly to nonbank borrowers and CBBC by countries in the latter three countries interbank credit. This turns out not to be the case, as the figures in Table 3 show. The oil exporters, not surprisingly, lent their petro-dollars almost exclusively to banks. But there were countries in the first two categories with relatively high proportions of interbank lending (Canada, Spain, but also USA and

Netherlands) and countries in the third and fourth categories with surprisingly low ones (Belgium-Luxembourg, Singapore, Panama, Cayman Islands).

TABLE 3

RATIO OF INTERBANK TO TOTAL CROSS BORDER BANK CREDIT, END OF 1986

	%		%
Saudi Arabia	100[a]	Bahamas	73.0
Venezuela	100	Bahrain	73.0
Hong Kong	85.3	Netherlands	69.2
Canada	84.0	Germany	65.7
United Arab Emirates	82.4	France	62.7[a]
Switzerland	80.7	Belgium-Luxembourg	60.8
Spain	78.4	Cayman Islands	56.8
United States	78.3	Netherlands Antilles	50.0
Singapore	76.2	Austria	49.0
Japan	75.4	Panama	30.3
United Kingdom	73.7		

Note: [a] 1984.
Source: Table 1.

This is as far as available statistics take us in identifying "revealed comparative advantage" in trade in financial services and, for all the reasons given before, it is not very far.

CBBC outstandings measure assets of lending banks. Even year-to-year changes in these could be accepted as a proxy for the banks' exports of financial intermediation services only if net lending could be assumed to be proportionate to gross lending and if the latter provided a reliable indicator of the value of financial services provided by the lending banks to the foreign borrowers. This would still leave out of account the value of all other financial services provided by banks to non-residents, such as payment and foreign exchange facilities and all the other ancillary services mentioned before, as well as financial services to non-residents by non-bank financial intermediaries, insurance companies, etc. Until, if ever, the problems of measuring all these kinds of trade in financial services can be overcome, the pattern indicated by CBBC is probably as close as we can get towards identifying the major trade flows.

There is yet another complication. Any attempt to explain the pattern of trade in financial services needs to allow not only for the great variety of such services other than those of financial intermediation services captured by CBBC but also for the fact that international financial intermediation itself covers a range of activities which differ in many respects relevant to different countries' comparative advantage.

Demattè has distinguished five roles and five functions of banks in the chain of international financial intermediation, each requiring specific kinds of expertise and capacities (Demattè, 1981). At the beginning of the chain, banks perform a collecting role, collecting funds from ultimate surplus units almost on a retail scale. At the end of the chain, they perform a final lending role which requires local knowledge of borrowing areas and expertise in credit evaluation. In between, there is the interbank intermediation role which can involve maturity, risk and currency transformation, as well as a "packaging" function (raising funds in certain amounts and placing them in larger or smaller amounts) and a spatial transmission function (funding in one geographical interbank market and lending in another). This classification provides a useful guide to likely determinants of comparative advantage.[1]

Comparative advantage

What determines the pattern of international trade in financial services? In principle, the answer should be found in texbook theory of international trade. The explanations most relevant to financial services will differ from those relevant to textiles, but so will those relevant to cereals and pharmaceuticals. It is, however, important at the outset to emphasise once more that we are concerned with the determinants of trade in financial services, not with those of international capital movements or DFI in banking.

Of course, much of the international business of financial enterprises is connected with international lending and borrowing, so that one would expect important links between the two patterns. But international banks handle purely domestic business in their home and foreign

---

[1] Demattè also identifies a "transmission" role which, unlike the transmission function incidental to financial intermediation, is undertaken, independently of any intermediation, by financial enterprises acting merely as brokers and a "speculation" role presumably on the assumption that speculation by financial intermediaries is, on balance, stabilising (DEMATTÈ, 1981, p. 98).

countries, and the concentration of international financial centres by no means corresponds to the patterns of international capital flows. Shipping services provide an analogy. Shipping industries naturally grew first, and are still dominant, in countries with large foreign trade requiring shipping services; their large home market has provided a natural base for export of shipping services. But there are countries, such as Greece and Norway, which have specialised in shipping and have developed shipping industries far out of proportion to their own demand; and there are countries, such as Panama and Liberia, which have secured a modest foreign exchange income from the provision of flags of convenience. In finance, Britain, the USA, France and Germany correspond to the first category of maritime nations; Switzerland, Luxembourg, Hong Kong and Singapore to the second; the Bahamas and Cayman Islands to the third.

Manufacturing, as we suggested before, provides the better analogy for the distinction between trade in financial services and multinational banking. Trade in manufactures occurs when a firm in country A sells its products to residents of country B; direct foreign investment occurs when the firm decides instead to produce its product in country B, whether for the domestic market in B or for export. The same holds for financial services. The factors giving a country a comparative advantage in trade in financial services, as explained in the theory of international trade, differ from those which induce and enable individual banks to establish branches or subsidiaries abroad, as explained in the theory of direct foreign investment (Grubel, 1983). But here, too, there are links since the conditions which make a country a major exporter of financial services overlap with those which make it a major source of direct foreign investment by and in financial enterprises.

As in the theory of merchandise trade, it will be useful to divide the discussion of determinants of the pattern of trade in financial services into two parts: first, the basic determinants of comparative advantage in a free competitive market and, secondly, the effects of market power and government intervention; or, as it is sometimes put, "natural" comparative advantage and "distortions".

"Natural" comparative advantage

The standard neo-classical explanation of comparative advantage, the Heckscher-Ohlin explanation in terms of different factor endowments among countries and different factor proportions among products, has little relevance to trade in financial services. The reason why countries with abundant capital have a comparative advantage in trade in financial services is not that the banking industry is capital-intensive. It is true that a comparative advantage in financial intermediation has normally developed where there was an initial concentration of wealth, such as to give rise to a domestic banking system and capital market. In all the major financial-service exporting countries, international banking grew out of domestic banking which, in turn, had developed in rich cities — Florence, Amsterdam, Paris, London, New York, Zurich, Frankfurt (Kindleberger, 1974; Reid, 1981). But the source of comparative advantage was not a cost advantage due to abundance of capital but a large domestic market for financial services and consequent economies of scale and development of specialised skills.

Nor, rather obviously, is the extension of the factor-proportions explanation to natural resource endowment which is so important for a large part of commodity trade (Garnaut-Anderson, 1980) of much use here. But it is not entirely irrelevant. Just as a waterfront is obviously crucial to a country's comparative advantage in shipping, so location can be significant for comparative advantage in trade in financial services. Proximity is important at the retail ends of the chain of financial intermediation, both in fund-collecting and in ultimate lending (Johnson, 1976; Demattè, 1981); and Singapore's offshore currency market owes its existence in part to Singapore's time-zone advantage, the fact that its business hours overlap with those on the US West Coast and Tokyo and for an hour or two with London (Hewson, 1982).

But this is something of a *curiosum*. Much more important for a country's comparative advantage in trade in financial services is its endowment with man-made conditions and resources favourable or necessary to efficient performance of financial services. Among the conditions are political stability, including peace and effective law enforcement, economic stability and a good infrastructure of complementary services. Paris is said to have lost its pre-eminence as a financial centre to London when France suspended specie payment during the 1870/1 war (Kindleberger, 1974, p. 61); and the Philippines'

efforts to develop an offshore currency market in the 1970s failed, and
Hong Kong lost some of its comparative advantage in the 1980s, partly
because of political uncertainties. Among aspects of economic stability
sometimes mentioned as relevant to comparative advantage in international financial intermediation is exchange rate stability (Johnson, 1976,
p. 2; Reid, 1981, p. 5; Kindleberger, 1974, p. 7), but this is debatable.
Important elements of a good infrastructure of complementary services
are, most obviously, telecommunications, but also accounting and
specialised legal services. Hong Kong had an advantage over Singapore
in developing loan syndication because it had the requisite legal skills
(Lee, 1986, p. 216).

But however much the Heckscher-Ohlin factor-proportions explanation is stretched, it clearly cannot adequately account for comparative
advantage in trade in financial services, any more than in intra-industry
trade in manufactures, and for similar reasons (Grubel-Lloyd, 1975;
Giersch, 1979). As Corden has pointed out, it makes little sense to say
that "Switzerland has a comparative advantage in watches because she
is watchmaker-intensive... Factor proportions theory refers to factors of
production that are generally available to be used in the production of
many different products and are (allowing for adjustment lags) available
to be used in the production of many different products. It does not
apply to factors specific to one activity" (Corden, 1979, pp. 5, 8).

As in the case of intra-industry trade in manufactures, the main
explanation of "natural" comparative advantage in trade in financial
services has to be sought elsewhere, chiefly in economies of scale
combined with product differentiation (Grubel-Lloyd, 1975; Corden,
1979). In banking, the major sources of immense economies of scale are
the possibility of clearing of debits and credits, and of centralised
decision-making through modern telecommunications technology.
Another contributing factor is the fact that international trade in
financial services is largely wholesale trade (Demattè, 1981, p. 95). In
addition, it reaps economies of scale from a large domestic market, *i.e.*
demand by residents for banking and other financial services. Specialisation, whether or not based on product differentiation, yields further
scale economies and promotes the development of a wide range of
specialised skills.

Economies of scale may be offset by countervailing factors. Local
knowledge is essential at the final lending end of the intermediation
chain and will usually favour DFI (the establishment of local branches
of foreign banks) rather than trade in financial services. For somewhat

similar reasons, there may be diseconomies of centralisation in international banking, and advances in telecommunications technology may be reducing economies of scale in some respects (Kindleberger, 1974, p. 54; Reid, 1981, p. 2).

Individual banks and other financial enterprises may achieve competitive superiority through links with trading and manufacturing companies, through the provision of ancillary (payment, travel, advisory) services and through goodwill based on reputation for soundness and efficiency and on skilful marketing. If these qualities characterise the average, or leading, financial enterprises of a country, they will collectively give the country a comparative advantage in trade in financial services.

Whether product cycle theory (Vernon, 1966) is also relevant to trade in financial services is perhaps more doubtful. Innovations in financial service techniques and instruments have revolutionised international trade in financial services in recent times, but few if any are patentable. Comparative advantage based on temporary technological superiority must therefore be rare in this field.

"Distortions"

So far we have assumed a free competitive market (already somewhat qualified by references to product differentiation and patents). In the real world, the pattern of international trade, in financial services as in merchandise trade, is modified or "distorted" by private market power and government intervention. It is not easy to think of examples of open resort to private market power, in the form of cartels or restrictions on entry, in international finance. It is a highly competitive, though oligopolistic-competitive, industry. But banks are powerful and are therefore often able to invoke the help of government to protect their interests. Governments, moreover, have their own motives for intervention. Private market power is therefore a much less important influence on the pattern of trade in financial services than government intervention. Such intervention can be classified under two headings, barriers to trade and inducements to trade. Since DFI is often an alternative to trade in financial services, and both are often complementary, the distinction between government intervention, whether barriers or inducements, aimed at the one or the other is not always clearcut.

Barriers to Trade. Barriers to trade in financial services, as to trade in manufactures, are mainly protectionist in intent; but some of the protection is of a special kind.

There is, first, straightforward protection of the domestic banking industry from foreign competition. This can take the form of partial or complete prohibition of entry of foreign banks into domestic banking or into the foreign exchange market (as until recently in Australia) or into domestic banking outside the national capital (as still in Indonesia). The instruments of intervention may be licensing (equivalent to QRs) or discriminatory taxation (equivalent to tariffs). There is, secondly, protection of the national monetary authorities (or, in their view, of the national interest) from external shocks or other undesirable market developments. Examples are the use of foreign exchange controls to insulate domestic money supply and the exchange rate from volatile international capital movements or to support an overvalued currency by restrictions on capital outflow, and the often unintended effects on international trade in financial services of domestic monetary and banking policies.

The effects of such intervention on international trade in financial services may be to inhibit, to distort or even to stimulate it. Protection of domestic banks from foreign competition undoubtedly limits direct foreign investment in banking; whether it necessarily reduces the volume of international trade in financial services (*i.e.* the sale of such services to non-residents by domestic or foreign financial intermediaries) is perhaps more doubtful. The use of exchange control to prevent destabilising short-term international capital movements has generally met with limited success, being easily undermined or evaded by "leads and lags" and other devices. The effect of the emergence of grey or black markets is to distort the pattern of trade in financial services, rather than to reduce its volume. In the years preceding deregulation in Australia, the Australian trading banks were not permitted to hold foreign currency, beyond minimum working balances (so they established overseas branches which were able to participate in loan syndication); foreign banks were excluded from domestic banking business in Australia (so they established merchant bank subsidiaries which were able to do everything except to accept deposits) and from the spot and forward foreign exchange market (so, through merchant bank subsidiaries, they promoted the Australian hedge market).

More significant for the growth and pattern of international trade in financial services in recent times than either of these two kinds of deliberately restrictive intervention have been the unintended consequences of domestic monetary policy measures. The most striking example, of course, is the emergence of the Eurodollar market in the late 1950s because British banks were prohibited from lending sterling abroad (so they began to lend dollars) and because the US banks were subjected to restraints on lending abroad and to interest ceilings at home (so they set up branches in London which were free from both restraints).[2] But these are only specific instances of what McKinnon has called the more general phenomenon of "regulatory imbalance" whereby domestic lending by banks is constrained through reserve requirements and other instruments of domestic monetary policy which do not apply to foreign operations (McKinnon, 1984; also Grubel, 1983). The result has been a wholly unintended enormous increase in the volume of international trade in financial services, as well as major changes in the geographic and institutional pattern of this trade, with a much larger role for banks in long-term capital flows than in earlier times (McKinnon, 1984; Arndt-Drake, 1985).

Inducements to trade. Governments have also in some cases offered special inducements to both trade and investment in financial services. The usual method to attract foreign banks, as in the case of other direct foreign investment, has been the use of special tax concessions and exemption from controls, such as reserve requirements, applicable to domestic banks. Examples have been the efforts of many governments in small countries to foster an offshore currency market, whether as in the case of Singapore to strengthen an already considerable comparative advantage in this field (Hewson, 1982) or to conjure a tax-haven industry into existence, as in various West Indies and Pacific island booking centres. Other countries — Luxembourg and Hong Kong are outstanding examples — have successfully promoted a vigorous export-oriented finance industry by creating a congenial environment in the form of "liberal banking laws" (Johnson, 1976, p. 262).

---

[2] KINDLEBERGER (1974, p. 58) mentions that British foreign lending at short-term was stimulated by the usury laws of 1571.

Conclusion

The purpose of this and the preceding paper on trade in financial services has not been to make policy recommendations. It has been to carve a small niche in positive economics for an important but hitherto neglected component of world trade, both in balance of payments statistics and in trade theory.

As regards trade theory, it appears that the theory developed to explain the pattern of trade in terms of natural comparative advantage is as applicable to trade in financial services as to trade in goods. But because distortions of trade in financial services are frequently by-products of policies with other objectives, such as domestic monetary policy, trade in financial services, unlike trade in goods, is not necessarily reduced by such distortions but often merely diverted or even expanded.

Canberra

H.W. ARNDT

REFERENCES

ARNDT, H.W. (1984), "Measuring Trade in Financial Services", in this *Review*, June.

ARNDT, H.W. & DRAKE, P.J. (1985), "Bank Loans or Bonds: Some Lessons of Historical Experience", in this *Review*, December.

CORDEN, W.M. (1979), "Intra-Industry Trade and Factor Proportions Theory" in Giersch (1979).

DEMATTÉ, C. (1981), "International Financial Intermediation: Implications for Bankers and Regulators", in this *Review*, March.

GARNAUT, R. & ANDERSON, K. (1980), "ASEAN Export Specialisation and the Evolution of Comparative Advantage in the Western Pacific Region" in Garnaut, R. (ed.), *ASEAN in a Changing Pacific and World Economy*, Australian National University Press, Canberra.

GIERSCH, H. (ed.) (1979), *On the Economics of Intra-Industry Trade*, Mohr, Tuebingen.

GRUBEL, H.G. (1983), "The New International Banking", in this *Review*, September.

GRUBEL, H.G. & LLOYD, P.J. (1975), *Intra-Industry Trade*, Macmillan, London.

HEWSON, J.R. (1982), "Offshore Banking in Singapore — A Case Study" in *Commissioned Studies and Selected Papers*, Part 2, Macroeconomic Policy: External Policy, Australian Financial System Inquiry, AGPS, Canberra.

JOHNSON, H.G. (1976), "Panama as a Regional Financial Centre: A Preliminary Analysis of Development Contribution", *Economic Development and Cultural Change*, Vol. 24 (2), January.

KINDLEBERGER, C.P. (1974), *The Formation of Financial Centres: A Study in Comparative Economic History*, Princeton Studies in International Finance, No. 36.

LEE, S.Y. (1986), "Developing Asian Financial Centres" in Tan, H.H. & Kapur, B. (eds.), *Pacific Growth and Financial Interdependence*, Allen & Unwin, Sydney, p. 216.

MCKINNON, R.I. (1986), "Issues and Perspectives: An Overview of Banking Regulation and Monetary Control" in Tan, H.H. & Kapur, B. (eds.) *Pacific Growth and Financial Interdependence*, Allen & Unwin, Sydney.

REID, H.C. (1981), *The Preeminence of International Financial Centres*, Praeger, New York.

VERNON, R. (1966), "International Investment and International Trade in the Product Cycle", *Quarterly Journal of Economics*, Vol. 80 (2), May.

[3]

Trade in Financial Services

Fariborz Moshirian

1. INTRODUCTION

IN the last decade, there has been an increased interest in trade in services both in academic and official circles. The Uruguay Round of trade negotiations has also placed a special emphasis on trade in services. The current account balance of payment of some of the OECD countries record trade in a number of service industries including travel, passenger transportation, shipping, shipment, insurance, telecommunication, construction, and financial services. Trade in financial services is one of the service industries which has grown significantly in the last 15 years partly due to financial deregulation, new telecommunication technology, and financial innovations. The international assets of banks, one of the main sources of growth of trade in financial services, grew strongly since the mid-1970s. Table 1A in the appendix shows that international bank lending grew by an average of ten per cent annually over the period 1975–1990.

Despite the growth of trade in financial services, inadequate data in this area has been a major constraint for empirical analysis of this industry. Recently, however, the OECD (1989–1990) has published some statistics on trade in financial services from 1984–1985 which are currently in restricted distribution. While the OECD statistical data cannot be used for a time series analysis, they have opened an opportunity to reassess the IMF definition of various components of international financial services and to evaluate what is traditionally called international financial services. This presents an opportunity for an analysis of the nature of trade in financial services and the ways in which trade in financial services takes place and some of its implications for the recent conclusions of the Uruguay Round of trade negotiations.

The remaining part of this paper is structured as follows: Section 2 analyses the traditional and recent definition of trade in financial services; Section 3 distinguishes between trade in factor services and financial services; Section 4 discusses how trade in factor and financial services are generated; Section 5 considers trade in financial services provided to non-residents by foreign and domestic financial institutions; and Section 6 evaluates the prospect of trade

FARIBORZ MOSHIRIAN is from the School of Banking and Finance, the University of New South Wales, Sydney, Australia.

348   FARIBORZ MOSHIRIAN

liberalisation, following the Uruguay Round, in financial services by dividing the
activities of financial institutions into four separate categories.

2. TRADITIONAL VERSUS NEW DEFINITIONS OF INTERNATIONAL FINANCIAL SERVICES

International financial services, according to the OECD (1989–1990)
definition, comprise of the receipts (exports) from or expenditures (imports) by
financial institutions (banks and other credit institutions) in providing or
receiving the following services:

(i)   Income from direct investments, received and paid. This item has two
       sub-categories: (a) undistributed income; and (b) interest.
(ii)   Income from other (financial) investments received and paid. This item
       has one sub-category which is 'interest or dividends received and paid'.[1]
(iii) Commissions and/or fees received or paid.[2]

The available data on financial services are divided into three major categories:

(i)   Financial services provided to or received from non-residents by all the
       resident financial institutions.
(ii)   Financial services provided to or received from residents by all the non-
       resident financial institutions.[3]

---

[1] The IMF *Balance of Payment Manual* defines other investment income flows as 'dividends on
equity securities and interest earned on bank deposits, debit securities and loans'.
[2] The IMF *Balance of Payment Manual* defines this item as 'the brokerage and commission charged
on non-merchandise transactions, the financial services performed by banks, underwriters, and
finance houses, as measured by the amounts of their charges.' According to the OECD (1990) this
item is derived from the following activities: foreign exchange transactions; international
payments, including the drawing and payment of cheques, promissory notes, credit cards, letters of
credit and bills of exchange; management of cash balances; factoring; operations in securities:
management, guaranteeing and placing of security issues; brokerage, payment of coupons,
safekeeping; redemption; conversions; asset management; fiduciary funds; guarantees and
endorsements; financial leasing; counselling on the reorganisation of firms: takeovers, mergers
etc.; participation in barter arrangements; other financial transactions not elsewhere specified.
Walter (1985 and 1988) defined international financial services and mentioned some of the
activities later defined by the OECD as 'commissions and fees'. According to Walter, deposit
taking in the onshore market abroad and in the offshore market as well as the international lending
activities are the mainstay of generation international financial services. In addition to the above
terms comprising 'commissions and fees', one can include travel cheques and travel-related
services provided by banks, as defined by Walter.
[3] Institutions owned by residents are those institutions located in the reporting country which are not
subsidiaries/branches owned by non-residents. A subsidiary/branch according to the OECD, is
considered to be owned by non-residents when non-residents control ten per cent but have an
effective voice in its management. Institutions located abroad which are not subsidiaries/branches
owned by residents are referred to as institutions owned by non-residents.

TRADE IN FINANCIAL SERVICES   349

(iii) The last category relates the above two categories to all inflows and outflows of capital recorded in the corresponding items of the balance of payments.

In recent years, the direct and financial investment income flows have been referrred to as factor services and/or factor incomes (see Grubel, 1987) as they are presumably provided by capital as a factor of production. However, the OECD (1989–1990) has broadened the definition of 'international financial services', which formerly covered only those activities related to 'commissions and fees', to embrace 'direct investment income flows' and 'foreign financial income flows' for three reasons: (a) the size of the commissions and fees relative to the size of the activities of financial institutions in the area of factor incomes is very small, (b) some of the financial services are embodied in other activities of the financial institutions, for instance, the OECD argues that the bulk of financial services consist of the granting of credit on borrowed funds (an activity measured by factor services); and (c) a number of services are free as they are compensated for by the main activities of the financial institutions.

The distinction between total financial investment income flows and the interest attributed to them by the OECD (1989–1990) has now offered an opportunity for researchers to know the size of the international financial services charges associated with these financial assets and liabilities. This in turn may capture the amount of international financial services which, as the OECD argued, appear to be free on face value and/or be part of the major financial activities of institutions (i.e. lending activities).

3. THE DISTINCTION BETWEEN TRADE IN FACTOR SERVICES AND FINANCIAL SERVICES

The available data in the OECD (1989–1990) restricted publications have certainly provided the opportunity for researchers to distinguish better between trade in factor services and financial services. The data for 1988, the latest data available for this purpose, will be used as a benchmark for this analysis.[4] A number of observations can be made from Table 1 which is constructed on the basis of the available data in the OECD (1990) records.

a. Foreign Financial Investment Income Flows

Foreign financial income flows, as mentioned earlier, comprise both interest received (paid) from (to) foreign financial assets (liabilities) as well as the

---

[4] Please note that the available data for 1984–1988 have very similar growth trends.

350   FARIBORZ MOSHIRIAN

TABLE 1

The Components of Trade in Financial Services, as Defined by the OECD, for Nine OECD Countries for 1988 in Millions of US Dollars*

Country	Income from Direct Investment (1)		Financial Investment Income Flows (2)		of which Interest (3)		Difference between Columns (2) and (3) (4)		Commissions and Fees (5)		Commissions and Fees and Financial Services Associated with Financial Investment Income Flows (6)		Percentage of Total Financial Trade (Columns 1, 2, 5) with Respect to Total Non-merchandise Trade (7)		Percentage of Column (6) with Respect to Total Non-merchandise Exports and Imports (8)	
	R[1]	E	R	E	R	E	R	E	R	E	R	E	R	E	R	E
US	48408 (46)	15882 (20.5)	52840 (50.2)	59746 (77.3)	52129 (49.6)	55901 (72.3)	711	3845	3835 (3.6)	1656 (2.1)	4526 (4.3)	5501 (7.1)	49.3%	39.1%	2.1%	2.7%
UK	22599 (21.4)	13123 (14.7)	76166 (71.2)	75648 (85.2)	n.a.	n.a.			8121 (7.6)	n.a.	8121 (7.6)	n.a.	71.3%	66.9%	5.4%	n.a.
Japan	3750 (4.5)	2001 (3.5)	74837 (89.8)	53805 (94.7)	66358 (72.4)	48808 (85.9)	8479	4997	46861 (5.6)	10028 (1.8)	13165 (15.8)	5999 (10.5)	49.3%	47.5%	4.0%	4.8%
Switzerland	3220 (13.4)	27.3	17604 (73.6)	7433	n.a.	n.a.	n.a.	n.a.	3069 (12.8)	n.a.	3069 (12.8)	n.a.	66.5%	35.9%	8.5%	n.a.
Germany	2723 (8.2)	6362 (22.9)	29595 (89.5)	21269 (76.6)	28582 (86.4)	19699 (71.0)	1013	1570	749 (2.3)	122 (2.7)	1762 (5.3)	1692 (6.1)	37.9%	44.5%	2.0%	3.3%
Italy	221 (2.4)	1620 (9.9)	7102 (78.4)	12553 (76.8)	6553 (72.4)	11923 (73.0)	549	630	1730 (19.0)	2153 (13.0)	2279 (25.0)	2783 (17.0)	21.3%	35.4%	5.3%	6.0%
France[2]	232 (1.1)	162 (0.08)	20383 (91.9)	19867 (91.5)	n.a.	n.a.	n.a.	n.a.	1542 (6.9)	1679 (7.7)	1542 (6.9)	1679 (7.7)	25.2%	28.5%	1.7%	2.2%
Netherlands	5452 (30.6)	12117 (29.2)	12117 (68.1)	11848 (69.6)	9149 (51.4)	7680 (45.1)	2968	4168	198 (1.1)	190 (1.1)	3166 (17.7)	4358 (25.6)	42.6%	41.2%	7.6%	10.5%
Spain	229 (7.4)	2209 (29.7)	2158 (54.4)	3798 (51.2)	2076 (51.7)	3167 (42.6)	109	631	1529 (38.0)	1414 (19.0)	1638 (40.0)	2045 (29.0)	14.6%	41.8%	5.9%	11.5%

Notes:
* The numbers in parentheses are the percentage of each item of trade in financial services with respect to total amount of trade in financial services.
[1] R = Receipts and E = Expenditure.
[2] For France the available data covers only trade in financial services provided to and received from non-residents by resident financial institutions.
Sources: Calculated on the basis of the available data in the OECD (1990) *Statistics on International Trade in Financial Services* and *Bank of Japan: Balance of Payment Statistics*.

TRADE IN FINANCIAL SERVICES   351

associated financial services charges. To the author, columns (1) and (3) can now be considered as factor or capital services and the difference between the total financial investment income flows from the interest attributed to these assets can be added to the item called 'commissions and fees' (column (5) of Table 1), which is measuring precisely what is traditionally called international financial services.

As can be seen from column (3) of Table 1, the amount of interest received (paid) from (to) foreign financial assets (liabilities) is the largest component of trade in financial services. The size of this item led the OECD to include factor services as part of trade in financial services.[5]

b. Commissions and Fees

The amount of 'commissions and fees' (column (5) of Table 1) as part of the trade in financial services is relatively high for a few countries. As can be seen from column (6) of Table 1, once the commissions and fees from holdings of foreign financial assets and liabilities (column (4)) are added to column (5), the percentage of commissions and fees increases markedly for all these countries. It is worth noting that once the size of commissions and fees are adjusted for other financial services incorporated in the foreign financial investment income flows (i.e. column (6)), the percentage of commissions and fees becomes more significant than the direct investment income flows (column (1)) for Japan, France, Italy and Spain. Furthermore, column (8) indicates that 'commissions and fees' are a significant component of the current account balance of some of the OECD countries. This implies that the recent definition of trade in financial services by the OECD, which assumes that the amount of 'commissions and fees' are very small, is not quite justified. Interestingly, the IMF definition of columns (1) and (2) used in the last forty years, as factor services, is not justified either. Given the OECD statistical data, one can now argue that columns (1) and (3) cover the factor services, whereas columns (3) and (4) can be considered as trade in financial services.

Table 2A in the Appendix shows the possible impact on the prices of financial products should the European internal market be realised. This table is prepared by Price Waterhouse (1988) to measure the cost differentials of financial services among the European countries. As can be seen from Table 2A, there are significant variations in the cost of financial services among the European

---

[5] Please note that the data on 'direct investment income flows' and 'other investment income flows' (i.e., the sum of columns 2 and 3 of Table 1) published by the OECD have been compared with those corresponding items recorded in the current account balance of the above nine OECD countries published by the IMF. This comparison shows that, with the exception of Spain's 'other investment income inflows', the recent data published by the OECD are consistent with those available in the IMF, *Balance of Payments Yearbook*.

FARIBORZ MOSHIRIAN

TABLE 2
Percentage of 'Financial Investment Income Inflows with
Respect to the Current Account Balance'

Country	1975	1980	1986	1991
Japan	4.48	3.64	8.14	24.1
Germany	2.14	3.1	4.0	10.2
US	4.8	10.7	11.2	10.3
France	5.2	9.8	12.0	16.5
Italy	3.5	5.0	4.2	8.2
UK	5.45	20.2	27.0	31.0
Switzerland	11.9	12.3	19.6	21.0

Source: Calculated on the basis of data available from the IMF
Balance of Payments Yearbook.

countries. It is therefore clear from Table 1A that private investors will not only take into account the rate of return on their foreign financial investment (i.e. column (3) of Table 1), but will also consider the financial services cost associated with their investment abroad (i.e. column (6) of Table 1). If the cost of foreign financial services is higher than domestic services, *ceteris paribus*, the decision to invest abroad will be affected. Therefore, the model of international 'financial investment income flows' will have to take into account the effect of the cost of financial services as one of the determinants of foreign financial investment income flows. One of the implications of the new statistical data from the OECD (1989–1990) is that one can now distinguish between columns (2) and (3) and hence the empirical results of the previous models designed to measure the determinants of foreign financial investment income flows are no longer accurate enough. Researchers like Kawck (1972), Kenen (1978), Bond (1977 and 1979), and Helkie and Stekler (1988) have assumed that interest or dividends (i.e., column (3)) are the only components of 'financial investment income flows' and hence their models ignored the financial services charges. This meant that their model estimated the investment income flows as products of financial assets and a rate of return. This type of model simply measured an identity and had no significant implications and/or interpretations for trade in financial services.

4. HOW THE EXPORTS AND IMPORTS OF FINANCIAL AND FACTOR SERVICES ARE DETERMINED

Table 2 shows the significance of 'financial investment income flows' in the balance of payments of the seven OECD countries in this study. As can be seen, the growth in international factor and financial services made financial investment income flows a significant component of the current account balance of payment in the 1980s. However, according to the IMF *Balance of Payments Yearbook*, for the majority of OECD countries including those countries reported

TRADE IN FINANCIAL SERVICES   353

TABLE 3
Percentage of Banks' International Assets by Nationality of Banks

Country	1985	1986	1987	1988	1989	1990	1991	Growth Rate[1]
Japan	26.1	32.4	35.4	38.1	38.2	35.5	31.4	9%
Germany	7.0	7.8	7.9	7.6	8.4	10.0	10.3	10%
US	21.7	17.3	14.8	14.6	14.1	11.9	11.5	3%
France	9.0	8.4	8.6	8.3	8.4	9.2	8.8	8%
Italy	4.2	4.2	4.2	n.a.	n.a.	5.4	5.0	8%
UK	7.1	6.1	5.8	5.1	4.8	4.5	4.2	4%
Switzerland	4.0	4.4	4.5	n.a.	n.a.	n.a.	n.a.	10%
Others	20.9	19.4	18.8	25.8	25.7	23.1	27.9	

Note: [1]Average annual growth rate of banks' international assets during the period from 1985 to 1991.

Source: Constructed on the basis of the data from *Bank for International Settlements*, various annual reports.

in Table 2, at least two thirds of the stock of private capital which generates 'financial investment income flows' (factor services) and 'commissions and fees' (financial services) belongs to the stock of their banks' international assets and liabilities. Banks' international assets have grown strongly since the mid-1970s. As mentioned earlier, Table 1A in the appendix shows that international bank lending grew by an average of ten per cent annually over the period 1975 – 1990, yet only seven OECD countries (see Table 3) are responsible for over 80 per cent of banks' international assets. These countries are the main generators and beneficiaries of trade in factor and financial services. As can be seen from the available data, their banks' international assets have increased significantly during the period from 1985 to 1991. Thus, this section will focus mainly on banks' international assets and liabilities in explaining trade in factor and financial services.

The following two major groups contribute to the receipts and expenditures of factor services and financial services: (a) the services provided to or received from non-residents by resident financial institutions and (b) the services provided to or received from residents by non-resident financial institutions. To clarify the nature of some of the financial services generated by these two groups, one may assume that if a Japanese investor borrows funds from the Citibank in New York, the interest payment to Citibank is considered as interest receipts for the US,[6] (receipts side of column (3) of Table 1) and the other financial services associated with this lending will be considered as exports of financial services which is measured by the difference between the total financial income receipts and the total interest receipts (column (4) of Table 1). Alternatively, there may not be an

---

[6] This example is the case of non-resident (Japanese investor) financial services provided by a resident financial institution (Citibank) for the US.

explicit financial services charge to this Japanese borrower, but an implicit cost embodied in the lending rate charged to her. In this case the implicit financial charge may appear in column (4) of Table 1. Note that there may be other financial service activities associated with the assets (liabilities) of non-residents for (from) those resident financial institutions which form either the difference between the total financial income receipts (expenditures) and interest receipts[7] (expenditures) or the separate item called 'commissions and fees' (column (5) of Table 1). It is noteworthy that as bank charges associated with lending activities of investors were considered relatively expensive, the investors have found the international bond market more attractive for fund raising and investment, as they avoid bank charges.

Table 1A, in the appendix, shows the growth in international lending activities and the international bond market. As can be seen, in the 1980s, the international bond market was a very popular market for investors/borrowers. While the ratio of bond financing with respect to total bank and bond financing was 4.4 in 1974, this ratio increased to 32.4 by 1990. As financial institutions are required to be the underwriters of bonds issued, this activity will increase the amount of trade in 'commissions and fees' (column (5) of Table 1), whereas it may reduce the size of financial services associated with lending activities (i.e. column (4) of Table 1). Thus, whether the international bond market contributes positively to the expansion of trade in international financial services (i.e., commissions and fees) remains an empirical question. However, regardless of the net outcome of the amount of trade in financial services, it should be noted that, in the case of funds raised in the international bond market, the interest associated with the buying and selling of bonds will still be part of the 'financial investment income flows' as recorded in column (3) of Table 1.

Furthermore, American residents may also be involved in the import and export of financial services. An American resident who deposits her money in the Tokyo Bank in Tokyo receives some interest which is part of the interest receipts of the US financial[8] income receipts (column (3) of Table 1). On the other hand, if some financial services are rendered to this American resident by the Tokyo Bank, it is considered as an import of financial services by the US (expenditure side of column (4) of Table 1) and an export of financial services by Japan (receipts side of column (4) of Table 1). On the other hand, if the above American investor asks for travellers cheques from the Tokyo Bank and/or that this bank be the underwriter of her company's bond issues, then the financial services charges will be recorded in the separate item called 'commissions and fees' as expenditure of the US (column (5) of Table 1). In addition, if an

---

[7] Column (4) of Table 1.
[8] This is an example of financial services provided to a non-resident (an American investor) by a non-resident financial institution for the US.

TRADE IN FINANCIAL SERVICES   355

TABLE 4
Cross-Border Interbank Claims as the Percentage of Total
Banks' International Assets

Country	1981	1984	1988	1990	1991
Japan	75.0	70.8	80.9	80.9	79.6
Germany	53.4	56.9	69.3	71.6	56.5
US	72.6	73.1	82.8	86.3	87.9
France	61.9	59.5	65.3	67.7	67.5
UK	69.7	70.4	76.3	75.6	71.3
Switzerland	78.2	82.5	81.4	83.4	83.2
Netherlands	75.7	73.5	70.4	73.3	74.2

Source: Constructed on the basis of data published in the IMF *International
Financial Statistics*, various annual issues.

Amercian resident borrows money from the Tokyo Bank, the interest paid will be
recorded as interest expenditure which is part of the total financial income
expenditures of the US (column (2) of Table 1). Note that it is also possible for a
branch of the Tokyo bank in Paris to offer some financial services to an American
multinational operating in France. In this case, export of financial services by the
Tokyo Bank will be recorded in Japan's current account balance and hence the
US current account records a corresponding import in her current account
balance. This type of trade corresponds to 'financial services to foreigners' (yet
resident in France) by non-resident (foreign) financial institutions.

Not all banks' activities are with non-bank groups. Interbank activities are a
significant part of the international operation of the banking industry and hence
they contribute heavily to trade in international financial services. As can be seen
from Table 4, over 75 per cent of banks' international assets for the major
countries is in the form of inter-bank activities. The cross-border *interbank*
claims of Japanese banks relate to the borrowing of funds by the American banks
from the Japanese ones, which in turn will be used by the American banks to
provide exports in financial services. Similarly, the cross-border *interbank*
deposits of American banks held in the Japanese banks are part of the American
banks' international liabilities. These liabilities could well be used to generate
American banks' lending related services and hence exports in financial services.

5. FINANCIAL SERVICES PROVIDED TO OR RECEIVED FROM NON-RESIDENT
BY RESIDENT FINANCIAL INSTITUTIONS

Given the above discussion on how resident and non-resident financial
institutions contribute to the expansion of trade in factor and financial services,
the question to be answered is this: what fraction of imports and exports of
financial services are generated through non-residents dealing with resident

356   FARIBORZ MOSHIRIAN

financial institutions and what fraction through residents dealing with non-resident financial institutions? Table 5 shows the financial services provided to and received from non-residents by resident financial institutions for four OECD countries for which these data are available for the period 1984—1988. As can be seen from the receipts side of Table 5, unlike Germany and Switzerland, for the UK and the US, a very large proportion of their financial income receipts are generated from resident (domestic and foreign) financial institutions dealing with foreigners. The figures from the receipt side in Table 5 reveal that German and Swiss residents (with the percentage of 41.9 and 48.2 respectively) are the largest users of international financial services from foreign (non-resident) financial institutions[9] and yet the British and the American residents' financial institutions are very active in fulfilling the needs of non-residents' for international financial services, (with the percentage of 91.7 and 72.3 respectively in 1988).

The expenditure side of Table 5 shows the percentage of financial income expenditure generated via resident financial institutions as international financial services provided for foreigners (non-residents). From this column, one can see that German and American residents are more active (with the ratio of 46.1 and 58.1 respectively in 1988) than Swiss or, in particular British residents in dealing with foreign institutions outside their countries.

From Table 5 one can argue that even if financial institutions are allowed to invest directly in foreign countries, some financial institutions do prefer to be present in certain countries only. In other words, they are selective in their presence, despite financial deregulation. On the other hand, domestic consumers always have certain demand for factor and financial services from financial

TABLE 5

The Percentage of Financial Services Provided to and Received from Non-resident by Resident (Domestic and Foreign) Financial Institutions with Respect to Total Financial Services

	1984		1985		1986		1987		1988	
	R	E	R	E	R	E	R	E	R	E
US	80	81.6	77.4	75.0	74.5	64.5	74.6	61.1	72.3	58.1
UK	86.8	90.3	85.5	90.0	83.8	87.5	83.0	84.6	91.7	86.2
Switzerland	n.a.	n.a.	49.7	73.4	51.3	67.9	54.0	67.9	48.2	67.1
Germany	36.8	48.3	37.6	44.0	39.7	41.3	42.8	42.4	41.9	46.1

Note: R = Receipts and E = Expenditures.

Source: Calculated from the OECD data 'Trade in Financial Services, 1989 and 1990'.

[9] However, note that not all resident financial institutions are domestic institutions and hence for the UK and the US, one may argue that the presence of a large number of foreign financial institutions operating in these two countries contributes significantly to their volumes of trade in financial services.

institutions outside their own country. Therefore, the next section of the paper will discuss the various places that trade in factor and financial services can take place and some of the implications for trade liberalisation in financial services.

6. TYPOLOGY OF TRADE IN FINANCIAL SERVICES

As can be seen from the above discussion, factor and financial services are heterogeneous products which may be quite distinct from other types of trade in services recorded in the current account balances of the OECD countries such as travel services, shipping services, and passenger services. Sampson and Snape (1985) have divided services into four categories based upon the consideration of whether the movement of the provider and receiver of the service is required between countries and whether or not the principal of comparative advantage can be applied. While some of the service industries may only belong to one or two of the following four categories, international financial services will cover all the four categories discussed by Sampson and Snape.

a. No Movement of Providers or Receivers

Transactions may occur without movement of the receiver of the service or of the factors of production. Sampson and Snape (1985) called this category 'separated services' which is analogous to what Bhagwati (1984) has called disembodied services. Since these services do not need the proximity of service providers and receivers, they can be traded like goods. For financial services (commissions and fees), Walter (1985) refers to a number of international financial services some of which can be placed in this category. For example, financial advisory services to institutions or individuals that involve a high degree of proprietary expertise and can generate larger profits than can be passed on via correspondence from one country to individuals or institutions situated in another country.

Other examples are international trade advisory services, legal and investment advisory services and tax advisory services. This category of trade in financial services belongs to 'financial services provided to or received from non-resident by resident (domestic and foreign) financial institution'. Furthermore, interbank activities are part of this category. Citibank in New York can lend money to Westpac bank (an Australian bank) in Sydney (without having any Office in Australia).[10] This fund can be used by Westpac to finance a project for a

---

[10] If direct transfer of funds is not possible a financial centre such as London may be used for this purpose.

Japanese company operating in Australia.[11] In this process the US will record an export factor and financial services, Australia will record a corresponding import in her current account. This type of trade in factor and financial services, which was overlooked by the OECD (1989–1990) belongs to 'financial services provided to or received from non-resident (foreign) financial institution by resident (domestic and foreign) financial institution'. This category, as can be seen from Table 4, forms a very significant proportion of the trade in factor and financial services.

As early as 1981, prior to financial deregulation in various countries, and as late as 1991, inter-bank loans were a very significant part of international financial services, and hence one can argue that international financial services have grown despite some national financial regulations in the 1980s, thanks to advances in telecommunication technology, offshore and Euro market centres, financial innovations and possibly the expansion of foreign direct investment. Thus, given the magnitude of inter-bank activities, it is not clear whether the conclusion of the Uruguay Round of trade negotiations will necessarily increase the *volume* of trade in factor and financial services, a point already raised by Ryan (1991).

b. Movement of Providers Only

In this example, trade in services takes place because of the movement of the factors of production from the exporting country in the form of capital and/or labour. Thus, there may be direct foreign investment in the form of the movement of physical capital and financial capital. The presence of foreign financial institutions in the host countries and the financial services provided to consumers in the host countries are part of this category. For example, lending activities from an American bank operating in Germany to a German resident can be considered as the movement of provider only. This category of trade in financial services belongs to 'financial services provided to or received from resident (foreign) by resident (foreign) financial institution'. In this case, the interest charges as well as the financial services charges will be recorded as the export of factor services and 'commissions and fees' in the US current account balance respectively. On the other hand, the money paid by German residents for financial services will be recorded in the German current account balance as the import of factor and financial services as well as commisisons and fees.

Note, however, that the protection of domestic financial institutions from foreign financial institutions may prevent foreign financial institutions from entering the domestic financial market, and yet the *volume* of trade in financial

---

[11] Note that, Wespac activities with the Japanese company will be associated with Australia's exports in factor and financial services and Japan's import of factor and financial services. This type of trade will be part of the 'movement of receivers only' discussed in part *c* of this section.

services may not necessarily be affected. For instance, as Arndt (1988) argued, prior to 1985, when foreign banks were prevented from domestic banking business in Australia, they established merchant bank subsidiaries which were able to do everything except to accept deposits. Thus, given the ways in which trade in factor and financial services takes place, one would argue that trade liberalisation may not necessarily increase the volume of trade in this industry.

c. Movement of Receivers Only

Trade in services takes place when the receiver of the service travels physically to the exporting country. Examples of such services are tourism (including business travel), medical services and education. In the case of financial services, this would include those associated with foreign tourist needs such as the purchase of travellers' cheques and financial services to satisfy the needs of wealthy foreigners travelling overseas. If these services (in the country in question) are not provided by financial institutions of the same country that the tourist and the wealthy travellers come from, they will be considered as trade in financial services. The above example belongs to 'financial services provided to or received from non-resident by resident (domestic) financial institution'. Another type of trade in this category relates to clients who satisfy their financial needs from the Euro-markets or offshore markets (or demand financial services from these centres via financial institutions or correspondence).[12] Interestingly, Euro Markets and some of the offshore markets have been created due to the national financial regulations. In other words, while the location of some trade may possibly change in the years ahead due to the successful conclusion of the Uruguay Round of trade negotiations, the *volume* of trade in factor and financial services may still continue its steady growth. Furthermore, foreign direct investment (FDI) in the host countries may be associated with trade in financial services. An American multinational company operating in Australia may borrow funds from an Australian bank. In this case, Australia will record an export and the US will record an import in their current account balance respectively. This example belongs to 'financial services provided to or received from resident (foreign) by resident (domestic) financial institution'. In the case where FDI is allowed by the host country and yet foreign financial institutions are prevented from operating in that country, foreign companies may demand financial services from domestic financial institutions. This will increase the volume of trade[13] generated by the domestic financial institutions. Thus, in a

---

[12] In this case trade in financial services will belong to category 1 (i.e. no movement of providers or receivers).
[13] Provided that foreign companies are neither able or willing to satisfy their financial needs from outside the host country nor able or willing to use foreign merchant bank subsidiaries in the host country.

360   FARIBORZ MOSHIRIAN

TABLE 6
Development in Individual Reporting Market Centres as a Percentage of Total Banks'
International Assets

Position of Banks in:	1984	1985	1986	1987	1988	1989	1990	1991
Japan	5.8	7.7	10.7	13.8	16.3	21.3	20.0	26.6
Germany	3.0	3.9	4.9	4.9	4.5	4.4	5.2	5.2
US	18.9	16.8	14.5	12.2	12.3	9.7	8.1	7.8
France	6.5	6.5	5.8	6.4	6.1	6.6	6.9	6.3
Italy	2.4	1.9	2.9	n.a.	n.a.	n.a.	n.a.	n.a.
UK	22.7	21.9	22.1	21.0	19.6	19.4	19.1	17.9
Switzerland	2.4	2.8	3.8	3.1	2.6	2.3	2.2	5.5
Netherlands	2.6	2.8	2.9	2.7	2.7	2.8		n.a.
Luxembourg	3.9	4.2	4.9	4.3	4.2	4.8	2.8	4.8
Belgium	3.2	3.7	4.3	3.9	3.1	3.4	3.5	3.4
Sweden	n.a.	0.7	0.7	0.8	0.8	1.1	1.3	1.3
Others	23.7	22.0	21.3	21.1	21.3	24.0	20.1	20.4

Source: Constructed on the basis of the data from *Bank for International Settlements*, various annual reports.

deregulated international financial market, to the extent that some multinational corporations may switch to the financial institutions of their own countries now able to operate in the foreign countries, trade liberalisation in financial services may in fact decrease the volume of trade in factor and financial services.

d. Movement of Providers and Receivers

In this case, trade in services takes place when both the providers and the receivers move to a third country where a service is made. For example, the provision of a medical service in country (c), provided to a patient from country (a) by a surgeon from country (b). In the case of financial services one can well consider the example of an American multinational operating in France, borrowing funds from a Japanese bank situated in Paris. In this case, Japan would record the export of commissions and fees as well as capital services in her current balance and the US would record the import of commissions and fees as well as capital services in her current account balance. This category of trade in financial services belongs to 'financial services provided to or received from resident (foreign) by resident (foreign) financial institution'. Note that, in the above example, if an American company borrows funds from an American bank in Paris, services provided will not be considered as trade in either factor or financial services.

The conclusion of the Uruguay Round of trade negotiations prompted some commentators to argue that in the future financial institutions may be based anywhere in the world. However, as can be seen from Table 6, the major OECD countries were the main centres of activity for financial institutions during the

TRADE IN FINANCIAL SERVICES   361

1980s. Whether trade liberalisation in financial services will increase the *volume* of trade in this sector, in particular in the Asia-Pacific region, will depend on whether the financial institutions envisage new opportunities for trade beyond the existing volume of trade in financial services that is already occurring regardless of the various national financial restrictions.

7. CONCLUSION

The OECD incorporates factor services as a part of trade in financial services, as they presume that the size of what is defined as 'international financial services' is very small. However, statistical analysis of the available data on factor services and international financial services reveals that the size of international financial services, as distinct from factor services, forms a significant component of the current account balance of some of the OECD countries and hence should be treated separately from the factor services.

The distinction between trade in factor services and financial services makes it clear that private investors consider, in addition to the real interest differential, the cost differential in financial services between domestic and foreign countries when they decide to invest abroad. Therefore, one would expect that financial deregulation and trade liberalisation in factor and financial services, following a successful conclusion of the Uruguay Round of trade negotiations, would reduce the cost differential in financial services. This would reduce the volume of trade which currently takes place due to the differences between the various national financial regulations and would also increase the volume of trade in financial services due to more financial product differentiation and the availability of greater varieties. In other words, the national financial regulations of the 1960s, 1970s and the 1980s, advances in telecommunication technology, and financial innovations have resulted in an expansion of the trade in factor and financial services occurring beyond national boundaries already, and one would expect that trade liberalisation in factor and financial services would not accelerate the growth of trade in financial services, but would rather increase the consumers welfare because of the availability of more and better differentiated financial products, and a greater variety of financial products.

FARIBORZ MOSHIRIAN

APPENDIX

TABLE 1A

Estimated Net Lending in International Markets — Exchange Rate Adjusted Flow[a]

	1974	1975	1976	1977	1978	1979	1980	1981	1982	1983	1984	1985	1986	1987	1988	1989	1990
(1) Net International Bank Lending	510	550	620	695	785	910	1070	1235	1330	1415	1505	1610	1770	1227	2043	2330	2601
(2) Growth of International Bank Lending		7%	11%	10%	11%	13%	15%	13%	7%	6%	5.9%	6.5%	9%	8.8%	6%	14%	11.6%
(3) Net International Bond Financing	23.5	43	73	102	131	159	187	219	278	336	419	544	700	807	945	1119	1250
(4) Total Bank and Bond Financing	534	593	693	798	917	1070	1258	1455	1608	1751	1924	2154	2470	2734	2988	3449	3851
(5) Ratio (3:5)	4.4	7.2	10.5	12.7	14.2	14.8		17.4	17.2	19.1	21.7	25.2	28.3	29.5	31.6	32.4	32.4

Note: [a]Non-dollar bank credits are converted into dollars at constant end-of-quarter exchange rates, non-dollar bonds at rates ruling on accouncement dates.

Sources: Calculated on the basis of the data available in the *Bank for International Settlements*, various annual issues.

TRADE IN FINANCIAL SERVICES   363

TABLE 2A

Possible Impacts on the Prices of Financial Products Through
Completion of the Internal Market — Per Cent

	Theoretical, Potential Price Reductions	*Indicative Reductions*	
		Range	*Centre of Range*
1. Spain	34	16−26	21
2. Italy	29	9−19	14
3. France	24	7−17	12
4. Belgium	23	6−16	11
5. Germany	25	5−15	10
6. Luxembourg	17	3−13	8
7. UK	13	2−12	7
8. Netherlands	9	0−9	4
EUR 8	21	5−15	10

Source: Price Waterhouse, *The Cost of Non-Europe in Financial Services*
(1988).

REFERENCES

Ardnt, H.W. (1988), 'Comparative Advantage in Trade in Financial Services', *Banca Nationale del Lavoro Quarterly Review*, **1**(164), 62−78.

Bhagwati, J.N. (1984), 'Splintering and Disembodiment of Services and Developing Nations', *The World Economy*, **7**(2), 133−44.

Bond, M.E. (1977), 'A Model of International Income Flows', *IMF Staff Papers*, **24**, 344−379.

Bond, M.E. (1979), 'The World Trade Model: Invisible', *IMF Staff Papers*, **26**, 257−333.

Clark, C. (1957), *Conditions of Economic Progress* (Reprinted, London: Macmillan).

Fisher, A.C.B. (1933), 'Capital and the Growth of Knowledge', *Economic Journal*, **43**, 379−389.

Grubel, H.G. (1987), 'All Traded Services are Embodied in Materials or People', *The World Economy*, **10**(3), 319−330.

Helkie, W. and L. Stekler (1988), 'Modelling Investment Income and Other Services in the US International Transactions Accounts, *International Finance Discussion Papers*, No. 319.

Kenen, P. (1978), *A Model of the US Balance of Payments*, Washington, DC (Heath and Company, Lexington, Mass).

Moshirian, F. (1993), 'Determinants of International Financial Services', *Journal of Banking & Finance*, **17**(1), 7−18.

Moshirian, F. (1994), 'What Determines the Supply of International Financial Services', *Journal of Banking & Finance* (forthcoming).

OECD. (1989−1990), *Statistics on International Trade in Financial Services* (Paris: OECD).

Ryan, C. (1991), 'Trade Liberalisation and Financial Services', *The World Economy*, **14**(3), 349−366.

Sampson, G.P. and R. Snape (1985), 'Identifying Issues in Trade in Services', *The World Economy*, **8**(2), 171−82.

Walter, I. (1985), *Barriers to Trade in Banking and Financial Services*, Thames No. 41.

Walter, I. (1988), *Global Competition in Financial Services* (Cambridge, Massachusetts/ Bellinger).

[4]

Journal of Banking and Finance 7 (1983) 597–609. North-Holland

PROTECTIONISM AND INTERNATIONAL BANKING

Sectorial Efficiency, Competitive Structure and National Policy*

Ingo WALTER

New York University, New York, NY 10006, USA

H. Peter GRAY

Rutgers University, New Brunswick, NJ 08903, USA

This paper deals with barriers to trade in services. More specifically, the paper deals with competition and its absence in the provision of international intermediation services by banks. Section 2 of the paper examines the substitutability of international trade and FDI (foreign direct investment) in the services sector as a basis for international competition. It also considers the overlap between commercial policy measures and regulations governing the entry and operations of foreign affiliates. Section 3 describes the types of restrictions imposed on foreign banks and evaluates their effects. Existing practices in some countries are outlined in the fourth section. The countries are the U.S., the U.K., Switzerland, Australia, Brazil and Taiwan. Section 5 evaluates competitive conditions in offshore banking centers, and compares them with conditions in onshore markets. The last section evaluates the costs and the benefits of an 'open' (free-trade) banking system. Such a system will tend to improve world welfare as well as the welfare of those countries who have a comparative advantage in international banking. The results are not clear with regard to the countries who have a comparative disadvantage in banking.

1. Introduction

Greater international trade and competition in the services sector represents one area in which a substantial gain in allocative efficiency of global resources is still to be achieved. Following considerable pressure from the United States, the General Agreement on Tariffs and Trade (GATT) identified services as a future field of emphasis for trade negotiations among signatories at a ministerial meeting in November 1982. Since international trade in services encompasses a wide range of rather heterogeneous activities, negotiations leading to an amelioration of international competitive distortions will require detailed assessments of national interests, new negotiating strategies and substantial familiarity with the specific characteristics of individual service industries. International competition in banking services, and particularly the treatment of foreign based banks in national financial systems, represents an important dimension of this issue.

*An abbreviated version of a paper was presented at the International Conference on Multinational Banking in the World Economy, Tel Aviv University, 13–15 June 1983.

0378–4266/83/$3.00 © 1983, Elsevier Science Publishers B.V. (North-Holland)

International banking exemplifies a central characteristic of international trade and competition in services generally. Foreign direct investment (FDI) is likely to prove a more important means of servicing foreign markets than conventional channels of international trade.

This paper develops the theme of the substitutability of foreign direct investment (FDI) for international trade, and argues that commercial policy measures and controls over FDI are alternative means of achieving the same goal. This suggests the following hypothesis: a nation's attitude towards foreign entrants into its national banking market will echo the country's position on international trade and protectionism in general. The hypothesis receives some qualitative, evidential support, but it is not proven. Even if it can be substantiated in some quantitative sense, the hypothesis would not be a reliable guide for future business or public policy decisions because of the rapidity of developments in international financial linkages, and because of broader ongoing changes in the regulation of multinational banks and in commercial policy generally.

The history of the great banking houses, dating back to the Italian banks of the fifteenth and sixteenth centuries, illustrates the importance of a direct presence through FDI in the foreign markets to be served. Whereas suppliers of internationally-traded goods have traditionally found exporting a perfectly satisfactory way to compete in foreign markets — with the role of offshore manufacturing activities being relatively recent — pressures for FDI in banking for purposes of business development have always been present. The multinationalization of industry and the integration of international capital markets merely amplified these pressures.

Trade-policy debates have traditionally focused on goods- rather than investment-related issues, and thus have largely missed problems relevant to international banking. With the burgeoning role of FDI in industry and services, the policy environment has changed, and it has become much more likely that distortions of international trade in banking services will be addressed in a systematic manner.

We examine here both the substitutability of international trade and FDI in the services sector as a basis for international competition, and the overlap between commercial policy measures and regulations governing the entry and operations of foreign affiliates. Section 3 of the paper describes the restrictions imposed on foreign banks and evaluates their effects. Section 4 reintroduces the hypothesis and adduces some institutional evidence in its support.

2. Market penetration via exports or foreign direct investment?

The argument for liberal international trade is that it will promote maximum efficiency in the global output of goods and services by allocating production among nations according to comparative-cost advantage. In practice, the argument is limited by the assumptions inherent in the static model on which it is based. With its exclusive emphasis on allocative efficiency, it may understate the damage that can be done by the imposition of trade distortions. In addition to conventional resource-allocation gains, international trade will benefit global production by reducing tendencies on the part of secluded national industries to become 'X-inefficient'. X-inefficiency here implies that firms do not minimize inputs in production or can secure excessive returns (either to labor or capital) over long periods of time. Similarly, industries sheltering behind trade distortions may prove laggard in the introduction of new products and processes. And, in a world characterized by rapid changes in technologies and patterns of demand, locking-in resources to existing economic structures via protection will surely retard national growth.

International trade in the classic sense promotes global productive efficiency because inputs are available in different countries at different opportunity costs. Some inputs may not be universally available and, in the absence of trade, a national market could be deprived of their benefits. In comparison with manufacturing, these inputs in the service industries are more likely to be proprietary, and to consist of product- and process-related technologies and industry-specific human capital. A nation can avail itself of these inputs by having them migrate — international factor mobility and technology transfers are substitutes for trade. Proprietary inputs are most efficiently introduced into a foreign country by multinational corporations (MNCs), which can be viewed as having control over factors of production that are internationally mobile. MNCs achieve their maximum contribution to the private allocation of resources globally when these mobile resources are so located among nations and so combined with local factors of production that the firm maximizes the present value of its equity [Gray (1982)]. The mobile resources involved will tend to be those unavailable in foreign countries except through international trade or international investment activities. The MNC's creation of a production affiliate abroad is responsive to the availability of such mobile factors, since it must overcome the 'costs of being foreign' in competition with indigenous firms in a local environment. The proprietary, mobile assets are 'ownership advantages' [Dunning (1979)].

If international trade and FDI serve similar purposes in improving global allocative efficiency, as well as generating dynamic gains, then measures that inhibit the establishment and the activities of foreign affiliates must have parallel effects as well. Consider a situation in which the advantages of serving a foreign market through FDI or exports are identical. The MNC will choose an approach to serving that market which is less restricted, and hence impediments to investment and trade will be seen as close substitutes.

In contrast, when unimpeded trade would yield a higher expected return than FDI, an MNC will only resort to the latter if the barriers to trade are prohibitive, and vice versa. However, competing host-country firms will be made more efficient by their exposure to foreign competition and the foreign availability of proprietary inputs no matter which way the MNC chooses to compete in the local market.

In banking, we have already noted a natural predisposition to serve foreign markets by establishing local banking offices rather than seeking to provide services from a home base of operations. Thus, we explicitly recognize the substitutability of controls over the establishment and operation of local banking offices by host-country authorities for conventional trade barriers. The presumption is that international trade in banking services, involving the production of a service in one country and its utilization by a client in a foreign country, is unusually disadvantaged by a lack of geographic proximity between the client and the bank [Pastré (1981)]. The existing bank–client relationship in the home country creates a cognitive imperfection that gives the bank an ownership advantage in dealing with the client in the foreign country. The foreign banking office can acquire the expertise on local conditions needed by the client's foreign affiliate. Beyond this, banks are able to provide competitive services to indigenous clients in foreign countries. These include foreign exchange, advisory, money transfer, syndicated lending, project financing, letters of credit as well as consumer banking services wherein a competitive advantage may exist over indigenous banks, based on proprietary technologies, information advantages or operational efficiencies. Foreign-bank competitiveness may also extend to the deposit-gathering and trading functions.

If foreign banks enjoy a proprietary-technology advantage, any impediment to the establishment of foreign banking offices or controls over their freedom of operation in a national market will reduce efficiency in that national market to the detriment of users of banking services.

In banking, then, it is controls over the establishment and operation of foreign banks that will determine the degree to which a national market is exposed to the potential benefits of external competition. And because banks provide a broad range of services, particularly in an advanced economy, it is quite possible that such controls can have selective effects — protecting domestic banks in some activities while allowing free rein to competition in others.

It is important to note that the case for 'trade liberalization' in banking services refers only to the absence of regulations and controls that *discriminate* between foreign and domestic banks. The argument for unrestricted competition does not necessarily support laissez-faire climate in the industry. The financial sector, especially in those aspects in which individual enterprises hold assets in trust, as it were, for clients with consequent extremely high leverage, raises the possibility of serious negative externalities and suggests the need for regulation. Grubel (1977) points out that regulation of banking systems has evolved in response to a tendency of unregulated banking to endemic financial crisis. Similarly, Hindley (1982) in an assessment of the benefits that will accrue from greater international competition in the insurance industry, explicitly recognizes the need for fiduciary regulation. Still, regulation must apply equally to all firms competing in the regulated market in order to avoid unnecessary efficiency losses while retaining the gains in banking system safety.

There exists one dimension of the comparability between traditional commercial policy and FDI controls over foreign subsidiaries that is not exact. Commercial policy is mainly non-discriminatory among foreign nations. Most favored nation (MFN) treatment still governs much of world trade, as a cornerstone of the General Agreement of Tariffs and Trade. In banking regulation, such a policy would be one dimension of 'national treatment' which would neither discriminate among foreign banks by the nationality of the parent bank nor between foreign and domestic banks. The principle of national treatment is by no means generally accepted. The alternative to non-discrimination among foreign banks is 'reciprocity'. Reciprocity implies that a nation accords to each foreign firm exactly the same treatment that the country's own firms receive in the individual foreign country. Reciprocity is analogous to retaliation in commercial policy. By treating the foreign firms as the foreign government treats home firms, a nation may hope to improve the mutual investment climate and will, it is hoped, maintain overall discrimination (or trade barriers) at a lower level than passive acceptance of unilateral increases in impediments to trade.

3. Treatment of foreign banks

Controls over foreign banks affect their entry into the national market or their freedom of operation. Both are of concern only if the treatment discriminates between foreign and domestic banks and according to the nationality of the (parent) bank.

3.1. Entry restrictions

Barriers to the entry of foreign banks vary greatly among countries. At one end is exclusion — the complete prohibition of all foreign banking presence extending even to representative offices.[1] Frequently, such an embargo

[1] Representative offices are the most passive form of foreign banking presence. They may not hold deposits nor make loans, and are useful mainly for developing new business contacts, conveying local market information to head offices, maintaining liaison with correspondents, and for providing a visible presence of the parent bank to the clients. In traditional terms, they can be thought as sales offices which promote trade by referring leads and orders to the parent corporation.

coincides with the existence of a nationalized domestic banking industry in which all private banking, domestic or foreign, is prohibited. More common is some form of conditional restriction on foreign bank entry, normally relating to the type of presence that is permissible and the associated banking powers. Even conditional restrictions are not entirely unambiguous. Within a set of banking regulations and laws there usually exists a discretionary element. In the same vein, policies may mean different things in different situations, and precedent is not an infallible guide to future policy responses.

Reciprocity is often espoused as the most equitable standard for foreign bank entry. However, in practice full reciprocity encounters a number of pitfalls that make it virtually impossible to administer in its narrowest form, and very few countries appear to adhere strictly to such a policy — although many include reciprocity among other factors considered. For example, in drafting the International Banking Act of 1978, the U.S. Congress in effect rejected reciprocity in favor of national treatment, which essentially provides equal opportunity for foreign banks in the U.S. and puts them on the same basis as domestic banks. To apply the concept of reciprocity in its strictest sense would conceivably have required 33 different policies for the foreign banks from the 33 countries represented in the United States at the time. Such a policy would necessarily have been largely reactive in nature, resulting in an incoherent amalgam of petty regulations entirely inconsistent with the objectives of the U.S. banking system.

While reciprocity may be impractical as a policy for large and internationally oriented banking systems, it is still nevertheless frequently used as a justification for various policy actions concerning foreign bank entry. Brazil, for instance, applies the concept to U.S. banks on a one-to-one basis, permitting a U.S. bank in Brazil for every Brazilian bank in the United States. Or suppose the assets of American banks in France were nationalized. It would be very surprising indeed if the U.S. government failed to retaliate against French state-owned banks in the United States. Some countries apply the principle of reciprocity to sub-national units, as do several U.S. states. Japan has denied Texas-based banks permission to establish branches in Tokyo because Texas does not allow foreign bank branches — although there are a number of Japanese representative offices in the state. But most countries seem to favor some form of national treatment of foreign banks once they have overcome whatever entry barriers exist. Thus, the principles of reciprocity and national treatment in fact co-exist and are often complementary. The former is largely negative and often punitive, while the latter is generally positive and constructive.

A study of regulations governing foreign commercial bank entry [U.S. Treasury (1979)] surveyed 150 countries. In addition to 24 former colonies of European powers, 13 countries had no explicit restrictions on foreign banks, and three others prohibited only the acquisition of a majority interest in an existing indigenous bank.[2] Eighteen countries prohibited additional foreign presence, or allowed none at all, and 23 countries limited foreign banks to representative offices.

3.2. Operating restrictions

Operating restrictions on foreign banking activity can generally be classified according to economic impact. First, there are policies that increase the cost of funds by denying or restricting foreign banks' access to certain interbank or central bank credits, or which keep them from accepting certain types of deposits — or any deposits at all. Such restrictions put foreign banks at a competitive disadvantage with respect to domestic banks, and are comparable to tariffs or quotas in their effects. Second, there are limitations imposed on the types of business open to foreign banks. These may take the form of qualitative or quantitative limits on lending activities, and restrictions on offering certain bank services.

Not all regulations imposed on foreign banks are intended to discriminate against them. Even under such circumstances, however, a handicap may still exist. An unintentional differential impact can occur because of differences between domestic and foreign bank operations. For example, some countries set maximum permissible limits on the size of loans made to individual borrowers. These limits are usually specified in terms of the size of the bank's capital. If a bank's local office is treated as a separate entity, instead of on a consolidated basis with its parent, its ability to extend loans to large corporate borrowers can be severely constrained — although direct loans from the parent may be a way of circumventing this problem. Moreover, if local requirements include minimum capital/asset ratios, treatment of foreign banks as separate entities may deprive them of a significant advantage, if not impose a severe handicap. General constraints on foreign bank growth and on certain types of lending, as well as limits on bank profitability, may represent de facto discrimination against foreign banks because (a) they tend to be among the later market entrants, except perhaps in ex-colonies, (b) they tend to have a heavier concentration of their business in the wholesale end of the market, and (c) they often have the potential of attaining a faster rate of growth than indigenous banks. Another unintended discrimination exists when limits are placed, for balance-of-payments reasons, on the repatriation of bank profits. At the same time, 'foreignness' can indeed be beneficial if liabilities denominated in other currencies are excluded from the base used to compute required reserves. Similarly, exclusion of foreign banks from the requirement to make (unprofitable) priority-sector loans or to support government debt issues will have a benign effect.

[2]Respectively, Argentina, Austria, Belgium, Bolivia, Federal Republic of Germany, France, Israel, Italy, Luxembourg, Panama, Paraguay, Spain, Switzerland; and Greece, Japan and Italy.

On balance, foreign banks can probably expect to operate at a disadvantage with respect to indigenous banks in most countries because of intentional and accidental discrimination against them. Sometimes these disadvantages will wane with time. Foreign banks generally seek entry into national markets in the wholesale end of the business, and will pursue activities that have some trace of internationality — either involving more than one currency (e.g., foreign loans) or lending to multinationals. Retail business will tend to become important only after the bank has been fully integrated into the national banking environment. This may give pioneer international banks a competitive edge over new entrants into the international banking arena and over new banks in general. Yet even when foreign banks have long been established as retail competitors, local banks often resist innovations involving new technologies, or innovations that promise to radically alter banking practices, such as automated teller machines and credit cards.

Foreign banks thus operate in one of the most restrictive environments in international trade. Restrictions are justified by the needs of effective economic-policy control, but often reflect strong protectionist pressure emanating from indigenous banks and political pressures relating to national control of the 'commanding heights' of the economy. When countries are indeed opened to foreign banks, it is sometimes only for a brief period for new entrants, and these 'windows' can lead to a mad scramble for establishment before the opportunity disappears. Operating restrictions often severely limit the activities of foreign banks as well, and both types of barriers clearly constrain the efficiency gains to the host country. Yet the restricted competition can itself be highly profitable to those foreign banks that have found a niche in the market. This explains the ambiguity that even the most international of banks have exhibited toward the prospects of aggressive liberalization of international trade in banking services.

4. Benefits and costs of open banking systems

The hypothesis of this paper is that, because of the close substitutability between conventional barriers to trade and restrictions imposed on entry and operations of foreign subsidiaries, a nation's position on foreign participation in its national banking market will closely reflect its posture towards international trade in general. A fair degree of rationality may well be reflected in this behavior, implying informal cost–benefit analysis. It is useful, therefore, to examine the hypothesis in terms of three sets of countries — slowly developing, rapidly developing and industrial.[3]

---

[3]The inclusion of Australia in the rapidly developing category is based more on the degree of protection traditionally afforded to its secondary and tertiary economic sectors than to such conventional measures as economic sophistication, per-capita GNP or literacy rate.

I. Walter and H.P. Gray, Protectionism and international banking   605

Slowly developing countries are likely to be highly suspicious of the benefits to be derived from the presence of foreign banks. They may be seen to impede the effectiveness of governmental policies aimed at economic development by virtue of their size and dominance in the local market, their externally determined business objectives, and their attainment of a possible collective quasi-monopoly in international transactions. Foreign banks' policies may reflect conditions at head offices (or in the home country) rather than those in the host economy [Letiche (1974)]. This is the 'economic policy' rationale for exerting tight control over foreign banks in the domestic financial market. The relevant cost is that the protected industry will tend to be relatively inefficient and slow to innovate and will, in this way, tend to impede economic development.

Rapidly developing countries will be particularly sensitive to the last point. As economic development takes place, particularly when the process of development is export-driven and involves ever greater integration with the global economy, the costs of an inefficient domestic industry will quickly begin to outweigh the benefits of a tighter control over foreign presence in the domestic banking market.

Industrial countries have little in the way of rational argument to warrant restrictions on foreign banks. Foreign banks are unlikely to represent serious challenge to national policies because, even in the absence of such restrictions, they are not usually able to control a major share of the national market. Moreover, local banks in developed countries should be much better able to compete with foreign banks, even in the face of imported innovations and banking practices. Similarly, techniques of central banking, supervision and control, as well as antitrust policy, will be much more highly developed. Hence the efficiency losses associated with restricted banking competition are far more difficult to justify in terms of compensating gains.

The attitudes of the United States, the United Kingdom and Switzerland all reflect countries with exceptionally well developed and sophisticated banking systems. They enjoy a comparative advantage in banking relative to nearly all other nations in the world. Major banks in all three countries are likely to support an open domestic banking environment in the expectation that this will provide a more receptive climate for their overseas affiliates or when they seek to establish new ventures abroad. Given similar advantages in manufacturing, one would expect that affected industries would likewise argue for free trade or, at a minimum, not to seek protection. Banks in such situations see an advantage in a free international banking climate, and are prepared to accept the irritation of enhanced competition in their home markets in order to achieve broader international goals. Perhaps even more importantly, their respective countries see liberal trade as being fundamentally in the national interest, and this clearly extends to the services sector as well as to manufacturing.

Other advanced countries likewise have relatively liberal policies toward foreign banks, although each has its own techniques of bank supervision and monetary control, which may bear differentially on foreign banks. Exceptions include Canada — with the traditional fear of dominance by U.S. banks gradually eroded by strong performance of Canadian banks in the American market and intensified pressure for reciprocity — and Sweden, which since 1955 has prohibited all forms of foreign bank entry except representative offices.

Australia, Brazil and Taiwan provide examples of countries with a history of protectionism and concern for the establishment of indigenous 'infant' industry. But they are now rapidly developing, and the costs of an inefficient domestic banking system are becoming increasingly onerous.

Australia has always been very protective of its manufacturing sector because of an inability to reap economies of scale, high domestic wages, and a consequent vulnerability to foreign competition. Australia's comparative advantage in natural resources and the small size of the indigenous market makes any secondary or tertiary economic activity vulnerable to foreign competition. In the interests of developing a domestic manufacturing sector, Australia has chosen to protect that activity. Its treatment of banking has been quite similar. Recognizing the static and dynamic costs of that protection, Australia had, until a change in government in May 1983, contemplated allowing a controlled level of foreign competition. But at the same time, it is preserving for indigenous banks those markets in which the socioeconomic costs of inefficiency are least — the gains from international competition are perceived to be small — and is likely to limit foreign banks to areas in which Australian banks are laggard in technology.

Brazil has been protectionist in its behavior toward foreign banking since 1964. This is fully consistent with its general stance in commercial policy during the period. Foreigners are excluded except where specific interests are served in key industries. In keeping with its impressive record of economic growth, Brazil has generated a banking system which, although benignly treated by the authorities, is reasonably efficient in serving domestic markets. It is seen as an important policy tool in economic development, and effective control of the system by the authorities is therefore deemed important. Nevertheless, the efficiency losses, seen in the high profitability of Brazilian banking, are quite apparent — as are the prospective gains from liberalization. Whereas this tradeoff is clearly evident in recently proposed shifts in Australian policy, it may still be some way off in Brazill.

Taiwan also supports the hypothesis that a country's treatment of foreign banks is likely to resemble closely its position on commercial policy in general. Taiwan is one of the newly industrializing countries in which rapid economic growth has been achieved in large part by recognizing the costs of allowing inefficient industries to be protected and pursuing an export-led development strategy. At the same time, the need for control over the domestic banking system and an active concern for the viability of certain import-competing sectors have traditionally argued for protection. Yet changed economic and political circumstances have more recently suggested a careful opening of the certain domestic sectors to increased foreign competition. Foreign banks are being introduced selectively. The rate at which new banking offices can be established is tightly controlled, their geographic spread is carefully restricted, and their activities are aimed at international activities.

None of the three countries, unlike those in the first group, has an international competitive advantage in banking services. Hence one would have expected relatively protectionist policies to restrict the entry and operation of foreign banks. Yet with economic development the costs of such a policy became progressively more apparent in relation to the benefits of international competition and specialization, with resulting pressure for policy change.

Slowly developing nations tend to restrict the entry and operation of foreign banks in ways which our hypothesis would suggest. In Egypt, for example, in order to accept local currency deposits, a foreign bank must have 51% Egyptian ownership. Moreover, foreign banks are required to deposit 15% of hard-currency deposits with the central bank, and foreign branches are limited to international trade and hard-currency lending. Domestic banking in India is completely nationalized and establishment of new subsidiaries or branches by foreign banks is prohibited. As a statutory measure, 12% of all bank lending must be to the Food Corporation of India for government food and fertilizer programs at concessionary rates. Taxes are also discriminatory in India, with foreign banks taxed at 75.25% versus 60% for Indian banks. All government and semi-government entities are under 'implied directives' not to deal with foreign banks. Nonetheless, existing foreign banks in India do have a distinct advantage in being exempt from rural branching requirements, and hence from having to maintain the costly rural offices that plague their domestic counterparts. And in Nigeria, local ownership of existing and new bank branches is mandatory under that country's indigenization policy. Moreover, 40% of total advances must be extended to local residents.

Apart from considerations of national interest, such policies are clearly the product of a political process that embodies both protection-seeking activities of domestic banks and the political 'sensitivity' of banking as a critical industry — the fear of a loss of national economic control and sovereignty through the activities of foreign banks. As countries develop, not only do the costs and benefits of protectionism in banking begin to change, but the degree of sophistication in monetary policy and bank supervision rises, so that such fears give way to political self-confidence in the presence of expanded foreign banking.

But even in high protectionist national banking systems, 'windows' of opportunity are often created for foreign banks. We know from the theory of multinational corporations that there are many ways to serve national markets through licensing, turnkey and management contracts, minority equity holdings, joint ventures, technology agreements, and other forms of 'unbundling' the traditional MNC package of services that goes well beyond invested capital. The same is true in banking. A foreign bank may be called in to rescue a failing domestic institution. Or a minority ownership may be coupled to a *de facto* management contract. Such involvements may be highly profitable and, on a risk/return basis, may dominate direct involvement via a branch or subsidiary in a much more competitive national banking environment. This may explain in part why banks have managed to contain their enthusiasm for aggressive initiatives for global banking liberalization.

5. Conclusions

The theory of commercial policy can be applied directly to international banking services, once it has been modified to take into account the tendency of banks to compete via FDI and a direct presence in the host country.

Countries lacking a competitive advantage in international banking services, pressured by indigenous banks and subject to specific social and political goals, will tend to pursue protectionist policies in this sector. These will take the form of quota-like entry restrictions, wherein a given policy, although perhaps clearly stated, may mean different things in different situations — even immediate past history may not necessarily be a reliable guide. Similarly, protectionism may be applied via operating restriction, usually targeted to affect the size of funding costs, lending growth, and profitability.

At the opposite extreme are countries with a clearly established competitive advantage in banking, which tend to favor essentially free competition, and tend to support an open system in the hope of promoting their own activities abroad. The principle of national treatment represents a cornerstone of this approach, although reciprocity may be used to pry open foreign markets.

Whereas the latter group of countries are clear beneficiaries from static and dynamic efficiency in banking markets, countries in the first group must equally weigh the costs and benefits of protectionism. As they develop, this relationship undergoes substantial change, which may give rise to shifts in attitudes toward the appropriate role of foreign banks in the national economy.

There is no doubt that a heterogeneous global competitive environment will remain in the banking sector. The offshore market will continue to set an overall benchmark for competitiveness and efficiency, albeit perhaps with somewhat greater home- or host-country supervision, closely linked to the more competitive onshore markets benefiting from liberal policies toward foreign banks. At the other extreme, some countries will continue to maintain essentially exclusionary policies, while still others fall in-between. Banks will find this a not uncongenial setting, as windows of opportunity develop from time to time, as new and innovative forms of involvement in national banking systems present themselves, and as restrictive policies at the national level create significant profit opportunities by their very existence.

References

Davis, Steven I., 1979, The Euro-bank, 2nd ed. (Macmillan, London).

Diebold, William, Jr. and Helena Stalson, 1983, Negotiating issues in international service transaction, in: William Cline, ed., Trade policy in the eighties (Institute for International Economics, Washington, DC).

Dunning, John H., 1979, Explaining changing patterns of international production: In defence of the eclectic theory, Oxford Bulletin of Economics and Statistics 41, Nov., 269–296.

Giddy, Ian H. and Gunter Dufey, 1982, The legal risks of Eurocurrency deposits, forthcoming.

Gray, H. Peter, 1982, Toward a unified theory of international trade, international production and foreign direct investment, in: J. Black and John H. Dunning, eds., International capital movements (Macmillan Press, London) 58–83.

Gray, H. Peter, 1983, Negotiating freer international trade in services, Journal of World Trade Law 17, Sept./Oct., 377–388.

Grubel, H.G., 1977, A theory of multinational banking, Banca Nazionale del Lavoro Quarterly Review, Dec.

Hindley, Brian, 1982, Economic analysis and insurance policy in the third world, Thames Essay no. 32 (Trade Policy Research Centre, London).

Letiche, J.M., 1974, Dependent monetary systems and economic development, in: W. Sellekaerts, ed., Economic development and planning (Macmillan, London).

Pastré, Olivier, 1981, Multinationals: Banking and firm relationships (JAI Press, Greenwich, CT).

Tschoegl, Adrian E., 1982, Foreign bank entry into Japan and California, in: Alan M. Rugman, ed., New theories of multinational enterprise (Croome Helm, London).

U.S. Treasury, 1979, Report to the congress on foreign government treatment of U.S. commercial banking organizations (Department of the Treasury, Washington, DC).

Is National Treatment Still Viable? US Policy in Theory and Practice

SYDNEY J. KEY

Sydney J. Key, Division of International Finance, Board of Governors of the Federal Reserve System, Washington D.C.

National treatment, which precludes the use of rules that discriminate between foreign and domestic firms, seeks to ensure equality of competitive opportunity for foreign firms entering or operating in a host country. National treatment is a generally accepted principle for international trade in financial services. It is the basis for commitments by the 24 countries belonging to the Organisation for Economic Co-operation and Development (OECD) and for the current negotiations on trade in services in the Uruguay Round of the General Agreement on Tariffs and Trade (GATT). The banking sector provides a useful example for considering national treatment and alternative principles. Under a policy of national treatment, foreign banks are treated, as nearly as possible, like domestic banks: they have the same opportunitie for establishment that domestic banks have, they can exercise the same powers in the host country, and they are subject to the same obligations.

Difficulties in implementing national treatment arise primarily from differences in regulatory structures between the home and host countries. Some of the most difficult problems stem from the lack of agreement among the major industrial countries regarding the permissible activities of

A number of individuals have offered valuable comments and suggestions. The author wishes to express her thanks for their generosity in this regard to Robert F. Gemmill, Edward J. Green, Dale W. Henderson, Karen H. Johnson, James S. Keller, Robert W. Ley, Kathleen M. O'Day, Fernando Perreau de Pinninck, William A. Ryback, Gilbert T. Schwartz, Hal S. Scott, and Gary M. Welsh. The views expressed in this paper are those of the author and should not be interpreted as representing the view of the Board of Governors of the Federal Reserve System or anyone else on its staff.

This paper was presented at a 'Conference on World Banking and Securities Markets after 1992', International Center for Monetary and Banking Studies, Geneva, 15–16 February 1990, and will be published in the conference proceedings.

banks, for example, whether to separate commercial and investment banking. Problems also arise in trying to apply rules developed for the domestic banks of a host country to branches of foreign banks.

The increasing international integration of financial services and markets is making the difficulties in applying the policy of national treatment more acute. At the same time, however, this process of integration is also creating pressures for the convergence of national regulatory structures that would make national treatment more viable. Within the European Community, the principle of mutual recognition is being used to achieve, in interaction with market forces, a single, unified regulatory structure. Such a structure involves removing barriers created even by non-discriminatory differences in national rules, that is, by differences in national rules that do not discriminate between foreign and domestic firms.

But the EC policy of mutual recognition is predicated on negotiated harmonisation of essential rules and on political agreement among the Member States on goals for regulatory convergence. Moreover, the policy is being developed and carried out in the context of a supranational structure to which Member States have already transferred a significant degree of sovereignty. Nowhere outside the Community is there a comparable supranational structure or, with the exception of capital-adequacy requirements for banks, comparable agreement on regulatory convergence. In their absence, one might ask whether the increasing difficulties in applying national treatment and the market pressures resulting from multinational banks operating under rules that differ significantly among countries could lead to a unification of national regulatory structures commensurate with the internationalisation of financal services and markets. In other words, could these forces lead to anything like the result being sought within the Community, although perhaps over a somewhat longer time period than that acceptable within the Community?

All of this assumes that national treatment is the starting-point for discussion of a country's policies towards foreign banks. A policy of national treatment applied, as in the United States, without regard to whether other countries also provide it, is based on the belief that open and competitive markets facilitate a more efficient, innovative, and financially sound banking system, and that the welfare of consumers of banking services in the host country will therefore be increased. A country may also provide national treatment in the hope that it will encourage other countries to do likewise. However, some countries, particularly some of the developing countries, still do not offer national treatment for foreign banking institutions. As a result, in addition to concern about the increasing difficulties in implementing national treatment and the interest in principles beyond national treatment,

366   KEY: IS NATIONAL TREATMENT STILL VIABLE: US POLICY IN THEORY AND PRACTICE: [1990] 9 JIBL

the policy of national treatment is also being criticised for its unilateral character by those who see reciprocity as a vehicle for encouraging more openness abroad.

The first section of this paper presents a conceptual analysis of national treatment and of principles that go beyond national treatment that have been used or proposed to govern domestic market access for foreign firms. The second section discusses the development and application of the US policy of national treatment in the context of the conflicting demands created by the internationalisation of banking and a host-country regulatory structure that differs significantly from that of other major industrial countries. The treatment of non-banking activities and interstate activities of foreign banks that operate banking offices in the United States are used as examples of the US approach. The final section presents the conclusions.

Conceptual Framework

The principle of national treatment

A policy of national treatment, applied *de facto* as well as *de jure*, attempts to provide equitable treatment for entry and operation of foreign banks within a host country.[1] The OECD National Treatment Instrument defines national treatment as treatment under host-country 'laws, regulations, and administrative practices no less favorable than that accorded in like situations to domestic enterprises'.[2] The expression 'no less favorable' allows for the possibility that exact national treatment cannot always be achieved and that any adjustments should favour the foreign firm. The wording is not meant to endorse a systematic policy of 'better than national treatment'. Instead, it emphasises the need for national treatment to be provided on a meaningful, common-sense basis as opposed to a rigid, mechanical application of host-country rules.

1. In this paper, *national treatment* refers to both entry and operation. Thus barriers to entry of foreign banks, such as quantitative restrictions, would be considered a violation of the principle of national treatment. Some use *national treatment* to refer only to operation within a host country and *market access* to refer to entry on a national-treatment basis, that is, without any discrimination against foreign firms.

2. Organisation for Economic Co-operation and Development, *Declaration by the Governments of OECD Member Countries and Decisions of the OECD Council on International Investment and Multinational Enterprises*, OECD, 1984 (rev. ed.). See also Organisation for Economic Co-operation and Development, *National Treatment for Foreign-Controlled Enterprises*, OECD, 1985, for a discussion of the National Treatment Instrument and its application in the OECD member countries.

National treatment has been characterised as creating 'equal opportunities to achieve unequal results'. The legal structure determines whether the opportunities are equal, but the market determines the results. *De facto* and *de jure* national treatment are sometimes distinguished on the basis of 'effects'. But here 'effect' does not refer to the end result of market performance as measured, for example, by market shares. Rather, it refers to the adverse effect that rigid application of host-country rules, that is, *de jure* national treatment, might have on the *regulatory environment* for foreign institutions and thus on their ability to compete. The practical meaning of *de facto* national treatment is illustrated by the discussion of the US experience in the second section of this article.

A conceptual difficulty with national treatment is that the appropriate market for achieving equality of competitive opportunities for multinational banking institutions may be broader than that of a single country. Because such banks compete on a global basis, barriers to international trade in banking services may also result from *non-discriminatory* differences in national rules, such as differences in permissible activities for banks or differences in the types of products that may be offered.[3] National treatment, which is limited to ensuring the absence of *discriminatory* barriers, does not address the problem of practical barriers created by the lack of multinational harmonisation of regulatory structures. National treatment also does not address the extent to which multinational co-operation and agreement is necessary to regulate and supervise financial activities conducted internationally.

Policies, goals, and obligations

Before considering principles that go beyond national treatment, it may be useful to identify the ways in which national treatment and other principles can be applied. First, national treatment could be a unilateral *policy* used by a host country for treatment of foreign banking organisations. As discussed below, with one exception, this is the current policy of the United States. Second, national treatment could be a *goal* set by an individual country, such as the United States, in negotiations regarding treatment of its banks abroad; such a goal could also be adopted in a multilateral agreement. Third, national treatment could be a legally binding *obligation*. Unlike a goal, such an obligation could involve sanctions.

3. In this context, *non-discrimination* refers to the absence of discrimination between domestic and foreign firms. By contrast, in the context of trade and capital movements, non-discrimination usually refers to the absence of discrimination among foreign residents of different nationalities; the concept is similar to that of a most-favoured nation (MFN) clause, under which benefits of any negotiated liberalisation must be extended to all countries granted MFN status.

One type of obligation is *imposed* unilaterally on another country by an individual host country as a condition of entry. For example, if a host country used national treatment as an obligation that a foreign country had to fulfil in order for its banks to be granted national treatment, the host-country's policy would be *reciprocal national treatment*. As explained below, the policy of reciprocal national treatment is used in the EC's Second Banking Directive.

A second type of obligation is *undertaken* by a host country as part of its participation in a bilateral or multilateral agreement or in a supranational structure. In this situation, some type of international body or supranational authority, not an individual nation, would determine whether the obligation had been fulfilled. The OECD Codes of Liberalisation are an example of an international agreement under which national treatment is an obligation, although the Codes do not provide effective sanctions.[4] If the current Uruguay Round of GATT negotiations results in agreement on national treatment as the principle governing international trade in financial services and effective sanctions support such an agreement, national treatment could become a much stronger international obligation among a broader group of countries.

Principles that go beyond national treatment

Various principles that go beyond national treatment, that is, principles that presuppose national treatment and seek something more, have been used or proposed as host-country policies for entry and operation of foreign banks, as goals for treatment of a country's banks abroad, or as obligations imposed by national reciprocity policies or undertaken in connection with international agreements or a supranational structure. Principles that go beyond national treatment include: *mutual recognition, effective market access* and *treatment comparable to that of the home country*. These principles, which are not always precisely defined, can be most easily understood in terms of which country's rules apply to the operations of foreign banks in a host country. Specifically, national treatment and the principles that go beyond it can be analysed in terms of three basic components: (1) *host-country rules*; (2) *home-*

country rules; and (3) *harmonised rules* that apply in both countries.[5] For example, national treatment involves application of host-country rules to foreign banks on a non-discriminatory basis.

Mutual recognition

Mutual recognition, which is the basis of the EC internal market programme, involves both harmonisation of essential rules and, in the absence of harmonisation, acceptance by host countries of home-country rules.[6] Even if rules are harmonised, a further issue is who administers and enforces the rules. In the banking sector, this question is particularly important because harmonisation of rules does not by itself guarantee the quality of supervision. The European Community is using *home-country control*, which requires acceptance of the home-country's administration and enforcement of rules.

Mutual recognition goes beyond national treatment in that it precludes the use of even non-discriminatory differences in national rules to restrict access to host-country markets. Under a policy of mutual recognition, a country might be required to offer treatment more favourable than national treatment to firms from other countries.[7] Mutual recognition, however, cannot simply be decreed among a group of countries with widely divergent legal systems, statutory provisions, and regulatory and supervisory practices. Mutual recognition of rules that differ as to what a country regards as essential elements and characteristics would be politically unacceptable. As a result, a crucial aspect of mutual recognition is the harmonisation of *essential* rules. Moreover, unless sufficient de facto harmonisation already exists, it must be explicitly negotiated among countries. Within the European Community, such negotiated harmonisation is far advanced and will provide the basis for mutual recognition and home-country control for financial services provided through branches and across borders beginning in 1993.

The European Community determined that national treatment (that is, host-country rules) would

4. See Organisation for Economic Co-operation and Development, *Introduction to the OECD Codes of Liberalisation*, OECD, 1987, for an overview of the OECD Codes of Liberalisation of Capital Movements and Current Invisible Operations.

5. For an analysis of the applicability of host-country rules, home-country rules and harmonised rules to different public policy goals and to different forms of provision of banking services internationally, see Sydney J. Key and Hal S. Scott, 'A Conceptual Framework for International Trade in Banking Services' (forthcoming).
6. See Sydney J. Key, 'Mutual Recognition: Integration of the Financial Sector in the European Community', (September 1989) *Federal Reserve Bulletin* (Volume 75) at 591 to 609.
7. In theory, under a policy of mutual recognition it is also possible that if, for example, home-country rules did not permit a broader range of activities abroad than at home, a host country (by relying on home-country rules) might effectively offer treatment less favourable than national treatment.

368 KEY: IS NATIONAL TREATMENT STILL VIABLE: US POLICY IN THEORY AND PRACTICE: [1990] 9 JIBL

not be adequate to achieve its goal of a single, unified market because even though each country's rules would have been applied on a non-discriminatory basis, twelve separate, autonomous jurisdictions with different rules in each would still have existed. An alternative approach of complete harmonisation, which the Community originally used with regard to products, was abandoned as involving too much detailed legislation at the Community level and totally impractical to achieve within any reasonable period.

Within the Community, the approach of mutual recognition is being used as a pragmatic tool that, together with market forces, is expected to result in a more unified, less restrictive regulatory structure. The process is interactive: mutual recognition requires initial harmonisation, and additional harmonisation results from mutual recognition. The expectation, indeed the overall strategy, is that any short-run competitive inequalities and fragmentation of markets created by mutual recognition will lead to pressures on governments for a convergence of national rules and practices that have not been harmonised at the EC level. In adopting the approach of mutual recognition in the financial area, the Community is in effect using trade in financial services to speed convergence of the regulatory policies of the Member States.

Strictly speaking, unilateral recognition is the principle used as a host-country policy, and mutual recognition involves the additional step of using this principle as an obligation imposed on or undertaken by another country. Within the European Community, in certain areas each country has undertaken an obligation to recognise the validity of the laws, regulations and administrative provisions of other Member States. Supranational Community institutions determine whether a country has fulfilled its obligation and are responsible for ensuring compliance. An individual Member State would not be permitted to impose unilateral sanctions on another Member State.

Effective market access

Effective market access, another principle that goes beyond national treatment, has been used in the EC's Second Banking Directive and in the Riegle-Garn bill in the United States, which was favourably viewed by both houses of Congress in 1990 but was not enacted before adjournment.[8] A major difficulty with the term effective market access is that it is undefined and has therefore been used in ambiguous and contradictory ways in the context of international trade in financial services. Effective market access can be defined (1) very broadly, in terms of liberalisation of a host-country's financial structure; (2) less broadly, as *de facto* national treatment; or (3) in terms of measures of performance, such as market shares.

8. See text accompanying Note 20 below regarding the Riegle-Garn bill.

The broad definition of effective market access involves both use of host-country rules and also harmonisation of rules among nations. In this usage effective market access encompasses two elements, namely, national treatment and progressive *liberalisation* of laws and regulations relating to banking and other financial services. Progressive liberalisation is another term that has different meanings. In the OECD, it refers to removing discriminatory barriers over time. In the context of the GATT, it was originally used with regard to developing countries to refer to overall liberalisation taking place over time. Among the industrial countries, progressive liberalisation could be viewed as the equivalent of an informal process of harmonisation. Because the degree of liberalisation in a particular industrial country would be measured against that existing in other major industrial countries, progressive liberalisation would involve an attempt to bring more restrictive structures into rough conformity with more liberal structures.

For example, suppose that a host country provides national treatment, that is, host-country rules do not discriminate between foreign and domestic firms. Nevertheless, the host-country's rules may be so restrictive in comparison with the regulatory framework for banking services in other industrial countries that market distortions and inefficiencies may be created. The latter issue could be addressed by the concept of progressive liberalisation. However, agreement among nations on the liberalisation required by the broad definition of effective market access would, in effect, mean agreement on goals for regulatory convergence in areas such as the permissible activities of banks or the types of products that may be offered.

Progressive liberalisation also differs from the harmonisation being accomplished under the Community's approach of mutual recognition because the latter explicitly includes the harmonisation of minimum prudential standards to ensure safety and soundness. As a result, progressive liberalisation in the abstract, without, for example, adherence to the standards of the Basle risk-based capital accord, could lead to less regulation than might be desirable on prudential grounds. Accordingly, meaningful harmonisation presupposes a consensus among nations regarding the distinction between national rules that have primarily the effect of imposing barriers to trade in services and national rules that are necessary for prudential purposes or for consumer protection. For example, a consensus exists within the European Community that permitting all forms of securities activities to be conducted in a bank or its subsidiary is a positive, liberalising measure.

In another usage, effective market access is defined less broadly as *de facto* national treatment, that is, non-discriminatory application of host-country rules. In this usage, effective market access is just a different label for national treatment, not a different concept. As mentioned earlier (see Note 1), some use national treatment to refer only to operation within a host country and market access to refer to entry on a national-treatment basis. In that case, under its less expansive definition, effective market access would mean nothing more than market access, that is, entry on a national-treatment basis.[9]

A third usage of effective market access involves measuring progressive liberalisation not by the regulatory frameworks of other industrial countries but by measures of market performance of foreign banks in a host-country market. This definition of effective market access cannot be analysed in terms of host-country rules, home-country rules or harmonised rules. The reason is that the definition is based on end results in the market rather than on the type of regulatory environment that is necessary to provide equal opportunities.

For example, figures for relative market shares are often cited as an indicator of openness of markets, that is, whether a host country provides effective market access. For example, the share of banking activity in France accounted for by US banks might be compared with the share of banking activity in the United States accounted for by French banks. But such a comparison does not measure 'access' to the respective banking markets because the relative shares depend on a variety of economic as well as regulatory factors. These include the size of the host-country market, the extent of international banking activity conducted in the host country, the extent of direct investment in the host country by home-country firms, the volume of bilateral trade, the relative skills and expertise of different banks and banks from different countries, and host-country consumer preferences, which might include holding deposits at domestic banking institutions. Only differences in relative market shares that could *not* be explained by such economic factors could be interpreted as the impact of host-country barriers to entry or restrictions on the operation of foreign banks.

Treatment comparable to that of the home country

Treatment comparable to that of the home country also goes beyond national treatment in that it could involve reverse discrimination in favour of foreign institutions.[10] Under this principle, entry and

9.   Whatever term is used for entry on a non-discriminatory basis, there remains the issue of determining whether a barrier is discriminatory. For example, quotas that apply to all new entrants, whether foreign or domestic, could be considered discriminatory if foreign firms had previously been barred from the market.
10.   In theory, treatment comparable to the home country could involve less favourable treatment than that provided for a host-country's domestic banks, but in that event the home country would not seek such treatment.

operation of foreign banks in a host country would be governed by home-country rules. For example, under such a policy, EC banks with US banking operations, would, unlike US banks, be allowed to conduct securities activities in the United States without regard to the limitations imposed on domestic banks by US law. If the principle of treatment comparable to that of the home country is used as an obligation, this amounts to *mirror-image reciprocity*.

Treatment comparable to that of the home country differs from mutual recognition because it does not involve harmonisation of home- and host-country rules. As a result, if, for example, the European Community were to seek treatment comparable to the home country (that is, the Community) for its banks abroad, such a goal could be viewed as the equivalent of an attempt to extend the principle of mutual recognition to countries outside the Community without having established on a more international basis the foundation for mutual recognition that exists within the Community. In the absence of agreement upon goals for regulatory convergence, systematically more favourable treatment of foreign firms resulting from the application of home-country rules in a host-country market would likely be unacceptable because of the resulting overall competitive inequality between foreign and domestic firms.

In practice, however, treatment comparable to that of the home country might be granted in certain limited areas if, for example, sufficient *de facto* harmonisation already existed or the resulting competitive inequality would not be great and would be outweighed by other factors. In such cases, the *host* country might adopt and enforce rules for foreign banks that would in certain respects conform to those of the home country. By contrast, under a policy of mutual recognition, specific rules comparable to those of the home country would not be incorporated into the host-country's legislative framework, and enforcement would be the responsibility of the home country.

Treatment comparable to that of the home country also differs from the broad definition of effective market access, that is, national treatment plus progressive liberalisation of a host-country's financial structure. The latter liberalisation is conducted on a national treatment basis, that is, it applies to both foreign and domestic firms. By contrast, if a host country were to grant treatment comparable to that of the home country, a foreign firm would receive better than national treatment in the host country. In other words, a country pursuing the goal of treatment comparable to that offered at home would be seeking liberalisation only for its own banks within a host country, rather than for the sake of overall efficiency of markets as in the case of progressive liberalisation.

The EC's Second Banking Directive

In its provisions regarding relations with non-EC countries the EC's Second Banking Directive uses three of the principles discussed above, namely, national treatment, effective market access and treatment comparable to that of the home country. The Second Banking Directive uses national treatment and what appears to be the less expansive definition of effective market access as an obligation that non-EC countries may be required to fulfil to obtain national treatment for their banks within the Community. The Second Banking Directive also includes a principle that could be interpreted as either the broad definition of effective market access or treatment comparable to that of the home country. But this principle is used only as a negotiating goal, not as an obligation that non-EC countries may be required to fulfil. The use of the principle as an obligation would have amounted to a policy of mirror-image reciprocity.

The ambiguities in the provisions of the Second Banking Directive regarding non-EC countries arise from the Community's use of the term effective market access in two different contexts. First, effective market access is mentioned in addition to national treatment as an obligation that may be imposed on non-EC countries. The directive refers to a situation in which EC banks in a non-EC country 'do not receive national treatment offering the same competitive opportunities as are available to domestic credit institutions and . . . the conditions of effective market access are not fulfilled'. The EC Commission has stated that the standard will be 'genuine national treatment', that is, *de facto* as well as *de jure* national treatment.

Second, effective market access is used as part of the phrase 'effective market access comparable to that granted by the Community' to refer to a goal for negotiations with non-EC countries. This phrase appears to refer to the principle of treatment comparable to that of the home country (that is, the European Community). Alternatively, it could be viewed as the broad definition of effective market access (national treatment plus progressive liberalisation), with progressive liberalisation defined in terms of the degree of liberalisation existing within the Community.

Treatment of direct branches of foreign banks

In addition to regulatory convergence, two other issues that should be considered in relation to national treatment and the principles that go beyond it are the treatment of direct branches of foreign banks and need for increased co-operation and co-ordination internationally among bank supervisors.

Direct branches of foreign banks, unlike subsidiaries, are an integral part of their foreign parent banks and are not separately incorporated in the host country. Therefore, even under a policy of national treatment, host-country rules designed for separately incorporated entities cannot be literally applied to branches. Provisions recently adopted in the OECD Codes of Liberalisation regarding the establishment of agencies and branches of financial firms take such considerations into account by referring to 'equivalent treatment'.[11] This is defined to mean that rules different from those applicable to domestic institutions may be applied to agencies and branches but only in such a manner that the requirements are no more burdensome than those applicable to domestic enterprises. The OECD's use of the term equivalent treatment serves to emphasise the need for *de facto* national treatment for branches.

Moreover, as applied to direct branches of foreign banks, even the policy of national treatment inherently involves some reliance on home-country rules and enforcement procedures. Permitting branch entry *per se* implies some recognition of the adequacy of home-country rules and supervisory practices. In most cases this amounts to implicit unilateral recognition of only certain aspects of the home-country framework rather than an explicit policy of more general unilateral or mutual recognition of a country's laws and regulations that have not been harmonised.

The differences between subsidiaries and branches are reflected in their different treatment within the European Community. Separately incorporated subsidiaries will continue to be governed by national treatment, while services provided through branches, together with those provided across borders, are to be governed by the principle of mutual recognition and its corollary, home-country control. However, even within the Community, home-country control is not absolute. In practice, the division of responsibilities between home- and host-country authorities may be rather complicated. In general, the home country will be responsible for initial authorisation and for ongoing prudential supervision. However, various aspects of the day-to-day conduct of business may be subject to host-country control on a national treatment basis under, for example, consumer protection laws necessary to protect 'the public interest', a rather stringent standard that has been established by the European Court of Justice. The conduct of monetary policy is an explicit exception to the principle of home-country control, and the host country also retains responsibilities, in co-operation with the home country, for branch liquidity.

11. Organisation for Economic Co-operation and Development. *Decision of the Council amending the Code of Liberalisation of Current Invisible Operations* (10 May 1989) C(89)82.

KEY: IS NATIONAL TREATMENT STILL VIABLE: US POLICY IN THEORY AND PRACTICE [1990] 9 JIBL 371

An important issue that arises because of the special characteristics of direct branches of foreign banks involves capital requirements and what measure to use as the equivalent of capital for such branches in, for example, formulating rules for access to domestic payment systems. Within the European Community, mutual recognition requires that so-called endowment capital requirements for branches of banks authorised by any Member State be abolished. By contrast, under a policy of national treatment host countries typically impose some type of branch capital requirement that is considered equivalent to the capital requirements imposed on domestic banks.

However, some countries such as the United Kingdom do not impose any endowment capital requirement on direct branches of foreign banks. Also, under provisions of the Financial Services Act, the UK authorities have entered into a series of 'understandings' with regulatory authorities in other countries that exempt branches of firms conducting an investment business in the United Kingdom from UK capital requirements, subject to the sharing of supervisory and financial information by home-country regulators with UK authorities. These policies could be viewed as the equivalent of unilateral recognition of home-country capital requirements for UK branches of foreign financial firms.

A further issue involves geographical expansion by a foreign bank that wishes to establish multiple direct branches within a host country. It is clear that if a foreign bank had a subsidiary commercial bank in, for example, the United States, the domestic branches of that subsidiary should be treated in the same manner as those of a domestically owned commercial bank. But, at least with regard to limitations on geographical expansion, the appropriate parallel for a direct US branch of a foreign bank is less clear. Such a branch might be regarded as the equivalent of a domestic branch of a US bank or as the equivalent of the bank itself.

The role of national supervisory authorities

The application of any principle for entry and operations of foreign banks in a host country is facilitated by the informal network of relationships among national supervisory authorities. The increasing internationalisation of financial services and markets has both necessitated and facilitated greater international co-operation and co-ordination with regard to supervision and regulation. To some extent, this process is independent of the principle used for treatment of foreign banks in a host country. For national treatment or any of the principles that go beyond national treatment to be viable, contacts among national bank regulatory authorities are

essential. Such contacts promote both harmonisation of rules and supervisory practices and also trust among supervisory authorities. The latter issue is important regardless of whether rules have been harmonised. Even under the principle of national treatment, but particularly under the principles that go beyond it, a critical element is reliance by the host country on the competence of home-country supervisory authorities in other countries in administering and enforcing rules.

The international harmonisation of rules governing banking that has been achieved to date has been accomplished by bank regulatory authorities in a relatively informal way. For example, the 1975 Basle Concordat, which set forth principles regarding the relative roles of home- and host-country supervisors in an effort to ensure that all banking organisations operating in international markets were supervised institutions, represented an accord reached by the bank regulatory authorities of twelve major industrial countries. It was negotiated under the auspices of the BIS Committee on Banking Regulations and Supervisory Practices, which was established in December 1974 as a mechanism for regular consultation among the banking authorities of the major industrial countries. The revised Concordat, released in 1983, incorporates the principle of home-country supervision of multinational banking institutions on a consolidated worldwide basis.

Similarly, the 1988 Basle risk-based capital framework is an accord among the banking authorities of the major industrial countries rather than a formal international agreement or treaty. Moreover, questions relating to implementation of the capital guidelines or adaptation of guidelines to changes in market practices will be dealt with as part of the continuing work of the BIS Committee. This agreement should facilitate evaluation of capital adequacy of foreign institutions seeking to enter a host country because, for countries that are a party to the agreement, home- and host-country capital requirements will be very similar once the harmonisation of minimum requirements has been achieved by year-end 1992.

Under the approach of mutual recognition being used within the European Community, the role of the banking authorities is even more critical. Mutual recognition and home-country control require *inter alia* that the supervisors of other Member States be recognised as capable. In addition, for mutual recognition and home-country control to be acceptable there will have to be sufficient harmonisation of supervisory procedures and practices beyond the general guidelines set forth for national laws or regulations in EC directives. Co-operation and co-ordination among national authorities will be essential in defining and implementing a reasonable and generally accepted line between home- and host-country control. As part of a longstanding tradition of such contacts, EC bank supervisors meet formally in a *Groupe de Contact*.

The US Policy of National Treatment

Overview

The United States provides an interesting example of the application of the policy of national treatment to international trade in banking services. The current US regulatory structure is both complex and significantly different from that in other industrial countries but, at the same time, the United States is committed by policy and by statute to allow foreign banks to compete on an equal basis with domestic banks in the United States. At present, the United States uses the principle of national treatment both as a policy for treatment of foreign banking institutions and also as a goal in bilateral negotiations. However, with respect to operating as a primary dealer in the government securities market, the United States also uses national treatment as an obligation that it imposes on foreign countries, that is, it has adopted a policy of reciprocal national treatment.[12]

The US policy of national treatment for foreign banking institutions was formally established in the International Banking Act of 1978 (IBA). Although this policy had not previously been established by statute, it has been the US practice towards foreign direct investment in general.[13] Foreign banks operate in the United States primarily through three types of banking offices: agencies, branches and subsidiary commercial banks.[14] Unlike subsidiary

commercial banks, agencies and branches are integral parts of their foreign parent banks and are not separately incorporated entities. Both agencies and branches may conduct full-scale lending operations, but agencies generally may not accept deposits. Prior to the IBA, US agencies and branches of foreign banks were licensed and supervised only by individual states. There was no federal regulatory framework for foreign banks that operated only agencies or branches.

As a result, foreign banks enjoyed a number of advantages over their US counterparts. For example, foreign banks were able to establish full-service branches in more than one state, so long as such branches were permitted by state law. Agencies and branches were not required to hold reserves with the Federal Reserve System. Moreover, only foreign banks that operated commercial bank subsidiaries in the United States were subject to the provisions of the Bank Holding Company Act (BHCA) restricting non-banking activities.[15] As a result, many foreign banks without US subsidiary banks were able to operate both securities affiliates and deposit-taking branches in the United States.

The IBA addressed the issue of parity of treatment with statutory provisions regarding federal and state licensing, interstate activities, non-banking activities, federal reserve requirements and access to the discount window, federal deposit insurance, and ownership and powers of Edge corporations. However, because of differences in regulatory frameworks in the United States and in foreign countries, it was not always possible to achieve exact equality of treatment. The problem was to avoid applying US law on an extraterritorial basis, that is, to avoid applying host-country rules to home-country activities, but at the same time to avoid giving foreign banks in the United States a competitive advantage over their domestic counterparts.

As a result, in enacting the IBA, Congress allowed certain deviations from national treatment that generally resulted in more favourable treatment for foreign banks. The major adjustments involved the treatment of existing and future non-banking and interstate activities. The IBA grandfathered existing non-banking and interstate activities of foreign banks. With regard to future non-banking activities, the IBA applied the non-banking provisions of the BHCA to the direct and indirect US operations of foreign banks with US agencies and branches.[16] However, the statute provided foreign banks an exemption from BHCA rules regarding the separation of banking and commerce for certain commercial, but not financial, activities conducted

---

12. See text accompanying Note 17 below. Only primary dealers, which are designated by the Federal Reserve Bank of New York, may engage in government securities transactions with the Reserve Bank of New York, which carries out the Federal Reserve System's open market operations.
13. International Banking Act of 1978, Pub. L. No. 95-369, 92 Stat. 607 (codified as amended in scattered sections of 12 USC). The term national treatment appears in the IBA only in a section dealing with reports on the denial of national treatment to US banks in foreign countries. However, the term was used repeatedly in the Committee reports and hearings and in the floor debates to describe the purpose of various sections of the Act.
14. Foreign banks also operate two less common types of banking offices in the United States: so-called New York state investment companies and Edge corporations. The former, which the IBA refers to as commercial lending companies, are separately incorporated entities with powers similar to those of agencies. (The non-banking provisions of the IBA that are discussed in this paper also apply to foreign banks operating New York investment companies.) Edge corporations are chartered by the Federal Reserve Board under the Edge Act, a 1919 amendment to the Federal Reserve Act, to engage in international banking and financial operations. An Edge corporation may be established in any state regardless of the location of its owner's other banking operations. An Edge corporation may also establish branches in any state.

15. Section 4 of the BHCA deals with non-banking activities of bank holding companies. Bank Holding Company Act of 1956, 12 USCA § 1843 (West 1989).
16. An example of an 'indirect' US operation of a foreign bank would be a US subsidiary of a foreign affiliate of the foreign bank.

in the United States by an affiliated foreign non-banking company. With regard to future interstate activities, the IBA limited the deposit-taking powers, but not the lending powers, of new branches established outside a foreign bank's 'home state' (see below) to those permissible for Edge corporations, that is, only deposits related to international activities.

Since enactment of the IBA, the question of what constitutes national treatment for foreign banking organisations has arisen in a number of areas. These include capital adequacy standards for foreign banks seeking to establish or to acquire banks in the United States, access to US payment systems for agencies and branches of foreign banks, treatment of foreign banks under interstate banking laws enacted by the states, treatment of securities subsidiaries of foreign banking organisations and the treatment of foreign financial conglomerates. Indeed, the difficulties faced by US authorities in determining the appropriate adjustment of foreign banks' reported capital to take into account differing concepts of capital was one factor leading the United States to pursue an international agreement on capital adequacy.

In enacting the IBA, Congress was also concerned about the treatment of US banks in foreign countries. Although the overall policy of the IBA is national treatment for foreign banking institutions without regard to home-country treatment of US banks, Congress was desirous that such an approach would promote similar attitudes on the part of foreign governments. To this end, the IBA required the Secretary of the Treasury, in conjunction with other agencies, to study and report to Congress on the extent to which US banks are denied national treatment in foreign countries. The first National Treatment Study was completed in 1979, and the study has been updated twice at the request of Congress. These studies have been used as the basis for bilateral negotiations with authorities in those countries where US banks see the greatest benefits from some relaxation of restraints on entry and operation of foreign banks. Under trade legislation adopted in 1988, reports on denial of national treatment for US banks and securities firms will be required every four years, with the first report due in December 1990.

Although at the time it enacted the IBA Congress specifically rejected a policy of reciprocity, in recent years there has been increasing Congressional concern about the competitive position of US banks both at home and abroad. Some of the issues that were originally addressed in the IBA, particularly with regard to non-banking activities, were re-opened during Congressional consideration of banking legislation in 1987. The outcome of this re-examination was, in general, to codify existing Federal Reserve rules and practices with respect to non-banking activities of foreign banks operating in the United States. However, the Omnibus Trade and Competitiveness Act of 1988 contains an exception to the US policy of national treatment by requiring reciprocal national treatment for the granting of primary dealer status to foreign firms operating in the US government securities market.[17]

The primary dealer legislation requires that the Federal Reserve determine whether US firms are granted 'the same competitive opportunities' as are available to domestic firms in the foreign country's government debt market, in other words, whether US firms are granted *de facto* national treatment. A country's failure to meet this obligation would result in a denial or revocation of primary dealer status for firms from that country in the United States.[18] In implementing this provision, the Federal Reserve made a judgment as to what constitutes *de facto* national treatment in foreign countries on much the same basis as the United States has itself defined *de facto* national treatment for foreign banks operating in the United States.[19]

In June 1990 the Senate Banking Committee approved a bill that would change the overall US policy of national treatment for foreign banking and securities firms from national treatment to reciprocal national treatment.[20] Both houses of Congress viewed the bill favourably, but it was not enacted prior to adjournment. It is expected that similar legislation will be introduced in the next Congress. The bill would have required foreign countries to grant US banks and securities firms 'the same competitive opportunities (including effective market access)' as are available to the country's domestic banks. The section-by-section analysis of the bill prepared by the committee in effect equated 'same competitive opportunities' (the primary dealer language), 'national treatment to ensure equality of competitive opportunity', '*de facto* national treatment' and 'effective market access'.[21] Thus effective market access appears to have been used in its less expansive definition as *de facto* national treatment.

Non-banking activities

Congress found it particularly difficult to define the policy of national treatment with respect to non-

17. Omnibus Trade and Competitiveness Act of 1988, 22 USC §§ 5341 to 5342 (1988).
18. Grandfathering was provided for primary dealers designated or acquired by foreign banks prior to 31 July 1987.
19. See Federal Reserve press release, 22 August 1989, and 'Primary Dealers Act of 1988', memorandum from the staff to the Board of Governors of the Federal Reserve System, 16 August 1989. See also 'Switzerland and the Primary Dealers' Act', memorandum from the staff to the Board of Governors of the Federal Reserve System, 22 November 1989.
20. S. 2028, as reported 13 July 1990, Senate Report 797, 101st Cong. 2d Sess. (1990).
21. US Senate, Committee on Banking, Housing, and Urban Affairs, The Fair Trade in Financial Services Act of 1990, Senate Report 797, 101st Cong. 2d Sess. (1990).

banking investments in the United States by foreign banks and their non-banking affiliates. US rules for activities that are permissible for banks and affiliated companies are established primarily by the Glass-Steagall Act and the BHCA.[22] The Glass-Steagall Act separated commercial and investment banking by generally prohibiting a bank or its affiliated company from underwriting or dealing in 'ineligible' securities.[23] The BHCA established the further principle of separating banking and commercial activities by generally prohibiting a bank holding company from engaging directly, or indirectly through a subsidiary, in non-banking activities and by restricting investments in non-banking companies to not more than 5 per cent of the voting shares.

The BHCA provides an exemption from this prohibition for activities determined by the Federal Reserve Board to be 'closely related to banking', although application or prior notice to the Board is required to engage in such activities.[24] Companies whose activities are not considered closely related to banking include not only commercial enterprises but also full-service securities firms and insurance companies. Within the restrictive statutory limitations of the Glass-Steagall Act on domestic securities activities of US banks and their affiliates, in 1989 the Federal Reserve Board authorised so-called section 20 subsidiaries of bank holding companies to engage to a limited extent in underwriting and dealing in debt and equity securities on

the basis that such subsidiaries are not 'engaged principally' in securities activities.[25] However, with regard to insurance activities, the BHCA, as amended by the Garn-St Germain Act, specifically prohibits US bank holding companies from engaging in most insurance activities in the United States and thereby precludes the Federal Reserve Board from determining that insurance activities are closely related to banking.[26]

By contrast, in many foreign countries banks may engage directly or indirectly in securities activities, and affiliations between banks and other financial or commercial enterprises are not prohibited. For example, the EC's Second Banking Directive does not place any restrictions on the type of company that may own or be affiliated with a bank through a holding company structure, although it does place limitations (in terms of a percentage of bank capital) on bank investments in non-financial enterprises. Insurance companies are considered non-financial firms under EC law, but the directive permits Member States to exempt insurance companies from these limitations.

The goal of achieving parity in treatment between domestic and foreign banking organisations in individual host countries has been further recognised by US law in that US banking organisations operating abroad are not subject to the same restrictions that apply domestically. In order to enable US banking organisations to compete more effectively with foreign banking organisations outside the United States, Congress gave the Federal Reserve Board the authority to approve certain exemptions for foreign activities that are not available for domestic activities.[27] Through bank holding companies and Edge corporations, US

22. Sections 16, 20, 21 and 32 of the Banking Act of 1933, 48 Stat. 162 (codified at 12 USC §§ 24, 377, 378, 78, respectively), are collectively known as the Glass-Steagall Act.

23. 'Ineligible' securities as used in this context include most debt and equity securities other than US and Canadian government securities.

24. The exemption is set forth in section 4(c)(8) of the BHCA. The activities that the Board has determined to be closely related to banking are listed in Regulation Y, Bank Holding Companies and Change in Bank Control, 12 CFR § 225.25 (1990).

The US statutory and regulatory structure for banks and bank holding companies is complex. The BHCA, which is implemented by the Federal Reserve Board, covers bank holding companies and their non-bank subsidiaries, but not the direct activities of banks themselves. The BHCA generally defines banks as institutions that (1) make commercial loans and accept transaction accounts, or (2) accept insured deposits.

Specific powers of banks depend on the bank's chartering authority (individual states for state-chartered banks and the Comptroller of the Currency for national, that is, federally chartered, banks), on federal statutes such as the Federal Reserve Act and the Glass-Steagall Act, and on rules established by the bank's primary federal regulator. The Federal Reserve is the primary regulator for state-chartered member banks, the Federal Deposit Insurance Corporation for state-chartered non-member banks, and the Comptroller of the Currency for national banks. However, the Federal Reserve also has authority over some foreign activities of national banks.

25. *J. P. Morgan & Co. Incorporated et al.*, 75 *Federal Reserve Bulletin* 192 (March 1989). See also Federal Reserve System, Review of Restrictions on Director and Employee Interlocks, Cross-Marketing Activities and the Purchase and Sale of US Government Agency Securities, Request for Public Comment, 55 *Fed. Reg.* 28,295 (10 July 1990). 'Section 20' refers to a section of the Glass-Steagall Act that provides that member banks may not be affiliated with companies that are 'engaged principally' in underwriting or public sale of ineligible securities. Although section 20 does not technically apply to non-member banks or to foreign banks operating only branches or agencies in the United States, the Board has used the BHCA to apply the same restrictions to affiliates of non-member banks that are subsidiaries of bank holding companies and to affiliates of US agencies and branches of foreign banks.

26. Section 4(c)(8) of the BHCA, as amended by the Garn-St Germain Depository Institutions Act of 1982, Pub. L. No. 97-320, § 601, 96 Stat. 1536. States, however, may set their own rules for powers of state-chartered banks. For example, in 1990 Delaware enacted legislation that would permit banks chartered in Delaware to conduct most insurance activities outside Delaware and limited insurance activities within Delaware (see Note 39 below).

27. Section 4(c)(13) of the BHCA and sections 25 and 25(a) of the Federal Reserve Act, 12 USC §§ 601 to 632 (1988).

banking organisations may engage abroad in any of the activities listed in the Board's Regulation K.[28] This list is broader than the domestic list of activities permissible for bank holding companies contained in the Board's Regulation Y. Under Regulation K, the standard for engaging in an activity abroad is whether it is 'usual' in connection with the business of banking or other financial operations in the host country and not inconsistent with US supervisory standards.

Abroad, subsidiaries of US banks and bank holding companies may engage in underwriting and dealing in debt and equity securities, subject to certain prudential limitations, such as those on the exposure to any single issuer of securities. By contrast, in the United States, underwriting and dealing in 'ineligible' debt and equity securities may only be conducted in a subsidiary of the bank holding company and may not account for more than 10 per cent of the subsidiary's revenues. Moreoover, such a subsidiary may not be funded by its affiliated bank and is subject to numerous other prudential restrictions (so-called firewalls) designed to insulate the securities subsidiary from the bank.[29] Although branches of US banks abroad are prohibited from underwriting or dealing in non-governmental securities, they are permitted to engage in some activities that are not permitted domestically, such as issuing guarantees.

The difference between foreign and domestic powers of US banks, which results from defining the powers of US banking organisations operating abroad partly on the basis of activities that are permissible in the host country, enables US banks to take advantage of national treatment offered by foreign countries to the extent determined to be consistent with US supervisory standards. This approach is consistent with the US goal of obtaining national treatment for its banks abroad; without different rules for foreign and domestic operations of US banking organisations, US banks would not

be able to compete on an equal basis in the host country. This difference is a necessary result of the internationalisation of banking, divergent regulatory structures in the United States and abroad and a governing principle that treats each country in the world as a separate playing field with national treatment accorded to foreign banks within each single host-country market.

In enacting the IBA, Congress also faced the problem of different regulatory structures in the United States and abroad. Defining de facto national treatment for foreign banks operating in the United States required a balancing of two potentially conflicting goals: (1) avoiding the extraterritorial application of US law, that is, the application of host-country rules to home-country activities; and (2) not giving foreign banks a competitive advantage over their domestic counterparts in the conduct of non-banking activities in the United States. Congress made different judgments as to the appropriate balancing of these factors depending upon the extent of the foreign bank's US non-banking operations, the degree of control the foreign bank exercised over foreign affiliates conducting non-banking operations in the United States and whether the US operations involved commercial/industrial activities or securities and other non-banking financial activities.

The situation most easily addressed arose when a foreign bank became subject to the BHCA because of its US banking operations but neither the bank nor its foreign affiliates conducted non-banking operations in the United States. Under a strict policy of national treatment, such a foreign banking organisation, like domestic institutions, would need Board approval for most activities conducted abroad even if the foreign activities did not extend into the United States. Clearly, an adjustment was needed to limit the extraterritorial aspect of a literal policy of national treatment. Accordingly, the BHCA requirements for notice or approval are not applied to the non-US activities of 'qualifying foreign banking organisations'.[30]

The most difficult situation to address arose when a foreign bank with US banking operations also engaged in activities in the United States that would not be permissible for domestic bank holding companies. If a foreign bank or its affiliate had a greater than 5 per cent ownership interest in a US company engaging in such activities, de jure national treatment would require that the US non-banking operations be divested, that such activities be conformed to those on the Regulation Y list of domestically permissible activities closely related to banking, or that the foreign bank refrain from operating banking offices in the United States. If this result were to be avoided, host-country (US) rules would need to be modified significantly to take

---

28.   This list, established under the authority of section 4(c)(13) of the BHCA and sections 25 and 25(a) of the Federal Reserve Act, is set forth in Regulation K, International Banking Operations, 12 CFR § 211.5(d) (1990). Additional activities may be approved by order. See also Federal Reserve System, Regulation K – International Banking Operations, Proposed Rule, 55 Fed. Reg. 32,424 (9 August 1990).

29.   In January 1989 the Board determined that underwriting and dealing in both debt and equity securities would be permissible activities for section 20 subsidiaries if conducted subject to proper controls and procedures (see Note 25 above). The Board authorised debt securities activities to begin in 1989, but postponed authorisation of equity securities activities, pending reviews of policies and procedures of individual companies. In September 1990 such authorisation was granted for J. P. Morgan & Co. As of this writing (November 1990), reviews for other companies have not yet been completed. In July 1990 the Board issued a proposal to relax certain of the firewalls (see Note 25 above).

30.   See Note 34 below and accompanying text regarding 'qualifying foreign banking organisations' (QFBOs).

account of home-country rules. As discussed below, because of different levels of concern about the competitive impact on domestic markets, different solutions were adopted for commercial/industrial activities, and for securities and other non-banking financial activities.

Prior to the IBA, the non-banking provisions of the BHCA applied only to foreign banks with subsidiary commercial banks in the United States. A 'foreign bank holding company' exemption was provided by the Federal Reserve Board's regulations under the BHCA.[31] In the absence of this exemption a foreign bank with a subsidiary commercial bank in the United States (which was by law a bank holding company) would, like a domestic bank holding company, have been subject to Board notice or application requirements for investments and activities abroad. Although the criterion for eligibility for the exemption was quite liberal, the exemption for US activities of controlled foreign affiliates (defined as an ownership interest of at least 25 per cent) was quite limited.[32] Specifically, a controlled foreign affiliate could engage only in either 'incidental' activities in the United States, that is, those activities permissible in the United States for an Edge corporation, or those which would be permissible under Regulation Y.[33]

Foreign banks wishing to conduct a banking business in the United States were able to avoid these limitations by operating in the United States through branches or agencies rather than subsidiaries. As a result, foreign banks were able to engage in both banking and non-banking activities in the United States. Moreover, these non-banking activities included both commercial/industrial activities and securities and other financial activities not permissible domestically for US banks. This created a situation of disparity in treatment between foreign and domestic banks that was addressed in the IBA.

Commercial/industrial activities

The approach adopted by Congress involved not only bringing foreign banks whose only US presence was an agency or a branch within the coverage of the non-banking prohibitions of the BHCA but also introducing a new exemption for the US activities of controlled foreign non-banking affiliates.[34] The exemption is available under the Board's regulations for affiliates of 'qualifying foreign banking organisations' (QFBOs). The benefits of the QFBO exemption for US activities of such an affiliate are considerably greater than those provided by the previous exemption, but the test for eligibility for the exemption is more stringent.[35] As under the former exemption, a foreign bank meeting the QFBO test may engage in foreign activities without the necessity of application or notice to the Board that would be required for a domestic bank holding company.

For US activities, the QFBO exemption permits a controlled non-banking affiliate of a foreign bank to engage in the same commercial non-banking activities in the United States that it conducts abroad, provided more than half of the affiliate's assets and revenues are outside the United States. The test is designed to ensure that the US commercial/industrial operations are a legitimate part of the foreign banking organisation's customary multinational business, not a structure whose primary purpose might be to evade US rules and thereby gain an unfair competitive advantage over domestic banks. As a result of this exemption, a German bank with a controlling interest in a German automobile company could conduct banking operations in the United States through agencies, branches or subsidiary commercial banks, and its affiliated automobile company could manufacture automobiles in the United States. Even if the German bank had a subsidiary bank in the United States, the German automobile company could invest in, for example, an Italian automobile company that engaged in the same line of business (that is, the automobile business) in the United States without the prior notice or approval that would have been required in the absence of the QFBO exemption.

The solution adopted by Congress for US commercial/industrial activities of foreign affiliates of foreign banks involved a modification of host-country (US) rules to reflect elements of foreign banking organisations' home-country rules. This limited use of treatment comparable to that of the home country underscores the complexities of

---

31. The exemption was granted under the authority of sections 2(h)(2) and 4(c)(9) of the BHCA.
32. The criterion for eligibility for the exemption was that over half of a foreign bank's consolidated assets and revenues must be derived from outside the United States.
33. The US activities of a *non-controlled* foreign affiliate were not restricted, except that the affiliate was permitted to engage in the securities business in the United States only to the extent permitted to US bank holding companies.

34. This exemption is contained in section 2(h)(2) of the BHCA, as amended by the IBA, and is implemented by section 211.23(f)(5)(i) to (iii) of Regulation K. For non-controlled foreign non-banking affiliates, if the foreign banking organisation meets the QFBO test, the pre-IBA exemption remains applicable (see Note 33 above) as long as more than half of the non-banking affiliate's consolidated assets and revenues are outside the United States. Regulation K, § 211.23(f)(5)(i) to (ii).
35. In general, to qualify for this exemption, the bank's foreign banking activities must be greater than its consolidated non-banking activities *and* more than half of its banking business must be located ouside the United States. Regulation K, § 211.23(b).

applying a policy of national treatment in a world of internationalisation of banking and divergent regulatory structures.

Securities and other financial activities

Congress adopted a different solution for foreign banks seeking to conduct non-banking financial activities in the United States. The primary reason was that, in comparison with commercial/industrial activities, US securities and other non-banking financial activities of foreign banking organisations caused a much greater concern about competitive equality between domestic and foreign banks within the US market. As a result, the principle of national treatment was applied to new activities in this area without adjustments to take into account home-country structure.

Like existing commercial/industrial activities, securities activities and other non-banking financial activities conducted in the United States prior to enactment of the IBA were grandfathered. The grandfathering of the securities activities, however, was controversial. Most of the grandfathered commercial/industrial activities would have been permissible under the exemption provided by the IBA, even without the grandfathering provision. By contrast, the IBA contained no special exemption for new securities activities or other non-banking financial activities of foreign banks in the United States. As a result, even if a foreign bank meets the criteria for a QFBO, the rules with regard to US securities activities are the same as those applicable to a US bank holding company. Specifically, a foreign bank with US banking offices or its foreign affiliate may not own more than 5 per cent of the shares of a US full-service securities firm.[36]

Some US banks believe that the grandfathered US securities subsidiaries of foreign banking organisations (which would not meet the limitations imposed on section 20 subsidiaries) give such banks an unfair advantage over US banks. Of course, US banks would prefer that this competitive disadvantage be remedied by obtaining similar powers for themselves, not by restricting the activities of foreign banks.

In 1989, as mentioned above, the Federal Reserve Board authorised so-called section 20 subsidiaries of bank holding companies to engage to a limited extent in underwriting and dealing in debt and equity securities.[37] In so doing, the Board sought to achieve a strict separation between the section 20 subsidiary and its affiliated banks. As a result, the section 20 subsidiaries are subject to a framework of structural and operating limitations (so-called firewalls) that were established to avoid the potential for conflicts of interest, unsound banking practices, unfair competition, loss of public confidence in affiliate banks and other adverse effects from the conduct of the ineligible securities underwriting and dealing activities.

In January 1990 the Board faced the issue of how to apply the US policy of national treatment in approving applications by foreign banks with US banking operations to establish section 20 subsidiaries in the United States.[38] Foreign banks requested a number of modifications of the firewalls to take into account home-country rules that do not require the separation of commercial and investment banking. The issue of competitive equality in the United States market was further complicated by the fact that the US bank holding company structure does not exist abroad. As a result, while foreign banks are banks, they have also, as discussed above, been treated as bank holding companies under US law.

In order to avoid imposing the US holding company structure on foreign banks, the Board determined to treat foreign banks as holding companies for purposes of the section 20 rules even though the result would be that a foreign bank (as a holding company) could fund its section 20 subsidiary while a US bank could not. With a few modifications, the other firewalls imposed on section 20 subsidiaries of US bank holding companies were also imposed on section 20 subsidiaries of foreign banks but not on the non-US operations of the foreign bank. A further issue involved the treatment of US agencies and branches of a foreign bank. The solution was, with limited exceptions, to treat these offices as US banking affiliates subject to the firewalls, not as part of the foreign parent bank in its capacity as a bank holding company.

---

36. Regulation K, § 211.23(f)(5)(ii). This limitation applies regardless of whether the foreign bank controls its foreign affiliate because the relevant pre-IBA exemption for *non-controlled* foreign affiliates does not apply to US securities activities (see Note 33 above). By contrast, for other non-banking financial activities (such as insurance), if the foreign banking organisation meets the QFBO test, its *non-controlled* foreign affiliate is eligible for the same exemption that applies to commercial/industrial activities (see Notes 33 and 34 above).

37. Under the BHCA, if the Federal Reserve Board determines that an activity is closely related to banking and a proper incident thereto, the Board may approve such activities by individual order or by adding them to the list in Regulation Y. However, the Glass-Steagall Act severely limits the extent to which the Board may approve the securities activities of a company affiliated with a member bank (see Notes 22 and 23 above). As a result, the Board's approval is subject to the requirement that the gross revenues from ineligible securities activities may not exceed 10 per cent of the section 20 subsidiary's total gross revenues on average over any two-year period. A subsidiary whose securities activities conform to this limitation is not 'engaged principally' in ineligible securities activities in violation of the Glass-Steagall Act.

38. *Canadian Imperial Bank of Commerce, The Royal Bank of Canada, Barclays plc,* 76 *Federal Reserve Bulletin* 158 (March 1990).

378 KEY: IS NATIONAL TREATMENT STILL VIABLE: US POLICY IN THEORY AND PRACTICE: [1990] 9 JIBL

With regard to insurance activities, as already noted, the BHCA, as amended by the Garn-St Germain Act, specifically prohibits US bank holding companies (including their non-banking subsidiaries) from engaging in most insurance activities in the United States.[39] Accordingly, under the BHCA non-US banks and insurance companies that operate offices in the United States and subsequently establish controlling relationships with each other outside the United States would be required to divest either existing US banking or insurance operations. Although Congress has granted the Federal Reserve Board the authority to exempt non-US banks from the non-banking restrictions of the BHCA, the Board has generally used this authority to approve such activities only on a temporary basis, that is, until the activities can be conformed to those permissible under Regulation Y for US bank holding companies.[40]

Interstate activities

The issues involved in defining and applying a policy of national treatment to the US non-banking and interstate activities of foreign banks are rather different. Because interstate activities involve geographical expansion only within the United States, a policy of national treatment based on achieving a level playing field within a single host-country market can, at least in theory, be more easily defined. The problem of conflicting home- and host-country rules faced with regard to non-banking activities is absent. However, a major complexity in defining national treatment for interstate activities of foreign banks is introduced by the US federal structure and the dual banking system.

Prior to the IBA, a number of states provided 'national' (that is, state) treatment to foreign banks by permitting the establishment of agencies and branches of foreign banks. Moreover, there were no federal restrictions on the establishment of agencies and branches by foreign banks. A foreign bank was therefore able to establish agencies and branches in more than one state, even if it also had a subsidiary commercial bank in the United States. At the same time, states either could not or did not provide each other with 'national' treatment. In contrast to the principle of non-discrimination among nationalities adopted at the federal level, some states treated foreign (that is, non-US) out-of-state banks more favourably than domestic out-of-state banks.[41] As a result, from the perspective of the United States as a whole, the non-US banks were receiving better than national treatment.[42]

The resulting ability of foreign banks to establish domestic deposit-taking offices in more than one state was perceived by the US Congress as a major competitive advantage for foreign banks. At the time of the IBA, domestic banks were unable to establish interstate branch networks in the United States, and this is still the case. Individual states are basically powerless to provide 'national' treatment with respect to establishment of *branches* by out-of-state domestic banks because of the McFadden Act, a federal statute that effectively prohibits interstate branching regardless of state law. As a result, even if state law permitted establishment of branches by out-of-state banks, federal law would preclude national banks and state-chartered member banks from taking advantage of such a provision.[43]

In addition, at the time the IBA was under consideration, bank holding companies (both domestic and foreign) were generally unable to acquire subsidiary commercial banks outside their principal state of operations. Only in the last decade have a number of states chosen to provide 'national' treatment to out-of-state bank holding companies

39. However, even within the United States, there is lack of agreement between the federal and state governments regarding permissible activities for banks. For example, some states permit banks to conduct insurance activities directly. In May 1990 Delaware enacted a law that empowers state-chartered banks to engage in a full range of insurance underwriting and agency activities in a segregated department of the bank or in a subsidiary of the bank. In September 1990 the Federal Reserve Board, acting on a petition filed by various insurance trade associations, determined that insurance activities conducted by Citicorp under the Delaware statute were not consistent with the Board's regulations implementing the BHCA. See 76 *Federal Reserve Bulletin* 977 (November 1990). Subsequently, Citicorp requested judicial review of this order. Regardless of the outcome of this review, the FDIC, as the primary federal regulator of Citicorp's Delaware bank, has the authority to order the bank to cease activities that the FDIC determines constitute unsafe or unsound practices. In addition, in its role as insurer, the FDIC has the authority to terminate the deposit insurance coverage of any federally insured depository institution that engages in activities that the FDIC determines constitute unsafe or unsound practices.

40. Under section 4(c)(9) of the BHCA, the Federal Reserve Board has discretionary authority to approve US activities of foreign banks that would not be permissible domestically for US bank holding companies. However, to use this authority, the Board must determine that 'the exemption would not be substantially at variance with the purposes of [the BHCA] and would be in the public interest'.

41. Some state statutes refer to any out-of-state bank, including a bank from another US state, as a 'foreign' bank.

42. State laws with respect to establishment of state-chartered subsidiaries of foreign banks differ. However, even if a state did not allow a foreign bank to establish a state-chartered bank, a foreign bank could, subject to the interstate restrictions of the IBA and BHCA, establish a national bank in that state. A national bank, as noted above, is a bank that is chartered by federal rather than state authorities.

43. The McFadden Act authorised national banks to branch only within their state of establishment. McFadden Act (1927), 12 USC § 36 (1988). Section 9 of the Federal Reserve Act applies the same rules to state-chartered member banks. See Note 49 below regarding state-chartered non-member banks. See Note 50 below regarding proposed legislation that would repeal the interstate branching restrictions of the McFadden Act.

with regard to acquisition of *subsidiaries*. In contrast to the McFadden Act, which is an outright prohibition, the federal law restricting the interstate acquisition of subsidiaries may be overcome by state laws.[44] Bank holding companies are prevented by the BHCA from acquiring subsidiary commercial banks outside their principal state of operations unless host-state law explicitly permits them to do so. When the IBA was enacted (with the exception of a few institutions grandfathered by the BHCA), bank holding companies did not have banking subsidiaries in more than one state. However, as discussed below, changes in state laws beginning in the 1980s are significantly altering the geographical structure of banking in the United States.

In enacting the interstate provisions of the IBA, Congress had essentially three choices for rules governing new activities of foreign banks: (1) preserving the existing situation (that is, not applying host-country rules at the federal level), which as explained above was considered unacceptable on the basis of competitive equality; (2) prohibiting establishment of any new interstate agencies or branches; or (3) prohibiting only those interstate activities that were the perceived source of the competitive inequality, namely, the ability to accept domestic deposits in more than one state. The IBA used the last approach. Congress tried to achieve national treatment with respect to interstate activities of domestic and foreign banks by limiting the interstate expansion of domestic deposit-taking capabilities of foreign banks. To this end, a foreign bank with a US branch or subsidiary was required to select one of the states in which it operated (including any state in which it operated only an agency) as its 'home state'.[45] A foreign bank may establish new agencies or branches outside its home state, but the deposit-taking powers of such branches are limited to those permissible for an Edge corporation (that is, deposits related to international activities). No restrictions are placed on the asset side of the branch's balance sheet. The IBA grandfathered existing deposit-taking offices of a foreign bank outside its home state.

The selection of a home state by a foreign bank also affects its ability to do a banking business in the United States through a subsidiary commercial bank. A foreign bank is precluded by the IBA from acquiring a subsidiary bank outside its home state if such an acquisition would be prohibited by the BHCA for a domestic bank holding company based in that state.[46] For example, a foreign bank with an IBA home state of New York may not acquire a bank in Massachusetts unless Massachusetts law allows bank holding companies based in New York to acquire banks in Massachusetts. A foreign bank may, however, acquire a bank within its home state.[47] Prior to the IBA, only foreign banks that were bank holding companies by virtue of operating subsidiary commercial banks in the United States were covered by federal limitations on interstate activities.

Some have asserted that the issue of restrictions on interstate activities of foreign banks will become moot because the United States will effectively have nationwide banking by 1991. As always under the US dual banking system, the situation is more complex. Beginning in the early 1980s, a number of states in the United States began to adopt regional reciprocity laws, often referred to as regional compacts. Under such laws, states permit, on a reciprocal basis, interstate acquisitions of banks by bank holding companies that operate chiefly within the region. This is, in effect, a policy of reciprocal 'national' treatment among the states within a region. Some of these state laws have so-called nationwide triggers that either are already in effect or will go into effect on a certain date, that is, they will offer reciprocal 'national' treatment to bank holding companies based in any of the 50 states. Moreover, some states do not have reciprocity provisions or will eliminate such provisions on a specified date and thereby provide 'national' treatment to out-of-state bank holding companies.

The upshot of this process is that, under existing state laws, by 1 January 1991 (when California's nationwide trigger is scheduled to go into effect), 46 states plus the District of Columbia will permit

---

44. Section 3(d) of the BHCA, known as the Douglas Amendment. See Note 50 below regarding proposed legislation that would repeal the Douglas Amendment.
45. Under Regulation K, a foreign bank may change its home state one time only. Regulation K, § 211.22(c).

46. Section 3(d) of the BHCA, the so-called Douglas Amendment, effectively prohibits a bank holding company from acquiring a bank (including establishment of a *de novo* bank) outside its principal state of operations unless the other state's law expressly permits acquisition of banks in that state by out-of-state bank holding companies. The principal state of operations is the state in which total deposits of the holding company's banking subsidiaries are largest.
47. However, if a foreign bank with a US subsidiary commercial bank had chosen a state other than its BHCA principal state of operations as its IBA home state, acquisition of a bank in the home state would be prohibited. In practice, foreign banks with US subsidiary commercial banks have generally selected the BHCA principal state of operations as the IBA home state.

out-of-state bank holding companies from some or all other states to acquire banks within the state.[48] Of these, 13 will have an interstate policy of more or less unrestricted 'national' treatment. Another 19 states, including New York, California and Illinois, will have an interstate policy of reciprocal 'national' treatment. An additional 15 states will have a policy of reciprocal 'national' treatment limited to states within their region. It is important to realise that, in general, the state interstate banking laws apply only to subsidiaries, not to branches.[49] In this context, the term 'nationwide banking' has been used to refer to nationwide expansion through acquisition of subsidiaries and has not included nationwide branching.[50]

This change in the geographical structure of US banking presents two different questions for the policy of national treatment for foreign banks within US offices. The first issue concerns foreign banks operating subsidiary commercial banks in the United States. Under most circumstances, it appears that a foreign bank would be treated as if it were a domestic bank holding company having its principal state of operations in the state that the foreign bank has chosen as its home state. However, in some states, interstate banking laws have either expressly or implicitly excluded non-US banks or their US bank holding company subsidiaries from taking advantage of regional acquisition opportunities. To date, Congress has not addressed this issue of possible discrimination against non-US banks.

48. As of that date, the four states without any type of interstate banking statute in effect will be Hawaii, Kansas, Montana and North Dakota. See 'Interstate Banking Legislation by State', Financial Structure Section, Board of Governors of the Federal Reserve System, November 1990. See also 'Trigger Dates: A Look at Laws Granting Interstate Powers to Banks', (7 February 1990) *American Banker* (Volume 155, No. 26) at 15. See Note 50 below regarding federal legislative proposals that would permit nationwide banking, including interstate branching.

49. The interstate laws in some states do provide for the establishment of branches by out-of-state banks. However, such provisions currently have little practical effect. Because of the prohibitions on interstate branching in federal law, only state-chartered banks that are not members of the Federal Reserve System may take advantage of interstate branching provisions in state law. For example, Bank of America Arizona, a non-member bank chartered by Arizona, has established a branch licensed by Utah. (Only one bank currently has interstate branches grandfathered under the McFadden Act.)

50. In July 1990 Senator Dodd and Representative Schumer introduced legislation to permit nationwide banking, including interstate branching. S. 2922 and H. 5384, respectively, introduced 26 July 1990, 101st Cong. 2d Sess. (1990). These bills would have the effect of permitting interstate acquisitions of banks on a nationwide basis by the beginning of 1992 and establishment of de novo banks by the beginning of 1993; regional compacts would thereby be eliminated. The bills would also permit interstate branching by the beginning of 1994, subject to an 'opt-out' provision for individual states. Banks from a state that chose to opt out of interstate branching would not be permitted to branch outside their own state.

The second, more theoretical issue involves the relevance of the change in the geographical structure of US banking to the restrictions imposed on establishment of new interstate branches by foreign banks. One question is whether national treatment in this context should be on the basis of function (that is, accepting domestic deposits) or structure (that is, branches versus subsidiaries). It could be argued that the rationale for the IBA restriction was based generally on the inability of US banking organisations to establish domestic-deposit taking offices (branches or banks) in more than one state rather than on the inability of US banks to establish interstate branches. Even if branching had been the crucial factor, there is still the question of how national treatment should be defined for direct branches of foreign banks. As discussed above, this involves the question of whether, for purposes of geographical restrictions, direct US branches of foreign banks should be regarded as the equivalent of a domestic bank or of a domestic branch of that bank.

Conclusion

National treatment is a generally accepted principle for a country's treatment of foreign banks. Despite its federal structure, dual banking system and a regulatory framework significantly different from that of other countries, the United States provides an example of the way *de facto* national treatment can be achieved within the jurisdiction of a host country. For non-banking activities, however, the issues are complex and involve a balancing of often conflicting goals: ensuring equality of competitive opportunity between domestic and foreign banks in the host country and avoiding the imposition of host-country rules beyond its own borders. As the international integration of banking increases and as the problems of defining a market by national boundaries intensify, this balancing will become even more difficult.

National treatment is based on the regulatory perspective of the host country and its sovereignty over its own territory. In a world in which banks operate internationally by providing services across borders and through branches and subsidiaries located in foreign countries, the strains in applying national treatment are becoming more intense. From a global perspective, the meaning of equality of competitive opportunity is not clear when multinational banks compete throughout the world but with different powers in different jurisdictions – when, for example, US banks compete in Europe with powers broader than those permitted at home, and European banks compete in the United States without certain powers permitted in their home countries.

KEY: IS NATIONAL TREATMENT STILL VIABLE: US POLICY IN THEORY AND PRACTICE: [1990] 9 JIBL. **381**

The continued viability of national treatment as a generally accepted principle for host-country treatment of foreign banking institutions may depend on the extent to which national regulatory structures converge. But the search for viable principles beyond national treatment can be viewed as a search for a means of achieving such convergence. The principles of effective market access broadly defined and treatment comparable to that of the home country raise the question of whether convergence exists or could occur. The use of mutual recognition within the European Community must be understood in the context of a political movement to liberalise the economic relationships among a group of countries. The Community is using mutual recognition in an environment of substantial co-ordination and common obligations established through a supranational structure. As a result, national regulatory structures can be expected to converge.

National treatment, by contrast, does not imply explicit or implicit international harmonisation.

However, as has been noted above, a process of relatively informal co-operation and co-ordination among bank supervisory authorities has yielded an accord on international capital standards. Even in a world of host-country policies of national treatment, one can envisage a process whereby such co-operation, together with market pressures in response to the anomalies created by substantial differences in national regulatory structures, could lead to further regulatory convergence. However, without deliberate co-ordination, the process of convergence, particularly with regard to bank powers, is likely to be substantially slower internationally than the process that is now under way within the European Community. Nevertheless, the use of national treatment for international trade in financial services remains an essential step towards competitive and efficient markets, and it lays a strong foundation for further efforts to achieve international harmonisation of regulatory and supervisory structures.

[6]

Obstacles to International Trade in Insurance

Robert Carter

THE CHARACTERISTICS OF INSURANCE

Insurance provides a means whereby a person or organisation exposed to possible financial losses arising from the occurrence of uncertain events may, in return for the payment of a premium, transfer that risk to an insurer. It satisfies a demand for financial security, and life insurance is also an important form of long-term personal saving. All private insurances operate by:

1. spreading the risk of loss over time, and between persons and organisations,[1] and, unlike social security schemes,
2. pooling the premiums collected from policyholders to create a fund from which claims can be paid at a later date.

The spreading of risks through insurance can take place at several levels. In the case of the smaller personal and commercial risks a single insurer may agree to provide the whole of the insurance required, any ensuing loss being paid from the funds he holds. Alternatively, if the risk is too large for one insurer to handle, other insurers may participate in the insurance, each taking an agreed share through a 'co-insurance' arrangement, so effectively spreading the risk over a larger body of policyholders. Even wider spreading of a risk may be achieved through 'reinsurance' when an original insurer transfers part of an insurance he has accepted to another insurer, known as a reinsurer, who in turn may pass on part of his liability to other reinsurers by 'retrocession' contracts. So, through the international insurance and reinsurance markets very large risks are spread widely over a large number of insurers, reinsurers and retrocessionaires located throughout the world. The essential difference between co-insurance and reinsurance is that whereas the original insured has a direct claim against each co-insurer for its share of any claim that arises, generally he has no right of recovery against a reinsurer but equally he has no liability to pay the premium(s) for any reinsurance(s) arranged by the original insurer(s).

Reinsurance is arranged not only in respect of individual large risks but also to protect insurers against accumulations of claims arising from events

206   *Obstacles to International Trade in Insurance*

such as earthquakes or other natural or man-made disasters, or against abnormally large accumulations of claims occurring in any one year.

Insurance business falls into two broad categories – life and other long-term insurances, and general or non-life insurances. The cashflow characteristics of all forms of insurance (that is the collection of premiums when policies are issued to pay for claims which may arise during the period of insurance) lead to the accumulation of funds which provide insurers with investment earnings in addition to the premium collected. In the case of non-life insurances, besides the funds held to pay claims which may occur, the delays between the occurrence and settlement of claims (which for liability and some other classes of business can be a year or longer) mean that funds must also be held to cover outstanding claims. Life insurances generate relatively larger funds because the majority of the contracts are for periods of more than one year; most premiums are payable at regular intervals throughout the period of the insurance, and being fixed at a constant level, the premiums initially exceed the amount required to cover the mortality risk in the early years; most contracts include a savings as well as a protection element, thereby generating additional funds. Therefore, insurers accumulate substantial funds to meet the claims payable upon the death or the survival of a life insured until a predetermined date, or during an annuitant's lifetime. Consequently, in many countries life insurers are major institutional investors.

TRADE IN INSURANCE

Insurance is supplied internationally in two ways; through the 'establishment' by insurance companies of overseas branch offices, subsidiaries and associated companies to supply insurances locally; and through 'cross-frontier trade' where an insurer located in one country will supply insurance services across national frontiers to a resident of another country

Marine, aviation and other transport insurances do not fit neatly into these definitions because, for example, in the case of cargo both the location of the goods will change, and the insurance may be assigned to a new owner during the period of insurance, so that what started as a domestic insurance becomes a foreign insurance. Therefore, transport insurances are usually separately classified in trade statistics.

It is difficult to estimate the volume of either type of trade because of the lack of adequate statistics. However, the data that are available indicate that:

1. international trade in non-life insurance is far larger than in life business, with the latter being conducted mainly through local establishements (Table 12.1);

207

Table 12.1 Numbers of insurance companies by continent

	Life companies		Non-life companies		Composite companies		Total	
	Number	% of foreign companies	Number	% of foreign companies	Number	% of foreign companies	Number	% of foreign companies
Europe	687	16.4	3411	27.7	407	7.4	4505	24.1
North America	2278	5.5	3809	4.6	6	33.3	6093	5.0
Latin America	210	62.9	413	41.6	462	2.8	313	10.6
Africa	84	40.5	241	27.8	138	10.1	463	24.8
Asia	119	47.1	633	43.8	158	21.5	910	40.3
Australasia	99	41.4	326	30.4	9	55.6	434	33.3
Total	3477	14.4	8833	24.4	1182	8.3	13177	15.9

Note: The total number of companies for Latin America excludes Puerto Rico and Trinidad so that the countries covered are the same as for Table 12.2.

Source: Swiss Reinsurance Co., *Sigma*, November/December 1985.

2. the restructuring of insurance markets worldwide has been accompanied by a more than proportionate reduction in the numbers of foreign insurance companies established in the domestic insurance markets of many countries, particularly in Africa, Asia and Latin America (Table 12.2);
3. cross-frontier trade in general insurance has been growing as establishment business has declined, though there has been some reversal of the trend for reinsurance as major international reinsurance companies have opened branch offices and formed subsidiaries in North America and Europe;
4. reinsurance supplied by foreign companies has risen relative to the growth of global demand for non-life insurance over the last twenty years. This reflects not only an increase in the barriers to establishment by foreign insurers but also the growth in the size of both individual transportation and industrial risks, and of conurbations, many in areas exposed to natural disasters.

RESTRAINTS ON TRADE

Since the 1950s there has been a progressive liberalisation of trade in goods under the aegis of the General Agreement on Tariffs and Trade (GATT). Simultaneously trade in services generally, and insurance in particular, has become subject to increasing restrictions. The Communist bloc countries totally exclude foreign insurers from their domestic markets and generally only reinsure internationally those risks with a high potential foreign currency cost. The industrialised countries range from the United Kingdom, the Netherlands and the United States which have traditionally pursued liberal trade policies, to countries such as France, Germany, Italy and Japan which place many restrictions on foreign insurers who seek to supply insurance services to their markets. It is however, the developing countries that have been the most active over the last thirty years in raising the barriers to trade. Many have sought to domesticate their insurance industries, wholly or partially excluding foreign direct insurers from their markets, and setting up state reinsurance corporations to reduce imports of reinsurance from the international market.

REASONS FOR PROTECTIONIST POLICIES

A variety of arguments have been advanced in support of protectionist trade policies in relation to services in general and insurance in particular. Strong support has come for many years from the United Nations Conference on Trade and Development (UNCTAD)[2] and from its of-

Table 12.2 Changes in the structure of insurance markets by continent

	1968 Domestic companies Number	1968 Foreign companies Number	% of total	1985 Domestic companies Number	1985 Foreign companies Number	% of total	Percentage change in numbers 1968–85 Domestic companies	Percentage change in numbers 1968–85 Foreign companies
Europe	3950	1580	28.6	3419	1086	24.1	−13.4	−31.3
North America	4967	360	6.8	5791	302	5.0	16.6	−16.1
Latin America	749	257	25.5	690	82	10.6	−7.9	−68.1
Africa	229	674	74.6	348	115	24.8	52.0	−82.9
Asia	382	705	64.9	543	367	40.3	42.1	−47.9
Australasia	409	195	32.3	289	145	33.4	−29.3	−25.6
Total	10686	3771	26.1	11080	2097	15.9	−3.7	−44.4

Source: Swiss Reinsurance Co., *Sigma*, July 1983 and November/December, 1985.

210   *Obstacles to International Trade in Insurance*

ficials.[3] The reasons given can be grouped under the following three headings[4]:

1. Protection of domestic consumers: In all countries insurance industries are subject to government supervision aimed at protecting the interests of policyholders from the failure of insurance companies to provide at a fair price insurance of the type and quality demanded by personal and business consumers, and to meet their contractual obligations. Such supervision includes restrictions on the entry of new companies to national markets.
2. Economic reasons: This includes attempts to avoid wasteful and destructive competition between insurers; build up local insurance industries by protection domestic insurers from foreign competition; promote domestic employment; retain funds generated by insurance operations for investment through local capital markets; and limit the drain on the balance of payments from insurance and reinsurance imports.
3. Socio-political reasons, including not only socialist political ideology but also religious, cultural and national security considerations.

Skipper adds to the list the status quo factor. Not all governments share the presumption that 'in the absence of strong arguments to the contrary, liberalisation [of trade] is desirable from an economic point of view'.[5] Therefore, until they are convinced that their economies will benefit from the lowering of protective barriers, they believe in maintaining the status quo.

TYPES OF OBSTACLES TO TRADE

The obstacles to insurance trade can be grouped into two types:

1. those measures which 'directly restrict' foreign insurers in supplying insurance services either through local establishments or on a cross-frontier basis, or which prevent the residents of a country from buying their insurances from foreign insurers;
2. those measures which 'indirectly' reduce foreign supply of insurance and reinsurance by making it either less advantageous for foreign insurers to supply their services or more costly for local residents to purchase them. Insurance supervisory regulations (such as minimum capitalisation and deposit requirements, and controls on the investment of funds) and the taxation of insurance companies and insurance transactions may deter a foreign insurer from establishing in or trading with a country. However, provided that foreign insurers are subject

Robert Carter   211

only to the same conditions as local companies, they cannot object to
them being discriminatory from a trade policy standpoint.

RESTRICTIONS ON ESTABLISHMENT

A study by the Organisation for Economic Co-operation and Development
(OECD) concluded that the most serious restrictions were those relating to
the establishment in a country of foreign insurers.[6] The ultimate obstacle is
complete prohibition which may arise from either the nationalisation of a
country's industry or the total exclusion of agencies, branch offices and
subsidiaries of foreign insurers from its market. Some forty countries,
including all of the socialist states and many other developing countries
(for example India, Iraq, Syria and Zambia) fall in the first category; and
an increasing number of developing countries, while retaining a competitive market, have excluded foreign insurers (for example, Indonesia,
Mexico and Thailand). In other countries, such as Korea and Taiwan,
foreign-owned companies are limited in the classes of insurance they are
authorised to write.

Indirect restrictions can be grouped under a number of headings:

1. Measures that adversely affect companies' operations, including the
   amount of control they can exercise over their business, such as:
   — domestication policies that require foreign companies to operate
     through locally incorporated subsidiaries with a local, sometimes
     majority, ownership interest and with the management too in the
     hands of local nationals. (Colombia, Ecuador, Peru and Venezue-
     la, for example, each require all insurers to be locally incorpo-
     rated and for foreigners to hold no more than a 20 per cent
     interest.)
   — employment restrictions which prevent foreign companies from
     using the services of expert expatriate staff.
   — reinsurance regulations which interfere with a company's reinsu-
     rance arrangements by requiring it to cede part of its business to a
     local reinsurer or place restrictions on its ability to reinsure with
     its parent company.
2. Measures that increase capital or operating costs, or reduce investment
   earnings, including minimum capital and/or deposit requirements, or
   restrictions on investments, that discriminate against foreign-owned
   insurers or reinsurers.
3. Measures that restrict access to the market such as:
   — government procurement policies that restrict the available
     market for foreign insurers by requiring central and local govern-

212   *Obstacles to International Trade in Insurance*

     ment departments, government contractors and other organisa-
tions in which the government has a financial interest, to be
placed with a state-owned insurer or wholly locally owned insurance companies.

— exclusion of foreign insurers from trade associations, which may
not only exclude them from benefiting from the services provided
by an association but also possibly deterring intermediaries from
placing business with them. (This criticism has in the past been
levelled against the Institute of London Underwriters.)

4. Exchange controls that prevent foreign insurers from remitting profits
back to parent companies.

5. Differential tax treatment in the assessment of taxes on income as
compared with locally-owned companies.

RESTRICTIONS ON CROSS-FRONTIER TRADE

Cross-frontier trade is subject to an equally wide range of direct and
indirect obstacles. Some industrialised nations (for example Italy) and
many developing countries prohibit residents from placing abroad with
foreign insurers any domestic risks, and others (such as France and the
United States) allow such cross-frontier trade only for risks that cannot be
placed locally. Most countries require residents to purchase insurances for
certain types of risk, notably motor liability and workers' compensation,
and normally recognise only insurances issued by locally authorised
insurers. Many developing countries likewise require imports, and in some
cases exports too, to be insured with local insurers.

    Even when cross-frontier insurances are not directly prohibited the same
result may be achieved by exchange control restrictions on the remittance
abroad of premiums. Although fewer restrictions are applied to local
insurers placing their reinsurances abroad with foreign reinsurers, some
governments, by obliging local insurers to transfer a part of the risks they
have written to a local (usually state-owned) reinsurer, reduce the volume
of business available to foreign reinsurers.

    The indirect obstacles to cross-frontier trade include:

1. tax rules that penalise residents who insure abroad; for example, by
imposing discriminatory taxes either on premiums paid to foreign
insurers, or on claims paid by them, or by excluding insurances
effected with foreign insurers from tax relief on premiums.

    Reinsurance transactions are similarly subjected to tax distortions.
Sometimes additional costs are imposed on the ceding companies, for

example by limiting the tax deductibility of premiums paid to foreign reinsurers (as in Malaysia). In other cases it is the foreign reinsurer who is penalised by taxes being withheld from premiums receivable. The United States imposes a federal excise tax on premiums paid abroad, and Australia withholds tax on imputed profits of reinsurances placed with foreign reinsurers.

2. insurance supervisory regulations which penalise companies that place their reinsurances abroad; for example by not allowing them, when calculating their solvency margins, to take credit for liabilities transferred to foreign reinsurers.

3. legislation requiring the deposit of funds locally to cover the value of provisions for unearned premiums and outstanding claims in respect of reinsurances ceded to foreign reinsurers.

4. measures that restrict market access for foreign insurers such as regulations that prohibit non-admitted insurers from advertising, or ban local brokers from either assisting local residents in placing their insurances abroad or from servicing such insurances.

How effective restrictions have been in achieving the objectives enunciated by governments in implementing them, and what other costs and benefits have flowed therefrom, is a matter for debate. Two examples will illustrate this point. Firstly, governments that have sought to cut the balance of payments costs of insurance imports by excluding foreign direct insurers from their domestic insurance markets usually have succeeded only in generating larger, offsetting reinsurance imports as local insurers have been forced to turn to international reinsurers not only to provide the capacity required to underwrite large risks but also to provide the technical expertise required for underwriting specialist classes of insurance and handling claims. Secondly, restrictions on foreign insurers participating in domestic markets have encouraged major commercial buyers of insurance, and in particular the multinationals, to find alternative ways of arranging their global insurance programmes. It has led to 'fronting' arrangements whereby a locally established insurer issues the required policies and then reinsures a large proportion of the risk back to a chosen foreign reinsurer, often the client's own captive insurer (that is, an insurance company established by the parent group primarily to write its own insurances).[7]

MOVES TO LIBERALISE INTERNATIONAL TRADE IN INSURANCE

Steps to reverse the trend of protectionism have taken place at three levels.

At the regional level there have been a number of examples of co-operation between countries to promote trade within the region, though in many instances at the expense of wider international trade. UNCTAD, for example, has encouraged developing countries to form regional reinsurance pools (such as the five Arab reinsurance pools) and regional reinsurance corporations (such as the African Reinsurance Corporation and the Asian Reinsurance Corporation).[8] More significant has been the progress made, albeit slowly, by the governments of the European Community towards the creation of a common market in insurance within the Community.

Secondly, the industrialised countries that are members of the Organisation for Economic Co-operation and Development have from time to time discussed within a special Insurance Committee the question of freedom of insurance transactions and the related payment and capital flow issues. In 1972 a High-level Group on Trade and Related Problems considered in its report the subject of trade in services and recommended that:

> Insurance probably deserves first attention not only because of its economic significance, but also because more than elsewhere progress towards real liberalisation is held up by involved technical arrangements.[9]

The Committee noted that the Rules of the Code of Liberalisation of Current Invisible Operations concerning insurance were incomplete, that member countries had lodged numerous reservations on liberalised operations, and that they were opposed to liberalisation until such time as national insurance supervisory regulations were harmonised. Given that negotiations were under way within the European Community dealing with those same issues, negotiations within the OECD were then largely suspended. However, following the initiative of the US government in raising the question of services during the Tokyo round of negotiations on the General Agreement on Tariffs and Trade (GATT), the OECD reactivated its Insurance Committee. In 1983 it produced a joint report with the Capital Markets and Invisibles Transactions Committee detailing the existing obstacles within member states to establishment and cross-frontier trade in insurance.[10]

Thirdly, discussions have commenced at a multilateral level within the GATT. Although the attempt by the American government to bring trade in services within the GATT negotiating framework was opposed mainly by developing countries, led by Brazil and India, it was agreed at the GATT ministerial meeting in November 1982 that individual countries with an interest in trade in services should be invited to prepare national studies on the barriers to trade in services. Following the submission of several national studies it was agreed at a further ministerial meeting in

September 1986 that a special Group of Negotiations on Services would be set up to look into how GATT principles and procedures should be applied to trade in services with the aim of establishing:

> a multilateral framework of principles and rules for trade in services, including elaboration of such trade under conditions of transparency and progressive liberalisation and as a means of promoting economic growth of all trading partners and the developing countries. Such framework shall respect the policy objectives of national laws and regulations applying to services and shall take account of the work of relevant international organisations.[11]

Whether trade in services will be brought eventually into the GATT negotiating framework and, if so, how it will be achieved, is far from clear at present. Although the various types of services have different character-istics it would be sensible for negotiators to work towards an arrangement that would embrace services rather than dealing with each type of service separately. On the other hand, one of the major difficulties that will have to be overcome in relation to insurance is how establishment issues can be handled within the GATT. Rodney Gray, who was the head of the Canadian delegation at the Tokyo Round, has pointed out that the 'right to deny a foreign entity access to the national territory is an important aspect of sovereignty'.[12] He concluded that most governments probably will be unwilling to accept a 'right of establishment' in treaty terms, though they may be prepared to accept the establishment of locally incorporated subsidiaries of foreign companies.

Clearly if progress is to be made the lead must be taken by the industrialised countries which still generate over 90 per cent of the total world expenditure on insurance (excluding the Communist bloc). In order to assess what are the prospects for a multilateral agreement covering both establishment and cross-frontier insurance trade, the final part of this chapter will examine the case for liberalisation and the difficulties that have been encountered in bringing about a common market in insurance within the European Community.

THE CASE FOR LIBERALISATION OF INSURANCE TRADE

The economic case for international trade rests on the theory of comparat-ive advantage, which demonstrates that countries should specialise in the production of those commodities in which they have a comparative advantage and rely on trade to meet their other needs. By so doing all of the trading partners will benefit from an increase in efficiency and thus

216   *Obstacles to International Trade in Insurance*

higher output, though the benefits need not necessarily be spread evenly either between each of the trading partners or between different social groups. Moreoever, during a period of resource reallocation, some short-term losses may be incurred. However, there is ample research evidence that over the long term countries do benefit from trade, and the theory is well understood by policy-makers and trade negotiators so that both bilateral and multilateral trade negotiations have been able to progress on the basis of sound economic principles.

Although the theory of comparative advantage was developed to explain the benefits to be derived from international specialisation and trade in 'goods', there is no apparent reason why some countries should not likewise enjoy comparative advantages in the production of one or more services, including insurance.[13] Few countries possess all of the attributes required for the successful conduct of insurance business internationally, including good communications, adequate supplies of well-educated and trained labour, access to international banking and other services, favour-able exchange control regulations, and so on. Furthermore, examples could be cited to support the claim that consumers, and in particular large industrial buyers of insurance, frequently could benefit by obtaining from foreign insurers lower premiums and/or insurance contracts more suited to their needs than local companies are willing to offer.[14] Also domestic insurance industries may gain from access to the advanced technical know-how and expertise of major foreign insurers and reinsurers.[15]

To date the amount of theoretical and applied research that has been undertaken has been insufficient to prove conclusively that the theory of comparative advantage is as equally valid for services as for goods. In addition, attempts to analyse the role and economic significance of services to both individual countries and within the international economy are confronted by conceptual and data limitation problems. For example, insurance services embrace both 'trade' and 'investment' activities which raise separate issues, and few countries possess detailed information regarding either the volumes of international business conducted by their own domestic insurers, or of insurance services supplied to residents by foreign insurers and reinsurers either through local establishments or across frontiers. Equally, few governments appear to understand fully the extent and net balance of payments effects of insurance services supplied by foreign insurers through local establishments or across frontiers.[16] It is therefore not surprising that adequate accurate data is hard to find other than for a very few countries.[17]

In 1963 the Organisation for Economic Co-operation and Development undertook a survey of insurance supervision in Europe which, among other things, detailed the obstacles to establishment by foreign insurers.[18] However, it was not until the pioneering work of the Trade Policy

Research Centre, the International Chamber of Commerce and a few individuals[19] in the mid-1970s that any serious attempt was made to assess the obstacles to services trade.

So it is that negotiations on trade in services will proceed without the firm theoretical and empirical research underpinning that has marked the negotiations on trade in goods, though to quote one observer: 'The weight of evidence – such as it is – falls on the side of liberalisation.'[20]

THE LESSONS FROM EUROPE

As noted earlier, the most ambitious plans for liberalising insurance trade have been those of the European Community where, according to the provisions of the Treaty of Rome, a common market in insurance should have been achieved by 1969. The twin freedoms of establishment and of 'services' (that is cross-frontier trade) were to be brought about by directives that, amongst other things, would approximate the laws of the member states 'to the extent necessary for the proper functioning of the common market'.

Agreement was quickly reached on reinsurance because throughout the Community reinsurance transactions were already relatively free. Therefore, both freedoms were implemented by a directive issued in 1964, whereby EC reinsurers were subject to insurance supervision only in their country of establishment. Direct insurance, however, has presented far more difficulties, to the extent that almost twenty years after the original deadline, agreement on freeing cross-frontier trade still has not been achieved.

Not least of the problems confronting the negotiators has been the widely differing views of member governments regarding the protection of insurance consumers.

At the one extreme the British government traditionally had been content to regulate only the financial solvency of insurance companies and, although a number of company failures in the 1960s has led to more extensive controls on the entry of companies to the market and the conduct of business, few constraints were imposed on the ways in which well-managed, financially prudent companies ran their businesses. Also the Lloyd's market continued to operate under a system of self-regulation. The situation in other countries was very different. French, German and Italian insurers, for example, enjoyed far less commercial freedom in that premium rates, policy terms, marketing and the investment of funds were all subject to supervisory control. Their governments took the view that the

218   *Obstacles to International Trade in Insurance*

interests of consumers were best served by regulating competition between insurers.

There were differences, too, in the treatment of foreign insurers. Britain, because of its own extensive overseas insurance operations, did not discriminate against foreign companies wishing to establish there and its residents were permitted to insure abroad. Other countries, to varying degrees, protected their domestic markets from foreign competition. For example French, German and Italian residents could not freely place their insurances abroad, so that established insurers also were protected against competition from non-admitted foreign insurers. Therefore, when negotiating on the freedoms for Community insurers the member governments have also had to agree on what rights of access external (that is non-Community) insurers shall have to the markets of member states, and on what terms.

Other obstacles to agreement have been the substantial differences between member states in regards to such matters as insurance contract law; the rights of contracting parties to choose which laws shall govern the contract; the rights of policyholders on the winding-up of an insurance company; and the tax treatment of insurance companies and insurance contracts.

Consequently it was not until 1973 that the Non-Life Establishment Directive was issued providing the right for direct insurers incorporated and authorised to write non-life insurance in one member state to establish branch offices elsewhere within the Community. It took another six years of negotiations and two judgements of the European Court of Justice before an establishment directive was issued for life insurance.

'Freedom of services' has still to be achieved. An attempt to free cross-frontier trade in the direct insurance of large risks (the Co-insurance Directive of 1978) had little practical effect because of the restrictive interpretations of the Directive's provisions by some member states. This led the European Commission in 1985 to instigate proceedings in the European Court of Justice against the governments of Denmark, France, Germany and Ireland. Although the Court's judgement, delivered in 1986, went some way towards promoting freedom of cross-frontier insurance it nevertheless accepted the right of member governments to maintain some restrictions on insurers supplying insurances to residents across national frontiers.

In December 1987 the Council of Ministers agreed to a draft Non-Life Services Directive, which was adopted in June 1988, to free cross-frontier trade in large industrial and commercial risks where the policyholder is above a specified size. Before freedom of services can be achieved for smaller risks additional consumer protection measures will have to be agreed and incorporated in a further Directive. A target date of 1991 was set in the Commission's 1985 White Paper *Completing the Internal Market* for achieving freedom of services for life insurance. However, there were still considerable obstacles to be overcome due to differences in national supervisory regulations and taxation before all governments could agree that the interests of both insurers and policyholders would be adequately protected.[21] Therefore, the first draft directive issued in February 1989 only provides for individuals, acting on their own initiative, to buy life insurances across EC state frontiers.

What the European Community negotiations have demonstrated is that even when there is political agreement on the principle of trade liberalisation many differing interests have to be reconciled before progress towards it can be achieved. The stages towards the creation of a common market in insurance within the Community do, however, provide a pointer to the possible ways forward for trade liberalisation on a wider stage.

STAGES IN TRADE LIBERALISATION

The first obvious candidate for negotiation is trade in reinsurance, particularly since there is a growing demand for insurance protection against increasingly larger risks. There is less need to supervise reinsurance contracts which are arranged between equally knowledgeable parties. The one necessary condition for consumer protection is confidence in the security of the reinsurer which essentially means confidence in the supervision exercised by the reinsurer's country of domicile. Next should come freedom of establishment; not only does it place a smaller balance of payments strain on a host country's economy but it also assists in the process of technology transfer between countries. As for consumer protection and fair competition between insurers, the European solution has been to adopt common authorisation, solvency and reserve localisation regulations, but to allow member states, if they so desire, to regulate other aspects of insurers' operations, any regulations applying equally to both domestic and foreign companies.

Liberalising cross-frontier trade poses the most difficult problems. The insurance buyers with the most to gain from access to the international insurance markets are the large industrial and commercial companies. especially those who themselves trade internationally and for whom there should be less concern with issues of consumer protection. Two key issues are insurer security, and matters of jurisdiction and the enforcement of court awards. As far as the former is concerned, an international agreement on solvency standards for insurers would be a major step forward in solving that problem.

220   *Obstacles to International Trade in Insurance*

Finally, it is worth reiterating that if the industrialised nations wish to bring about greater freedom of trade in services it is up to them to set the lead.

Notes

1.   J. S. Revell, *The British Financial System* (London: Macmillan, 1973) p. 401.
2.   United Nations Conference on Trade and Development, *Reinsurance Problems in Developing Countries* (Geneva: UNCTAD Secretariat, 1975); *Third World at the End of the 1970s* (Geneva: UBCTAD Secretariat, 1980).
3.   W. R. Malinowski, 'European insurance and the Third World', *Journal of World Trade Law*, August-September 1971; and José Ripoll, 'UNCTAD and insurance', *Journal of World Trade Law*, January-February 1974, and 'Some thoughts of development and insurance', *Best's Review* (Oldwick, New Jersey) February 1976.
4.   R.L. Carter and G.M. Dickinson, *Barriers to Trade in Insurance* (London: Trade Policy Research Centre, 1979), ch. 2; and Harold D. Skipper Jr, 'Protectionism in the provision of international insurance services', *Journal of Risk and Insurance*, vol. 54 no. 1, March 1987.
5.   Harold D. Skipper Jr, ibid.
6.   Organisation for Economic Co-operation and Development, *International Trade in Services: Insurance – Identification and Analysis of Obstacles* (Paris: OECD Secretariat, 1983).
7.   United Nations Conference on Trade and Development, *The Impact of Captive Insurance Companies on the Insurance Markets of Developing Countries* (Geneva: UNCTAD Secretariat, 1984).
8.   UNCTAD, *Reinsurance Problems in Developing Countries*.
9.   Organisation for Economic Co-operation and Development, *Policy Perspectives for International Trade and Economic Relations*, High Level Group on Trade and Related Problems (Paris: OECD Secretariat, 1983).
10. See note 6.
11. *GATT Press Release*, 25 September 1986.
12. Rodney de C. Gray, 'A not so simple plan for negotiating trade in services', draft paper (London: Trade Policy Research Centre, 1985).
13. Paul F. Butler, *Statement to the President's Export Council* (Washington), 10 February 1983; and R. L. Carter and G. M. Dickinson, op cit.
14. Carter and Dickinson, *Barriers to Trade in Insurance*.
15. Harold D. Skipper Jr, 'Entering a foreign country's marketplace', *Journal of the American Society of CLU*, vol. 40, May 1986.
16. G. M. Dickinson, 'International insurance transactions and the balance of payments', *Geneva Papers on Risk and Insurance*, no. 6, October 1977.
17. Britain's balance of payments data for insurance transactions, although good, still suffer from the distortion of the annual estimates of earnings from the underwriting of overseas insurances by the treatment of claims payments and the additions to reserves for the payment of claims in future years.
18. *Supervision of Private Insurance in Europe* (Paris: OECD Secretariat, 1963).
19. Brian Griffiths, *Invisible Barriers to Invisible Trade* (London: Policy Research Centre, 1975); and Ronald Shelp, 'The proliferation of foreign insurance laws: reform or regression', *Law and Policy in International*

Robert Carter   221

Business, no. 8, 1976, and *Beyond Industrialization: Ascendancy of the Global Service Economy* (London: Praeger, 1981).

20. Harold D. Skipper Jr, 'Protectionism in the provision of international insurance services'.

21. R. L. Carter and E. V. Morgan, *Freedom to Offer Life Insurance Across EEC State Boundaries*, report prepared for the European Commission, 1986 (private circulation).

Part II
Multinational Banking

[7]

A Theory of Multinational Banking

Multinational banking involves the ownership of banking facilities in one country by the citizens of another. It has been described and analysed broadly in a number of books [Baker and Bradford (1974), Baum (1974), Lees (1974 and 1976), Robinson (1972)]. Specific and more narrowly defined problems related to multinational banking have been analysed in a sizeable number of journal articles, most of which are noted in the appended bibliography.[1]

This paper represents a first attempt to develop a general theory of multinational banking capable of explaining the phenomenon with the help of a few price-theoretic principles. Such theorizing is useful in the discussion of policy issues raised by the recent rapid growth of multinational banking and by proposed U.S. legislation designed to curb it.[2]

The growth of multinational banking is reflected in some U.S. statistics. In 1965 foreign banks had 19 branches in the United States. By 1974 their number had increased to 39. During this period the assets of branches and agencies of these foreign banks in the United States rose from 1.4 per cent to 5.4 per cent of total U.S. bank assets. At the same time, 13 U.S. banks with 211 branches abroad grew to 129 banks and 737 foreign branches. The assets of these U.S. banks abroad represented 2.6 per cent and 17.7 per cent of total U.S. banking assets at the beginning and end of the period, respectively.[3]

The growth of multinational banking involved all countries,

---

[1] The *Columbia Journal of World Business* had a special issue devoted to multinational banking (Winter 1975) containing papers by ALIBER, CARSON, EDWARDS and ZWICK, FRANKEL, HUTTON, PERKINS, RUCKDESCHEL and WELSH. A special issue on the subject was also issued by the *Federal Reserve Bank of San Francisco Economic Review* (Spring 1976), containing papers by ALIBER and JOHNSTON. Two of the earliest and important papers, drawing on previously unavailable official statistics are by BRIMMER (1975) and KLOPSTOCK (1973).

[2] The U.S. legislation has been discussed by EDWARDS (1974), GARROE (1975), DEAN and GRUBEL (forthcoming), as well as by several of the authors cited in footnote one.

[3] These statistics were taken from ALIBER (1975), p. 10 and BRIMMER (1975), p. 345.

though data are difficult to obtain and present. However, Lees (1974, p. 15) shows for the year 1968-69 a 14×10 matrix listing the nationality of the parent banks and the region of their foreign banking activity along the horizontal and vertical axes, respectively. In this matrix, about 70 per cent of all cells are filled with a total of 2,744 entries. As the U.S. data indicate, since 1969 there has been further rapid growth in the activity.

Multinational banks are attracting the attention of law-makers because in most countries they have escaped the regulation and supervision to which their domestic rivals are subjected and because their activities can be argued to entail negative externalities through absence of requirements to publish adequate information, the lack of deposit insurance and lenders of last resort and their functioning as a conduit for international short-term capital flows which reduce national monetary sovereignty.

The basic analytical question to be answered by a theory of multinational banking is identical to that present in the case of direct foreign investment: [4] What is the source of comparative advantage accruing to a U.S. bank in a place like Singapore, which is in competition with local banks having obvious advantages in their familiarity with local customers, capital markets, employees and the government? Put differently and applied to the special problem of banking, the basic phenomenon to be explained by the theory of multinational banking is why a bank abroad can profitably offer lower lending *and* higher borrowing rates than its domestic competitors and thus attract customers away from them.

The theory of multinational banking to be presented in the next three parts of this paper distinguishes three analytically distinct functions of such banks, which in practice may or may not be undertaken by the same firm. Thus, in succession I analyse the phenomenon of multinational retail, service and wholesale banking. The paper closes with a brief sketch of welfare and policy implications derived from the theoretical analysis.

I. Multinational Retail Banking

In California, Canadian, British and Japanese banks have opened branches serving local customers by providing the same deposit and

---

4 See, for example, CAVES (1971), KINDLEBERGER (1969) and VERNON (1966).

A Theory of Multinational Banking 351

loan facilities as the branches of the Bank of America and other commercial banks. Branches of U.S. and Canadian banks have constituted for many years the only network of commercial banks in the Caribbean and some South American countries.[5] The Chase Manhattan Bank once was in the retail banking business in Great Britain through a chain of " Money Boutiques ".

Retail banking by foreign-owned firms is a relatively unimportant phenomenon quantitatively, though it is growing in California. It is declining rapidly in Latin America and the Money Boutiques in London were closed after they had been in operation only a few years.

The theoretical explanation of multinational retail banking is almost identical to that of direct foreign investment in manufacturing advanced by Kindleberger (1969), Vernon (1966) and Caves (1971). These banks use management technology and marketing know-how developed for domestic uses at very low marginal cost abroad. Of special importance is the marketing know-how necessary to penetrate domestic markets in which banks offer slightly differentiated packages of services appealing to chosen groups of customers. The location of branches and advertising are important components of marketing strategies in this field.

The growth of U.S. and Canadian retail banking in Latin America was based on these principles in an extreme form, as the banks entered the countries at early stages of economic development and there was no domestic competition to speak of. The growth of foreign retail banks in California and the episode of those Money Boutiques in London, on the other hand, seems almost purely to be based on the product differentiation principles of oligopolistic markets noted above.

Multinational retail banking in developing countries has diminished sharply as policies motivated by economic nationalism led to restrictive legislation and take-over by nationals. Competitive advantage based purely on product differentiation is rather precarious and can easily be curtailed by innovative responses from the domestic industry, as has happened in Britain where local banks entered previously unserviced loan fields and forced the closure of the Money Boutiques. The management technology of banking is relatively stable and modern systems built on the use of computers, which are marketed internationally by specialized firms rather than developed by every

---

[5] A detailed study of this type of Banking is found in BAUM (1974).

bank individually, so that this source of comparative advantage in multinational retail banking is minor.

As a final motive for multinational retail banking and the other forms of multinational banking discussed below are the benefits from geographic diversification manifesting themselves in more stable earnings. These benefits arise from the less than perfect synchronization of business cycles throughout the world and the absence of price arbitrage on non-tradable factor inputs, such as labor, where costs fluctuate in response to largely local random influences. As Rugman (1976) has shown for the case of banks and a growing literature in international finance explains,[6] these benefits from diversification can be substantial and are prized by wealthholders.

II. Multinational Service Banking

The rapid growth of direct foreign investment in the world since the end of the second World War is well known and documented. Multinational banking has grown in parallel with this direct investment as the banks tried to meet the demand for banking services of these firms abroad. Bankers describe this move abroad as a defensive measure necessary to assure the continued business with the domestic parents of the foreign subsidiaries. Failure to accompany the subsidiaries abroad would force them to turn to foreign banks or domestic rivals with branches abroad for deposits, loans and other services. Eventually, such growing commercial relationships might expand to where domestic business is taken over by local or foreign banking competitors.

This explanation of motives by bankers can be interpreted in price-theoretic terms. The continuous business carried on between, for example a U.S. bank and U.S. manufacturing firm in the United States, is made highly efficient by the use of informal operations procedures built on trust, which in turn is based on continuous personal contacts and the resultant flow of information vital for decision-making. The continuous commercial contacts between the bank and manufacturing firm permit the bank to have access to information about the firm's financial conditions at such a low cost and high speed that it is in a better position than any other competitor to evaluate and respond to the firm's demand for loans.

---

6 One of the earliest empirical studies of this phenomenon is GRUBEL (1968).

A Theory of Multinational Banking 353

The ability to draw on the information and personal contacts between the bank's and manufacturing firm's parents in the United States at very low marginal cost represents the main source of comparative advantage that the bank's foreign branch has in dealing with the firm's subsidiary abroad in competition with the local banks. Failure to use this comparative advantage leads to the development of information capital and personal relationships between foreign-owned manufacturing subsidiaries and local banks which can eventually be used to take away business from the U.S. bank in dealing with the manufacturing firm in the United States and its subsidiaries in other countries. Because of this risk, the move abroad is " defensive ".

The preceding analysis of motives for multinational service banking explains the phenomena that all industrial countries' banks have penetrated each others' markets along with their national manufacturing firms. Combined with the fact that U.S. multinational manufacturing firms are the most important source of direct investment, the preceding analysis also explains the relative dominance of U.S. multinational banks. For the same reason, of course, British multinational banking had been dominant in the period before the second World War.

Multinational service banks also do some business with local firms and wealthy individuals by offering them specialized services and information required for trade and capital market dealings with their native countries. These local firms and wealthy individuals often are attracted to the large multinational banks by their prestige and the perceived high liquidity and safety of deposits with these banks. Furthermore, the banks provide convenient opportunities for diversification of portfolios.

Finally, it should be mentioned that multinational service banks do business with tourists and travelling business men. The banking divisions of the American Express Company are best known for their activities in this field. The motive for this type of business and the implicit source of comparative advantage is very similar to that found in connection with service banking for multinational enterprises: The banks can draw on knowledge of tourists' and business men's domestic banking connections and tastes and preferences. Tourists and business men are attracted to multinational service banks because of the greater assurance that their specific needs are known and met and because familiarity with the bank's business methods lowers implicit transactions costs for them. The banks' offering of services to tourists and business men tend to be at least in part defensive in connection with the lucrative business of issuing travellers' checks. If it were not possible to cash or obtain new checks from U.S. banks in key tourist centers abroad, their users might turn to and continue to use competitive substitutes provided by foreign banks. The importance of this fact is evidenced by the supply of free tourist services by American Express banks abroad — mail deposits, clean rest-rooms — designed to attract the U.S. tourists.

III. Multinational Wholesale Banking

Multinational wholesale banking provides an efficient network for international capital flows. It leads to the arbitrage of funds between countries of relatively tight and easy monetary policy, functioning mainly through the institution of the Euro-dollar [7] market and international loan consortia. Individual banks typically carry on simultaneously the service and wholesale banking functions, but because the two functions are based on different motives and have different welfare effects, it is useful to discuss them separately.

An analysis of the Euro-dollar market and the role of multinational banks in it can best be undertaken by focusing on explanations of the following phenomenon introduced above in a slightly different form: Why would residents of France (individuals, French companies, multinational companies) deposit with and borrow dollars from a multinational bank in Paris rather than deposit with and borrow francs from a French bank?

The answer to this question is a truism, but nevertheless important to spell out. French depositors of dollars receive a higher return and French borrowers of dollars pay a lower price than they do by dealing in their domestic currency. In other words, the spread between effective lending and borrowing rates in the Euro-dollar market must be narrower than that in the domestic currency market. This particular description of the phenomenon leads us to the analysis of the following three basic causes of this narrower spread.

---

[7] Banks deal in currencies other than just dollars, but to keep the exposition simple, only Euro-dollars will be mentioned in this paper. For the most comprehensive analysis of the Euro-dollar market see LITTLE (1975). For the « new view » of Euro-dollar markets see HEWSON (1975).

First, the dollars may have attached to them an intrinsic service of value, which would make it cheaper to borrow and give of a higher real yield even if the nominal borrowing and lending rates on dollar and French francs in Paris were the same. Implicit service values of this sort arise from the dollar's use as the key currency in international trade and finance. For example, firms having export and import dealings denominated in dollars may find themselves with temporary excess supplies or demand for dollars. By lending or borrowing these dollars the firms save transactions costs and eliminate exchange risks.

There are some additional intrinsic benefits from holding and borrowing dollars already mentioned in connection with the multinational service bank functions: portfolio diversification against risk of loss due to interest and exchange rate changes and default and the greater liquidity of dollar assets.

Second, historically most important in the development of the Euro-dollar market and multinational wholesale banking have been government policies resulting in lower costs of operation and permitting multinational banks to operate on narrower spreads between borrowing and lending rates than their domestic counterparts. In this category of policies are the absence of legal minimum reserve requirements on deposits denominated in foreign currencies,[8] and of compulsory deposit insurance.

Since in most countries there are interest payments on minimum reserves and only a small fraction of them serve as a liquidity buffer, minimum reserve requirements constitute an implicit tax on domestic but not Euro-dollar business.[9] Compulsory deposit insurance similarly has a differential impact on the cost of the two types of banking business, though the advantage to multinational banks in operating costs should at least in part be offset by the greater riskiness of deposits with them, suggesting the need for the payment of marginally higher rates on deposits.[10]

Two government regulations favoring multinational wholesale banks in the United States are the prohibition of nationwide branching and of merchant banking activities by regular commercial banks. Since

---

[8] Germany has a minimum reserve requirement on foreign currency deposits of German banks.

[9] These issues are discussed by TOBIN (1960) and JOHNSON (1976), together with proposals for institutional changes.

[10] Most countries have an upper limit on the size of deposits insured, so that with these kinds of deposits there is no need to pay a compensatory rate.

foreign banks are not covered by this prohibition, they gain a competitive advantage permitting them to operate on narrower profit margins. In many European countries, but especially Britain, banking business with domestic residents is burdened and made more expensive by foreign exchange controls. Euro-currency dealings and business with non-residents is relatively free from such controls and can therefore be operated at lower cost.

Third, multinational wholesale banks have sources of comparative advantage arising from a type of product differentiation they offer. They tend to deal only with large customers and among themselves, thus avoiding the high marginal costs associated with retail banking. In a sense, they act not as banks but primarily as brokers between lenders and borrowers.

The deals with large customers take place through loan consortia and typically are denominated in Euro-dollars. They have as ultimate borrowers and lenders, governments, quasi-governmental agencies and utilities and large multinational corporations. The operation through consortia and dollars enable individual banks to diversify their risks, keep placement costs low and avoid legal limitations on loans to individual customers. The multinational wholesale banking business is very efficient, transmitting large sums of funds around the world from areas with temporary excess liquidity to those with temporary shortages, dealing in large sums per transaction on extremely small margins. The speed and low cost of these transactions is made possible because the banks are well known to each other and for the strength and prestige of their parents, so that they can forego costly credit investigation.

Recent studies of Euro-dollar banks balance sheets in Britain by Hewson (1975) have shown that these banks typically have nearly matched amounts of assets and liabilities in every maturity class.[11] Furthermore, they have adjustable interest rates on both loans and deposits. As a result of these characteristics of their portfolios, these banks do not engage in the maturity transformation typical of normal commercial banks or many other financial intermediaries. They therefore analytically are behaving more like brokers and do not have the liquidity and exchange risks of normal banks. The implication of these facts for our purposes of analysis is that the multi-

---

[11] This may be a statistical illusion, as is argued by MAYER (1976). Many short-term loans are rolled over almost automatically and for all practical purposes are long term.

national wholesale banks' business is less risky and can be operated on a narrower spread between lending and borrowing rates than that of regular banks whose gross profit margin must cover a larger rate of expected losses.

The preceding analysis implies that the special wholesale type of business in which the multinational banks specialize can as well be taken up by regular domestic banks. In most countries this is indeed the case, but the multinationals as a group have an additional function. They represent the conduit for capital flows among nations by drawing on special knowledge capital. For example, a small French firm in the provinces may have a temporary excess supply of funds which it deposits with its local bank. The provincial bank then may place the funds with one of its correspondent multinational French banks which in turn deposits them with one of the branches of an American multinational bank. Sometimes going through a number of banks in the multinational wholesale market, the excess funds originating in a French province may eventually end up as a loan to a small Japanese borrower dealing with a relatively unknown provincial Japanese bank.

All of the dealings in the chain of lending just described are done quickly and at low cost since in each link of the chain the partners in the transactions know each other very well and are in normal, regular business contact. In a sense, the multinational wholesale banking network represents the equivalent of a global federal funds market, assuring an efficient use of the existing stock of money capital, giving rise to the well-known large quantity of inter-bank deposits and raising the velocity of circulation of money.

IV. Welfare Effects of Multinational Banking

The benefits from multinational banking appear in three forms. First, in countries where retail banking by foreign banks is permitted legally, the multinationals constitute an actual or potential source of competition, reducing the power and wastes of the typical national banking oligopolies. Second, the multinational banks are using existing stocks of knowledge capital at very low marginal cost to provide socially valuable services. This type of welfare effect is the same as that brought about by multinational manufacturing enterprises.

Third, the multinational banks increase the efficiency of capital flows, especially through the speed with which capital moves and the types of customers that are served.

The costs of multinational banking can also be considered to take three basic forms. Stated uncritically and in the strongest way possible, they are as follows. First, there are those arising from the discriminatory treatment of multinational and other banks by government regulations, which were designed to eliminate certain perceived externalities. For example, the U.S. prohibitions on merchant banking and nation-wide branching were instituted to prevent the excessive concentration of financial power. Compulsory deposit insurance in many countries was designed to prevent runs on banks. Compulsory membership in a national banking system with minimum reserve requirements, a lender of last resort and disclosure regulations were instituted to reduce the incidence of financial crises to which banking systems used to the subject. By being excluded from these regulations, multinational banks can produce externalities which were considered worth eliminating through the control of domestic banks.

Second, a special type of externalities which national banking systems attempt to eliminate through compulsory minimum reserve requirements and control over the reserve base are those arising from cyclical fluctuations in the money supply, income, employment, prices and the balance of payments. Since foreign currency deposits of domestic and multinational banks in most countries are not subject to minimum reserve requirements, the monetary authorities do not have effective control over the liquidity created by these institutions, especially through the Euro-dollar market.

Multinational banks as conduits of international short-term capital flows have made it more difficult for national monetary authorities to set interest rates or control the quantity of credit and money for optimal national demand management. Multinational banks therefore have contributed to the loss of national monetary sovereignty through both the creation of additional liquidity and the intensification of disturbing capital flows.

Third, multinational banks have caused inflation throughout the world by increasing liquidity through the multiple expansion of deposits in the Euro-dollar market. Furthermore, by the increased efficiency in the use of existing capital, they have raised the global velocity of money and created inflationary pressures in all countries.

V. Policy Implications of the Analysis

At the simplest level the policy issue surrounding the development of multinational banking is whether it should be brought under the regulations umbrella of national and perhaps an international agency, such that the discriminatory exclusion of multinational banks from national regulation noted above is terminated. Proposed U.S. legislation is aimed at the establishment of neutrality in the effects of regulation on domestic and multinational banks and the enactment of this legislation " ...will inevitably have repercussions in other countries and may be used as a precedent for new legislation elsewhere." [Hutton (1975), p. 109]. Without going into details about the legislation, the issues can be sketched briefly.

The arguments in favour of controls are that they would curtail the costs noted in the preceding section without reducing appreciably the benefits. The existence of domestic banking legislation is evidence of the fact that countries wish to have the benefits from the internalization of externalities they were designed to bring about, even if experts are not fully agreed on the net benefits after costs from these policies. Until such agreement is reached among experts and policies are changed for domestic banks, it is sensible to attempt the elimination analogous externalities brought on by multinational banks. The real economic advantages of these banks noted above are strong enough to assure their continued existence even after they have ceased to be the beneficiaries of favourable, discriminatory legislative treatment.

The arguments against any controls on multinational banking are that they yield great benefits in terms of increased capital-market efficiency noted above, while the alleged costs are small or non-existent. The probability of development of concentrated financial power in the United States through nation-wide branch-banking and merchant-banking activities by multinationals is extremely small, since competition among financial intermediaries is so strong that it would be very unlikely that new, foreign-owned banks can make great inroads even with the legislative advantages they now possess.

In the United States, the Euro-dollar business is not important. Recent studies of Euro-dollar markets in the rest of the world have shown that they are unlikely to have resulted in a multiplication of original dollar deposits, primarily because of leakages and the balance-sheet characteristics noted above. Therefore, they probably have added little to net world liquidity and increased velocity of circulation.

Whatever the ultimate conclusion will be concerning the ability of multinational banks to create money through the Euro-dollar market, even if they could create quite large amounts, their activities do not necessarily cause inflation. Like in the case of technical innovations in domestic money markets which increase the velocity of circulation, central banks can and do adjust their policies to reach assigned demand management objectives. Making correct monetary policy may be more difficult as a result of the exogenous growth of new financial institutions, but it is not made ineffective.[12]

The loss of national monetary sovereignty through international short-term capital flows has been worsened only marginally by the operation of multinational banks. It is quite certain that if they were eliminated, new institutions would quickly take their place. At the same time, the alleged loss of monetary sovereignty discussed so widely during the 1960s and early 70s has been curtailed through the abandonment of the parity exchange rate system and may never have been serious. Recent research has shown that Germany, the most important country that allegedly had lost its sovereignty, in fact had retained effective control over its money base, except during a few isolated episodes of extremely heavy speculative capital inflows. [See Herring and Marston (1977)].

At a most fundamental level, moreover, serious doubts are arising over the benefits of having national monetary sovereignty. During the sixties it was believed that such sovereignty was necessary to reach independently chosen national targets on the inflation-unemployment trade-off curve. Failure to reach these targets was blamed on fixed exchange rates and short-term capital flows. Recent research suggests, however, that this blame for the failure to attain Phillips-curve targets has been due to the basic absence of a longer-run inflation-unemployment trade-off. If this analysis is correct, then the primary argument for increased control over multinational banks as conduits for short-term capital flows has lost its merit.

---

[12] This appears to have been the conclusion reached by most analysts after the Radcliffe Committee Report in Britain and the book by J. Gurley and E. Shaw in the 1950s in the United States had argued that all financial intermediaries need to be treated in almost the same way as commercial banks in order to retain control over aggregate demand through monetary policy.

While the proposed controls over multinational banks are likely to yield few benefits, they can be expected to result in additional costs and a resultant curtailment of the benefits brought by the multinational banks. The imposition of minimum reserve requirements raises the cost of banking in all countries where no interest or below-market interest rates are paid on these reserves. The tax on multinational banking implicit in such reserve requirements can thus be expected to decrease its size. Compulsory deposit insurance raises important problems of moral hazard,[13] which may be especially serious in the case of multinational banks which typically deal in large deposits. The creation of a lender of last resort specifically for multinational banks will create the opportunity for the abuse of discount facilities, which in national banking systems has complicated monetary control.

Finally, one of the inevitable results of government control of banks appears to be the strengthening of oligopolistic market structures, as regulatory authorities are influenced by the industry and tacit agreements between the authorities and the industry result in restrictions on entry in return for ready compliance.

VI. Summary and Conclusions

In this paper I have analysed the nature of the activities undertaken by multinational banks in the retail, service and wholesale business. This analysis has provided the price-theoretic background for the presentation of the social benefits created by multinational banks. The welfare costs of these banks' activities were seen to arise primarily from their exclusion from national policies designed to capture externalities from banking generally, but especially those arising from financial instability, inflation and control over the money supply.

The broad sketch of arguments for and against the regulation and control of multinational banking has to be modified to account for the special circumstances of individual countries. Yet, the basic arguments are likely to be the same in all countries. They are clear

---

13 For a discussion of these issues see EDWARDS and SCOTT (1977).

in principle, but extremely difficult to evaluate in practice. The case for the control of multinational banks is weakened considerably if in fact Euro-dollar markets do not create liquidity and national monetary sovereignty is irrelevant for the pursuit of independent national unemployment-inflation targets.

Burnaby, B. C.

HERBERT G. GRUBEL

REFERENCES

ALIBER, R. Z., "International Banking: Growth and Regulation," *Columbia Journal of World Business*, Winter 1975.

ALIBER, R. Z., "Towards a Theory of International Banking," *Federal Reserve Bank of San Francisco Economic Review*, Spring 1976.

BAKER, J. C. and M. G. BRADFORD, *American Banks Abroad: Edge Act Companies and Multinational Banking* (New York: Praeger Publishers), 1974.

BAUM, J. D. *The Banks of Canada in the Commonwealth Caribbean* (New York: Praeger Publishers), 1974.

BRIMMER, A. F., "Growth of American International Banking: Implications for Public Policy," *Journal of Finance*, May 1975.

CARSON, D., "Government Policies and the Eurodollar Market," *Columbia Journal of World Business*, Winter 1975.

CAVES, R. E., "International Corporations: The Industrial Economics of Foreign Investment," *Economica*, 1971.

DEAN, J. and H. G. GRUBEL, "Regulatory Issues and the Theory of Multinational Banking" in *Issues in Financial Regulation*, F. Edwards, ed. New York: Columbia University Press, forthcoming.

EDWARDS, F., "Regulation of Foreign Banking in the United States: International Reciprocity and Federal-States Conflicts," *Columbia Transnational Law Review*, 13, 2, 1974.

EDWARDS, F. and J. ZWICK, "Activities and Regulatory Issues: Foreign Banks in the United States," *Columbia Journal of World Business*, Spring 1975.

EDWARDS, F. R. and J. SCOTT, "Regulating the Solvency of Depository Institutions: A Perspective for Reform," Columbia University, Graduate School of Business, Discussion Paper, 1977.

FRANKEL, A. F., "The Lender of Last Resort Facility in the Context of Multinational Banking," *Columbia Journal of World Business*, Winter 1975.

GANOE C., "Controlling the Foreign Banks in the U. S.," *Euromoney*, June 1975.

GRUBEL, H. G., "Internationally Diversified Portfolios: Welfare Gains and Capital Flows," *American Economic Review*, December 1968.

HELLER, H. R., "International Reserves and World Wide Inflation," *IMF Staff Papers*, March 1976.

HERRING, R. and S. MARSTON, *National Monetary Policies and International Financial Markets*, (Amsterdam: North Holland), 1977.

HEWSON, J., *Liquidity Creation and Distribution in the Eurocurrency Markets*, (Lexington, Mass.: D. C. Heath and Co.), 1975.

HUTTON, H. R., " The Regulation of Foreign Banks - A European Viewpoint," *Columbia Journal of World Business*, Winter 1975.

JOHNSON, H. G., " Reserve Requirements and Monetary Control," Economic Council of Canada, Discussion Paper #66, 1976.

JOHNSTON, R. A., " Proposals for Federal Control of Foreign Banks," *Federal Reserve Bank of San Francisco Economic Review*, Spring 1976.

KINDLEBERGER, C. P., *American Business Abroad*, (New Haven, Conn.: Yale University Press), 1969.

KLOPSTOCK, F., " Foreign Banks in the United States: Scope and Growth of Operations," *Federal Reserve Bank of New York, Monthly Review*, June 1973.

LEES, F. A., *International Banking and Finance*, (New York: John Wiley and Sons), 1974.

LEES, F. A., *Foreign Banking and Investment in the United States: Issues and Alternatives*, (London: Macmillan), 1976.

LITTLE, J. S., *Euro-Dollars: The Money Market Gypsies*, (New York: Harper and Row), 1975.

MAYER, H., " The BIS Concept of the Net Size of the Euro-Currency Market, and its Relation to the World Money Supply," *Euromoney*, 1976.

PERKINS, J. H., " The Regulation of Foreign Banking in the United States," *Columbia Journal of World Business*, Winter 1975.

ROBINSON, S. W. Jr., *Multinational Banking*, (Leiden, A. W. Sijthoff), 1972.

RUCKDESCHEL, F. B., " Risk in Foreign and Domestic Lending Activities of U. S. Banks," *Columbia Journal of World Business*, Winter 1975.

RUGMAN, A. M., " Multinational Banks have Stable Earnings," Discussion Paper of University of Winnipeg, Manitoba, 1976.

TOBIN, J., " Towards Improving the Efficiency of the Monetary Mechanism," *Review of Economics and Statistics*, 42, August, 1960.

VERNON, R. " International Investment and International Trade in the Product Cycle," *Quarterly Journal of Economics*, May 1966.

WELSH, G. M., " The Case for Federal Regulation of Foreign Bank Operations in the United States," *Columbia Journal of World Business*, Winter 1975.

[8]

Journal of Banking and Finance 5 (1981) 33–63. North-Holland Publishing Company

THE MULTINATIONAL BANK:

A Financial MNC?

Jean M. GRAY*

Rider College, Lawrenceville, NJ 08648, USA

H. Peter GRAY

Rutgers University, New Brunswick, NJ 08903, USA

The theory of non-financial multinational corporations is applied to the multinational commercial bank. The incentives toward multinationality that characterize the expansion of non-financial firms have their counterparts in multinational banks. The theory of the MNC provides a useful basis for the development of a theory of the multinational bank when the subsidiary offices operate in foreign financial markets. When banks' foreign subsidiaries operate in supranational markets (such as the Eurocurrency markets), there is little or no equivalence because the multinational banks compete only among themselves: there is no competition with indigenous firms. The supranational markets give rise to a distinct type of subsidiary. These banking offices and the markets in which they operate serve to integrate national capital and money markets with some possible endangerment to the stability of the international financial system.

1. Introduction

The multinational corporation is a non-financial corporation which operates productive assets in a number of different sovereign states. Usually these separate operations are integrated to the extent that the operations of an MNC can be said to transcend national boundaries. In the process, efficiencies are generated which are not available to firms limited to national operations. The tremendous growth of multinational corporations in the post-war period attests to the superiority of this organizational form. [Hawkins and Walter (1979)] The sources of its growth and enhanced efficiency have been the focus of considerable research over the past twenty years and a fair consensus has now been obtained.

The last fifteen years have seen the multinational form adopted by financial corporations — most notably commercial banks. However, the growth of multinational banking has received significantly less analytic

*The authors gratefully acknowledge the copious comments on earlier drafts by Ian Giddy. The authors alone are responsible for any remaining shortcomings.

attention than that accorded to non-financial corporations: multinational banking lacks a theoretical framework such as exists for the MNC. If multinational banking, as opposed to national banking extended internationally by arm's length correspondent relationships, is to be understood and its contribution to global efficiency assessed, there must be an accepted theory of MNB behavior. This paper seeks to evolve such a theory by asserting that the conditions which generate efficiency gains and augment profits in multinational banking are the same as those which apply to non-financial multinational corporations. Evaluation of the hypothesis should result in a better understanding of the gains that accrue to MNBs from their organizational form and, by extension, of the costs and benefits that the emergence of MNBs presents for the efficiency of the international financial system.

The idea of comparing the structure and sources of efficiency gains of the MNB with that of the MNC is not original here. Grubel (1977, p. 350) posed the same question in the following way:[1]

'The basic analytical question to be answered by a theory of multinational banking is identical to that present in the case of foreign direct investment: what is the source of comparative advantage accruing to a U.S. bank in a place like Singapore, which is in competition with local banks having obvious advantages in their familiarity with local customers, capital markets, employees and government? Put differently and applied to the special problem of banking, the basic phenomenon to be explained by the theory of multinational banking is why a bank abroad can profitably offer lower lending rates *and* higher borrowing rates than its domestic competitors and thus attract customers away from them.'

In his paper, Grubel approached the problem by examining different types of operations of commercial banks and contrasts each with the theory of the MNC. This paper will take the theory of the MNC and apply each feature of that theory to the phenomenon of multinational banking. Identification of the similarities and distinctions which foster multinationality in banking as compared to non-financial MNCs should cast light on the behavior of MNBs and on the advantages to be derived in financial markets by the multinational organizational form.

Section 2 presents a summary of the consensus view regarding the conditions and enabling factors which induce non-financial MNCs to adopt the multinational organizational form. Section 3 defines multinational banking and applies the components of the consensus theory to it.

---

[1]As section 3 shows, direct competition between MNB and local banks in the 'host-country' market is not a necessary activity for the MNB. Section 4 shows that sites of supranational markets (such as Singapore) make such competition even more improbable.

Commercial banks appear to require an additional set of incentives to have foreign branches and/or subsidiaries and these are developed in section 4. These new factors are only indirectly related to the theory of the MNC and show the MNB to be the more complex organism. Section 5 summarizes the theory of the MNB and identifies its role as the main linkage among financial markets. Finally, section 6 provides a short survey of the costs and benefits derived by the global financial system from the existence of MNBs. The distinction between the two sets of motivations developed in sections 3 and 4 shows the hypothesis to be partially valid. The approach to a theory of multinational banking through the theory of MNCs is a productive one.

2. Sources of efficiency gains for MNCs

In his eclectic theory of international production, Dunning (1977, 1980) identifies three categories of enabling factors or incentives which lead to the creation of multinational enterprise. They are: ownership-specific advantages, internalization incentive advantages and location-specific variables.

Ownership-specific advantages are those features which make it possible for a corporation of one nation to compete in foreign markets with foreign, indigenous firms. They are prerequisite to multinationality. The ownership advantages consist mainly of intangible assets which derive from the size and established position of the corporation. They show themselves in the corporation's access to inputs on favored terms: access to skilled personnel, financing, the ability to integrate the operation of a subsidiary with the other parts of the MNC, access to an inventory of patented techniques and technology as well as to experience. These advantages will confer a competitive edge to a subsidiary of an MNC which will usually allow it to compete with *de novo* or small foreign firms even in the foreign market. These advantages are further enhanced if the corporation is already multinational in scope since it will then have the additional ability to exploit any potential efficiency gains inherent in international differences in factor markets as well as in access to better and broader commercial intelligence.

The ability to internalize the ownership-specific advantages and to avoid the risks and costs of transactions conducted at arm's length are the driving force toward multinationality. These are the advantages derivable from the existence of imperfect markets around which the early formal theory of the MNC was built [Hymer (1976), Rugman (1980)]. At the risk of simplifying a very complex concept, it is useful to distinguish three different kinds of internalization which will provide incentives to adopt a multinational form. The first exists when an MNC has an ownership-specific advantage in terms of access to an input in which it enjoys a monopoly. The monopoly can derive either from past expenditures on R&D or from sheer experience in the industry. This advantage permits either a cost reduction exclusive to the owner or the creation of an improved or preferable product at a cost competitive with that of other firms in the industry. It is the need to maintain the property rights inherent in the firm-specific knowledge that will lead a firm to exploit the advantage in many countries in preference to licensing it to local, indigenous corporations. This is the appropriability concept. The second source of gain from internalization derives from imperfections in product markets which an MNC is able to exploit as a result of its size, economies of scale, flexibility in joint supply in marketing, purchasing or finance and possibly by control over the supply of inputs to potential competitors. The third source of internalization gains is the inefficiency of an arm's length market system compared with the workings of a single unit. They include those gains that derive from single operational control over different levels of operations and imply some degree of vertical integration and, probably less importantly, some horizontal integration. In addition, the sheer quality of communication and empathy among employees may allow information to be transmitted more effectively within a corporation than is possible among different organizations. This state of affairs could only be explained within the traditional internalization arguments by forcing the meaning of avoidance of transaction and negotiating costs among separate corporations. There may exist within a single corporation a degree of homology among the employees that can yield a quality of communications and of commercial intelligence that exceeds anything that can be transmitted among people employed in separate organizations.[2]

The third set of forces identified within the eclectic theory are location-specific variables. These variables stress the influence of spatial phenomena such as transportation costs and other barriers to the exchange of goods among countries as well as to differences in culture and the availability of knowledge of markets and commercial practice in foreign nations. Influences of this kind are necessary if a foreign market is not to be served by exports from the home country where the ownership-specific advantages are located. The most obvious location-specific advantage is the possibility that foreign countries offer different, and more favorable, prices of immobile factors of production than are available in the home country. Mobile ownership-specific advantages can be married with the more favorable factor prices abroad of immobile factors to generate lower costs of production. Location-specific variables also include the so-called psychic differences among nations which imply different marketing strategies and different design of goods for a particular market. The role of transportation costs and commercial policy barriers to international trade may also be crucial in the determination of

---

[2]The source of the efficiency gain identified can be seen as the advantage reaped by a team of players used to each others' habits and strategies over a scratch team of opponents however individually gifted the latter may be.

how a particular foreign market will be served and lead to foreign direct investment.

All three sets of enabling factors or incentives are necessary for an MNC to evolve. But they are sequential in the sense that internalization efficiencies are available for exploitation only if ownership-specific advantages exist. Equally, multinationalization will not take place unless there is some positive location-specific inducement to create a foreign subsidiary.

Dunning's eclectic theory, while undeniably the single most satisfying theory of the causes of the existence of MNCs, is more complex and more general than is necessary for a first approach to multinational banking. For this reason, the assumption is made that ownership-specific advantages accruing to the established position of a banking firm in the industry exist. The theory can then be simplified and its main features separated. Six conditions which give rise to direct foreign investment are singled out for analysis: three concern internalization efficiencies and three relate to location-specific considerations. The application of these conditions to banking retains the essential features of the eclectic theory, but does not develop either their sequential nature nor their interdependence:

(1) Imperfections in product markets.
(2) Imperfections in factor or input markets.
(3) Economies of internal operation.
(4) Preservation of established customer accounts (preserving a market share).
(5) Entry into a growing or high-growth market.
(6) Ensuring control over a raw material source.

Because the process of financial intermediation differs significantly from that of manufacturing, the conditions inducing multinationality among banks will not parallel exactly those delineated for non-financial corporations. The correspondence is sufficiently close, however, for the application to be usefully made.

3. MNC incentives applied to multinational banks

A multinational bank is defined as a financial corporation which acquires deposits and initiates loans from offices located in more than one country. For the purposes of this paper organizations providing non-bank financial services, such as investment banking and leasing, are excluded, although the ability of a foreign subsidiary to foster such profit-enhancing activities may well prove important in the decision to establish a foreign office.[3] Included

---

[3]For U.S. banks, investment banking and commercial banking activities cannot be lodged in the same corporate entity: each requires a special subsidiary. This paper is concerned only with the commercial banking activities of foreign offices.

are all branches, subsidiaries and affiliate organizations which provide direct deposit and loan services. Banking organizations whose foreign activities are restricted to shell branches in offshore centers are not included: deposits and loans are assigned to the shell by the home office but the shells themselves have no contact with bank clients and do not initiate bank business.[4] However, banks with representative offices and agencies located in foreign countries are multinational to the extent that these offices produce banking services directly, that is, they may hold customers' credit balances, borrow and lend in host countries and solicit loans and deposits for transfer to other banking offices within the organization. Banks participating in a consortium that owns a foreign bank and the foreign bank itself are multinational in so far as their behavior meets the above criteria. However, consortia-owned banks and their owners must meet an additional criterion: the individual owner-banks and the consortium-owned bank are multinational if the members have an effective voice in the control of the syndicate's foreign operations so that co-operation between the members and the owned bank encompasses anything that will be advantageous to both banks concerned. The essential characteristic of multinational banking is that the existence of foreign offices creates scope for, and results in, intracorporate gains in efficiency and profit.

Just as the gain from multinationality accruing to a non-financial firm depends to a significant degree upon the differences among the national economies in which it possesses subsidiaries, so too does the MNB gain from being represented in different kinds of markets. Two types of multinational banking markets may be distinguished. The first is the supranational market in which activities are restricted to so-called off-shore banking. The other includes the national banking markets of countries which host offices of foreign banks. One of the functions of the MNB is to link different national markets to its own advantage, but it also benefits from its ability to integrate national markets with the supranational market.

A substantial portion of supranational market activities consists of inter-bank loans and deposits. Non-bank clients include the larger multinational corporations, parastatals and governments requiring extra-national depository services and/or loans in amounts or currencies that are not available at comparable terms from banks operating solely in national markets. Banks participating in the supranational market are not homogeneous and customers make subjective appraisals of qualitative differences in bank service, personnel, experience and safety. Even so, the supranational market is highly competitive. It is subject to minimal regulation and, for banking markets, is relatively efficient in that interest rate differentials on loans and on deposits which are not warranted by market

[4]Shell branches are more appropriately regarded as one form of the international banking arm (or department) of a domestic bank.

expectations or perceived risk, are likely to be quickly eliminated by arbitrage.[5] Because the market is supranational, no banks are indigenous and the only effective barrier to entry would appear to be the lack of size/reputation to warrant a supranational clientele.

With this background, the list of conditions which induce non-financial firms to become multinational can be applied to the operations of commercial banks. As noted above, the list focuses on the main facets of Dunning's second and third categories.

Dunning's first and prerequisite category is the existence of ownership-specific advantages. These are assumed to exist for any banking organization which makes the decision to become multinational. That is the bank must be able to provide some specialized service which extends beyond its domestic market, or it must have a reputation for efficiency, creditworthiness or the quality of the information it purveys which will enable it to profit from an extension of its operations into the supranational or other national markets. Achieving economies of scale will not be an important ownership advantage accruing to multinationality. Economies of scale appear to be exhausted at a relatively small size of banking firm, and all MNBs can be assumed to have reached the critical size. Differences in the size of a bank's capital base or the extent of its international network may influence some customer's choice of MNB, but they will not preclude multinationality.

3.1. Imperfections in product markets

Imperfections in product markets are generally attributed to barriers to entry, product differentiation and segmented markets. As noted above, these qualities are more characteristic of regulated national banking markets than they are of the supranational market. To the extent that they are permitted access to national markets, foreign MNBs will benefit from market imperfections in the same ways as non-financial corporations. For multinational banks, however, the question is whether the differential returns among national financial markets which can be attributed to market imperfections are sufficient to induce direct foreign investment.

Government regulators limit market access to some degree for both domestic and foreign banks in virtually every country. For MNBs which succeed in gaining access, the benefits will depend on the ease with which other banks can enter the market, the degree to which domestic market penetration is allowed, and whether operations can be carried out through a wholly-owned facility or are restricted to minority ownership participations

---

[5]Because they are negotiated and not open markets, banking markets cannot meet the criteria of efficient markets. However, as Dufey and Giddy (1978, p. 226) suggest, the active trading of deposits among banks may be an effective way to trade information about individual banks and to measure the ebb and flow of supply and demand.

with local institutions. Governments in countries with less developed financial markets may be amenable to some competition with domestic banks when it lowers the cost of international trade financing and the management of the country's foreign exchange reserves [Baum (1974), Letiche (1974)]. They are likely to be politically more sensitive to competition from any source in purely domestic wholesale and retail banking markets. Regulators may also be sensitive to an MNB's nationality or its bank 'brand name' insofar as these reflect current political alliances, trade patterns and perceptions of bank soundness and experience.[6]

Product differentiation can result from superior marketing techniques, research and development and the qualitative differences associated with experience in a particular product line. It can provide MNCs and established MNBs with a competitive edge in foreign markets. However, opportunities to develop and to retain proprietary control over differentiable products in banking are extremely limited. Innovations in the design of credit instruments and in the introduction of new services can be quickly emulated by other banks, domestic or foreign, and such knowledge is simply not appropriable. Profits and prestige may be enhanced by innovation, but any advantages due to sole ownership will be short-lived as competitors adopt the new techniques or invest in the requisite information capital.

The inducements for direct investment in foreign banking markets offered by product market imperfections are positive, but they do not appear to be significant. MNBs which succeed in penetrating restricted national markets will benefit to the extent that they share the available quasi-rents from barriers to entry, segmented markets and product differentiation with institutions already in the market. The limits to which oligopolistic practices can enhance earnings will be set by the degree of penetration allowed, regulators' attitudes toward new entrants, the quickness with which new services are emulated and the ease with which potential clients can escape to the supranational market. In general, the more competitive the national financial system and the more fully it is integrated with the supranational system the fewer will be the opportunities for banks to package or 'bundle' multiple services in ways which obscure the prices of individual components, and the smaller will be the gains attributable solely to product market imperfections.

3.2. Imperfections in factor markets

The two most important inputs into the provision of banking services are funds and knowledge (information capital). In modern banking markets both can be transferred within or among banking organization quickly and at low

---

[6]The significance of the firm-specific advantages to be derived from 'nationality' and 'bank' brand names in Eurobanking is developed by Giddy (1981).

cost. Once in place, modern communications and funds transfer facilities are available to all banks within a system. Even with equal access, however, MNBs retain a small cost advantage over non-MNBs.

MNBs manage liabilities on a global basis, raising funds in domestic and other national markets as well as in the supranational market. Since a substantial portion of the funds transferred internationally are made through the MNB's own network of foreign offices, the costs are internal to the organization. Non-MNBs' access to global funds is indirect, through correspondent relationships with MNBs. Because they are external to the firm, non-MNB costs will be higher: a positive spread over the global cost of funds will accrue to MNBs for providing intermediary services to non-MNB respondents.

Unlike the case for MNCs, the advantage from internalizing a factor cost is not firm-specific. All MNBs operating in national markets will enjoy this comparative imperfection in the supply of global funds. The degree to which any one benefits will depend on the global market's perception of its creditworthiness and the number of other MNBs competing in the same national markets. The advantage will be minimal in developed financial markets without significant barriers to entry in which a large number of MNBs compete for respondent and wholesale banking market clients.[7]

MNBs also derive advantages from imperfections in factor markets through the possession of information capital relevant to the individual corporations and industries which they serve. Banks acquire a considerable stock of commercial intelligence from long-standing corporate-client relationships. Dunning (1977, p. 403) defines this phenomenon as a 'cognitive imperfection' which arises whenever information about the product or service being marketed is not readily available or is costly to acquire. In so far as banks follow home country clients who locate abroad, they may be able to retain or even to expand this knowledge advantage. To the extent that they are able to do so a cognitive imperfection exists: the MNB can supply more suitable or lower cost financial services than can foreign banks unfamiliar with the customer's problems. Banks which fail to open foreign offices to serve their multinational corporate clients may lose the cognitive advantage abroad *and* at home. Other MNBs familiar with the rules and regulations in the country in which the MNC subsidiary is located can, in time, develop new specializations and serve the MNC globally.

The need to preserve information capital is an important condition leading to multinationality in banking. Direct access to global funds does provide MNBs with a small, cost advantage over domestic banks, but, by itself, is unlikely to be a critical element in the decision to become a multinational.

---

[7]Giddy and Allen (1979, p. 315) predict that international banking will soon merge with domestic banking to form a single, global wholesale banking market for the United States.

3.3. Economies of internal operation

The notion that a single firm may reduce its cost of operation by substituting its own internal organization for the costs inherent in the use of arm's length markets is attributable to Coase (1937). It is developed in a multinational context in Gray (1972, pp. 77–81). These cost savings are usually enjoyed as a result of vertical integration when different processes of a total operation are all carried on under the same executive control. They can also result from horizontal integration when operations are carried out in different countries with different underlying attributes, especially when the potential gains are more likely to be exploited because of the more efficient information linkages available within an MNC than in an arm's length market.

Cost reductions can take the form of either lower money outlays or of improved quality of service with no increase in money outlays. MNBs operating in a number of national markets can enjoy both forms of 'Coase economies'.

Many of the economies of internal organization available to banks have been achieved in a national market before the bank becomes multinational. Management is coordinated under central executive control, liability management procedures use a wide variety of different segments of the financial markets, and the marketing of the bank's services extends well beyond its local or 'natural' banking area. Becoming multinational merely extends these economies of operations to new markets. Potential savings may increase, but the essential difference lies in the breadth and scale of operations rather than in the techniques themselves.

Additional economies of internal organization from multinationalization can be achieved in four separate areas: efficiency in marketing and account management, availability and cost of funds transfers within the MNB, larger and improved networks of market information and commercial intelligence, and the potential for reduced earnings variability.

Banking is a service industry. Banks which compete for non-bank deposit and loan customers on a global basis need to develop facilities for direct and personal contact with potential clients wherever they are located. Foreign offices in important — and in not so important — national banking markets become the vehicle for the marketing and management of customer accounts. The activities of foreign offices parallel those of the home office, but they are location-specific: the home office cannot provide them as efficiently. Depending on the scale of operations in different countries, foreign offices can develop personal contacts with existing and potential clients, tailor loan and deposit contracts to meet clients' needs, provide the home office with information on the local business climate and customs, make credit evaluations and negotiate loan terms. The costs of establishing a presence in a new foreign market are generally low relative to the resources of the organization and there is no external market for making intracorporate decisions.

Offices in different national markets also allow MNBs to substitute intrabank funds transfers for some of those made through the external market. Insofar as they do, transactions costs and risks that are external to the firm are reduced. The ability to centralize control over internal funds flows should improve the earnings stream of the MNB for two reasons. First, by reducing external transactions costs it narrows marginally the spread required between the cost of funds and their use. Secondly, it provides the organization with great flexibility in global asset and liability management. Centralized coordination of internal transfers should increase the opportunities for arbitraging favorable interest rate differentials and for shifting funds globally to their most profitable use [Moskowitz (1979)].

If MNBs as a class have only one advantage over non-MNBs it has to be their ability to develop an internal global communications and intelligence network beyond the capabilities of purely domestic banks. Presumably, the more broadly-based the bank, the better will be its information capability. The sheer number of separate sources of commercial intelligence can provide a more efficient network of information with consequent increased profit opportunities.[8] In the same way, individual foreign offices will be able to provide a source of identification of special opportunities or risks in (foreign) national markets before they are generally known. For example, the physical presence of an MNB may influence a host government's choice of bank of deposit for its foreign exchange reserves or its choice of a lead bank in arranging a syndicated loan in the supranational market. The MNB may also able to create an external market in information by intermediating between a government seeking foreign investment and a corporate client in search of particular geographic, climatic, or labor force combinations.

Operations coordinated among a network of foreign offices could also contribute to lower variability in earnings for MNBs as compared to non-MNBs. This additional stability would derive from the broader asset diversification available internationally on the condition that credit market cycles are not perfectly correlated among nations. Earnings variability would also be reduced by the practice of international asset and liability management which would shift funds from offices with slack loan demand to those with strong loan demands [Rugman (1979, ch. 10)].

The types of gains to MNBs attributable to Coase economies are essentially the same as those obtained by non-financial MNCs. Operations among units in economies or markets with different characteristics are coordinated to maximize the goals of the firm. While information is not

---

[8]Giddy (1981) has performed a simple test of this advantage by regressing the foreign exchange profits of U.S. banks on the number of foreign countries in which each bank has offices. The regression shows the relationship to be strong, positive, and statistically significant.

appropriable for banks, its accumulation and transmission provide the linkages which enable them to identify profitable opportunities wherever they arise.

3.4. Preserving established customer accounts

The importance of cognitive imperfections in inducing direct foreign investment in banking has already been developed. Information capital provides opportunities for MNBs to internalize a firm-specific advantage so long as client relationships remain intact. However, unlike proprietary knowledge in manufacturing which can be protected by patents and other means, commercial intelligence can be acquired by any bank with an interest in developing specializations in specific markets or industries. The loss of a key customer for any reason would expedite the information transfer and could mean the loss of any advantage the bank may have had from a market specialization. Therefore, preserving established accounts by opening foreign offices becomes the means for protecting non-appropriable knowledge. If a bank's global share of a market is to be maintained, it must perpetuate and extend its specialized knowledge by providing on-the-spot information and intermediary services for its domestic clients in foreign markets. If it does not become an MNB there is a good chance that market share and information capital will both be eroded as more MNBs compete in specialized international markets.[9]

The tenuous nature of control over information capital in banking as compared to manufacturing may explain the sharp differences in attitudes towards joint ventures and minority equity participants on the part of MNBs and MNCs. MNCs are generally reluctant to share ownership or enter into licensing arrangements abroad for fear these will lead to a dissipation of proprietary knowledge. In contrast, joint ventures and consortia arrangements with other MNBs, national market banks and government sponsored financial institutions are common among MNBs. Shared intelligence in one national market may still be an important intermediate product in another, and group banking arrangements can extend the benefits of multinationality and the preservation of established customer accounts at low cost, tighten control over correspondent relationships and provide entry into national markets which might otherwise be closed by government fiat.

3.5. Entry into growth markets

The desire to participate in the high growth Euromarkets at least partially

---

[9]Giddy and Allen (1979) foresee an increase in the number of smaller banking institutions entering multinational markets to provide specialized banking services as lower costs of participation combine with fewer regulatory barriers to lower the costs of entry.

explains the rush to open off-shore banking offices between 1968 and 1974. Insuring participation in national banking markets with a potential for growth has also contributed importantly to the expansion of on-shore banking facilities.

MNBs are multiple product firms with great flexibility to tailor their products to specific client needs. Extending and adapting an existing product line in new markets present no technological or supply problems. MNBs also have great flexibility in tailoring the size and nature of their investments in national markets to the existing regulatory structure and to a set of risk-adjusted expected returns. Despite the facts that firm specific advantages may not be long retained and expected returns may be highly uncertain, the decision to enter a new market should almost always be positive. The incremental costs and risks of establishing a representative office or acquiring a minority equity participation are low relative to the total capital of an established and diversified MNB organization. Thus, the initial investment decision may be more one of determining the appropriate size of the outlay to assure a positive net present value than one of making a determination as to whether or not to enter the market.

Evidence of the importance which MNBs attach to establishing at least a minimal presence in national markets is provided by the large number of representative offices, joint ventures and minority equity participations undertaken in newly independent and developing countries. There is always the possibility that the first-comers into small, relatively stable markets with a potential for generating some business may pre-empt entry by other MNBs and preserve for themselves any benefits from market imperfections that exist. Depending on ease of entry, the likelihood that such a favored position would be retained in markets is small: it is also relatively unimportant.

3.6. Ensuring access to raw materials

Corporations need readily-available supplies of raw material if they are to provide customers with an uninterrupted flow of products. When these raw materials are available only in specific geographic locations outside the home country, MNCs often seek direct control over such supplies by establishing foreign subsidiary companies. The subsidiaries may be established whether or not the firm expects to reap Coase-economies from the vertical integration and without reference to the efficiency of arm's length international markets. The intent is simply to ensure continuity of supply.

The benefits of gaining direct access to indigenous supplies of key currencies provides an analogous inducement for banks to become multinational. In the process of providing currency transformation services for customers, MNBs acquire liabilities and assets in a variety of currencies. The foreign exchange risks to which these services may give rise can be eliminated by hedging in foreign exchange markets. To the extent that an MNB can establish stable deposit bases in the currencies in which their international assets are denominated, the costs of hedging can be reduced or eliminated. The greater the share of assets in a bank's portfolio denominated in a single currency, and the greater the rate of roll-over, the greater the potential gain from a reliable and stable source of that currency. Deposit bases which originate in home-country operations of a particular currency are less subject to supply vagaries which may plague foreign exchange and even the supranational markets.

Ensuring a stable dollar deposit base and source of access to dollar credits is an important reason for non-U.S. MNBs to establish themselves in the United States. As long as the dollar remains the pre-eminent currency in which international banking assets are denominated, a domestic deposit base will provide direct access to funds which can be used to finance clients in American as well as in international markets. Simply put, liability management in a particular currency is more efficiently accomplished by operations in that currency's home market.

The international Banking Act of 1978 imposes on foreign banks in the United States, the same regulatory costs *and benefits* as apply to domestic banks. Foreign subsidiaries in the United States have access to the Federal Reserve discount window and the other services of the System at the cost of being required to hold reserves against deposits and being subject to the same limitations on branching as domestic banks. The regulatory costs of having a banking subsidiary operating in the United States have increased, but the benefits of an improved dollar source clearly outweigh them. A German banker [Dicken (1979)] expressed his bank's motivation for establishing a New York subsidiary in the following way:

'[W]e would like to be importantly included in the Fed's open market operations. Also we would like to have access to the Fed as a lender-of-last-resort. We need such direct access to dollar funds because we intend to be in business here not for the next few weeks..., but for the next fifty to one hundred years. We need New York for our international banking business.'

Equally, the existence of a New York subsidiary and the benefits that it confers, adds to the prestige and perceived credit worthiness of the bank.

Because most of their operations are conducted in dollars, American MNBs will attach relatively less importance to securing currency bases by opening offices in the home markets of foreign currencies. Nonetheless, the argument does apply: deposit bases in important (key) currency countries can provide relatively low-cost and low-risk sources of these currencies.

4. The escape motivation

The main ingredient in Stephen Hymer's seminal theory of forces motivating non-financial firms to become multinational was the existence of imperfect markets. When the imperfection exists in a factor market as a result of the development of a firm-specific technological input through R&D expenditures, an ownership advantage has been created. This ownership advantage will be exploited by an MNC if it can be internalized and if there exists a locational advantage to utilizing the input in a foreign country. When the imperfection exists in a product market, the MNC will attempt to establish itself in this market in order to share in any existing quasi-rents. Net ownership assets (in Dunning's terms) are directly prerequisite to the exploitation abroad of an imperfection in a factor market. They are indirectly necessary to exploit an imperfect product market in the sense that it will be difficult for even an established foreign corporation to effect entry into a foreign oligopoly in the absence of net ownership advantages. The emphasis in the theory of MNCs is the lure of some pure or quasi-rent available from the establishment of a foreign subsidiary: it is a 'pull' theory. They are indirectly necessary to exploit an imperfect product market in the sense that it will be difficult for even an established foreign corporation to effect entry into a foreign oligopoly in the absence of net ownership advantages. The emphasis in the theory of MNCs is the lure of some pure or quasi-rent available from the establishment of a foreign subsidiary: it is a 'pull' theory whereby an MNC is drawn to a potentially-advantageous imperfectly-competitive foreign market.[10]

The theory that imperfect markets are the main *raison d'être* of MNCs can also be applied to MNBs, but with an important difference! Commercial banks operate in their domestic markets under the *aegis* of a supervisory or regulatory body and in a *milieu* subject to disruptive jolts that follow from the discretionary conduct of monetary policy by the central bank. While the regulatory climate does make it difficult for an established bank to fail or to make less than some minimally-satisfactory rate of return on invested capital, there is also an implicit upper bound to profit rates. Thus, established banks (those with net ownership advantages *vis-à-vis* foreign banks) may perceive the regulatory climate as a market imperfection which restrains rather than enhances profit-rates. To the extent that a bank can visualize higher rates of return on capital to be obtainable in an unregulated supraregulated supranational market, banks will be tempted into multinationallity by escaping from imperfect and into foreign *competitive* markets. Provided that the supranational market allows banks to escape the regulatory strictures,

---

[10]Dunning (1977, pp. 410–411) distinguishes between the net social contribution of an MNC when it has created a piece of knowledge and transferred it and when it is merely exploiting an oligopolistic product market. However, both Hymer (1976) and Kojima (1973) lump all imperfections in a single efficiency-reducing category.

MNBs can earn higher rates of return on capital (adjusted for risk) in *laisser-faire* markets in which competition will be more severe, by compensating any reduction in the net profit rate on earning assets with increased leverage.[11]

This motivation for becoming multinational is generally different from those analysed in the previous section and has quite different implications for the contribution of multinational banking to global welfare and for the policy implications which follow. The main distinction is that the motivations considered in section 3 are incentives to establish a host-country office in a foreign, regulated market in addition to the home market. The manner and the degree of regulation may differ among nations but these distinctions are of secondary importance. The *laisser-faire* and more competitive markets that attract MNBs are better described as 'supranational' financial markets. Of these the Eurocurrency markets are the obvious example.

Another dimension of the 'escape motivation' applied peculiarly to U.S. Banks. The Glass-Steagall Act prohibits the combination of investment and commercial banking and the McFadden Act prohibits a bank from opening a branch outside of its home state. Both of these restrictions were tempered by the Edge Act which allows U.S. commercial banks to set up Edge corporations abroad which can act as an investment banker. Because the focus of this paper is on commercial banking, Edge corporations engaged in other than commercial banking activities are not considered in detail but their existence will obviously contribute to the Coase-economies available from an international network of offices.

The advantages of escaping into an unregulated market (as distinct from operating within a system of national regulations) can best be considered by examining the determinants of the rate of return on bank capital potentially available. These determinants can be expressed as an identity of a set of component ratios reminiscent of the du Pont system of financial analysis:

$$\frac{P(1-t)}{E} \equiv \frac{P(1-t)}{EA} \cdot \frac{EA}{TA} \cdot \frac{TA}{E},$$

where P is profits before taxes, E is the value of bank equity (paid-in capital and surplus and retained profits), t is the marginal tax rate, and EA and TA measure earning assets and total assets respectively. The rate of return on equity (P/E) is clearly very sensitive to variation in the rate of return on earning assets, variation in the ratio of earning assets to total assets and variation in the ratio of total assets to equity. (In banking circles, this last ratio is sometimes referred to as 'capital gearing' and in the theory of finance

[11]In practice, MNBs are liable to regulation of their activities in supranational markets through the regulation of the parent bank . . . This point is considered below in this section.

developed for non-financial corporations, it is known as financial leverage or the leverage factor.)

The greater competitiveness that exists in unregulated supranational financial markets will be likely to provide an MNB with a ratio of profits to earning assets below that available domestically. But freedom from regulation will permit banks to have higher ratios of earning to total assets and of total assets to capital than are likely to be sanctioned by domestic regulatory authorities. Overall rates of return to equity will tend to be higher for bank activities in unregulated markets if the favorable effects of the two ratios, EA/TA and TA/E, more than offset any diminution in $P(1-t)/EA$. After-tax profits will also be enhanced to the extent that a multinational network of offices permits the organization to distribute total profits among different profit centers located in countries with different rates of corporate taxes. Any gains in the total rate of return on equity to the MNB which result from operations in an unregulated banking market must be adjusted for any increased variability in profit rates that may result from the unregulated activities. Higher leverage factors, greater maturity mismatching and greater rate-of-exchange exposure can all contribute to increased year-to-year variability in profits. Any variability in profit rates is generally assumed to be an undesirable characteristic and is likely to be seen as a partial offset against any increase in average or expected rates of return on equity. This source of variability in profit rates derives from the positions which a bank operating in an unregulated market may be expected to adopt and does not depend upon the unregulated market having greater intrinsic instability. To the extent that an unregulated market also exposes a bank to some greater likelihood of financial crisis than a regulated market, some allowance for higher risk may also need to be set against any increase in rates of return on equity.

The amount of capital gearing (the ratio of total assets to equity) permitted to banks by regulatory authorities grows with the size of the bank. This, by itself, provides an incentive for growth in the size of the bank if the other two ratios on the right-hand side of the identity were held constant or deteriorate by less than the ratio of assets to equity increases. Regulatory authorities are prepared to countenance lower ratios of capital to liabilities for large banks because these are, presumably, blessed with better-diversified portfolios of assets and almost negligible non-systematic risk. Multinationalization may take place as an engine of growth if the conditions for higher overall rates of return on equity can be met. In addition to the absence of regulation, sheer growth might provide greater financial leverage. In much the same way, growth may be seen as an end in itself and multinationalization may be motivated solely by a desire for growth. However, it is not immediately clear that the argument of allowing higher gearing with domestic growth can be automatically extended to growth which is achieved by operations in unregulated banking markets. Unregulated international or supranational markets are likely to be exposed to larger shocks than regulated national markets because of their greater exposure to political and economic disruptions. This greater exposure to market risk, coupled with the higher variability in profit rates that may be expected to derive from procedures in unregulated markets, may mean that the ideal amount of capital should be higher for international banks than for national banks of similar size.

Activities in supranational banking markets are an extremely important attraction for the establishment of foreign offices. This is testified to by the relatively large numbers of foreign offices that exist in supranational banking centres: London has 275 foreign banks located there, Hong Kong has 105, Luxembourg 100, and Singapore has 95. While London is an important financial center in its own right as well as being at the main location of Eurocurrency activities, the other centers are almost exclusively associated with supranational banking centers. In contrast, such large national centers as New York, Paris, and Tokyo have, respectively, only 100, 50, and 70 foreign banks.

Unregulated banking markets allow banks to enhance profits by creating foreign offices to

(i)   Enjoy freedom to maintain capital funds only to the extent that a dearth of capital might inhibit the supply of deposits.
(ii)   Maintain liquid reserves only to the extent dictated by prudence.
(iii)   Indulge in foreign exchange positions and maturity mismatch exposure freely.
(iv)   Take advantage of inter-market arbitraging (liability management).
(v)   Utilize any tax havens that might be available.
(vi)   Avoid domestic restrictions on foreign exchange transactions.
(vii)   Avoid interest rate regulations in national markets.
(viii) Serve as an intra-bank source of funds for offices operating in national markets.

The gains that are to be obtained from reasons (i) and (ii) have already been described in the identity given above. The absence of regulatory oversight will enable banks to avoid the burden imposed upon national banks by authorities concerned with avoiding instability in financial markets. Any compulsory deposit insurance also fits in this particular category. [Grubel (1977, p. 358).] In the same way, the gains from reasons (iii), (iv), and (v) are straightforward examples of the profit-enhancing potential that derives from operation in a *laisser-faire* market. Any potential for taking advantage of global rate differentials in different markets, particularly between a supranational and a national market, and to take positions which involve some degree of exposure to risk of loss on which regulatory authorities would frown, offer an incentive to establish a foreign office in a supranational market.

The avoidance of specific restrictions, usually associated with domestic monetary policy goals [reasons (vi) and (vii)] have been important causes of the growth of multinational banking as far as both the number of foreign offices and the volume of deposits are concerned [Dicken (1979)]. The surge in the establishment of foreign branches and subsidiaries by large U.S. banks in the late 'sixties can be attributed to the existence of the interest equalization tax which impeded the acquisition of foreign assets and to Regulation Q which limited the rate of interest payable on time deposits. High reserve requirements on deposits in German banks imposed by the Bundesbank in an effort to stifle the inflow of deposits into West Germany in 1969, were an important stimulus to West German banks to establish branches outside of the sphere of influence of the Bundesbank.[12] Swedish and Swiss banks have both created foreign offices in order to be able to avoid the handicaps that domestic regulations over foreign exchange caused in servicing clients foreign requirements.

Finally, the existence of a subsidiary or branch in a supranational market allows easier and (probably) cheaper access to international funds during periods of national monetary stringency. The history of short-term capital inflows into the U.S. MNBs in 1969 as a release from monetary stringency invoked in Washington by the Federal Reserve System is well documented: the failure of the System to have foreseen this phenomenon is difficult to understand since the mechanism had been used on a smaller scale during the crunch of 1966 [Brimmer (1973) and Gray (1979, pp. 635–661)].

While supranational markets themselves may be virtually unregulated, the participants can be subjected to some form of supervision by the national regulatory. authorities through the parent bank. The actual degree of supervision of supranational subsidiaries varies sharply among different nations. Walter (1981) provides a thorough description of the way in which this supervision is handled and indicates that the American regulatory authorities are the leaders in this emerging practice. But the fact that the regulatory authorities do inspect the international asset and liability positions of banks with subsidiaries operating in supranational markets does not necessarily imply effective regulation. Commercial banks, particularly very large banks, often fail to heed well-intentioned comments made by the regulatory authorities in the seclusion of the executive offices — particularly when highly profitable activities are 'at issue'. The appeal of entry into an unregulated market as a cause of multinationality stands but it may require qualification for banks of certain countries. To the extent that it constitutes a

---

[12]Luxembourg has the additional advantage of an almost complete lack of concern with the bank's capital base.

vehicle for growth and growth enables commercial banks to pay less attention to regulators, participation in an unregulated market becomes *pro tanto* more attractive.

Because supranational financial markets became quantitatively significant in the early sixties, the 'supranational subsidiary' is a fairly new species and a recent contributor to the drive to multinationality. But the growth of the supranational financial markets has been such that the importance of this type of subsidiary, measured in terms of assets, has grown to exceed that of 'host-country' offices of the type considered in section 3 above.

The original hypothesis that the incentive for multinationality on the part of banks is closely analogous to that of non-financial MNCs was originally correct but its validity has waned in the last twenty years. No longer is the 'pull' theory of multinational banking the more important strand (as it remains for MNCs). Large and fast-growing subsidiaries of MNBs exist in response to the escape motivation. Rather than seeking imperfections abroad which they are capable of exploiting, MNBs seek to escape from government-imposed regulations at home and in other national markets and flock to the supranational markets.

5. The theory of the multinational bank: Summary

The theory of the MNB, like that of the MNC, can be described in terms of the motivations that induce multinationality. Once these causes are identified and understood, the pattern of operational behavior of the MNB (or the MNC) is effectively determined.

Commercial banks evolve into MNBs for two quite distinct sets of reasons. In this they differ from MNCs whose multinationality tends to derive from a single cohesive, though complex, set of forces. The first set of reasons for multinationality (leading to the establishment of host-country branches or subsidiaries) allows the parent bank to reap the gains available from a presence in foreign national markets. The second inducement to multinationalization (establishing supranational branches or subsidiaries) allows the bank to operate in a supranational financial market. The two different types of foreign offices will have different operating criteria.

Early MNBs relied completely on host-country offices abroad and evolved in response to the motivations identified in section 3. Established banks in one country with some net ownership-specific advantages were able to establish themselves in foreign national financial markets. The ownership-specific advantages were mainly connected with working relationships with multinational (non-financial) corporations and the banks were able to retain the very close relationship with their home-based clients and with the clients' foreign subsidiaries (the location-specific aspect of host-country offices). The pecularities of the banking industry — regulation, virtually-assured minimum profit rates, low costs of entry — made it possible for economies of internalization to be achieved with little exposure to risk of loss. These economies of internalization came mainly in the form of commercial intelligence, possibilities for foreign-exchange dealings, arbitrage operations and the expansion into the international sphere of a set of domestic correspondent relationships. In developed financial markets, the MNB penetrated the foreign market only to a limited degree, usually eschewing direct competition with local indigenous banks in the retail banking market and emphasizing wholesale and international banking transactions.[13]

The second class of MNB activity generates supranational branches or subsidiaries which provide direct representation in a (virtually) unregulated supranational market. The motivation underlying this type of expansion has been detailed in section 4. It mainly seeks the higher rates of return on equity that are associated with operations in an unregulated market. Such operations are likely to involve unrestrained liability management, acceptance of exchange-rate risks and maturity-mismatching as well as the ability to achieve high ratios of earning assets to total assets and of total assets to equity. In supranational markets, the MNB competes with other giant banks in a large, wholesale banking market. Competition among the banks is keen, sheer size of parent is a precondition for entry into this market but, in contradistinction to the establishment of host-country offices in national markets, *net* ownership-specific advantages are not needed since there are no indigenous banks in a supranational market.

While this dichotomy of types of MNB is analytically correct and useful, it is quite blurred in the real world. Nearly all MNBs will have foreign offices of both kinds. Indeed, in financial centers in which supranational markets are located (such as London, Luxembourg, or Hong Kong), a single branch may fulfill both functions.[14] The distinction between the two types of foreign office and between their operational criteria, implies potentially different contributions to the world's financial system as well as potentially different problems.

MNBs establish financial linkages which closely integrate national and supranational banking markets. This integration of financial markets is schematically depicted in fig. 1 which shows one supranational market and three national markets. All banks in a national market are deemed to be subject to similar pressures through the operation of national money markets. The supranational market is shown as being directly linked with each national market by that nation's MNB's supranational offices (though, in practice, foreign-owned MNBs will also serve as important direct linkages

---

[13]This does not mean that all foreign branches or subsidiaries did not compete for local deposits — merely that such competition was not pursued to the same degree that local banks would pursue it among themselves.

[14]Internally, in such offices, there will be quite separate operating divisions.

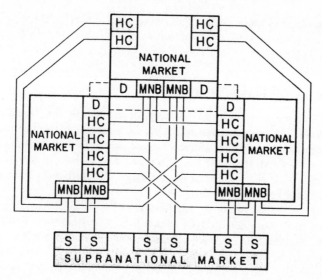

Fig. 1. Schematic representation of MNB linkages. (Key: MNB signifies head office, HC indicates host-country office and S, supranational office. D identifies domestic banks and dotted lines show correspondent relationships: these contrast with intra-bank linkages indicated by the solid lines. All banks within a single market react in the same way to demand and supply pressures. In practice, HC offices may have a direct link with the parent's supranational office.)

in some markets). National markets are linked with each other indirectly through the supranational market and directly through host-country MNB offices and correspondent relationships (shown as dotted lines between pairs of domestic banks). Linkages generated by host-country offices probably now dominate the older and weaker linkages forged through networks of international correspondent relationships and foreign exchange dealers. Any change in conditions in a single financial market will be quickly transmitted to the other markets in the system — both directly and indirectly. For example, a sudden change in the conditions prevailing in the supranational market will quickly be transmitted to the national markets by the linkage between MNB head offices and their supranational foreign offices. Any tendency for the direct linkage to be slow in transmitting the change in conditions to one national market will be made up for by linkages among head offices and host-country branches or subsidiaries in other national markets. The transmission of changes in conditions in the supranational market is also likely to be aided by changed patterns of borrowing by large firms (and governments) with access to both the national and the supranational market.

It is possible to preserve some degree of independence for a national financial market but the difficulty of such a task is enhanced by the existence of the sophisticated financial linkages developed by MNBs. Positive measures to be taken toward breaking such linkages are considered in Frydl (1979 1980) and Tobin (1978).

6. The welfare implications of MNBs

The theory of multinational banking developed in the three preceding sections is useful because it permits a new distinction to be introduced into any assessment of the global efficiency gains which follow from the existence of networks of MNBs. What is important is that the two separate motivations which encourage the development of MNBs may have difference implications for economic welfare.

Any analysis of the welfare contributions of a set of financial institutions will need a more complex analytic model than is customarily used in welfare economics. Traditional welfare-economic analyses are set in a general equilibrium framework: they presuppose the attainment of an equilibrium and contrast the efficiency of the different equilibria that are generated by different sets of initial conditions. The concern is with allocative efficiency. An important attribute of a set of financial institutions (and of the financial system within which it operates) is that it may affect the probability that an equilibrium will be reached without some intervening crisis being generated. The allocative-efficiency aspects of a set of financial institutions must be weighed against any tendency for the set of institutions to contribute to or endanger the attainment of the equilibrium stability efficiency. One question which must be addressed is whether or not allocative-efficiency is likely to be achieved at the expense of stability-efficiency (or *vice versa*) and, secondly, whether the distinctions inherent in host-country and supranational offices play a role in any trade-off between the two kinds of efficiency.

For some purposes, it will be useful to distinguish between two kinds of stability efficiency in financial systems. A system will have one kind of stability efficiency when it is able to prevent an external shock from bringing about deterioration in financial markets: a second, stronger kind of stability efficiency would be attained if a system were to take a set of financial markets which were in disarray and to return them to a state in which it functions smoothly. A system of flexible exchange rates may well have the first, weaker capability but not the second. Current disappointment with flexible exchange rates may derive, in part at least, from the fact that fixed parities were renounced after the international financial system was in substantial disarray. When the global financial system is operating under severe strain, the stability-efficiency qualities of multinational banks may be more important than any allocative efficiency which they may generate [Minsky (1977a, b)].

In this context, it is useful to define some terms which help to characterize the different conditions which will exist in international financial systems. A financial system is defined as 'fragile' when a large number of economic units is hostage to the continued availability of refinancing so that any severe disruption of financial markets will be self-aggravating. Minsky (1977a) terms such positions as 'speculative'. He argues that fragility can be endemic to an economic system so that it becomes self-reinforcing. The opposite of fragility is 'robustness' and a robust financial system will be able to withstand a severe disturbance (real-sector or financial in origin) without allowing the impact to be magnified and without allowing repercussions from that disturbance to cause deterioration into an economic collapse or financial crisis. Whether a system is fragile or robust is not determinable in the absence of the conditions which prevail in the world when the system is being assessed. Define a 'tranquil world' as one in which an important number of economic units is not required by past errors of judgment or current disturbances to change the liability and asset mix of their portfolios by more than can be accomplished by adjustment of flows within a single planning period. Turbulence is the antonym of tranquility and implies the existence of a succession of judgmental errors and shocks that come upon each other in historical time at a rate greater than economic units can adapt to without changing both the mix and the size of their asset and liability holdings. Thus, turbulence implies the possibility of suppressed financial disequilibria and failure to adapt to new circumstances as well as ongoing disturbances. A third possibility is a super-tranquil world in which shocks occur which assist in the adjustment process needed to eliminate suppressed disequilibria.[15] The more tranquil the world, the less is the intrinsic robustness needed for a financial system to achieve its potential level of allocative efficiency. Similarly, the more turbulent the world, the greater must be the original robustness of the financial system if a crisis is to be averted. In a turbulent world, welfare criteria must emphasize stability efficiency above allocative efficiency.

It is difficult, as the world enters the decade of the 1980s, to conclude that the international financial system is anything but fragile and any current assessment of the welfare effects of multinational banking will place great weight on their stability efficiency. Certainly with continued growth in OPEC surpluses, the world is turbulent.[16] We shall, however, consider the allocative efficiency of MNBs first. Grubel (1977) identifies three kinds of efficiency gains of this kind which can be attributed to MNBs: increased competition in domestic banking markets, Coase-economies in servicing

---

[15]Thus, a decline in oil prices brought about by a weakening of OPEC would be a super-tranquil disturbance.

[16]*New York Times* (1980, p. D 1) reports concern on the part of central bankers from the Group of Ten that continued recycling of OPEC surpluses would require excessive lending to deficit nations by commercial banks and bring the risk of a financial crash.

MNCs, and greater allocative efficiency as a result of better integration of national capital and money markets.

The contribution of foreign banks to improved competition in a national retail market in a developed economy is likely to be substantial only if the authorities allow multinational banks to compete actively with local banks. Even where retail markets are open to entry by foreign multinational banks, these banks are unlikely to upset any prevailing level of competition and will merely insert themselves to compete in the accepted pattern. Retail banking is a regulated industry and this, by itself, will limit the contribution which new entrants can make to benefit the industry's clients. Any possible gain in allocative efficiency should be compared with the efficiency gain resulting from an increase in the number of domestic banks. Multinationals are only likely to benefit the efficiency of a retail market on balance if they bring knowhow and banking expertise with them and if they enter into a size range different from that which new domestic banks will be able to achieve. By contrast, multinational banks can make significant contributions to the efficiency of financial markets in developing countries by introducing modern, sophisticated techniques more quickly than these could be developed by indigenous bankers.[17]

The ability to serve the foreign activities and/or subsidiaries of domestic clients more expertly than local banking in host-country markets is a one-shot gain. The gain derives from a familiarity with the problems and desires of the parent company and its industry: this knowledge provides the multinational bank with a competitive advantage over local competitors. But local, competing banks have only to serve the client for a short period of time before they will enjoy the same bank–client familiarity and relationship. Other activities that accrue to multinational banks such as better commercial intelligence, increased expertise in arbitrage and foreign exchange transactions are continuing gains.

Finally, there is the gain that derives from the integration of capital and financial markets. This is a time-honored source of efficiency gains in so far as the terms and availability of credit tend to be equalized in different countries. Supranational markets, such as the Eurocurrency market, also indicate some gain in efficiency in the cost-reduction sense in that spreads between borrowing and lending rates are smaller than in national, regulated markets. The smaller spread encourages the efficiency gains derived from financial intermediation.

The only possible cost in terms of allocative efficiency is that multinational

---

[17]The establishment of sophisticated international banking in primary-producing countries may be a response to the need for the provision of international banking services in nations exporting to the developed world. This is merely an example of financial linkage supplementing communication and information linkages that were created in response to international trade in primary products.

banks tend to encourage the growth of large banking units and tend to bias the allocation and terms of credit toward giant corporations and away from small borrowers.

The potential gains and losses in stability-efficiency are likely to prove more substantial. Most of these gains and losses can be attributed to the existence of MNBs in supranational markets. Host-country banking offices play a smaller role in stability-efficiency as linkages among national markets but their role is minor in comparison with the integrating effects achieved by supranational offices. Given this fact, the welfare effects of MNBs, at least in the stability dimension, become difficult to distinguish from the welfare effects derivable from the existence of the supranational markets themselves. There are four main aspects of stability-efficiency that derive from the existence of multinational banks: the benefit of the ability of institutional evolution and growth to contribute to the robustness of the international financial system, the costs of erosion of national control for monetary aggregates and the possibility that the supranational markets have created credit so freely that they have contributed to global inflation, the implication of failure by one or more large MNBs (Eurobanks), and the costs of enhanced instability of exchange rates [Frydl (1979–1980, p. 11)].

The evolution and growth of the supranational market in the years immediately following the fourfold increase in the price of oil in 1973/4 contributed greatly to the robustness of the international financial system. This evolution allowed the deficits of oil-importing nations to be financed without severe short-run adjustments to the new international trading conditions, without regressions of long duration or depression and without severe financial crisis. It would be hard to overestimate the welfare gain that MNBs contributed at that time. The MNBs proved themselves capable of absorbing huge amounts of financial risk but their capacity to absorb risk is, at any given time, finite. The capacity may grow slowly through time as the institutions acquire increased equity bases but the fact that the capacity to intermediate between debtor and creditor is limited, means that the efficiency gain in the form of latent robustness that allowed MNBs to tame the turbulence of 1974, may not be available in the 1980s. MNBs have exhausted their potential for rapid evolution and for large increases in the volume of intermediation.

A financial system becomes increasingly fragile when the capacity of the set of financial institutions to absorb risk does not increase with the risks inherent in making loans to deficit units. Fragility depends on the latent capacity of the financial system to withstand shocks as well as on the ongoing turbulence of events. If deficit units resist making the adjustments required by conditions in the goods and financial markets and continue to finance deficits, the suppressed disequilibria grow more serious. Any set of financial institutions which facilitates continued financing or impedes efforts by the national authorities to bring about adjustment, will contribute to the fragility of the system. This is stability-inefficiency. MNBs can contribute to increased fragility by creating linkages which make financing the deficit easy and which allow borrowers to bypass monetary restriction.

If MNBs, in their search for profit, have created excessive amounts of credit in supranational markets and the deficit nations have used this credit to postpone adjustment, the MNBs contribute to fragility. If the creation of credit allows deficit nations not only to finance deficits but also to inflate so that the competitiveness of their tradable goods and services is reduced, the situation becomes more turbulent. In the same way, making credit available to debtor nations, with or without the approval of the monetary authorities, will be stability-inefficient. In 1969 in the United States, monetary stringency was partially circumvented by the inflow of funds to the U.S. market from the Eurocurrency market under the *aegis* of the MNBs [Brimmer (1973)]. This is a classic example of MNBs evolving more quickly than the perceptions of the central bankers. What is of concern here is the weakening of the national control over the money supply and the role of supranational offices of MNBs in that process.

The second way in which MNBs can aggravate the fragility of the international financial system is for banks to expose themselves to excessive risk. This can occur when supranational offices seek to maintain target rates of profitability and take risks that are (collectively) imprudent. Under these conditions, rescheduled loans to near-bankrupt clients play a larger part in bank portfolios without contributing to revenues (and retained profits) at an appropriate risk-adjusted rate. Weak loans can force banks to roll over maturing debt, sometimes unwisely, in an attempt to save funds already committed [Walter (1981)]. Banks with important amounts of funds tied up in assets of this kind will be less well able to withstand any financial crisis that may strike the system. Supranational offices of MNBs have license to reduce their liquidity cushions and, possibly, their ratios of equity to assets so that the entire system becomes more vulnerable. They engage in liability management (as do many domestic and host-country offices) and liability management is the essence of 'speculative finance'. Minsky (1977a, p. 144) stresses the role of banks in the creation of fragility.

> 'Commercial banks . . . typically engage in speculative finance: the term to maturity of their debts is shorter than that of their assets. . . . The shorter term of debts than of assets in bank means that banks are vulnerable to financial market developments: untoward developments can increase the carrying cost of assets in position without necessarily improving their cash flows.'

All of these factors reduce the robustness of the financial system by reducing the size of any adverse impact which a supranational office can withstand before being in danger of collapsing. The almost universal practice in the Eurocurrency market of syndicating loans reduces the exposure of individual banks to any default by a borrower. The benefits of this practice of syndication may be countered by the accompanying very high rates of inter-bank deposits: such deposits can cease very quickly to be assets, particularly liquid assets, when a bank comes close to insolvency. In addition to bank failures caused by turbulence, banks could also fail because of mismanagement or because of the severity of competition. Provided that the parent banks are strong, this eventuality seems unlikely.

The final attribute of supranational markets and MNBs which may lead to systemic fragility is the potential role played by banks in creating unstable foreign exchange markets. Any such instability will be the responsibility of both host-country and supranational offices. If banks' positions in foreign exchanges lead to self-fulfilling expectations and create swings in exchange rates of great amplitude, then the system of MNBs may have both a stability and an allocative cost. The allocative cost derives from the reduced ability of business to make rational investment decisions when the foreign exchange market is not providing some stable indication of the competitiveness of foreign and domestic industries. The stability cost derives from the fact that unstable foreign exchange markets can lead to bankruptcies by clients and severe trading losses by some commercial banks. Bankruptcies and losses by banks are the essence of fragility.

The potential of supranational offices for stability-inefficiency raises the question of what can be done to increase the robustness of the international financial system — particularly given the ongoing turbulence in world affairs. One solution is to reduce the turbulence and this can be done by forcing deficit nations to accept the adjustments required of them by new international economic conditions. There is little evidence at this time that the deficit nations are doing more than make small and grudging adjustments in their economies. Frequently in developing nations, the prospect of political upheaval is too strong for stringent measures to be put in place. The tight money policy of the Federal Reserve Board may betoken some reduction in the rate at which the United States will increase its indebtedness but the policy may not be able to withstand the political pressures it will arouse. Agreements by central bankers have added robustness to the supranational markets. By agreeing in effect to act as lender of last resort to supranational markets and to insure deposits of foreigners in failed banks, the central banks have increased the capacity of the Eurocurrency market to attract liabilities and, therefore, to intermediate.

A third measure might be to attempt to reduce the stability-inefficiency of the supranational markets by exercising some control over the MNBs. This will be difficult to accomplish. Giddy and Allen (1979, pp. 321–323) argue that MNBs are not subject to regulation by national authorities and that there will be competition among regulators to maintain their sphere of influence. If this be true, regulation could only come about by collusion and co-operation among regulators. Tobin (1978) suggests that the violence of fluctuation in foreign exchange markets and national control over the monetary aggregates could be improved if a wedge were to be interposed between national capital markets. He suggests that a tax be levied on all spot conversions from one currency to another and is presumably thinking mainly in terms of host-country offices or interbank lending. His proposal could be refined to eliminate small transactions and transactions that are backed by documents indicating that the funds flow is tied to the transfer of goods or to direct investment. When funds are acquired from supranational offices the tax might not be applicable. A reserve requirement imposed by the authorities on 'managed liabilities' is already in force in the United States and would serve equally well as the wedge between a national and the supranational market. This solution presupposes a willingness on the part of the authorities in deficit countries to impose adjustment on their citizenry (and electorates).

7. Conclusion

The existence of two distinct causes of multinationality in banking separates the theories of multinationality in financial and non-financial corporations. While the welfare gains derived from MNCs are subject to a great deal of dispute, many unbiased analysts would identify the gains as quite positive and as growing through time. The growth through time derives, in part, from the increased ability to harness the potential contributions of this new organizational form. The welfare gains of MNBs are much less notable. With the exception of the integration of national capital markets, the allocative gains are small and the stability-efficiency of MNBs is likely to be negative in the future.[18]

The answer does not seem to lie in the regulation of MNB offices operating in supranational markets. National financial markets may have to learn to co-exist with very large, unregulated financial markets and with the risk of periodic crisis or mini-crisis. Relief from this situation will not be easy to achieve and will probably require initiatives on several fronts. Some of these have already been instituted [Giddy (1980)]. First and foremost, the world needs a reduction in the degree of turbulence to be instigated by positive adjustment policies in deficit (debtor) nations. A second means is to reduce the penalty aspects of domestic controls which enhance the attraction of supranational markets. A third is in line with Tobin's suggestion of

---

[18]As Grubel (1977, p. 358) points out, the regulation of domestic or national banking systems evolved in response to a tendency of unregulated banking to endemic financial crisis. Escape from regulatory oversight is, therefore, likely to increase the likelihood of financial crisis.

thwarting some of the linkages which contribute to stability-inefficiency. The final measure is for the world's central banks to increase the robustness of the financial system by instituting new measures to that purpose — such as enforcing parent responsibility for foreign offices and central bank responsibility for foreign deposits in offices of commercial banks under their domestic jurisdiction.

References

Baum, D.J., 1974, Banks of Canada in the Commonwealth Caribbean: Economic nationalism and multinational enterprise of a modern power (Praeger, New York).
Brimmer, A.F., 1973, Multinational banks and the management of monetary policy in the United States, Journal of Finance 28, 439 454.
Coase, R.H., 1937, The nature of the firm, Economica 4, 386 405.
Dicken, E., 1979, Forthcoming challenges to multinational banking, Paper presented at Port Chester, NY, Oct. 27, 1979, to a Conference on United States-European Economic Perspectives for the 1980s.
Dufey, G. and I. Giddy, 1978, The international money market (Prentice-Hall, New York).
Dunning, J.H., 1977, Trade, location of economic activity and the MNE: A search for an eclectic approach, in: Bertil Ohlin et al., eds., The international allocation of economic activity (Macmillan, London) 395 418.
Dunning, J.H., 1980, Explaining changing patterns of international production: In defence of the eclectic theory, Oxford Bulletin of Economics and Statistics.
Frydl, E.J., 1979–1980, The debate over regulating the Eurocurrency markets, Federal Reserve Bank of New York Quarterly Review 4, 11–20.
Giddy, I., 1980, Moral hazard and central bank rescues in an international context, The Financial Review 2, 50 56.
Giddy, I., 1981, The theory and industrial organization of international banking, in: R.G. Hawkins, R. Levich and C. Wihlborg, eds., Internationalization of financial markets and national economic policy (JAI Press, New York).
Giddy, I. and D.L. Allen, 1979, International competition in bank regulation, Banca Nazional Del Lavoro Quarterly Review, 2110326.
Gray, H.P., 1972, The economics of business investment abroad (Macmillan, London).
Gray, H.P., 1979, International trade, investment and payments (Houghton Mifflin, Boston).
Grubel, H.G., 1977, A theory of multinational banking, Banca Nazional del Lavoro Quarterly Review, 349–364.
Hawkins, R.G. and I. Walter, 1979, Multinational corporations: Current trends and future prospects, Prepared for the Joint Economic Committee of the U.S. Congress.
Hymer, S.H., 1976, The international operations of national firms: A study of foreign direct investment (MIT Press, Cambridge, MA).
Kojima, K., 1973, A macroeconomic approach to foreign direct investment, Hitotsubashi Journal of Economics 14, 1–21.
Letiche, J.M., 1974, Dependent monetary systems and economic development, in: W. Sellekaerts, ed., Economic development and planning (Macmillan, London).
Minsky, H.P., 1977a, A theory of systematic fragility, in: E.I. Altman and A.W. Sametz, eds., Financial crises: Institutions and markets in a fragile environment (Wiley Interscience, New York) 138–152.
Minsky, H.P., 1977b, The financial instability hypothesis: An interpretation of Keynes and an alternative to 'standard' theory, Nebraska Journal of Economics and Business, 5–16.
Moskowitz, W.E., 1979, Global asset and liability management at commercial banks, Federal Reserve Bank of New York Quarterly Review, 42–48.
New York Times, 1980, Central bankers warn on oil prices, April 16, D 1.
Rugman, A.M., 1979, International diversification and the multinational enterprise (Lexington, MA).

Rugman, A.M., 1980, Internalization: The general theory of direct foreign investment, Weltwirtschaftliches Archiv.

Tobin, J., 1978, A proposal for international monetary reform, Eastern Economic Journal 4, 153–160.

Walter, I., 1981, International capital allocation: Country risk, portfolio decisions, and regulation in international banking, in: R.G. Hawkins, R. Levich and C. Wihlborg, eds., Internationalization of financial markets and national economic policy (JAI Press, New York).

[9]

Journal of Banking and Finance 7 (1983) 583–595. North-Holland

INTERNATIONAL BANKS AS LEADERS OR FOLLOWERS OF INTERNATIONAL BUSINESS

An Historical Perspective

Charles P. KINDLEBERGER

MIT, Cambridge, MA 02139, USA

International banking and international trade have been partners since the beginning of world trade and world finance. Indeed, the distinction between international trade and international finance as two separate functions and institutions is relatively recent. Banks and business firms are two parts of a world network. Therefore there is no easy answer to the question as to whether banks follow or lead international business. It is probable that where banks are aggressive in building world networks, and industries focus on single projects, banks lead and industry follows. But under the opposite conditions, the roles will reverse. There is no way to determine which of the two processes is dominant.

Textbook myth to the contrary notwithstanding, domestic banking has many origins, not just evolution from goldsmiths. Private banks also evolved from tax farmers who dealt in the king's money for a time and lent out funds temporarily in their possession; from manufacturers issuing to workers tokens which continued to circulate; from scriveners and notaries; from money-changers and merchants. International banking developed primarily from merchants and money-changers. International trade and international banking were widely overlapping activities until the middle of the nineteenth century. Before that period not all traders undertook banking roles, but most bankers indulged in trade, international, domestic including retail, and even in production. Italian bankers from the thirteenth century on, German in the sixteenth, Dutch in the seventeenth and eighteenth and British in the eighteenth and early nineteenth centuries all furnish examples of a wide variety of operations:

> 'The outstanding trait of Francesco Marco di Datini, a merchant of Prato outside Florence over the turn of the fourteenth to fifteenth century, was the variety of his activities as clothmaker, armourer, mercer, shopkeeper, import and export business, dealer in wool, cloth, veils, wheat, metals and hides, in spices, pictures and jewels. He joined the guild of cloth merchants, took over the city's tolls for meat and wine, did some underwriting (in insurance), and finally against the advice of his friends, set up a bank' [Origo (1957, p. 78)]. 'A

conservative banker, Datini did not lend to princes, popes, or Communes.' (ibid., p. 152).

The Tuscan bankers of the thirteenth and fourteenth centuries who loaned to the English kings did so with an eye to obtaining licenses for the export of wool [Kaeuper (1970)]. In the fifteenth century:

'The leading staples of the Medici were wool, alum, cloth, spices, olive oil, citrus fruits, but they equally dealt in aristocratic luxuries such as silks, brocades, jewelry and silver plate, in addition to selling letters of credit to pilgrims, travelers, students, diplomats, and churchmen, and handling the papal remittances from Europe to Rome.' [de Roover (1966, pp. 135, 142).]

At the end of the eighteenth century and a short distance into the nineteenth, John Hope and Company of Amsterdam clung proudly to the tradition of a wide range of operations at a time when other merchant bankers were well along the path to specialization:

'Hope made loans to the Russian court, and to the United States for the Louisiana purchase, helped transfer funds owed by Spain to Napoleon by way of Vera Cruz, Baltimore, New York, London and Amsterdam. As merchants the bank dealt at first hand and second hand in "all articles: money, grain, colonial produce, ships' articles, gold, silver, drysaltery, ordnance, textiles, tobacco, tea, wine, flower bulbs, in short anything that could be traded at a profit".' [Buist (1974, p. 53).] 'The firm operated the monopoly of Portugese diamonds, together with a monopoly of imports of brazilwood for dyeing, bought Talleyrand's library when he was strapped for funds, speculated in Russian hemp and flax by buying and storing it in St. Petersburg when the blockade cut off its export to the west.' (ibid., pp. 75, 212, 245).

Nathan Rothschild went first to Manchester when he left the Frankfurt ghetto and began speculating in cotton and cotton textiles before moving to pure banking and to London [Corti (1928)]. At the end of the nineteenth century even J.P. Morgan bought up a distress cargo on speculation and sold it at a profit before converting to his family's more sedate mode of operation.

The Italian bankers did specialize somewhat by area. Venice dealt particularly with the Levant and Germany, exporting silver and importing spices, silk, alum. Genoa was the rival of Venice in the east, but also active in Spain, Portugal and Lyons. When the Genoan bankers were expelled from Lyons in 1464, they moved their operations to Besançon, which they gradually transferred to Piacenza in Italy [da Silva (1969)]. The Tuscan bankers of the thirteenth to fifteenth century dealt more with northern Europe. With a head office in Florence, the Medici had a network of branches all over Italy:; abroad they had branches at London, Bruges, Geneva, Lyons and Avignon [de Roover (1966)].

This paper deals with private banking and neglects the roles of public banks which were connected mainly with the provision of standard money, building capital markets for government debt, and, to a limited extent, supporting the great chartered trading companies such as the East India Company, the Dutch East India Company, and the French East India Company. This last connection between international business and banking was on the whole minimal. It proved fatal in the case of the Bank of Amsterdam [van Dillen (1934)]. A deposit bank, and presumably forbidden to make loans, it came to the rescue of the Dutch East India Company which had been sorely hurt by the 4th Anglo-Dutch War in 1782. In the course of providing this support, both institutions went bankrupt. Despite some ostensible connection of the Sword Blade Bank with the South Sea Company, and of John Law's Banque Royale with the Compagnie d'Occident, giving rise to the South Sea and Mississippi bubbles respectively, the mercantile aspects of these operations were unimportant as compared with government finance on the one hand, and private speculation on the other. [Dickson (1967), Carswell (1960), Levasseur (1854).]

Specialization occurred gradually both in domestic and in international banking. The process can be followed in many business histories. William Braund, for example, started out in the early eighteenth century as a general merchant selling cloth in Germany and Portugal, and bringing back mixed cargos. He later specialized in cloth exports to Portugal and imports of gold and silver. Gradually he gave up on exports, bought bills of exchange on Lisbon from other exporters, and with the proceeds bought specie for importation into England. Trade with Portugal flourished under the treaty of Methuen of 1704. In due course, he found it less strain to focus his attention on insurance underwriting in London [Sutherland (1933)]. The same process can be seen a century later in the history of Brown Brothers. Alexander Brown migrated to Baltimore from Northern Ireland, and began his career by importing Irish linen into the United States. He switched to exporting cotton for his own account, and financing cotton exported by others along with selling letters of credit on his Liverpool office to American importers of British goods. He and his sons at one time owned a shipping line, and the sons later dabbled in government and railroad investment. The Brown brothers spread to Philadelphia, New York and Liverpool, gave up selling cotton for their own account except to fill out a ship's load, then gave up shipping. After specializing in advances on cotton exports and letters of credit for imports, the Liverpool office moved to London and took on a general banking business [Perkins (1975)].

Both international business and international banking got a stimulus about the middle of the nineteenth century from the far-reaching changes in transport and communication. International banking had long been handicapped by the slowness and uncertainty of communication. At the beginning of the sixteenth century, usance from Genoa — the time allowed for a sight bill of exchange before payment was required — was five days to Pisa, six to Milan, 15 to Ancona, 20 to Barcelona, 50 to Valencia and Montpellier, two months to Bruges, and three months to London [Braudel (1949, trs. 1973, p. 375)]. Usance between London and Antwerp was one month, a period that remained unchanged from the fourteenth century to 1789 [de Roover (1949, p. 109)]. Innovation in domestic transport proceeded earlier. In the 1630s, the cities of Holland evolved a system of passenger barges, drawn in canals by horses at an average speed of 3 miles an hour. This may not have been a drastic increase in average speed, but it reduced the variance of the time taken by merchants journeying between cities on business, as it eliminated the occasions when a sailing lugger had to wait for a favorable wind [de Vries (1979)]. In the international field, dependability was the purpose of an innovation which took place in 1819 — the liner, or sailing vessel which left New York for Liverpool every Saturday whether it had a full cargo or not [Albion (1939)]. Turnpikes had sped internal transport in the eighteenth century at a rate which has been described for Britain as a 'transport revolution' [Deane (1965, ch. iii)].

By the middle of the nineteenth century, however, international transport and communications achieved a series of quantum leaps with the development of the railroad, steamship, telegraph, transatlantic cable (1866), Suez canal (1868), Alpine tunnels, and the domestic telephone (1880s). Before the twentieth-century innovations of radio, transatlantic telephone and airplane had the same effect, and after World War II, the jet aircraft, telex, and satellite television were added. The first use of airplanes (instead of trains) for transporting central bankers in emergency was made in 1931, when President Hans Luther of the Reichsbank flew about Europe trying to borrow funds to stave off crisis, the same year that United States and British government officials first negotiated on the transatlantic telephone. The Bank for International Settlements, established by the Young Plan of 1930, and located at the central railroad junction of Europe, Basel, was from the viewpoint of transport an immediate relic of a bygone day.

The industrial revolution, and especially the railroad and steamship, also increased the demand for capital from business. One innovation was the spread of the joint stock company from the mid-1850s. Domestic banking changes took place everywhere, starting with joint-stock banks in England in 1826 and 1833, and on the Continent the first 'mixed bank', lending to industry beyond mere short-term financing of shipments and inventories, in the Société Generale of Brussels, founded in 1825. The real upsurge, however, came in the '50s, with the establishment of the Crédit Mobilier in France in 1852, the Bank of Darmstadt in Germany in 1856, and a host of imitations in France, Germany, Austria, Italy, Sweden and Spain [Cameron (1961)]. The inspiration for this development came from Saint-Simonism, a system of thought that attached importance in economic growth to the expansive effect of new and vigorous banks. As it turned out, intimate relations between business and banking flourished more in Germany, Austria and Italy than they did in France after the failure of the Crédit Mobilier in 1868. Great new deposit banks of the 1960s like the Crédit Lyonnais and the Société Générale (of France) turned away from industrial lending to short-term credits on the English pattern and to security speculation [Bouvier (1961)]. Some industries in Germany such as chemicals fought shy of close collaboration with banks, as Henry Ford was to do later in the United States [Riesser (1911)]. For the most part, however, banks and industry were intimately associated in Germany, Austria and Italy, with inter-locking directorates and bank directors voting the shares of clients securities deposited with them.

There was a faint imitation of the Crédit Mobilier in England that failed in the financial crises of 1866. In domestic banking, the 'fifties and 'sixties saw the development of larger and stronger banks through mergers and absorptions, and the beginning of the formation of national networks. Most worked along the traditional lines financing trade and inventories, although in north England, a number of banks made longer-term loans to industry, sometimes disguised as short-term loans the frequent renewal of which was understood [Cottrell (1980)].

In international banking, the nineteenth century brought about the creation of specialized institutions like the acceptance houses and bill brokers in England, the hautes banques and merchant banks of Paris, Frankfurt and Hamburg. In 1872 the Germans formed the Deutsche Bank with the express purpose of moving into the British quasi-monopoly in foreign-exchange transactions. The newly-formed Reich expressed disgust that the German navy bought the foreign exchange needed for overseas disbursements in London [Helferrich (1956, pp. 32–33, 53)]. As it turned out, the Deutsche Bank got caught up in the boom that followed the founding of the greater Reich and turned to domestic lending (ibid., 63–66). It later sought to rival British foreign banking in Southeastern Europe and Turkey, but never became a formidable threat in the foreign exchange field.

Major thrusts of international banking of the period were concerned with lending to foreign governments, or for public works such as railroads. The Crédit Mobilier established subsidiaries in Austria, Italy and Spain, and James de Rothschild, despite his disdain for the principles that motivated the Pereire brothers' operation of the Crédit Mobilier, followed suit. Anglo-Italian and Anglo-Austrian banks were established without conspicuous success. The period was marked, however, by a general turning of British investor interest away from the Continent after the Revolution of 1848, and the development of specialized British regional banks, largely to finance trade, operating in Latin America, Australasia, South Africa and the Far East [e.g., Joslin (1963), Butlin (1961)].

The movement of United States banks abroad like Brown Brothers, George Peabody which evolved into J.P. Morgan, and Welles and Co. in Paris was originally motivated by trade. Gradually they turned to selling U.S. securities. Some firms such as J. and W. Seligmann pioneered in selling United States government securities about the time of the Mexican war (1846) and thereafter of railroad bonds. A number of institutions serving tourists and American expatriates went abroad toward the close of the nineteenth century — lawyers in Paris, stockbrokers in such a watering place as Pau, and the American Express Company [Kindleberger (1976)]. A number of banks set up branches in France in World War I but most were withdrawn during or after the 1921 recession [Abrahams (1967)]. The beginning of United States direct investment in Europe can be traced back to the 1850s, but it is unlikely that American banks paid serious attention to it until the 1920s and especially after World War II.

For Latin America one hint may present a representative picture. J.G. Fodor and Arturo O'Connell state that United States foreign direct investment in Argentina began early in the twentieth century with shoe machinery and sewing-machine factories, moved in the 1920s to automobile manufacture, pharmaceutical and toiletry specialties, elevators, cement, and oil refining. 'With the coming of more trade and the establishment of branch operations, banks and shipping followed.' [Fodor and O'Connell (1973).] This makes service industry follow manufacturing, not lead it.

The location of banks is generally dictated by the nature of their business. Merchant bankers were originally at ports, court bankers at the capital or seat of power. Major banks were typically pulled to the money and capital market. The London and Westminster Bank formed in 1833 under an interpretation of the Bank Act of 1833 that permitted joint-stock banks in London if they did not issue notes, was a combination of money-and-capital market bank (the London of the name) and a bank seeking to serve the aristocrats of Mayfair and benefit from their deposits. In the last twenty years, a new source of attraction for bank location has arisen — the multinational corporation. The movement of a number of the great New York money market banks uptown to the Grand Central area north along Park Avenue is a response to the agglomeration of headquarters of multinational corporations there. The Chase Manhattan Bank with a new building downtown resisted the move, and tension between the two locations representing the multinational corporation on the one hand and the capital markets on the other remains unresolved. An earlier example of the magnetic attraction of multinational corporations was the winning out of Frankfurt over Hamburg and Düsseldorf as the financial center of the German Federal Republic after the enforced separation of banks by Lander had lapsed.

Hamburg, the port, was the financial center for international trade, Düsseldorf the center of securities trading. Frankfurt had been the headquarters of the United States occupation forces, and attracted United States corporations setting up subsidiaries in West Germany.

In most countries, domestic banks have created national networks, usually headquartered in the financial center. Banks with excess funds are drawn to the center to find outlets in the capital market; banks with strong demands for funds at home are attracted to obtain additional resources. the process is usually long-drawn out; it may move in waves. It is seen especially clearly in Italy after unification in 1860, and in Germany following its unification in 1871 and again after 1948 when authority was turned over to the German government by the Allied occupation authorities [Kindleberger (1974)]. The felt need for assured sources of funds or outlets rests on a fear that markets may at a time of need be insufficiently broad and competitive for money to be lent or borrowed in needed amounts at existing or near rates.

Domestic banks may create subsidiaries abroad for separate foreign operations for the same basic reasons — mainly to find outlets for surplus funds, but on occasion to find funds to meet needs at home, and for two more reasons: to apply abroad a lending technique developed at home, or even one newly developed gathering funds in the foreign market and dispensing them there, and to gain access to banking techniques already developed abroad or likely to be developed there. The first of these reasons takes banks to less competitive markets, the second to more competitive. There is one more reason a bank may wish to establish a branch in a foreign country, i.e., to have a presence there. This is called 'defensive investment', investment designed not so much to make a profit in that place as to prevent a loss somewhere else, or in the system as a whole. The First National City Bank of New York branch in Paris was at a severe disadvantage as compared to local banks, which attracted low-interest deposits whereas it had to pay market rates for funds, but went ahead because it was fearful that the day might come when some customer would want to talk to his bank in Paris, and might choose to take his account elsewhere if the National City were not on hand [Kozul (1971)].

Niehans (1978) has claimed to find the essence of the multinational corporation in vertical integration across national boundaries for fear of bilateral monopoly. He uses a series of case studies of Swiss multinational corporations to derive this conclusion, but a handier illustration perhaps comes from the international oil industry. The refiner fears being cut off from access to crude upstream; the producer of crude in turn worries that he may be cut off from transport or markets downstream. The effective way to overcome these fears is to integrate vertically. If there were assured competitive markets at each stage of production with limited price variability, or alternatively, if it were cheap to store inputs or to sell outputs forward, the possible losses from monopoly or monopsony could be insured against in other ways which did not run the risk of diseconomies of scale in administration. In oil, coal, bauxite and perishable products such as electricity, however, storage costs are high and/or forward markets undeveloped beyond the near term.

The stockpiling alternative to vertical integration has been used by international business and finance. A firm deciding on a capital expenditure frequently borrows the funds in the Eurocurrency market and holds them until needed. Money can be stockpiled in this way in the same way that companies building the Alaskan pipeline stockpiled pipe. The cost of assured liquidity and not depending upon the good will of bankers at a later time when money may be tight has been the difference between the borrowing and the deposit rate. With floating borrowing rates, this moved within a narrow range. In any event the risk of a price change today seems less worrisome to business than the risk of inability to count on quantity. This accounts for the acceptability of floating rates on long-term borrowing to borrowers, and explains why foreign-exchange risk has had such little effect in cutting off international capital flows [Kindleberger (1981)].

The first solution, vertical integration between banks and industry, has been adopted, so far as I am aware, mainly in Japan. There a single complex may combine producer companies in a number of fields such as iron and steel, shipbuilding, chemicals, and heavy engineering with a trading company for engineering designs and marketing, and a bank plus life and casualty insurance companies to furnish the finance. Provided that the bank and insurance companies are successful in attracting business, the industrial complex is reasonably assured of being in a position to finance new projects as they come along.

After Japan, the relations between banks and business in Germany and Austria are the closest thing to vertical integration. The possibilities of such close collaboration were abandoned by France in the nineteenth century, and excluded by law in the United States and Italy by the Glass-Steagall act of 1933, requiring banks to sell off investment-banking affiliates, and by the 1936 Banking Law in Italy to the same effect. German and Austrian banks ran into as much trouble on their business investment in the 1930s as the Italian and American, but were bailed out by government in the short run, and allowed over the longer period to accumulate resources while armament and the war were financed by government [Hardach (1981), Notel (1981)]. The intimate connections that still prevail in Germany between business and the banks after more than a century are ironically underlined by the fact that the Dresdner Bank is widely blamed for the troubles of AEG-Telefunken, the two companies sharing a common chairman in their separate boards of directors.

There is, to be sure, the possibility of close collaboration between business and banking in Italy at the official level through the governmental Istituto Riconstruzione Italiana (IRI) and the Istituto Mobiliare Italiana (IMI), the former taking over the equities in a vast number of firms in the deflationary crises of 1923 and 1933, and the latter raising funds for distribution to industry through access to government credit. IRI and IMI on the whole leave operating industrial firms to their own devices except in emergency situations, or where some important social purpose is to be served. Vertical integration between government-owned finance and industry in Italy is therefore more potential than actual.

A more interesting development from the viewpoint of international networks is the merger movement across national lines. Early in the development of the Eurocurrency market, there was a movement to form consortia banks sponsored by leading banks in say four countries. This seems to have petered out, probably because the parent banks preferred to keep good loans for themselves, and parents of other banks were unwilling to take only the less attractive credits. Recently, however, there have been international mergers and acquisitions, especially by foreign banks in the United States, as for example, that of the Marine Midland Bank by the Hongkong and Shanghai Co. and the purchase of a 40 percent position in the equity of the Crocker National Bank of San Francisco by Barclays of London. United States banks have long been forbidden to undertake branch banking across state lines, and in the usual case before the bank holding company spread, across county lines. Foreign banks are under no such restriction so long as they conform to the separate laws of each state. If many foreign banks take advantage of the gap in American banking legislation which exempts them from the prohibition against interstate banking, the regulation may be relaxed for American banks also. Likewise there is talk of relaxing the Glass–Steagall act to enable U.S. banks to constitute investment affiliates, and legislation is in process to enable New York banks to establish a sort of free zone in which they can attract international business without regulation from the U.S. authorities, after the pattern of the Eurocurrency market. Returns on these and similar changes are not all in, but it is possible to detect the sentiment that the pace of innovation — NOW accounts, CDs, money funds, the Eurocurrency market, bank-holding companies, and full-line financial operations by non-banks — has been too rapid in recent years to enable secure judgements to be made about their consequences. At one extreme is the view that the system of regulation should be tightened up and returned to the position of a decade or so ago; at the other the serious suggestion that any regulation of money is a disaster, and all regulation should be abandoned. Vaubel in particular argues in favor of private competitive monies on the ground that good monies will drive out bad — the opposite of Gresham's law [Hayek (1977), Vaubel (1977)].

Whether banks then follow or lead international business admits of no easy answer. National networks follow different laws and traditions: International networks have been created by some national banking units, and seem to be in formation with international ownership. Similarly in some industries manufacturing firms have been building world networks. The movement is not universal: there are none in competitive industries such as farming or textiles, and none in coal or steel. In chemicals, pharmaceuticals, petroleum, computers, and other electrical appliances, however, world networks continue to be filled out, although losses since 1974–1975 have required many companies to sell off good assets to keep going, and the composition of networks is in some flux. A recent modification of the theory of the multinational corporation observes that the advantage of such companies should be calculated not on the features which enable them to make their separate investments, but on their capacity overall to arbitrage on a world basis [Kogut (1982)]. The same is true of world banking networks. To return to the original question, it is likely that where bank networks are aggressive in building world networks, and industry focuses on single projects and defensive investment, banks lead and industry follows. On the other hand, where industry is aggressive and banks are defensive, the order is reversed. I see no way to determine which the dominant tendency is now, and I suspect that it is subject at the moment to substantial change.

Two types of world banking networks can be distinguished, at least in theory. Citicorp claims to operate with the first, an integrated world network in which the dollar goes round the world each day and world activities are dominated from New York. All branches are exposed to the possibility that they may be directed with little or no notice to transfer a sizeable proportion of their lendable funds to another branch. The other type that applies to most banks is to assign a certain capital to a branch, and to make changes slowly, step by step, expanding successful branches by small increments as the system gains resources and contracting less successful ones the same way. While the two systems are different in theory, they probably converge in practice.

Are banks more or less international than firms? Some years ago I suggested a classification of degrees of internationalism for industrial firms (which did not meet with favor in the literature and has not been adopted). Three categories were distinguished: (1) national firms with foreign operations, (2) multinational firms, and (3) international firms. The distinction rested in theory not on size or system of organization, but on behavior. In foreign exchange, for example, the first group was disposed to feel completely easy only in its own currency, and minded going long but not short of foreign currencies. The second group trying to be a good citizen of every country in which it had operations, was reluctant to go short of any currency. The international corporation, on the other hand, was prepared to maximise worldwide by taking long positions in strong curriencies, and short in weak, without regard to which currency was that of the firm headquarters [Kindleberger (1969)]. In employment, the first group hired mostly its own nationals in positions of responsibility, the second nationals of the host countries, the third the best people it could find regardless of nationality. Similar classifications could be made for capital budgeting, new products, location of research and development, and a host of other functions.

It is probably fair to say that there are no truly international corporations by these criteria. To a major or minor degree all are conscious of government policy of the home country, and find themselves exquisitely embarrassed when they are pulled two ways by different governments as in the case of the GE rotors for the compressors for the Soviet pipeline. The home country counts even for the giants such as Ford or Shell.

There are probably no truly international banks, either. I have not attempted to devise criteria on which a scale of internationalism for banks could be rated. The foreign-exchange criterion is unsatisfactory, since most banks have learned on the basis of such episodes as the speculative losses of the National City Bank of Brussels in the 1950s that short-term monetary assets and liabilities in separate currencies are best balanced daily. Total liabilities owed to foreigners? Or to foreigners and compatriates outside the borders of the country of headquarters? Numbers of branches? Rank in assets in each country among foreign banks, in each country outside the home country? Even though one can classify banks as local, regional, money-market and international, the lines between the truly international banks and those regional and national banks with foreign branches or representation are hard to draw. A few banks continue to specialize in limited foreign operations without forming world networks. And even world banks are examined by national authorities since such authorities have a residual responsibility for the world operations of banks headquartered in their jurisdictions under the Bank for International Settlements concordat of 1975 that followed the Herstatt episode.

I suspect that there is no way to judge whether the 20 leading banks of the world measured by assets are more or less international than the 20 leading corporations on the *Fortune* world 500 list. It is clear, however, that at the moment banks are probably becoming more international, as foreign banks come to the United States, even if some American banks with interests abroad shrink them a little, and that there is at the moment a decline in the spread of international firms.

World banks are sufficient in size and number, however, that monetary policy should be made on a world basis, starting no doubt with money supplies, interest rates and moving perhaps ultimately to such questions as regulation and taxation.

One final point. I very much doubt that the rise of international banking and business networks in the next period of recovery and those that succeed it, will ever eliminate the need for the local knowledge which is the advantage of the local bank or the local firm. The return to general non-specialized business and finance that comes with world economic integration still requires someone to specialize in understanding local credit and local ways of doing business. Not everything in the way of relevant information can be punched into the computer and transported with complete understanding to company or bank headquarters, as the troubles of the Continental Illinois, the Chase Manhattan and the Seattle First National Bank in the Penn Square fiasco illustrate. In addition, some specialized networks will continue to develop, subordinate to the world network: Whichever leads in the increasing non-specialized world, banking or business, there will be no getting away from the need for a minimum of specialization in local knowledge by some unit or units.

References

Abrahams, Paul P., 1976, The foreign expansion of American finance, 1907–1921 (Arno Press, New York).

Albion, Robert G., 1939, The rise of New York port (1815–1860) (Scribners, New York).

Bouvier, J., 1961, Le Crédit Lyonnais de 1861 à 1882, two vols. (S.E.V.P.E.N., Paris).

Braudel, Fernand, 1949 (1973), The Mediterranean and the Mediterranean world in the age of Philip II, vols. 1, 2 (Harper and Row, New York).

Buist, Marten G., 1974, At spes non fracta: Hope and Co., 1700–1815 (Martinus Nijhoff, The Hague).

Butlin, S.J., 1961, Australia and New Zealand bank (Longmans, Green and Co., Croydon, Australia).

Cameron, Rondo, 1961, France and the economic development of Europe (Princeton University Press, Princeton, NJ).

Carswell, John, 1960, The South Sea Bubble (Cresset Press, London).

Corti, Egon Caesar, 1928, The rise of the House of Rothschild (Blue Ribbon Books, New York).

Cottrell, P.L., 1980, Industrial finance, 1830–1914, The finance and organization of English manufacturing industry (Methuen, London).

da Silva, Jose-Gentil, 1969, Banque et crédit en Italie au XVII siècle, vols. 1, 2 (Editions Klincksieck, Paris).

Deane, Phyllis, 1965, The first industrial revolution (Cambridge University Press, Cambridge).

de Roover, Raymond, 1949, Gresham on foreign exchange (Harvard University Press, Cambridge, MA).

de Roover, Raymond, 1966, The rise and fall of the Medici Bank (W.W. Norton, New York).

de Vries, Jan, 1978, Barges and capitalism: Passenger transportation in the Dutch economy, 1632–1839 (A.A.G. bijdragen 21, Wageningen) 33–398.

Dickson, P.G.M., 1967, The financial revolution in England: A study in the development of public credit, 1688–1756 (St. Martin's Press, New York).

Ehrenberg, Richard, 1896 (1928), Capital and finance in the age of the Renaissance (Harcourt Brace, New York).

Fodor, J.G. and Arturo O'Connell, 1973, Argentina and the Atlantic economy in the first half of the 20th century, English version of an article in Spanish in Desarollo Economico 13, no. 49.

Hardach, Gerd, 1981, Banking & industry in Germany in the interwar period, 1919–1939, Paper submitted to a conference on Banks and Industry in the Interwar Period, sponsored by the Banco di Roma held at M.I.T., October 23–24.

Hayek, Friederich A., 1977, Choice in currency, a way to stop inflation, Occasional paper no. 48. (Institute of Economic Affairs, London).

Helferrich, K., 1956, Georg von Siemens, Ein Lebensbild aus Deutschlands grosser Zeit (Richard Serpe, Krefeld).

Joslin, D., 1963, A century of banking in Latin America, to commemorate the Centenary of the Bank of London and South America.

Kaeuper, Richard H., 1970, Bankers to the Crown: The Ricciardi of Lucca and Edward I (Princeton University Press, Princeton, NJ).

Kindleberger, C.P., 1969, American business abroad (Yale University Press, New Haven, CT).

Kindleberger, C.P., 1974, The formation of financial centers: A study in comparative economic history, Princeton Studies in International Finance no. 36 (Princeton University, Princeton, NJ).

Kindleberger, C.P., 1976, The origins of U.S. direct investment in France, Journal of Business History, 383–413.

Kindleberger, C.P., 1981, Quantity and price, especially in financial markets, in: C.P. Kindleberger, International money (Allen and Unwin, London). 256–266.

Kogut, Bruce, 1983, Foreign direct investment as a sequential process, in: David Audretch and C.P. Kindleberger, eds., The multinational corporation in the 1980s (M.I.T. Press, Cambridge, MA) 38–56.

Kozul, Julien-Pierre, 1971, Paper on banking, in: C.P. Kindleberger, ed., The international corporation (M.I.T. Press, Cambridge, MA). 273–289.

Levasseur, E., 1854 (1970), Recherches historiques sur le système de law (Burt Franklin, New York).

Niehans, Jurg, 1978, Benefits of multinational firms for a small parent economy: The case of Switzerland, in: T. Agmon and C.P. Kindleberger, eds., Multinationals from small countries (M.I.T. Press, Cambridge, MA) 1–39.

Notel, Rudolf, 1981, Money, banking & industry in inter-war Austria and Hungary, submitted to the conference on Banks & Industry sponsored by the Banco di Roma, held at M.I.T. Oct. 23–24.

Origo, Iris, 1957, The merchant of Prato (Knopf, New York).

Perkins, Edwin J., 1975, Financing Anglo-American trade: The House of Brown, 1800–1880 (Harvard University Press, Cambridge, MA).

Riesser, Jacob, 1911, The Great German banks and their concentration in connection with the economic development of Germany (National Monetary Commission, Washington, DC).

Sutherland, Lucy, 1933, A London merchant, 1699–1774 (Oxford University Press, London).

Van Dillen, J.G., ed., 1934, History of the principal public banks (Martinus Nijhoff, The Hague).

Vaubel, Roland, 1977, Free currency competition, Weltwirtschaftliches Archiv. 113, 435–459.

[10]

ROBERT Z. ALIBER

International Banking

A Survey

INTRODUCTION

TWO DISTINCT SETS of issues are involved in the analysis of international banking; one set, the industrial organization issues, centers on the patterns of expansion of foreign branches and subsidiaries of banks headquartered in the United States, Great Britain, Japan, and a few other industrial countries and on the nature of the advantage that these branches and subsidiaries have in relation to their host-country competitors. The second set, the international finance issues, involves the role of banks in cross-border and cross-currency financial flows, both from their head offices and from their foreign branches and subsidiaries.

Despite the attention to international banking, there are few uniquely international institutions; rather international banks are a subset of domestic banks with significant numbers of foreign branches and subsidiaries. Moreover, there are few uniquely international banking activities; although foreign exchange trading may seem to be one, in many countries most or all foreign exchange trading involves domestic banks with few if any foreign branches.

The growth of foreign branches and subsidiaries of major banks occurred in two waves. The first occurred in the decades before World War I; when the war started,

This paper was prepared for the Eighth Annual Economic Policy Conference of the Federal Reserve Bank of St. Louis, held on November 4–5, 1983. Eleanor Blayney has been extremely helpful in finding many of these articles. Her comments on the central ideas in these articles and on the various drafts of this paper have been most helpful.

ROBERT Z. ALIBER *is professor of international trade and finance, University of Chicago.*

Journal of Money, Credit, and Banking, Vol. 16, No. 4 (November 1984, Part 2)

banks headquartered in Great Britain had two thousand foreign branches, and banks headquartered in France and Germany together had five hundred. The foreign branch networks of the U.S. and Canadian banks were modest. The second major wave has occurred since 1960; now the foreign branches, subsidiaries, and other entities total forty-five hundred (United Nations 1981).

That there are few uniquely international banks should not obscure the fact that there are scores of international banks. By one measure there were 84 in 1975 "defined as deposit-taking banks with branches or majority-owned subsidiaries in five or more different countries and/or territories" (United Nations 1981, p. 4). Twenty-two of these had head offices in the United States, ten each in Great Britain and in Japan, seven in France, five each in Canada and Germany.

The expansion of the foreign branches and subsidiaries of domestic banks might seem a logical extension of the consolidation of local and regional banks into national banks that has been underway for more than a century. Banking in most countries is highly concentrated, so that a few banks account for at least 80 percent of the market for deposits and loans, both in large and small countries. The United States is a notable exception for the 100 largest banks account for less than 50 percent of the market (Committee of London Clearing Bankers 1971).

According to the traditional view, U.S. banks engage in domestic banking when they sell deposits or make loans within the United States, and they engage in international banking when they do business in other countries from branches or subsidiaries. One implication of this view is that the sale of sterling-denominated deposits in New York by U.S. banks or of dollar-denominated deposits in London by British banks would be considered domestic banking transactions from the U.S. and British points of view. The rationale for this view of the boundary is that it parallels the traditional view of the boundary in many other areas, such as the scope of regulation, taxation, and exchange control.

An alternative view is based on the association between the countries where individual banks are headquartered or chartered and the domestic currencies in these countries. According to this view, U.S. banks are involved in domestic banking transactions when they sell deposits and buy loans denominated in the U.S. dollar in other countries as well as in various U.S. centers. In constrast, these banks are involved in international banking when they buy loans and sell deposits denominated in a currency other than the U.S. dollar — both in financial centers in the United States and in various foreign countries. The rationale for this view is that there is a significant currency clientele effect — that the owners of deposits prefer to match the currency of denomination of deposits and the branches of banks headquartered in countries identified with this currency.

A third view is that the boundary should be based on whether the bank and the depositor or borrower have the same or different national identities. If this view is accepted, then U.S. banks are involved in domestic banking when they buy a loan from a U.S. firm, regardless of where the transaction occurs or the currency in which the transaction is denominated. Moreover, U.S. banks would be involved in international banking when they buy a loan from a foreign borrower, regardless of the currency involved or the center in which the loan is repayable.

The choice of the boundary between domestic banking and international banking may vary with the question being analyzed. The organizing principle used in this paper is the association between national currencies and the country of charter. Thus the sale of dollar-denominated deposits in London by British and German banks has little to do with domestic banking, regulatory issues, and monetary issues from the British point of view; London is a haven for the sale of dollar and other nonsterling deposits. From the point of view of most monetary and regulatory questions, dollar-denominated deposits in London are much more closely related to dollar-denominated deposits in New York than they are to sterling-denominated deposits in London. When the focus is on competition among banks headquartered in different countries, the sale of dollar-denominated deposits in London is more nearly a geographic extension of U.S. domestic banking than a foreign banking activity. If these distinctions are accepted, then, from the point of view of industrial organization, U.S. banks engage in international banking when they sell deposits and buy loans denominated in currencies other than the U.S. dollar.

The analysis of the expansion of banks into foreign countries is facilitated by using analogies from other fields of international economics. Thus the usual questions raised in the theory of international trade can be applied to international banking activities. In a competitive world economy, which countries produce bank deposits or financial intermediation services at the lowest possible cost?

The central question of theory of direct foreign investment can be applied to the international banking industry to determine whether the ownership pattern of international banks is random or systematic with respect to the size or number of banks headquartered in different countries. If the pattern of international banking is non-random, then one of the major challenges is to identify the factors that explain ownership patterns in international banking.

One observation from industrial organization is that the ability of a firm to grow depends on its ability to raise capital on more attractive terms than its competitors. Because banks are so highly leveraged, the terms on which they can attract capital may be of central importance in explaining the patterns of international banking, since small differences in either the efficiency of particular banks or in the environment in which they operate may have significant differences on their profit rates. Hence the pattern of expansion of international banks should be related to the question of whether banks headquartered in some countries find it easier to attract capital than others. Is the source of this profit or cost advantage internal to the banks, or is the advantage inherent in their domestic environment, either in terms of some regulatory features or in terms of some market phenomena?

The theory of international banking is reviewed in section 1, especially efforts to provide a rationale for the expansion of banks abroad and their advantage relative to host-country competitors. The papers that examine the patterns of expansion of international banks are considered in section 2. The impacts of national regulations on the competitive ability of banks operating in different countries are reviewed in section 3. The profitability of banks operating in various countries and the cost of capital to banks headquartered in different countries are reviewed in section 4.

The last three sections of this paper review articles that deal with the role of banks in international financial flows. The efficiency of the international payments process is discussed in section 5. The role of international banks in the cross-border financial flows is evaluated in section 6; special attention is given to why bank loans to the developing countries increased at such a rapid rate in the late 1970s and the early 1980s. The adequacy of lender-of-last-resort arrangements for international banks is considered in section 7.

1. THE THEORY OF INTERNATIONAL BANKING

One question under this heading is why banks headquartered in particular countries set up branches or subsidiaries in foreign countries; this question is directed to the nature of the advantage that these banks have that enable them to compete with host-country banks. The second is whether banks headquartered in a particular country are underrepresented or overrepresented abroad; this question is directed at whether the number of foreign branches or banks headquartered in particular countries is systematic.

The traditional answer to the first question is that banks go abroad to serve their domestic customers who have gone abroad, which is sometimes called the gravitational pull effect (Metais 1979). In some cases the story is that the domestic banks within the host countries are poorly equipped to serve the local branches of source-country firms, which is used to explain the growth of the overseas branches of colonial banks in the nineteenth century. However, in the last few decades many of the foreign branches established by the international banks have been in the industrial countries that have been well served by host-country banks. The modified rationale is that banks follow their domestic customers abroad to reduce the likelihood that they might lose their business to host-country banks. These foreign branches are likely to lend to foreign affiliates of the same firms they lend to at home and to provide these affiliates with various services. Caves (1977) noted that each bank had a differentiated package of services; its close link with a group of firms is one differentiated product.

This "follow-the-leader" explanation leads to an identification problem, for the factors that explain why firms headquartered in one country set up foreign subsidiaries might also explain why banks headquartered in this same country also set up branches abroad, quite independent of whether domestic firms are investing abroad.

Casual observation suggests that the expansion of various foreign markets of banks headquartered in particular countries occurs in waves that parallels the foreign expansion of industrial firms headquartered in the same countries. Thus in the late 1960s and early 1970s, U.S. banks expanded rapidly abroad at the same time that

U.S. firms were expanding rapidly abroad. In the late 1970s and the early 1980s, in contrast, banks headquartered in various countries in Western Europe and Japan expanded in the United States.

One view of the pattern of expansion is that banks based in countries with relatively low spreads between the interest rates they pay on deposits and the interest rates they receive on loans would be more likely to establish branches abroad because they had developed low-cost technologies for intermediation (Aliber 1976). On the other hand, the low spreads might be a location-specific advantage that reflects the factor endowments of a country rather than a firm-specific advantage owned by a group of firms that operate within a particular country.

Several authors have distinguished among activities of foreign branches of domestic banks and have sought to provide an explanation for each; these activities include offshore banking, host-country retail or domestic banking, and multinational and wholesale banking (Giddy 1981). Grubel (1977) claimed to present a first attempt to develop a general theory of multinational banking capable of explaining the phenomenon with some simple price theory principles. His explanation for multinational retail banking is almost identical with that for direct foreign investment advanced by Kindleberger (1969); these banks use management technology and marketing know-how developed for domestic uses at very low marginal cost abroad. Grubel's explanation for the growth of multinational wholesale banking is that the multinational banks operate on narrower spreads between borrowing and lending rates than their domestic counterparts, but he does not provide a convincing story for the source of this advantage.

Gray and Gray (1981) apply Dunning's eclectic theory of production, which combines ownership-specific and location-specific advantages, to explain the growth of international banks. Dunning's theory appears to have had limited ability to predict the rapid growth of European and Japanese investment in the United States in the late 1970s, as does this theory of multinational banking.

The theory of international banking has built heavily on the theory of direct foreign investment. One of the major shortcomings of the latter is the extensive attention to conceptualization and the modest attention to testing. Similarly, the theory of international banking has been handicapped.

2. PATTERNS OF EXPANSION OF INTERNATIONAL BANKS

The articles on empirical patterns in the development of international banks can be placed into one of several groups. One group traces the historical development of international banks; Born's *International Banking in the 19th and 20th Centuries* is the classic. Then there are global surveys of the pattern in the current structure of international banking, such as the UN's *Transnational Banks* and the OECD's *The Internationalization of Banking*. Finally, some studies focus on one country as a source country or on one country as a host country; in the former case, most of the studies deal with the foreign expansion of U.S. banks, and, in the latter, most center on the growth of foreign banks in the United States.

Some of these studies like *Transnational Banking* are primarily number-counting activities. The 84 banks considered to be transnational had a total of 4,000 branches, subsidiaries, affiliates, and representative offices in 1974. About 1,100 of these entities were in financial or offshore centers; 84 were in London, and from 45 to 60 entities were in each of the following centers—Luxembourg, Switzerland, the Caribbean, Hong Kong, Singapore, and Lebanon. About 1,600 entities were in the developing countries. One-third of the 4,000 entities were branches and subsidiaries of U.S. banks, 15 percent were branches and subsidiaries of British banks, and slightly less than 10 percent were the branches and subsidiaries of French and of Japanese banks.

The deposits and loans of foreign branches of banks headquartered in particular countries can be placed into one of three groups, depending on whether the currency of denomination of these deposits or loans matches the currency of the country in which the parent is headquartered, the currency of the host country, or the currency of a third country. Both the second and the third types of transactions are international; the first is domestic.

Many banking offices in offshore financial centers participate in all three types of transactions, though the relative importance of these types of transactions differs by center. Thus the volume of host-country banking business in the Caribbean is very small. Even the sterling-denominated transactions of the foreign banks in London comprise a small part of their total transactions. In contrast, outside financial centers most of the transactions of the foreign banks are of the second type.

A major problem in developing inferences about the patterns of international expansion of major banks arises because of inadequate data. Individual banks report their total deposits and loans of their foreign branches with modest attention to the distinction between deposits and loans denominated in the domestic currency and deposits and loans denominated in a foreign currency. National monetary authorities provide data on the deposits and loans of banks operating within their jurisdictions denominated in their own currencies and in various foreign currencies; however, few authorities provide information on whether the deposits and loans are those of domestic banks or of foreign banks. The Bank of England, however, does present data on the sterling-denominated deposits and loans (with separate entries for U.S. and Japanese banks) of non-British banks in Great Britain, as well as their deposits and loans denominated in currencies other than sterling. These data permit analysis of the market share of non-British banks in the domestic market for sterling-denominated deposits and loans. The shares of U.S., Japanese, and other foreign banks in this market are small, especially in the sterling-deposit market; the foreign banks fund their sterling loans by borrowing from British banks. One inference from the contrast between the large volume of deposits and loans that the non-British banks have in London and the small volume of sterling deposits and loans is that most of their deposits and loans are denominated in the U.S. dollar. The combination of the small share of the London branches of U.S. banks in the sterling-deposit market and their large share in the dollar deposit in London is strong evidence in support of a currency clientele effect.

Most literature on patterns of foreign banking discusses the number of foreign branches or entities of banks headquartered in different countries, but without any attention to their share of a market for deposits or loans denominated in foreign currencies. Focusing on these ratios would be more useful as a way to determine whether banks in a particular country are more nearly international than banks headquartered in other countries.

Yannopoulos (1983) noted that the assets in the foreign branches of U.S. banks are twice as large as the assets of U.S. branches of European banks. The economic significance of this finding is questionable and for several reasons. Yannopoulos accepts the political jurisdiction approach to the boundary between domestic and foreign deposits and loans of U.S. and of foreign banks, and he groups the offshore loans of U.S. banks denominated in U.S. dollars with their loans denominated in various foreign currencies; similarly he groups the dollar and nondollar loans of U.S. branches of European banks. The incentives for the growth of offshore deposits denominated in the U.S. dollar are substantially larger than those for the growth of offshore deposits in the currencies of most other industrial countries. Hence it is likely that the dollar loans of European banks in the United States are as large or larger than the nondollar loans of U.S. banks in Europe.

Mills (1980) focused on the changes in the market share for loans of banks chartered in each country; he concluded that since the end of 1977 the market share of U.S. banks has declined. His study was directed at the dollar-denominated loan market; hence no inference can be made about whether banks headquartered in other countries are also losing share in the markets for loans denominated in their currencies.

Returns earned by the foreign branches of domestic banks have been related to returns on their domestic activities. Metais (1979) noted that the return on international assets was less than the return on domestic assets and attributed these lower returns to increased competition in international banking. Fieleke (1979) concluded that the return on assets of the foreign branches of U.S. banks compared favorably with the return on their domestic assets if an adjustment is made for the necessary return on the parent's investment in the branches. He was unable to find evidence that the return on the assets abroad of U.S. banks reduced the variance of their total return. Since he did not distinguish the return on the dollar business of foreign branches of U.S. banks from the return on their nondollar business, it is not surprising that the returns abroad are highly correlated with domestic returns.

Terrell (1979) identified several characteristics of U.S. branches of foreign banks; the branches relied extensively on advances from their parents to fund their U.S. loans; their commercial and industrial loans were a larger proportion of their total loans than was the case for U.S. banks; and their U.S. deposit base was growing rapidly. In a subsequent article (Terrell and Key 1977), it was noted that foreign banks were more extensively involved in the interbank market than U.S. banks were. Terrell (1979) compared the expansion of U.S. banks in Japan with the expansion of Japanese banks in the United States as a way to evaluate the various hypotheses about the multinationalization of banking. He accepted the "follow-the-leader" hypothesis as the explanation for the initial establishment of foreign branches and noted that both U.S. and Japanese banks relied extensively on the interbank market rather than on deposits as a source of funds. He noted that the correlation between the growth in domestic and foreign lending is much higher for Japanese banks in the United States than for U.S. banks in Japan.

Horvitz and Shull (1982) sought to explain why, when the International Banking Act of 1978 reduced the advantages accorded to foreign banks in the U.S. market, the rate of growth of foreign banks in the United States did not decline, even though foreign banks had subpar returns in the U.S. market. The suggestion was that they continued to expand in the United States to maintain secure access to dollar funds should access to dollars in offshore markets become more limited, because of the limited growth prospects at home and because the price of the shares of U.S. banks was low.

No significant conclusion can be made from these studies about changes in the share of U.S. and various foreign banks in the markets for deposits and loans denominated in various currencies. Banks headquartered in Canada, Western Europe, and Japan appear to have been increasing their share of the market for loans denominated in the U.S. dollar. The share of U.S. banks in the markets for loans denominated in the currencies of these countries is not available. In both cases the foreign banks have been increasing their loans with funds obtained primarily in the interbank market. Data about the changes in the position of U.S. and foreign banks in the loan market do not provide an adequate basis for explaining the competitive position of U.S. banks in deposit markets denominated in various foreign currencies and of foreign banks in the market for U.S. dollar deposits.

3. REGULATION AND THE STRUCTURE OF INTERNATIONAL BANKING

Regulations may restrict the ability of domestic banks to establish foreign branches; and, where entry is permitted, regulations may restrict the range of activities of foreign banks relative to domestic banks. Walter and Gray (1983) suggest that countries that have a comparative advantage in the production of banking services are likely to favor an open system. The problem is to go from the list of diverse national regulations applied to the entry of foreign banks into various national markets to the size distribution of international banks and the shares for deposits and loans denominated in individual currencies of foreign banks. Regulations may affect the size distribution through their impacts on the profitability of or return to a particular type of transaction in a particular center; differential regulation is the primary factor in the expansion of offshore financial centers. Regulations also limit the ability of foreign banks to enter cartelized—and profitable—protected national markets for banking services.

Several different themes are evident in regulation studies. One involves the impact of restrictions on entry of foreign banks into national markets, and the conflict between the principle of reciprocity and the principle of most-favored-nation treatment. The International Banking Act of 1980 was based on the most-favored-nation theme.

A second theme involves the impact of national regulations on the establishment of foreign branches. Domestic limitations on the branching of U.S. banks — both national legislation such as McFadden Act and state legislation — channel U.S. banks to expand in deposit and loan markets outside the United States. Similarly national reserve requirements, interest rate ceilings, and examination procedures have motivated banks to establish foreign branches. These regulations explain the rapid growth of offshore deposits relative to domestic deposits in the 1970s, a decade of sharply higher interest rates (Aliber 1980).

Even though the offshore market for domestic deposits and loans should be considered as an extension of the domestic market, the expansion of offshore banks raises several questions. One involves the selection by a bank of the financial center in which offshore deposits might be sold.

Another question involves the significance of currency clientele effects in the offshore market for deposits. If German or Swiss residents acquire a dollar-denominated deposit, are they likely to prefer a deposit sold by a branch of a U.S. bank? A third question is whether banks headquartered in particular countries have a "home-turf" advantage, especially in relation to the currency clientele effect.

4. PROFITABILITY, THE COSTS OF CAPITAL, AND THE STRUCTURE OF INTERNATIONAL BANKING

In August 1983, Mitsubishi Bank Ltd., the fourth largest bank in Japan, acquired the Bancal Tristate Corporation from its U.S. owners. The *New York Times* reported that "banking specialists say the subsidiaries of Japanese banks have been able to attract business by offering lower interest rates for borrowers and higher rates for depositors. They are aided, in part, by the lower cost of capital to their parent banks in Japan that enables them to undercut their American competitors."

Firms are able to expand their market share when their cost of capital (or any other input) is lower than that of their competitors. The cost of capital is given to the firm by investors, who price the capital on the basis of the risk they associate with the firm and the returns available to them on other securities. Individual firms can seek to reduce their cost of capital by undertaking less risky activities or by diversifying their activities.

Because of the high leverage in banking, modest differences in the interest rate spreads between deposit and loan rates that several banks might achieve would be reflected in a significant difference in their returns on equity. A counterpart proposition is that differences among countries in the cost of capital would have an impact on the ability of banks headquartered in the countries identified with low costs of capital to increase their share of world markets. National differences in the cost of capital can be inferred from national differences in real rates of interest which arbitrage has not competed away.

One commercial, nonacademic study estimated the real profitability of 150 international banks for 1978, 1979, and 1980, where real profitability was measured by the return on equity adjusted for changes in the national consumer price index. The conclusion was that banks headquartered in Switzerland, Belgium, the Netherlands, Italy, Canada, and the United States had positive real returns; banks headquartered in Spain and France had negative real returns; and banks in Great Britain, Germany, and Japan were marginally profitable (ICBA Banking Analysis Ltd., 1982). Revell (1981) concluded from a comprehensive study on bank margins for eighteen countries that the costs of bank intermediation have risen with the rate of inflation. He noted that if the authorities seek to maintain traditional spreads between their deposit and loan rates as costs increase, the capital ratios would decline.

Little attention has been given to the cost of capital in attempting to explain the patterns of expansion or changes in market shares of firms and banks. Porzecanski (1981), Goldberg and Saunders (1981), and Houpt (1980) noted that foreign banks were expanding in the United States because U.S. bank stocks were depressed, but they did not explain why U.S. bank stocks were depressed. The low levels of prices of U.S. equities in general and bank stocks in particular might be explained by the increase in the cost of capital to U.S. firms and the decline in the cost of capital to Japanese and European firms. Changes in the cost of capital to firms and banks headquartered in different countries can be inferred from changes in their Q ratios, which relate the market value of the firm (or of its shares) to its book value (or the book value of its shares). Increases in the Q ratios might reflect increases in anticipated profitability or reductions in the cost of capital. Firms expand when their Q ratios exceed one, and they contract when their Q ratios are lower than one. Differences across countries in Q ratios might be important because banks headquartered in countries with higher Q ratios would be in a more favorable position to expand abroad than banks headquartered in countries with lower Q ratios.

Average Q ratios for 1974–82 in the United States and eight other industrial countries, both for major banks and for industrial firms, are shown in Table 1. The Q ratios for international banks as a group have fallen relative to the Q ratios for all listed firms. In most countries the Q ratios for banks approximate those for all firms, although in Japan and Switzerland the Q ratios for banks are higher than for industrial firms, whereas in the United States and Great Britain the Q ratios for the banks are lower than for industrial firms. The Q ratios for Japanese banks and firms are higher than those for any other country.

The attractiveness of the Q-ratio hypothesis is that the same economic argument that explains the patterns of direct foreign investment by industrial firms applies to the banks headquartered in different countries.

5. INTERNATIONAL BANKS AND THE INTERNATIONAL PAYMENTS PROCESS

Virtually all payments between any two currency areas involve transactions that go through the foreign exchange departments of major commercial banks. Transactions in foreign exchange incur both explicit and implicit costs. The lower these costs, the smaller the difference between international payments and domestic payments. International investments encounter two risks that are not encountered on domestic investments, including the risk of changes in exchange rates and the risks of changes in exchange controls. The lower the costs and risks of international transactions, the smaller the segmentation of money and capital markets denominated in various national currencies. If these costs are insignificantly low and the forward exchange market facilities are readily available (or if implicit hedges can be created through the bonds denominated in domestic and foreign currency), then the several national money markets can be considered components of one integrated international market. Because trader and investor concern about future changes in exchange rates would be hedged, interest rates on similar assets denominated in different currencies would not differ significantly after adjustment for the hedging costs; international payments would not be significantly more costly than domestic payments.

Traditionally the foreign exchange market has been described by studies of markets in national financial centers such as New York, London, and Tokyo. These center-oriented studies provide useful descriptive information on market participants and trading practices. The foreign exchange market differs from all other markets in that neither of the items traded — demand deposits denominated in the domestic currency and demand deposits denominated in a foreign currency — is unique to the market in the same way that particular commodities such as coffee or individual securities such as IBM shares are unique to the markets in which each is traded. No one buys foreign exchange to hold foreign exchange; rather, transactions in foreign exchange — in one national money in terms of another — are an intermediate transaction as traders and investors seek to acquire foreign goods and securities. Moreover the foreign exchange market is organized as a series of bilateral markets in demand deposits denominated in the domestic currency and one other currency, usually the U.S. dollar. One metaphor is a wheel with the U.S. dollar at the hub or center of the system and each national currency at those points where the spokes join the rim of the wheel. Thus the market in the U.S. dollar–German mark demand deposits is represented by one spoke in the wheel, and the market in the U.S. dollar–British pound by another spoke. Payments between Great Britain and Germany may involve an intermediate transaction in the U.S. dollar.

The principal center for trading foreign exchange in each currency pair is in the center identified with the foreign currency; London is the principal center for trading sterling against the dollar and Frankfurt is the principal center for trading marks against the dollar. New York is a secondary center for trading each of these currencies against the dollar. The mark price of the dollar in Frankfurt cannot differ significantly from the mark price in New York for the banks with offices in each center and for the largest commercial customers.

The cost of international payments to traders and investors in particular countries almost certainly varies with their size and relative importance, and with the scope of competition among the banks. Price competition among banks in particular financial centers for foreign exchange business may be limited by various conventions and agreements, especially in countries where entry of branches of foreign banks may be restricted. The significance of these anticompetitive practices needs

TABLE I

Q RATIOS FOR NATIONAL BANKING SYSTEMS

	1974	1975	1976	1977	1978	1979	1980	1981	1982
Canada N	NA	NA	6	6	6	6	6	5	5
Agg. Q	NA	NA	1.37	1.24	1.33	1.22	1.50	1.19	1.10
$\overline{Q}$ (s.d.)	NA	NA	1.33(0.26)	1.21(0.11)	1.29(0.19)	1.19(0.20)	1.43(0.34)	1.19(0.14)	1.11(0.20)
Nat. Q	1.19	1.23	1.20	1.07	1.25	1.63	1.64	1.25	1.11
France N	6	6	6	5	6	5	7	7	3ᶜ
Agg. Q	1.11	1.19	0.83	0.89	0.94	1.06	0.67	0.52	0.76
$\overline{Q}$ (s.d.)	1.09(0.26)	1.18(0.28)	0.83(0.30)	0.91(0.32)	0.98(0.52)	1.16(0.55)	0.86(0.51)	0.62(0.29)	0.89(0.50)
Nat. Q	0.72	0.94	0.69	0.64	0.80	0.82	0.75	0.58	0.62
Germany N	12	12	12	12	12	12	12	12	11
Agg. Q	1.45	1.81	1.44	1.55	1.43	1.17	1.09	1.02	1.10
$\overline{Q}$ (s.d.)	1.41(0.24)	1.65(0.34)	1.30(0.31)	1.50(0.23)	1.49(0.18)	1.18(0.18)	1.20(0.28)	1.09(0.24)	1.21(0.24)
Nat. Q	1.24	1.63	1.44	1.44	1.49	1.24	1.16	1.10	1.22
Italy N	5	5	5	4	5	4	5	5	5
Agg. Q	1.98	1.01	0.71	0.54	0.50	0.59	1.64	1.92	1.18
$\overline{Q}$ (s.d.)	1.93(0.34)	1.18(0.62)	0.87(0.56)	0.56(0.21)	0.56(0.26)	0.65(0.39)	1.65(0.21)	1.89(0.67)	1.10(0.36)
Nat. Q	1.08	0.99	0.71	0.58	0.67	0.74	1.22	1.26	1.02
Japan N	10	10	11	17	17	17	17	17	17
Agg. Q	1.92	1.82	1.82	1.67	1.62	1.77	1.88	2.52	2.30
$\overline{Q}$ (s.d.)	1.92(0.18)	1.87(0.31)	1.81(0.21)	1.63(0.31)	1.60(0.30)	1.68(0.32)	1.76(0.40)	2.31(0.81)	2.09(0.61)
Nat. Q	1.59	1.77	1.98	1.87	1.95	1.90	1.88	2.15	1.97

continued overleaf

TABLE 1 continued

Netherlands N	4	4	4	5	5	5	5	5	5
Agg. Q	0.89	1.13	0.99	1.00	1.04	0.92	0.78	0.65	0.61
$\underline{Q}$ (s.d.)	0.86(0.17)	1.36(0.54)	1.20(0.45)	1.14(0.24)	1.16(0.25)	0.97(0.29)	0.72(0.26)	0.52(0.25)	0.50(0.21)
Nat. Q	0.51	0.72	0.71	0.74	0.67	0.71	0.71	0.54	0.60
Switzerland N	6	6	9b	9	9	9	9	9	10
Agg. Q	1.19	2.08	1.84	1.70	1.61	1.83	1.83	1.44	1.33
$\underline{Q}$ (s.d.)	1.24(0.10)	1.92(0.30)	1.77(0.23)	1.70(0.18)	1.62(0.20)	1.82(0.33)	1.83(0.47)	1.40(0.43)	1.33(0.31)
Nat. Q	0.67	1.07	1.02	0.97	0.95	1.03	1.00	0.85	0.91
United Kingdom N	8	8	7	7	7	7	7	7	7
Agg. Q	0.33	0.73	0.59	0.66	0.68	0.62	0.59	0.59	0.50
$\underline{Q}$ (s.d.)	0.39(0.13)	0.85(0.27)	0.61(0.08)	0.68(0.09)	0.68(0.07)	0.61(0.08)	0.59(0.22)	0.64(0.16)	0.49(0.17)
Nat. Q	0.45	1.01	0.92	1.03	1.02	0.89	0.97	0.96	1.05
United States N	25a	25a	33	34	34	34	32	31	35
Agg. Q	0.94a	0.97a	1.20	0.84	0.87	0.85	0.86	0.77	0.80
$\underline{Q}$ (s.d.)	NA	NA	1.06(0.38)	0.81(0.20)	0.80(0.23)	0.80(0.23)	0.81(0.28)	0.76(0.20)	0.84(0.30)
Nat. Q	1.17	1.43	1.60	1.22	1.22	1.21	1.38	1.13	1.27
World Q	1.08	1.35	1.41	1.20	1.22	1.21	1.32	1.18	1.25
Int'l Bank Q	1.29	1.51	1.35	1.24	1.24	1.19	1.23	1.27	1.17

SOURCE: Capital International.

NOTES: For every year except 1977, table values are based on year-end data; in the case of 1977, values are based on data as of first quarter 1978. NA = not available.

N = number of country banks (excluding merchant banks but including consumer financial institutions) for which data are given in Capital International.

$\underline{Agg}$. Q = composite measure derived by dividing total market value of listed banks by total book value; this measure weights individual Q values by size (in terms of book value). $\sum_{i=1}^{N} MV_i / \sum_{i=1}^{N} BV_i$.

$\underline{Q}$ (s.d.) = mean Q (standard deviation).

Nat. Q = national industrial Q as computed by Capital International.

World Q = world price index to book value as computed by Capital International.

Int'l bank Q = international banking industry Q as computed by Capital International.

aAs given in Maisel (1981). Capital International does not give data for North American banks before 1976.

bSample size increase reflects division into "Inhaber" and "Namen" capitalizations for the larger Swiss banks.

cDecrease in sample size reflects nationalization of all French banks with deposits ≥ $125 m.

to be determined, since the largest buyers of foreign exchange in these countries may be able to use their ability to take their transactions to a foreign center to obtain more favorable exchange rates. As a consequence, the cost of international payments is likely to vary by center, by the size of the transaction, and by whether the payment involves the U.S. dollar directly or as an intermediate transaction.

The costs of international payments are frequently inferred from studies directed toward estimating transactions costs. One set of studies estimates these costs from the deviation of the actual price of a transaction and a price inferred from triangular arbitrage (Frenkel and Levich 1977). Another approach — which provides much lower estimates of these costs — infers transactions costs from the measures of the correlation between changes in the price of a futures contract of one maturity and changes in the price of a futures contract of a nearby maturity (Aliber 1983b).

The studies of transaction costs in foreign exchange show the minimum costs incurred by the largest or most efficient investors that are willing to arbitrage between U.S. and foreign money markets, primarily those in London, Toronto, Frankfurt, and Tokyo. However, information on these transactions costs is likely to be a poor proxy for the costs incurred not only by traders who deal in smaller amounts, but also by those who make payments between the United States and other foreign centers or between two non-U.S. centers.

6. INTERNATIONAL BANKS AND INTERNATIONAL CAPITAL FLOW

One of the puzzles of the last decade is that such countries as Argentina, Brazil, and Mexico were able to greatly increase their debt denominated in the U.S. dollar and the currencies of several other industrial countries, following the first and especially the second oil price shock. Because of the combination of the subsequent surge in nominal and real interest rates and the decline in their export revenues, external liquidity of many of these countries declined seriously, so that a significant part of the annual interest obligations on the external debt are paid on time only because the lenders are compelled to capitalize these payments into principal. If the external debt of these debtor countries continues to increase more rapidly than their national incomes, their external solvency may be jeopardized. Although explanations can be offered for why individual borrowing countries have encountered debt-servicing problems, so many countries have encountered these problems that the debt problem should be considered systemic.

The external debt of the developing countries increased from less than $100 billion in 1972 to $500 billion in 1981; the debt due private creditors increased from $17 billion in 1972 to $210 billion in 1981. One explanation for the rapid growth of bank lending to the developing countries — about $50 billion of new loans in 1979, 1980, and 1981 — despite the decline in lending spreads, was the anticipated profitability on this business; another was the slackness in domestic loan demand in the industrial countries.

Two competing explanations have been offered. One centers on the combination of the severe decline in export proceeds in the recession and the surge in real interest rates. The core of this argument is that the lenders could not reasonably have been expected to anticipate such a massive shock. The other explanation is that the borrowers were involved in Ponzi finance. Since new loan inflows were more than adequate to pay the interest on outstanding loans, this process could not be sustained indefinitely. Thus an adjustment from a period of Ponzi finance to post-Ponzi finance was inevitable (Minsky 1977). Either the lenders believed that this adjustment could be readily accomplished without jeopardizing the market value of their loans, or, perhaps because they were caught up in the dynamics of the credit allocation process, they failed to foresee such an adjustment.

The key question is whether competition for market share led international banks to lend too much to the developing countries and to charge markups for the cross-border risks that were too low. Such competition — the herd effect — might explain why the major international banks became overcommitted on their loans to the developing countries (Guttentag and Herring 1983a).

Friedman (1977) described Citibank's approach to estimating or measuring country risk and provided examples of the bank's checklist for evaluating developing country borrowers. This scorecard approach toward evaluating the creditworthiness of the developing country borrowers was typical of those used to reduce the concern that the debt-servicing problems of particular developing countries were becoming increasingly precarious (Friedman 1979).

Zecher (1983) noted that the loan portfolios of U.S. banks and their foreign branches were increasingly internationalized in the period from 1951 to 1981 and suggested that international diversification was efficient because total returns increased while the risk of their portfolio declined. Zecher attributed the severity of the external debt problem of the developing countries to the general failure to predict the sharp drop in the rate of U.S. and world inflation and the combination of the increase in interest rates and the decline in commodity prices.

Agmon and Dietrich (1984) asserted that the growth in bank lending to the developing countries on a country-by-country basis cannot be explained by traditional credit standards or the creditworthiness of the borrowers. They developed a model that suggests that bank loans are a convenient way to redistribute income from the developed to the developing countries, but they provide no convincing explanation of why the banks should be interested in redistributing income. Teeters (1983) noted there is no simple explanation for the combination of rapid growth in international lending and relatively low markups.

Inevitably the large losses that the major international banks might incur on their loans to the developing countries and the potential threat to their own solvency have led to proposals for regulation of bank lending abroad and for additional information on the external indebtedness of individual borrowing countries. The adequacy of these proposals is necessarily conjectural.

7. THE LENDER-OF-LAST-RESORT IN AN INTERNATIONAL CONTEXT

The failure of Bankhaus Herstatt in the mid-1970s led to renewed concern about the adequacy of lender-of-last-resort facilities for international banks. One source of uncertainty involved whether Eurobanks — those banks that sold deposits denominated in a currency other than that of the country in which they were located — had access to a lender-of-last-resort. Would that lender be the central bank of the country where the offshore bank was located, the central bank identified with the currency of the deposit, or the central bank of the head office of the Eurobank? The worldwide financial collapse of the early 1930s had been attributable to the absence of an international lender-of-last-resort (Kindleberger 1978). The IMF was established with the view that it might operate in this capacity.

Three different problems associated with the application of the lender-of-last-resort concept to international financial and banking arrangements should be noted. The first involves clarification of the identity of the lender-of-last-resort for particular banks or banking offices that might encounter liquidity problems. The second involves the adequacy of the lender-of-last-resort for each country — if the Bank of France is the lender-of-last-resort for domestic French banks, who is the lender-of-last-resort for the Bank of France; and when might such a lender be necessary? The third question is whether the availability of an international lender-of-last-resort would mean that the external debt problems of developing countries could be resolved if this lender provided required liquidity on demand.

The resolution of the first problem, the identity of the lender-of-last-resort for offshore banks, is a legal issue. Frankel (1975) notes that the choice of lender-of-last-resort for offshore banks might be based on the country where jurisdiction of the banking office is located, the currency needed by the banking office to satisfy the demands of depositors, or the national identity of the parent of the offshore bank. The offshore branches of U.S. banks are sales points for deposits of these banks; the depositors have a claim on the bank as an institution rather than on the local branch. The responsibility for providing liquidity to the foreign subsidiaries of U.S. banks (including consortia banks) has been less clear, since the subsidiaries have their own capital. The ambiguity appears to have been resolved by requiring the parent to provide liquidity for the subsidiary (Blunden 1977). What happens if the parent is unable or unwilling to provide the liquidity is unclear.

The second problem, the need for a lender-of-last-resort for various national central banks, was only partially resolved by the establishment of the IMF. The usual story is that an international lender-of-last-resort is needed in the international system as a counterpart to the lender-of-last-resort in the domestic system. The principal reason for the need for a lender-of-last-resort in the domestic system is that financial institutions are obliged to convert their liabilities into some other asset, usually central bank liabilities at a fixed price. However, if the price of their liabilities were permitted to vary, they would be less likely to encounter liquidity problems. An analogy for the international system is that a lender-of-last-resort is needed when countries peg their currencies — and seek to maintain their parities in the event of large payments deficits, especially those attributable to capital outflows. The need for an international lender would be less pressing with floating exchange rates.

The third question is whether international financial crises could be avoided if an international lender-of-last-resort is ready to provide external liquidity to countries on demand. The traditional rationale for a lender-of-last-resort is to minimize the likelihood that a liquidity crisis might escalate into a solvency crisis. The principal reason that countries encounter liquidity problems is that lenders are skeptical about their solvency.

Three options are open to an international lender-of-last-resort if interest payments are so large that some debtor countries appear insolvent. One is to provide liquidity as an indirect way to reduce the interest burden; to the extent that the interest rate on loans from the lender-of-last-resort are below those from private lenders, the interest payments that borrowers must make decline. The second is to pursue more expansive monetary policies in an effort to reduce the interest rates on the external debt. The third is to raise the commodity price level and perhaps the level of income in the developing countries—and hence raise their ability to pay interest. Guttentag and Herring (1983b) recognize that a major credit shock could "wipe out most or all of the capital of major international banks." They raise the distinction between the availability of a lender-of-last-resort for particular countries, which is the implication of the term "international lender-of-last-resort," and the availability of domestic lenders-of-last-resort for those international banks whose solvency and liquidity may have been jeopardized by their loans to foreign countries. To the extent, however, that the U.S. Federal Reserve System can have an impact on the interest rate on loans from the international bank to developing countries, and on the world price level, the Fed is the surrogate for an international lender-of-last-resort. The capital of major international banks has declined significantly because of the credit shock; the lender-of-last-resort must evaluate the cost and benefits of more expansive policies to "float-off" the solvency or capital adequacy problem with alternative approaches toward ensuring that the banking system has adequate capital.

8. CONCLUSION

Two major themes have been identified in the international banking literature. The first involves organizational patterns in international banking and the second the role of the international banks in international financial flows. Banks participate in international banking transactions when they sell deposits and buy loans denominated in a currency other than that of the country where they are headquartered. The key industrial organization question is whether the expansion of foreign branches and subsidiaries of banks headquartered in different countries conforms to a pattern. Previous empirical studies have provided no insight into this question, since they tend to group deposits and loans of foreign offices in domestic currency with deposits and loans in foreign currencies. Data presented in this paper suggest that banks headquartered in countries in which Q ratios (the ratio of market value to book or replacement value) are high appear better positioned to expand abroad.

The key question about the role of banks in international capital flows centers on why their loans to the developing countries increased so rapidly in the late 1970s. Many developing countries now have a severe external liquidity problem, and some may be insolvent. One hypothesis is that the rapid expansion in loans of international banks to developing countries may have reflected that their attention was riveted on maintaining market share regardless of its cost. An alternative is that the lenders based their lending on estimates of the creditworthiness of the borrowers on what proved to be incorrect assumptions about continued low real interest rates and high commodity prices. In any event, international banks have an associated capital adequacy problem and lenders-of-last-resort in turn have a problem of how to uphold the international financial system.

References

Agmon, Tamir, and J. Kimball Dietrich. "International Lending and Income Distribution: An Alternative View of Country Risk." *Journal of Banking and Finance*, (1984), in press.

Aliber, Robert Z. "Towards a Theory of International Banking." Federal Reserve Bank of San Francisco *Economic Review* (Spring 1976), 5–8.

————. "The Integration of the Offshore and Domestic Banking Systems." *Journal of Monetary Economics* 6 (October 1980), 509–26.

————. "Transactions Costs in the Foreign Exchange Market." Mimeographed. 1983(b).

Blunden, George. "International Cooperation in Banking Supervision." *Bank of England Quarterly Bulletin* 17 (September 1977), 325–30.

Born, Karl Erich. *International Banking in the 19th and 20th Centuries*. Leamington Spa, Warwickshire: Berg Publishers, 1983.

Caves, Richard E. "International Corporations: The Industrial Economics of Foreign Investment." *Economica* 38 (February 1971), 1–27.

Committee of London Clearing Banks to the Committee to Review the Functioning of Financial Institutions. *The London Clearing Banks*. London, 1971.

Fieleke, Norman S. "The Growth of U.S. Banking Abroad: An Analytical Survey." In *Key Issues in International Banking*, Conference Series No. 18, pp. 9–40. Boston: Federal Reserve Bank of Boston, October 1979.

Frankel, Allen F. "The Lender of Last Resort Facility in the Context of Multinational Banking." *Columbia Journal of World Business* 10 (Winter 1975), 120–28.

Frenkel, Jacob A., and Richard M. Levich. "Covered Interest Arbitrage: Unexploited Profits?" *Journal of Political Economy* 85 (December 1977), 1209–26.

Friedman, Irving. "Evaluation of Risk in International Lending: A Lender's Perspective." In *Key Issues in International Banking*, Conference Series No. 18, pp. 115–30. Boston: Federal Reserve Bank of Boston, October 1979.

Giddy, Ian H. "The Theory and Industrial Organization of International Banking." In *The Internationalization of Financial Markets and National Economic Policy*, edited by Robert Hawkins, pp. 195–243. New York: JAI Press, 1981.

Goldberg, Lawrence G., and Anthony Saunders. "The Determinants of Foreign Banking Activity in the United States." *Journal of Banking and Finance* 5 (March 1981), 17–32 (a).

————. "The Growth of Organizational Forms of Foreign Banks in the United States." *Journal of Money, Credit, and Banking* 13 (August 1981), 365–74 (b).

Gray, Jean M., and H. Peter Gray. "The Multinational Bank: A Financial MNC?" *Journal of Banking and Finance* 5 (March 1981), 33–63.

Grubel, Herbert G. "A Theory of Multinational Banking." *Banca Nazionele del Lavoro Quarterly Review* 123 (December 1977), 349–63.

Guttentag, Jack M., and Richard Herring. "What Happens when Countries Cannot Pay Their Bank Loans? The Renegotiation Process." *Journal of Comparative Business and Capital Market Law* 5 (May 1983), 209–31 (a).

————. "The Lender-of-Last Resort Function in an International Context." *Essays in International Finance* 151 (May 1983) (b).

Horvitz, Paul M., and Bernard Shull. "Foreign Bank Growth Has Accelerated Despite IBA." *American Banker*, July 15, 1982, pp. 4–12.

Houpt, James V. "Foreign Ownership and the Performance of United States Banks." Board of Governors of the Federal Reserve System *Staff Studies* 109 (July 1980).

ICBA Banking Analysis Ltd. "The Profitability of Banking." Mimeographed. London: ICBA, 1982.

Kindleberger, Charles P. *American Business Abroad: Six Lectures on Direct Investment*. New Haven, Conn.: Yale University Press, 1969.

————. *Manias, Panics, and Crashes: A History of Financial Crises*. New York: Basic Books, 1978.

Maisel, Sherman J. "The Theory and Measurement of Risk and Capital Adequacy." In *Risk and Capital Adequacy in Commercial Banks*, edited by Sherman J. Maisel, pp. 19–186. Chicago and London: University of Chicago Press.

Metais, Joel. "The Multinationalization of the Large Commercial Banks: An Industrial Economics Approach." *Revue Economique* (May 1979).

Mills, Rodney H., Jr. "U.S. Banks Are Losing Their Share of the Market." *Euromoney* (February 1980), 50–62.

Minsky, Hyman P. "The Financial Instability Hypothesis: An Interpretation of Keynes and an Alternative to 'Standard' Theory." *Nebraska Journal of Economics and Business* 16 (Winter 1977), 5–16.

OECD, Committee on Financial Markets. "The Internationalization of Banking." (Monograph by R. Pecchioli.) Mimeographed. Paris: OECD, 1983.

Porzecanski, Arturo C. "The International Financial Role of U.S. Banks, Past and Future." *Journal of Banking and Finance* 5 (March 1981), 5–16.

Teeters, Nancy H. "The Role of Banks in the International Financial System." Mimeographed. Washington, 1983. Presented at the International Conference on Multinational Banking in the World Economy, Tel Aviv, 1983.

Terrell, Henry S. "U.S. Banks in Japan and Japanese Banks in the United States: An Empirical Comparison." Federal Reserve Bank of San Francisco *Economic Review* (Summer 1979), 18–30.

Terrell, Henry S., and Sydney J. Key. "The Growth of Foreign Banking in the United States: An Analytical Survey." In *Key Issues in International Banking*, Conference Series No. 18, pp. 54–86. Boston: Federal Reserve Bank of Boston, October 1979.

United Nations Centre on Transnational Corporations. *Transnational Banks: Operations, Strategies, and Their Effects in Developing Countries*. New York: United Nations, 1981.

Walter, Ingo, and H. Peter Gray. "Protectionism and International Banking." Presented at the International Conference on Multinational Banking in the World Economy, Tel Aviv, 1983.

Yannopoulos, George N. "The Growth of Transnational Banking." In *The Growth of International Business*, edited by Mark Casson, London: Allen and Unwin, 1983.

Zecher, J. Richard. "Financial Innovation and Multinational Banking in the 1980s." Presented at the International Conference on Multinational Banking in the World Economy, Tel Aviv, 1983.

[11]

POSITIVE THEORIES OF MULTINATIONAL BANKING: ECLECTIC THEORY VERSUS INTERNALISATION THEORY

Barry Williams

University of Queensland

Abstract. The choice of an appropriate paradigm to consider banks' motivation to enter a new market and their subsequent performance is an important issue in multinational banking. This paper discusses this issue within the context of two competing theories of the multinational enterprise and the special theories of banking as applied to the multinational enterprise. The conclusion of this paper is that while it may not be possible to empirically distinguish between the propositions of Eclectic theory and Internalisation theory, Internalisation theory offers a framework with greater internal consistency for the study of the multinational bank. Further, any empirical studies must be conducted within the framework of the appropriate special theories consistent with internalisation theory. These special theories have developed over time in an unstructured fashion, and the application of internalisation theory provides a cohesive framework within which to analyse these theories.

Keywords. Internalisation Theory, Eclectic Theory, Multinational Banking.

1. Introduction

In studying international banking Aliber (1984) considered two related issues are raised. The first is the factors that determine the pattern of expansion of multinational banks. The second is the role of banks in international capital flows. The focus of this paper will be upon the first of these issues; however in discussing the problems raised in this area, some problems that are related to the second of these issues will be examined. This paper aims to consider two alternative paradigms that have been proposed for the study of the multinational enterprise. These paradigms are Eclectic Theory and Internalisation Theory. Both are positive theories in that they attempt to provide a theoretical structure to study the observed behaviour of multinational banks. As such, these theories are aimed at providing predictions about the behaviour of the multinational firm.[1] These issues have been argued by Aliber (1984) to be a subset of the issues determining the performance of domestic banks, and so are the application of industrial organisation theory, on a cross-border basis. However, the study of multinational banking is more appropriately studied as a subset of the study of the Multinational Enterprise (MNE), and thus is considered by Casson (1990) to have a wider focus than industrial organisation theory. This wider study of the MNE incorporates

0950-0804/97/01 0071-30   JOURNAL OF ECONOMIC SURVEYS Vol. 11, No. 1
© Blackwell Publishers Ltd. 1997, 108 Cowley Rd., Oxford OX4 1JF, UK and 350 Main St, Malden, MA 02148, USA.

many elements of industrial organisation theory, or alternatively, the theory of the firm. The aim of this paper is twofold, firstly it will consider these two theories and determine which of these paradigms is most appropriately applied to the study of multinational banks, secondly it will demonstrate that internalisation theory provides a unifying paradigm to encompass the previously disparate approaches to multinational banking.

The paper is organised as follows, first, the multinational bank will be considered as a subset of multinational corporations. Then both internalisation theory and eclectic theory will be defined, and their applications to multinational banking will be discussed. Next, the debate between internalisation theory and eclectic theory will be considered. This paper will take the viewpoint that internalisation theory has greater internal consistency, and so provides the most appropriate framework for considering the multinational bank, or the multinational corporation.[2] Following this, other theories of multinational banks and multinational corporations will be considered. Firstly, those theories that are subsets of internalisation theory will be discussed, together with their application to multinational banking. These theories have developed in an unstructured fashion, and it is partly the intention of this paper to demonstrate that internalisation theory provides a framework to unify these approaches. Second, some theories that have been supplanted by internalisation theory will be discussed. While these theories have been supplanted by more recent developments, they retain elements that contribute to the discussion of multinational banks and the multinational firm. The paper will conclude with some comments providing direction for further research.

1.1 *The multinational enterprise and international banks*

A multinational enterprise has been defined by Buckley and Casson (1991) as '... an enterprise that owns and controls activities in different countries.' (pg 33). Developments in the institutional and technological features of multinational banking have resulted in banks owning and controlling banking activities in one country from geographical locations removed from the assumed location of that activity. Participation in Euromarket activity can result in loans being made to sovereign nations or foreign corporations, denominated in foreign currencies, without the lender leaving its country of original incorporation.[3] Originally the study of the multinational enterprise emphasised the ownership of assets physically present in a foreign county, particularly in the manufacturing industries. This extension of the examination of multinational enterprises to circumstances where a physical presence is not required for multinational activity to occur is consistent with the broader definition of the multinational enterprise.

The taxonomy issues relating to the products offered by multinational banks are also not well defined. Initially, multinational banking was characterised by Edwards (1975) as participation in the Euromarkets. This definition was expanded by Aliber (1977) to include both Euromarket activity and traditional foreign banking, which was defined as competing with the incumbent domestic banks in the provision of banking services, while Robinson (1972) defined multinational banking as '... operating a bank in and conducting banking operations that derive from, many different countries and national systems' (pg 4). The Robinson definition is drawn so widely that it encompasses some forms of banking activity that are purely domestic in nature (Lewis and Davis, 1987). The definition provided by Lewis and Davis (1987) is the one that will be adopted in this paper, 'Multinational banking embraces both the Eurocurrency banking activities of foreign banks and their banking in host country currencies' (pg 248). This definition is the closest to the sprit of the previous definition of the multinational corporation provided by Buckley and Casson (1991). There have been attempts to categorise the sub markets involved in banking across borders, for example Giddy (1983) and Hirtle (1991). While this categorisation aids understanding at the broad level of product markets, such as provided by Johnston (1983) and Lewis and Davis (1987), the distinctions between individual product markets across borders have become smaller. As a result, multinational banking is not considered by Casson (1990) to be a homogenous activity, but rather a series of activities which are distinct, but interrelated.

The economic functions of multinational banks are considered by Davis and Lewis (1982) to be threefold. First, multinational banks mismatch assets and liabilities across currencies. The preferred currency of borrowers may not be identical to that preferred by savers, and multinational banks act to overcome this difference in preferences. Second, multinational banks transform these preferences across borders. The final function is common to all banks, and to most financial institutions, and is that of transforming the maturity of deposits into the preferred maturity of borrowers. The role of multinational banks in this context has been the subject of some discussion; however, that discussion is not central to this paper. The theory of the multinational enterprises and the related theory of multinational banks have evolved to explain why multinational banks offer these transactions services via a direct presence rather than by using the open market.

2. Internalisation theory

2.1 *A general overview of internalisation theory*

Internalisation theory draws upon the Coasian theory of the firm and location theory. The multinational firm is regarded as an extension of the Coasian firm, in which market failure occurs not only in the domestic market, but also across borders. The Coasian approach explains the why and how of the production decision, while location theory provides the where. Coase (1937) considered that transactions costs lead the firm to prefer outright ownership of complementary assets, rather than bearing the costs of contracting in the open market. Under the Coasian approach the functioning of the perfect market is impaired by externalities, in particular the transactions costs associated with negotiating contracts. By owning complementary assets the firm is able to internalise these externalities and so reduce its transactions cost. Within the Coasian approach there are four types of market costs associated with an external market that can be avoided by using an internal market, (i) brokerage costs, (ii) costs of defining the obligations of the contracting parties, (iii) the risk of scheduling and the related input costs, and (iv) the taxes paid on the transactions.

Internalisation theory retains the conventional assumption of profit maximising behaviour by firms and continues the assumption of imperfect markets. The orthodox theory of production is outdated by the nature of the intermediate products the multinational enterprise deals with. Buckley and Casson (1991) considered that the firm is no longer solely a producer of goods, it also conducts research and development, trains labour, procures financial assets, and then sells these intermediate products within the multinational network, using administrative fiat via transfer pricing. The traditional Heckscher–Ohlin model of free trade is violated by exogenous market imperfections.[4] To overcome external market failure, the multinational firm organises an internal market and so avoids excessive transactions costs. The multinational enterprise is a second-best solution to international trade. When the firm organises an internal market, the country-specific advantages of the Heckscher–Ohlin model become firm specific advantages internal to the firm, which results in foreign direct investment. Under the conditions of non-increasing returns to scale and perfect markets, the independent operation of separate plants, even if interdependent (i.e. manufacturing intermediate products) cannot be improved upon. Thus, Buckley and Casson (1991) considered a necessary condition for internalisation to be a superior solution is that the external market be imperfect. The administrative cost of the internal market is greater than that of using a well-functioning market. The internalisation approach replaces the market mechanism with managerial allocation, thus Buckley (1993) considered management co-ordination has a central role in internalisation theory. Buckley (1988) considered internalisation theory produces two implications: (1) firms will choose the lowest cost location for any activity, and (2) firms grow via internalisation, up to the point where the costs of internalisation equal its benefits.

Within the internalisation framework, the knowledge advantage becomes a public good within the firm, which can be best exploited by expanding offshore. The internal market avoids the imperfections of the external market but imposes costs upon the firm, as it now must act as the allocative and price setting mechanism. The optimal solution is where the marginal costs of internalisation equal the marginal benefits. This issue is related to the issue of the scale of the firm and the issue of returns to scale of internalisation. The failure of the market for knowledge is regarded by Rugman (1981) to be a key factor in the internalisation approach.

A number of types of market imperfections generate benefits to internalisation. In activities where time lags occur between decision and output, futures markets are often necessary for the production decision to occur. Otherwise there will be insufficient price signals for the short-term production decision and the long-term investment decision to be coordinated. In this case, the firm may create futures markets internally, especially for intermediate products, via ownership of the complementary assets and the use of long-term contracts. Efficient exploitation of market power may require discriminatory pricing. This is often not feasible in an external market, due to the anti-trust laws. Discriminatory pricing may be best conducted via internal markets. If the external market is organised such that there is a concentration of power between the two main players, a potentially unstable bargaining situation results. This potential instability is determined by Buckley and Casson (1991) as best resolved by merger or takeover between the firms involved.

The internalisation of intermediate products is a key characteristic of the multinational firm, and information is a crucial intermediate product for the firm. By generating an internal market for information, the multinational firm is able to recoup the costs of generating that information, and the scope for an internal market is greater across country borders than domestically, see for example Rugman (1980 and 1981). If there is asymmetric information, where the seller has superior knowledge about the product, it may be difficult for the seller to persuade the buyer of the equity of the price asked for the product. This situation is best resolved by the seller taking over the buyer, or setting up a subsidiary in competition to the buyer. A specific international case of internalisation is where tariffs, or restrictions on capital flows, or differences in taxation regimes exist. This situation generates incentives to organise an internal market, within the limits of practice acceptable to the relevant custom and taxation authorities. The internal market for information allows the firm to retain control of the product and transform it into a product that is specific to that firm. The maintenance of the internal market enables the firm to retain control of the product and so prevent dissipation of its information advantage. Within the internalisation framework, the market for knowledge is one regarded by Buckley and Casson (1991) to be where the incentive to organise an internal market is strongest.

The costs of internalisation are potentially higher resource costs, higher communication costs, and the potential for increased political interference. Once a market is internalised, the scale of each of the constituent production facilities must be consistent with the scale of each other. In a perfect market, each plant would operate at the optimal scale without reference to the scale of any other plant. The result of internalisation is to restrict the scale of the operating units to the lowest common denominator of the operating scales of the constituent plants. This can be alleviated to some degree by allowing partial internalisation and allowing surplus output to be sold on the open market, however, this will be dependent upon the specificity of the intermediate products. Communication costs increase as a function of geographical factors. These factors are not confined to distance. In an international context, there are the potential costs associated with country risk. Further, the internal market will need to be competently organised and managed, which are not free commodities.

Due to the costs of internalisation, the pattern of expansion of the MNE will reflect the pattern of world social, political, and economic relations. Buckley and Casson (1991) assert 'The source countries most prominently represented in a given host country will be the ones whose structure is closest — in a very broad sense — to that of the host country' (pg 44). The relationship between internalisation and internationalisation is that internationalisation occurs whenever internalisation occurs across a national boundary. Internalisation is most likely to occur across national borders due to the nature of knowledge as a public good. Other existing theories of the multinational enterprise are regarded by Rugman (1981) as sub-cases or examples of the internalisation approach to internationalisation. Some example of these theories are comparative advantage theory, surplus entrepreneurship, defensive expansion, Grubel's theory of Euromarkets, international investment theory, and product life cycle theory. All of these approaches will be discussed later in this paper.

2.2 Internalisation theory as it applies to international banking

The defensive expansion approach to multinational banking is a specific application of internalisation theory. The approach was originally applied to the reaction of United States banks to restrictive domestic regulations. These regulations, the Interest Equalisation Tax (IET) and the Voluntary Foreign Credit Restraint Program (VFCRP), restricted the ability of U.S. banks to service the requirements of the overseas' subsidiaries of existing clients. The U.S. banks expanded offshore to avoid the impact of these regulations, particularly by operating in London to gain access to the Euromarkets. In this context, the U.S. banks were considered by Brimmer and Dahl (1975) to be seeking to internalise existing bank-client relationships before being supplanted by a new banking relationship. This approach has been expanded to a more general principle. There are considerable costs associated with learning the banking requirements of a particular corporation. This knowledge can be applied abroad at relatively low marginal costs. The non-banking presence of corporations abroad is regarded by Fieleke (1977) as an initial entrance from which banks can adapt to local conditions. The long-term bank-client relationship is important to the bank, and the bank is willing to adjust the location mix of its branches to respond to the changing locations of the client's operations. Khoury (1979) believed this implies the presence of an internal market for information about that client, which the bank feels it is best placed to exploit via physical co-location with the client rather than via an external market. Due to information asymmetries, Grubel (1977) argued that the bank cannot sell its knowledge about the client and receive a fair price.

In discussing the defensive expansion issues several other points have been raised which are supportive of internalisation theory. Branches of U.S. banks were observed by Fieleke (1977) to charge bad loans off against their parent rather than against the branch. This indicates that these banks are using administrative fiat to generate an internal market in loans. Additionally, foreign branches of U.S. banks paid interest for funds borrowed, including from their parents, but were not charged for the capital used to back their operations. Further, the foreign branches often had lower levels of capital than the domestic operations of the parent. This points to the banks using transfer pricing to operate an internal market in loanable funds and capital. Within the internalisation approach, a mix of regulatory arbitrage, market failure and location-specific factors are regarded by Buckley and Casson (1991) to be the motivating factors for offshore expansion by banks. Multinational banks are regarded by Grubel (1977) as developing technology and management expertise domestically and then applying them overseas at low to zero marginal cost. This approach is characterised as the surplus entrepreneurship theory, which is discussed in more detail later in this paper. Multinational retail banking has been suggested as offering scope for portfolio diversification and earnings stabilisation. Both reasons for multinational retail banking are in effect the bank internalising market failure.

When operating in the Euromarkets, the multinational bank is regarded by Grubel (1977) as able to internalise the benefits certain currencies have due to their institutionalised role in world trade and investment. Further, these banks can internalise the effects of operating on a transnational basis, and so are able to operate outside of cost-increasing government regulations. Finally, wholesale multinational banks gain a comparative advantage due to the nature of the product they deal in. By dealing with large clients only, they can operate on a lower fixed costs basis and so internalise this comparative advantage. Rugman (1981) regarded internalisation of information as the principal advantage of the multinational bank. The bank-client relationship consists of a set of information flows. This flow of information becomes a public good within the firm that Buckley and Casson (1991) believed is best exploited via foreign direct investment. According to Rugman (1981), internalisation is increased by scale economies, market power, and regulatory protection. Banks further gain from international investment by internalising portfolio diversification benefits.

Internalisation is also regarded by Tschoegl (1987) as part of the economies of scope exploited by a bank both domestically and internationally. Knowledge is an important input in multinational retail banking, particularly knowledge of the local conditions. The regulatory structure is also an important determinant of multinational retail banking, thus incorporating the location factors of internalisation theory. In multinational retail banking there exist factors which are considered by Tschoegl (1987) as not saleable, such as economies of scale, or which can only be sold in a well-functioning market. These markets do not currently exist in some cases, such as the market for knowledge, which is not well functioning due to information asymmetry problems. These factors are examples of inputs to multinational banking that are appropriately internalised by the multinational retail bank.

One of the main advantages of an multinational bank is regarded by Casson (1990) as personal contact. There are few opportunities for monopolistic advantages for banks, as the products are difficult to patent and expertise can be hired away from the innovating bank by paying a market-clearing wage. This personal contact is regarded as the multinational bank's information network and its infrastructure of skills. These advantages can be enhanced by owning information-gathering centres in a variety of locations. The ability to institutionalise and learn from this network of information is an advantage for the multinational bank. It has been argued by Casson (1990) that U.S. banks expanded offshore to follow the expansion of U.S. manufacturing films. This was done so that the existing flow of information resulting from the bank-client relationship would not be pre-empted by a competitor bank or a potential competitor bank. The bank's need to establish a physical presence overseas was increased by the rise in firms owned as listed companies rather than family owned. The result is an increased need for delegated monitoring in large projects. This has meant that banks have required increased information flows about debt funded non-banks. This requirement can best be met by establishing a physical presence close to the client. In this context the bank is internalising the information flows that go to make up the bank-client relationship.

Drawing upon previous studies, transactions costs are regarded by Buckley (1988) as high in '... vertically integrated process industries, knowledge-intensive industries, quality assurance-dependent products and communications-intensive industries' (pg 182). This results in a profile of industries that internalisation theory predicts to be dominated by multinational firms. Included in this profile is multinational banking. To generate a bridge between the general theory of internalisation and the study of a particular industry, special theories must be employed that provide empirically testable propositions. Banking is one industry that Buckley (1988) considered internalisation theory expects to be multinational in scope, as it is skill, knowledge and communication intensive. In particular, the key issue in the modern multinational firm is a network of contracts binding the strategy of the firm to its control of key functions. Thus, the multinational bank is viewed as a vehicle for internalisation of transactions costs, with transactions costs being defined in a Coasian sense.

3. Eclectic theory

3.1 *General overview*

Eclectic theory, or ILO theory, views the foreign direct investment decision to be a combination of three factors. These factors are (i) Internalisation, (ii) Location, and (iii) Ownership. This applies Dunning's (1977) model of multinational corporations. The theory is a combination of industrial organisation theory, internalisation theory, and location theory. Each of the three elements of eclectic theory is regarded to have an important role in the investment decision by the multinational, and each of these roles is considered to be interconnected with the other two. Figure 1, from Dunning (1988, p. 12) illustrates the conceptual framework used in the eclectic approach.

Ownership-specific advantages are usually defined as intangible assets. It is the possession of these assets that Cho (1985) regarded as allowing the multinational to compete effectively with its domestic competitors who have the advantage of incumbency. Ownership advantages are determined by three factors, according to Dunning (1988); (i) access to markets or materials, (ii) access to endowments of the parent at low to zero marginal cost, and (iii) those arising from

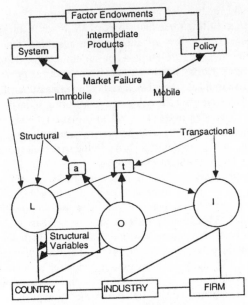

Figure 1. Dunning's (1988) eclectic theory.

multinationality *per se*, which allows the multinational to take advantage of any factors unique to the host country. Examples of ownership advantages include product differentiation, innovation, economies of scope, experience, and favoured access to inputs. Such advantages may be transitory due to the nature of the innovation process or changes in property rights. Further, ownership advantages resulting from a specific asset, (O_a), are distinguished from transaction advantages that arise from the multinational's allocative mechanism, (O_t). Dunning (1988) considered transaction advantages arise from the multinational's ownership of an organisational hierarchy, which can act to replace the market mechanism in the event of market failure.

Internalisation advantages of the multinational enterprise originate in market failure and are of Coasian form. The reasons for internalisation are threefold. The first is risk and uncertainty, resulting in the multinational firm internalising risks and the risk management process. The second is the result of economies of scale in an imperfect market. The third is due to the market not pricing externalities to transactions. The distinction between ownership and internalisation is believed by Dunning (1988) to be important and logically correct. While this distinction appears minor in cases where there is no external market for the factor being internalised, Dunning argues that it is market failure that leads to internalisation, while it is the ownership of a particular asset or set of assets, (O_a), that explains why one firm is a multinational rather than another.

Location advantages relate to both the home country of the multinational firm and the host country for its investments. The location decision is regarded by

Dunning (1988) as interdependent with the ownership and internalisation decisions. Examples of location advantages include input prices, barriers to trade, tax regimes, institutional arrangements, the prospects of the economy, and socio-political situations. It is these location advantages that explain why the multinational enterprise chooses to be represented in a particular host country by direct investment, rather than by trading with the country at arms length. These advantages are sequential. Thus, an ownership advantage must be present before market failure leads to internalisation. Following internalisation, location factors will dictate the site of the investment. Internalisation factors, when combined with location factors, determine the form of the investment.

3.2 *Eclectic theory applied to international banking*

Initial application of eclectic theory to multinational banking, by Gray and Gray (1981), found it too complex and too general. As a result, eclectic theory was applied to banking activities across borders, but competing in market segments located within national borders only. This approach excluded the Euromarkets, which were characterised as the result of an escape motivation.[5] In this application, it was assumed that ownership advantages exist. The discussion focussed upon three factors relevant for internalisation advantages and three factors relevant for location advantages. The internalisation advantages discussed were (i) product market imperfections, (ii) factor market imperfections, and (iii) economies of internal operations. The location factors discussed were (i) preserving customers, (ii) entry into growing markets, and (iii) control of raw materials. Economies of scale were not regarded as important ownership advantages in multinational banking, as they appear to be exhausted in banking at a size below that attained by most banks prior to multinationality.[6] This approach suffers from the limits placed upon the generality of eclectic theory as applied to multinational banking. This is an inconsistency, as it attempts to apply a general theory of the multinational enterprise to multinational banking, yet regards the same theory to be too general to be freely applied to multinational banking. This initial application of eclectic theory to multinational banking was believed to be incomplete and so was expanded, by Yannopoulos (1983). Eclectic theory was argued to be sufficiently general to deal with the different markets of multinational banking, including the supra–national markets such as the Euromarkets.

Location-specific factors are regarded as a necessary but not sufficient conditions for internationalisation. Dunning (1981a) argued that location factors alone do not explain why a foreign bank can compete effectively with the domestic incumbents. Location advantages in multinational banking include a variety of factors, according to Yannopoulos (1983), including differences in regulatory structures, the desire of investors to separate currency from political risk,[7] the geographical dispersion of the bank's client base, labour migration leading to banks following their retail customers, information collection, and access to a skilled pool of labour.

Ownership advantages are crucial in the eclectic framework, as it is the possession of these advantages that allow the foreign bank to overcome the advantages possessed by the domestic banks due to incumbency. A significant ownership advantage in banking is product differentiation, which according to Yannopoulos (1983), comes from two sources: (i) the importance of certain key currencies in international trade and finance, and (ii) the importance of non-price competition in the market for banking services. The first of these sources of product differentiation is Aliber's (1984) currency clientele argument. With a currency clientele, customers will prefer to transact with bank incorporated in the country of origin of the transaction currency due to that bank's established mechanisms for those transactions.[8] However, as argued by Lewis and Davis (1987, p. 263) this advantage could be exploited via correspondent banking, and does not require a physical presence overseas for a bank to utilise this advantage. Further, in the presence of a well functioning inter-bank market this advantage will not be as critical.[9]

Yannopoulos (1983) argued that the multinational bank can generate short-term advantages for itself via apparent product differentiation and longer term advantages via perceived differentiation. Apparent differentiation is associated with the terms of the services offered by the multinational banks. Dufey and Giddy (1981) considered that long-term product differentiation in the international finance markets is not feasible due to the difficulties of patenting such products and because most new products are combinations of existing products. Additionally, Merrett (1990) found that it is difficult to retain skilled staff in the face of labour market pressure for those staff.[10] Perceived differentiation is associated with the bank's size, its credit rating, and the perceived probability of loan renewal. These factors are not as readily tradeable in the market place and are more difficult to emulate than intermediated products. Thus, it is these advantages that will generate a longer term advantage for the multinational bank.

Internalisation in multinational banking is largely sourced from the role of information. Industries that rely on proprietry information are considered by Casson (1979) to reap larger gains from internalisation. Both Tschoegl (1987) and Yannopoulos (1983) considered information has a crucial role in banking, with the bank-client relationship consisting primarily of flows of information. Information inputs are difficult to obtain at arms length due to failures in the market for information. Such failures are regarded by Buckley and Casson (1991) to include the relatively short effective life of much information and the scale and learning advantages gained from owning the information collection process.

Combining the role of banks in the maturity transformation process with the importance of information as an intermediate input, there is a need for banks to maintain direct representation in foreign countries. Given the nature of the bank's portfolio, internalisation allows further gains to be made in their maturity transformation process. When banks are large relative to their clients, Yannopoulos (1983) considered that they can exploit stochastic principles when managing their asset-liability exposures. In providing loans in foreign currencies, particularly when following clients, the banks desire deposit bases in those same currencies.[11] This allows the banks to internalise any gains made by providing maturity transformation from the liabilities of generally short maturity to providing assets of relatively longer maturity. If multinational banks cannot raise this deposit base domestically in the preferred currency, they must raise their liabilities in the interbank market. As a result of using the interbank market, some of the gains to be reaped from maturity transformation will be shared with this market.

Further application of the eclectic framework to multinational banking has provided more specific examples of internalisation, ownership, and location advantages. Ownership advantages are potentially transitory. Cho (1985 and 1986) categorised them to include access to skilled personnel and managerial resources, favourable financial sources, widespread and efficient banking networks, knowledge and experience in multinational operations, expertise in servicing a particular customer type, established creditworthiness, differentiation of banking products, and prestige. Information provides an opportunity for the bank to differentiate itself via positioning its products to a particular market or customer group on the basis of superior knowledge. Location advantages are categorised by Cho (1985 and 1986) into five types: (i) regulatory frameworks, (ii) effective interest rate differences, (iii) different economic situations, (iv) nationality of banks, and (v) socioeconomic differences. Internalisation advantages are categorised into five groups, (i) availability and cost of fund transfers within the multinational banks, (ii) efficient customer contacts, (iii) transfer pricing manipulation, (iv) improved networks for information gathering, and (v) potentially reduced earning variability.

4. The debate between eclectic theory and internalisation theory

The development of eclectic theory and internalisation theory has generated some controversy. Casson (1987) considered that there are three weaknesses underlying the alternatives to internalisation theory. These are (1) too much is claimed for the theory, (2) too much effort is devoted to artificial differentiation from other theories, and (3) logical errors remain, even after development. A key point in the debate between the two theories is whether ownership is a necessary condition for multinationality. Proponents of eclectic theory, such as Dunning (1973, 1977, and 1988) argue that the ownership of some advantage over domestic incumbents is necessary. This approach draws upon Hymer-Kindelberger theory from Hymer (1976) and Kindleberger (1969) and product-cycle theory, from Vernon (1971). Eclectic theory asserts that the multinational firm must have monopoly advantage to overcome the incumbents' natural advantage. The ownership advantage is developed domestically by the multinational enterprise and then applied overseas, following product-cycle theory. Eclectic theory continues the Hymer-Kindleberger tradition of emphasising the role of costs of operating in a foreign environment.

Proponents of internalisation theory are found by Casson (1987) to contend that eclectic theory focuses upon a single cost-benefit relationship. Eclectic theory retains the HK theory assumption that the multinational corporation incurs additional costs when investing abroad.[12] These costs are the costs of overcoming the domestic firm's advantages of incumbency, in the eclectic framework these are overcome by the application of the firm's ownership advantage. Internalisation theory considers the cost of overcoming the domestic firm's incumbency to be one component of the costs of global operations. The decision to invest is not made on the basis of the incumbency costs versus ownership benefits, but rather on the basis of total costs versus total benefits. The limited analysis by eclectic theory on this point continues the Hymer-Kindleberger theory discussion of why the multinational will, or will not, use a licensing agreement when operating in a foreign country. However, its implications do not proceed beyond this point. Hymer (1976) considered the issue of why US firms did not transfer their technology abroad via licensing, but instead used direct investment. It was concluded that licensing was not used due to market failure. However, Hymer (1976) failed to distinguish between market failure due to market structure and market failure due to transactions costs. Eclectic theory continues this focus and focuses upon the issue of whether to expand offshore via licensing, and fails to distinguish between different types of market failure. (Casson, 1987).

It is incorrect to assume that a multinational firm needs an ownership advantage relative to the domestic incumbents. Casson (1987) considered it is appropriate to consider the advantage the multinational possesses relative to its competitor firms. This advantage may well be a non-monopolistic advantage relative to other multinational enterprises, yet be a monopoly advantage relative to the domestic incumbents with which the multinational is also competing. The benefits of internalisation alone can overcome the Hymer-Kindleberger type costs without the need for a firm to own any other advantage. However, the eclectic approach does offer a contribution to the study of the multinational enterprise, by recognising the monopolistic advantage it possesses. This advantage is superior management and superior technology, which Casson (1987) considered the multinational has internalised in the Coasian sense. Buckley (1993) regarded internalisation theory as placing a greater emphasis upon the role of management in co-ordinating transactions previously allocated via the market mechanism.

The boundary drawn by eclectic theory between ownership advantages and internalisation has been the focus of significant debate. Eclectic theory argues that the possession of an ownership advantage is necessary before it can be internalised. However the use of ownership of assets, (O_a), and ownership of transaction advantages, (O_t), is an artificial distinction. In generating this distinction, a tautology has in fact been used and Casson (1987) found any distinctions between ownership and internalisation had been removed. Eclectic theory argues that it is necessary and correct to distinguish between asset generation and asset use, in the same context as product cycle theory. Much of this debate is centred upon the boundaries drawn around the respective definitions of internalisation.[13] Eclectic theory, argued Dunning (1988), defines internalisation as largely transactions market failure. Authors such as Casson (1987) considered that internalisation theory regards internalisation to have a larger definition drawn out of the Coasian theory of the firm. Casson (1987) argued that the emphasis of eclectic theory results in the full implications of internalisation theory being ignored, in particular, the eclectic approach limits the application of internalisation theory to exploring the issue of why the multinational will, or will not, use a licensing agreement when operating in a foreign country. As discussed by Casson (1987), the application of Eclectic Theory's concept of ownership provides explanatory power regarding the growth of the multinational corporation. However, the concept of ownership is one more correctly applied to the analysis of performance post entry, rather than to the analysis of choice pre entry.

Both Hymer's (1976) original thesis and Vernon's (1971) product-cycle model were developed using data gathered from multinational firms based in the United States, with an emphasis upon manufacturing and extractive enterprises with a research and development focus. Both theoretical frameworks were thus influenced by the observed pattern of multinationality of this particular subset of multinationals in the era following World War II. This generates difficulties in applying these theories to multinational enterprises not in that particular subset. However, internalisation theory draws upon the generality of Coasian theory of market failure and so is capable of application to a wider variety of circumstances without foregoing any internal consistency. The predictions yielded by each theory are generally similar.

The issue of the choice between the two theories is not one of which theory yields a superior forecast of the multinational corporations activities, but rather, which of these two theories will enable the researcher to consider the multinational corporation with the greatest degree of internal consistency. At the level of abstraction represented by internalisation theory and eclectic theory, it is not possible to generate empirically testable hypotheses. (Buckley, 1988) As discussed by Buckley (1988), analysis of the multinational corporation requires the use of special theories specific to the issue being considered. Internalisation theory provides the general framework for the application of these theories. As internalisation theory draws upon the generality of Coasian theory, the application of these special theories within the internalisation framework offers those researching the multinational bank the scope to consider a wider variety of issues, and retain internal consistency. The following section will discuss the special theories of the multinational bank within the internalisation framework.

5. Other theories that are subsets of internalisation theory

Prior to the development of internalisation theory, and subsequent to its development, other theories were proposed to explain the existence of multinational banking. Each focussed upon a particular issue or set of issues. These foci can now be seen to have been subsets of the general theory of internalisation. Each approach has a common element of some form of market failure that is being internalised in the Coasian sense. Buckley (1988) considered discussion of these theories provides a bridge between the general theory of internalisation and the special theories applicable to multinational banking that allow testable hypotheses to be developed. Figure 2, adapted from Buckley

THEORIES OF MULTINATIONAL BANKING   85

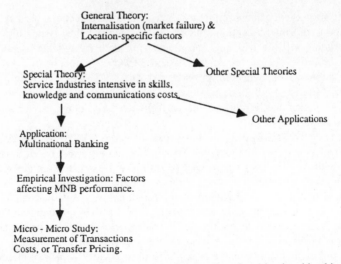

Figure 2. Internalisation theory to special theories of multinational banking.

(1988) illustrates this process. These theories have developed over time and there has previously been little to act as a unifying framework. It is partly the intention of this article to demonstrate that internalisation theory acts to integrate these previously disparate theories into a cohesive model.

5.1 *Comparative advantage theory*

Comparative advantage theory was the application of traditional neo-classical Heckscher-Ohlin trade theory to multinational banking by Aliber (1976). Banks with a comparative advantage in producing bank products (deposits and loans) will tend to dominate the world banking market. In this approach interest rates (price) are the primary factor in choosing a bank product.[14] The banks with a comparative advantage in producing bank products will gain access to the world capital markets on increasingly favourable terms due to their higher relative profits. This will accelerate their increased market share due to lower costs, and as a result, further increase profits.[15] Due to market failure, the bank will not sell its advantage and will instead internalise it via various forms of representation overseas. This approach has been criticised on several grounds. It explains the optimal producer of a certain bank product, however, according to Cho (1986) it does not explain the method or location of production. Further, it does not discuss the issues of convenience, the nature of the capital used to fund the cross-border expansion or the transactions costs associated with the banking relationship. An important omission is the failure of the theory to discuss the nature of a risk-return trade off in finance. In expanding offshore the bank will expose itself to risks not present in its domestic market. Further, clients of the bank, particularly depositors will be concerned with the riskiness of their ongoing relationship with the bank.

Bank of Credit and Commerce International (BCCI) offered attractive rates to its depositors, however these rates did not represent BCCI's comparative advantage in intermediation, or prevent its ultimate downfall as a multinational bank.[16] (Adams and Frantz, 1992) Further, the borrower will be also concerned regarding the riskiness of the bank, as an interruption in the client's line of credit will also generate disruptions. Thus, prices are not the only criteria that are important to the clients of multinational banks. This failure to discuss the risk-return trade-off multinational banking is a one that is prevelant in all of the theories discussed in this section.

5.2 *Surplus entreprenuership*

This theory is the application of Kindleberger's (1969) surplus entrepreneurship approach to multinational retail banking by Grubel (1977). Multinational retail banks apply entrepreneurial skills such as technology and management expertise to overseas markets at low to zero marginal costs. By applying its skills overseas, the bank has chosen to internalise its advantage rather than sell it on the market. The approach has much in common with the product cycle theory and Hymer-Kindelberger theory. Additionally, the theory contains the intuition of eclectic theory, that the multinational enterprise has a monopoly access to skills and technology. However, the role of market failure is not well developed. In particular the theory does not explain well why the firm chooses to use foreign direct investment as overseas representation rather than exporting its advantage. The surplus entrepreneurship approach implies that information technology and management expertise are generic, while such factors may in fact be specific to the environment where they were developed. The issues of capital and risk are not evaluated. Thus the theory contains elements of internalisation theory but lacks its generality.[17]

5.3 *Defensive expansion*

Defensive expansion was initially the discussion of the impact of specific regulations upon the incentives for U.S. banks to expand offshore by Brimmer and Dahl (1975). This approach was been expanded to a more general theory by Grubel (1977). The growth in multinational banking is due to foreign direct investment abroad by corporations. Banks respond to the expansion of their clients abroad to defend their client-bank relationship. If the banks do not accompany their client abroad, the client will establish a banking relationship that could expand to supplant any domestic banking relationships. A banking relationship consists of a flow of information. This flow of information enables the bank to assess any new loan proposal at low marginal cost, as most of the assessment has occurred previously. This lower marginal cost gives a bank's offshore subsidiary a competitive advantage over its incumbent competitors. Due to market failure, this information flow cannot be traded or priced within the market and so must be exploited by the owning banks. This expansion may not be aimed at generating profits in the new location, but is instead considered by Kindleberger (1983) as aimed at preventing losses in some pre-existing activity. However, Caves (1977) considered that the bank's clients will also face transactions costs when changing banks. Further, defensive expansion does not analyse the costs of international expansion and the role capital plays in an international expansion. International expansion should only be undertaken when the expected marginal cost of expansion does not exceed the expected marginal gain. This theory can be regarded as a specific application of the general theory of internalisation. In this case the bank is investing offshore to internalise its existing contractual and information relationships.[18]

5.4 *Multinational wholesale banking theory*

In this theory Grubel (1977) argued that the Euromarkets exist solely because of narrower interest margin spreads. There are three sources of these narrower spreads. First, intrinsic service value is associated with certain key currencies such as the US dollar. This intrinsic service value makes multinational firms unwilling to convert surplus balances in these currencies. This results in lower transactions costs. Second is the lack of government enforced externalities in the Euromarkets. Such externalities are regarded by Grubel (1977) to include compulsory deposit insurance for U.S. dollar deposits, reserve assets acting as implicit taxes, and minimum reserve requirements. The third source is the comparative advantage generated by the Eurobank's product. This is due to economies of scale and Hewson's (1975) argument of a lower asset-liability mismatch risk in the Euromarkets.[19] Aliber (1984) also considered that there could be a currency clientele effect in the Euromarkets. In a currency clientele effect, depositors prefer to transact with banks incorporated in the country of origin of that currency. It has been argued that the currency clientele effect is due to access to lender of last resort facilities in that particular currency. The currency clientele effect has been regarded by Tschoegl (1987) as limited in multinational retail banking due to a lack of conformity across borders of lender of last resort facilities.[20] The multinational wholesale banking theory provides an explanation for the existence of the Euromarkets, and the reasons for the dominance of particular nationalities of banks, but it does not explain which individual banks will tend to dominate the Euromarkets.[21]

5.5 *International investment theory*

International investment theory applies the principles of portfolio diversification to foreign direct investment by the multinational enterprise. However, Buckley and Casson (1991) argued that this is an inappropriate application. The application of modern portfolio theory to the multinational enterprise fails to allow for the ability of the individual investor to assemble an internationally diversified portfolio and does not consider the size of investments needed to generate an optimally diversified portfolio. Only if the individual is unable to assemble an

88 WILLIAMS

internationally diversified portfolio the multinational enterprise act as a second-best alternative.[22] This approach assumes the absence of international mutual funds and the existence of obstacles to individuals assembling internationally diversified portfolios, without explicitly stating this assumption. If the firm is using foreign direct investment to assemble an internationally diversified portfolio on behalf of its' shareholders, then Buckley and Casson (1991) regarded the resulting portfolio as being non optimal. Using the direct investment method, the multinational will usually own a few large assets, unless the firm is very large. To obtain an efficiently diversified asset portfolio, the multinational should eschew the direct investment approach and instead assemble a portfolio of equity interests in a variety of firms in a number of locations. The portfolio diversification argument does not justify the need for a physical presence offshore to obtain risk diversification.[23]

5.6 *Horizontal and vertical integration*

In considering the role horizontal and vertical integration plays in multinational banking, economies of scale and economies of scope must also be considered. The application of horizontal integration to the multinational enterprise is based upon Hymer's (1976) conclusion that multinational firms may benefit from cross-border collusion. (Casson, 1987) If two local monopolists can each price according to the local price elasticities, then joint profits will be maximised. Horizontal integration across borders results in the creation of multinational enterprises, with Casson (1985a) stating 'The typical horizontal foreign direct investor is a firm producing a differentiated product and protected by limited barriers to entry' (pg 186). Horizontal integration provides an example of internalisation, as arms-length market-based relationships are replaced by managerial coordination (Casson, 1987). In multinational banking, horizontal integration provides a mechanism for the allocation of technology and knowledge to new locations at low marginal costs (Lewis and Davis, 1987). This approach has much in common with the surplus entrepreneurship approach to banking discussed previously (Kindleberger, 1969; Grubel 1977). In multinational banking, horizontal integration is considered by Casson (1990) to be the creation of '... self contained domestic banking operations in different countries' (pg 15). As a result Casson (1990) argued that vertical integration is more common in multinational banking, although it often has the appearance of horizontal integration.

Vertical integration provides the multinational firm the opportunity to internalise the trade of intermediate products. This may be the result of the desire to control the upstream quality control process, the desire to reap economies of scale, due to perishable intermediate products, the desire to exercise market power, to control product innovation and so control the underlying technology,[24] the desire to minimise tax,[25] or vertical integration may be the response to irregular purchases of the final product.[26] The distinction between ownership and internalisation used in eclectic theory has difficulty in dealing with vertical integration. Vertical integration is both an ownership advantage and internalisation. As these occur simultaneously, the sequential approach of eclectic theory does not deal well with the factors which originally produced the vertical integration (Casson, 1987). The gains from vertical integration across borders by banks are particularly apparent in foreign exchange trading, trade finance, and risk management. When trading foreign exchange, the use of a global banking network by the multinational bank internalises the alternative arrangement, that of correspondent banking. This results in reduced transactions costs due to increased interest from the interbank float, reduced transactions processing charges and the use of netting exposures amongst the branch network (Lewis and Davis, 1987). Further, an extensive branch network across borders allows the multinational bank potentially to provide trade finance at both ends of the transaction and so internalise the fees from the transaction, allows the multinational bank to manage any exposures across time zones and allows netting and possible arbitrages when making a market in risk management products (Lewis and Davis, 1987). Trade financing could occur entirely via correspondent banking, however, if the multinational bank is concerned as to the security of the correspondent banking relationship, it will establish its own facilities. (Casson, 1990).

In explaining horizontal and vertical integration, economies of scale and economies of scope are often provided as explanatory factors (Casson, 1987). The multinational enterprise is regarded by Casson (1987) as a more efficient alternative to cartels for industries characterised by economies of scale. Economies of scale may be exploited by the use of both horizontal integration, and vertical integration. Vertical integration may allow economies of scale by allowing the use of large scale technology in production, together with the control of labour intensive production. Vertical integration ensures that a continuing flow of inputs is not interrupted to technology intensive production, allowing the economies of scale to be exploited. However, vertical integration may also generate diseconomies of scale by limiting the constituent plants are limited to the lowest common multiple of efficient output (Casson, 1987). In multinational banking vertical integration allows the exploitation of economies of scale, particularly in foreign exchange trading, risk management and trade finance. Economies of scope can also be realised in multinational banking, particularly when providing more than one service either to the same client, or at the same location. By providing both trade financing and foreign exchange trading there is considerable potential for economies of scope in both dealing and settlement, as well as in assisting the multinational bank's global risk management (Lewis and Davis, 1987). In providing both lending services and trade finance to the client, both the multinational bank and the client can benefit from economies of scope.

The horizontal and vertical integration approaches to multinational banking provide explanations as to why a bank would wish to achieve multinationality. These explanations are consistent with internalisation theory, as they involve the replacement of external markets with managerial allocation. However, these approaches do not provide any guidance as to which banks will become multinational and which banks will operate in their domestic markets only. Further, these theories do not assist in the understanding of why a particular country will be chosen by a multinational bank over any other. These theories do not consider the alternative organisational forms that a multinational bank can adopt when achieving multinationality, other than to discuss why correspondent banking would be rejected. This rejection of correspondent banking does not assist in the understanding which alternative organisational forms would be adopted by multinational banks and why that form would be chosen over any other. Further, the theory does not provide sufficient scope for the discussion of the issues of risk and capital, both of which are important in multinational banking. Thus, as with the other theories in this section, horizontal and vertical integration theories are at best a partial explanation of multinational banking.

5.7 *Oligopolistic competition*

Many multinationals compete in markets with oligopolistic characteristics and some multinationals are formed to profit from collusion across borders (Casson, 1987). The multinational enterprise and the international cartel are alternative arrangements to exploit local or international monopolies (Casson, 1985c). The multinational firm with multiple production facilities has been considered by Casson (1985c) as the method by which the multinational enterprise internalises the gains that could alternatively be made via international cartel membership. The conditions under which the firm will choose international cartel membership rather than stand alone multinationality were considered by Casson (1985c) as ' ... product homogeneity, absence of economies of scale, low-capital intensity, static technology, a general absence of innovation and a high risk of expropriation of foreign assets' (pg 90). If the reverse conditions occur, then the firm will choose to adopt the form of a multinational firm with multiple production facilities. Of these conditions, Casson (1985c) considered that the presence or absence of innovation is the most important determining factor, with cartels operating best in conditions of static rather than dynamic products.

Multinational banks frequently operate in domestic banking markets which are characterised by oligopolistic structures. Banking as an industry is often highly regulated, with the industry often being characterised by lack of competition, excess profit and cartel agreements (Lewis and Davis, 1987). In Australia the domestic banks exchanged agreed pricing lists amongst themselves until the introduction of the Trade Practices Act in 1974 made such activities illegal (Pauly, 1987). Upon deregulation, the entry of foreign banks has been used as a policy to weaken the effect of the local monopolies that had been established under the previous regulatory structure (Davis and Lewis, 1982). Lack of innovation in products has been considered to be an important prerequisite for the formation of international cartels. Multinational banking has experienced a decade in which both the products offered and the regulatory framework has undergone significant change, which is continuing. The range of products available to multinational banks has expanded significantly, and is continuing to expand. At the same time many of the domestic banking markets, within which the multinational banks also compete, have undergone significant regulatory reforms.

As a result, multinational banking is not characterised by cartels, but rather by multinational firms, consistent with the expectation of Casson (1985c). Multinational banks compete within domestic markets which are often oligopolistic in nature, however, the same reforms that have made it difficult to form multinational banking cartels are also gradually undermining the relative power of many of these domestic oligopolies. Further, many of these oligopolies are the outcome of barriers to entry, which multinational banks seek to exploit by operating behind the barrier. In this way the multinational bank can internalise the market imperfection, which is often imposed by the government in the form of licensing restrictions. However, by exploiting the market imperfection, the multinational bank has weakened the oligopolistic structure of the industry.

The existence of oligopolies in domestic banking markets provides the multinational bank with both an opportunity for expansion into that market, while at the same time acting as a deterrence to that expansion. If the multinational bank can operate behind the barriers to entry that originally generated the oligopoly, it is able to internalise the advantage that results from its membership of that oligopoly. However, in attempting to enter that market, the multinational bank will first have to surmount those barriers to entry. In such a circumstance the multinational bank will operate at a disadvantage compared to the domestic banks. The advantages the domestic bank faces due to incumbency are discussed by eclectic theory and were originally drawn from Hymer-Kindleberger theory, the existence of these costs are not denied by internalisation theory.

The application of the theories of oligopolistic competition to multinational banking is again a partial explanation for multinational banking. The discussion of oligopolies provides an insight as to why a firm would choose to become multinational, rather than join an international cartel. However, it does not provide an insight as to why one bank will become multinational, while another will not. The theory does provide an insight into why some nations will be chosen over others by the multinational bank, but it does not provide any guidance as to the organisational form that will be adopted upon multinationality, nor does it provide guidance as to how the multinational bank is able to overcome any of the barriers to entry in a new market. Further, the issues of the risks associated with the expansion, and the capital used to fund the expansion are not considered in this theory, both of these issues are important in any theory of multinational banking.

6. Other theories of multinational enterprise/international banking

The theories discussed in this section have been supplanted by more recent theories such as internalisation theory. However, these theories do retain elements that are relevant for an overview of the theory of the multinational enterprise, while other theories of the multinational enterprise do exist, the theories that are discussed here are those that have some relevance to the debate between eclectic theory and internalisation theory. In particular, eclectic theory has been influenced by Hymer-Kindleberger theory and by Vernon's product-cycle theories. All of these earlier theories have been criticised as not adequately discussing the relevant issues. Most are early attempts at generating a theory of the MNE and are often specific to a particular case and cannot be generalised. Others have problems with the logic, or the conclusions as based on the assumptions.[27] Due to their antecedent of generating theories from specific cases, and attempting to apply these theories to a more general case, there is a lack of structure in these approaches. Each of these theories have provided insights that have been useful in later study of the multinational enterprise, however they are now superseded by the generality of internalisation theory. Further, the theories discussed in this section contain elements that are relevant for the debate between eclectic theory and internalisation theory.

6.1 Concentration ratio theory

Concentration ratio theory assumes that profits and numbers of firms in an industry are inversely related. Aliber (1976) argued that banks based in countries with higher concentration ratios are more able to satisfy the capital needs of offshore expansion. More profitable banks will have higher retained earnings. This approach is compatible with the neo-classical comparative advantage theory, as low cost of production of bank products, or a high deposit—loan interest rate spread, provides a necessary but not sufficient condition for high profits. This approach, however, has its weaknesses. International expansion is not necessarily funded internally. The link between concentration ratios and profits taken by this approach has also been criticised by Demsetz (1973) among others.

6.2 Hymer—Kindelberger theory

Hymer-Kindelberger (HK) theory attempts to determine the advantages a foreign-owned firm has over the domestic incumbents. HK theory assumes the domestic incumbents have innate advantages over any foreign entrant due to (i) a knowledge of consumer preferences and the institutional features; and (ii) the costs associated with distance from the parent, including communications costs, time in travel, and distance leading to errors. To overcome these costs, the foreign firm must posses some compensating advantage. These may be advantages specific to a particular nationality, or usually in HK theory, a firm-specific advantage. These are regarded by Kindleberger (1969) to include ownership of a brand name, possession of marketing skills, patents, technology, lower cost finance, managerial skills, economies of scale, and economies of vertical integration. In HK theory, these advantages are not sold or licensed due to imperfections in the patents markets and other market failures. The production is conducted overseas to (i) overcome tariff barriers and the cost of transportation, and (ii) adapt the product to local conditions.[28]

Buckley and Casson (1991) regard internalisation theory as differing from the HK theory on a number of points. First, HK theory takes the firms endowment as given and does not explain the source of those endowments. The planning and investment functions are ignored. This overstates returns from the investment as any costs are ignored. Internalisation theory, however, emphasises the role of a total cost-benefit trade off. Secondly, as costs of acquisition are ignored, the HK theory does not explain why one form of investment is preferred over another. The cost advantages vary with the scale of research and development, according to Buckley and Casson (1991), and as a result the HK theory does not explain the optimal level of investment in offshore operations. Finally, HK theory, by implication, examines a single innovation or patent. The internalisation approach emphasises a stream of innovations or the ability to innovate, to generate growth. Thus, HK theory is essentially static, while internalisation theory emphasises the dynamics of the multinational enterprise. HK theory has been applied to multinational banking, by Tschoegl (1987), but the approach used was consistent with internalisation theory.

6.3 *Currency-area theory*

Currency-area theory from Aliber (1970 and 1971) discusses a specific advantage of the foreign firm over the domestic incumbents. In this context it has much in common with HK theory. It assumes the foreign firm operates at a disadvantage to the domestic incumbents and that the multinational enterprise needs to possess some specific advantages to overcome the costs of foreign operations. Some currencies will carry a premium to compensate holders of that currency for bearing exchange rate risk. Investors of different nationalities will evaluate the premium of that currency differently. As a result, investors attach different costs of capital to multinational firms compared to the domestic incumbent firms they are competing with. These capital market imperfections have several potential sources. One is that investors are myopic, and so the investors assume all foreign investments are denominated in the same currency as the home currency of the parent corporation. If the host currency is at a premium, then portfolio investors will allow the MNE to borrow at advantageous terms in the host currency in anticipation of making exchange rate gains. The investors believe they are acquiring home currency denominated assets, which will generate exchange rate gains for the host-country investor. Alternatively, the multinational may be regarded as efficient in hedging its exchange rate risk. However, hedging alone would generate equilibrium with any domestic incumbent firm. This theory does not discuss how the multinational has a cost of capital advantage over the domestic incumbent. Alternatively, investors are willing to price into the multinational's cost of capital any advantages gained from international diversification and so reward the multinational with a lower cost of capital.[29]

Well-informed investors would not persist with myopia regarding the multinationals' cash flows, once they have learnt of large-scale offshore investment by the multinational enterprise. Thus, this model holds at best in the initial stages of offshore investment by the multinational enterprise. Additionally, this theory cannot explain the pattern of multinational enterprise behaviour within a currency area that is, within a region where the same currency is used for most transactions. Further, according to Buckley and Casson (1991), it cannot explain the pattern of cross investment, i.e., United States firms investing in Europe at the same time as European firms investing in the United States. It is argued by Aliber (1971) that the theory deals with the cross hauling of investment, by considering that the investments occurred at different points in time. Thus, at one point in time one currency is at a premium and so investment flows into that country. At a different point in time the currency is at a discount and so investments flow out of that country. This theory can only explain a single direction of investment flow at any one time, but it does allow for dynamics in the direction of the flow over time. The reasons for cost of capital differences across borders are not well argued, and as a result the currency-area theory can be regarded as at best a special case of particular types of offshore activity by the multinational enterprise. Aliber's (1970; 1971) theory best explains the takeover of going concerns by MNEs from currency areas where the currency is at a premium at the time of the takeover. However, it cannot explain why a firm would set up a new operation and incur the associated capital costs, as opposed to simply taking over the domestic incumbent firm.

6.4 Product-cycle theory

Product cycle theory from Vernon (1966, 1971) assumed first that tastes differ with income. Second, the theory assumed that communication costs within the firm, and between the firm and the market, are significant and will increase with distance. Third, there are predictable changes in product technology and product marketing methods. Finally, an imperfect market for technical knowledge is assumed.

In the first phase of a product, entrepreneurs wish to be close to the markets due to communication costs. Technical innovation will occur in advanced markets and so production stays in the advanced market. Innovation will occur close to the consumers, so that it can be responsive to the consumers' needs. Additionally local monopolies can be exploited and product differentiation developed. In this phase the attributes of flexibility and responsiveness are valued above lower cost inputs. These attributes can be best achieved by proximity to consumers. In phase 2, the participants operate behind barriers to entry generated by economies of scale and marketing and research advantages. Inside this market, the participants conduct vigorous competition, and potentially a price war, until market shares are stabilised. During this phase overseas markets will be serviced by exporting. The final stage is *senescent oligopoly*. Economies of scale no longer act a barrier to entry, and after attempts to generate new barriers to entry, mainly by product differentiation, the market becomes in effect contestable. The production-location decision will be based upon the cost of inputs. It is during this phase that production will move offshore and the firm will develop into a multinational corporation, using foreign direct investment.

The product cycle theory, like internalisation, emphasises innovation and production improvement. However, this theory does not explain foreign direct investment that is not import substituting and does not explain investment in industries where product innovation is ongoing, or the product is non-standardised. Recent trends in the theory of multinational enterprise have outpaced this theory, as product innovation is ongoing, rather than initial phase, and products are differentiated for each market. Product cycle theory considers each phase of the process as separate, rather than as an integrated process. Additionally, product cycle theory does not give a time patterns for the phases. According to Buckley and Casson (1991), it says what will be next but not when. However, it should be noted that internalisation theory, while dynamic, does not provide a precise time line either. The internalisation approach, however, is more sophisticated, as it discusses the dynamics of the multinational enterprise in the context of exogenous shocks. Given a particular exogenous shock, internalisation theory is able to provide a dynamic for the next phase of development. Internalisation theory does not provide any guidance as to the timing of each exogenous shock.

7. Conclusions

Internalisation theory offers a superior framework for the study of multinational banks. This is particularly due to its framework not prejudging any issues. In contrast, eclectic theory retains the assumption of Hymer-Kindleberger theory that the multinational enterprise operates at a disadvantage to the incumbent firms and this disadvantage generates a need for a compensating advantage. Internalisation theory considers the total cost-benefit relationship to be the investment determining factor, rather than eclectic theory's single cost-benefit relationship. Additionally, eclectic theory assumes that a firm develops an ownership advantage domestically for international application. Internalisation theory, however, allows multinationality *per se* to be a characteristic of a firm. Further, the boundaries drawn by eclectic theory in defining internalisation have ignored the larger implications of the Coase (1937) theory of the firm. However, as general theories of the multinational enterprise, Internalisation theory and eclectic theory do not generate any testable hypotheses that enable their falsification. To operationalise internalisation theory, special theories specific to the issue being studied must be employed. However, following Buckley (1988), they must be consistent with the general theory of internalisation. As a result, the choice between these competing paradigms must be made on the basis of the internal validity of each. Theories offered as alternatives to internalisation theory have been (i) a subset of internalisation theory; (ii) not fully discussed the range of issues relevant for the multinational enterprise, or; (iii) have been normative rather than positive in content.

Acknowledgements

The author is grateful for comments from Chris Adams, Don Anderson, John Foster, Ron Weber, Ian Zimmer, the participants at the Syme Department of Banking and Finance Research Seminar, Monash University, and two anonymous referees. All errors remain the responsibility of the author.

Notes

1. As the focus of this paper is positive theories, the Dynamic Comparative Advantage Approach proposed by Kojima (1973, 1982) will not be discussed as it has normative as well as positive content, see Dunning (1988).
2. Both internalisation theory and eclectic theory yield similar predictions regarding the general form of the multinational corporation. These can only be tested by the application of special theories, specific to the issue being studied (Buckley, 1988). Internalisation theory offers the framework with greatest internal consistency for consideration of these special theories. This issue will be discussed in more detail in sections 4 and 5.
3. This type of Eurocurrency banking is discussed in Lewis and Davis, (1987), page 221.
4. Sodersten (1980), and Caves, Frankel and Jones (1990) discuss the Heclescher–Ohlin model.
5. The escape motivation is the motivation to remove banking activities from the ambit of restrictive regulations.
6. McAllister and McManus (1993) find economies of scale in banking exhausted at the level of USD 500 m in assets, and constant returns to scale in banking afterward.
7. This factor is one that has been argued to have lead to the development of the Euromarkets, as it led to the USSR holding its dollar balances outside of the United States for fear of a politically motivated accounts freeze, see for example Shapiro (1992) page 579.
8. Aliber (1984) also argued that depositors would have a preference for these banks due to their access to lender of last resort facilities in that currency. However the existence of lender of last resort facilities are not uniform across national boundaries. The currency clientele argument is also discussed in section 5.4 of this paper.
9. I am indebted to an anonymous referee for this point.
10. Merrett (1990) considered British colonial banks in Australia, and found that competitive advantages based on staff or products were eroded by competitor banks actively recruiting away trained staff, see page 67–68.
11. This argument could explain why, for example, Midland Bank purchased Crocker National in California. As argued by Shapiro (1992, pg 662) Midland brought little to the takeover other than the deal itself, and so the takeover ultimately failed. The reason for this failure could well be that the deregulation of the U.S. banking market in the 1980s made retail deposits more expensive than previously. Thus, a retail presence in the U.S was no longer necessary for access to low cost U.S. dollar funding. (I am indebted to an anonymous referee for this point.) Given the failure of many cross border acquisitions in banking, (Shapiro 1992), it appears that the need to control information flows is more important than the need to establish a direct deposit base in every currency that the bank transacts. Additionally, increased efficiency of the interbank market may have further weakened the deposit base argument.
12. This assumption is not rejected by internalisation theory, however its application by Eclectic theory is considered to be too limited.
13. This problem is in part sourced in the failure of Hymer (1976) to distinguish between market failure resulting from market structure and market failure resulting from transactions costs (Casson, 1987).
14. The theory ignores the importance of a risk return trade off in finance.
15. Hirtle (1991) has argued that a lower cost of capital for Japanese banks has helped establish their international position. Zimmer and McCauley (1991) have argued that the relative decline of US banks in multinational banking is partly due to increased costs of capital. Zimmer and McCauley considered that this apparent relative decline seems to be reinforced by the increased emphasis of US banks on off-balance sheet activities. This relative decline may be more apparent than real. Despite the dominance of the *Euromoney* top 10 and top 100 by Japanese banks, the Euromoney awards for

THEORIES OF MULTINATIONAL BANKING   97

excellence in 1993 and 1994 have been dominated by US-based firms (Euromoney, June 1994, July 1994; Jain 1994). Jain (1994) argued that some of this apparent domination is due to foreign exchange driven factors.

16. I am grateful to an anonymous referee for this point.

17. This theory would be consistent with the domination of the derivatives markets by banks, particularly U.S banks (Jain, 1994, pg 386). These banks have established expertise in this market which they are unable and unwilling to sell in the market, preferring to internalise the advantage. However, this application goes beyond the original scope of multinational retail banking, and thus, probably acts as a partial explanation of this phenomenon, together with defensive expansion and multinational wholesale banking theory.

18. Defensive expansion could act as a partial explanation of the domination of world banking size tables by Germany and Japan, as these nations are both currently experiencing balance of payments surpluses, thus these banks may be accompanying their clients trading and investment activities abroad. Jain (1994) considered this is particularly appropriate for Japanese banks. Lewis and Davis (1987) found that half of the foreign currency lending abroad by Japanese banks was to Japanese enterprises. Hirtle (1991) found that customer relationships are particularly important for Japanese and German banks. Lewis and Davis (1987) argued that the decision of Japanese firms to locate production offshore in the 1970s is linked to the rise of Japanese multinational banking.

19. The idea of a lower asset liability mismatch risk in the Euromarkets has been criticised by Davis and Lewis (1982).

20. Also deregulation has allowed foreign owned banks access to some domestic banking markets.

21. The dominance of the world top 100 banks by Japanese, U.S. and German banks is consistent with this theory, as it is likely that there is an institutionalised preference for particular currencies, however other reasons have also been advanced for this dominance that are consistent with other theories such as defensive expansion and surplus entrepreneurship. Jain (1994) also argues that this apparent dominance of Japanese banks is due to appreciation of the Yen, resulting in the U.S. dollar value of these bank's assets being increased. Jain (1994) found US banks dominate many activities conducted in multinational banking, Hirtle (1991) found US banks to be particularly strong in areas such as foreign exchange trading and derivative products.

22. The literature on this point is mixed, see Jacquiliat and Solnik (1978), Agmon and Lessard (1977) and Logue (1982).

23. It has been suggested that banks, due to the nature of their assets, offer portfolio diversification benefits not available from investment in traded securities. If this held then it would be priced into domestic bank's share prices in an efficient market.

24. This may be particularly important in cases where patents are difficult to enforce, (Casson, 1987), the difficulties in patenting products in the banking market has been discussed by Dufey and Giddy (1981).

25. All of these points are drawn from Casson (1987).

26. This issue is discussed by Casson (1987b), together with the desire to vertically integrate due to transportation costs, and the associated desire to co-locate production.

27. Behavioural Process Theory (Aharoni, 1966) will not be discussed in this section as it has had no influence on the theories being applied in this paper, it is discussed in Buckley and Casson (1991), Appropriability Theory (Magee, 1977) will also not be discussed.

28. This second reason is especially important according to Caves (1971), who considered product differentiation to be important.

29. This issue is not yet resolved, see, for example, Jacquillat and Solnik (1978), Agmon and Lessard (1977) and Logue (1982).

98 WILLIAMS

References

Adams, J. R. and Frantz. D. (1992) *A Full Service Bank*. New York: Pocket Books.

Agmon, T. and Lessard, D. (1977) Investor recognition of corporate international diversification. *Journal of Finance*, 32, 1049–1056.

Aharoni, Y. (1966) *The Foreign Investment Decision Process*. Boston: Harvard University Press.

Aliber, R. Z. (1970) A theory of direct foreign investment. In C. P. Kindleberger (ed.) *The International Corporation*, (pp. 17–34). Massachusetts: M.I.T Press.

— (1971) The multinational enterprise in a multiple currency world. In J. Dunning (ed.), *The Multinational Enterprise*, (pp. 49–57). London: Allen and Unwin.

— (1976) Towards a theory of international banking. *Economic Review*. Federal Reserve Bank of San Francisco, Spring 1976, 5–8.

— (1977) Discussion. *Key Issues in International Banking*. Proceedings of a Conference. Federal Reserve Bank of Boston, 45–50.

— (1984) International banking, a survey. *Journal of Money, Credit and Banking*, 16, 661–678.

Brimmer, A. and Dahl, F. (1975) Growth of American international banking: implications for public policy. *Journal of Finance*, 30, 341–363.

Buckley, P. J. (1988) The limits of explanation, testing the internalisation theory of the multinational enterprise. *Journal of International Business Studies*, 19, 181–193.

— (1993) The role of management in internalisation theory. *Management International Review*, 33, 197–207.

— and Casson, M. (1991) *The Future of the Multinational Enterprise*, 2nd Edition. London: MacMillan.

Casson, M. (1985a) Entrepreneurship and the dynamics of foreign direct investment. In P. Buckley and M. Casson (eds.), *The Economic Theory of the Multinational Enterprise*, (pp. 172–191) London: MacMillan.

— (1985b) Multinational and intermediate product trade. In P. Buckley and M. Casson (eds.), *ibid*, (pp. 144–171).

— (1985c) Multinational monopolies and international cartels. In P. Buckley and M. Casson (eds.), *ibid*, (pp. 60–97).

— (1987) *The Firm and the Market*. London: Allen and Unwin.

— (1990) Evolution of multinational banks: a theoretical perspective. In G. Jones (ed.), *Banks as Multinationals*, (pp. 14–29) London: Routledge Publishing.

Caves, R. E. (1971) International corporations: the industrial economics of foreign investment. *Economica*, 38, 1–27.

— (1977) Discussion. *Key Issues in International Banking*. Proceedings of a conference. Federal Reserve Bank of Boston. pp. 87–90.

—, Frankel, J. and Jones, R. (1990) *World Trade and Payments: an Introduction*, Fifth Edition, Illinois: Scott Foresman.

Cho, K. R. (1985) *Multinational Banks: Their Identities and Determinants*. Michigan: UMI Research Press.

— (1986) Determinants of international banks. *Management International Review*, 26, 10–23.

Coase, A. H. (1937) The nature of the Firm. *Economica*, 4, 386–405.

Davis, K. and Lewis, M. (1982) Foreign banks and the financial system. *Australian Financial System Inquiry, Commissioned Studies and Selected Papers, Part 1*. Canberra: Australian Government Publishing Service.

Demsetz, H. (1973). Industry structure, market rivalry and public policy. *Journal of Law and Economics*, 16, 1–9.

Dufey, G. and Giddy, I. H. (1981) Innovation in the international financial markets. *Journal of International Business Studies*, Fall 1981, 33–51.

Dunning, J. (1973) The determinants of international production. *Oxford Economic Papers*, 25, 289–336.

THEORIES OF MULTINATIONAL BANKING   99

— (1977) Trade, location of economic activity and the MNE: a search for an eclectic approach. In B. Ohlin, Hesselborn, P. and Wijkman, P. (eds.), *The International Allocation of Economic Activity*, (pp. 395–431), proceedings of a Nobel Symposium held in Stockholm. London: MacMillan Press.

— (1981a) *International Production and the Multinational Enterprise*. London: Allen and Unwin.

— (1988) The eclectic paradigm of international production: a restatement and some possible extensions. *Journal of International Business Studies*, 19, 1–32.

Edwards, F. (1975) International banking: an overview. *Columbia Journal of World Business*, Winter 1975, 7–8.

Euromoney (1994a) What a difference a decade makes: Euromoney five hundred. *Euromoney*, June 1994, 137–169.

— (1994b) Euromoney awards for excellence. *Euromoney*, July 1994, 41–66.

Fieleke, N. (1977) The growth of US banking abroad: an analytical survey. *Key Issues in International Banking*, Proceedings of a Conference. Federal Reserve Bank of Boston, 6–40.

Giddy, I. (1983). The theory and industrial organisation of international banking. *Research in International Business and Finance: a Research Annual*. London: JAI Press. 3, 195–243.

Grubel, H. (1977) A theory of multinational banking. *Banca Nazionale del Lavoro, Quarterly Review*, December, 349–363.

Hewson, J. (1975) *Liquidity Creation and Distribution in the Eurocurrency Markets*, Lexington: Lexington Books.

Hirtle, B. (1991) Factors affecting the international competitiveness of internationally active financial institutions. *Quarterly Review, Federal Reserve Bank of New York*. 16, 38–51.

Hymer, S. H. (1976) *The International Operations of National Firms: a Study of Direct Foreign Investment*. Cambridge, Mass: MIT Press.

Jacquillat, B. and Solnik, B. (1978) Multinationals are poor tools for diversification. *Journal of Portfolio Management*, Winter 1978, 8–12.

Jain, A. (1994) *International Financial Markets and Institutions*. Boulder, Colorado: Kolb Publishing.

Johnston, R. (1983) *The Economics of the Euro-Market: History. Theory and Policy*. London: MacMillan Press.

Khoury, S. J. (1979) International banking: a special look at the foreign banks in the US. *Journal of International Business Studies*, 18, 67–88.

Kindleberger, C. P. (1969) *American Business Abroad*, New Haven: Yale University Press.

— (1983) International banks as leaders or followers of international business. *Journal of Banking and Finance*, 7, 583–595.

Kojima, K (1973). A macroeconomic approach to foreign direct investment. *Hitotsuhashi Journal of Economics*, 14, 1–21.

— (1982) Macroeconomic versus international business approach to direct foreign investment. *Hitotsubashi Journal of Economics*, 22, 1–19.

— and Ozawa, T. (1984) Micro- and macro— economic models of direct foreign investment: towards a synthesis. *Hitotsubashi Journal of Economics*, 25, 1–20.

Lewis, M. and Davis, K. (1987) *Domestic and International Banking*, Oxford: Philip A Allan.

Logue, D. E. (1982) An experiment in international diversification. *Journal of Portfolio Management*, Fall 1982, 22–27.

MacAllister, P. H. and McManus, D. (1993) Resolving the scale efficiency puzzle in banking. *Journal of Banking and Finance*, 17, 389–405.

Magee, S. P. (1977) Information and multinational corporations: an appropriability theory of direct foreign investment. In J. N. Bhagwati (ed.), *The New International Economic Order* (pp. 317–340), Massachusetts: MIT Press.

Merrett, D. T. (1990) Paradise lost? British banks in Australia. In G. Jones (ed.) *Banks as Multinationals*, (pp. 62–84). London: Routledge.

Pauly, L. (1987) *Foreign Banks in Australia: The Politics of Deregulation*. Sydney: Australian Professional Publications.

Robinson, S. (1972) *Multinational Banking*. Leiden: A. W. Sijthoff.

Rugman, A. M. (1980) Internalisation as a general theory of foreign direct investment; a re-appraisal of the literature. *Weltwirtschaftliches Archiv*. 115, 365–379.

— (1981) *Inside the Multinationals*. London: Croom Helm.

Shapiro, A. C. (1992) *Multinational Financial Management*, 4th edition, Boston: Allyn and Bacon.

Sodersten, B. (1980) *International Economics*, 2nd Edition. London: MacMillan Publishing.

Tschoegl, A. E. (1987) International retail banking as a strategy: an assessment. *Journal of International Business Studies*, 18, 67–88.

Vernon, R. (1966) International investment and international trade in the product cycle. *Quarterly Journal of Economics*, 80, 190–207.

— (1971) *Sovereignty at Bay: the Multinational spread of U.S. Enterprises*. New York: Basic Books.

Yannopoulos, G. N. (1983) The growth of transnational banking. In M. Casson (ed.), *The Growth of International Business*, (pp. 236–257) London: Allen and Unwin.

Zimmer, S. A. and McCauley, R. N. (1991) Bank cost of capital and international competition. *Quarterly Review*. Federal Reserve Bank of New York, Winter, 33–59.

Part III
Eurocurrency Banking

[12]

The Eurocurrency Market

Statement by Henry C. Wallich, Member, Board of Governors of the Federal Reserve System, before the Subcommittee on Domestic Monetary Policy and the Subcommittee on International Trade, Investment and Monetary Policy of the Committee on Banking, Finance and Urban Affairs, U.S. House of Representatives, July 12, 1979.

It is a pleasure to testify before these subcommittees today on behalf of the Federal Reserve Board. You have asked for our views on the rapidly growing and now sizable Eurodollar market and on the possible need for legislation to deal with it.

U.S. monetary authorities have monitored the development of the Eurodollar market since its birth in the 1950s and its expansion into a market for several Eurocurrencies. The Federal Reserve obtains data from affiliates of U.S. banks operating abroad and has worked with foreign central banks and the Bank for International Settlements (BIS) to develop a reporting network that provides information on the market as a whole. The Federal Reserve and Comptroller of the Currency also obtain information as bank supervisors. Thus, we are well placed as an institution to observe the working of the market and to assess both the benefits it provides and the problems it poses.

I would like first to address some general questions about the Eurocurrency market that are often asked. I will then turn to the possible need for better control of the market from a monetary policy standpoint since the issues raised in your invitation to present testimony relate primarily to monetary policy. In addition, since concern is also expressed from time to time regarding the adequacy of supervision to assure the safety and soundness of banks participating in Eurocurrency banking, I shall briefly touch on this aspect.

PRINCIPAL FEATURES OF THE EUROCURRENCY MARKET

The Eurocurrency market is an international banking market in bank deposits and loans that are denominated in currencies other than the currency of the country where the bank is located—for example, dollar deposits and loans of banking offices in London. The phrase "Eurocurrency" developed because the market originated in Europe, chiefly as a market for Eurodollars. Eurodollars still account for about three-quarters of the Eurocurrency market, with about half of the remainder being Euromarks. Also, some deposits in the market are denominated in pounds sterling, Swiss francs, and other major currencies. I will focus my comments on the Eurocurrency market as a whole with the reminder that at present it is largely, but not exclusively, a market in dollars.

What is now considered the Eurocurrency market extends beyond Europe to include banking activities in major industrial countries worldwide and in offshore banking centers such as the Bahamas, the Cayman Islands, Hong Kong, and Singapore. Still, the Eurocurrency market does not embrace all of international banking activity. Traditionally, international banking has been conducted through the taking of deposits from foreigners and lending to foreigners in the currency of the country where the bank is located. This form of banking continues. On the other hand, some Eurocurrency activity is not international at all and occurs within a country's domestic market; deposits are taken from residents and loans made to residents denominated in dollars or other foreign currencies.

The Eurocurrency liabilities of banks usually take the form of time deposits of large size. Eurocurrency deposits are not generally used to make payments directly, and only a relatively small part are in immediately available funds that can be used directly to economize on conventional checking account balances. Thus, for the most part they cannot be considered money in the narrow sense of M-1. The closest analogy, in U.S. monetary statistics, is perhaps with large negotiable certificates of deposit, which are included in M-4. However, negotiable CDs can be issued by U.S. banks only with a maturity of one month or more while one-third of all Eurocurrency deposits have a remaining maturity of less than one month. Thus, Eurocurrency deposits may be said to have more of a money-like quality than large CDs.

How Large is the Eurocurrency Market?

The scale of the Eurocurrency market is often misunderstood. For instance, one measure of size often cited—its so-called gross size—represents the total of foreign currency liabilities of banks in industrial countries reporting to the BIS plus those of certain offshore branches of U.S. banks. This figure exceeded $800 billion at the end of 1978. However, it is inflated by a large volume of interbank activity that neither contributes to the liquidity of the nonbank public nor is associated with any extension of credit to nonbanks. On these grounds, we exclude interbank liabilities such as correspondent balances and federal funds from U.S. domestic money and credit aggregates. One should similarly adjust downward the stock of Eurocurrency liabilities. Commonly cited measures produced by the BIS and others put the net size of the Eurocurrency market in the neighborhood of $400 billion. However, these measures still overstate the monetary significance of the market because they net out only banks' liabilities to other banks within the reporting area. Eliminating, insofar as possible, liabilities to banks and central banks outside the reporting area yields a measure of net monetary liabilities in the Eurocurrency market of roughly $150 billion to $175 billion as of the end of 1978. Of this amount, about one-third is counted in the monetary statistics of some country. Thus, today the so-called stateless money in the Eurocurrency market, that which is not counted in

national monetary statistics, is on the order of $100 billion to $120 billion.

The net credit provided to nonbanks through the Eurocurrency market, estimated at about $225 billion to $250 billion as of the end of 1978, is larger than its net monetary liabilities. The difference arises largely because of sizable deposits of central banks in the market. While these deposits do not constitute part of the net monetary asset holdings of nonbanks, they do provide a source of funds that can be used to make loans and, to the extent that they are largely deposits of central banks of smaller countries, they are more likely to be shifted among currencies.

The numbers I have cited tend to shrink one's perception of the Eurocurrency market compared with the impression that is often conveyed, but the importance of the market should not be underestimated. The absolute numbers involved are large. Moreover, Eurocurrency holdings and credits have been growing more rapidly than the domestic monetary and credit aggregates of the United States and of most other countries. For example, from the end of 1974 to the end of 1978, Eurocurrency liabilities to nonbanks are estimated to have grown at an average annual rate of about 18½ percent, compared with growth in M-1 and M-4 in the United States at average annual rates of 6.3 percent and 8.5 percent respectively over the same four-year period. This trend can be expected to continue unless checked. Thus, the existence of the Eurocurrency market increasingly will have to be taken into account in formulating and executing domestic monetary policies; issues of surveillance, supervision, and control of the Eurocurrency market will continue to be in the foreground of domestic and international financial policy.

Is the Eurocurrency Market Out of Control?

Because Eurocurrency banking is not subject to reserve requirements or various other restrictions, such as liquidity ratios or credit ceilings, which various monetary authorities employ to facilitate the execution of domestic monetary policies, it is often alleged that the Eurocurrency market is a source of uncontrolled liquidity. However, because of its close links with domestic markets for bank funds, the Eurocurrency market is, in fact, directly subject to the influence of domestic monetary policies in countries of financial importance.

Observation of interest rates confirms the prediction of economic theory that Eurocurrency interest rates should be closely tied to interest rates in the domestic market for comparable assets denominated in the corresponding currency. Relatively stable differentials are normally observed, and these differentials reflect costs in the domestic market arising from reserve requirements and other regulations that do not exist in the Eurocurrency market.

These close links between domestic and "Euro" interest rates are maintained by flows of funds between domestic markets and the Eurocurrency market. For example, when domestic U.S. interest rates rise, depositors have an incentive to switch funds from Eurodollar deposits to domestic U.S. bank deposits and commercial paper. Some borrowers shift their borrowing to the Eurodollar market, and banks themselves move funds raised in that market to the U.S. credit market. These responses put upward pressure on Eurodollar interest rates until the normal relationship with domestic U.S. rates is restored. In practice, the adjustment is virtually instantaneous. Thus, the dampening effect of higher U.S. interest rates on credit demand and spending is felt in the Eurodollar market as well as in the U.S. market.

Limitations on the free flow of funds internationally, such as the Voluntary Foreign Credit Restraint program—in effect until January 1974 as part of the U.S. balance of payments program of the 1960s—can weaken the tie between Eurocurrency and domestic interest rates. But because controls on capital movements inevitably have significant leakages, a fairly close correspondence can usually be observed even when such measures are in force.

While the transmission of domestic monetary influences to the Eurocurrency market is very real and effective, there is a somewhat paradoxical tendency for the growth of the market to accelerate relative to the domestic banking market when monetary policy becomes more restrictive and interest rates rise. In the case of Eurodollars this phenomenon is a consequence of two features of the U.S. monetary system: first, requirements that member banks hold non-interest-bearing reserves and, second, restrictions on deposit interest rates (particularly the prohibition of interest payments on deposits of less than 30 days' maturity).

As a result of reserve requirements, member banks incur additional costs in bidding for large deposits domestically compared with the costs of raising funds in the Eurodollar market since a portion of funds raised at home must be held in nonearning form. Monetary restraint in the United States, either in the form of a higher federal funds rate or in the form of higher reserve requirements, pushes up these additional costs of domestic banking and induces banks to shift their funding efforts to the Eurodollar market even though deposit interest rates for dollars in that market may rise by at least as much as in the domestic market. With higher market interest rates generally, demand deposits tend to be attracted from the U.S. banking system to the Eurodollar market since such deposits cannot, by law, earn interest in the United States. Similar reactions occur in the response to monetary tightening in other countries although the specific factors differ from country to country. These effects constitute one reason, although by no means the only reason, why the Eurocurrency market has grown so rapidly over the past decade when inflation has risen and brought with it historically high nominal interest rates.

As interest rates rise, the Eurocurrency market is not the only financial channel that gains a competitive advantage. Domestic U.S. financial flows through channels not subjected to member bank reserve requirements or interest rate restrictions—such as the commercial paper market, finance companies, and money market mutual funds—are also favored.

Despite the tendency of the Eurocurrency market to grow relatively more rapidly when domestic interest rates rise, it is still true that monetary restraint is effective. When the Federal Reserve tightens monetary policy, it forces interest rates to rise and growth of domestic member bank deposits to slow. The expansion of the Eurodollar market will slow less than that of the domestic market in response to higher interest rates, and the Eurodollar market may grow faster than it otherwise would if enough banking activity shifts to it from the U.S. market. Nevertheless, it will normally be the case that the application of domestic restraint will reduce the growth of the two markets taken together.

DOES THE EUROCURRENCY MARKET CREATE PROBLEMS FOR DOMESTIC MONETARY POLICY?

While the Eurocurrency market is linked to domestic markets and subject to control through the impact of domestic monetary policy on interest rates, it does pose problems for monetary policy. My judgment is that these problems have been of only moderate significance to date, but they are increasing. Moreover, the Eurocurrency market adds to inflationary pressures because liabilities to nonbanks in this market are rising faster than domestic money supplies. In the present inflationary environment we must look closely at every source of inflationary tendency.

Let me identify some of the ways in which the Eurocurrency market complicates the execution of monetary policy. The presence of a Eurocurrency market confronts domestic monetary authorities with a dilemma. They could, in principle, act in such a way as to provide for the desired growth of liquidity, taking account of both the domestic market and the Eurocurrency market. One problem that the Federal Reserve would encounter in following such an approach would arise because we cannot gauge well the extent to which growth in the Eurocurrency market affects spending in the United States. Dollars held or borrowed in the Eurocurrency market could be spent anywhere in the world, not just in the United States. On the other hand, it is likely that growth in the nondollar portion of the market would stimulate spending in the United States at least marginally. Other monetary authorities face the same uncertainties.

Perhaps an even more serious problem in carrying out a monetary policy that takes ex-

plicit account of the Eurocurrency market would arise because of the uneven effects of restrictive policy on the domestic and Eurocurrency markets. Those smaller domestic banks and their customers that have less access to the Eurocurrency market than the large international banks and their U.S. and foreign customers would absorb a disproportionate share of the burden of a restrictive policy. This inequity, in turn, would undermine support for an appropriate counterinflationary monetary policy.

Moreover, if monetary authorities focus exclusively on the growth of domestic aggregates, ignoring the effects of the more rapid growth of liabilities to nonbanks that is occurring in the Eurocurrency market, they may facilitate more expansionary and more inflationary conditions than they intend, or may be aware of. Indeed, there is a risk that, over time, as the Eurocurrency market expands relative to domestic markets, control over the aggregate volume of money may increasingly slip from the hands of central banks. Thus, it would be prudent to have available instruments for controlling the Eurocurrency market as we have for controlling domestic monetary aggregates. This is one of the principal reasons for seriously considering the need for reserve requirements against Eurocurrency deposits on an international basis.

WHAT ROLE DOES THE EUROCURRENCY MARKET PLAY IN EXCHANGE-RATE DEVELOPMENTS?

The existence of the Eurocurrency market as a liquid and efficient mechanism for international financial dealings has certainly had an important influence on exchange-rate developments in recent years. It would be wrong, however, to view the market itself as having given rise to new stabilizing or destabilizing forces. Rather it has acted as a conduit and amplifier through which both stabilizing and destabilizing financial flows have been felt in exchange markets with greater speed and intensity.

In recent years the size of current-account deficits has been unprecedented. Without an efficient international financial market to channel funds from countries in surplus to those in deficit, exchange-rate pressures at times would have been even greater than they were. The Eurocurrency markets have played an important role in moving excess savings to private and official borrowers in countries with current-account deficits.

At other times international capital flows have exacerbated pressures in exchange markets that have arisen to some extent from the need to finance current-account deficits. In some of these episodes the capital movements undoubtedly have reflected a reasonable market view that authorities were attempting to maintain untenable exchange-rate relationships. In other episodes, however, market psychology has appeared to drive exchange rates to unwarranted levels—movements that have subsequently been reversed. The international character and the liquidity of the Eurocurrency market have tended to swell the volume of funds moving through exchange markets at such times.

WHAT MEASURES COULD BE TAKEN TO DEAL BETTER WITH THE EUROCURRENCY MARKET?

The thrust of my discussion of the Eurocurrency market has been to reject as unfounded the extreme view that the market is an unrestrained source of monetary and exchange-market instability but to recognize that its existence makes the execution of monetary policy more difficult. There is a danger that, if measures are not taken to moderate the growth of the Eurocurrency market, the problem will grow over time and the prospects for controlling inflation will worsen correspondingly. Thus, careful monitoring of the Eurocurrency market is in order, and careful consideration should be given to making monetary restraints on the Eurocurrency market move more in parallel with restraints on domestic markets. In considering various approaches we should be mindful of several factors.

First, any approach adopted should take account of and seek to preserve the benefits that flow from the existence of the market. I have only alluded to these benefits, but they are considerable. The market is extremely competitive and efficient. It facilitates movements of large volumes of funds from savers to investors

across national borders at low cost. In doing so it helps to finance temporary current-account imbalances and improve the efficiency of investment worldwide. It also exerts competitive pressure on domestic banking systems to be more responsive to their customers and to become more efficient.

Second, any approach adopted should have a good prospect of contributing significantly to broad control over the volume of international liquid assets and credit. Little would be achieved, and a great burden would be placed on some institutions, if part of the market were restricted and another part were left unrestrained to take up the slack, or if Eurocurrency banking activity could easily be shifted into new unrestricted forms. Similarly, any burden imposed should be as low as possible and should apply equally and equitably to all banks operating in the Eurocurrency market. Thus, for example, it has not seemed desirable to restrict the scale of U.S. banks' participation in the Eurocurrency market so long as banks of other major countries were unfettered.

The Federal Reserve has, of course, the responsibility to consider the safety and soundness of U.S. banks abroad when reviewing proposals of banks to expand their international operations. Together with the Comptroller of the Currency, the Federal Reserve also examines the lending, funding, and management of U.S. banks abroad and considers the consolidated worldwide positions of U.S. banks in assessing their overall condition. Foreign central banks often believe that they do not have the authority to oversee the foreign operations of their banks as closely as we do in the United States, but they are moving, in some cases with the support of new grants of authority, to adopt approaches similar to ours.

Third, measures that were applied only to Eurodollars and not to all Eurocurrencies would have limited effectiveness and might well introduce new instabilities into international financial markets. Although depositors and bankers see Eurodollars, Euromarks, and Eurosterling as being quite different and are not indifferent among these Eurocurrencies, forward markets in foreign exchange offer a ready means of achieving any desired foreign exchange position regardless of the actual currency of a deposit. Hence, restrictions on the availability of one Eurocurrency would induce some who wished to hold that currency to move into deposits denominated in other currencies and then to acquire the desired currency through a forward contract.

Taking account of these considerations, the Federal Reserve has been examining the advantages and disadvantages of various ways that the Eurocurrency market might be brought under greater control. One technique we have explored would entail placing reserve requirements on the Eurocurrency liabilities of banks' head offices, branches, and affiliates no matter where located. Those countries whose banks and banking affiliates have a significant, or potentially significant, presence in international markets would be expected to act in concert with respect to their banks. Deposits accepted from banks that were subjected to the requirement could be exempted. The objective would be to slow down the growth of deposits from outside the covered banks and the corresponding growth of credit by putting the Eurocurrency market more nearly in a position of competitive equality with domestic banking markets. If this approach were accepted by the important countries, it would minimize the likelihood that large, parallel, but reserve-free markets would emerge through banks with head offices in nonparticipating countries. I am submitting with my testimony a paper prepared by the Federal Reserve Board staff that explores this approach in more detail.[1]

The reserve requirement approach seems to be the most effective of several that might have merit. An alternative, unilateral approach would be to reduce the competitive advantage of the Eurocurrency market by removing reserve requirements and interest rate restrictions on those domestic deposits for which Eurocurrency deposits are close substitutes. However, this would have the disadvantage of giving up an important monetary policy instrument. Other possible international approaches might be to

impose special restraints on Eurocurrency loans or deposits in relation to capital, or to specify some kinds of liquidity ratios that would have to be observed in Eurocurrency banking.

Federal Reserve representatives have discussed our thinking concerning the use of reserve requirements in the Eurocurrency market with representatives of other central banks of the Group of Ten countries and Switzerland. These central banks have shown a willingness to discuss this and other possibilities. A plan of work has been established to examine reserve requirements and other techniques over the next several months. The technical difficulties are considerable. Neither the Federal Reserve nor other central banks will be in a position to decide whether reserve requirements or any of the alternatives are sufficiently promising to press for their adoption until the work now under way is completed.

WHAT LEGISLATIVE INITIATIVES WOULD FACILITATE BETTER CONTROL OVER THE GROWTH OF THE EUROCURRENCY MARKET?

At the present time the Federal Reserve has no firm basis on which to make recommendations concerning legislation to enable U.S. participation in an international program to control better the growth of the Eurocurrency market. The work we will be doing and the discussions we will be engaged in with other central banks over the coming months may give us a better basis on which to make such recommendations in the future.

H.R. 3962, introduced by Congressman Leach, envisions a system of reserve requirements that would be adopted in concert by major countries. To this extent, the bill parallels the thinking in the Federal Reserve on how the issue of the growth of the Eurocurrency market might be addressed. However, to embed in legislation a specific approach based on reserve requirements at this stage could impede efforts to reach agreement on an international solution. While not favoring specific legislative limitations with respect to Eurocurrency reserve requirements, the Board does believe that its reserve requirement authority over banks in the international

---

1. The discussion paper for this statement is available on request from Publications Services, Division of Support Services, Board of Governors of the Federal Reserve System, Washington, D.C. 20551.

sphere should be broadened, given the rapid and unpredictable changes that can occur in international markets. The Federal Reserve has been given the authority by the Congress in past legislation to place reserve requirements on foreign branches and affiliates of member banks. This authority should be extended to branches of U.S. banks that are not members of the Federal Reserve System, as provided in H.R. 7.

H.R. 3962 contains two other provisions in addition to those concerning reserve requirements on Eurocurrency deposits. It would call for the Federal Reserve Board to prepare a report to the Congress on the role of U.S. banks and other financial institutions in the Eurocurrency market and in foreign exchange markets. I would like to assure the subcommittees that even without legislation the Board will assess carefully all of the related issues in formulating its approaches to Eurocurrency markets and exchange markets and will keep the Congress informed through regular channels.

The bill would also prohibit Board approval of the establishment of any international banking facility in the United States before December 31, 1980, and would require the Board to report to the Congress before June 30, 1980, on the advisability of adopting such proposals. The Board has not yet considered what action it should take with respect to the international banking facility proposal. It intends to do so soon, and when it does, it will weigh all the factors that affect the competitive position of U.S. banks, large and small, relative to foreign banks. The Board should be free to give due weight to matters of equity, monetary control, and relations with foreign banking institutions in considering what action to take.

These hearings and the introduction of H.R. 3962 demonstrate well-directed congressional interest in the problems posed by the Eurocurrency market. I hope my presentation will prove useful to the members of the subcommittees in the conduct of your oversight responsibilities and in the further consideration of legislation. In view of the discussions among central banks, which I have indicated will be proceeding in the coming months, you may wish to ask the Federal Reserve to inform the Congress of progress in this area at the start of the next session of the Congress. We would welcome the opportunity to do so. □

[13]

The Euro-Dollar Market: Some First Principles

The following article was written by Professor Milton Friedman of the University of Chicago. It presents the author's views on certain aspects of the Euro-dollar market. Publication in The Morgan Guaranty Survey *does not imply agreement by the bank in every respect with Dr. Friedman's analysis. The article is published as an interesting and provocative contribution to discussion of this important subject.*

THE Euro-dollar market is the latest example of the mystifying quality of money creation to even the most sophisticated bankers, let alone other businessmen. Recently, I heard a high official of an international financial organization discuss the Euro-dollar market before a collection of high-powered international bankers. He estimated that Euro-dollar deposits totaled some $30 billion. He was then asked: "What is the source of these deposits?" His answer was: partly, U.S. balance-of-payments deficits; partly, dollar reserves of non-U.S. central banks; partly, the proceeds from the sale of Euro-dollar bonds.

This answer is almost complete nonsense. Balance-of-payments deficits do provide foreigners with claims on U.S. dollars. But there is nothing to assure that such claims will be held in the form of Euro-dollars. In any event, U.S. deficits, worldwide, have totaled less than $9 billion for the past five years, on a liquidity basis. Dollar holdings of non-U.S. central banks have fallen during the period of rapid rise in Euro-dollar deposits but by less than $5 billion. The dollars paid for Euro-bonds had themselves to come from somewhere and do not constitute an independent source. No matter how you try, you cannot get $30 billion from these sources. The answer given is precisely parallel to saying that the source of the $400 billion of deposits in U.S. banks (or for that matter the much larger total of all outstanding short-term claims) is the $60 billion of Federal Reserve credit outstanding.

The correct answer for both Euro-dollars and liabilities of U.S. banks is that their major source is a bookkeeper's pen.[1] The purpose of this article is to explain this statement. The purpose is purely expository. I shall restrict myself essentially to principle and shall not attempt either an empirical evaluation of the Euro-dollar market or a normative judgment of its desirability.

Another striking example of the confusion about Euro-dollars is the discussion, in even the most sophisticated financial papers, of the use of the Euro-dollar market by U.S. commercial banks "to evade tight money," as it is generally phrased. U.S. banks, one reads in a leading financial paper, "have been willing to pay extremely high interest rates...to borrow back huge sums of U.S. dollars that have piled up abroad." The image conveyed is that of piles of dollar bills being bundled up and shipped across the ocean on planes and ships—the way New York literally did drain gold from Europe in the bad—or good—old days at times of financial panic. Yet, the more dollars U.S. banks "borrow back" the more Euro-dollar deposits go up! How come? The answer is that it is purely figurative language to speak of "piled

[1] The similarity between credit creation in the U.S. fractional reserve banking system and in the Euro-dollar market has of course often been noted. For example, see Fred H. Klopstock, "The Euro-Dollar Market, Some Unresolved Issues," *Essays in International Finance*, No. 65 (Princeton, March, 1968), p. 6. A recent excellent analysis is given in an article by Joseph G. Kvasnicka, "Euro-Dollars—an Important Source of Funds for American Banks," *Business Conditions*, Federal Reserve Bank of Chicago, June, 1969. A useful but analytically less satisfactory examination of the Euro-dollar market is Jane Sneddon Little, "The Euro-Dollar Market: Its Nature and Impact," *New England Economic Review*, Federal Reserve Bank of Boston, May/June, 1969.

up" dollars being "borrowed back." Again, the bookkeeper's pen is at work.

What are Euro-dollars?

Just what are Euro-dollars? They are deposit liabilities, denominated in dollars, of banks outside the United States. Engaged in Euro-dollar business, for example, are foreign commercial banks such as the Bank of London and South America, Ltd., merchant banks such as Morgan Grenfell and Co., Ltd., and many of the foreign branches of U.S. commercial banks. Funds placed with these institutions may be owned by anyone—U.S. or foreign residents or citizens, individuals or corporations or governments. Euro-dollars have two basic characteristics: first, they are short-term obligations to pay dollars; second, they are obligations of banking offices located outside the U.S. In principle, there is no hard and fast line between Euro-dollars and other dollar-denominated claims on non-U.S. institutions—just as there is none between claims in the U.S. that we call "money" and other short-term claims. The precise line drawn in practice depends on the exact interpretation given to "short-term" and to "banks." Nothing essential in this article is affected by the precise point at which the line is drawn.

A homely parallel to Euro-dollars is to be found in the dollar deposit liabilities of bank offices located in the city of Chicago—which could similarly be called "Chicago dollars." Like Euro-dollars, "Chicago dollars" consist of obligations to pay dollars by a collection of banking offices located in a particular geographic area. Again, like Euro-dollars, they may be owned by anyone—residents or nonresidents of the geographic area in question.

The location of the banks is important primarily because it affects the regulations under which the banks operate and hence the way that they can do business. Those Chicago banks that are members of the Federal Reserve System must comply with the System's requirements about reserves, maximum interest rates payable on deposits, and so on; and in addition, of course, with the requirements of the Comptroller of the Currency if they are national banks, and of the Illinois State Banking Commission if they are state banks.

Euro-dollar banks are subject to the regulations of the relevant banking authorities in the country in which they operate. In practice, however, such banks have been subject neither to required reserves on Euro-dollar deposits nor to maximum ceilings on the rates of interest they are permitted to pay on such deposits.

Regulation and Euro-dollars

The difference in regulation has played a key role in the development of the Euro-dollar market. No doubt there were minor precursors, but the initial substantial Euro-dollar deposits in the post-World War II period originated with the Russians, who wanted dollar balances but recalled that their dollar holdings in the U.S. had been impounded by the Alien Property Custodian in World War II. Hence they wanted dollar claims not subject to U.S. governmental control.

The most important regulation that has stimulated the development of the Euro-dollar market has been Regulation Q, under which the Federal Reserve has fixed maximum interest rates that member banks could pay on time deposits. Whenever these ceilings became effective, Euro-dollar deposits, paying a higher interest rate, became more attractive than U.S. deposits, and the Euro-dollar market expanded. U.S. banks then borrowed from the Euro-dollar market to replace the withdrawn time deposits.

A third major force has been the direct and indirect exchange controls imposed by the U.S. for "balance-of-payments" purposes—the interest-equalization tax, the "voluntary" controls on bank lending abroad and on foreign investment, and, finally, the compulsory controls instituted by President Johnson in January 1968. Without Regulation Q and the exchange controls—all of which, in my opinion, are both unnecessary and undesirable—the Euro-dollar market, though it might still have existed, would not have reached anything like its present dimensions.

Fractional reserves

Euro-dollar deposits like "Chicago deposits" are in principle obligations to pay literal dollars —i.e., currency (or coin), all of which consists, at present, of government-issued fiat (Federal Reserve notes, U.S. notes, a few other similar issues, and fractional coinage). In practice, even Chicago banks are called on to discharge only an insignificant part of their deposit obligations by paying out currency. Euro-dollar banks are called on to discharge a negligible part in this form. Deposit obligations are typically discharged by providing a credit or deposit at another bank—as when you draw a check on your bank which the recipient "deposits" in his.

To meet their obligations to pay cash, banks keep a "reserve" of cash on hand. But, of course, since they are continuously receiving as well as paying cash and since in any interval they will be called on to redeem only a small fraction of their obligations in cash, they need on the average keep only a very small part of their assets in cash for this purpose. For Chicago banks, this cash serves also to meet legal reserve requirements. For Euro-dollar banks, the amount of literal cash they hold is negligible.

To meet their obligations to provide a credit at another bank, when a check or similar instrument is used, banks keep deposits at other banks. For Chicago banks, these deposits (which in addition to facilitating the transfer of funds be-

tween banks serve to meet legal reserve requirements) are held primarily at Federal Reserve banks. In addition, however, Chicago banks may also keep balances at correspondent banks in other cities.

Like cash, deposits at other banks need be only a small fraction of assets. Banks are continuously receiving funds from other banks, as well as transferring funds to them, so they need reserves only to provide for temporary discrepancies between payments and receipts or sudden unanticipated demands. For Chicago banks, such "prudential" reserves are clearly far smaller than the reserves that they are legally required to keep.

Euro-dollar banks are not subject to legal reserve requirements, but, like Chicago banks, they must keep a prudential reserve in order to be prepared to meet withdrawals of deposits when they are demanded or when they mature. An individual bank will regard as a prudential reserve readily realizable funds both in the Euro-dollar market itself (e.g., Euro-dollar call money) and in the U.S. But for the Euro-dollar system as a whole, Euro-dollar funds cancel, and the prudential reserves available to meet demands for U.S. dollars consist entirely of deposits at banks in New York or other cities in the U.S. and U.S. money market assets that can be liquidated promptly without loss.

The amount of prudential reserves that a Euro-dollar bank will wish to hold—like the amount that a Chicago bank will wish to hold—will depend on its particular mix of demand and time obligations. Time deposits generally require smaller reserves than demand deposits—and in some instances almost zero reserves if the bank can match closely the maturities of its dollar-denominated liabilities and its dollar-denominated loans and investments. Although a precise estimate is difficult to make because of the incompleteness and ambiguity of the available data, prudential reserves of Euro-dollar institutions are clearly a small fraction of total dollar-denominated obligations.

This point—that Euro-dollar institutions, like Chicago banks, are part of a fractional reserve banking system—is the key to understanding the Euro-dollar market. The failure to recognize it is the chief source of misunderstanding about the Euro-dollar market. Most journalistic discussions of the Euro-dollar market proceed as if a Euro-dollar bank held a dollar in the form of cash or of deposits at a U.S. bank corresponding to each dollar of deposit liability. That is the source of such images as "piling up," "borrowing back," "withdrawing," etc. But of course this is not the case. If it were, a Euro-dollar bank could hardly afford to pay 10% or more on its deposit liabilities.

A hypothetical example

A Euro-dollar bank typically has total dollar assets roughly equal to its dollar liabilities.[2] But these assets are not in currency or bank deposits. In highly simplified form, the balance sheet of such a bank—or the part of the balance sheet corresponding to its Euro-dollar operations—must look something like that shown in the adjoining column (the numbers in this and later balance sheets are solely for illustrative purposes).

It is the earnings on the $9,500,000 of loans and investments that enable it to pay interest on the $10,000,000 of deposits.

Where did the $10,000,000 of deposits come from? One can say that $700,000 (cash assets minus due to other banks) came from "primary deposits," i.e., is the counterpart to a literal deposit of cash or transfer of funds from other

[2] Which is why it is not subject to any special foreign exchange risk simply by operating in the Euro-dollar market. The balance sheet of its Euro-dollar operations balances in dollars; if it is, for example, a British bank, the balance sheet of its pound sterling operations balances in pounds. It is operating in two currencies but need not take a speculative position in either. Of course, it may take a speculative position, whether or not it operates in the Euro-dollar market.

EURO-DOLLAR BANK H OF LONDON

Assets		Liabilities	
Cash assets*	$1,000,000	Deposits	$10,000,000
Dollar-denominated loans	7,000,000	Due to other banks	300,000
Dollar-denominated bonds	2,500,000	Capital accounts	200,000
Total assets	$10,500,000	Total liabilities	$10,500,000

*Includes U.S. currency, deposits in N.Y. and other banks, and other assets immediately realizable in U.S. funds.

banks.[3] The other $9,300,000 is "created" by the magic of fractional reserve banking—this is the bookkeeper's pen at work.

Let us look at the process more closely. Suppose an Arab Sheik opens up a new deposit account in London at Bank H (H for hypothetical) by depositing a check for $1,000,000 drawn on the Sheik's demand deposit account at the head office of, say, Morgan Guaranty Trust Company. Let us suppose that Bank H also keeps its N.Y. account at Morgan Guaranty and also as demand deposits. At the first stage, this will add $1,000,000 to the deposit liabilities of Bank H, and the same amount to its assets in the form of deposits due from New York banks. At Morgan Guaranty, the transfer of deposits from the Sheik to Bank H will cause no change in total deposit liabilities.

But Bank H now has excess funds available to lend. It has been keeping cash assets equal to 10% of deposits—not because it was required to do so but because it deemed it prudent to do so. It now has cash equal to 18% (2/11) of deposits. Because of the $1,000,000 of new deposits from the Sheik, it will want to add, say, $100,000 to its balance in New York. This leaves Bank H with $900,000 available to add to its loans and investments. Assume that it makes a loan of $900,000 to, say, UK Ltd., a British corporation engaged in trade with the U.S., giving corporation UK Ltd. a check on

[3] Note that even this is an overstatement, since most of the deposits at N.Y. banks are themselves ultimately "created" rather than "primary" deposits. These are primary deposits only vis-à-vis the Euro-dollar market separately.

Morgan Guaranty. Bank H's balance sheet will now look as follows after the check has cleared:

Assets		Liabilities	
Cash assets	$1,100,000	Deposits	$11,000,000
Dollar-denominated loans	7,900,000	Due to other banks	300,000
Dollar-denominated bonds	2,500,000	Capital accounts	200,000
Total assets	$11,500,000	Total liabilities	$11,500,000

We now must ask what UK Ltd. does with the $900,000 check. To cut short and simplify the process, let us assume that UK Ltd. incurred the loan because it had been repeatedly troubled by a shortage of funds in New York and wanted to maintain a higher average level of bank balances in New York. Further assume that it also keeps its account at Morgan Guaranty, so that it simply deposits the check in its demand deposit account.

This particular cycle is therefore terminated and we can examine its effect. First, the position of Morgan Guaranty is fundamentally unchanged: it had a deposit liability of $1,000,000 to the Sheik. It now has a deposit liability of $100,000 to Bank H and one of $900,000 to UK Ltd.

Second, the calculated money supply of the U.S. and the demand deposit component thereof are unchanged. That money supply excludes from "adjusted demand deposits" the deposits of U.S. commercial banks at other U.S. commercial banks but it includes deposits of both foreign banks and other foreigners. Therefore, the Sheik's deposit was included before. The deposits of Bank H and UK Ltd. are included now.

Third, the example was set up so that the money supply owned by residents of the U.S. is also unchanged. As a practical matter, the financial statistics gathered and published by the Federal Reserve do not contain sufficient data to permit calculation of the U.S.-owned money supply—a total which would exclude from the money supply as now calculated currency and deposits at U.S. banks owned by nonresidents and include dollar deposits at non-U.S. banks owned by residents. But the hypothetical transactions clearly leave this total unaffected.

Fourth, Euro-dollar deposits are $1,000,000 higher.

However, fifth, the total world supply of dollars held by *nonbanks*—dollars in the U.S. plus dollars outside the U.S.—is $900,000 not $1,000,000 higher. The reason is that interbank deposits are now higher by $100,000, thanks to the additional deposits of Bank H at Morgan Guaranty. This amount of deposits was formerly an asset of a nonbank (the Arab Sheik); now it is an asset of Bank H. In this way, Bank H has created $900,000 of Euro-dollar deposits. The other $100,000 of Euro-dollar deposits has been transferred from the U.S. to the Euro-dollar area.

Sixth, the balance of payments of the U.S. is unaffected, whether calculated on a liquidity basis or on an official settlements basis. On a liquidity basis, the Arab Sheik's transfer is recorded as a reduction of $1,000,000 in short-term liquid claims on the U.S. but the increased deposits of Bank H and UK Ltd. at Morgan Guaranty are a precisely offsetting increase. On an official settlements basis, the series of transactions has not affected the dollar holdings of any central bank or official institution.[4]

Clearly, there is no meaningful sense in which we can say that the $900,000 of created Euro-

---

[4] It is interesting to contrast these effects with those that would have occurred if we substitute a Chicago bank for Bank H of London, i.e., suppose that the Arab Sheik had transferred his funds to a Chicago bank, say, Continental Illinois, and Continental Illinois had made the loan to UK Ltd., which UK Ltd. again added to its balances at Morgan Guaranty. To simplify matters, assume that the reserve requirements for Continental Illinois and Morgan Guaranty are the same flat 10% that we assumed Bank H of London kept in the form of cash assets (because, let us say, all deposit changes consist of the appropriate mix of demand and time deposits).

First, the position of Morgan Guaranty is now fundamentally changed. Continental Illinois keeps its reserves as deposits at the Federal Reserve Bank of Chicago, not at Morgan Guaranty. Hence it will deposit its net claim of $100,000 on Morgan Guaranty at the Chicago Fed to meet the reserves required for the Sheik's deposit. This will result in a reduction of $100,000 in

dollar deposits is derived from a U.S. balance-of-payments deficit, or from dollars held by central banks, or from the proceeds of Euro-dollar bond sales.

Some complications

Many complications of this example are possible. They will change the numbers but not in any way the essential principles. But it may help to consider one or two.

(a) Suppose UK Ltd. used the dollar loan to purchase timber from Russia, and Russia wished to hold the proceeds as a dollar deposit at, say, Bank R in London. Then, another round is started—precisely like the one that began when the Sheik transferred funds from Morgan Guaranty to Bank H. Bank R now has $900,000 extra deposit liabilities, matched by $900,000 extra deposits in New York. If it also follows the practice of maintaining cash assets equal to 10% of deposits, it can make a dollar loan of $810,-000. If the recipient of the loan keeps it as a demand deposit at Morgan Guaranty, or transfers it to someone who does, the process comes to an end. The result is that total Euro-dollar deposits are up by $1,900,000. Of that total, $1,710,-000 is held by nonbanks, with the other $190,-000 being additional deposits of banks (the $100,000 extra of Bank H at Morgan Guaranty plus the $90,000 extra of Bank R at Morgan Guaranty).

If the recipient of the loan transfers it to someone who wants to hold it as a Euro-dollar deposit at a third bank, the process continues on its merry way. If, in the extreme, at every stage, the whole of the proceeds of the loan were to end up as Euro-dollar deposits, it is obvious that the total increase in Euro-dollar deposits would be: $1,000,000 + 900,000 + 810,000 + 729,000 + \ldots\ldots\ldots\ldots = 10,000,000$. At the end of the process, Euro-dollar deposits would be $10,000,000 higher; deposits of Euro-dollar banks at N. Y. banks, $1,000,000 higher; and the total world supply of dollars held by nonbanks, $9,000,000 higher.

This example perhaps makes it clear why bankers in the Euro-dollar market keep insisting that they do not "create" dollars but only transfer them, and why they sincerely believe that all Euro-dollars come from the U.S. *To each banker separately in the chain described, his additional Euro-dollar deposit came in the form of a check on Morgan Guaranty Trust Company of New York!* How are the bankers to know that the $10,000,000 of checks on Morgan Guaranty all constitute repeated claims on the same initial $1,000,000 of deposits? Appearances are deceiving.

This example (involving successive loan extensions by a series of banks) brings out the difference between two concepts that have produced much confusion: Euro-dollar creation and the Euro-dollar multiplier. In both the

Morgan Guaranty's reserve balance at the New York Fed. Its deposits have gone down only $100,000 (thanks to the $900,000 deposit by UK Ltd.) so that if it had no excess reserves before it now has deficient reserves. This will set in train a multiple contraction of deposits at Morgan Guaranty and other banks which will end when the $1,000,000 gain in deposits by Continental Illinois is completely offset by a $1,000,000 decline in deposits at Morgan Guaranty and other banks.

Second, the calculated money supply of the U.S. and the demand deposit component thereof are still unchanged.

However, third, the money supply owned by the residents of the U.S. is reduced by the $900,000 increase in the deposits of UK Ltd.

Fourth, there is no change in Euro-dollar deposits.

Fifth, there is no change in the total world supply of dollars.

Sixth, the balance of payments of the U.S. is affected if it is

calculated on a liquidity basis but not if it is calculated on an official settlements basis. On a liquidity basis, the deficit would be increased by $900,000 because the loan by Continental Illinois to UK Ltd. would be recorded as a capital outflow but UK Ltd.'s deposit at Morgan Guaranty would be regarded as an increase in U.S. liquid liabilities to foreigners, which are treated as financing the deficit. This enlargement of the deficit on a liquidity basis is highly misleading. It suggests, of course, a worsening of the U.S. payments problem, whereas in fact all that is involved is a worsening of the statistics. The additional dollars that UK Ltd. has in its demand deposit account cannot meaningfully be regarded as a potential claim on U.S. reserve assets. UK Ltd. not only needs them for transactions purposes; it must regard them as tied or matched to its own dollar indebtedness. On an official settlements basis, the series of transactions does not affect the dollar holdings of any central bank or official institution.

simple example and the example involving successive loan extensions, the fraction of Euro-dollars outstanding that has been created is nine-tenths, or, put differently, 10 Euro-dollars exist for every U.S. dollar held as a cash asset in New York by Euro-dollar banks. However, in the simple example, the Euro-dollar multiplier (the ratio of the increase in Euro-dollar deposits to the initial "primary" deposit) is unity; in the second example, it is 10. That is, in the simple example, the total amount of Euro-dollars goes up by $1 for every $1 of U.S. deposits initially transferred to Euro-dollar banks; in the second example, it goes up by $10 for every $1 of U.S. deposits initially transferred. The difference is that in the simple example there is maximum "leakage" from the Euro-dollar system; in the second example, zero "leakage."

The distinction between Euro-dollar creation and the Euro-dollar multiplier makes it clear why there is a definite limit to the amount of Euro-dollars that can be created no matter how low are the prudential reserves that banks hold. For example, if Euro-dollar banks held zero prudential reserves—as it is sometimes claimed that they do against time deposits—100% of the outstanding deposits would be created deposits and the potential multiplier would be infinite. Yet the actual multiplier would be close to unity because only a small part of the funds acquired by borrowers from Euro-dollar banks would end up as additional time deposits in such banks.[5]

(b) Suppose Bank H does not have sufficient demand for dollar loans to use profitably the whole $900,000 of excess dollar funds. Suppose, simultaneously, it is experiencing a heavy demand for sterling loans. It might go to the Bank of England and use the $900,000 to buy sterling. Bank of England deposits at Morgan Guaranty would now go up. But since the Bank

[5] This is precisely comparable to the situation of savings and loan associations and mutual savings banks in the U.S.

of England typically holds its deposits at the New York Federal Reserve Bank, the funds would fairly quickly disappear from Morgan Guaranty's books and show up instead on the Fed's. This, in the first instance, would reduce the reserves of Morgan Guaranty and thus threaten to produce much more extensive monetary effects than any of our other examples. However, the Bank of England typically holds most of its dollar reserves as Treasury bills or the equivalent, not as noninterest earning deposits at the Fed. It would therefore instruct the Fed to buy, say, bills for its account. This would restore the reserves to the banking system and, except for details, we would be back to where we were in the other examples.

The key points

Needless to say, this is far from a comprehensive survey of all the possible complications. But perhaps it suffices to show that the complications do not affect the fundamental points brought out by the simple example, namely:

1. Euro-dollars, like "Chicago dollars," are mostly the product of the bookkeeper's pen—that is, the result of fractional reserve banking.

2. The amount of Euro-dollars outstanding, like the amount of "Chicago dollars," depends on the desire of owners of wealth to hold the liabilities of the corresponding group of banks.

3. The ultimate increase in the amount of Euro-dollars from an initial transfer of deposits from other banks to Euro-dollar banks depends on:

(a) The amount of their dollar assets Euro-dollar banks choose to hold in the form of cash assets in the U.S., and

(b) The "leakages" from the system—i.e., the final disposition of the funds borrowed from Euro-dollar banks (or acquired by the sale of bonds or other investments to them). The larger the fraction of such funds held as Euro-dollar deposits, the larger the increase in Euro-dollars in total.

4. The existence of the Euro-dollar market increases the total amount of dollar balances available to be held by nonbanks throughout the world for any given amount of money (currency plus deposits at Federal Reserve Banks) created by the Federal Reserve System. It does so by permitting a greater pyramiding on this base by the use of deposits at U.S. banks as prudential reserves for Euro-dollar deposits.

5. The existence of the Euro-dollar market may also create a greater demand for dollars to be held by making dollar balances available in a more convenient form. The net effect of the Euro-dollar market on our balance-of-payments problem (as distinct from our statistical position) depends on whether demand is raised more or less than supply.

My own conjecture—which is based on much too little evidence for me to have much confidence in it—is that demand is raised less than supply and hence that the growth of the Euro-dollar market has on the whole made our balance-of-payments problem more difficult.

6. Whether my conjecture on this score is right or wrong, the Euro-dollar market has almost surely raised the world's nominal money supply (expressed in dollar equivalents) and has thus made the world price level (expressed in dollar equivalents) higher than it would otherwise be. Alternatively, if it is desired to define the money supply exclusive of Euro-dollar deposits, the same effect can be described in terms of a rise in the velocity of the world's money supply. However, this effect, while clear in direction, must be extremely small in magnitude.

Use of Euro-dollars by U.S. banks

Let us now turn from this general question of the source of Euro-dollars to the special issue raised at the outset: the effect of Regulation Q

and "tight money" on the use of the Euro-dollar market by U.S. banks.

To set the stage, let us suppose, in the framework of our simple example, that Euro-dollar Bank H of London loans the $900,000 excess funds that it has as a result of the initial deposit by the Arab Sheik to the head office of Morgan Guaranty, i.e., gives Morgan Guaranty (New York) a check for $900,000 on itself in return for an I.O.U. from Morgan Guaranty. This kind of borrowing from foreign banks is one of the means by which American banks have blunted the impact of CD losses. The combined effect will be to leave total liabilities of Morgan Guaranty unchanged but to alter their composition: deposit liabilities are now down $900,000 (instead of the $1,000,000 deposit liability it formerly had to the Sheik it now has a deposit liability of $100,000 to Bank H) and other liabilities ("funds borrowed from foreign banks") are up $900,000.

Until very recently, such a change in the form of a bank's liabilities—from deposits to borrowings—had an important effect on its reserve position. Specifically, it freed reserves. With $1,000,000 of demand deposit liabilities to the Arab Sheik, Morgan Guaranty was required to keep in cash or as deposits at the Federal Reserve Bank of New York $175,000 (or $60,000 if, as is more realistic, the Sheik kept his $1,000,000 in the form of a time deposit). With the shift of the funds to Bank H, however, and completion of the $900,000 loan by Bank H to Morgan Guaranty, Morgan Guaranty's reserve requirements at the Fed fell appreciably. Before the issuance of new regulations that became effective on September 4 of this year, Morgan Guaranty was not required to keep any reserve for the liability in the form of the I.O.U. Its only obligation was to keep $17,500 corresponding to the demand deposit of Bank H. The change in the form of its liabilities would therefore have reduced its reserve requirements by $157,500 (or by $42,500 for a time deposit) without any change in its total liabilities or its total assets, or in the composition of its assets; hence it would have had this much more available to lend.

What the Fed did effective September 4 was to make borrowings subject to reserve requirements as well. Morgan Guaranty must now keep a reserve against the I.O.U., the exact percentage depending on the total amount of borrowings by Morgan Guaranty from foreign banks.[6] The new regulations make it impossible to generalize about reserve effects. A U.S. bank losing deposits to a Euro-bank and then recouping funds by giving its I.O.U. may or may not have additional amounts available to lend as a result of transactions of the kind described.

If Bank H made the loan to Chase instead of to Morgan Guaranty, the latter would lose reserves and Chase would gain them. To Chase, it would look as if it were getting additional funds from abroad, but to both together, the effect would be the same as before—the possible release of required reserves with no change in available reserves.

The bookkeeping character of these transactions, and how they can be stimulated, can perhaps be seen more clearly if we introduce an additional feature of the actual Euro-dollar market, which was not essential heretofore, namely, the role of overseas branches of U.S. banks. In addition, for realism, we shall express our example in terms of time deposits.

Let us start from scratch and consider the head office of Morgan Guaranty in New York and its London branch. Let us look at hypothetical initial balance sheets of both. We shall treat the London branch as if it had just started and had neither assets nor liabilities, and shall restrict the balance sheet for the head office to the part relevant to its CD operations. This set of

circumstances gives us the following situation:

NEW YORK HEAD OFFICE

Assets		Liabilities	
Deposits at F. R. Bank of NY	$ 6,000,000	Time certificates of deposit	$100,000,000
Other cash assets	4,000,000		
Loans	76,000,000		
Bonds	14,000,000		
Total assets	$100,000,000	Total liabilities	$100,000,000

(Note: Required reserves, $6,000,000)

LONDON OFFICE

Assets		Liabilities	
	$ 0		$ 0

Now suppose a foreign corporation (perhaps the Arab Sheik's oil company) which holds a long-term maturing CD of $10,000,000 at Morgan Guaranty refuses to renew it because the 6¼% interest it is receiving seems too low. Morgan Guaranty agrees that the return should be greater, but explains it is prohibited by law from paying more. It notes, however, that its London branch is not. Accordingly, the corporation acquires a time deposit at the London office for $10,000,000 "by depositing" the check for $10,000,000 on the New York office it receives in return for the maturing CD—or, more realistically, by transfers on the books in New York and London. Let us look at the balance sheets:

NEW YORK HEAD OFFICE

Assets		Liabilities	
Deposits at F.R. Bank of NY	$ 6,000,000	Time certificates of deposit	$ 90,000,000
Other cash assets	4,000,000		
Loans	76,000,000	Due to London branch	10,000,000
Bonds	14,000,000		
Total assets	$100,000,000	Total liabilities	$100,000,000

(Note: Required reserves, before issuance of new regulations, $5,400,000; since issuance of new regulations, between $5,400,000 and $6,400,000).

LONDON OFFICE

Assets		Liabilities	
Due from N. Y. office	$10,000,000	Time certificates of deposit	$10,000,000

---

6 The required reserve is 3% of such borrowings so long as they do not exceed 4% of total deposits subject to reserves. On borrowings in excess of that level the required reserve is 10%.

Clearly, if we consolidate the branch and the head office, the books are completely unchanged. Yet these bookkeeping transactions: (1) enabled Morgan Guaranty to pay a rate in London higher than 6¼% on some certificates of deposit; and (2) reduced its required reserves by $600,000 prior to the recent modification of Regulation M. The reduction in required reserves arose because until recently U.S. banks were not required to keep a reserve against liabilities to their foreign branches. With the amendment of Regulation M, any further reduction of reserves by this route has been eliminated since the Fed now requires a reserve of 10% on the amount due to branch offices in excess of the amount due on average during May.[7]

Hypocrisy and window dressing

This example has been expressed in terms of a *foreign* corporation because the story is a bit more complicated for a U.S. corporation, though the end result is the same. First, a U.S. corporation that transfers its funds from a certificate of deposit at a U.S. bank to a deposit at a bank abroad—whether a foreign bank or an overseas branch of a U.S. bank—is deemed by the Department of Commerce to have made a foreign investment. It may do so only if it is within its quota under the direct control over foreign investment with which we are still unfortunately saddled. Second, under pressure from the Fed, commercial banks will not facilitate direct transfers by U.S. corporations—indeed, many will not accept time deposits from U.S. corporations at their overseas branches, whether their own customers or not, unless the corporation can demonstrate that the deposit

7 An amendment to Regulation M effective September 4 established a 10% reserve requirement on head office liabilities to overseas branches on that portion of such liabilities in excess of the average amount on the books in the four-week period ending May 28, 1969.

is being made for an "international" purpose. However, precisely the same results can be accomplished by a U.S. holder of a CD making a deposit in a foreign bank and the foreign bank in turn making a deposit in, or a loan to, the overseas branch of a U.S. bank. As always, this kind of moral suasion does not prevent profitable transactions. It simply produces hypocrisy and window dressing—in this case, by unnecessarily giving business to competitors of U.S. banks!

The final effect is precisely the same as in the simple example of the foreign corporation. That example shows, in highly simplified form, the main way U.S. banks have used the Euro-dollar market and explains why it is that the more they "borrow" or "bring back" from the Euro-dollar market, the higher Euro-dollar deposits mount. In our example, borrowing went up $10,000,000 and so did deposits.

From January 1, 1969 to July 31, 1969 CD deposit liabilities of U.S. banks went down $9.3 billion, and U.S. banks' indebtedness to their own overseas branches went up $8.6 billion. The closeness of these two numbers is not coincidental.

These bookkeeping operations have affected the statistics far more than the realities. The run-off in CD's in the U.S., and the accompanying decline in total commercial bank deposits (which the Fed uses as its "bank credit proxy") have been interpreted as signs of extreme monetary tightness. Money has been tight, but these figures greatly overstate the degree of tightness. The holders of CD's on U.S. banks who replaced them by Euro-dollar deposits did not have their liquidity squeezed. The banks that substituted "due to branches" for "due to depositors on time certificates of deposit" did not have their lending power reduced. The Fed's insistence on keeping Regulation Q ceilings at levels below market rates has simply imposed enormous structural adjustments and shifts of funds on the commercial banking system for no social gain whatsoever.

Correcting a misunderstanding

A column that appeared in a leading financial paper just prior to the Fed's revision of reserve requirements encapsules the widespread misunderstanding about the Euro-dollar market. The Euro-dollar market, the column noted, has:

". . . ballooned as U.S. banks have discovered that they can ease the squeeze placed on them by the Federal Reserve Board by borrowing back these foreign-deposited dollars that were pumped out largely through U.S. balance-of-payments deficits. Of this pool of $30 billion, U.S. banks as of last week had soaked up $13 billion . . .

"Thanks to this system, it takes only seconds to transmit money—and money troubles—between the U.S. and Europe. . . The Federal Reserve's pending proposal to make Euro-dollar borrowing more costly to U.S. banks might make their future demands a shade less voracious, but this doesn't reduce concern about whether there will be strains in repaying the massive amounts already borrowed."

Strains there may be, but they will reflect features of the Euro-dollar market other than those stressed by this newspaper comment. The use of the Euro-dollar market by commercial banks to offset the decline in CD's was primarily a bookkeeping operation. The reverse process—a rise in CD's and a matching decline in Euro-dollar borrowings—will also require little more than a bookkeeping operation.

[14]

JÜRG NIEHANS and
JOHN HEWSON

The Eurodollar Market and Monetary Theory

INTRODUCTION

The question of how and to what extent the Eurodollar market creates liquidity continues to intrigue both experts and laymen. This paper presents a critical review of the principal issues from the point of view of money supply theory. The authors hope that this will both contribute to a better understanding of the Eurodollar market and stimulate further analytical work.

The discussion about the Eurodollar market can be seen as an illustration of Kuhn's model of scientific progress through the struggle for survival of competing paradigms. The models scientists build to explain the world depend on the species they choose as their paradigms. In the theory of money supply, the traditional paradigm for banks is the intermediary that uses monetary deposits to buy non-monetary assets, holding a fraction of deposits in reserve. This typically results in a model of the money supply in which an increase in central bank money or an increase in the demand for bank deposits results in an increase in the money supply several times as large. This has been the dominant money supply model for the last half century.

When new, initially puzzling observations turn up, scientists first try to assimilate them to the dominant theory. When, in the course of the sixties, the rapid expansion of the Eurodollar market seemed to confront economists with a "mystery" [9], their natural reaction was to meet the challenge by explaining the new phenomena in terms of the familiar model, assimilating the Eurobank to the paradigm of the dominant money supply theory [3]. Yet, characteristically, each of these assimilation efforts raised new puzzles, and the debate continued.[1]

[1] It is symptomatic of the unsettled state of the discussion that estimates of the Eurodeposit multiplier range as high as 18.45 [10] and as low as 0.5-0.9 [8].

Jürg Niehans is professor of political economy, The Johns Hopkins University. John Hewson is on the staff of the Reserve Bank of Australia.

2 : MONEY, CREDIT, AND BANKING

It is the basic contention of this paper that the bank that accepts monetary liabilities to buy nonmonetary assets is an inappropriate paradigm for the Eurodollar market, and that this market is more fruitfully interpreted in terms of an antithetical paradigm, at once older and newer, of a bank borrowing and lending funds of approximately the same "moneyness" in a perfect market. Once this is recognized, the Eurodollar market in turn becomes the paradigm for an important basic function of financial intermediaries which the dominant model tends to suppress, namely, the function of efficient distributors of funds. This could set the stage for a synthesis incorporating the features of both the ruling paradigm and its antithesis, but this is beyond the scope of the present paper.

In describing financial intermediation in the Eurodollar market, many economists felt compelled to fall back on what could be called the "case method." It consists of constructing sequences of T-accounts showing alternative chains of events starting from some initial disturbance (e.g. [17]). Inevitably, this results in a bewildering variety of possible cases, which leads to the conclusion that no general statements can be made. In other fields, economics has long progressed beyond this primitive (though indispensable) stage by recognizing certain constraints on the behavior of economic agents. One type of constraint familiar from monetary theory is the assumption that banks and nonbanks maintain certain fixed proportions between the items in their balance sheets. This results in the fixed-coefficient approach to money supply theory with the multipliers made familiar by Phillips [16]. The "new view" generalized the fixed-coefficient approach to a general equilibrium model of financial intermediation in which balance-sheet structures are determined simultaneously with interest rates from the optimizing behavior of economic agents [21]. Part 1 of this paper will first review the efforts to interpret the Eurodollar market in terms of the fixed-coefficient approach and second examine the modifications introduced by the explicit recognition of the interest mechanism. In part 2 it will be argued that a correct understanding of the Eurodollar market requires a distinction between deposit creation and liquidity creation, and that liquidity creation is probably much smaller than even a general equilibrium approach to deposit creation would suggest. Part 3 presents an alternative interpretation of the Eurodollar market as a system not of credit creation but of efficient credit distribution.

I. DEPOSIT CREATION

1. The Fixed-Coefficient Approach

We begin by restating the elementary model.[2] Assume that the paradigmatic bank accepts deposits from nonbanks D which are, for their owner, money. A proportion σ of the deposits is held in the form of reserves R with the central bank, while the remainder is used to buy nonmonetary assets. Assume also that the de-

---

[2] Equity capital and the default risk for which it serves as a reserve are disregarded throughout.

mand for deposits by the nonbank public is a linear function of the money supply M, while the remainder consists of currency C. Currency and bank reserves make up the monetary base B. The model can thus be written

$$R = \sigma D$$

$$D = \gamma M + \beta$$

$$M = C + D$$

$$C + R = B;$$

and, for given B, the effect of a shift in demand from currency to demand deposits, measured by $d\beta$, on the volume of deposits is

$$\frac{dD}{d\beta} = \frac{1}{1 - \gamma(1 - \sigma)}.$$

This model of a two-stage banking system can be applied to the Euromarket by assuming that Eurobanks hold deposits r with U.S. banks amounting to a fraction ρ of their deposit liabilities e, while the Eurodeposits the nonbank public wishes to hold are a linear function of their total liquid assets M^*, defined as the U.S. money supply M minus the U.S. bank deposits held by Eurobanks plus Eurobank deposits. The model thus reads

$$r = \rho e$$

$$e = \epsilon M^* + \alpha$$

$$M^* = M - r + e$$

$$C + D + r = M.$$

For given M, the effect of a shift in asset preferences from U.S. dollars to Eurodollars, measured by $d\alpha$, on the volume of Eurodeposits is thus given by the multiplier

$$\frac{de}{d\alpha} = \frac{1}{1 - \epsilon(1 - \rho)},$$

which is of exactly the same form as the elementary deposit multiplier, with the U.S. money supply playing the role of the monetary base. This is the prototype of the paradigm assimilation referred to in the introduction. It is, as far as we can see, the only analytical basis for the belief that the Eurodollar system has created, or has the potential to create, a considerable amount of liquidity, and is, for the same reason, subject to the risk of cumulative destruction of liquidity.

4 : MONEY, CREDIT, AND BANKING

Once this reinterpretation is accepted, the attention shifts to the probable size of ρ and ϵ for the Eurodollar market. It is generally recognized that reserve ratios in Eurodollar banks are very low, certainly much below 5 percent and possibly as low as 1–2 percent.[3] This would tend to make the Eurodollar multiplier higher than, say, the U.S. deposit multiplier. On the other hand, it has also been recognized that the fraction of incremental dollar holdings the nonbank public wishes to hold in the form of Eurodollars is much smaller than the fraction of an increment in the U.S. money supply the nonbank public wishes to hold in the form of U.S. demand deposits [8], .10–.15 perhaps being a plausible order of magnitude.[4] This low volume of ϵ tends to make the Euromultiplier relatively low. Assuming, as an illustration, $\rho = 1/30$ and $\epsilon = 1/8$, the multiplier becomes approximately 1.1 (it should be noted that with such low values of ρ, ϵ is practically all that matters for the result). This means that only a very small fraction of all Eurodollar deposits are created through the multiplier process "by the bookkeeper's pen."

The process of paradigm reinterpretation can be carried further. It was realized early that Eurobanks, since their deposits do not serve as a medium of exchange and their reserves (if any) are held with U.S. commercial banks and not with the central bank, are more like nonbank financial intermediaries than like commercial banks. In addition, it is not strictly legitimate to treat the U.S. money supply as the exogenously given base of the Eurodollar market, for a shift in the demand for Eurodollars, by changing the U.S. dollar deposits of Eurobanks, may have repercussions on the supply of U.S. money. What we have to use, therefore, is the model of a three-stage banking system in which nonbank intermediaries hold fractional reserves with banks, while the banks, in turn, hold fractional reserves with the central bank. Such a model can be written as follows:

$$R = \sigma(D + r)$$

$$D = \gamma M^* + \beta$$

$$r = \rho\, e$$

$$e = \epsilon M^* + \alpha$$

$$M^* = C + D + e$$

$$C + R = B.$$

[3]The Eurodollar liabilities of the banks in the eight countries reporting to the BIS, after netting out interbank deposits, were estimated to be $97 billion at the end of 1973. Total demand deposits of *all* foreign commercial banks with U.S. banks at the same time are given as $5.4 billion. However, what matters for the reserve ratio are the U.S. dollar holdings of reporting Eurobanks alone as a fraction of the *gross* amount of Eurodeposits, including interbank deposits. It is also important to note that U.S. dollar deposits of foreign banks have only about doubled from 1966 to 1973, while Eurodeposits increased about sevenfold. This indicates that those U.S. deposits are not, in the main, reserves for Eurodeposits.

[4]According to the *Survey of Current Business*, September 1974, the sum of the U.S. money supply and time deposits at the end of 1973 was $641.3 billion. A volume of (net) Eurodeposits of $97 billion would account for about 13 percent of the total amount of currency, demand deposits, and time deposits. It is clear that Eurodollars should not be related to M_1 but to M_2.

If asset preferences shift from U.S. dollars to Eurodollars ($d\alpha = -d\beta$), the effect on the volume of Eurodollars can be shown to be

$$\frac{de}{d\alpha} = \frac{1}{1 - \dfrac{\sigma}{1 - (1 - \sigma)(\gamma + \epsilon)}\epsilon(1 - \rho)} = \frac{1}{1 - \mu\epsilon(1 - \rho)} .$$

μ must be a proper fraction, with $\frac{1}{2}$ being in the plausible range. This means that the Eurodeposit multiplier, corrected for the three-stage aspects of the system, turns out to be even smaller than in a two-stage model. It is unlikely that it will be much different from unity. This means that even in a fixed-coefficient model, if plausible parameter values are used, an autonomous shift in asset preferences in favor of Eurodollars is not likely to create a significant amount of additional Eurodeposits. The analogy of Eurobanks with nonbank intermediaries thus gives no basis for concern about their deposit-creating potential. At the same time it should be noted that with the fixed-coefficient approach the multiplier cannot fall below unity.

2. The General-Equilibrium Approach

As we have learned from Tobin [20], the paradigm of the fixed-coefficient approach is a bank which can, because of imperfections in the credit market, change its balance sheet without affecting the various interest rates. There may be institutional aspects in the U.S. credit market that lend considerable validity to this paradigm. The Eurodollar market, on the other hand, is highly perfect in the sense that interest rates on all assets and liabilities are determined from day to day in a highly competitive process without significant elements of credit rationing. As a consequence, a simple reinterpretation of the fixed-coefficient multiplier is illegitimate. What we have to use as a paradigm is a bank in a perfect credit market. The relevant framework has been provided by the "new view" or "Yale approach" [21]. The question is still about the creation of Eurodeposits due to a spontaneous shift in asset preferences, but now the interest mechanism moves to the center of the stage.[5]

If an economist trained in general equilibrium analysis tried to give an intuitive answer to this question, this answer might run about as follows. Basically, the relationship between the markets for U.S. dollars and Eurodollars is analogous to the relationship between the markets for any two substitutes like, say, butter and margarine. If there is a spontaneous shift in preferences from butter to margarine, the ultimate increase in the quantity of margarine in the new equilibrium will be smaller than the spontaneous shift, because the relative increase in the price of margarine will induce some former users to shift to butter. The "margarine multiplier" would thus be less than unity. Similarly, a shift in asset preferences from

---

[5]Other attempts to apply the Yale approach to the Eurodollar markets, including empirical estimates of the resulting multipliers, are to be found in [4, 5].

6 : MONEY, CREDIT, AND BANKING

U.S. dollars to Eurodollars, since it triggers a relative decline in Eurodollar interest rates, would induce a shift of funds previously invested in Eurodollars into the U.S. market. As a first approximation, our general equilibrium economist would thus tend to expect a Eurodollar multiplier of less than unity, a divisor rather than a multiplier.

However, this argument would probably be qualified by some further considerations. First, the general equilibrium analogy disregards the very element that forms the backbone of the fixed-coefficient approach, namely, the fractional-reserve mechanism. Our economist is likely to feel that a shift in preferences to an asset with a relatively lower reserve requirement (in terms of base money) would tend to increase the multiplier. Second, he would probably expect that marginal asset preferences must play a role. In particular, if out of every additional dollar of M^* a large part is held in Eurodeposits, the multiplier should be higher, ceteris paribus, than if additional money is held largely in the form of currency and/or U.S. dollars. As a result of these conflicting forces, the Eurodollar multiplier, it seems, can be either higher or lower than one, with a value below one being likely for a low marginal propensity to hold Eurodollars and a low reserve ratio of U.S. banks.

This intuitive argument will now be made more precise. The model used is a straightforward generalization of the three-stage fixed-coefficient model. The basic definitions are unchanged:

$$M^* = C + D + e$$

$$C + R = \overline{B}.$$

Both D and e are assumed to be homogeneous and interest bearing. The balance-sheet identities of U.S. banks and Eurobanks, respectively, are

$$L + R = D + r$$

$$l + r = e,$$

where L and l denote loans. The Eurobanks hold all reserves with U.S. banks. There are two interest rates, one for U.S. dollars I, the other for Eurodollars i. In reality there are also differences between borrowing and lending rates in each market, but these are assumed to be given and constant. This can be rationalized, if desired, on the basis of constant costs in each of the two banking industries.

The demand for reserves by U.S. banks depends on the volume of their deposit liabilities, both to the public and to the Eurobanks:

$$R = R(D + r) \quad 0 < R_D < 1.$$

The influence of interest rates on reserve demand is disregarded. For Eurobanks, we use the radical assumption that their reserves are independent of any other variables in the model and thus relatively exogenous. In view of the low level of these reserves and their lack of sensitivity to the growth of Eurodollars noted above, the price of this simplification in terms of realism does not seem excessive. If anything, it would tend to bias the result in favor of a higher multiplier.

The supply of deposits by the nonbank public depends on the two interest rates and the quantity of money:

$$D = D(I, i, M^*) + \beta \qquad D_I > 0, D_i < 0, 0 < D_M < 1$$

$$e = e(I, i, M^*) + \alpha \qquad e_I < 0, e_i > 0, 0 < e_M < 1.$$

The demand for loans is assumed to depend on interest rates:

$$L = L(I, i) \qquad L_I < 0, L_i > 0$$

$$l = l(I, i) \qquad l_I > 0, l_i < 0.$$

In equilibrium, the two interest rates will be such that the supply of deposits, after due allowance for reserves, is equal to the demand for loans in each market.

Suppose now the demand for Eurodollars increases by $d\alpha$, while the demand for U.S. deposits falls by $d\beta = -d\alpha$. It is then a standard comparative-statics problem to determine the Eurodollar multiplier $de/d\alpha$. The result can be written

$$\frac{de}{d\alpha} = 1 + \frac{A}{\Delta},$$

where A and Δ are determinants of partial derivatives. Stability requires that an excess demand for loans in the U.S. market is reduced by the increase in I it tends to bring forth. This can be shown to imply $\Delta > 0$. Whether the Eurodollar multiplier is more or less than one thus depends on the sign of A. A straightforward, but somewhat laborious, chain of operations reveals

$$A = (1 - R_D) \{ [e_I D_i - e_i D_I] + (1 - D_M)[e_i(L_I + l_I) - e_I(L_i + l_i)]$$

$$+ e_M [D_i(L_I + l_I) - D_I(L_i + l_i)] \} + R_D [e_M(L_I l_i - L_i l_I) - e_I L_i - e_i L_I].$$

In interpreting this result, we can use the plausible assumption that the U.S. interest rate has a stronger effect on demand and supply of U.S. dollars than on Eurodollars, while the reverse is true for the Eurodollar rate. Thus

$$|L_I| > |l_I| \quad |l_i| > |L_i|$$

$$|D_I| > |e_I| \quad |e_i| > |D_i|.$$

This permits us to assign negative signs to the first two square brackets. These are the components that tend to push the multiplier below unity. The third square

8 : MONEY, CREDIT, AND BANKING

bracket, however, is positive. This means that a high marginal propensity to hold Eurodollars as reflected in e_M tends to raise the multiplier. The last square bracket is also positive.

If we abstract from the marginal propensity to hold Eurodollars ($e_M = 0$) and U.S. reserves ($R_D = 0$) and also assume that all additional money is held in U.S. banks ($D_M = 1$), the multiplier is sure to be below one, since A reduces to

$$A = e_I D_i - e_i D_I < 0.$$

This shows that a multiplier above one is due to e_M and R_D. More precisely, by taking the partial derivatives of A with respect to e_M and R_D, it is simple to show that the Eurodeposit multiplier is indeed higher the higher the reserve ratio of U.S. banks and the higher the marginal propensity to hold Eurodollars.

By determining the effect of $d\alpha$ on i, I, and M^*, we can also ascertain that a shift of preferences from U.S. dollars to Eurodollars (1) lowers the rate of interest on Eurodollars, (2) is likely (but not quite certain) to raise the rate of interest on U.S. dollars, (3) produces a fall of the Eurorate relative to the U.S. rate, and (4) cannot be relied upon to increase the aggregate money supply M^*. By and large, the intuitive argument is nicely confirmed by the formal analysis. The main point is that the interest mechanism is quite likely (though not certain) to convert the multiplier into a divisor. Since this is true if the reserves of Eurobanks are completely independent of interest rates and the deposit volume, it must be even more likely if these reserves do react.

II. LIQUIDITY CREATION

1. Gross versus Net Liquidity

So far, the analysis of the Eurodollar market has been in terms of the approaches familiar from money supply theory. We now come to a more radical departure. The preceding discussion implied that the contribution of the banking system to the liquidity of the nonbank sector can be measured in terms of a suitably defined monetary aggregate like M_1, M_2, or, if the Euromarket is included, our M^*. In each case, total liquidity is measured by adding to currency the relevant liabilities of the banking system. The assets of the banking system—and thus the liabilities of the nonbanks—do not matter. We may call such a concept "gross liquidity."

However, what matters for the spending decisions of households and firms is, in general, not gross liquidity. In addition to their assets, a great deal may also depend on their liabilities to banks. If a man gets a loan of \$1,000, which he has to repay tomorrow, his reaction will presumably be quite different from what it would be if he had to repay the loan gradually over twenty years. If assets and liabilities have exactly the same degree of liquidity or "moneyness," their net effect will be approximately zero: if two men exchange IOU's with identical due dates, they will hardly feel more liquid than before. If they did, the nonbank sector could increase its liquidity ad infinitum just by the exchange of IOU's, and prices would go to infinity. Liquidity creation cannot be quite that simple. What we need is a concept reflecting both assets and liabilities. We shall call it "net liquidity."

To quantify aggregate net liquidity, we have to assign weights to different assets and liabilities intended to reflect the degree of their "moneyness."[6] This is not the place to discuss the possible derivation of such numbers in detail. It seems plausible to imagine that they are derived by estimating the effect on, say, money national income of an exogenous $1 increase in the supply of each asset and liability. The resulting numbers could then be scaled in such a way that the weight for M_1 is unity. Conjectures about such weights will depend on one's views about the macroeconomic system. A monetarist would tend to argue that there is a marked fall in the weights once we go beyond M_2 and that there is a large difference in the weights assigned to demand deposits and, say, treasury bills. A "Radcliffian" would see a very gradual decline in weights from monetary to nonmonetary assets. A nonmonetarist would feel that the difference in weights between demand deposits and treasury bills is relatively small and probably smaller than between treasury bills and, say, mortgages. For the purpose of the following discussion it will simply be assumed that the weights have somehow been determined.

In terms of these concepts it can be said that the traditional money supply theory assumes that currency and deposits (either including or excluding time deposits) have liquidity one, while bank claims (except reserves) have liquidity zero. With this assumption, net and gross liquidity coincide; the creation of money is equivalent to the creation of liquidity. For the U.S. banking system with its large monetary liabilities without corresponding monetary claims, this may be a fruitful first approximation. Suppose, however, a bank accepts time deposits to make short-term loans in such a way that the maturities and other contractual conditions are exactly matched. In this case, the liquidity coefficients of assets and liabilities would be equal. The creation of gross liquidity would not be accompanied by the creation of net liquidity, and the gross liquidity measure would be a misleading indicator of the macroeconomic effects. It is submitted that this case is closer to the realities of the Eurodollar market than the first. If this is so, the whole debate about money creation in the Euromarket is largely beside the point. It may even happen that a bank makes loans with a higher liquidity than the deposits it accepts. In this case, the expansion of gross liquidity is accompanied by an actual reduction in net liquidity. The Euromarket has provided examples of this sort, too.

This argument can be stated in terms of the balance sheet of a representative bank. We shall assume that the liquidity of deposits and loans is monotonically related to their maturity. This clearly does some violence to reality, liquidity in general being a much more complex concept. However, in an investigation of the Eurodollar market the simplification seems to be justified, at least as a first approx-

---

[6] The need for such liquidity weights can be avoided by writing the relevant macromodel not in terms of aggregate variables, but in terms of the whole array of different assets and liabilities. In such a model, the question about liquidity creation, being a question about a certain aggregate, would be devoid of meaning.

imation, because the other aspects of loans and deposits are standardized to a relatively high degree. It is consistent with this observation that maturity is the only aspect of liquidity about which extensive data have been collected.

The bank accepts deposits of various maturities $D_0, D_1 \ldots D_n$, the subscripts indicating the maturity, beginning with checking deposits. It uses the borrowed money to make loans $L_0, L_1 \ldots L_n$ (L_0 includes central bank reserves), where the subscripts refer to the same maturity classes as for deposits. The contribution of this bank to the gross liquidity of the nonbank sector would be measured by

$$\Delta M = \lambda_0 D_0 + \lambda_1 D_1 + \cdots + \lambda_n D_n = \sum_i \lambda_i D_i,$$

where the λ's are the liquidity coefficients (with $\lambda_0 \equiv 1$). The contribution to *net* liquidity, however, would be

$$Q = \sum_i \lambda_i D_i - \sum_i \lambda_i L_i = \sum_i \lambda_i (D_i - L_i),$$

with

$$\sum_i (D_i - L_i) = 0.$$

Creation of net liquidity for the nonbank sector clearly requires that assets and liabilities are "mismatched" (i.e., $D_i \neq L_i$ for some i) in the sense that the bank "borrows short" in order to "lend long." This may be called positive maturity transformation. If funds are matched for each maturity, there is no net liquidity creation, and the balance sheet may be called perfectly matched. If the bank "borrows long" in order to "lend short," that is, with negative maturity transformation, net liquidity of the nonbanks is reduced. The typical U.S. commercial bank, which served as the paradigm for money supply theory, is clearly engaged in positive maturity transformation. The question is whether the typical Eurobank behaves in the same way and, if so, to what extent.

2. The Maturity Structure of Eurobanks

An effort to answer this question must begin with the maturity statistics published periodically by the Bank of England. The totals for September 1973 reveal a remarkable degree of matching of maturities (see Table 1). For the four maturity classes from 8 days to 1 year, comprising roughly 75 percent of the balance sheet, the matching is just about as perfect as could be expected if it were a carefully monitored rule. For the shortest maturity, however, liabilities exceed claims, while for the maturities of 1 year or more claims exceed liabilities. This is consistent with

TABLE 1

Maturity Structure of Claims and Liabilities in Nonsterling Currencies,
All U.K.–based Eurobanks
(September 30, 1973)

Maturity	Total		With Banks		With Nonbanks	
	Claims	Liab.	Claims	Liab.	Claims	Liab.
	(percent)					
1. Less than 8 days	14.9	19.1	17.1	17.4	8.9	28.4
2. 8 days–<1 month	18.9	19.4	20.6	19.8	13.5	17.6
3. 1 month–<3 months	24.8	26.2	25.7	26.8	22.3	22.3
4. 3 months–<6 months	20.8	20.9	21.6	22.0	18.8	14.9
5. 6 months–<1 year	8.2	8.8	8.8	8.8	6.6	8.8
6. 1 year–<3 years	4.8	2.5	2.9	2.5	9.8	2.7
7. 3 years and over	7.7	3.1	3.3	2.8	20.0	5.4
All maturities	100.0	100.0	100.0	100.0	100.0	100.0
	(millions of £s)					
All maturities	49,774	49,664	36,354	42,313	13,420	7,351

Source: Bank of England *Quarterly Bulletin* (March 26, 1974).

some positive maturity transformation,[7] but the overall degree of liquidity creation seems to be very small. Suppose, as an illustration, we assign to the various maturity classes the following liquidity coefficients:

Maturity Class	λ
1. less than 8 days	.9
2. 8 days–<1 month	.8
3. 1 month–<3 months	.7
4. 3 months–<6 months	.6
5. 6 months–<1 year	.4
6. 1 year–<3 years	.2
7. 3 years and over	.1

Applying these coefficients to the balance-sheet figures leads to the conclusion that for every dollar of total deposits, liquidity creation amounts to just 4.45 cents. Of course, the above coefficients are arbitrary, but other reasonable assumptions would produce about the same result.

However, it is wrong to base such conclusions on the total balance sheet. From the point of view of liquidity creation for the nonbank sector, interbank transactions are immaterial. What matters are claims and liabilities of Eurobanks relative to nonbanks.[8] We note at once that in U.K. Eurobank dealings with nonbanks,

[7]It is worth noting that the totals of claims and liabilities coincide almost exactly, indicating that the Euromarket entries of the banks concerned can indeed be treated as if they formed a separate balance sheet. It also indicates that Eurobanks had not transferred sterling funds into other currencies to any significant extent.

[8]It may be noted in passing that in their transactions with other banks, accounting for about three-fourths of claims and more than five-sixths of liabilities, London Eurobanks appear to observe a rather strict matching rule for *all* maturity classes (see Table 1). The interbank market seems neither to create nor to destroy liquidity.

12 : MONEY, CREDIT, AND BANKING

TABLE 2

Maturity Structure of Claims and Liabilities in Nonsterling Currencies, with
Nonbanks, Subgroups of U.K.-based Eurobanks
(September 30, 1973)

Maturity	British Claims	British Liab.	American Claims	American Liab.	Japanese Claims	Japanese Liab.	Other Foreign Claims	Other Foreign Liab.	Consortium Claims	Consortium Liab.
				(percent)						
1. Less than 8 days	10.7	28.0	9.1	29.8	3.0	38.1	14.7	28.3	4.2	24.4
2. 8 days– <1 month	14.7	17.7	15.1	18.4	10.3	10.7	14.6	13.6	7.4	17.2
3. 1 month– <3 months	22.5	19.9	25.8	24.2	19.2	29.8	25.4	25.3	13.7	19.1
4. 3 months– <6 months	20.3	14.7	20.3	14.9	15.8	4.8	21.8	15.5	11.1	16.8
5. 6 months– <1 year	7.1	9.4	6.7	8.1	2.1	. . .	6.4	10.4	7.4	9.2
6. 1 year– <3 years	10.8	2.3	5.9	2.7	4.3	4.8	6.9	1.7	21.4	7.6
7. 3 years and over	13.8	8.0	17.1	1.8	45.4	11.9	10.1	5.1	34.8	5.7
	100.0	100.0	100.0	100.0	100.0	100.0	100.0	100.0	100.0	100.0
				(millions of £s)						
All ma- turities	5,122	3,284	4,580	2,920	971	84	838	801	1,909	262

Source: Bank of England *Quarterly Bulletin* (March 26, 1974).

liabilities are little more than half as high as claims. The remainder is made up by net borrowings from other banks, serving as feeders for the London center. The liability structure of these other banks is not known. However, it seems reasonably safe to conjecture that it is not drastically different from the structure of nonbank liabilities of London banks. This conjecture can be based on two observations. First, the structure of nonbank liabilities is remarkably similar in each of the five subgroups of U.K.-based Eurobanks (Table 2), suggesting that there is something like a representative maturity structure of nonbank deposits. Second, the structure of nonbank deposits is also remarkably similar to the structure of deposits from banks. It will thus be assumed that the nonbank liabilities that the London banks obtained indirectly through other banks had the same maturity structure as those they received directly.

The figures for nonbanks in Table 1 show a significant excess of liabilities over claims at the short end of the scale, while claims exceed liabilities at the long end. Using the same illustrative liquidity coefficients as before, we can calculate a liquidity creation of 16.49 cents for every dollar of deposits. Under the alternative assumption that maturities up to 1 year have a liquidity equal to one, whereas longer maturities have zero liquidity, the liquidity creation would be about 22 cents per dollar of deposits. These are considerably higher numbers than those for the total balance sheet, to be sure, but still liquidity creation is only about one-fifth of deposit creation.[9] Unfortunately, there are no comparable data for national

[9] As Table 2 shows, a large part of long-term lending is done by Japanese and consortium banks, while British, American, and other foreign banks, accounting for 78.5 percent of non-

banking systems. Taking the Eurobank statistics at their face value, it would seem that the amount of maturity transformation, while significant, is probably much lower than in, say, the U.S. banking system.

The next question is whether these statistical data can indeed be taken at face value. We believe that they still give an exaggerated picture of maturity transformation.[10] The main reason is that the actual maturity of loans to nonbanks is often much shorter than the recorded maturity. In recent years, about 90 percent of all loans to nonbanks seem to be floating-rate loans, which are "rolled over" every 3–6 months. Even if the commitment period is several years, the actual credit instrument, usually a promissory note, has a maturity of only 3 or 6 months at a time. With each renewal, the interest rate is adjusted to the market rate. Most agreements also provide that the loan has to be repaid in full if the lender is unable to borrow in sufficient quantity.[11] With these roll-over provisions, the lender, in fact, limits his liquidity risk to the roll-over period and shifts the long-term liquidity risk to the borrower. In most of these agreements, the roll-over period thus seems to be a better measure of the actual maturity of the loans than the commitment period.

It is not known to what extent the maturity tabulations of the Bank of England reflect, respectively, commitment periods and roll-over periods. Indications are that a very substantial part of the loans, particularly among the longer-term loans (granted by consortium and Japanese banks), are recorded by commitment period.[12] This implies that the maturity statistics of the Bank of England give an exaggerated picture of maturity transformation in the Euromarket, particularly at the upper end of the maturity scale. In addition, we have to take account of the fact that the shortest claims include some demand deposits with U.S. banks, while no demand deposits are included among the liabilities. This introduces an element of negative transformation at the short end of the scale. Overall it is probably fair to say that the typical Eurobank provides very little maturity transformation and thus creates very little liquidity to the nonbank sector.[13] The recent difficulties of the Euromarket with the "recycling" of short-term petrodollars is consistent with this view.

3. The Determinants of Maturity Transformation in a Perfect Market

What may be the reason for the low degree of maturity transformation in the Eurodollar system? Any answer to this question can only be tentative at the present time. First we note that in U.S. commercial banks a large part of liabilities

---

bank claims and no less than 95 percent of nonbank deposits, exhibit a much lower degree of maturity transformation.

[10] The following discussion is based on Hewson [4, chap. 2].

[11] This does not help the bank if the debtor is insolvent, but such default risks, common to all banks, do not make the initial loan long term.

[12] Only about 10 percent of the loans of all maturities are fixed-interest loans, and we know these to be concentrated among the short maturities. On the other hand, about 30 percent of all loans are *recorded* to be for 1 year or more. It follows that more than two-thirds of the latter, possibly almost all of them, are actually of the roll-over type.

[13] This is precisely the reason why the U.S. deposits held by Eurobanks are so small and virtually independent of their deposit liabilities.

14 : MONEY, CREDIT, AND BANKING

consists of deposits with an indefinite withdrawal date. While demand deposits can be drawn upon any day, their actual duration is indefinite, subject to stochastic considerations. While a savings deposit can perhaps be withdrawn any day, subject to certain penalties or waiting periods, it may actually remain in the account for decades. In Eurobanks the volume of such funds is very small. Most deposits have definite maturity dates, and the banks do not rely on the law of large numbers to determine the expected withdrawals. At every moment, they can borrow any relevant amount at the going (but variable) rate in a nearly perfect market. Uncertainty must thus be assumed to be concentrated in the expected interest rates.

Under such conditions, any maturity transformation, be it positive or negative, increases risk, as measured by the variance of bank profits (see the Appendix, on which the following argument is based). Such a risk will only be incurred if it is accompanied by a higher expected return, arising from a difference between the longer-term rates and the compounded short-term rates. In the absence of significant deviations of the term structure from parity, the bank will always tend to match maturities. If the long-term rates are far enough above the short-term rates, it becomes profitable to engage in positive maturity transformation. If, on the other hand, the long-term rate is far enough below the short-term rates, it is advantageous to borrow long to lend short. The larger the variability of interest rates, the more likely it is, other things equal, that the bank will maintain a matched balance sheet. From this point of view, the low level of maturity transformation in the Euromarket would find an explanation in the small margin between long and short rates associated with a relatively high degree of uncertainty about future interest rates.

The problem may be pursued one step further. Why, we may ask, should Eurobanks not solicit deposits with indefinite duration, relying on the law of large numbers? The answer is probably that in a market which, compared with the domestic market, relies on a relatively small number of large deposits (usually upward from $100,000), the law of large numbers does not provide a sufficient reduction of risk. But why, then, do Eurobanks not try to attract large numbers of small deposits, including checking deposits? Well, probably because most of the small deposits are held by households and firms who do not wish to hold external assets, while most of the external dollar holdings belong to relatively few firms and households. Thus it seems that the structural differences between the Euromarket and the U.S. credit market are basically due to the inherent differences between external and internal markets for funds. To the external market, the Edgeworth-Orr/Mellon[14] model of banking, with its stochastic reserve losses, does not apply. What is needed is rather a model derived from the term-structure literature. If future developments lead to an international diversification of dollar holdings even by the large number of small wealth holders, perhaps the structure of the Euromarket would become more similar to that of a domestic banking system.

This discussion of liquidity creation (or its absence) in the Eurodollar market

[14]See [2, 14].

would be seriously incomplete without a reference to a group of banks that have indeed engaged in massive maturity transformation. These are the central banks. Whenever a central bank invests dollar holdings in 3-month Eurodollars, it creates liquidity for the nonbank sector in the same way as the Federal Reserve, buying 3-month treasury bills in the open market, or as a commercial bank, investing excessive reserves in short-term assets. In a fixed-exchange rate system, the newly created liquidity will be distributed over the international system in the familiar way in all these cases. It should be noted that this effect has nothing to do with any special features of the Eurodollar market. Except for transitional phenomena, the results for world liquidity in a fixed-rate system are practically the same if the central bank in question, instead of buying Eurodollars, conducts open-market operations in its own currency, buys U.S. treasury bills, Euromarks, or gives discount credit to its banks. It is not the Eurodollar market that is inflationary or deflationary, but perhaps the policies of the central banks.

III. LIQUIDITY DISTRIBUTION

1. A Transactions-Cost Model of Liquidity Distribution

For half a century, economists have been accustomed to see the main function of the banking system in its ability to create money, liquidity, or credit. In part 2 it was argued that in the Eurodollar system liquidity creation plays but a minor role. What, then, is the major economic function of the Eurodollar market, to which, presumably, it owes its existence and spectacular growth? It will be argued on the following pages that the Eurodollar system is, in the main, a network for the efficient distribution of liquid dollar funds. This argument reintroduces into banking theory an idea that actually dominated the literature until the beginning of the present century,[15] when it was gradually pushed into near-oblivion by the Phillips multipliers [16]. In a typical banking system, creation and distribution of liquidity are combined. In the Eurodollar market, we are confronted with a system in which the distribution function clearly dominates. This market is interesting and, to some, "mysterious" precisely because it requires an understanding of aspects that recent monetary theory has tended to overlook.

It will now be shown how these distribution aspects can give rise to the emergence of a system like the Eurodollar market. To simplify the analysis we shall assume, not quite realistically, that Eurodollar banks maintain perfectly matched balance sheets, thus avoiding any creation or destruction of liquidity. What exactly is the economic function of such banks? A general answer will be given in terms of a network model in which transactions costs are assigned a crucial role. This will be followed by an interpretation of some specific features of the Euromarket in terms of this model.[16]

[15]For a representative example, see [15].
[16]The model is an adaptation of one used in [11]. A version similar to the present one has been used by [4].

16 : MONEY, CREDIT, AND BANKING

Suppose there are agents $1 \ldots i \ldots n$, who can be visualized as being scattered all over the globe. Some of them are ultimate lenders of dollars, with $\overline{x}_i > 0$ denoting supply by agent i. Others are ultimate borrowers, with $\overline{x}_i < 0$ denoting the amount demanded. We may assume that no agent is both an ultimate borrower and an ultimate lender, but this is not essential. There will generally be agents who are neither ultimate borrowers nor ultimate lenders; these can nevertheless be active as intermediaries.

Since maturity transformation is excluded, we may just as well assume that there is only one homogeneous credit instrument of a given maturity. To isolate the credit market from the rest of the economic system, we use the fiction that the system is dichotomized. The ultimate borrowings and lendings are imagined to have been determined in a first stage, together with consumption and production, in such a way that $\Sigma_i \overline{x}_i = 0$. This equilibrium of supply and demand has been brought about by adjustments in what will be called the basic rate of interest. In the second stage it only remains to be decided who lends to whom and at what interest differential relative to the basic rate. The solution to this second problem is not allowed to have any repercussions on consumption and production and the ultimate demand and supply of credit. This separation is artificial, and in reality all aspects of the system are interdependent. For the present purpose, however, the gain in generality of an integrated general equilibrium system would not be worth its vastly higher complexity.[17]

The dollars may flow from an ultimate lender to an ultimate borrower through any number of intermediaries. The actual borrowing or lending of an agent may thus be larger than his ultimate borrowing or lending. The actual amount i lends to j will be denoted x_{ij}. For each agent there is a balance-sheet constraint which says that the excess of his actual lending over his actual borrowing must equal his ultimate lending:

$$\sum_j x_{ij} - \sum_j x_{ji} = \overline{x}_i \qquad (x_{ij} \geqslant 0).$$

Each credit transaction imposes costs on both the lender and the borrower. These transactions costs include the costs of collecting market information, the costs of communication, taxes, the costs of obtaining information about the borrower and the expected value of default losses on the side of the lender, and the costs of administering accounts. These costs are generally different for each borrower and lender *pair*. Between certain private individuals and firms they may be low, but between others they are very high and in any case much higher than between the same agents and certain banks. Also, a firm in Minneapolis probably has lower transactions costs on loans to other firms in Minneapolis than on loans to firms in Hongkong, and a lender in Sweden will often find it more efficient to have a

[17]For integrated systems of similar type, see [12].

deposit with his Stockholm bank than one in Rome at the same rate of interest. Abstracting from liquidity creation, it is a function of the banking system to channel the dollars from ultimate lenders to ultimate borrowers in such a way that transactions costs for a given lending program are minimized.

This is easy to formalize. Suppose transactions costs are proportionate to the amount of the loan, thus having the dimension of an interest rate. The transactions costs on the loan x_{ij} for the lender are denoted by c_{ij}, and for the borrower c_{ij}^*. What should be minimized are total transactions costs in the system, thus

$$\min T = \sum_i \sum_j (c_{ij} + c_{ij}^*) x_{ij},$$

subject to the balance-sheet constraints given above. This is a simple linear programming problem. Its optimal solution determines the whole network of credit flows.

To realize the optimal solution we do not have to rely on some imaginary central planning. From duality theory we know that the same solution can be found by assigning appropriate values to the dollars in the hands of each agent in such a way that the total gain in value of the funds on their way from the ultimate lender to the ultimate borrower is maximized, subject to the constraint that the gain on each transaction be no greater than the transactions costs involved. The resulting shadow prices (positive or negative) can be interpreted as additions to, or subtractions from, the basic interest rate, reflecting the fact that the lending rate for the ultimate lender in Rio de Janeiro is typically below the London interbank rate, while the borrowing rate of an Italian manufacturing firm is above it. For many banks, the difference between borrowing and lending rates will probably be smaller than for almost all nonbanks, and for firms with a high credit standing it will be lower than for those with a low rating. The shadow prices have the property that for each transaction in the optimal solution, the interest differential between lender and borrower just covers the transactions costs between them, while all transactions not belonging to the optimal solution would involve a loss. The optimal solution is thus the only solution consistent with perfect competition in a system in which each agent maximizes profit, considering the market-determined interest differentials.[18] It is, therefore, plausible to assume that a highly competitive financial system would tend to approximate the optimal solution at least in its rough outline.

2. A Transactions-Cost Interpretation of the Eurodollar Market

In such a model just about any sort of credit network (consistent with the constraints) can be produced by making appropriate assumptions about the

[18]If there is concern about the assumption of perfect competition in a system in which agents are different from each other, it may be interpreted as a group of identical agents large enough to rob each member of any appreciable influence on interest rates.

18 : MONEY, CREDIT, AND BANKING

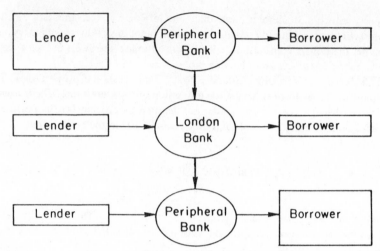

Fig. 1. Internal Structure of the Eurodollar Market

ultimate flows and the transactions costs. In particular, the distribution of the ultimate supply and demand for dollars and the transactions costs between different classes of borrowers and lenders are able to explain the main features of the Eurodollar market. This will first be illustrated by the internal structure of the market. The Eurodollar market is a market for bank deposits and bank loans, not for loans among nonbanks. It is also largely an interbank market. For the London Eurobanks, nonbank business is only a fraction of interbank business, but for peripheral banks the reverse may be true, at least for one side of the balance sheet. We thus obtain the picture of a system in which dollars are channeled from ultimate lenders to ultimate borrowers through banks, with a large part of the credit flows passing through several banks, often including the London center (see Fig. 1).

Such a picture can easily be made to emerge from the network model by assuming that (1) there are large excess demands or excess supplies of funds in individual local areas (if this were not so, there would be a number of separate markets and the flows through the center would be small); (2) transactions costs between nonbanks are very high (if this were not so, nonbanks would contract directly); (3) transactions costs between nonbanks and banks vary widely, often being lower between parties in the same area (if this were not so, each bank would balance its own nonbank business); and (4) transactions costs between peripheral banks, particularly if they are in different areas, are often considerably higher than between a peripheral bank and the London center (otherwise there would be no center or centers and funds would flow through at most two banks). This shows that the above model can account for the main outlines of the internal structure of the Euromarket.[19]

[19]It may also be noted that the development of shell banks in such centers as the Caymans and the Bahamas can also be explained by reference to the transactions cost model; in most

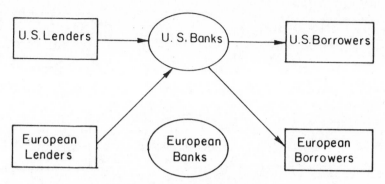

Fig. 2. Absence of Eurodollar Market

A more fundamental question concerns the relationship between the Eurodollar market and other segments of the market for dollar funds, particularly the U.S. market.[20] Swoboda has tried to explain the emergence of the Eurodollar market by the increasing cost of supplying dollar money and the consequent "denomination rents" [18]. He assumed that U.S. banks are low-cost producers of dollar funds, while Eurobanks are high-cost producers. With an increase in the demand for dollars, Eurobanks would find it increasingly profitable to enter the market. While this argument, unlike so much of Eurodollar literature, has at least the virtue of having an analytical basis, we find it unconvincing. While individual banks may possibly have increasing costs (though costs are more likely to be diminishing), we find it hard to believe that the U.S. banking system as a whole should have markedly increasing costs. Swoboda would also find it hard to explain why, say, Swiss banks should find it profitable to enter the dollar market at the time when the emergence of an external market for Swiss francs would presumably have to be taken as an indication that they can meet an increased demand for Swiss francs only at rapidly increasing costs.

The network model can explain the same phenomena in a straightforward way without recourse to increasing costs (see Fig. 2). Suppose there are nonbank borrowers and lenders of dollars both in the United States and in "Europe" (where "Europe" refers to the non-U.S. part of the world). There are also banks, both in the United States and in Europe. If transactions costs are much lower for dealings between banks and nonbanks than for dealings of nonbanks among themselves, all credits flow through the banks. But if transactions costs of European banks on dollar transactions are generally higher than those of U.S. banks, all dollar transactions will go through U.S. banks; there will be no Eurodollar market. It should be

---

part these centers have developed as "tax havens" for international banks and corporations, etc. The development of these centers is discussed in more detail in [4], where numerical illustrations of the linear programming problem can be found.

[20] Still another segment would be the foreign exchange market, in which dollar funds are exchanged for other currencies.

20 : MONEY, CREDIT, AND BANKING

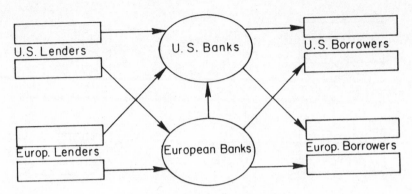

Fig. 3. Integrated Dollar Market

noted that this case is consistent with any amount of European borrowing, European lending, or European net lending.

If transactions costs of European banks in such a situation are gradually lowered relative to U.S. banks, an increasing part of the dollar transactions of nonbanks, both in the United States and in Europe, will begin to flow through European banks (see Fig. 3). Within the U.S., some lenders will still find it profitable to deposit their funds in U.S. banks, while others find better conditions in Europe. An analogous statement can be made for European nonbanks. Even small changes in transactions costs may conceivably result in large shifts in credit flows. The upper limit of the potential size of the Eurodollar market would only be reached when all dollars flow through European banks, U.S. banks being reduced to accepting deposits from European banks and holding U.S. government assets. All we have to do to produce this extreme case is to imagine transactions costs sufficiently high for U.S. banks and sufficiently low for European banks. If costs are high on transactions between the U.S. and Europe, perhaps because of government intervention, while they are low within each area, the credit system would tend to be-

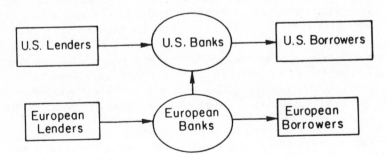

Fig. 4. Fragmented Dollar Market

come fragmented along the lines of Figure 4, the only link between the two parts being some deposits of European banks in U.S. banks.

It should be clear from this discussion that we should not expect to find any particular relationship between the size of the Euromarket and the U.S. balance of payments or U.S. indebtedness.[21] If the U.S. has a deficit, European dollar lending will probably grow relative to European dollar borrowing, while the reverse will be true for the U.S. The effect of this on the relative size of the flow passing through European banks is not clear. What would indeed produce an expansion of the Euromarket, given plausible patterns of transactions costs, is a rise in both European dollar demand and European dollar supply. It is hard to see, however, what this should have to do with the U.S. balance of payments. It is primarily a question of the inequality of dollar distribution *within Europe,* and not of the claims or liabilities of the United States vis-à-vis the rest of the world.

In the light of this analysis, the main determinants of the size of the Eurodollar market are the different transactions costs of U.S. banks and Eurobanks as expressed in the deviations of their borrowing and lending rates for different customers. These differences can be explained mainly by three groups of factors.

1. Differences in Location. Ceteris paribus, a firm on the Pacific Coast can probably borrow at a lower rate from a California bank than from a Swiss bank, but the transactions costs for a Swiss firm are probably higher if it holds its time deposits in a San Francisco bank than if it holds them in Zürich. This would be enough to give U.S. banks a comparative advantage for some transactions, while Eurobanks would have an advantage for others.

2. Differences in Legislation. If the margin between borrowing and lending rates for U.S. banks is widened by interest ceilings, reserve requirements, taxes, limitations to entry, and other aspects of banking regulation, while in Europe this is true to a much lesser extent this would tend to enlarge the Euromarket at the expense of the U.S. market, and vice versa. One of the most notable examples in this respect was the imposition of the Voluntary Foreign Credit Restraint Program (VFCR) in the United States, which established ceilings on loans to foreigners by U.S. financial institutions, banks and nonbanks. Since assets of foreign branches were not subject to VFCR guidelines, U.S. banks were encouraged to shift their foreign credits from the books of their head offices to the books of their foreign branches.[22]

3. Differences in Operating Efficiency. These would, of course, have the same effects as the two preceding factors. Though they may play some role, we find it hard to believe that a major part of the growth of the Eurodollar market can be attributed to the higher efficiency of European banks.

The main determinants of the size of the Euromarket thus have to be sought not

[21]This view has been given early prominence by Klopstock [8, fn. p. 17]; see also [18, p. 24].

[22]For a discussion of this development, see [1, 7]. It is of interest to note that similar considerations apply to the development of the Euromark market following the imposition of a minimum reserve requirement on bank borrowing from nonresidents by the German authorities in 1968 and 1970. For a discussion of this development, see [6, chap. 3].

22 : MONEY, CREDIT, AND BANKING

in the theory of money creation, but in the basic theory of the division of labor on the basis of comparative advantage.

SUMMARY AND CONCLUSION

In the first part of this paper it was shown that even the fixed-coefficient approach to money supply theory, using the paradigm of a bank that accepts monetary deposits to buy nonmonetary assets in imperfect markets, produces a Eurodeposit multiplier that is quite small. If the theory is generalized by using the paradigm of a bank operating in a perfect market with flexible interest rates, the resulting multiplier tends to be still lower and quite likely below one. It was argued in the second part, however, that even the general equilibrium approach as used for domestic monetary theory is not, in fact, appropriate for the analysis of the Eurodollar market, since it still assumes that the banks essentially use monetary deposits to buy nonmonetary assets, thus creating liquidity for the nonbank sector, whereas the typical Eurobank performs only a minimum amount of credit transformation and thus creates little liquidity. The proper paradigm, so it was argued, is a bank which, while roughly matching the maturities of assets and liabilities, contributes to. the efficiency of credit distribution. In this case, the deposit multiplier loses its significance, because it can no longer be used as an indicator of liquidity creation. This line of reasoning, if valid, leads to two general conclusions.

On one hand, monetary theory sheds new light on the Eurodollar market. For early 1975, seemingly competent observers predicted an acute liquidity crisis of the Eurodollar market with what, in at least one case, was called "mathematical certainty." The fact that these predictions were dramatically falsified by events suggests that they resulted from a fundamental lack of understanding of the Eurodollar market. In the light of the present analysis, the Eurodollar market appears much more stable than those observers assumed; in fact, it would seem more stable than many national banking systems. This does not mean that Eurobanks have no default risks. They are no less subject to misjudgments about the solvency of their debtors than other banks. It means that Eurobanks are less subject to liquidity risks than the banks appearing in traditional money supply theory. They contribute less to the creation of liquidity and are less subject to the cumulative destruction of liquidity known from the history of bank "panics." It is still true that the size of the Euromarket is subject to large variations, but these would be due not so much to the creation or destruction of money as to the changing competitiveness of Eurobanks relative to U.S. banks.

On the other hand, the case of the Eurodollar market gives reason for a reexamination of the paradigm of money supply theory. Of course, a bank with perfectly matched maturities in a perfect market is again an extreme case that would not be appropriate for, say, the U.S. banking system. However, the analysis of the Eurodollar market provides an incentive to incorporate the distributive function of the banking system into a more general theory of the money supply.

APPENDIX

Maturity Transformation in a Perfect Market

This appendix provides the analytical basis for section 3 of part 2. It considers maturity transformation for a bank operating in a perfect credit market. The analysis is restricted to two periods. There are just two types of credit instruments, called "short" and "long," respectively. The following notation will be used:

x_0^s: short-term claims, bought at t_0, due at t_1
x_1^s: short-term claims, bought at t_1, due at t_2
x_0^l: long-term claims, bought at t_0, due at t_2

y_0^s: short-term liabilities, accepted at t_0, due at t_1
y_1^s: short-term liabilities, accepted at t_1, due at t_2
y_0^l: long-term liabilities, accepted at t_0, due at t_2

i_0^s: actual interest rate on short-term funds at t_0, with $g_0^s = 1 + i_0^s$
i_1^s: expected interest rate on short-term funds at t_1, with $g_1^s = 1 + i_1^s$
i_0^l: actual interest rate on long-term funds at t_0, with $g_0^l = 1 + i_0^l$.

In reality, the bank would not borrow and lend at the same rate, the margins between borrowing and lending rates reflecting the bank's marginal operating costs. However, this element is not essential for the present analysis and will thus be disregarded.

At t_0 the bank's balance-sheet constraint is

$$x_0^s + x_0^l = y_0^s + y_0^l = W_0. \tag{1}$$

The bank will have to decide which part of its assets and liabilities shall be held in the form of short-term funds. These decision variables can be defined as

$$a = \frac{x_0^s}{x_0^s + x_0^l} = \frac{x_0^s}{W_0} = \text{"short ratio" for assets}$$

$$b = \frac{y_0^s}{y_0^s + y_0^l} = \frac{y_0^s}{W_0} = \text{"short ratio" for liabilities.}$$

The difference $b - a$ can be used to measure maturity transformation: $b > a$ would indicate positive maturity transformation, with an extreme at $b - a = 1$; $b < a$ would reflect negative transformation with an extreme at $a - b = 1$, and perfect matching would be defined by $b = a$.

At t_0 the bank also has to consider its refinancing operations at t_1. It will then have at its disposal the proceeds from x_0^s including interest plus the newly borrowed short-term deposits y_1^s. From this it will have to repay y_0^s with interest, while the remainder can be invested in x_1^s. This refinancing constraint can be written

$$g_0^s (x_0^s - y_0^s) = x_1^s - y_1^s. \tag{2}$$

The net worth of the bank when "liquidated" at t_2 will be

$$
\begin{aligned}
W_2 &= g_1^s x_1^s + g_0^l x_0^l - g_1^s y_1^s - g_0^l y_0^l \\
&= g_1^s (x_1^s - y_1^s) + g_0^l (x_0^l - y_0^l) \\
&= g_1^s g_0^s (x_0^s - y_0^s) + g_0^l (y_0^s - x_0^s) \\
&= g_1^s g_0^s (a - b) W_0 + g_0^l (b - a) W_0 \\
&= (g_1^s g_0^s - g_0^l)(a - b) W_0. \tag{3}
\end{aligned}
$$

What the bank wants to optimize is the expected value of $P = W_2/W_0$. g_0^s and g_0^l are known. The only uncertain element is g_1^s, with an expected value $E(g_1^s)$ and variance σ_g^2. We thus have

$$E(P) = [g_0^s E(g_1^s) - g_0^l] \, (a - b). \tag{4}$$

If the bank wanted to maximize $E(P)$ without considering risk, it would be confronted with one of the following cases:

1. $g_0^s E(g_1^s) < g_0^l$. In this case, the long-term rate is higher than the compounded short-term rates. The bank would maximize expected profit by borrowing only on short term ($b = 1$) and lending only on long term ($a = 0$). It would choose a corner solution with what could be called complete positive mismatching of maturities.

2. $g_0^s E(g_1^s) > g_0^l$. In this case, it would be profitable to do all borrowing on long term ($b = 0$) and all lending on short term ($a = 1$). The result would be complete negative mismatching of maturities.

3. $g_0^s E(g_1^s) = g_0^l$. In this case the maturity structure does not matter, every choice of a and b promising the same (zero) expected profit.

In reality, the bank is likely to consider risk alongside the expected profit. This risk can be measured by

$$
\sigma_\pi = \begin{cases} g_0^s (a - b)\sigma_g & \text{if } a \geqslant b \\ g_0^s (b - a)\sigma_g & \text{if } b \geqslant a. \end{cases} \tag{5}
$$

Risk is thus proportional to the degree of maturity transformation as measured by $a - b$ or $b - a$. The bank may be assumed to maximize utility

$$U = U[E(P), \sigma_\pi]$$

subject to an opportunity locus obtained by solving (5) for $a - b$ or $b - a$ and substituting into (4):

$$E(P) = \begin{cases} \left[E(g_1^s) - \dfrac{g_0^l}{g_0^s} \right] \dfrac{\sigma_\pi}{\sigma_g} & \text{if } a \geqslant b \\[2ex] \left[\dfrac{g_0^l}{g_0^s} - E(g_1^s) \right] \dfrac{\sigma_\pi}{\sigma_g} & \text{if } b \geqslant a. \end{cases} \tag{6}$$

$E(P)$ can thus be represented by a pair of linear functions of σ_π. The relevant function, for given interest expectations, will be the one that makes the square bracket positive. It is clear from (4) that it never pays to choose $b \geqslant a$ if the long rate is below the compounded short rates, and it will never pay to choose $a \geqslant b$ if the long rate is above the compounded short rates.[23]

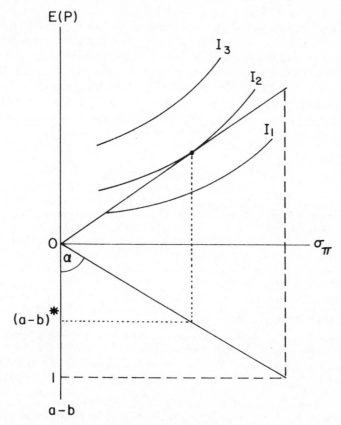

Fig. 5. Portfolio Equilibrium

[23]Note that both $E(P)$ and σ_π only depend on the *difference* $a - b$. The absolute level of a and b are immaterial. To take an extreme case, with perfect matching ($a = b$), the bank does not care what proportion of its balance sheet is "short."

26 : MONEY, CREDIT, AND BANKING

This portfolio problem can be visualized in terms of Tobin's [19] well-known graph (see Fig. 5). There is a set of indifference curves $I_1, I_2 \ldots I_n$ depicting the utility function in terms of $E(P)$ and σ_π. Suppose for the moment $g_0^s E(g_1^s) \geqslant g_0^l$. In this case, the downward axis measures $a - b$, where $a - b = 0$ would reflect perfect matching, while $a - b = 1$ is the case of perfect negative mismatching. The line sloping downward to the right in the SE quadrant represents (5), with $\tan \alpha$ measuring $g_0^s \sigma_g$. The opportunity locus (6) is graphed in the first quadrant. The bank will choose $(a - b)^*$. If $g_0^s E(g_1^s) - g_0^e$ is gradually lowered, the opportunity locus will become flatter. There will be a point at which $(a - b)^*$ goes to zero; maturity transformation will cease to be profitable, perfect matching will be maintained. The same is true if σ_g is gradually increased. Absence of maturity transformation is thus seen to be the consequence of interest rates that are (*a*) close to term structure parity or (*b*) highly uncertain.

If $g_0^s E(g_1^s) \leqslant g_0^l$, the second lines of (5) and (6) become relevant, and the downward axis measures $b - a$. In this case, the bank engages in positive maturity transformation. From the side of the bank there is no presumption that positive transformation is more likely or more frequent than negative transformation. If banks habitually borrow short in order to lend long rather than the reverse, the reason would have to be sought in a persistent tendency for long rates to be above the compounded short rates, caused by institutional or market factors exogenous to the present model.

LITERATURE CITED

1. Brimmer, A. "Capital Outflows and the U.S. Balance of Payments: Review and Outlook." Paper delivered at the Federal Reserve Bank of Dallas, Texas, February 11, 1970.

2. Edgeworth, F. Y. "The Mathematical Theory of Banking." *Journal of the Royal Statistical Society,* 51 (1880), 113–27.

3. Friedman, M. "The Euro-Dollar Market: Some First Principles." *Morgan Guaranty Survey,* October, 1969.

4. Hewson, J. "Liquidity Creation and Distribution in the Euro-Currency Markets." Ph.D. dissertation, The Johns Hopkins University, 1974 (to be published 1975).

5. Hewson, J, and E. Sakakibara. "The Euro-Dollar Deposit Multiplier: A Portfolio Approach." *IMF Staff Papers,* 21, No. 2 (July, 1974), 307–28.

6. ____. *The Eurocurrency Markets and Their Implications: A "New" View of International Monetary Problems and Monetary Reform.* Lexington: D.C. Heath, 1975.

7. ____. "The Impact of U.S. Controls on Capital Outflows and the U.S. Balance of Payments: An Exploratory Study." *IMF Staff Papers* (forthcoming).

8. Klopstock, F. "The Euro-Dollar Market: Some Unresolved Issues." Essays in International Finance, No. 65, Princeton University, 1968.

9. Machlup, F. "Euro-Dollar Creation: A Mystery Story." Reprints in International Finance, No. 16, Princeton University, 1970.

10. Makin, J. H. "Demand and Supply Functions for Stocks of Euro-Dollar

Deposits: An Empirical Study." *Review of Economics and Statistics,* 54 (November, 1972), 381–91.

11. Niehans, Jürg. "Money in a Static Theory of Optimal Payments Arrangements." *Journal of Money, Credit, and Banking,* 1 (November, 1969), 706–26.

12. _____. "Money and Barter in General Equilibrium with Transactions Costs." *American Economic Review,* 61, No. 5 (1971), 773–83.

13. _____. "Geldschöpfung und Kreditvermittlung im Eurodollarmarkt." In *Verstehen und Gestalten der Wirtschaft,* Essays in Honor of F. A. Lutz, 1971.

14. Orr, D., and W. G. Mellon. "Stochastic Reserve Losses and Expansion of Bank Credit." *American Economic Review,* 5 (September, 1961), 614–23.

15. Palgrave, R. H. I., ed. "Dictionary of Political Economy." *Banking,* Bd. I, 1901.

16. Phillips, C. A. *Bank Credit.* 1920.

17. Scanlon, C. J. "Definitions and Mechanics of Eurodollar Transactions." In *The Eurodollar,* ed. H. V. Prochnov. Chicago, 1970, pp. 16–41.

18. Swoboda, H. "The Euro-Dollar Market: An Interpretation." Essays in International Finance, Princeton University, 1968.

19. Tobin, J. "Liquidity Preference as Behavior Towards Risk." *Review of Economic Studies* (1957/58), 65–86.

20. _____. "Commercial Banks as Creators of Money." In *Banking and Monetary Studies,* ed. Carson. 1963, pp. 408–19.

21. _____. "A General Equilibrium Approach to Monetary Theory." *Journal of Money, Credit, and Banking,* 1 (February, 1969), 15–29.

[15]

Multipliers and the Portfolio Approach: A Geometric Exposition

For this analysis we assume that $R_E/E = q = 0$: in other words, Eurobanks hold no reserves (except perhaps temporarily in the interim between receiving deposits and making loans). The public's preferences are represented by:

$$E/(E + D) = p(i_e, X) \tag{9.13}$$

where E is Eurodollar deposits, D is US bank deposits, i_e is the interest rate on E and X stands for other relevant variables such as other interest rates. Then, p lies between 0 and 1. The US money supply is given by $M = E + D$, and $D = B/r$ where B is the stock of base money and r the reserve ratio of US banks. Consequently

$$M = \frac{1}{1-p}\frac{B}{r}$$

We are considering two specific situations: in the first the authorities peg B so that M varies directly with p; in the second M is assumed constant, an expository device for deriving the results of this analysis.

In the north-west quadrant of Figure 9.5 is shown the relationship between i_e and p, that is, the portfolio preferences of depositors for some given set of values of the X variables. The south-east quadrant is simply a construction line. The south-west quadrant is based upon the relationship:

$$E = pM = \frac{p}{1-p}\frac{B}{r} \tag{9.14}$$

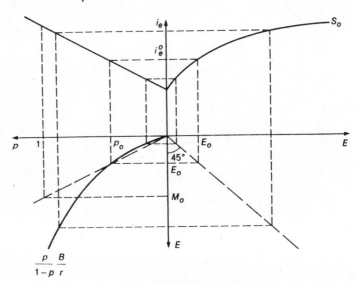

Figure 9.5

Two lines are shown. The curved line, which shifts only if B/r changes, shows the relationship between E and p when B/r is held constant and M is allowed to vary. The straight (broken) line is drawn for a particular initial value of $M=M_o$ and initial value of $p=p_o$ and assumes M constant at M_o. It has a slope of M_o and intersects the other line at $p=p_o$. The line thus represents positions of disequilibrium immediately following changes in p from $p=p_o$ such as in the first step of the multiplier process when the private sector converts US bank deposits into Eurodollar deposits. Initially no change in M occurs, but once loans are made by Eurobanks, M will increase (and the line rotate until it intersects the other at the new value of p).

The supply curve of Eurodollar deposits in the north-east quadrant is derived using the construct line shown by starting at particular i_e values in the north-west quadrant and tracing through the figure counter-clockwise, using the solid (curved) line in the south-west quadrant. The straight line in the south-west quadrant is not at this stage relevant to the analysis but is drawn assuming a current interest rate of i_E^o, portfolio ratio of p_o and money stock of M_o.

Figure 9.6 illustrates the effects of an autonomous shift in portfolio preferences towards Eurodollars, depicted by a leftward shift of the line in the north-west quadrant. Here, the two lines in the south-west quadrant come into play. At the initial interest rate of i_e^o which we temporarily hold constant, the immediate effect on Eurodollar deposits (before any credit creation) is determined from the broken line in the south-west quadrant as an increase from E_o to E_p corresponding to the increase in p from p_o to p_1. (US

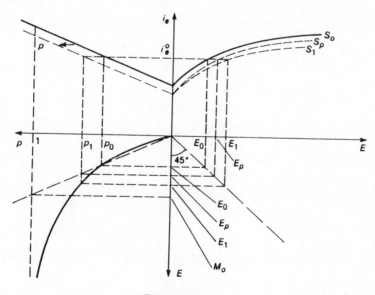

Figure 9.6

deposits have fallen correspondingly so that M is constant.)[1] This initial shift is depicted by the movement from S_o to S_p in the north-east quadrant. However, the process of credit creation by Eurobanks leads to an increase in M (as described in the text) until, at the initial interest rate i_e^o, equilibrium is achieved at p_1 with $E=E_1$. The supply curve thus shifts to S_1.

In the context of the formula used in the text, $(E_1-E_o)/(E_p-E_o)$ corresponds to the multiplier $\frac{1}{1-p(1-q)}$ of equation 9.6 and (E_p-E_o) to the initial autonomous deposit. The analysis of a change in base money and US bank deposits involving a shift in the solid line in the south-west quadrant is left as an exercise to the reader.

Figure 9.7 takes the north-east quadrant of Figure 9.6 and augments it by a curve representing the demand for loans from Eurobanks. To do this, it is assumed that a fixed spread exists between Eurodollar loan and deposit rates, enabling us to depict the demand for loans against the deposit interest rate. Initial equilibrium is thus at point A, after the shift in portfolio preferences, interest rates change, leading to a moderation of that shift and to equilibrium at E_2 rather than at E_1.

As drawn, the ultimate change in E is (E_2-E_o) which is less than the initial change (E_p-E_o), but this need not necessarily be the case. Thus, the initial deposit multiplier *could* be less than unity if interest rate changes were sufficiently large. But this is not the appropriate analogue of the 'margarine multiplier' referred to by Niehans and Hewson and discussed in the text. That example and multiplier is more appropriately interpreted as referring to $(E_2-E_o)/(E_1-E_o)$ which *must* be less than unity. As emphasised in the text, the appropriate definition of the multiplicand is critical for a clear understanding of the issues involved.

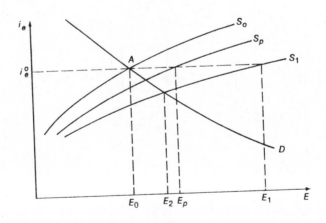

Figure 9.7

Note

1. While, for reasons listed later in the paragraph, the result is an analytical device, it can be assumed that this is brought about by US depositors withdrawing cash from US banks which is redeposited with Eurobanks. The initial impact, prior to Eurobanks expanding their loans, is a reduction in D and an increase in E, with M constant.

[16]

Some aspects of the determination of euro-currency interest rates

This article has been prepared mainly by R. B. Johnston of the Bank's Overseas Department.

Summary

This article discusses some systematic relationships which have been observed between domestic and euro-currency interest rates. It describes a model to explain these relationships, based on the extra costs which banks incur from holding reserve requirements against domestic deposits. Statistical tests have been used to compare the marginal cost of three-month money (after allowing for the extra cost of reserve requirements) in the euro-dollar and domestic US markets, and in the euro-deutschemark and domestic West German markets. These tests confirm that, in the absence of disruptions to the free flow of capital, the differences in these costs are virtually zero and that domestic banks effectively arbitrage between the euro and domestic money markets. The article concludes that the euro-currency market is not independent of domestic money markets and that its rôle as a channel for short-term capital flows appears to be very closely linked to the activities of domestic banks.

Introduction

Because of the close substitutability between assets in domestic and in external money markets, it is clear that, in the absence of restrictions on the free flow of capital, interest rates in the two markets should be closely related. Also, because of the availability of forward cover in the foreign exchange market and the close association of the euro-currency market with the foreign exchange market, there should clearly be a very close relationship between the interest rates offered, on different currency deposits, in the euro-currency market, and the costs of forward cover. Such relationships are well known.[1] Analysis of the movement of euro-currency interest rates, however, within this general framework, has revealed more specific and systematic relationships between domestic and euro-currency deposit rates; indeed some of the observed margins between interest rates in the domestic and external money markets have been so stable as to be termed a technical differential.

This article attempts to rationalise some of the observed relationships within a fairly general framework of the supply of, and demand for, individual euro-currencies. The first section considers a simple model of a single euro-currency deposit market and recent empirical experience which illustrates how

restrictions and imperfections can cause systematic deviations from the model. The model is then extended, in the second section, to discuss how two euro-currency deposit markets and the spot and forward exchange markets interact. This section also considers why interest-rate parity appears to hold between euro-currency interest rates for different currencies but not between nominal interest rates in different domestic markets, and also the rôle of the euro-markets in channelling short-term capital flows. Recent empirical experience is reported in support of the model. In the final section, some of the wider implications for the analysis of the euro-currency markets are briefly presented.

A model of the relationship between the euro-currency and domestic markets

The initial assumptions of the model are that:

1 euro-currency deposits and domestic deposits are, in terms of the number of settlement days and marketability, perfect substitutes;

2 there are no capital controls on the movement of funds between the domestic money market and the euro-currency market;

3 domestic banks are required to hold non-interest-bearing reserve balances against domestic currency deposits;[2]

4 institutions which take deposits and make loans in a currency other than that of the country in which they are operating—hereafter termed euro-banks[3]—are not legally obliged to hold reserves against such foreign currency deposits;[4]

5 private non-bank holders of funds may have strong, non-pecuniary preferences for holding either a domestic or a euro-currency deposit; and

6 for domestic banks, loans to euro-banks are no more risky than loans made in the domestic inter-bank market.

The first four assumptions are factual in nature and, therefore, may be easily verified. In general, assumptions 3 and 4 hold for most currencies in the euro-currency market; the validity of assumption 2 varies as between currencies and over time; assumption 1 need not strictly hold, but it does not seem an unreasonable simplification.[5]

[1] See, for example, R. J. Herring and R. C. Marston, *National Monetary Policies and International Financial Markets* (Amsterdam: North-Holland, 1977), chapters 4 and 8; and G. Dufey and I. H. Giddy, *The International Money Market* (Englewood Cliffs, New Jersey: Prentice-Hall, 1978), especially pages 48–77.

[2] The conclusions from the model would be unchanged if an uncompetitive rate of interest were paid on reserve balances held with the central bank, although this would have to be allowed for in the subsequent analysis.

[3] The distinction between domestic banks and euro-banks is of course artificial but is made for convenience of analysis. In practice, an institution which is primarily concerned with taking deposits and making loans in foreign currencies may also be permitted to take deposits and make loans in the currency of the country in which it is resident. However, such transactions may be viewed, without loss of generality, as domestic banking operations.

[4] It might, however, be expected that some margin of reserves would be held against the possibility of withdrawals. The analysis requires only the assumption that this margin is less than the legal domestic reserve requirement, or that these reserves can be employed at a rate of interest greater than the domestic interest rate payable on obligatory reserves.

[5] A deposit between euro-banks in London is normally for the delivery of funds on the second business day after the deal has been made, and may therefore be somewhat longer than for a domestic agreement, which is usually for the delivery of funds on the same day as the deal or the day after.

Private non-bank holders of funds are assumed to have non-pecuniary preferences for depositing in one market rather than the other (assumption 5). This may reflect different perceived degrees of political or financial risk in the two markets.

The validity of assumption 6 is likely to depend on domestic banks' perceived degree of risk in lending to the euro-currency market. This may vary over time. One reason for expecting this risk to be small is that euro-banks have very close links with domestic banks—in many cases euro-banks are the wholly or partly-owned subsidiaries or branches of domestic banks in a foreign country—which may, as a matter of routine, make loans to or take deposits from their overseas affiliates. Whether, in fact, domestic banks' perceived degree of risk in lending to the euro-currency market is small is an empirical question investigated below. For the purposes of exposition, it is assumed here to be zero.

It is now possible to derive the supply and demand curves for euro-currency deposits under this set of assumptions and four simple propositions about the behaviour of non-bank holders of funds, domestic or parent banks, and euro-banks.

- Non-banks' supply of funds to the euro-currency market will depend, among other things, on the relative return on deposits in the two markets, and it is likely that, *ceteris paribus*, for a given domestic deposit rate, the supply of currency to (demand for deposits from) the euro-market will be positively related to the euro-currency deposit rate. This may be simply written as:

$$S_{ec}^{nb} = f_1(i_{ec} - i_d) \qquad (1)$$

with

$$\frac{\delta S_{ec}^{nb}}{\delta i_{ec}} > 0$$

where i_{ec} and i_d are respectively the euro-currency and domestic currency deposit rates; and S_{ec}^{nb} is the supply of euro-currency by non-banks.[1] This supply schedule is illustrated as segment 1 in Chart A. It is drawn so that even when the euro-currency deposit rate is below the domestic deposit rate there is a positive supply of currency to the euro-market, on the assumption that there exist investors who, even in these circumstances, would prefer a euro-currency holding to a domestic currency deposit.

- The supply of currency to the euro-market by domestic banks will depend on the cost to banks of raising deposits domestically and on the returns they receive from lending these in the euro-currency market. To a domestic bank, the effective

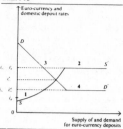

Chart A

cost it pays for loanable funds at the margin is not just the nominal deposit rate but this nominal cost adjusted for the extra costs it incurs from holding (non-interest-bearing) reserves against these deposits plus any extra costs, such as the cost of Federal Deposit Insurance in the United States. The effective cost per unit of loanable funds to a domestic bank is therefore:

$$i_d^e = \frac{i_d + x_d}{1 - r_d} \qquad (2)$$

where r_d is the domestic reserve requirement on resident deposits and x_d is any extra cost of domestic currency borrowing to domestic banks.

Given this effective cost to banks of raising funds in the domestic market, they would only on-lend funds to the euro-market if the rate they could obtain on euro-currency deposits exceeds this cost. This gives the supply condition for domestic banks:

$$S_{ec}^b = f_2(i_{ec} - i_d^e) \qquad (3)$$

with

$$S_{ec}^b = 0 \text{ when } i_{ec} \leqslant i_d^e$$
$$= f_2 \text{ when } i_{ec} > i_d^e$$

It might also be expected that this schedule would be highly elastic with respect to the euro-currency deposit rate: if this rate exceeded the effective cost to domestic banks of raising loanable funds, any domestic bank could obtain a profit simply by borrowing domestically and lending the proceeds in the euro-currency market. In the absence of capital controls and other imperfections in the market, arbitrage by banks between the domestic and euro-currency markets should therefore be such as to place an upper ceiling on the euro-currency deposit rate.[2] The supply schedule is therefore illustrated as being perfectly elastic at the effective cost of loanable funds to domestic banks—segment 2 of Chart A.

[1] Under the assumption that domestic and external deposits are imperfect substitutes to private non-bank wealth holders, equation 1 is viewed as a stock relationship, in line with the portfolio selection theory of capital flows. See J. H. Makin, 'Demand and supply functions for stocks of euro-dollar deposits: an empirical study'. *Review of Economics and Statistics*, Vol. LIV, November 1972, pages 381–91.

[2] This formulation of the supply schedule for domestic banks suggests a flow, rather than a stock-adjustment model of capital movements. The justification for this is that it is assumed that domestic banks, unlike non-banks, are largely indifferent between lending to euro-banks and lending in the domestic money market, and, therefore, while it might be appropriate to formulate equation of non-bank wealth holders, as a stock-adjustment relationship, it would seem more appropriate to view equation 3 as a flow relationship. For a model which analyses the supply of euro-dollar deposits by financial intermediaries in terms of a flow relationship, see P. H. Hendershott, 'The structure of international interest rates: the US Treasury bill rate and the eurodollar deposit rate'. *The Journal of Finance*, Vol. XXII, 1967, pages 455–65.

- The demand for funds (supply of deposits) by euro-banks will depend on the demand for loans from euro-banks by final users. We might expect, *ceteris paribus*, that this demand for loans, and the euro-banks' derived demand for funds, would be inversely related to the euro-currency deposit rate.[1] This demand curve for funds is therefore drawn downward-sloping (segment 3 of Chart A). The determinants of the relative position of this curve are likely to be fairly complex, but would be expected to depend upon the relative costs to final users of borrowing from banks in the euro-currency rather than the domestic market—this latter cost would depend, *inter alia*, on the cost of loanable funds to domestic banks (i_d^e)—and on the relative ability to borrow in the two markets.[2] This might be expressed algebraically as:

$$D_{ec}^{nb} = f_3(i_{ec} - i_d^e) + X \qquad (4)$$

with

$$\frac{\delta D_{ec}^{nb}}{\delta i_{ec}} < 0$$

which shows the derived demand for funds by euro-banks as a function of the relative effective cost of loanable funds in the two markets plus exogenous factors (X) such as relative lending margins.

- A domestic bank would only borrow its own currency from the euro-currency market if the effective cost of raising loanable funds from the euro-currency market were less than the effective cost of loanable funds in the domestic market. The euro-currency interest rate at which this becomes profitable will depend on relative interest rates in the two markets and on the relative reserve requirements on resident and non-resident deposits.

The effective cost per unit to a domestic bank of raising loanable funds in the euro-currency market is:

$$i_{ec}^e = \frac{i_{ec}}{1 - r_e} \qquad (5)$$

where r_e is the domestic reserve requirement on non-resident deposits, on the assumption that domestic banks do not pay any extra costs on their euro-currency borrowing. Combining equations 2 and 5, the euro-currency interest rate at

which it will become profitable for domestic banks to borrow euro-currency is given at:

$$i_{ec}^e = i_d^e \qquad (6)$$

or where

$$i_{ec} = i_{ec}^d = \frac{(i_d + x_d)(1 - r_e)}{(1 - r_d)}.$$

At this rate, the demand for funds from the euro-currency market by domestic banks should become nearly perfectly elastic with respect to the euro-currency deposit rate. This might be expressed algebraically as:

with

$$D_{ec}^b = f_4(i_{ec}^d - i_{ec}) \qquad (7)$$
$$D_{ec}^b = 0 \text{ when } i_{ec} \geqslant i_{ec}^d$$
$$= f_4 \text{ when } i_{ec} < i_{ec}^d$$

This is illustrated as segment 4 in Chart A.

This completes the simple analysis of the supply of, and demand for, a single euro-currency in isolation from the rest of the euro-currency market.

The equilibrium euro-currency deposit rate is then determined by the intersection of the demand and supply schedules at i_{ec}^* in Chart A. This chart also shows that the equilibrium euro-currency deposit rate is constrained within narrow limits by the arbitrage activity of domestic banks, the upper arbitrage limit (segment 2) depending on the nominal cost to domestic banks of raising deposits in the domestic market and the level of reserve requirements on resident deposits, and the lower arbitrage limit (segment 4) depending on the domestic deposit rate and the relative level of reserve requirements on resident and non-resident deposits.

A test of the model
As a test of this analysis, Chart B compares, from January 1973 to end-March 1978, the three-month euro-dollar bid rate[3] and the US secondary market three-month certificate of deposit (CD) rate, corrected for US domestic reserve requirements and the costs of Federal Deposit Insurance,[4] i.e. the effective cost to US banks of raising loanable funds in the domestic market.

The chart shows that the relationship between the two rates has been particularly close since end-1975, suggesting that, in this period, the three-month euro-dollar rate has been determined by the rate at which it was profitable for US domestic banks to supply funds to the euro-dollar market (i.e. at an intersection of the demand curve with segment 2 of the supply curve in

[1] Euro-bank loans are usually in the form of bank credits of a specified term. The interest rate on these credits is normally a fixed spread over LIBOR (London inter-bank offered rate)—the rate at which major banks are prepared to lend funds in the London inter-bank market. The above formulation of the demand curve for loans suggests that this demand is responsive to the total cost of borrowing, i.e. the euro-currency interest rate plus the spread.

[2] Because of the practice of syndicating loans in the euro-market, very large amounts ($2 billion is not unknown) may be raised on competitive terms in the euro-market, and there may be no close substitute for these in the domestic market.

[3] The bid rate is taken to approximate the rate which US banks would receive on their lending to the market. This is the rate at which a selection of large banks in the euro-market are prepared to borrow funds in the London inter-bank market. In practice, the bid rate would be the subject of negotiation between individual banks.

[4] The US domestic reserve requirement on large denominated CDs was, from 1st October 1970 to 12th December 1974, 5% and thereafter, until 2nd November 1978, 6%. The cost of Federal Deposit Insurance is approximately 0.036%. The formula used to calculate the effective cost to US banks of raising loanable funds in the domestic market was therefore:

$$i_d^e = \frac{i_d + 0.036}{1 - r_d}$$

where $r_d = 0.05$ 1st October 1970 to 12th December 1974
$= 0.06$ after 12th December 1974
and i_d was the dealers' offer rate in the secondary market for large denominated CDs in New York.

Chart B

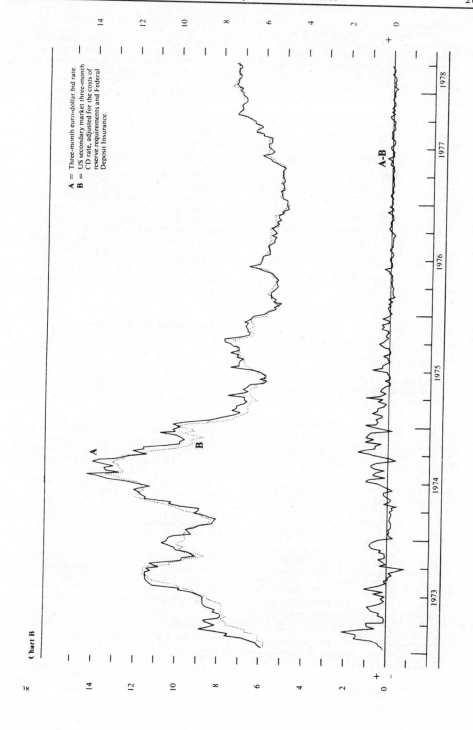

A = Three-month euro-dollar bid rate.
B = US secondary market three-month CD rate, adjusted for the costs of reserve requirements and Federal Deposit Insurance.

Chart A). Indeed the mean differential between the two rates after 1st January 1975 was only 0.07 percentage points with a variance of only 0.05 percentage points (see Table A).[1] Not surprisingly, published Bank for International Settlements statistics on the size of the euro-market also show US banks as large net suppliers of funds to the euro-market during this period (see Table B).

Table A

Three-month euro-dollar rate less effective cost to US banks of loanable funds in the domestic market[a]

	Mean	Variance	Number of observations
1 January 1973– end-December 1973	0.48	0.26	52
Mid-June 1974– end-December 1974	0.64	0.18	28
Mid-June 1974– mid-June 1975	0.53	0.16	52
1 January 1975– end-March 1978	0.07	0.05	169
Total sample	0.22	0.16	249

[a] Calculated as the US secondary market three-month CD rate corrected for the cost of reserve requirements and Federal Deposit Insurance.

Table B

External assets and liabilities of US banks

$ billions	Assets	Liabilities[a]
1974 December	46.2	60.4
1975 December	59.8	58.7
1976 December	81.1	70.7
1977 December	92.6	78.1
1978 March	98.8	79.3

Source: Bank for International Settlements statistics on international banking developments.

[a] Excluding US Treasury bills and certificates held in custody on behalf of non-residents.

This in itself might be accepted as sufficient evidence to support the model in terms of the efficiency of arbitrage flows from the US domestic market to the euro-dollar market.[2]

It is, however, worth considering why during 1973 and 1974 the differential between the two rates fluctuated sharply. One reason may be that during this period US domestic banks were either unable or unwilling to arbitrage between the two markets.

Until 1974, the United States enforced a capital restraint programme which included ceilings on US domestic bank lending to non-residents. This had the effect of making the upper arbitrage limit (segment 2 of Chart A) ineffective, allowing the euro-dollar rate to rise above the effective cost to US banks of domestic dollar borrowing.[3] After the removal of the controls in January 1974, the differential between the rates narrowed temporarily; however, during the summer of 1974 a crisis of confidence developed in the euro-currency market after the closure of the Cologne bank, ID Herstatt, on 26th June. Although this banking failure was due to heavy losses sustained in foreign

exchange dealings, it produced more general fears about the solvency of banks in the euro-currency market. In these circumstances, it would not have been unusual for depositors to require a significant risk premium for depositing in the euro-currency market or, as a consequence, for euro-dollar rates to move erratically and above the effective cost to US banks of borrowing domestically. In September 1974, the central bank Governors from countries of the Group of Ten and Switzerland stated that they were satisfied that means were available for the purpose of the provision of temporary liquidity to the euro-markets and would be used if and when necessary. Subsequently worries about the solvency of euro-banks appear to have largely evaporated, and by mid-1975 the differential between the rates had returned to its technical level.

In the year before the removal of capital controls, the mean and variance of the differential between the rates were respectively 0.48 and 0.26 percentage points, while, during the Herstatt crisis (mid-June to end-December 1974, or mid-June 1974 to mid-June 1975) the mean and variance of the differential were 0.64 and 0.18 percentage points respectively. For both these periods, the means and variances of the differential were significantly different from those found for the period after January 1975, thus tending to confirm the visual evidence (see Table C).

Table C

Analysis of variance: euro-dollar/domestic CD differential

	1 January 1973– end-December 1973	Mid-June 1974– end-December 1974
Mid-June 1974– end-December 1974	$F_{51, 27} = 1.4$	
1 January 1975– end-March 1978	$F_{51, 168} = 5.3$[a]	$F_{27, 168} = 3.7$[a]

[a] Indicates that the variances are significantly different at a 1% level of significance.

The movement in euro-dollar interest rates in recent years tends to give strong support for the simple model developed above and suggests that, in the absence of market imperfections such as capital controls, there is at the margin a very close relationship between the effective cost of loanable funds to banks in the euro-dollar and US domestic markets. This analysis also confirms that, in the absence of serious crises of confidence, domestic banks, do not generally regard the risks of depositing in the euro-currency market as significantly greater than those of depositing in the domestic market.

The analysis also tends to suggest that the euro-dollar rate is determined largely independently of both the forward exchange market and the interest rates on other euro-currencies. While this might not be unreasonable for the euro-dollar which is the dominant currency in the euro-market, making up about three

[1] While these statistics indicate that the population mean is significantly different from zero, this may only reflect measurement error or transactions costs in the markets. For example, the difference between the rates offered by dealers in the secondary market and the actual cost to US banks of borrowing high-denomination CDs, although subject to variations, might, in normal circumstances, amount to some 0.10–0.15 percentage points. Allowing for this difference could completely eliminate the mean differential observed between the rates during the period.

[2] This analysis does not test the efficiency of arbitrage flows from the euro-market to domestic markets. This is, however, considered in the next section.

[3] Such restraints may have also increased US corporations' external borrowing, since the capital controls restricted their raising capital domestically for use overseas. By increasing the demand for funds from the euro-currency market, this would also have tended to widen the differential between domestic and euro-dollar interest rates.

quarters of its gross size, and which also acts as the numeraire in the foreign exchange market, it is certainly not the case for other currencies in the euro-market.[1] The question of the inter-relationship between euro-currency interest rates and the foreign exchange market is considered in the next section.

An extension of the model

In fact, the supply of, and demand for, a euro-currency are not independent of the rate of interest on alternative currencies in the euro-market as assumed above. Euro-currency interest rates are instead directly related through the forward market, since an investor holding say euro-dollars could sell the dollars spot for say deutschemarks, invest the deutschemarks in the euro-deutschemark market and cover forward. Indeed, arbitrageurs would shift funds between currencies as long as it was profitable to do so. For equilibrium, the euro-currency rate should equal the euro-dollar rate less the forward discount on dollars *vis-à-vis* the currency—the familiar interest-rate parity theorem. To explain the determination of euro-currency interest rates, it is, therefore, necessary to discuss the forward exchange market and its relationship with the euro-currency market.

Before proceeding to this, it should be noted that it is usual practice in the euro-market for banks to determine a non-dollar euro-currency rate as simply the euro-dollar rate less the forward discount or plus the forward premium on dollars against that currency, implying that interest-rate parity holds between currencies in the euro-market. However, even in the absence of restrictions on capital flows, arbitrage flows between domestic money markets do not seem to bring

national interest rates into interest-rate parity. Indeed, to the extent that euro-currency interest rates are different from nominal domestic interest rates, interest-rate parity between euro-currency rates (and the forward exchange market) may be inconsistent with interest-rate parity between nominal domestic interest rates—and there has been considerable discussion among economists on the reasons for a less than perfectly elastic arbitrage demand schedule for forward exchange.[2]

To simplify the analysis, no discussion is made of the spot exchange market. The justification for this is that, following Walras' Law, the excess demand in the four markets (the spot and forward exchange market and two euro-currency markets) must sum to zero and therefore one market (here taken as the spot exchange market) is redundant.

An integrated model

In diagrams 1 and 2 of Chart C, the supply and demand curves for two individual euro-currencies—the euro-dollar market and one other euro-currency market (for example, the euro-deutschemark market)—have been redrawn under the assumptions described previously. These show the supply of, and demand for, the euro-currency, given the level of interest rates and reserve requirements in the two domestic markets.[3] For illustrative purposes it is assumed that West German domestic interest rates are less than US domestic rates.[4] The equilibrium euro-dollar and euro-deutschemark rates are assumed, initially, to be $i_{\cdot d}^{*}$ and $i_{\cdot c}^{*}$ respectively.

Diagram 3 of the chart illustrates the supply and demand for forward cover in the foreign exchange market.

Chart C

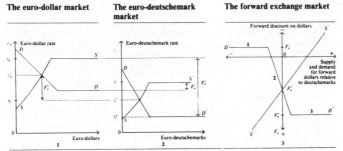

| The euro–dollar market | The euro-deutschemark market | The forward exchange market |

[1] Domestic and euro-market interest rates, and forward and spot exchange rates are jointly determined. While the size of the US domestic money market suggests that a causal chain from events there to the euro-dollar market, and thence to the forward exchange market, will often explain changes in all markets, this will not always, nor even generally, be the case. Euro-markets may at times affect US money markets: for example, if New York banks borrow domestically in order to lend in the euro-markets, this would tend to push up US CD rates.

[2] See, for example, L. H. Officer and T. D. Willett 'The Covered-Arbitrage Schedule: A Critical Survey of Recent Developments', *Journal of Money, Credit and Banking*, Vol. 2, May 1970, pages 247–57. Of particular interest is the paper by W. H. Branson, 'The Minimum Covered Interest Differential Needed for International Arbitrage Activity', *Journal of Political Economy*, Vol. 77 December 1969, pages 1028–35, in which it is suggested that transactions costs will produce a discontinuity in the arbitrageurs' demand schedule for forward exchange. This proposition is considered further below.

[3] For the purposes of simplifying the analysis, it is assumed that the level of domestic interest rates is given exogenously of short-term capital flows. In fact it has already been observed (footnote[1] above) that capital flows can affect domestic money markets, but this assumption may not be unreasonable in the short term if domestic monetary authorities set (interim) targets for the level of domestic short-term interest rates.

[4] This does not necessarily imply that the equilibrium euro-dollar rate need be greater than the euro-deutschemark rate. Instead it will depend on the relative interest rates at which US domestic banks find it profitable to borrow from the euro-dollar market (the perfectly elastic segment of *DD'* in diagram 1 of the chart) and West German domestic banks find it profitable to supply funds to the euro-deutschemark market (the perfectly elastic segment of *SS'* in diagram 2 of the chart). This model would therefore suggest that, even when there is a free flow of capital, perverse relationships could develop between domestic and euro-currency interest rates

The speculators' supply of forward exchange,[1] which is illustrated as $S^{*}S^{*}$ in diagram 3 of Chart C, will depend, *inter alia*, on their expectations about the future spot dollar/deutschemark exchange rate and on the forward discount on dollars. The shape of the supply schedule will reflect the aggregation of individual speculators' supplies, which may themselves depend on the size of individuals' outstanding forward contracts; the effect of one speculator's supply on another's; their wealth and their ability to borrow. Indeed there does not appear to be any reason why the total supply curve should even be stable. For simplicity, however, it is here assumed that, for a given set of expectations about the future spot exchange rate, speculators' supply of forward exchange is a linearly decreasing function of the forward discount on dollars. Thus if the forward discount on dollars is less than F_{d}^{*}, speculators will supply forward dollars relative to deutschemarks; if it is greater than F_{d}^{*}, they will supply forward deutschemarks relative to dollars.

The arbitrageurs' demand for forward exchange may be derived from an analysis of the supply and demand curves for the two euro-currencies—it is illustrated as $D'D'$ in diagram 3 of Chart C. Between the points $F_{d}^{'}$ and $F_{d}^{''}$, this schedule is shown to be nearly perfectly inelastic with respect to the forward discount on dollars (segment 2), i.e. in this range any change in the forward discount will produce only small capital movements, while beyond these points the schedule becomes perfectly elastic (segments 1 and 3). The reason for this is as follows: given US and West German domestic interest rates and reserve requirements, then domestic banks' arbitrage limits with the euro-currency market are fixed—and these are shown as the perfectly elastic sections of the demand and supply schedules in diagrams 1 and 2 of the chart. Therefore, provided domestic interest rates (and reserve requirements) are unchanged, the maximum possible euro-dollar rate is i_{s}^{e}, the rate at which US domestic banks find it profitable to supply dollars to the euro-dollar market, and the minimum possible euro-deutschemark rate is the rate at which West German domestic banks find it profitable to borrow euro-deutschemarks, i_{ec}^{d}. The maximum possible forward discount on dollars is therefore the difference between these rates, shown as $F_{d}^{'}$ in diagrams 2 and 3

of the chart, and arbitrageurs' demand for forward dollars must become perfectly elastic at this forward discount.

For if the forward discount on dollars were to rise and to become greater than $F_{d}^{'}$, then arbitrageurs in the euro-currency market would find it profitable to shift funds out of euro-dollars into euro-deutschemarks. These arbitrage flows between euro-currencies would tend to push the euro-dollar rate above i_{s}^{e} or the euro-deutschemark rate below i_{ec}^{d}. But at these euro-currency interest rates, domestic banks will find it profitable to arbitrage with the euro-currency market—US domestic banks will supply funds to the euro-dollar market and West German domestic banks will demand funds from the euro-deutschemark market. In equilibrium, the euro-dollar rate cannot remain above its upper arbitrage limit of i_{s}^{e} nor the euro-deutschemark rate fall below its lower arbitrage limit of i_{ec}^{d}, and the forward discount on dollars cannot exceed $F_{d}^{'}$. The demand for forward dollars will therefore become perfectly elastic at this rate.

Similarly, the equilibrium forward discount on deutschemarks cannot exceed $F_{d}^{''}$—the difference between US banks' lower arbitrage limit and West German banks' upper arbitrage limit. The demand for forward deutschemarks therefore must also become perfectly elastic at $F_{d}^{''}$.

Between the forward discounts, $F_{d}^{'}$ and $F_{d}^{''}$, movements in euro-currency interest rates are unconstrained by the arbitrage activity of domestic banks, and within this range euro-currency interest rates should adjust rapidly to a change in the forward discount. If the forward discount on dollars were to increase from its equilibrium level F_{d}^{*}, (say to $F_{d}^{''}$ in diagram 3 of Chart D), suppliers of funds to the euro-dollar market would find it profitable, at the initial rates of interest on euro-dollars and euro-deutschemarks, to transfer these funds to the euro-deutschemark market and cover forward; and arbitrageurs would find it profitable to borrow euro-dollars to lend on a covered basis as euro-deutschemarks. The combined effect is therefore to shift the supply curve for euro-dollars to the left (from

Chart D

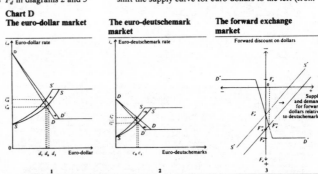

The euro-dollar market

The euro-deutschemark market

The forward exchange market

| 1 | 2 | 3 |

[1] 'Speculators' refers to any market operators taking an open position in the forward exchange market.

SS, to *SS'* , see diagram 1 of Chart D), and the demand curve for euro-dollars to the right (from *DD* to *DD'* in diagram 1 of Chart D), sharply increasing the euro-dollar rate from i_{ed}^* to i_{ed}^{**} (see diagram 1 of Chart D), while shifting the supply curve for euro-deutschemarks to the right (from *SS* to *SS'* in diagram 2 of the chart) and the demand curve for euro-deutschemarks to the left (from *DD* to *DD'* in diagram 2) as banks which had previously borrowed euro-deutschemarks would now find it profitable to borrow euro-dollars instead and switch these into deutschemarks and cover forward. These shifts in the supply and demand schedules for euro-deutschemarks will sharply decrease the euro-deutschemark rate from i_{ec}^* to i_{ec}^{**} (see diagram 2 of Chart D). The movements in the euro-dollar and euro-deutschemark rates, combined with some subsequent narrowing in the forward discount on dollars (from $F_d^{\tilde{}}$ to F_d^{**} in diagram 3 of Chart D), would re-establish equilibrium between the markets. At the new equilibrium, as Chart D shows, the euro-dollar rate is higher, the euro-deutschemark rate lower, and the forward discount on dollars somewhat wider.

Because both the supply and the demand curves shift in both euro-currency markets, however, the actual movement of funds between the markets need only be small to re-establish equilibrium—the shift out of euro-dollars is illustrated in the chart as d_0 to d_1;[1] the shift into euro-deutschemarks as c_0 to c_1—and therefore the arbitrageurs' demand curve for forward dollars is likely to appear to be nearly perfectly inelastic with respect to the forward discount on dollars between the points F_d and F_d'. It is the mobility of capital between euro-currencies, and the adjustment in euro-currency interest rates, which allows dealers to determine a euro-currency rate simply as the euro-dollar rate less the forward discount on dollars. If arbitrage between euro-currency markets were not perfect, and it took considerable time and movement of funds to remove disequilibrium between euro-currency interest rates, then other influences—the demand for the euro-currency by final users and the supply of the euro-currency by holders of funds—could determine a rate of interest on the euro-currency which was different from the euro-dollar rate less the forward discount on dollars, and covered differentials between euro-currency interest rates could emerge.

However, this model also shows that the range over which the demand schedule for forward dollars is inelastic is a limited one and therefore only over a rather narrow range can the euro-currency rate be determined independently of other influences. If, for example, the speculators' supply curve of forward exchange were to shift from *SS* to *S'S'*(see Chart E), this would widen, initially, the forward discount on dollars from F_d^* to F_d^{**} . If euro-banks determine the euro-currency rate as the euro-dollar rate less this forward discount, F_d^{**} , then euro-currency markets remain in equilibrium—there is no arbitrage flow

Chart E

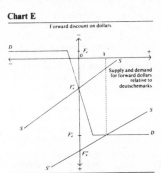

between euro-currencies—but euro-currency markets are now out of equilibrium with domestic currency markets. A forward discount of F_d^{**} forces the quoted euro-currency rate below the rate at which domestic banks find it profitable to borrow the euro-currency. Domestic banks would therefore find it profitable to borrow their domestic currency in the euro-market rather than in the domestic market or to borrow euro-dollars, swap these into the domestic currency and cover themselves forward; and they would continue to do so until the forward discount on dollars narrowed to F_d'(see Chart E)—the rate at which they no longer find it profitable to borrow euro-currency rather than domestic currency—or until domestic interest rates fell into line with the euro-currency rate. The net result would be that *X* forward contracts would have been made and that there would have been an inflow of *X* from euro-dollars into the domestic currency (see Chart E). This inflow would continue until either the forward rate or domestic interest rates adjusted. The main determinants of the euro-currency rate then comprise a wider set of variables than just the euro-dollar rate and the forward discount on dollars.

The euro-markets and short term capital flows
An interesting question concerns the rôle of the euro-markets as a channel for short-term capital flows. Some observers have suggested that, because there are no restrictions on flows between currencies in the euro-market and because arbitrage is nearly perfect between euro-currencies but not between domestic currencies, euro-markets have increased the volume of short-term capital flows, aggravating exchange rate pressures and decreasing the effectiveness of countries' domestic monetary policies. However, to the extent that euro-banks determine euro-currency rates as simply the euro-dollar rate less the forward discount on dollars, there is never any incentive for covered arbitrage flows between euro-currencies within the euro-market. Indeed, even if there were, the above framework suggests that very small flows would bring euro-currency interest rates back into equilibrium.

The main reason for short-term capital flows which are channelled through the euro-currency market is the

[1] If, as is likely, banks are the main arbitrageurs between euro-currencies, then there need be no decrease in the size of the euro-dollar market when the forward discount on dollars increases above its equilibrium level. If banks only arbitrage in the euro-dollar market, only the demand curve for euro-dollars will shift and the size of the euro-dollar market would increase as banks borrow dollars to lend covered in deutschemarks. In segment 1 of Chart D the size of the euro-dollar market would increase from d_0 to at least d_1.

arbitrage activity of domestic banks when euro-currency interest rates are pushed to the margins at which they find it profitable either to lend to, or borrow from, the euro-currency market. These margins are *exclusively* a function of domestic interest rates, reserve requirements or other domestic capital controls and independent of the existence of the euro-currency market. The rôle that euro-banks play is one of intermediating between currencies, e.g. matching demands for deutschemarks with dollar deposits. Euro-banks are not the cause of short-term flows; this is to be found in the misalignment of domestic interest rates, reserve requirements and exchange rate expectations.

One final question is why, even in the absence of restrictions on capital flows, interest-rate parity appears to hold between euro-currency interest rates but not between nominal domestic interest rates. One reason may be that whereas country and default risk may be quite different between domestic markets they need not differ between euro-currencies.[1]

An alternative way of answering the question is to consider why, given that interest-rate parity does hold between euro-currencies, the supply of currency to the euro-market is not perfectly elastic at the nominal domestic interest rate. This may simply reflect the imperfect substitutability between domestic and euro-currency (or external) deposits for non-banks: while the supply and demand curves for external deposits by domestic banks become perfectly elastic at certain euro-currency interest rates, the supply of currency to the euro-market by non-banks is not perfectly elastic at the nominal domestic rate of interest. Rather it appears upward sloping (as illustrated as *SS'* in diagram 1 of Chart C), first because non-bank holders of funds are likely to have strong preferences, other than pecuniary ones, for holding domestic currency rather than euro-currency and secondly, because they may have limited sources of funds with which to arbitrage. In other words, while it seems appropriate to view banks as flow-adjusters freely borrowing funds on competitive terms, it seems more appropriate to view non-banks in general as stock-adjusters allocating a given portfolio between domestic and external assets of varying risk and return.

A simple test of the integrated model
As a test of this integrated model, it would be instructive to see whether the euro-currency interest rate on a strong currency, such as the deutschemark, has been determined, in the absence of controls on the free flow of capital to the domestic market, at the rate at which it would have been profitable for domestic banks to borrow from the euro-currency market. To investigate this, the nominal three-month euro-deutschemark rate and the nominal West German domestic three-month inter-bank rate have been plotted, [2] in Chart F, together with the differential between the rates, for the period January 1973 to end-March 1978.

While this chart suggests that there was a very close relationship between the rates from mid-1975 to end-1977, there were also considerable deviations, particularly in 1973 and 1974, and again in 1978. However, at different times during this period the West German authorities have imposed controls, of varying severity, in an attempt to reduce capital flows into Western Germany, and only between August 1975 and December 1977 were West German domestic reserve requirements the same on West German banks' domestic and foreign-owned deutschemark liabilities (see Table D). Only for this period would the extra costs of raising loanable funds to West German banks have been the same in the domestic and euro-market, and therefore only for this period would the model suggest that there should be a close relationship between nominal domestic and euro-deutschemark rates. For this period, the calculated mean and variance of the differential (see Table E) were, respectively −0.15 and 0.03 percentage points, suggesting that the relationship between the rates was in fact very close.[3]

Table D
Minimum reserve ratios on time liabilities of West German banks[a]

	Liabilities to residents	Liabilities to non-residents	On growth of liabilities to non-residents
Applicable from the first day of			
1972 July		30.00	60
Aug.	11.75		
1973 Mar	13.55		
July		35.00	60
Oct.		35.00	60
Nov.	13.95		
1974 Jan.	13.25	30.00	0
Sept.	11.90		
Oct.	10.95	27.60	0
1975 June	10.40		
July	9.35	24.85	0
Aug.		9.35	0
1976 May	9.85	9.85	0
June	10.35	10.35	0
1977 Mar.	10.45	10.45	0
June	9.95	9.95	0
Sept.	8.95	8.95	0
1978 Jan.	8.95	15.00	80
Mar.	9.65		
June	9.00	9.00	0

[a] Reserve class DM 1,000 million and over from December 1970 to February 1977; thereafter DM 100 million and over.

Table E
Three-month euro-deutschemark rate less West German three-month inter-bank rate[a]

	Mean	Variance	Number of observations
1 January 1973– end-December 1973	− 6.42	5.89	46
1 January 1974– end-July 1975:			
Unadjusted for reserve changes	− 0.23	0.27	87
Adjusted for reserve changes	− 0.21	0.24	87
1 August 1975– end-December 1977	− 0.15	0.03	120
Total sample	− 1.32	6.97	253

[a] The interest rates used were Monday middle closing rates, where available.

Between January 1973 and January 1974, West German reserve requirements were discriminatory as between banks' domestic (13%–14%) and foreign-

[1] For example, euro-dollar and euro-deutschemark deposits could both be made with the same London bank.
[2] The interest rates used were the middle closing rates on Mondays where available.
[3] However, these statistics again indicate, contrary to that expected from the model, that the population mean was statistically different from zero. This may only reflect the fact that no allowance has been made for bid/offer spreads in either of the markets. These would be expected to increase the mean differential, i.e. to make it less negative, by about 0.13 percentage points depending on the spread margin in the West German inter-bank market.

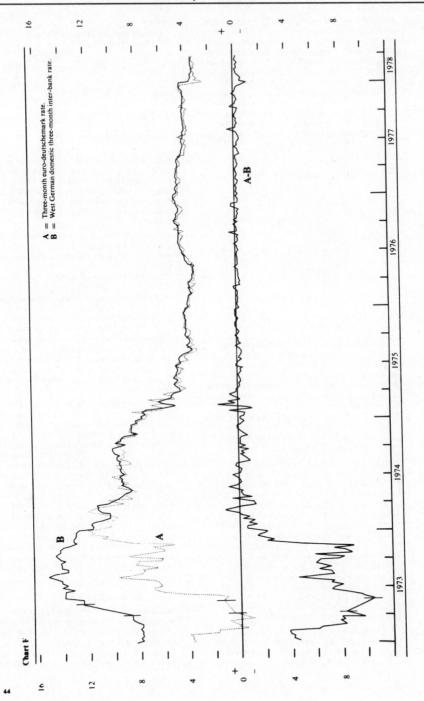

Chart F

A = Three-month euro-deutschemark rate.
B = West German domestic three-month inter-bank rate.

owned (35%) deutschemark liabilities. Further, a 60% reserve requirement was imposed on the growth of West German banks' time liabilities in deutschemarks to non-residents. Together these imposed a 95% reserve requirement on any increase in West German banks' time liabilities to non-residents and effectively discouraged West German domestic banks from borrowing deutschemarks from the euro-currency market. In terms of the model, these measures would remove the perfectly elastic segment of both the demand schedule for euro-deutschemarks and the demand schedule for forward dollars which would now become DD rather than DD (see Chart G). This latter

Chart G

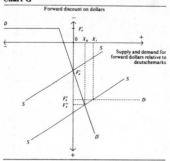

schedule is now inelastic over a much larger range, which allows the forward discount on dollars to widen in equilibrium, beyond F_d^*. The net effect is that the euro-deutschemark rate will fall below the rate at which domestic banks would have begun to find it profitable to borrow euro-deutschemarks in the absence of the discriminatory reserve requirement; the forward discount on dollars will widen to F_d^{**}; and there will be a smaller flow out of dollars into deutschemarks—X_0 rather than X_1 in the absence of the discriminatory reserve requirement (see Chart G).

Further, during the period February 1973 to February 1974 the West German Government under the Bardepot Law, imposed a 100% minimum reserve requirement (raised from 50% in February 1973; and subsequently reduced to 20% in February 1974 and removed in September 1974) against foreign loans contracted by West German companies, making it unprofitable for them to borrow externally. Together these measures appear to have effectively insulated the West German domestic market from short-term capital inflows during 1973, and there were very sharp deviations between the level of domestic and euro-deutschemark rates. The mean and variance of the differential during this period, -6.42 and 5.89 percentage points respectively, are sharply different from those in the 1975–77 period (see Table F).

In the immediate period after the removal of reserve requirements on the growth of West German banks' non-resident deutschemark deposits and the Bardepot regulations, the deviations between the rates were

Table F

Analysis of variance: euro-deutschemark/ domestic deutschemark differential

	1 January 1973– end-December 1973	1 January 1974– end-July 1975	
		Unadjusted for reserve changes	Adjusted for reserve changes
1 January 1974– end-July 1975:			
Unadjusted	$F_{68, 68} = 22.3$[a]		
Adjusted	$F_{68, 68} = 24.8$[a]	$F_{68, 68} = 1.1$	
1 August 1975– end-December 1977	$F_{65, 119} = 198.7$[a]	$F_{68, 119} = 9.0$[a]	$F_{68, 119} = 8.0$[a]

[a] Indicates that the variances, are significantly different at a 1% level of significance.

reduced, with the mean and variance of the differential narrowing to -0.23 and 0.27 percentage points respectively. However, these are still fairly large compared with the period after August 1975, possibly reflecting the discriminatory nature of reserve requirements on West German banks' foreign-owned liabilities.

In January 1978, when again faced with large capital inflows, the West German authorities once more imposed discriminatory reserve requirements on the level and growth of the deutschemark liabilities of West German banks to non-residents. A reserve requirement of 95% was once more effectively placed on any increase in West German banks' foreign-owned time liabilities. Following this, the euro-deutschemark rate dropped below the domestic inter-bank rate. However, it subsequently returned to a more 'normal' level. One possible reason may be that, in the absence of restrictions on foreign borrowing by West German companies, corporations may themselves have arbitraged between the domestic and euro-markets. The discriminatory reserve requirements were rescinded in June 1978.

These movements in the differential between the West German domestic and euro-deutschemark interest rates are broadly consistent with the model developed above. They suggest first that, in the absence of restrictions or discriminatory reserve requirements on foreign inflows, domestic banks will arbitrage with the euro-market to equalise the costs of borrowing in the two markets and consequently to place a lower limit on the euro-deutschemark rate and, when combined with the arbitrage activity of US banks, an upper arbitrage limit on the forward discount on dollars; and secondly that discriminatory domestic currency reserve requirements—particularly those which impose large penalties on the growth of foreign-owned liabilities—are effective in reducing flows to the domestic market, even though they may be, to some extent, circumvented by the arbitrage activities of corporations.

Some implications of the model

The above analysis has attempted to explain some of the systematic relationships which have been observed between domestic and euro-currency deposit rates. This has suggested that, in the absence of restrictions on the free flow of capital, domestic banks will arbitrage between the domestic and euro-currency markets so as to equalise. at the margin. the effective cost of loanable funds to banks in the two markets. Recent empirical experience is broadly consistent with this hypothesis.

An implication of this analysis relates to the applicability of certain frameworks which have been used to analyse the credit-creating potential of the euro-markets. Some of these treat the euro-market as if it were an autonomous or closed banking system;[1] or at least one with an independent set of interest rates.[2] Others suggest that, because euro-banks are not legally obliged to hold reserves against their deposits, any shift of deposits to the external market could increase, by the size of reserve balances released, the volume of loans that may be made from a given deposit base.[3]

The analysis of this article, however, suggests that the euro-currency market is not independent of domestic banking systems and that, if capital flows are unrestricted, interest rates in the two markets are extremely closely related. Indeed in such circumstances the euro-currency market appears very much as an integrated part of domestic banking systems, with even small changes in liquidity in one market generating compensating flows from the other. Furthermore, it is not the case that flows channelled through the euro-market automatically escape the imposition of domestic reserve requirements. A sizable proportion of euro-currency deposits are supplied by banks from their domestic currency deposits—as a rough and rather conservative estimate these may represent 20% of the market's net sources of funds—and at least some proportion of foreign currency deposits are lent by euro-banks to banks in the country of issue of the currency or converted by euro-banks into the domestic currency of the country where they operate. In either of these cases, the flows which pass through the euro-markets will attract domestic reserve requirements. Indeed funds which are channelled through the euro-currency market will only avoid domestic requirements when euro-banks intermediate directly between non-banks, and even then euro-banks will hold prudential reserves against the non-bank deposits.

One possible impact that the market may have—though one that is not readily measurable—is, like any efficient financial intermediary, to increase the velocity of circulation of money. However, if the euro-markets do have some impact on the velocity of circulation, it is not immediately clear that this is independent of domestic monetary policies—changes in domestic interest rates and reserve requirements will directly influence the level of euro-currency interest rates and hence the amount of credit extended by the euro-currency and domestic banking systems combined.

These considerations reinforce the main thesis of this article which is that the euro-markets are not independent of domestic banking systems and that it is misleading to study them in isolation.

[1] For example, models which attempt to apply fractional reserve multiplier analysis.
[2] For example, general equilibrium or portfolio balance approaches. See J. Niehans and J. Hewson. 'The Eurodollar Market and Monetary Theory'. *Journal of Money, Credit and Banking*. February 1976. pages 1–27, for a critical discussion of the various approaches.
[3] G. Dufey and I. H. Giddy. page 162 (see footnote [1] on page 35).

[17]

The Pricing of Syndicated Eurocurrency Credits

In recent years the syndicated Eurocurrency bank loan has become one of the most important instruments for international lending. These publicly announced loans have grown rapidly, totaling over $80 billion in 1979, and now comprise approximately half of all Eurocurrency credits. Syndicated credits are an important pillar in the recycling process whereby surpluses from oil-exporting countries (in the form of deposits) are channeled to oil-importing countries (in the form of loans) to finance their deficits.

The pricing of syndicated Eurocurrency credits is a subject of particular interest to banks and their supervisors. The loans are generally priced as a spread over the interbank interest rate in the Euromarkets. The interest rate paid by the borrower is adjusted every three or six months as market rates vary. Spreads for all borrowers have narrowed sharply from those prevailing in 1974-75, while maturities have lengthened. There are concerns that, at the rather narrow spreads currently prevailing (⅜ to 1½ percent, depending on the borrower), these loans may not yield an adequate return on bank capital after adjusting for risk and expenses. To the extent that this is true, the capacity of commercial banks to continue to play an important role in recycling could be impaired.

This article investigates the pricing of syndicated loans. It examines the factors which analytically should be important and empirically are important in determining the spread. The paper does not attempt to hypothesize whether the spreads are in some sense correct or reasonable; instead, it concentrates on the events and influences that have contributed to the currently narrow spreads.

An overview of the sydicated loan market

A syndicated credit is a loan in which a group of financial institutions makes funds available on common conditions to a borrower. This type of lending commonly occurs in both the Eurocurrency market and in the United States domestic market, although in the latter it is a bit less frequent and is done under slightly different institutional arrangements. In the domestic market, as a normal part of business practice, a corporation will usually have a banking relationship with a number of institutions. If the corporate borrower needs more funds than a single bank can or will provide, rather than opting for a syndication the borrower will often draw down its credit lines at other banks, sometimes at less favorable terms. By contrast, in the Eurocurrency market, if a given borrower needs a large amount of funds, a syndicate will usually be formed and all banks in the syndicate will participate in the loan on the same terms.

Growth and development of the market

The syndicated Eurocredit is a relatively new market development dating from the late 1960s. Prior to this innovation, large Euromarket financings were all in the form of Eurobonds. Bank credits were, just as now, priced as a percentage over the interbank interest rate but were issued by a single bank. Hence, the size of the credits were constrained by the prudent lending limits of the bank. Using the syndication mechanism, credits of over $1 billion have been handled with relative ease.

Since its inception, the market has grown rapidly from $4.7 billion in 1970 to $82.8 billion in 1979 as shown in the table. This twentyfold increase does not all represent new money being made available, since there were considerable refinancings in 1978 and 1979 when spreads narrowed. Nonetheless, the growth is impressive. Syndicated credits now provide somewhat more than half of the medium- and long-term borrowings in international capital markets. (Eurobonds and foreign bonds account for the rest.) However, they accounted for more than 85 percent of the medium- and long-term funds for developing countries and 98 percent for centrally planned economies in the 1973-79 period.

In the wake of successive oil price increases and the resulting balance-of-payments deficits for most nonoil-producing less developed countries (LDCs), the Eurocurrency market allows for recycling of funds to many governments that have little or no access to other international capital markets. The relative share of non-OPEC (Organization of Petroleum Exporting Countries) LDC borrowing follows very closely the pattern of aggregate current account deficits of these countries. Non-OPEC LDCs accounted for 21 percent of the market in 1972-73, rising to 39 percent in 1975, dropping to 32 percent by 1977, and rising again to 43 percent in 1979. The aggregate deficit for non-OPEC LDCs was approximately $7 billion in 1972-73, rising to $32 billion by 1975. As a result of the declining real price of oil, and the recovery of the developed countries from the 1974-75 recession, the aggregate deficit declined to $14 billion in 1977. But for 1979 the aggregate deficit is estimated at about $35 billion and is projected to go up to about $50 billion-$55 billion in 1980.

The Communist countries have also increased their commercial bank borrowing dramatically since 1972-73. The bulk of this borrowing has been done by East Germany, Hungary, and Poland. It was widely believed that the Soviet invasion in Afghanistan early this year would adversely affect the borrowing ability of the Communist countries. So far the evidence is inconclusive. Rumania and Hungary recently borrowed on terms which, taking into account market conditions, are no different from those they would have obtained in 1979. However, the volume of loans to Eastern bloc countries is much lower than in previous years.

Up until late 1979, OPEC countries were also active borrowers in the Eurocredit market. The bulk of the OPEC borrowing was done by the group of countries known as high absorbers, those with current account deficits and small current account surpluses. The low-absorbing group, consisting of the countries with the massive current account surpluses, namely, Saudi Arabia, Kuwait, Libya, Qatar, and the United Arab Emirates, do relatively little of the borrowing. OPEC borrowing is used primarily to finance energy-related and other development projects.

As the syndicated loan market has matured, it has become much less concentrated. While in 1970 the top ten borrowers accounted for 84 percent of total Eurocredits, by 1974 this figure had declined to 66 percent and by 1979 was only 54 percent (Chart 1).

Syndicated Eurocredits comprise only about half of Eurocurrency bank lending. The other 50 percent is lent by individual banks, is not publicized, and is contracted for a shorter maturity than its syndicated counterpart. These credits are primarily to the private sector for trade financing or internationally related business loans.

Why are syndications so prevalent in the Eurocurrency market?

Syndicated Eurocredits have emerged as a popular

New Syndicated Eurocurrency Bank Credits

In billions of dollars

Group	1970	1971	1972	1973	1974	1975	1976	1977	1978	1979	January-April 1980
Total	4.7	4.0	6.8	21.9	29.3	21.0	28.8	41.8	70.2	82.8	18.4
Industrialized countries	4.2	2.6	4.1	13.8	20.7	7.3	11.3	17.4	29.1	27.5	9.2
Non-OPEC LDCs	0.3	0.9	1.5	4.5	6.3	8.2	11.0	13.5	26.9	35.4	4.9
OPEC countries	0.1	0.4	0.9	2.8	1.1	2.9	4.0	7.5	10.4	12.6	3.1
Communist countries	0	0.1	0.3	0.8	1.2	2.6	2.5	3.4	3.8	7.3	0.8

Because of rounding, figures may not add to totals.

Source: Morgan Guaranty Trust Company, *World Financial Markets.*

vehicle for international lending because they contain advantages from the point of view of both lenders and borrowers. From the lenders viewpoint, the syndication procedure is a means for banks to diversify some of the unique risks that arise in international lending. In part, these risks reflect the heavy concentration of public-sector borrowers in the market. Information compiled by the World Bank since 1975 indicates that credits to the public sector comprise approximately 75 percent of the syndicated lending.

The legal protection available to a bank is much different if a private borrower defaults as opposed to the case in which a public borrower defaults. If a private borrower defaults or otherwise fails to fulfill the obligations stipulated in the loan agreement, creditors can pursue various legal remedies. There is a considerable legal framework in each country to safeguard the claims of creditors if a borrower has declared bankruptcy. When commercial banks lend to public-sector borrowers, there is much more uncertainty about legal recourse. For instance, there are questions about which public-sector borrowers are covered by sovereign immunity.

There also are special political uncertainties, including the risk, however remote, that a public-sector borrower will choose not to repay loans from individual banks or a group of banks in a particular country. The syndication process tends to magnify the penalty associated with selective defaults. In the case of a widely syndicated loan from banks in several nations, unwillingness to repay debts could effectively preclude the borrower from entering the credit market in the future. It would be surprising if a lender in the earlier syndicate would be willing to participate and other lenders would be reluctant. In addition, unwillingness to repay debts would bring political pressure from several countries as opposed to only one or two.

In addition to developing syndication procedures, banks have taken other steps to protect themselves against these risks. For example, the risk of selective default on credits encourages banks to include a cross-default clause in the loan agreement. This clause states that, if one public borrower from a country defaults, the loans of other public borrowers from that country may be called into default as well. In that case, the loans of those borrowers become due and payable.

To recapitulate, syndication of public credits allows banks to reduce risk in two ways. First, it allows banks to diversify their loans to the public sector, which is more essential than with loans to the private sector due to the banks' lack of control over and protection against default by sovereign entities. Second, it provides more protection against selective defaults.

The syndication procedure is advantageous from

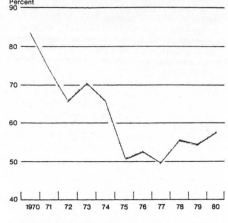

Chart 1

Percentage of Syndicated Eurocredit Market Captured by the Top Ten Borrowers

Percent

Source: Morgan Guaranty Trust Company, World Financial Markets.

the lenders' viewpoint as it allows different-sized banks to function in the market simultaneously. That is because a Eurocurrency loan is underwritten by a small group of banks who resell portions of the loan to other banks. The larger banks can underwrite a loan and earn underwriting fees. Smaller banks can simply purchase participations from the underwriting banks.

From the borrowers' viewpoint, syndication allows for the efficient arrangement of a larger amount of funds than any single lender can feasibly supply. This factor is crucial in explaining the popularity of shared credits in both the domestic market and the Eurocurrency market. In the latter, however, syndicated lending becomes less of a convenience and more of a necessity. The financing needs imposed by the recycling process, coupled with the lack of alternative financing arrangements in the Eurocurrency market, create the demand on the part of borrowers for huge bank loans. In the United States domestic market, if a business needs a large amount of long-term funding, bank loans are only one, albeit often the most viable, of several options. The firm may also arrange for debt or equity financing. In external markets, however, there are fewer options. Industrial country borrowers, both governmental and private, may have access to the international bond markets, but LDC borrowers by and large do not. The only alternative source of financing for the latter group is the syndicated Eurocredit market.

The underwriting procedure used in the syndication of Eurocurrency credits may allow the borrower to obtain better terms than those that would otherwise be available. The syndicated credit is essentially a hybrid instrument, a cross between traditional bank lending and the underwriting function of investment banking. By underwriting, major banks show their confidence in the credit, thereby making it more attractive to smaller financial institutions. This blending of the investment banking and commercial banking functions is prohibited in many national markets including the United States, Japan, and Italy. In recent years, however, there has been some blurring of these activities in the United States. There are several examples of commercial banking practices which are not strictly speaking underwriting activities but which involve syndication procedures. Moreover, municipal debt is often underwritten by commercial banks. In the London market, where a majority of the Eurocurrency syndications are arranged, underwriting is standard for both commercial banks and their merchant banking affiliates. These affiliates operate much like investment banks in the United States.

The syndication procedure[1]

There are generally three levels of banks in a syndicate: the lead banks, the managing banks, and the participating banks.[2] Most loans are led by one or two major banks who negotiate to obtain a mandate to raise funds from the borrower. Often a potential borrower will set a competitive bidding procedure to determine which lead bank or banks will receive the mandate to organize the loan.

After the preliminary stages of negotiation with a borrower, the lead bank will begin to assemble a management group to underwrite the loan. The management group may be in place before the mandate is received, or may be assembled immediately afterward, depending on the loan. The lead bank is normally expected to underwrite a share at least as large as that of any other lender. If the loan cannot be underwritten on the initial terms, it must be renegotiated or

the lead bank must be willing to take a larger share into its own portfolio than originally planned.

Once the management group is firmly in place and the lead bank has received a mandate from the borrower, a placement memorandum will be prepared by the lead bank and the loan will be marketed to other banks who may be interested in taking up shares (the participating banks). This placement memorandum describes the transaction and provides information about the borrower. The statistical information regarding the financial health of the borrower given in the memorandum is generally provided by the borrower. The placement memorandum emphasizes that reading it is not a substitute for an independent credit review by the participating banks. Bank supervisory authorities normally require sufficient lending information to be lodged in the bank to allow bank management to make a reasonable appraisal of the credit.

In a successful syndication, once the marketing to interested participants is completed, the lead and managing banks will keep 50 to 70 percent of their initial underwriting share.

Not all credits are sold to participants. In smaller credits to frequent borrowers, club loans are often arranged. In a club loan the lead bank and managers fund the entire loan and no placement memorandum is required. This type of credit is most common in periods of market uncertainty when all but the largest multinational banks are reluctant to do business.

It takes anywhere from fifteen days to three months to arrange a syndication, with six weeks considered the norm. Generally speaking, the more familiar the borrower, the more quickly the terms can be set and the placement memorandum prepared; the smaller the credit, the shorter is the time needed for negotiating and marketing.

After the loan is arranged, one of the banks serves as agent to compute the appropriate interest rate charges, to receive service payments, to disburse these to individual participants, and to inform them if there are any problems with the loan. The lead bank usually serves as agent, but another member of the management group may do so.

The most common type of syndicated loan is a term loan in which the funds can be drawn down by the borrower within a specified period of time after the loan agreement has been signed (the drawdown period). The loan is usually repaid according to an amortization schedule, which varies from loan to loan. For some loans it may begin as soon as the loan is drawn down. For other loans, amortization may not begin until as long as five years after the loan agreement has been signed. The period before repayment of principal begins is known as the grace period. This is one of the most

---

[1] A more detailed description of the syndication procedure can be found in an article by Henry Terrell and Michael G. Martinson, "Market Practices in Syndicated Bank Euro-currency Lending", *Bankers Magazine* (November 1978).

[2] In some of the larger credits, there are four or more levels of banks: the lead banks, the co-managers, the managing banks, and one or more levels of participating banks. The co-managing banks underwrite more than a prespecified amount of funds.

important points of negotiation between a borrower and a lead bank, and borrowers are normally willing to pay a wider spread in order to obtain a longer grace period.

Another type of loan less frequently used is a revolving credit. The borrower is given a line of credit which can be drawn down and repaid with more flexibility than the term loan. The borrower must pay a fee for the undrawn portion of the credit line.

The vast majority of syndicated credits are denominated in dollars, but loans in German marks, Swiss francs, Japanese yen, and other currencies are also available.

The pricing of syndicated loans
Interest on syndicated loans is usually computed by adding a spread to the London interbank offer rate (LIBOR). LIBOR is the rate at which banks lend funds to other banks operating in the Euromarket. Occasionally, however, a loan may be priced as a spread over the United States prime rate. Less frequently, pricing is done both as a percentage over LIBOR and over the United States prime rate; the banks have the option to shift from LIBOR to prime pricing at their discretion. Pricing over the United States prime rate occurs when the syndicate is comprised primarily of United States banks who prefer to book the loan out of their head office rather than at an offshore branch. Strictly speaking, dollar loans booked in the United States are not Eurocurrency loans. However, these loans may be organized by offshore merchant bank subsidiaries.

The spread is negotiated with the borrower at the outset and either remains constant over the life of the loan or changes after a set number of years.[3] For example, a fifteen-year loan was recently syndicated at a spread of ⅜ percent over LIBOR for the first five years, ½ percent for the next five years, and ⅝ percent for the last five years. Loans priced over the United States prime rate generally carry a spread of ⅛ to ¼ percent less than loans priced over LIBOR.

---

[3] An innovation in the pricing of syndicated credits has recently surfaced: a loan with a floating spread. This novel mechanism is being tested for a relatively small loan. For the first year the spread was set at ⅞ percent over LIBOR, but after the first year the floating concept takes over. Each year the banks in the syndicate will quote a spread based on their assessment of what the market would require of the borrower if it was to seek a loan for the amount and maturity outstanding. The actual spread will be a weighted average of the quotes, with a maximum of 1¾ percent and a minimum of ⅝ percent. If the borrower objects to the spread quoted by the banks, he has the option of repaying the loan without notice.

This floating rate spread has advantages for both borrower and lenders. The borrower will benefit because each requote will be for a shorter maturity, that is, seven years in twelve months, six years in twenty-four months, etc. Lenders, on the other hand, can adjust the spread if the creditworthiness of the borrower changes. In addition, the lenders will be in a position to take advantage of any widening of spreads that may occur in the market.

The LIBOR is changing continuously. However, the rate on any particular loan is readjusted only every three or six months. This is known as pricing on a rollover basis. The borrower is usually given the choice between a three-month or a six-month readjustment period. A six-month period is normally selected because in a period of generally rising interest rates, as had been the case until recently, it is desirable for a borrower to lock in rates for as long a period as possible. The new base rate is calculated two days prior to the rollover date as the average of the offer rates of several reference banks in the syndicate. The reference banks are carefully specified in the loan agreement.

The spread above the LIBOR paid by the borrower understates the bank's actual return on a loan. The LIBOR is generally ⅛ to ¼ percent above the rate at which banks purchase funds from large depositors (the bid rate). The London interbank bid (LIBB) rate is roughly equal to the interest rate on certificates of deposit (CDs) in the United States domestic market, adjusted for reserve requirements. In some situations the bid rate may even exaggerate the cost of funds to Eurobanks. The main example of this occurs when a single depositor (or group of closely related depositors) already hold significant funds in the bank and would like to deposit more.

Other fees
In addition to the interest costs on a Eurocurrency loan, there are also commitment fees, front-end fees, and occasionally an annual agent's fee. Commitment fees are charged to the borrower as a percentage of the undrawn portion of the credit and are typically ½ percent annually, imposed on both term loans and revolving credits. Front-end management fees are one-time charges negotiated in advance and imposed when the loan agreement is signed. Fees are usually in the range of ½ to 1 percent of the value of the loan.[4] These front-end fees include participation fees and management fees. The participation fees are divided among all banks in relation to their share of the loan. The management fees are divided between the underwriting banks and the lead bank.[5] The agent's fee, if applicable, is usually a yearly charge but may occasionally be paid at the outset. These fees are relatively small; the agent's fee on a large credit may run $10,000 per annum.

To protect their margins, banks require all payments of principal and interest to be made after taxes im-

---

[4] Borrowers are sometimes willing to pay higher fees in return for a lower spread on the loan.

[5] See Terrell and Martinson, *loc. cit.*, for a more complete description of the method by which the front-end fees are divided among the financial institutions.

posed in the borrower's country have been paid. If those taxes are not creditable against the banks' home country taxes, the borrower must adjust his payments so that the banks receive the same net repayment. The decision as to whether the borrower or lender absorbs any additional taxes imposed by the country in which the loan is booked is negotiated between the parties.

Also, usually inserted is a reserve requirement clause, stipulating that an adjustment will be made if the cost of funds increases because reserve requirements are imposed or increased. This clause was invoked for loans booked in the home office of United States banks when marginal reserve requirements were imposed in late 1979.

There is generally no prepayment penalty on Eurocredits. In 1978 and 1979 when spreads narrowed, many borrowers chose to refinance the loans initially obtained in 1975 and 1976 at a higher spread. Banks then tried to impose prepayment penalty clauses on new loans, but borrowers were reluctant to go along with these. At least for the moment, banks have backed off because prepayment penalties have little relevance in a period of low spreads.

The charges on syndicated loans may be summarized as follows:

Annual payments = (LIBOR + spread) ×
amount of loan drawn
+ (Commitment fee) ×
amount of loan undrawn
+ tax adjustment (if any)
+ Annual agent's fee (if any)

Front-end charges = participation fee ×
face amount of loan
+ management fee ×
face amount of loan
+ initial agent's fee (if any)

Front-end changes are an important component of the banks' total return on a credit. Consider a $100 million seven-year credit with no grace period. If the loan is priced at 100 basis points over a LIBOR of 10 percent, annual payments of interest and principal repayment total slightly over $21 million. A 1 percent fee requires that $1 million be paid to the banks in the syndicate at the outset. This raises the effective interest to the borrower from 11 percent to 11.31 percent per annum. If banks' paid, on average, 9.75 percent for their funds, the front-end fees increase their margin on the loan from 125 basis points to 156 basis points. This represents a 25 percent increment to their return on a credit.

Trends in spreads and maturities

The history of syndicated credits may be divided into four periods, two "borrowers markets" and two "lenders markets" depending on terms and conditions. During borrowers markets, spreads were low and maturities were long—attractive terms from the point of view of the borrowers. During lenders markets, the situation was reversed.

- Lenders market, 1970 to late 1972
- Borrowers market, late 1972 to mid-1974
- Lenders market, mid-1974 to mid-1977
- Borrowers market, mid-1977 to present.

This division is depicted in Chart 2 where a time series for spreads and maturities from 1972 through the third quarter of 1979 is shown for the four major groups of borrowers: industrialized, OPEC low absorbers, high-income developing, and low-income developing.[6] Information on loans syndicated prior to 1972 are not available on a basis consistent with later data.

The lenders market from 1970 through late 1972 is best characterized as a period of market development. Spreads remained relatively constant during 1970 and 1971, and many borrowers entered the market for the first time.

By mid-1972, lenders had developed confidence in the market, credit volume rose, spreads began to narrow, and maturities lengthened. Bullet loans—credits in which there is no amortization over the life of the loan and the principal is entirely repaid at maturity—made their debut in the market during this period. This borrowers market continued until the Herstatt collapse in June 1974. The market bottomed out in mid- to late 1973. In the third quarter of 1973, weighted average spreads for the industrialized and high-income developing countries were 0.68 and 0.93 percent, respectively, coupled with maturities of nine and eleven and a half years. After the quadrupling of oil prices, there was a small but perceptible tightening of terms, as loan demand outstripped the supply of funds at the record low spreads. Even so, by the summer of 1974, spreads were low and maturities were averaging about eight and a half years.

All this changed, however, after the failure of Bankhaus Herstatt and the subsequent demise of Franklin

---

[6] This classification scheme is similar to the one used by the World Bank. High-income developing countries are those the World Bank classified as high, upper, and intermediate middle developing at the end of 1978. Low-income developing countries are those the World Bank classified as lower middle developing as well as lower developing at end-1978. Industrialized and oil-exporting countries correspond to the World Bank group with those titles.

National Bank. Depositors reacted by seeking to hold only very short-term funds in the safest and largest banks. Responding to this sudden shift in depositors' attitudes, banks sought to shorten the maturity of their lending. They were unwilling to commit themselves to long-term loans at prevailing spreads. The result was a sharp tightening of lending terms; the weighted average spreads for industrialized countries doubled from 63 basis points in the second quarter of 1974 to 129 basis points in the fourth quarter. The deterioration in terms for the OPEC borrowers and the developing countries was equally dramatic.

In 1975, spreads widened further to the 1½ to 2 percent range and maturities dropped to about five and a half years. Very few new loans with a maturity longer than eight years were agreed to by lending institutions. This lenders market lasted until mid-1977. At that point, confidence in the market began to strengthen as a result of the banking system's successful role in the recycling process. In addition, German and Japanese banks entered the syndicated market on a large scale,

vigorously soliciting business. Hence, spreads began to narrow. The weighted average spread for industrialized countries dropped from 1.25 percent in the third quarter of 1977 to 0.79 percent in the first quarter of 1978. Spreads for the developing countries fell correspondingly. By the fourth quarter of 1977, average maturities had lengthened to nearly seven years.

The borrowers market which began in mid-1977 is still present. In 1978 and the first three quarters of 1979, maturities rose and spreads narrowed further. By the third quarter of 1979, spreads for high-income developing countries reached a record low of 0.86 percent. But, in the wake of the freeze on Iranian assets in November 1979 and the series of oil price increases in late 1979 and 1980, market perceptions of risk have been altered and a two-layered market has developed. In this period of market uncertainty as reflected in the slowing of new syndication activity, prime borrowers continue to borrow on terms not dissimilar to what they were receiving late last year (spreads of ⅜ to ⅝ percent). Other borrowers are, however, confronted with

Chart 2

Spreads and Maturities on Syndicated Loans

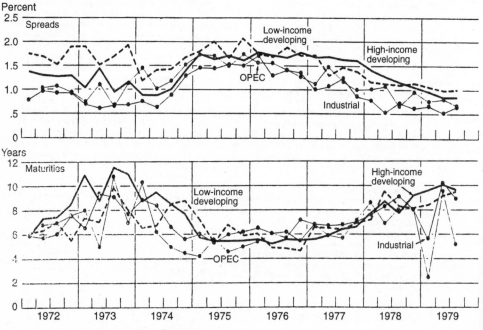

Source: World Bank, Borrowing in International Capital Markets.

somewhat higher spreads and lower maturities than in mid-1979.[7]

Determinants of spreads
There are several basic questions that consistently appear in any analysis of spreads.

- What causes a borrowers market or a lenders market?
- How are interest rates, spreads, and maturities related?
- What are the systematic differences in spreads between groups of countries?

This section considers certain economic factors which are important in the determination of spreads for syndicated Eurocredits: the level of interest rates, the volatility of interest rates, maturity, and risk. There are, however, other important factors which are difficult to quantify, such as increased competition from German and Japanese banks and relative loan demand pressures at home. These supply side influences were not explicitly included in the statistical analysis.

Level of interest rates
Narrow spreads are associated with a high level of interest rates for two reasons. The first reason is that banks would be expected to equate the marginal cost of all sources of funds. In periods of high nominal interest rates, the opportunity cost of reserve requirements is higher. Hence, the absolute differential between Euromarket and domestic market interest rates will widen because the former has no reserve requirements. Thus, more funds will be shifted into the Euromarket and, with an unchanged demand for funds, this would be sufficient to reduce spreads.

The second reason that a high level of nominal interest rates implies a narrower absolute spread relates to the return on capital. A bank should be concerned about the consolidated return on capital. It can be shown that, when LIBOR rises, the rate of return on capital increases. Thus, if the cost of capital remains

[7] Another factor contributing to the slight tightening of terms for some borrowers is the freeze and slowdown of Japanese bank participation in the market. In October 1979 the Japanese Ministry of Finance effectively banned Japanese participation in syndicated credit until April 1980. They were able to reenter the market in April, but they are limited to an estimated $5 billion in credits for April 1980-March 1981, only a small fraction of their participation in the first nine months of 1979. Since the market is relatively competitive, there have been enough non-Japanese banks willing to participate in syndicates so that this has had little influence on the spreads of most borrowers. However, because of internally imposed country exposure limits, the slowdown of lending by Japanese banks has had an adverse effect on the spread for some heavy borrowers.

constant, spreads will be lowered to maintain the same rate of return on capital. The rate of return on capital is computed by assuming the loan is funded proportionately by capital and borrowed funds. Thus, if we hypothesize a capital/total assets ratio of 5 percent, this implies that the average loan is funded 95 percent from deposits and 5 percent from capital. Assuming the bank has no overhead or loan-processing costs and it purchases funds in the interbank market at LIBOR, the return on capital is derived as follows:

$$\text{Return on capital} = [\text{return on the loan} - \\ (\text{the cost of deposits}) \times \\ (\text{deposits/assets})] \\ \times \text{assets/capital}$$

All terms are expressed in percentage per annum. If the capital/asset ratio is 0.05, the spread is 1 percent and the LIBOR is 16 percent, we have:

$$\text{Rate of return on capital} = [\text{LIBOR} + 1 - \\ (0.95 \times \text{LIBOR})] \times 20 \\ = 1.8 \times 20 = 36$$

Assuming a marginal tax rate of, say, 50 percent, this 36 percent pretax rate of return is equivalent to an aftertax rate of return of 18 percent. If the capital/asset ratio and spread remain constant, and the LIBOR increases to 20 percent, the before-tax rate of return is now 40 percent and the aftertax rate of return is 20 percent. If the bank wished to achieve an 18 percent aftertax return on capital with a LIBOR of 20 percent, it would charge a spread of 80 basis points.

Since both effects work in the same direction, in theory higher interest rates should be associated unambiguously with lower spreads. Empirical work, shown in the appendix, confirms the theoretical hypothesis. Each 100 basis point (or 1 percentage point) increase in the level of rates over the relevant range will, all other things being equal, narrow spreads by 7 basis points.

Variation of interest rates
The more volatile are interest rates, the larger should be the spreads on Eurocurrency loans because banks do not eliminate interest rate risk by perfectly matching assets and liabilities. Since liabilities on average have shorter maturity than the rollover period for assets, the bank may have to fund the assets for the remainder of the rollover period with more expensive money than anticipated. The evidence indicates that this is important. Bank of England data for November 1979 show that 23 percent of foreign currency liabilities

Risk Protection Features of Syndicated Eurocredits

One of the most interesting features of a syndicated Eurocurrency loan is the degree it is tailored to minimize the risks that financial institutions participating in this market would otherwise face. Compared with the fixed rate credit arranged by an individual bank, the rollover syndicated Eurocredit reduces risk in several notable ways, as summarized below.

Lending Risks

Risk	Source of risk	Risk reduction strategy
Country risk	The ability and willingness of borrowers within a country to meet their obligations	Syndication of the credit and diversification of bank's loan portfolio
Credit risk	The ability of an entity to repay its debts	Syndication of the credit and diversification of bank's loan portfolio
Interest risk	Mismatched maturities coupled with unpredictable movements in interest rates	Matching assets to liabilities by pricing credits on a rollover basis
Regulatory risk	Imposition of reserve requirements or taxes on the banks	A clause in the contract which forces the borrowers to bear this risk

of banks in the United Kingdom (including a number of United States bank and other Euromarket participants) was for eight days or less, 19 percent between eight days and one month, and 28 percent between one and three months. Thus, the vast majority of the liabilities which fund these loans are of a shorter maturity than the rollover period for the loans themselves. A bank will tend to demand a risk premium for incurring this interest rate risk.

Empirical work supports this supposition. Each 0.01 increase in the quarterly coefficient of variation (the standard deviation as computed from daily figures, divided by the mean) translates into a 3 basis point increase in spreads.

Maturity
The relationship between maturity and spread depends on whether one is examining individual loan data at a single point in time or aggregate data across time. In a cross-sectional analysis, which examines individual loan data at a single point in time, there should be a positive relationship between the two variables. With other factors constant, a longer maturity loan should carry a wider spread in order to leave the lenders indifferent. This is true because, if spreads widen, lenders are locked into a long maturity loan at the old spreads. If spreads narrow, the borrower can refinance. In addition, bankers attempt to analyze both the economic and

political risks associated with a loan. It is more difficult to analyze the economic and political risks over a twelve-year horizon than over a five-year horizon. Thus, for each additional year of maturity, lenders will require compensation in terms of spread, fees, or grace period. Borrowers also prefer longer maturities and are willing to compensate lenders for such a loan because they are assured of the availability of funds at a prespecified spread, even if market conditions tighten. If market conditions loosen, a borrower can often refinance.

However, by averaging spreads and maturities for each risk group in each quarter, the trade-off on an individual loan is not visible. At any point in time, a lender might be willing to make a six-year loan to the borrowers of a certain risk class at ⅝ percent, an eight-year loan at ¾ percent, or a ten-year loan at ⅞ percent. If equal numbers of borrowers opted for each maturity, in the aggregate we would simply observe an eight-year loan at ¾ percent.

Looking at aggregate data on spreads and maturities over time, as this article has done, there should be an inverse relationship between the two variables as maturity will serve as a proxy for market confidence. During periods of low confidence in the market, spreads should be wide and maturities short. For example, in the two years following Herstatt, banks were worried about the continued availability of funds. This was reflected in wide spreads and low maturities.

In fact, it was found that each one-year increase in maturity is associated with a 9 basis point decline in spread.

Risk

The higher the perceived risk associated with a borrower, the greater the debt service difficulties anticipated by the lenders, hence the wider the spread that would be required. Thus, low-absorbing OPEC borrowers would be expected to pay a bit more than industrialized countries, high-income developing countries would be expected to pay more for borrowings than OPEC borrowers, and low-income developing countries would be expected to pay more than high-income developing countries. The data seem to bear this out. Holding other factors constant, OPEC countries borrow at 15 basis points more than industrialized borrowers, high-income developing countries at 38 basis points more, and low-income developing countries at 48 basis points more.

Risk premiums may be related to maturity. Since there is less certainty about the economic and political state of a given economy ten years from now, as opposed to next year, a risk-averse bank may charge a maturity-related risk premium to less than prime customers. It was found that for high-income developing countries each additional year adds to the spread 5 basis points over what an industrialized country would pay. Thus, on a seven-year loan, a high-income developing country would pay 35 basis points more than an industrialized country. For low-income developing countries, each additional year adds to the spread 7 basis points over what an industrialized country would pay. Thus, for a seven-year loan, a low-income developing country would pay almost 50 basis points more than an industrialized country. For OPEC countries, each additional year adds 2 basis points or about 15 points on a seven-year loan.

The perceived risk of lending to nonoil LDCs declined during 1975-79, as reflected in the spread differential between industrialized countries and nonoil LDCs. The large OPEC surplus in 1974 evaporated more rapidly than even the optimists in the market had predicted, and nonoil LDC deficits declined sharply in real terms from their 1975 peak of $32 billion. In addition, a number of nonoil LDCs—major borrowers like Korea and Brazil, for example—have developed their export potential rapidly. However, with the renewed widening of the OPEC surplus, the corresponding deficits for the LDCs are likely to be larger and more long lasting than had been thought. This is leading to a reassessment of relative risk.

Summary and Outlook

This article has attempted to explore the factors which are theoretically and empirically important in the pricing of syndicated loans. It was found that, if the level of interest rates increases, the volatility of rates declines, or, if the maturities on loans lengthen, then the spreads on syndicated loans tend to narrow. Banks clearly recognize risk differentials between borrowers. Those from OPEC countries borrow at about 15 basis points more than those from industrialized countries. Those from high-income developing and low-income developing countries pay a risk premium of nearly 40 and 50 basis points, respectively.

Thus far in 1980 there has been a slight tightening of terms for many borrowers. With the United States moving into a recession, interest rates have fallen. This has caused spreads to widen. The October 1979 decision of the Federal Reserve to place greater emphasis on bank reserves in day-to-day operations and less emphasis on short-term movements in the Federal funds rate resulted in wider interest rate swings. This increased rate volatility has been reflected in wider spreads. Maturities have dropped as well, demonstrating concern on the part of some lenders about the effects on the banking system of another round of large-scale deficit financing.

In the next two or three quarters, spreads on loans to a number of LDC borrowers could widen considerably more than spreads for industrialized borrowers. Nonoil LDCs already have a large amount of debt which must be serviced, as the outstanding debt of developing countries has more than doubled since 1974. Furthermore, this debt is concentrated in the largest United States and foreign banks, some of which are reviewing lending limits for certain borrowers. Consequently, banks may be more hesitant to participate in large new syndications unless lending margins widen.

Laurie S. Goodman

Appendix: Spreads

It is postulated that spread depends upon the level of interest rates, the volatility of interest rates, the maturity of the credits and risk variables as shown in equation (1).

(1) Spread = f (interest rates, volatility, maturity, risk)

The construction of a series which captures the volatility of interest rates without also capturing their level presents a bit of a problem. Using the variance or standard deviation of interest rates over the quarter is not satisfactory, as we would expect either to be highly correlated with the level of interest rates. For example, a standard deviation of 0.5 may reflect a great deal of volatility when interest rates are 5 percent, and reflect relatively little volatility when interest rates are 13 percent. Using the coefficient of variation (which is the standard deviation divided by the mean) rather than the variance or standard deviation mitigates this problem.

To investigate the impact of the variables mentioned above, a pooled cross-section time series regression of the following form was performed:

(2) Spread = constant + b_1 rate + b_2 CV rate
         + b_3 mat + b_4 D_1 + b_5 D_2 + b_6 D_3

where:

rate	= the six-month Eurodollar interest rate
CV rate	= coefficient of variation of the six-month Eurodollar interest rate
Mat	= maturity
D_1	= 1 if the observation is that of a high-income developing country; 0 otherwise
D_2	= 1 if the observation is that of a low-income developing country; 0 otherwise
D_3	= 1 if the observation is that of an oil-exporting surplus country; 0 otherwise

The dummy variables were used to investigate if, on average, there are systematic differences in spreads between groups of countries. The coefficients on the dummy variables can be interpreted as risk premiums over what industrialized borrowers would pay.

The weighted average spread and maturity for each of the four groups (industrialized, OPEC, high-income developing, and low-income developing) were calculated from the World Bank's *Borrowing in International Capital Markets* data base. Regressions were performed from the third quarter of 1973 to the third quarter of 1979, and the results are given below (t statistics in parenthesis):

(3) Spread = 2.093 − 0.072 rate + 3.092 CV rate
         (16.00) (−5.59)   (2.49)
         −0.086 mat + 0.376 D_1
         (−5.25)   (5.62)
         + 0.484 D_2 + 0.147 D_3
         (7.25)   (2.09)

R^2 (adj) = 0.635; S.E. = 0.236; DW = 1.36

Note that all coefficients have the expected sign, all are significant at the 5 percent level, and the regression explains 64 percent of the spread. While strictly speaking this Durbin-Watson statistic is meaningless, as this is a pooled cross-section time series, it may indicate autocorrelation as, out of 99 error differences, only three are across groups.

This relationship is flawed because it does not take account of changes in relative risk over time. To handle that problem, a slightly different equation was estimated. The dummy variables were weighted by maturity, on the assumption that the risk premium for less than prime customers should be higher for longer maturities. The regression results are:

(4) Spread = 2.365 − 0.078 rate + 3.080 CV rate
         (10.32) (−6.13)   (2.51)
         −0.118 mat + 0.051 (D_1 x mat)
         (−6.97)   (5.74)
         +0.069 (D_2 X mat)
         (7.64)
         +0.023 ((D_3 x mat)
         (2.40)

R^2 (adj) = 0.644; S.E. = 0.234; DW = 1.42

Note that all the coefficients are the correct sign, all are significant at the 5 percent level, and the regression explains 64 percent of the dependent variable. The Durbin-Watson improves marginally and the R^2 and standard error remain basically unchanged.

[18]

"The Future of Banking"

by

M. K. Lewis
(Midland Bank Professor of Money and Banking,
University of Nottingham)

Presented 18th February, 1986

Introduction

It is often said that there is 'nothing new under the sun', and international banking has a long and chequered history. In the fourteenth and fifteenth centuries the Florentine banking houses – the Bardi, Peruzzi and the Medici – rose on the back of the growth of international trade in wool, cloth and silks and declined just as rapidly under the weight of sovereign debt. During the nineteenth century, British and European bankers financed the development of the 'new world' through the 'overseas' banks founded in London and other European centres for the express purpose of funnelling funds to colonies and other countries, and also by sponsoring and underwriting issues of foreign bonds. Defaulting bonds gave rise to periodic crises; in 1873 / 74, no less than twelve countries defaulted on bond interest and repayments. Earlier this century, nearly 100 US banks became heavily involved in loans to Germany much of which was locked up in standstill agreements during the 1930s.

Since the early 1970s extensive international bank lending has again taken place, as countries have used external borrowings on a scale unknown for decades to finance industrialization and development programmes and also to cushion the impact of adverse changes occurring in the world economy upon their international trading positions. Lending by banks between regions is often referred to as 'recycling'. Recycling attracted attention because of the vast size of the sums which have been

1

THE FUTURE OF BANKING

directed through the banks' balance sheets from members of OPEC (petro-dollars) to the non-oil exporting developing countries. But the position is much more general. Banks in fact lent to the developing countries more than twice the inflow of petro-dollars. Recycling of petro-dollars was only one part of the tremendous expansion, and recent decline, of international bank lending.

During the decade after 1973, international bank lending in net terms, i.e. net of interbank redepositing, increased at an average rate of 22% per annum. Growth slowed dramatically by 1983, and was only 7% in 1984. A sharp and continuing deceleration has occurred in lending to the developing countries. Following a 6% increase in 1983, bank credits to developing countries grew by only 2% in 1984. Increases in the claims of US banks fell from $36 billion in 1982 to $2 billion in 1984, and actually declined during the first three quarters of 1985 with new extensions more than offset by net repayments of existing loans.

At the same time, for some kinds of international financing, the banks' role has changed. Traditional deposit taking and lending by banks has been supplanted by issues of marketable paper and their placement to non-bank investors. A similar trend in domestic markets has given rise to what is called the 'securitization of lending', a process in which banks participate as arrangers of securities issues rather than as makers of traditional loans. This development prompts the question central to the title of this paper. Are we witnessing in the securitization of lending a reaction to current circumstances or the beginnings of a permanent alteration in the character of financing and thus in the business of banking?

Our starting point is the 'business of banking', and especially international banking. Like banks anywhere, international banks collect idle funds on a short-term basis from one region and activate them by lending to other regions often for much longer terms. But special problems arise because the lending is across countries, and also because the banking is 'wholesale' with individual loans ranging from millions up to billions of dollars. In examining these, we draw parallels with the principles and practice of insurance.

The Business of Banking

Despite ongoing changes in the style and structure of financial markets, banks have not changed greatly with respect to the economic functions which they perform. Indeed, banks can only be defined in a way consistent with international variations in financial structures, legislation and traditions in terms of the functions they perform as providers of payments

2

THE FUTURE OF BANKING

services, intermediation services and risk-sharing services. These services may be provided in different ways, and with different emphases, but by focusing upon the services a common ground can be found between apparently different national, as well as past and present, banking systems.

Banks supply the services by entering into loan and deposit contracts with various customers, and the differences between the characteristics of these contracts constitute the services produced. These differences are what is meant by banks 'creating liquidity'. For example, borrowers are able to obtain funds for longer periods and depositors lend for shorter periods than would occur in the absence of banking.

In terms of such 'maturity transformation' there is common ground between international and domestic banking. Deposits could be gathered from surplus regions of the world and on-lent by banks to the deficit regions without any essential alteration to the characteristics of the claims involved, other than that of the substitution of the bank's name for that of the borrower. But this is not the case, at least for the deposits and loans of British and American banks involved in international business. For British banks as at 1984, 90% of deposits in foreign currencies by non-bank customers were for maturities of less than 6 months, and 35% of deposits matured within one week. OPEC depositors have generally preferred to hold short term liabilities and this has been true also of other non-bank depositors. On the asset side, maturities have gradually lengthened and in 1984, 64% of claims outstanding to non-banks in foreign currencies had a maturity of 6 months and more, 41% had a remaining maturity of 3 or more years. Differences between the maturity of deposits and loans for British banks' domestic (sterling) banking business in 1984 did not differ greatly, especially for the non-retail i.e. wholesale banks. Table 1 gives details.

More generally, a common thread between domestic and international banking can be found in terms of the protection and guarantees which are provided contractually to customers. We find it instructive to visualize banks in both domestic and international operations as insurers; they provide customers with 'insurance' against certain portfolio risks and issue to customers financing options which can be exercised in various circumstances. To illustrate, a bank is visualized to buy securities issued by borrowers of funds and then offer them to lenders of funds with an insurance policy added. Costs of servicing the policy are recovered from the interest rate differential between loan and deposit rates and service

3

THE FUTURE OF BANKING

Table 1

Sterling and Foreign Currency Business of UK-based Banks with Non-bank Customers, Analysed by Maturity, as at February 1984

| | Sterling | | | | Foreign Currency | |
| | Retail Banks | | Non-retail Banks | | All Banks | |
	L	A	L	A	L	A
less than 8 days	82.44	2.48	49.37	11.44	35.11	7.14
8 days – < 1 month	8.18	4.33	20.32	5.55	21.23	8.99
1 month – < 3 months	5.91	8.25	15.98	9.75	21.72	12.20
3 months – < 6 months	1.73	4.58	6.06	7.22	12.28	8.01
6 months – < 1 year	1.14	5.75	2.93	9.87	4.92	6.50
1 year – < 3 years	0.25	11.72	2.10	17.64	1.45	16.43
3 years +	0.35	62.89	3.24	38.53	3.29	40.73
TOTAL	100.00	100.00	100.00	100.00	100.00	100.00

Source: Bank of England

4

THE FUTURE OF BANKING

charges. In this way, protection is provided should depositors have unexpected needs for cash, with banks guaranteeing that balances can be withdrawn on demand or at short notice, in full or in part, at face value. In short, banks provide liquidity insurance to depositors.

Banks as insurers allow for deposits to be withdrawn at short notice, despite holding assets of much longer maturity. Assurance of redeemability of deposits at full value is provided, while the banks themselves hold assets which fluctuate in value. Borrowers are insured against interest rates on their loans fluctuating daily, despite variations each day in the banks' cost of funds. Banks assure borrowers that loans will not have to be repaid within the period over which the funds are committed. They also provide for customers' – both borrowers and lenders – liquidity needs by issuing contingent claims in the form of overdraft facilities, standby credit facilities, lines and forward commitments to make loans, exercisable at the customers' volition. These 'insurance' contracts are much the same in all types of banking.

Banks are able to provide these guarantees by taking advantage of economies of scale in portfolio management arising from the law of large numbers. As such, the economies parallel those which form the basis of conventional insurance. Almost all insurance arrangements are based on the holding of reserves. Individuals could themselves lay up a fund to cover, say, ill-health and car accidents, and many in fact do so. Others prefer to purchase insurance, leaving the insurer to accumulate and manage the funds. They do so because the intermediary is able to pool reserves more economically, taking advantage of the fact that not all accidents occur at the same time. So it is with banks. Not all depositors want cash at once, nor do all loans fail, allowing savings in the amount of cash and liquid assets needed to insure against liquidity needs, and in capital reserves held to shield depositors from the risks of defaulting loans.

In both cases the economies of scale come from pooling enough individual risks so that the law of large numbers can operate, as insurers do with motor car insurance and banks do in *retail banking*, where the numbers of customers served by individual institutions run into thousands and millions. When large numbers of liquidity options are combined and large numbers of loans are pooled, regularities emerge which enable banks to guarantee the spendability of their assets while making a profit. More promises to pay out cash are issued than cash is held, in the same way that the total sums insured under the policies of insurance companies exceed the value of assets held.

5

THE FUTURE OF BANKING

Banks' liquidity insurance has a special characteristic in that confidence, as well as the natural hazards of life, governs the firms' exposure. Pooling of deposit withdrawals can work only if one depositor's decision to withdraw deposits is completely independent of the decision made by others, and that is the case only so long as depositors are fully confident that their cash needs will be met. The history of banking is littered with illustrations of a loss of confidence spreading like a contagion, and demonstrates also that such events cannot be predicted with accuracy. In most banking systems communal arrangements have been introduced to ensure the maintenance of the confidence needed for risk pooling, and these are themselves a form of insurance. This insurance also has a special feature, since the main aim is to prevent the event rather than to recompense people after its occurrence.

Stochastic principles cannot be applied so readily in *wholesale banking* business (including international banking). Whereas retail banks have a large number of little accounts, wholesale and international banks typically have a small number of big customers. The customers are large, often multinational companies, governments or governmental enterprises, and the institutions deal in large-valued transactions usually in small volumes. If the usual pooling principles are to be applied, banks would have to be very large indeed and there would be marked tendencies to concentration. A significant proportion of international banking world-wide is in fact undertaken by very large Japanese and US banks, but smaller banks survive in the international and domestic wholesale markets, many as specialist wholesalers. How are loans of five *years* to be matched with deposits of seven *days* maturity? How can the risk of large loan losses be diversified?

Essentially the same problems face insurance companies, where risks are often large relative to the resources of the firms. Natural disaster insurance, marine insurance for tankers, aviation insurance are examples. Individual firms are unable to get the full benefits of the 'pooling of risks' from amongst their own policyholders, in the same way that wholesale bankers cannot get sufficient risk diversification from their own balance sheet. In the insurance industry, the solution is for a number of companies to group together to form a pool. Pooling occurs in two main ways. With *co-insurance*, the insurance is split between one or more companies, while with *reinsurance* the initial insurer or co-insurer cedes or transfers some part (perhaps even the major part) of the risk to other insurance companies, i.e. to the reinsurers. They may in turn reinsure part of their

6

THE FUTURE OF BANKING

risk with other companies, and so on. When a claim is made, the insured is paid out by the leading underwriter, who in turn claims against the reinsurers for their proportion of the loss.

Pooling by co-insurance and reinsurance is an institutional response by private markets which has two main purposes. It spreads individual risks that are too big for even the largest insurance companies, and allows small companies to write more business than their own reserves or capital could safely support.

Wholesale banking is directly analogous. Institutional mechanisms have been established in private banking markets which enable liquidity creation to occur at a global level. These institutional responses involve loan syndication, the interbank market, and the development of balance sheet options. Loan syndicates are a formal subcontracting of lending risks, precisely equivalent to co-insurance and reinsurance arrangements in international insurance markets. Their purpose is the same; they enable the individual institutions to spread risks, avoiding too much exposure to individual cases. Inter-banks dealings can be looked upon, in part, as an informal means of risk-sharing. Loan risks are backed not just by the capital of the lending bank, but also indirectly by the capital of the banks which agree to lend to it and artificially expand its loanable capacity. When funds are lent interbank, there is also a sharing of potential funding requirements. As with reinsurance treaties, a 'claim' by the customer against the option of withdrawal in the deposit contract is met in part by the bank drawing upon its 'contracts' with the other banks. Finally, because of the options issued to customers, banks have developed 'options' on their balance sheets in the form of access to bought funds ('liability management') and the ability to sell off assets by converting loans into marketable paper.

By virtue of these collective devices, no one bank is left with a large share of the process by which large, risky and illiquid loans are transformed into short term, guaranteed deposits. Liquidity and lending risks are shared out in the system as a whole.

Thus the insurance principles stand; what differs between retail and wholesale banking is the arrangement for their achievement. With small (i.e. 'retail') insurance, risk pooling mostly occurs within the firm. For large ('wholesale') risks, risk pooling occurs outside of the firm but within the market. Lending and participating banks can be regarded as a combined risk carrier, with the equivalent of co-insurance and reinsurance arrangements creating a unit or pool which is large enough for the law of

7

THE FUTURE OF BANKING

large numbers to apply.

This is the position in aggregate, viewed in terms of the risks which are being insured. Looked at from the individual firm's viewpoint, the network of interfirm dealings has the objective of breaking up large risks into shares or participations which are, in the end, individually small enough to be encompassed, and pooled with other participations, in an individual firm's portfolio. In the absence of the network, customers would have to spread deposits and loans over a number of banks, arranging 'co-insurance' themselves. Banks carry out this task more conveniently and cheaply.

The collective arrangements provided by banks are far from costless. Decision rules must be formulated in syndicates, documentation prepared, and banks have to monitor their interbank exposures. As in retail banking, confidence is crucial; perhaps more so, because the backing for deposits is 'command' over funds from the wholesale funding markets. There must be confidence on the part of banks that the funds can be commanded, and confidence by depositors that the funds will be commanded.

Problems of International Banking

Banks in their international banking operations can be seen to have followed the classic rules of insurance; that is, that large risks can be covered more easily and cheaply the better they are spread over independent risk bearers. Funding risks inherent in guaranteeing that large deposits can be withdrawn at short notice have been spread across the 2,000 or so banks with a position in the international interbank market. The banks' method of handling the loan risks have followed the method used in international insurance markets, involving the equivalent of reinsurance arrangements to spread the risks as widely as possible around the globe amongst hundreds of participating firms. We now examine the adequacy of the classic principles of insurance for international banking. But first we look to experiences in the 1980s.

In any account, the altered circumstances of the non-oil developing countries must serve as a backdrop. They were major borrowers (see Table 2), and have featured most in the rescheduling of loans. A conjunction of three inter-related events has led to a changed environment. One is the second oil price cycle beginning in 1979 / 80. A second is the world recession and the consequences it has had for world trade and export growth. Finally, rising interest rates in the US increased sharply the interest payments of those borrowers with floating rate debt to

8

THE FUTURE OF BANKING

Table 2

Syndicated Lending Classified by Characteristics of Borrower, 1972 – 1982

	1972	1973	1974	1975	1976	1977	1978	1979	1980	1981	1982
Total syndicated lending distributed by country grouping (per cent)											
Western Industrialised countries	60.3	63.0	70.6	34.8	39.2	41.6	41.4	33.2	50.8	64.7	50.1
Non-OPEC developing countries	22.1	20.5	21.5	39.0	38.2	32.3	38.3	42.8	31.2	25.1	37.2
OPEC countries	13.2	12.8	3.8	13.8	13.9	17.9	14.8	15.2	14.3	8.9	11.8
Centrally planned economies	4.4	3.7	4.1	12.4	8.7	8.2	5.5	8.8	3.7	1.3	0.9
20 largest loans distributed by type of borrower (per cent)											
Sovereign	33.6	19.7	70.1	63.7	62.7	76.9	65.5	58.9	37.2	11.0	72.9
Public sector	20.1	61.8	24.6	30.6	30.3	20.6	29.9	38.6	37.9	13.7	8.8
Private sector	46.3	18.5	5.3	5.7	7.0	2.5	4.6	2.5	24.9	75.3	18.3
20 largest loans distributed by geographic region (per cent)											
Europe, Middle East and Africa	71.1	88.6	81.7	50.7	56.5	60.8	35.9	40.5	31.5	12.3	38.9
North and South America	27.0	9.9	5.0	23.5	39.5	36.1	57.2	34.4	68.5	84.9	51.9
Far East	1.9	1.5	13.3	25.8	4.0	3.1	6.9	25.1	–	2.8	9.2
Memo: 20 largest loans as a per cent of total syndications	54.4	45.2	40.6	40.5	32.3	38.0	40.6	43.1	34.1	48.8	51.9

Source: Euromoney

9

THE FUTURE OF BANKING

service. It has been estimated that perhaps 80% of the increased indebtedness of the non-oil exporting developing countries in the late 1970s and early 1980s can be attributed to these three 'external' circumstances.

In the face of such a marked revision in the underlying environment, it is inevitable that loans made in earlier circumstances will take on a different complexion. And it is easy to be wise afer the event. But looked at coldly from the viewpoint of risk management there were three 'problems' with the way banks handled international lending.

Banks pool risks on both sides of their balance sheet, but there was not independence between the two sides. Following the increases in oil prices, lending opportunities were presented on both sides of the balance sheet. Bankers were able to take funds from the present oil producing countries and lend them to countries financing projects which would make them either future producers of oil or producers of alternative energy resources, made viable by currently high oil prices. Both sides of the balance sheet rested to some extent on the continuance of high oil prices. When the impact of rises in oil prices lessened and prices actually began to fall, both sides of the balance sheet experienced deterioration. Deposit growth slowed down and borrowers fell behind in repayments.

Second, international bankers pioneered the now almost universal arrangements by which interest rate risks are passed on fully to borrowers at rollover dates. Pricing at the rollover period is based directly upon funding costs (e.g. LIBOR, CD rates) making it a cost-plus contract, like those employed for military purchases of new technology, when the government compensates the supplier for all costs plus an agreed profit margin. Such an arrangement can be visualised as a fixed-price (i.e. rate) contract combined with an 'insurance' contract by which the purchaser takes on the insurance function and reimburses the supplier for unexpected costs. In the case of military purchases, it is thought to be an appropriate distribution of risk bearing; risk is shifted to the agency best able to bear it.

For borrowers with low risk tolerance and incomes which decline when interest rates rise, the appropriateness of such insurance arrangements for loans can be questioned. What is undeniable is that the nature of the risk to a bank is changed more than shifted, since loan default risks are increased and, moreover, no longer have independent fates, rebounding onto the banks. Banks thought that they had shifted the refinancing and interest rate risk of lending onto borrowers, but it is the banks which bear the

THE FUTURE OF BANKING

ultimate credit risk should the borrower be unable to pay the higher interest costs.

Finally, in terms of the objective of risk-spreading, syndication had, in fact, created a fiction. Loans were syndicated, and participations spread across many banks. Each bank may have held a diversified portfolio of participations. But risk is not in terms of loans. It is in terms of independent fates. With rollover credits, risk is perhaps best measured by the amount of outstanding debt of countries on floating rate terms, net of bank claims held by those countries. The pattern of draw-down and repayments meant that by 1982, 75% of the *net* floating rate syndicated debt was held by four countries alone: Mexico, Brazil, Argentina and South Korea.

Syndication is meant to be an anti-accumulation device, to use a term common in insurance, preventing too much of an accumulation of risk in individual portfolios. But there was clearly accumulation in the aggregate loan portfolio; in a sense there was one risk. Adding interdependent participations does not improve the spread of risks in a bank's balance sheet. In insurance terms, it was as if each insurer sought after a diversified portfolio of houses insured for earthquake damage, but it just happened that each lay along the San Andreas fault.

This analogy with natural disaster insurance seems not inappropriate, and leads us on to the question of insurability; specifically whether the size of loans and the risks involved in lending to developing countries make the business 'uninsurable'. Insurers themselves think of risks falling into one of three categories: those risks which are insurable on a net basis; those uninsurable on a net basis but insurable in gross account; and those uninsurable on a gross basis. The first corresponds to retail banking, comprising risks which can be pooled on a net basis by an individual insurer. But larger risks can be accepted by individual insurers thanks to the ability to cede part of them to other insurers. By virtue of reinsurance, an insurance company is able to accept larger risks on a gross basis without having to assume larger risks on net account. This second category obviously corresponds to wholesale banking business. The question is whether some international banking spills over into the third category.

Risk spreading works for risks which are capable of being diversified. These are independent risks which may loom large for individual transactors but can be socially removed by the operation of the law of large numbers. Even if risks are *somewhat* interdependent, having a large number buy shares of the risk is usually adequate. But for 'social risks',

11

THE FUTURE OF BANKING

risks which derive from a change in the state of nature or state of the world and are directly significant for many risks, these pooling techniques do not help. They do not help because losses are interdependent; there is a large, undiversifiable background risk common to all participations which cannot be diversified away.

Economic depression, unemployment, natural disasters, and war are examples of cases where risks involve dependence, and insurers refuse to underwrite many such risks. Insurance cover provided by means of the 'reserves principle' would require a thick reserve holding by the underwriting companies and co-insurers to cover the large accumulation hazard, large average losses and infrequent loss experience. Once losses were experienced, costs of broking reinsurance would rise while attempts to rebuild reserves by raising premiums would see 'adverse selection' set in, i.e. the good risks would leave the pool and self-insure.

All of these hazards of insuring social risks may be seen to apply to loans made by banks to developing countries. Problems arose because of a change in the 'state of the world', as the world-wide economic decline took hold. Banks' holding of capital reserves are not 'thick' in comparison with exposures and banking authorities have also been looking to raise capital requirements. International banking, like reinsurance, has tended to be carried out under conditions of *uberrimae fidei*, and the many small banks needed for enhanced risk spreading tended, when buying participations, to rely on the country risk assessment of the syndicate leaders and correspondent banks. As concerns about capital adequacy and perceived credit risks has grown, many banks (US-owned banks in particular) have curtailed the extent of their interbank activity and are monitoring ongoing exposures more carefully, adding to costs of 'traditional' international bank deposit and lending business. Banks' search for off-balance sheet activities has coincided with many customers' preferences, and prime banking business has returned to securities markets.

In effect, banks have experienced the problem of 'adverse selection', whereby in the aftermath of losses insurance cover is dominated by bad risks. Depositors have undoubtedly revised their perceptions of the relative quality of bank-issued liabilities *vis-à-vis* bonds and notes issued by highly rated government and corporate borrowers. Because of lenders' changed preferences, the banks' best borrowers have found that they can issue bonds, floating rate notes and commercial paper in the international capital markets on better terms than they are able to obtain by bank loans. In 1984, new issues of international bonds caught up with new

12

THE FUTURE OF BANKING

international bank lending (see Table 3). In terms of outstanding stocks, however, bank loans are still much larger. But the loans with which banks are left are the 'worse' ones with lengthening maturities due to rescheduling. Large potential losses on these loans to their 'old' clients, the non-oil exporting developing countries, are being spread over a shrinking borrower base.

Here we have some factors encouraging the 'securitization' of lending and the move away from traditional bank intermediation. But other forces are at work and we now look to future prospects.

Future Prospects

Two engines of the growth of international banking in the 1970s have gone, and the weight of past behaviour continues to cloud the future. Demand for the intermediation services of banks depend both on the underlying distribution of wealth and the liquidity and risk preferences of wealthholders. During the 1970s both factors favoured bank intermediation. Many commentators have depicted the financial behaviour of OPEC countries, especially in the initial years of high surplus, as cautious, with a desire to hold funds in instruments having a high degree of liquidity. At the same time, the desire of developing countries to continue investment programmes by medium-term funding presented the banks with a tailor-made opportunity to intermediate the wealth transfer process.

The pattern of current account deficits and surpluses has altered dramatically in the mid 1980s. For 1985 the United States had the largest current account deficit (an estimated $115 billion) and other industrialised countries had the largest current account surpluses. With Japanese and German lenders preferring to acquire securities and other claims issued directly by the United States, the wealth transfer process has reverted to more 'traditional' channels. Capital flows are running in the main amongst the industrial countries.

Banks were able to sustain international lending during the 1970s by pulling in a steady stream of banks fresh to the international scene. On average over 60 new banks entered international banking every year. The opportunity which was thereby presented for risk spreading kept the margins for risk low, part of the spread being an 'insurance premium' levied by banks to cover the risks of funding and default. The average spread added to LIBOR declined each year from 1975 through to 1981. Here again matters have changed. For the moment, at least, it would seem that the process of international portfolio diversification by banks has run its course. The world has run out of additional banks willing to enter into

13

THE FUTURE OF BANKING

Table 3

New International Bond Issues and Bank Credit Commitments Publicly Announced, Medium- and Long-term

(billions of dollars)

	1981	1982	1983	1984
A. International Bond Issues				
Floating rate notes and CD's	11.3	15.3	19.5	38.2
Fixed rate instruments	41.5	60.2	57.6	73.3
Total	52.8	75.5	77.1	111.5
B. Syndicated Bank Loans				
Involuntary new money loans	–	–	14.3	11.3
Voluntary loans	94.6	98.2	52.9	50.7
Total	94.6	98.2	67.2	62.0
C. Other Bank Credits				
Merger-related standbys	39.1	–	4.0	28.0
Euronotes and other facilities*	14.0	5.4	9.5	27.3
Total	53.1	5.4	13.5	55.3

*Facilities extended by banks to back up the issuance of financial instruments such as short-term Euronotes, certificates of deposit, bankers acceptances, and commercial paper.

Source: Morgan Guaranty Trust Company

THE FUTURE OF BANKING

international loan syndicates.

By contrast, there seems to be no shortage of institutional and other investors seeking an internationally-diversified portfolio of good quality bonds and securities. Removal of exchange controls and the liberalization of capital markets in the UK, Japan and Europe has widened demand, while US corporations and financial institutions have looked to market issues of securities internationally.

Banks' activities may have unwittingly contributed to this trend in a number of ways. Financial intermediaries rely on transactions costs for their existence, yet historically have improved the workings of primary securities markets. Banking supports an infrastructure of security exchanges, dealers and brokers which reduce the operating costs and risks of banks' portfolios. More so than in domestic intermediation, banks in their international operations have relied upon money and securities markets to develop balance sheet and funding options matching those issued by them to deposit-holders. The switch from official financing to bank and other private financing of balance of payments imbalances has undoubtedly widened the range of internationally transferable private assets. In these ways, international banking has worked against the fragmentation of security markets.

A number of innovations in financial instruments has seen international securities markets take on some of the character of banking markets. There used to be sharp differences between the two. Bonds were issued at fixed interest rates, bank loans at variable rates. With bonds, the holding preferences of buyers must coincide with sellers, unless the securities are prematurely disposed of, whereas banks reconcile differences in holding patterns, borrowing short and lending long. While the risks of banks arranging security flotations was limited to that of underwriting the issue, banks making loans assume default and illiquidity risks on behalf of customers.

These differences were eroded first by the development of floating rate notes, which now represent over 40% of Eurobond issues. These are bonds (normally medium term in length) issued with an interest coupon which consists of a margin over a reference rate, such as Libid, plus a 'spread'. The coupon is paid at the end of each interest period, normally 3 or 6 months, and is revised in line with current market rates for the next interest period. This pricing arrangement makes them the direct counterpart in the bond market of the rollover technique pioneered in international bank lending. Banks are also involved as both issuers and

15

THE FUTURE OF BANKING

holders of notes, so that the market for floating rate notes has acquired some of the characteristics of an international interbank market.

The gap between short run supplies of funds and demands for medium to long run financing has been bridged by the emergence of a market for Euronotes based around note issuance facilities provided by the banks. Euronotes are unlisted securities with set maturities of one, three or six months, normally in units of $500,000, placed with investors by the arranging institution. A note issuance facility is a form of standby credit line arranged with a bank or a syndicate of banks (see Table 3 page 14). Facilities are normally medium-term, say 7-10 years, much the same length as loans, with funding by means of successive issues of the notes in variable quantities over the lifetime of the facility. In contrast with a loan, the participating banks are not necessarily obliged to fund or rollover the maturing notes. Instead, they guarantee the continuance of funding, standing ready over periods as long as 10 years to buy the notes which cannot be placed at the interest cost specified in the underwriting contract.

From the viewpoint of borrowers, Euronotes have the characteristics of loans: they are medium-term, flexi-rate and have guaranteed renewal. Yet holders of the notes have an investment avenue which is more flexible and more liquid than loans, more akin to certificates of deposit. Banks gain fee income and, so long as the notes are placed at each maturity date without difficulty, off balance sheet business.

This transformation of short term funds into long term lending is not unlike that which occurs on banks' balance sheets. Indeed, the parallel is almost complete if we return to the idea of banks as insurers, for banks provide insurance type services to borrowers. With loans, a bank can be visualized as accepting liquid deposits from lenders and offering them to borrowers with an insurance policy added. The policy, in effect, is a guarantee that the bank stands ready over a number of years to provide substitute deposits, on agreed terms, should lenders be unwilling to continue with their funding. With flexi-rate loans, the costs of servicing the policy are recovered from the 'spread' over funding costs and in service charges, much as with note issuance facilities.

When we view banks as issuers of guarantees and option contracts of various types, the switch to securitized lending seems less of a change and more an adaptation to prevailing market conditions. Banks in international lending have a remarkable record of innovation, as illustrated by Euro-banking, wholesale banking, rollover credits, flexi-rate loans, syndicated lending, multiple currency loans, international

16

THE FUTURE OF BANKING

banking facilities, and so on. On the score of adaptability, at least, one can be sanguine about future prospects.

But, as of 1986, the immediate future of international banking is clouded by the issue of how banks are able to handle their existing debt. Here again the comparison with insurance may be instructive. In terms of the large accumulation of risks, enormous sums involved, infrequent claims experience, and large potential losses, we have suggested that the risks of international loans may have much in common with natural disaster insurance. For disasters, the law of large numbers break down not only for individual insurers but for the system as a whole. Use of the standard risk-sharing arrangements helps but still leaves individual firms and the system as a whole with risks for which they are ill-equipped to bear.

The analogy with insurance is an apt one in another respect. Insurers *do* underwrite natural disasters. To cover natural catastrophes is seen to be one of the tasks of the insurance industry. Insurers face swingeing losses should there be a repetition of the San Francisco earthquake of 1906 or the Tokyo earthquake of 1923. In the event of a super-catastrophe or series of occurrences of great devastation, which could bring about the financial ruin of many national and international insurers, there is the expectation of supportive action and responsibility for compensation by governments, acting as insurers of last resort. Governments may provide assistance for reconstruction, waive solvency and capital requirements temporarily, and help insurers to dispose of their assets at reasonable prices.

Many argue that the same is true of banking today: that one answer is for governments and multilateral organizations such as the World Bank and IMF to step in and, by co-financing with the banks and re-financing their loans, aid more in the reconstruction process. There is undoubtedly much potential for 'moral hazard' in such a course. But there are risks in present arrangements: that the rush into prime paper will continue and that banks will be more cautious in new loans and less generous in repayment provisions than is desirable for world development and political stability.

Continuing the analogy with insurance, the insurance industry has experienced difficulties in handling 'wholesale' insurance, and underwriting results in the 1980s have greatly deteriorated, especially in reinsurance. Insurers have not found it easy to determine the premiums appropriate when providing insurance cover for large aeroplanes, supertankers, space satellites, advanced medical and bio-technology. They have learnt from experience that the reinsurance arrangements needed for the underwriting of large risks give rise to problems of

17

THE FUTURE OF BANKING

collective risk. When risks are shared up and subcontracted, overall exposure for the system as a whole is not easy for an individual underwriter or reinsurance participant to assess. Risk limits and exposure limits, like credit limits in interbank markets, are a help, yet international insurance has been prone to cycles of competitive rate-cutting and of optimism and pessimism.

What insurers call 'professional sinning' was also rife in international banking. Bankers undoubtedly overlent and followed the herd. Many banks failed to apply to participations the standards followed for ordinary loans, and risks were underrated. Information transmission in international banking was poor, and many of the participating banks ignored the evidence of a growing overall loan exposure to the developing countries.

Yet bankers deserve praise for lending to developing countries on scales which were beyond the capacity of the official institutions and the willingness of national governments to undertake. 'Recycling' was a considerable achievement. Continuance of lending to the developing countries into the early 1980s sustained growth in the world economy. However, recovery and thus repayment of the debt is not just a matter between banks and their customers, under the aegis of the IMF. It rests much on sustained and non-inflationary economic growth in the industrial countries, and actions taken by governments to reduce protectionism and expand trade opportunities for developing countries.

Unwillingly perhaps, banks both individually and collectively now have a direct pecuniary stake in the economic viability of the developing countries. By proxy, so do the citizens of their home countries either as shareholders of banks, depositors or taxpayers. That is an entirely new development, and a not unencouraging one for world progress, which poses a challenge to us all.

[19]

Developments in the international syndicated loan market in the 1980s

This article[1] surveys developments in the international syndicated loan market[2] during the 1980s. Although the market experienced high volumes of business at the beginning of the decade, there was a significant decline after the onset of the LDC debt crisis in 1982, which continued during the mid-1980s. From the end of 1986, activity revived and business has continued to strengthen. The article considers the advantages that syndicated loans possess over various capital market instruments, exploring two particular sources of demand for new credit facilities—merger and acquisition related activity and the arrangement of multiple-option facilities (MOFs).

General overview

At the beginning of the 1980s, the market for international syndicated loans was already well established and business was buoyant. New credit facilities worth almost $83 billion were announced in 1980, and a further $101 billion were announced in the following year. Many major international banks were heavily involved in extending loans to borrowers from the less developed countries (LDCs) and newly industrialising economies (NIEs) in the period 1976–82. Some of the assumptions which underlay the banks' policy of portfolio diversification through more overseas lending were, however, increasingly being questioned, particularly in relation to loans extended to state entities in the LDCs. With the intensification of the debt crisis resulting from the decision by Mexico to suspend interest payments to its creditors in August 1982, the euroloan market entered a phase of sharp contraction. Activity reached a nadir in 1985, when the value of new international syndicated loans amounted to only $19 billion.[3] In contrast, in the capital markets, gross eurobond issues increased from $74 billion in 1982 to $163 billion in 1985. Thus the decline in the use of the syndicated loan as a vehicle for international financial flows was very clearly associated with the process of securitisation which was then having a major impact on financial markets. This phenomenon was related to an increased investor preference for tradable claims and the desire of some borrowers—notably major industrial companies—to exploit the fact that their creditworthiness relative to the banking sector had improved markedly, so giving them an incentive to issue securities directly to end investors.

Since the last quarter of 1986, however, the market for syndicated loans, both international and domestic, has once more experienced high levels of activity, although the composition of borrowers has changed significantly from that at the beginning of the decade. This resurgence has been attributable to three salient factors:

● the desire of corporate institutions in the developed countries to restructure their existing lines of credit into more flexible financing arrangements, such as multiple-option facilities (see below);

● the growth in debt-financed takeovers and management buyouts, reflecting, in part, the reduction in the cost of debt finance resulting from the decline in inflation from the early 1980s; and

● more generally, the competitive funding opportunities that this sector offers to second-tier corporate borrowers which do not possess a sufficiently high credit rating to obtain access to the eurobond market and utilise interest rate swaps at favourable rates.

Chart 1
Announcements of international syndicated credits

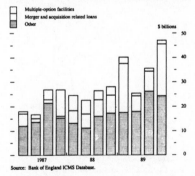

Source: Bank of England ICMS Database.

(1) Written by T J Allen in the Bank's International Division.
(2) The Bank of England's International Capital Markets Database records all announcements of syndicated credits other than those which represent banks' domestic currency lending to home country residents. It therefore includes both 'eurocurrency' credits, where banks resident in one particular centre arrange loans denominated in foreign currencies (from the banks' point of view) for either residents or overseas borrowers, and domestic currency loans (again from the banks' point of view) for non-residents.
(3) Domestic syndications, however, fell less precipitously over the period 1982 to 1985.

Bank of England Quarterly Bulletin: February 1990

The relative importance of multiple-option facilities and merger-related loans is illustrated in Chart 1. The syndicated loan market, together with its fixed-income competitors, has also benefited from the extended period of growth that the major OECD economies experienced after the economic slowdown of the early 1980s. In particular, investment expenditure has been strong over the past three years, increasing the demand for funds. During 1989, there also appears to have been a recovery in the value of commitments raised on behalf of developing countries. This increase was partly associated with project finance opportunities and lending related to commodity earnings, rather than reflecting new money packages to borrowers from heavily indebted countries requiring funds for general or unspecified purposes.

Conditions in the syndicated loan market, 1980–89

Until 1985, borrowers from the LDCs and the NIEs generally accounted for a more substantial share of the international syndicated loan market than did borrowers from the major OECD countries (see Chart 2 and Table A). The recovery in volumes which has taken place since the end of 1986, however, almost entirely reflects greater activity by borrowers from the major industrial economies. In recent years there has also been a change in the importance of industrial borrowers generally relative to sovereign borrowers, although the former have always represented the single most important group of borrowers since 1980. Borrowing by central governments and other government departments accounted for approximately 20% of all credits in the early 1980s. After 1982, this proportion declined significantly and is now around 5% of

Table A
International syndicated credits: borrowers, by region
$ billions

	1980	1981	1982	1983	1984	1985	1986	1987	1988	1989(a)
Major OECD countries	20.5	33.2	22.6	8.2	9.9	5.1	11.6	61.4	72.8	98.7
Minor OECD countries	19.4	15.7	18.4	13.6	6.2	4.4	6.5	14.9	18.3	23.9
Eastern Europe	2.8	1.1	0.5	0.5	2.2	3.6	2.3	1.9	1.2	2.2
International institutions	0.6	0.4	—	1.2	0.1	—	0.4	0.4	0.1	0.1
Less developed countries	15.0	22.5	19.7	5.1	4.0	1.5	3.7	6.5	6.2	15.0
Newly industrialising economies	11.1	14.7	11.8	3.5	3.5	3.0	1.1	1.1	1.5	3.7
Oil producing countries	13.0	12.9	13.8	5.5	3.8	1.2	3.3	2.0	1.6	5.3
Other	0.4	0.4	1.4	0.4	0.4	0.2	0.7	0.5	0.1	0.1
Total	82.8	100.9	88.2	38.0	30.1	19.0	29.6	88.7	101.8	149.0

Source: Bank of England ICMS database.

(a) Provisional.

the overall market: governments of LDCs have, in many cases, been excluded from the market altogether, and those of the industrial countries have increasingly turned their attention to bond financing and the euronote sector, where they have been able to obtain finer rates and pursue more precise debt management policies. For example, the Kingdoms of Belgium, Spain and Sweden developed large commercial paper or medium-term note programmes either in the US domestic market or in the euromarket. In contrast, credit facilities arranged on behalf of industrial borrowers have represented over 45% of all syndicated loans in every year since 1982, reaching 88% of all announcements in 1988 and 81% in 1989. US dollar denominated credits have always formed the most significant component of the total market; in every year since 1980 dollar facilities accounted for more than 60% of all international syndicated loans.

Table B
International syndicated credits: breakdown by type of borrower
$ billions

	1980	1981	1982	1983	1984	1985	1986	1987	1988	1989(a)
Industrial borrowers	48.5	65.1	53.3	22.0	17.1	8.5	15.2	67.8	89.4	120.6
Banks and financial institutions	16.9	18.9	16.9	5.0	9.0	8.2	9.0	15.0	8.9	21.1
Central banks	—	—	1.1	1.9	0.3	0.5	1.5	1.0	1.1	1.2
Central government	14.2	14.4	16.0	8.8	3.6	1.6	3.7	4.0	1.5	4.5
Other government	3.2	2.5	0.9	0.3	0.1	0.2	0.2	0.9	0.9	1.6
Total	82.8	100.9	88.2	38.0	30.1	19.0	29.6	88.7	101.8	149.0

Source: Bank of England ICMS database.

(a) Provisional.

Chart 2
Announcements of international syndicated loans, 1972–89

─── Total
─ ∙ ─ Developing country borrowers (a)
─ ─ ─ Major OECD borrowers

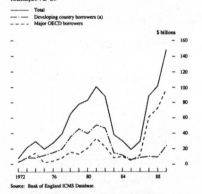

$ billions

Source: Bank of England ICMS Database.

(a) Includes less developed countries, newly industrialising economies and oil producing countries.

Margins[1] on international syndicated loans for major OECD borrowers underwent a general but not continuous decline from 1982 to the first half of 1988 (see Chart 3). The fall in average margins which took place after 1983 can be attributed to two main factors. First, with the onset of the debt crisis many prime corporate borrowers turned to the various securities markets to service their financing requirements. In particular, the growth of the eurocommercial paper and floating-rate note markets provided borrowers with alternative sources of short-term and floating-rate funding. The banks were therefore obliged to compete more aggressively for international

(1) International syndicated loans are generally priced with reference to the Libor benchmark, although other bases such as the Paris interbank offered rate (Pibor), the US prime rate or various CD rates are also used. As well as being influenced by market competition, the margin that is charged above this will essentially be a function of country and credit risk.

Chart 3
Spreads [a] **on major OECD and less developed country loans**

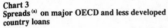

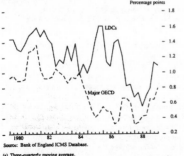

Source: Bank of England ICMS Database.

(a) Three-quarterly moving average.

and wholesale business as well as turning their attention to off-balance-sheet financing. Second, the major international banks became involved in arranging standby credit facilities designed to support the commercial paper activities of industrial companies or provide short-term cash advances for working capital purposes. As such loan facilities are not intended to be fully drawn upon in normal circumstances, the margins attached to them are comparatively low and the facility fee represents a more important element in the overall pricing. For almost all of the period from 1982 to 1988, the average margin on loans for borrowers from the major OECD countries was below that incurred by borrowers from the LDCs.

More recently, however, average margins have increased for both borrowers from the major OECD countries and those from LDCs, although they remain below the levels seen at the beginning of the decade. The new capital adequacy rules introduced under the auspices of the Bank for International Settlements represent one factor that should cause banks to negotiate higher margins. The increase in spreads may also be attributed to a change in the composition of loan facilities which have been arranged in recent quarters. For example, high margin business in the form of loans to finance acquisitions has become a greater component of the total market. The strength of potential competition among banks in the syndicated loan market, however, acts as a countervailing force, limiting the extent to which spreads may rise.

Market attributes

The demand for international syndicated credit facilities, which predominantly reflects private sector funding requirements, results from the fact that the syndicated loan market, or more generally the banking sector, is able to perform certain essential functions more satisfactorily than securities-based capital markets. The main advantages of a syndicated loan facility are:

● a credit facility provides the borrower with a stable source of funds—of particular value in the event that other capital markets are subject to some form of disruption;

● the syndicated loan sector generally allows borrowers to raise larger sums than they would be able to obtain through either the eurobond or the equity markets in the short term;

● the ability to arrange deals quickly and discreetly, which may be of value with certain transactions such as takeovers;

● the capacity to provide commitments to lend which can be cancelled relatively easily; it would be difficult to cancel borrowing in the securities markets without reducing investor confidence.

To some extent these advantages are relative rather than absolute. For example, the US domestic commercial paper market and the ECP market can offer a wide range of borrowers access to short-term funds, albeit on an uncommitted basis, and the medium-term note market can be regarded as a form of contingent bond financing. As dealers in these markets will only place notes on a 'best efforts' basis, such programmes do not offer the certainty of committed bank lines. For prime industrial corporate borrowers and well-regarded sovereign borrowers, this does not present a major problem as they will be able to place their paper and bonds at more competitive rates than they could obtain funding in the bank market under normal circumstances. But for a wide spectrum of companies, particularly in Western Europe where the domestic CP markets are less well developed than in the United States and an established 'below investment grade' bond market has not as yet emerged, the stability and certainty of banking relationships continue to be attractive.

Multiple-option facilities [1]

A multiple-option facility (MOF) is the general name for a number of credit and money-market fund-raising mechanisms which are documented in a single agreement and are administered by a single agent on behalf of a syndicate of banks. The MOF is typically based upon a committed revolving credit and incorporates other arrangements which allow the borrower to obtain finance on an uncommitted basis, such as tender panels for multicurrency cash advances and bankers' acceptances or facilities allowing for the issue of commercial paper or some other form of note. Such facilities therefore represent a more convenient packaging of existing banking services rather than a fundamental innovation; instead of managing a series of bilateral banking relationships, the corporate treasurer can arrange a significant part of his company's funding through one agent. Under normal circumstances borrowers will obtain funding through a tender panel mechanism or by issuing

(1) A more detailed discussion of this instrument is included in the May 1988 *Bulletin*, page 212.

Bank of England Quarterly Bulletin: February 1990

The syndication process

The syndicated loan market is able to provide a broad spectrum of borrowers with funding for a wide range of projects. Loans can vary in size from small club deals, where three or four relationship banks can participate in transactions for as little as £10 million, to very large acquisition or project-related credits worth in excess of a billion pounds. For example, Eurotunnel obtained two syndicated loans in the third quarter of 1987 with a combined value of £5 billion, where the syndicate comprised approximately 160 banks. More recently, RJR Acquisition Corp obtained a package of loan facilities worth $13.6 billion in order to provide a consortium headed by Kohlberg Kravis Roberts with the necessary finance to complete the leveraged buyout of R J R Nabisco.

The syndication process commences when either a borrower approaches a bank and invites it to become a syndicate arranger or when the bank itself approaches a corporate borrower which it believes to be seeking funds. The arranger, or in some cases the arrangers, once mandated will then set about co-ordinating a consortium of banks who are prepared to lend money given an initial set of terms. The borrower's relationship banks will usually form the basis of the syndicate and further invitations may be extended according to the size, complexity and the pricing of the loan as well as the desire of the borrower to increase the range of its banking relationships.

Eventually, the arranger or lead-manager may find itself at the apex of a whole hierarchy of institutions, who may accept positions as co-lead managers, managers, co-managers or just participant banks, depending on the amount of money that they are prepared to lend or commit and the input that they have in the syndication process. The larger the credit, the more complex the structure. The lead-management

role itself is occasionally undertaken by the treasury department of the company seeking to raise the loan.

The arranger may either undertake the syndication on a 'best efforts basis' or, if the borrower is prepared to pay an appropriate fee, put together an underwriting group to give the borrower a guarantee of committed finance. If the latter route is adopted, the syndication process will take place in two phases. The underwriting group will come together in the primary syndication and then subsequently their commitments may be reduced during a secondary syndication, when new banks will be invited into the consortium. If the terms of the loan are considered attractive or the borrower is well-regarded by the market, the loan may well be oversubscribed. In this case the arranger may either invite the borrower to increase the size of the total credit or the banks may find that the amounts they have committed are scaled down *pro rata*. The completion of a transaction is often evidenced by the publication of a notice, generally referred to as a 'tombstone', in the financial press.

As well as earning a margin over Libor (or any other benchmark) when the loan is drawn, banks in the syndicate will receive various fees. The arranger and other banks in the lead management team, who may be responsible for various aspects of documentation, will generally receive some form of front-end management fee. Other participants will usually expect to receive a participation fee for agreeing to join the facility; the actual size of the fee will vary with the size of the commitment. Once the credit is established, members of the syndicate will often receive an annual facility or commitment fee, again proportional to their commitments. Loan documents may sometimes incorporate a penalty clause, whereby the borrower agrees to pay a fee or give some consideration to the lenders in the event that it pre-pays its debts prior to the specified term.

---

short-term promissory notes, and will achieve finer rates than they would have to pay if they were to make drawings upon the committed credit component of their MOF. For many major companies the MOF has represented a rationalisation of existing banking services, rather than a net increase in bank intermediation. Moreover, available evidence suggests that drawings made under these facilities are generally modest when compared with the total value of funds that could potentially be obtained under the uncommitted portions.

During 1987 and the first half of 1988 there was a trend among many major industrial companies to consolidate their existing bilateral credit lines into more flexible arrangements such as MOFs, while refinancing debt at

favourable rates at the same time. This tendency was particularly evident in the United Kingdom and France, where borrowers took advantage of the greater flexibility provided by MOFs. The development of other banking products such as the revolving underwriting facility and the note issuance facility had already established the concept of competitive bidding mechanisms such as tender panels and the MOF sought to combine this feature with a standard credit. Banks decided to bid aggressively for mandates to arrange such transactions and strongly marketed the product, particularly as such arrangements gave them the opportunity to establish new business relationships after a period in which volumes in the syndicated loan market had been low. The fees and margins attached to these arrangements have generally been regarded as being fine—a number of well-regarded UK companies have been able to obtain MOFs where the annual facility fee was less than 10 basis points and the spread no more than 12.5 basis points over Libor.

As many major companies, both in the United Kingdom and elsewhere, have now acquired MOFs, the demand for such arrangements will increasingly come from second-tier corporate borrowers, for whom various eurocurrency options are less relevant. The implementation of the Basle capital convergence agreement by the United Kingdom and other countries should make banks more reluctant to participate in MOFs at the aggressively-priced margins which were common in the early part of 1988. Some banks may, however, choose to participate in this lower return business in order to establish or retain long-term relationships with customers. Moreover, the more cautious attitude which some bankers have adopted towards high yield mezzanine debt and leveraged transactions could result in a desire to reweight portfolios more towards lower-geared companies wishing to have access to funds for general corporate purposes.

Merger and acquisition related lending

The stock market crash of October 1987 led to speculation that new merger and acquisition activity would decline significantly, reflecting the perceived difficulties of raising new equity finance. The continued buoyancy of company profits within the major industrial economies during 1988, together with the depressed state of many companies' stock market valuations, however, provided a considerable stimulus to new acquisitions. In many cases the syndicated loan has been the vehicle through which such takeovers have been financed. As mentioned above, the banking sector, through consortium loans, allows borrowers to raise larger sums than they are able to obtain through either the eurobond or the equity market over the short term, and to do so quickly. Moreover, borrowers may subsequently refinance such debt by utilising other markets.

The value of international credits arranged to finance acquisitions or mergers increased from $8.8 billion in 1987 to $24.6 billion in 1988 and then expanded to $55.8 billion during 1989 (see Table C). UK companies together with their subsidiaries were the most important national group of borrowers in both 1987 and 1988. To a large extent, this reflected the arrangement of a small number of very large facilities for major UK companies. For example, three financings, arranged for Grand Metropolitan Finance ($6 billion), the Tate and Lyle Group ($1.3 billion) and BAT Industries ($3.2 billion), accounted for almost three quarters of the UK total in 1988. Many of the credits arranged in the period 1987–89 were intended to finance acquisitions of US companies. Consequently, merger-related syndicated loans have been overwhelmingly dollar-denominated—82% during 1989.

Merger-related business can provide banks with two major forms of income: fees from giving advice on the

Table C
Merger and acquisition related international syndicated loans
US$ millions

Country of borrower	1987	1988	1989(a)
Australia	641	2,311	1,247
Canada	750	150	2,100
France	—	2,447	789
Japan	—	1,472	—
United Kingdom	5,794	14,141	10,059
United States	900	1,705	33,703
Other	710	2,367	7,946
Total	**8,795**	**24,593**	**55,844**
of which:			
Sterling	*457*	*515*	*8,335*
US dollar	*7,788*	*22,898*	*46,292*
Other	*550*	*1,180*	*1,217*

Source: Bank of England ICMS database.

(a) Provisional.

mechanics of mounting a takeover (or defence) and interest charges and other fees from participating in any financing package arranged on behalf of the acquirer. While there is some debate on the subject of exactly how generous are the returns on merger and acquisition business, the greater emphasis which many banks have placed on this type of activity since the beginning of 1988 indicates that it has been perceived as a welcome source of income. While a prime corporate borrower might pay 12.5 basis points or less over Libor on drawings obtained under the committed portion of a MOF, the average margin attached to merger-related eurocurrency loans during the first three quarters of 1989 was 112 basis points; such returns do, however, involve banks assuming a higher risk/return profile. The spread of perceived risk is illustrated by the range of margins from which that average is calculated, which stretches from 15 to 600 basis points. Recently, a number of well-regarded borrowers who were not highly geared nor likely to become so after making their acquisitions were able to obtain large merger-related syndicated credits in the London market at relatively fine rates. There is perhaps a tendency for pricing on merger-related loans for major companies with limited debt levels to move closer to the rates that such companies could obtain on facilities intended to finance working capital.

Mezzanine debt

Another development which has received considerable attention during the last two years has been the growing use of mezzanine or subordinated debt. This instrument has generally been associated with the current wave of corporate restructuring that is taking place in Western Europe and North America, particularly in connection with leveraged buyouts, where companies are acquired with borrowed funds which result in the acquirer assuming a relatively high gearing ratio. Mezzanine funding can take a number of different forms and refers to the issue of any form of subordinated debt claim. In the United States, mezzanine debt often takes the form of 'below investment grade' bonds, while in Europe it is generally some form of bank debt with equity warrants attached. Although mezzanine debt is usually associated

Bank of England Quarterly Bulletin: February 1990

Announcements of international syndicated credits and international banking flows

Data on announcements of syndicated loans can yield useful information on a number of issues, such as the degree of competition within particular sectors of the banking market, the extent to which companies in certain countries are restructuring their financial commitments and the growth of new loan products (mezzanine finance, multiple-option facilities). It has also been suggested that announcements of new international syndicated credits could be used as a leading indicator of bank lending to non-banks. The arrangement of credit facilities, however, represents the establishment of commitments to lend and, therefore, it is not always possible to make direct inferences about the value of actual drawings; trends evident in the international syndicated loan market are not necessarily reflected in cross-border flows. A recent study at the Bank using univariate time series techniques came to the conclusion that there was only a weak statistical relationship between announcements of new international syndicated credits and international banking flows. The difficulty in relating the two data sets also arises from the fact that the Bank of England's data on international syndicated loans do not include facilities with a maturity of less than one year; moreover, data on international banking flows will also incorporate drawings upon bilateral lines of credit.

---

with financing acquisitions and buyouts, it could have other applications, such as certain forms of project finance, where the actual project involved is particularly cash-generative.

The subordinated debt packages arranged for European buyouts have generally been domestic transactions with relatively little intermediation taking place outside the capital market of the country in which the acquired company is located. This situation could change in the future. The completion of the leveraged buyout of R J R Nabisco at the beginning of 1989 demonstrated that even the very largest companies can be subject to a takeover. Mezzanine financings may also be structured to include layers of debt which possess varying degrees of subordination; the interest rate or the value of the equity warrants attached to more junior claims will be correspondingly higher. The mezzanine market has grown quickly in a comparatively short time and the potential returns from this type of lending are attractive to many banks who have been used to standard corporate credits carrying narrow margins over Libor in recent years. Banks are not the only participants in this market. A number of special-purpose funds have been set up since the beginning of 1988 to provide subordinated finance for

buyouts. The reduced creditor protection attached to these loans means that the margin over Libor may be 3% or more, somewhat higher than the margins which might be charged on the senior loan component of a LBO financing. At present, however, the current pattern of European short-term interest rates is having an adverse impact upon new lending opportunities. Nevertheless, if the market in leveraged buyouts were to develop further in Europe, as a result of prominent companies being subject to takeovers or management buyouts, the local markets in mezzanine debt might become insufficient to accommodate the demand for funds, resulting in greater cross-border activity.

Secondary market

Another major development since the early 1980s has been the increasing tendency for banks to trade credit participations in the secondary market. While there are few statistics on the total size of the secondary market, the LDC debt problem and more recently the growth in LBOs have encouraged banks to adjust the balance of their loan portfolios. The recent Basle agreement on capital adequacy has presented many banks with the choice of increasing capital or removing assets from their balance sheets; many appear to have chosen to adopt the latter option to some degree, using loan transfers or securitisation to effect the reduction. There are three main methods by which loan participations may be transferred: novation, assignment and subparticipation. Novation involves the replacement of one legal agreement with another, thus extinguishing the contractual relationship between the original creditor and the debtor; assignment and subparticipation are non-recourse funding arrangements which do not normally involve the borrower as they operate in parallel with, rather than instead of, the original loan. This heightened emphasis on marketability could result in the syndicated loan market assuming some of the characteristics of the FRN market. The existence of a well-developed market in participations in syndicated loans results in banks developing many of the same skills that are required to operate successfully in the bond market, namely the ability to market debt claims and to establish a major network of potential investors. This could be regarded as part of a more general process in the euromarkets, where in recent years innovation and securitisation have led to the gradual dissolving of the boundaries between money, credit and capital markets. The existence of an established market in loans or loan participations also raises some interesting issues for bank supervisors. After consultation with the markets, the Bank issued a Notice in February 1989 (BSD/1989/1) which sets out the Bank's supervisory policy on the treatment of loan transfers involving banks.

Conclusion

Over the last three years, the international syndicated loan market has clearly demonstrated its ability to mobilise substantial volumes of funds on behalf of a variety of different borrowers. The strength of investment spending over the past three years and the buoyant levels of merger and acquisition activity in recent years have generally provided international financial markets with a major stimulus on the demand side. In particular, acquisition-related lending has come to represent a major component of the overall market for international syndicated credits. More recently, there have been some indications that borrowers from the less developed countries are making greater use of the market in specific contexts. The market has also shown its ability to meet the increasingly complex needs of major corporate borrowers. While the demand for syndicated loans may fluctuate over time, this sector is likely to remain a significant and durable component of international financing.

Part IV
Offshore Services

[20]

Offshore Financial Centers

Statement by Henry C. Wallich, Member, Board of Governors of the Federal Reserve System, before the Subcommittee on Oversight of the Committee on Ways and Means, U.S. House of Representatives, April 25, 1979.

Mr. Chairman, as requested in your letter inviting the Federal Reserve to participate in these hearings, I shall discuss the role of U.S. banks in offshore centers and will comment on the types and adequacy of the information the Federal Reserve obtains on bank activities in such locations.

Offshore financial centers, some of which are also tax havens, are nowadays a highly important part of the international financial system. No picture of international financial developments is complete without taking into account the transactions that are made or booked in these centers. It is for this reason that activities in these centers are of interest to the Federal Reserve as a central bank when monitoring international flows of money and credit in relation to domestic monetary conditions. Furthermore, U.S. banks occupy a prominent place in these offshore centers. The Federal Reserve as bank supervisor must therefore be concerned with monitoring the activities of U.S. banks in these centers to assure itself that they are conducting their affairs in a safe and sound manner.

While tax considerations are frequently an important element in the operations of offshore financial centers and the kinds of transactions that take place or are booked in them, these considerations are not prominent in the concerns of the Federal Reserve about these centers. Other authorities exercise oversight on tax aspects of transactions in these centers and have the specialized expertise to deal with such matters. As I have just indicated, our interests run to the broad economic implications of activities in these centers and to the bank supervisory aspects of these activities. Therefore, in my statement I shall discuss first some general characteristics of offshore financial centers and of the operations of U.S. banks in them. I shall then turn to the role of the Federal Reserve in relation to these centers and I shall follow with a description of the kinds of information obtained by the Federal Reserve in the furtherance of its interests and responsibilities.

OFFSHORE FINANCIAL CENTERS

Offshore financial centers are easier to identify than to characterize. Broadly speaking, however, an offshore financial center is a location where funds are borrowed from nonresidents and lent to other nonresidents through the intermediation of banks and other financial institutions. These activities are recognized to have little effect on the domestic economy of the center or on domestic financial conditions. Some of these centers are fully operational, in the sense of actual dealings being conducted with customers with regard to obtaining funds and negotiating credits. Others are merely booking centers where deposits and loans are legally lodged, but where no transactions are physically made. The City of London is the preeminent example of an operational offshore financial center. The Bahamas and the Cayman Islands, on the other hand, are notable examples of booking centers.

What are the essential elements of offshore financial centers and what has spurred their growth? As for the former, tax considerations can of course have an important influence on a country's growth and appeal as an offshore financial center. Likewise very important, however, are factors such as exchange control laws, local reserve requirements, communication facilities, the country's time zone, its commercial laws, and its political and social stability. This is illustrated by the fact that London, the largest "offshore center," is located in one of the world's most heavily taxed countries. Secrecy laws are frequently another important consideration, but, like liberal tax laws, they are generally more important to the customers of banks than to the banks themselves.

The growth of offshore financial centers has been prompted mainly by the needs and demands of multinational business. As business has become more and more internationalized, needs for international financial services have expanded and become more diverse. Companies operating in a variety of countries have required funding sources in different currencies, outlets for temporarily idle funds, access to different kinds of credit facilities, and the means for the transfer of monies across international frontiers. Tax laws and foreign exchange restrictions are, of course, among the crucial factors influencing the ways international business is transacted. For multinational companies, therefore, locations where international financial transactions can be effected free of most tax consequences and of foreign exchange controls have a great attraction. Since bankers traditionally follow their customers and adapt to their needs, banks have been quick to locate in and promote such offshore centers.

U.S. BANKS IN OFFSHORE CENTERS

U.S. banks have long been located in and played a prominent role in the major financial centers of the world, such as London, where "offshore banking" is an important part of their business. U.S. banks have also played an important part in the development and rapid growth of offshore financial centers outside the major financial markets that have occurred in recent years. As recently as December 1972, for example, member bank branches in six major offshore centers had total claims on third parties of only $14 billion, or 20 percent of third-party claims at all their foreign branches. At the end of last year, those claims totaled more than $95 billion and represented 46 percent of third-party claims at all foreign branches of member banks.

The Bahamas and the Cayman Islands are by far the most important of these offshore centers

to U.S. banks. At the end of last year, U.S. banks had 139 branches in these two locations, with claims on third parties exceeding $70 billion. Details of the distribution of business among offshore centers and types of customers are shown in the accompanying tables.[1] As noted earlier, the Bahamas and the Cayman Islands are booking centers for financial transactions that have been negotiated elsewhere. Virtually all of the branches of U.S. banks in these centers are consequently "shell" branches—that is to say, they are a set of ledgers managed and kept by an agent rather than a physical location where business is transacted.

The growth of international banking is the underlying cause for the growth of these centers, but U.S. regulations were the initial catalyst for the establishment of branches of U.S. banks in these centers. The voluntary foreign credit restraint (VFCR) program and the interest equalization tax (IET), which were implemented in the mid-1960s to restrict the outflow of capital from the United States, limited the ability of U.S. banks to meet their customers' foreign needs and to otherwise engage in international banking. As a way of doing so, banks began to establish low-cost "shell" branches in these countries to obtain access to the Eurocurrency markets. Since foreign loans booked and funded in these branches did not affect the U.S. balance of payments, they were exempt from the restrictions on foreign credits that applied to domestic banking offices.

Although U.S. government programs to restrict capital outflows were ended in 1974, U.S. bank activity in the Bahamas and the Cayman Islands has continued to grow. For those banks that do not have full-service foreign branches in, say, London, these locations offer low-cost access to the Eurocurrency markets and, notably, the ability to raise funds for their international business free of domestic reserve requirements. For many bank customers, these locations provide advantages as tax havens, while for others secrecy laws are important in their decisions to place funds.

---

1. The attachments to this statement are available on request from Publications Services, Division of Support Services, Board of Governors of the Federal Reserve System, Washington, D.C. 20551.

For the banks themselves, operations in the Bahamas and the Cayman Islands also have certain tax advantages. U.S. banks operate abroad mainly through branches, and the earnings of branches are not deferrable but are immediately subject to U.S. income taxes after allowable credits for foreign income taxes paid. Generally, therefore, when a foreign tax rate is higher than the U.S. tax rate, there are advantages to shifting the business from the foreign country to tax-free countries. Another reason for shifting business into a tax-haven country is to enable banks to avoid double taxation of foreign branch earnings, as can occur when both foreign and U.S. tax authorities tax the same income. It should be noted that in neither of these cases is there an avoidance of U.S. federal taxes; in fact, in some instances the shifting of business to tax-haven countries results in greater tax revenues accruing to the U.S. government. Income earned in these locations, as with other income earned abroad, is not subject to U.S. state and local taxation.

The tables attached to this statement provide a general indication of the types of business booked at branches of U.S. banks in the Bahamas and the Cayman Islands. A large amount of purely interbank activity is booked in these branches, some of which involves the rechanneling of funds within a bank's organization and some of which involves purely market transactions of buying funds from some banks and selling them to others. Loans booked in these branches are preponderantly to foreign companies, including foreign subsidiaries of U.S. companies, and totaled $36 billion at the end of last year. Deposits from nonbank sources totaled $25 billion, and were divided almost equally between foreign customers and U.S. addressees. The latter are primarily U.S. corporations.

FEDERAL RESERVE ROLE

The Federal Reserve is interested in and monitors activities of foreign branches of member banks both in its role as the nation's central bank and in its role as a bank supervisor. Our interests differ somewhat according to these roles. In our central banking role, we monitor activities of foreign offices of U.S. banks in offshore centers and elsewhere as part of our general surveillance of international financial markets and international flows of funds. The growth of international lending through the Euromarkets and other markets has had important repercussions for capital flows throughout the world. Conditions and practices in those markets interact closely with conditions and operations in our domestic monetary and credit markets. In analyzing the condition of the U.S. economy and of its external position, as well as in assessing the consequences of various policy alternatives, much effort at the Federal Reserve is nowadays invested in following developments in international banking and financial markets and activities of U.S. banks in those markets.

As a bank supervisor, our interests are directed to the soundness of operations in these offices and to compliance with relevant banking laws and regulations. Most of our detailed knowledge of the operations of U.S. banks in offshore centers arises from our role as a bank supervisor. Since the branches in the Bahamas and the Cayman Islands are "shell" offices, virtually all of their records are maintained at the head office in the United States and thus are available for inspection at the time the bank is examined. Indeed, because of the special characteristics of these branches, the Board, when it authorized them, conditioned its approval on full records being maintained at the head office. Another condition attached to those authorizations was that these offices not be used to shift deposits and other business from the United States.

The supervisory interest in these operations runs, as I have already indicated, to their safety and soundness and their possible effects on the overall condition of the bank. They are scrutinized by bank examiners in connection with the overall examination of the bank and in the same fashion as other parts of the bank. The emphasis is accordingly on the quality of assets and the ability of borrowers to repay, in accordance with the terms and conditions of the credits. Virtually no attention is paid to the identity of depositors nor to depositor transactions. Thus, customer compliance with the tax laws of their various countries is not a consideration in the examination process. That compliance is covered by other authorities in this country and abroad. In any event, bank examiners are basically credit analysts and are not equipped to conduct tax audits.

INFORMATION ON OFFSHORE CENTER OPERATIONS

The Federal Reserve employs several sources of information on the activities of offshore offices that enable it to monitor compliance with sound banking practices and relevant U.S. regulations and that help in evaluating the impact of offshore offices on international financial flows. The information from these sources has been adapted to the Federal Reserve needs and interests that I have just discussed and are generally adequate for those purposes.

As I mentioned earlier, our most detailed information about the activities of U.S. banks in offshore centers is obtained from examination reports. These reports are the primary supervisory document. In addition, statistical reports are collected periodically on individual offices and are used mainly in our overall evaluation of banking activities in these centers. On a monthly basis, banks file reports for their major foreign branches showing their assets and liabilities by type of customer. Data compiled from

this report are published regularly in the FEDERAL RESERVE BULLETIN, including a separate section covering the Bahamas and the Cayman Islands. A second report is collected quarterly and shows foreign branch assets and liabilities by country.

Besides these reports on foreign branches, U.S. banking organizations also submit financial statements on their foreign subsidiaries on an annual basis. Subsidiaries of U.S. banks in the Bahamas and the Cayman Islands are much less important than their branch operations. At year-end 1977, total assets of these subsidiaries were only $3 billion, about one-third of which represented intercorporate transactions. Some of these subsidiaries conduct a wide range of activities similar to those of branches; others serve mostly to channel funds among affiliated offices. While some conduct trust activities, the volume is relatively small and is directed to foreign parties.

CONCLUSION

In this statement, I have tried to provide some insight into the general workings of offshore centers and into the nature of the Federal Reserve's interest and attention to developments in these centers, both in general and in particular relation to offices of U.S. banks. □

[21]

Tax havens explained

The wide publicity given to tax havens has led many developing countries to contemplate the adoption of similar status in order to speed up their development. This article defines both the dividends and drawbacks of such a status.

Milka Casanegra de Jantscher

What do the Bahamas, Bermuda, Hong Kong, Liberia, the Netherlands, the New Hebrides, Panama, and Switzerland have in common? They are all "tax havens." As such they are apt to excite either passionate praise or passionate denunciation, depending on the point of view of the commentator. Those who recommend the use of tax havens may cite with approval the remark of Lord Tomlin that "every man is entitled if he can to order his affairs so that the tax attaching under the appropriate Acts is less than it otherwise would be." Speaking of those who deplore their use, one writer observed that "many of the pronouncements on the subject were sufficiently vehement to convince one that nothing short of the destruction of the tax haven and a virtual embargo on [exports of] . . . capital would save the Republic."

What is a tax haven?

Essentially, a tax haven is a place where foreigners may receive income or own assets without paying high rates of tax upon them. Although strictly speaking not all tax havens are countries, we can refer to them as such here for the sake of convenience. In some havens the tax relief that foreigners enjoy stems from the absence of the chief forms of direct taxation—income, estate, and gift taxes; but in most countries the relief stems from special features of the tax system that result in a very low effective tax rate on certain forms of foreign investment. Some countries that enjoy a reputation as tax havens have cultivated it. In others the features that make them a tax haven are merely a consequence of their having followed certain principles of taxation, such as that of strict territoriality in applying income taxation, but without the intention

of establishing a tax haven. Such countries are likely to consider the tax haven label derogatory.

In the absence of reliable data on the use being made of tax havens, exaggerations flourish. The advantages that these countries offer to taxpayers are well described in guides written by professionals who specialize in carrying out operations in tax havens for their clients. But hard statistical information on the extent of the revenue losses suffered by high-tax countries and the benefits which tax haven countries derive from their status is woefully meager. There is general agreement on only a few facts, principally that the amount of business activity carried out in tax havens is considerable, even though exact figures are not available. Moreover, it appears that the use of tax havens by enterprises in high-tax countries—particularly by multinational enterprises—is growing.

Even though the list of tax havens includes several developed countries, most are developing countries. It is precisely their example that other developing countries are tempted to follow, in the hope that becoming a tax haven will help them solve some of their economic problems. While the tax haven status does bring some benefits to the tax haven country, it is one of the objects of this article to dispel the myth that the tax haven status is a panacea for a country's economic problems.

The modus operandi

Tax havens are used for a great variety of operations. The main purpose of those who patronize them is to minimize the taxpayer's total tax burden by subjecting at least a part of his income or wealth to a lower effective rate than would other-

wise be applicable. But care should be taken to distinguish between operations whose main purpose is that of diminishing a taxpayer's total burden and those that have a bona fide business purpose. The latter are generally not considered tax haven operations, even if they take place in a tax haven. Some industries located in tax havens are engaged in producing goods for the domestic or international market. Some royalties are paid from tax havens for patents or know-how actually being used in the country. Some foreign citizens work in tax haven countries. Even though these individuals or corporations benefit from the country's low tax rates, they do "real" business within its borders.

In contrast, much "tax haven" business is fictitious, in the sense that little or none of it is effectively carried out in the tax haven proper. Goods that are bought and sold by tax haven subsidiaries often do not pass through the tax haven's territory; they move directly from the country of origin to the country of destination. The assets of trusts that are established in tax havens are usually kept thousands of miles away; and neither the grantor nor the beneficiary is normally resident in the tax haven country.

Tax haven operations consist fundamentally in establishing within a tax haven country one or more legal entities, such as trusts, personal holding companies, or corporate subsidiaries, and attributing to them income earned elsewhere in order that it should be taxed at the country's low rates—or perhaps not taxed at all. This objective is usually accomplished by either (1) accumulating income in the tax haven country at low rates of tax, to be withdrawn later and invested elsewhere according to the investor's wishes; or (2) artificially shifting business profits from high-tax countries to a tax haven country.

In the case of passive investment, from which dividends, interest, or royalties are derived, trusts and personal holding companies are used as buffers or screens between the real investor and his assets. For many years the creation of these

31

legal entities for the purpose of obtaining a tax advantage was among the most popular uses of tax havens. As a result of countermeasures enacted during the past few years in certain capital exporting countries, the use of tax havens to shelter passive investment income has apparently not increased as fast as other tax haven activities.

At present, the most rapidly growing type of tax haven operation is that of shifting business profits from high-tax countries to tax haven countries. These profit shifting transactions are usually carried out by large corporations through tax haven subsidiaries, using sophisticated methods that are designed to diminish the tax base artificially in high-tax jurisdictions while increasing it in the tax haven country.

The most important of these methods involves transfer pricing: the setting of prices on goods and services that are bought and sold between a parent company and its foreign subsidiary. No "arm's length" bargaining takes place between these parties, so the prices that are set can be manipulated to minimize the enterprise's total taxes. (The "arm's length" relationship implies dealings between two independent and unrelated parties, where prices are determined according to market forces.) For example, instead of a company selling goods directly to a foreign buyer and realizing a profit that is fully taxable in its home country, it may sell the goods at an artificially low price to its subsidiary in a tax haven country. Thus, it shows only a small profit on which it has to pay a low tax, or perhaps even a loss! Its subsidiary then resells the goods to the ultimate buyer at the normal price, earning a large profit, all of which however is taxed at a low rate, or not taxed at all, because the subsidiary is located in a tax haven.

Another type of activity is carried out in tax haven countries by the financial sector. In most of these countries there exists a financial sector whose size and importance are out of proportion to the size and resources of the country itself. This sector usually comprises a large number of banks and trust companies, most of which are branches or subsidiaries of foreign-owned institutions. The reasons for their presence in tax haven countries are quite varied. These institutions manage trusts and holding companies that have been established to shelter foreign passive investment income; they hold deposits for foreign investors; they provide administrative facilities for a variety of corporate subsidiaries.

Foreign banks also use "shell" banks or branches located in tax haven countries to do Euro-currency business.

The activities of the financial sector are largely of an ancillary or dependent nature. The main object of many of these banks or trust companies is to provide services to other tax haven activities, such as administering tax haven trusts and corporate subsidiaries and holding deposits for foreign investors. Much of the business of this sector is "real" business in the tax haven. Banks and trust companies that administer trusts or holding companies do a large amount of the technical, audit, and legal work of administration in the tax haven country. In other cases, however, such as the Euro-currency branches of foreign banks, the "real" activity is carried out elsewhere, except perhaps for a nominal presence in the tax haven.

Tax havens also attract foreigners who come to work for foreign banks or other companies, and retirees, who decide to establish their residence where the advantage of a temperate climate is joined to that of a low-tax environment. In these cases there is "real" activity in the country—whether working or merely residing in it—and the tax factor is only one of several considerations that induce these individuals to settle in a tax haven country.

Tax and other advantages

Low tax rates are perhaps the principal attraction offered by tax havens. Usually these low rates are associated with income taxation; in fact, what springs to mind immediately upon hearing the words "tax haven" is the absence of income taxation, or the existence of a form of income taxation that exempts foreign investment. Though it is true that many of the ad-

vantages offered by tax haven countries are income tax advantages, these are by no means the only benefit that these countries offer to foreign investors.

Within the tax field, the absence of other taxes such as estate, inheritance, and gift taxes may be as important to certain investors as the absence of an income tax. Bilateral tax treaties between a tax haven country and some of the major developed countries are another feature that may attract investors. The existence of a tax treaty allows third-country investors to base their holding companies in tax havens and obtain a reduction in withholding taxes applied to the dividends and interest they receive from developed countries with which the tax haven country has the tax treaty.

Strict and well-enforced rules of banking secrecy and, in general, the possibility of doing business without close supervision by government agencies are additional attractions usually offered by tax haven countries. Other factors, such as the low cost of doing business, the existence of liberal banking regulations, and the absence of exchange controls are also important. These advantages were the chief reasons why foreign banks established Euro-currency branches in the Bahamas; the country's attractive tax climate was apparently of only secondary importance. Finally, a good communications service, a well developed legal system with an abundance of legal and accounting expertise, and, above all, a high degree of political and financial stability also help to make a country successful as a tax haven.

Countering tax loopholes

Are these all the elements necessary to enable taxpayers from high-tax jurisdictions to minimize their tax burdens? In fact, there is one other element without which they could not do so and that is the existence of features in the tax systems of developed countries that allow taxpayers to take advantage of the benefits offered by tax haven countries. Among these features are, for example, the more favorable tax treatment granted to trusts located abroad than to domestic trusts, and the mechanism of tax deferral that allows taxpayers of high-tax countries to defer income tax payments on income from foreign sources until it is repatriated. These and other mechanisms may be likened to escape valves left in their tax systems by high-tax countries, in order to grant taxpayers relief from the pressures of taxation. As long as these

Milka Casanegra de Jantscher

a Chilean national, has a law degree from the University of Chile, Santiago, and an LL.M. degree from Harvard University.
Mrs. Casanegra joined the staff of the Fund in 1972 and is now a Senior Tax Administration Analyst. She was formerly Assistant Commissioner for Planning and Research in the Internal Revenue Service of Chile.

provisions remain in effect, high-tax countries cannot place all the blame on tax havens for the losses of revenue they suffer.

During the past two decades some countries have moved to eliminate these safety valves. The United States has pioneered the way, with other countries, such as Australia, Belgium, Canada, the Federal Republic of Germany, and the United Kingdom following that example. The enactment of measures against the use of tax havens has not been easy and in each of these countries has produced an uproar among interested taxpayers in high-income brackets.

"there is a tendency to exaggerate the number of jobs created by tax haven activities"

In general, legislation on this subject is aimed at one or both of the following objectives: (1) preventing the tax-free accumulation by tax haven countries of certain forms of income, such as passive investment income and income derived from the assignment of service contracts to a foreign subsidiary; and (2) attacking the problem of transfer pricing, by attempting to tax a parent company on the profits it would have obtained if the transaction with its subsidiary had taken place at arm's length.

The tax systems of a number of industrialized countries, such as Canada, the Federal Republic of Germany, the United Kingdom, and the United States, permit domestic companies to postpone the payment of taxes on profits earned by foreign subsidiaries until those profits are repatriated. This has made attractive the establishment of foreign personal holding companies in tax haven countries that can accumulate income either free of tax or subject to a very low effective rate. The rules recently enacted in some developed countries to prevent this accumulation generally require the income of these foreign holding companies to be taxed on an accrual basis, thereby eliminating the tax deferral privilege that the owners previously enjoyed.

There are several reasons why these rules are complex. Perhaps the main one is the wish of the developed countries to soften their impact upon companies that are accumulating income in low-tax jurisdictions for normal business reasons, without intending to avoid taxes. In order to achieve this purpose, anti-accumula-

tion rules rely heavily on percentage criteria, which have the merit of being objective but which at the same time leave a wide margin for maneuvering by taxpayers. Thus the anti-accumulation rules usually apply only when the subsidiary established in a low-tax country is "controlled" by taxpayers in the high-tax country. "Control" is defined as ownership of more than 50 per cent of the stock of the foreign subsidiary. The United States and Canada, however, only count corporations or individuals, each of whom owns more than 10 per cent of the foreign corporation, toward the 51 per cent "controlling" share of the company. This latter rule attempts to exclude portfolio investment from the anti-accumulation provisions. The Federal Republic of Germany does not employ this provision. Obviously, these percentage criteria can be easily circumvented. A case in point is the recent increase in the number of subsidiaries in low-tax countries whose parent company legally owns only 50 per cent of the stock, but in practice exercises full control without being subject to the anti-accumulation provisions.

Apart from those loopholes due to the percentage criteria, there are other important exceptions to these rules that have usually been enacted in response to special interest groups. This is the case, for example, of the exceptions to these rules that until recently favored shipping interests in the United States.

Transfer pricing

In spite of the shortcomings of the rules that attempt to prevent the accumulation of tax-free income in tax havens through holding companies, these rules appear to have been more successful than the provisions designed to curb the use of transfer pricing to shift income from high-tax to low-tax jurisdictions. The tax laws of several developed countries contain provisions to ensure that sales and other operations carried out between domestic corporations and their foreign subsidiaries are transacted at arm's length prices. These provisions are difficult to administer, since the actual determination of the arm's length price is fraught with complexity.

As a result, the provisions against the use of tax havens that developed countries have lately introduced have mainly affected the accumulation of passive investment income in tax haven countries, not by banning accumulations outright, but by making them more costly and complex. Therefore, the accumulation of income by holding companies and trusts is still possible, but only for very wealthy investors or the large corporations. As the latter are also the corporations that use transfer pricing to shift income to tax havens, and as transfer pricing practices have not been much affected by the provisions against the use of tax havens, it is probable that the "clients" of tax havens are increasingly being drawn from higher-income and greater-wealth brackets. In fact, some of the movement against tax havens in developed countries has stemmed from medium or small corporations that claim that tax havens afford tax relief mainly to large corporations, making competition more difficult for other enterprises.

Benefits to the tax haven

But what are the benefits that tax havens may obtain from their status and what is the price they must pay for those benefits? For developing economies one of the main apparent advantages of being a tax haven is the possibility of achieving a higher employment level. This is particularly attractive to countries with a narrow resource base, which tend to have chronic unemployment problems.

However, there is a tendency to exaggerate the number of jobs created by tax haven activities. The establishment of hundreds and even thousands of corporations and trusts and the large number of transactions that technically take place in tax haven countries are generally accomplished by using little manpower within the tax haven country. The case of Norfolk Island, a possession of Australia and a former tax haven, illustrates this point. According to a survey quoted in a manual on tax havens, in 1972 more than 1,450 companies were incorporated in Norfolk Island—nearly one per inhabitant. Nevertheless, it appears that the tax haven sector was directly benefiting only 25 residents of the Island, as much of the business was being carried out by lawyers and accountants in Australia.

It should be remembered that the main purpose of tax haven activity is to avoid taxation and that no business or trade is actually carried out in the country. The main exceptions are the institutions in

33

the financial sector, which are the principal generators of employment opportunities and additional demand for services within the tax haven sector of the economy. However, these institutions usually prefer to staff their organizations with expatriates—particularly in the higher positions—so not all the jobs created by this activity will be available for nationals of the host country.

Other economic activities are also stimulated by tax haven operations. Construction is boosted, principally of commercial buildings. As in the case of employment, the number of new buildings

sources may be taxable while income from foreign sources is exempt. Moreover, in most tax haven countries indirect taxes such as customs duties, sales taxes, and others are fully applicable.

The drawbacks

Is there a price to be paid for all these advantages? Yes, and it is generally not fully apparent when countries set out to become tax havens but may become burdensome later.

The problems created and constraints imposed by the tax haven status vary according to the degree of development of

affairs. Secrecy and supervision do not go well together, and generally the latter suffers in tax haven countries; accordingly, it is not surprising when bank failures or other financial problems do occur.

Another circumstance that may frighten away investors is the suspicion that a country's leaders are considering important changes that may include nationalization or other radical measures. Even the smallest indication of this may precipitate a flight of depositors and other investors. A tax haven government must also be cautious about hinting that it may change its tax policies to meet revenue demands, for such hints may destabilize the tax haven sector. This seriously constrains the formulation of a coherent domestic tax policy, as there is a natural reluctance among authorities to jeopardize the tax haven sector by any changes, however necessary, in the tax system.

> ## "tax haven countries tend to be more vulnerable to external factors than developing countries that are not tax havens"

required is much smaller than the size of the tax haven sector might indicate, as hundreds of holding companies or other subsidiaries may require only enough office wall space on which to hang a nameplate. Only those enterprises that actually do something—again mainly enterprises in the financial sector—require sizable office space to carry out their activities. Another activity that may be stimulated is tourism, particularly if the country enjoys an agreeable climate and meetings of directors in the country are a requirement for incorporation. A tax haven country may also attract retired persons as residents, and their presence provides employment opportunities and helps bring in foreign exchange.

The existence of a large financial sector has other important effects too. It may help a country maintain a free and open foreign exchange and payments system. In addition, the advantage of having a readily accessible financial market is considerable. Government bond issues may be underwritten or subscribed to by foreign banks, thereby making funds available for public investment and economic development.

Finally, the tax haven sector is a source of revenue to the government. However liberal the tax system of a country may be, there will always be some form of tax or fee for which the foreign investor will be liable. These contributions range from a simple annual fee payable by all corporations established in the country to income tax on profits considered to be of domestic origin. For example, in the case of banks that do both domestic and foreign business, profits from domestic

the country, the size and composition of its tax haven sector, and the kind of benefits granted to this sector. In general terms, the most troublesome problems arise in developing countries where the tax haven sector contributes a relatively important share to the country's gross national product (GNP).

At first glance this may appear paradoxical. The fact that the tax haven sector is contributing substantially to GNP should mean that new economic activity is taking place, which is desirable. This is true, but the problem lies in the nature of tax haven activity. As its main purpose is that of tax avoidance, tax haven activity generates very little investment in tangible assets; therefore, tax haven business is extremely volatile and lacking in stability.

The one sector that does engage in real economic activity—the financial sector—is heavily dependent on what occurs in the rest of the tax haven sector. If this foreign business disappears, the domestic activity will not be sufficient to retain the large number of banks, insurance companies, and other organizations that form the financial sector of a tax haven country.

Tax haven activity is highly sensitive to national and international developments. Within a tax haven country itself, the slightest whiff of financial scandal—such as a prominent bank defaulting on its obligations—is enough to send investors in search of another tax haven that offers more security. Situations such as these are difficult to prevent, as one of the things investors look for in tax havens is absolute secrecy and as little prying as possible by government officials into their

International factors

Internationally, one of the factors that can influence tax haven investment is the attitude of developed countries toward this activity. The measures against the use of tax havens already taken by them have all had some impact. Future measures are already being studied by some developed countries that will make the use of tax havens more costly and complex than it is at present.

Fluctuations in the world economy and disturbances in international financial markets also affect tax haven activities. Competition among tax havens trying to outdo one another by offering more stability, lower taxes, and better commercial facilities accentuates the volatility of tax haven investment.

Tax haven countries tend to be more vulnerable to external factors than developing countries that are not tax havens. Not only are they sensitive to changes in international commodity prices like other developing countries, as well as to international economic fluctuations, but they are also directly affected by the tax policies of developed countries, which are beyond their control. Accordingly, the greater their dependence on tax haven activities, the more unstable is their economic situation. These considerations, together with the constraints that the tax haven status places on the formulation of national fiscal policies, suggest that developing countries should think twice before aspiring to become tax havens. Meanwhile, those that are already tax havens should try to diminish their dependence on the activities of this sector. ▪

34

[22]

Offshore banking centers: benefits and costs

Accompanying the explosive growth of the Eurocurrency market, there has been a proliferation of offshore banking centers. This article briefly analyzes why this proliferation has occurred and discusses the benefits to and costs for such centers.

Ian McCarthy

Over the last two decades, there has been a striking growth in international financial markets in general and the Eurocurrency market in particular. This growth has been facilitated by, and to some extent has precipitated, a marked increase in the number of offshore banking centers.

In 1965, the total Eurocurrency market was estimated at $9 billion (net), and the offshore centers accounted for a negligible share of this total. By 1978, the Eurocurrency market had grown to $375 billion (net), and the group of financial centers included under the rubric of offshore centers accounted for $45 billion of this. The striking increase in the importance of offshore centers largely reflects the advantages they offer vis-à-vis more traditional centers, although in many ways the offshore centers should be seen as adjuncts to these traditional centers rather than as solely competitors. Indeed the distinction between major international financial centers, such as London and New York, and offshore centers, such as Bahrain, Luxembourg, and Singapore, is to some extent an arbitrary one. For example, London offers many of the same advantages for Eurocurrency business, in terms of freedom from reserve requirements and interest withholding taxes, that Singapore does; while New York authorities have been exploring the possibility of establishing a "banking free zone" in which banks dealing with nonresidents would be exempt from minimum reserve requirements, interest rate controls, and interest withholding taxes.

This article analyzes the benefits and costs of hosting offshore banks in general terms, drawing, where appropriate, upon the experience of several offshore centers. The article does not, however, attempt to deal with the implications of offshore banking activities for other countries or for Eurocurrency markets, nor does it deal with the benefits and costs of operating tax havens. (See "Tax havens explained" by Milka Casanegra de Jantscher, **Finance & Development**, March 1976.)

An analysis of offshore banking centers finds the major benefit attached to hosting offshore banks to be their local operating expenditures, to the extent that these contribute to domestic welfare. Estimated operating expenditures are as high as 8 per cent of the host country's gross national product (GNP) in some centers. This benefit appears to be only loosely related to the volume of business routed through a center but closely related to the number of banks and the types of operations carried out. Countries with smaller economies gain proportionately more from offshore banking than those with larger ones. However, in addition to the benefits from local expenditure, there may also be substantial direct and indirect costs associated with the regulation and control of offshore centers. The major potential indirect cost is the possible adverse impact of offshore banks'

activities onshore. However, as long as offshore banks operate entirely offshore, it is impossible for flows of funds through them to influence the domestic monetary system; and if onshore activities are permitted, they will only cause problems if the authorities are unable to control them.

The offshore center

This article defines offshore banking centers as places—whether countries, areas, or cities—which have made a deliberate attempt to attract international banking business (nonresident, foreign-currency denominated assets, and liabilities) by reducing or eliminating restrictions upon operations as well as lowering taxes and/or other levies. Approximately 21 centers qualify under this definition (see Table 1 for more detailed information).

Offshore centers may be classified as either "paper" or "functional." A paper center acts as a location of record, but little or no actual banking is carried out there whereas a functional center is one where deposit taking or final lending is actually carried out. Functional centers serve as important links between Eurocurrency markets, helping to channel funds from major international financial centers (such as London and New York) to final borrowers; in contrast, paper centers are basically used by international banks to minimize overall taxes and other levies.

Despite the apparent heterogeneity of the centers, they do have some characteristics in common. First, in virtually all of the centers, local capital requirements—which must be held in the form of onshore assets, whether government paper or bank premises—are low or nonexistent for offshore banks. Second, license fees are generally low. Third, entry is relatively easy, especially for large international banks, in contrast to the situation in neighboring

Table 1
Fifteen offshore banking centers: some basic data

	Ease of entry	Local capital requirements	Taxes and levies	Annual license fees	Number of offshore banks	Total offshore assets (In billions of U.S. dollars)
Anguilla	Until now, unregulated.	None	None	EC$1,350	100	...
Bahamas	Relatively easy, even for new banks.	None	None	US$300–45,000[1]	263	70
Bahrain	Generally limited to branches of major international banks.	None	None	US$25,000	37	21
Bahrain	Generally limited to branches of major international banks.	None	None	US$25,000	37	21
Cayman Islands	Relatively easy, even for new banks.	None	None	C$5,000–15,000	260	12[2]
Hong Kong	Foreign banks are now being licensed after a 13-year moratorium. For the most part, only one branch of large international banks will be allowed.	None	10% withholding tax on interest paid. (proposed 17% offshore profit tax).	...	74[3] 200[4]	11
Jersey	Only large, reputable international banks have been admitted.	None	£ 300 per annum for corporate tax companies	...	33	2
Lebanon	Foreign banks must deposit LL7.5 million with the Treasury. Other new banks must have 50% Lebanese ownership and deposit LL4.5 million.	LL 15 million[5]	None[6]	...	78	...
Luxembourg	Only large, reputable international banks have been admitted.	Lux F 250 million	40% corporate tax 40% municipal business tax 30% liquidity ratio.	...	92	48
Netherlands Antilles	Extremely easy.	None	3–6% profit tax. No liquidity requirements.	...	43	...
New Hebrides	Extremely easy.	None	None	$A 1,000	13	...
Panama	Relatively easy for branches or subsidiaries of international banks.	US$250,000	None	None	66	7
Philippines	Limited entry until profitability of existing operations has been assured. Major international banks favored.	US$1 million[7]	5% profit tax (on offshore to offshore transactions) 10% profit tax (offshore to onshore).	US$20,000	17	1
Seychelles	Limited to branches of subsidiaries of major international banks.[8]	None	None	US$20,000[8]	1[8]	...
Singapore	Relatively easy. Major international banks favored.	S$3 million	10% profit tax (on offshore operations).	S$50,000	66	17
United Arab Emirates	Restricted licenses are limited, in theory, to reputable international banks.	None	None (at least in the Emirate of Sharjah).	None	55[9]	...

Sources: Material from *The Banker, Banker Research Unit, Euromoney, Far Eastern Economic Review, Sunday Times.*
Note: Six centers are not listed because data are either insignificant or unobtainable. These are Barbados, Costa Rica, Guernsey, the Isle of Man, Nicaragua, and St. Vincent.
... Indicate that data are either insignificant or unobtainable.
[1] US$300 (nonactive banks) to US$45,000 (authorized dealers and agents).
[2] Estimated assets in September of 1977 for the Cayman Islands and the Bahamas were US$82 billion. Estimated assets in the Bahamas were some US$70 billion.
[3] Full license banks.
[4] Deposit-taking companies.
[5] Minimum capital if LL 15 million of which LL 4.5 million must be deposited with the Treasury. New branches of foreign banks must deposit LL 7.5 million.
[6] Since the declaration of the "Banking Free Zone" in March 1977.
[7] US$1 million must be held in any foreign-currency debt instrument of the Philippine Government.
[8] Information provided by authorities.
[9] Twelve with Restricted Licenses (offshore licenses).

countries, which may strictly limit or prohibit the entry of foreign banks. Fourth, and most important, taxes and levies on offshore business are virtually nonexistent in these centers, in marked contrast to the situation in alternative locations. None of the centers imposes minimum reserve requirements on offshore liabilities or withholding taxes on internal income. Only four impose profit taxes, and these are very limited. Moreover, some, but not all, offer the advantage of proximity to important loan outlets or deposit sources; Bahrain, for example, is an offshore base for petrodollar transactions.

Demand

The demand for offshore centers by banks in general increases with the severity of taxes, levies, and restrictions imposed by authorities in onshore centers. For example, if New York—now an onshore center—were to exempt banks' operations with nonresidents from minimum reserve requirements and other charges, then banks would be less attracted to paper operations in offshore centers such as the Bahamas. Of course, in a sense, this would merely mean that New York had become a new offshore center rather than any diminution in overall offshore business.

Ian McCarthy

a U.K. citizen, is an economist in the Central Banking Service of the Fund. He was educated at the London School of Economics (U.K.) and joined the Fund in 1968.

If major countries coordinated their taxation, bank supervision, and application of reserve requirements, then tax avoidance via routing transactions through offshore banking centers would be more difficult and less rewarding, but even if this were to happen, functional offshore centers would still offer some advantages.

The volume of business routed through offshore centers has increased with the growth of Eurocurrency transactions of the participating institutions, at least so long as the offshore centers have provided fiscal advantages to offshore banks and enacted fewer regulations than elsewhere.

The demand for individual paper centers is quite sensitive to minor changes in local charges and regulations. Paper centers are obviously extremely close substitutes for one another in today's world of modern telecommunications. As long as a bank has little physical presence in a center, it is fairly easy to relocate operations if one center tries to impose slightly higher charges than the others. This is particularly the case where international banks have banking operations in several paper centers.

The demand for functional centers is less sensitive to local taxes and levies. Functional centers generate profits in their own right rather than solely via the avoidance of taxes and levies elsewhere. Moreover, they are not close substitutes for one another; and banks, because of their physical presence in the centers, will incur more substantial costs if operations are closed. The functional centers, therefore, have been able to impose profit taxes on offshore banks.

Lastly, once a center, particularly a functional one, attracts a sufficient number of banks, its attractiveness to other banks increases automatically. There is thus what might be seen as a takeoff point. Once a sufficient number of banks are attracted, substantial external economies may result—for example, it may become economic to provide newcomers with the services of accountants, lawyers, and moneybrokers, and communication with other trading or correspondent banks may become easier.

In recent years, there has been a proliferation of ministates, and many of them have developed an interest in hosting offshore banks, whether paper or functional. However, most of them are better fitted to act as paper centers, since they often lack both a favorable location and the requisite financial and communication facilities. Given the proliferation of paper centers and the broad-based coverage provided by existing functional centers, it is unlikely that the recent increase in their supply will be matched by an equivalent increase in demand for them. The prospects for new centers are therefore limited.

Operating expenditures

The number of countries willing to act as offshore centers is clearly related to their perceptions of the costs and benefits involved. Ideally, a country's decision to specialize in offshore business—to introduce the requisite amendments to legislation, to invest in telecommunications and infrastructure, and to accept the potential indirect costs—would depend upon an explicit assessment of the expected future net welfare gain, discounted over time. In practice, however, there are many uncertainties and inherent difficulties in quantifying many of these costs and benefits. All that a country's authorities can do is to list the potential costs and benefits and make an ad hoc assessment as the opportunities occur to host these banks.

Offshore banks pay salaries and incur local expenditures which contribute to the welfare of the host economy. Available

Table 2
Five host countries: gross direct benefits ascribable to offshore banking
(In thousands of U.S. dollars)

	Salaries	Other expenditures	Total expenditures	License and other fees	Profit taxes
Bahamas[1]					
1973	17,093	13,025	30,118	1,545	n.a.
1974	17,195	12,935	30,130	1,515	n.a.
1975	18,330	14,556	32,886	1,508	n.a.
Bahrain[2]					
1977	...	...	20,800–40,000	800	n.a.
1978	...	...	37,650–50,000	875	n.a.
Cayman Islands[1]					
1976	4,898	4,040	8,938	957	n.a.
1977	5,340	4,879	10,219	1,501	n.a.
Panama[3]					
1974	2,268–15,919	1,711–12,009	2,977–27,928	...	n.a.
1975	2,405–21,506	1,814–16,224	4,103–37,730	...	n.a.
1976	3,564	2,689	6,253	...	n.a.
Singapore					
1974	...	...	12,000[4]–127,900[5]	1,200	2,700–4,100[6]
1975	...	...	15,700[4]–131,000[5]	1,200	3,300–5,000[6]
1976	...	...	21,300[4]–151,100[5]	1,300	4,600–6,800[6]

n.a. indicates that data are not applicable.
... indicate that data are either insignificant or unobtainable.
[1] Information provided by the monetary authorities.
[2] Based on published estimates.
[3] Estimated on the basis of employment figures provided by the authorities.
[4] Estimated using the assumption that operating expenditures equaled 0.05 per cent of offshore assets (Bank of America's estimated cost of Eurocurrency business according to N. Colchester, "Counting the Cost of Lending," *Financial Times*, July 15, 1978).
[5] Estimated by prorating the share of Asian Currency Units (ACUs) in the financial sector's share of GNP according to ACUs' share of external assets.
[6] Estimated on the basis of commercial banks' company reports.

evidence suggests that this is normally the major contribution of offshore banking to the host country. Care must be taken, though, to distinguish between the *gross* and *net* benefits. If salaries are paid to expatriates who import most of their consumption needs, there is little or no benefit to the domestic economy other than profits for importers and import taxes paid to the government. On the other hand, if salaries are paid to local employees and they spend a relatively insignificant proportion of them on imports, the net welfare gain will be far greater.

Various estimates of the direct benefits attributable to offshore banks in the Bahamas, Bahrain, Panama, and Singapore are summarized in Table 2. These are relatively more important, as might be expected, for the smaller economies. Although the absolute amounts involved are unimpressive by the standards of international banking, they are not insignificant from the point of view of the countries involved.

For the Bahamas, offshore banks' expenditures amounted to 6.2 per cent of GNP and were second only to tourism in economic importance. For the Cayman Islands, these expenditures amounted to $10 million, whereas tourism, the major economic activity, contributed $22 million to the economy. The benefits do not appear

to have been closely related to the level of offshore assets held by the banks. For example, the Bahamas shared in the rapid growth of Eurocurrency markets between 1973 and 1975 (the Bahamas and the Cayman Islands together accounted for $26 billion in Eurocurrency assets in 1973 and $50 billion in 1975); yet, despite a 90 per cent increase in business routed through the two centers, the offshore banks' local expenditures increased only 9 per cent. Similarly, the assets of the offshore banks in Bahrain doubled between 1977 and 1978, while their estimated expenditures increased only 20–25 per cent.

Taxes and levies

By imposing charges upon the banks—through license fees, profit taxes, or liquidity and capital requirements (to be satisfied by holding onshore assets)—the local authorities may, in theory, appropriate some of the benefits which the international banks derive from locating their operations in the offshore centers. Their ability to do so will depend upon the magnitude of these benefits to the banks concerned and the pressure of competition from other offshore centers. Paper centers have generally found it difficult to levy any charges other than license fees, but four functional centers—Luxembourg, the Netherlands Antilles, the Philippines, and Singapore—have been able to levy profit taxes on offshore banks. (A fifth center—Hong Kong—has announced an intention to do so.) For three of the four centers, the amounts raised have not been impressive, with the exception of Luxembourg, where the Compagnie Luxembourgeoise de la Dresdner Bank is the largest single taxpayer and offshore banks contribute a major share of corporate taxes. For Singapore, the yield from its 10 per cent profit tax is probably between $5 and $7 million annually, while the Philippines has so far gained nothing, since its offshore banking units have been making negligible profits.

License and other fees, such as work permit and registration fees, have similarly yielded relatively low returns. None of the centers appear to have derived much more than $1.5 million per annum, and many have derived less. Other charges and levies are unimportant for the most part.

Even if the direct benefits of offshore banking are not as substantial as has generally been thought, there may still be significant indirect benefits. The centers may gain improved access to international capital markets; the domestic financial system may become more efficient, both through increased competition and through exposure to the practices of the offshore banks; and a cadre of local staff may be trained which will contribute to a faster growth of the domestic economy.

However, these benefits may not necessarily materialize. Since only "brass-plate" operations are being carried on in the paper centers, the larger functional centers will probably be better able to profit from improved interaction with international markets or from the competition to domestic banks from offshore operations. (Brass-plate operations refer to those where the only sign of a bank's presence is a brass-plate outside an office; such offices may administer the affairs of several banks.) However, countries which are able to act as functional centers generally have both excellent access to international markets and fairly well-developed domestic financial systems to start with.

As for the benefits from training a cadre of local staff, first, the expertise gained in offshore banking may not be relevant to the local financial system. Second, once bankers are trained, they may opt to stay with the offshore banks, in which case there may even be an internal "brain drain."

Costs

Many countries view offshore banking as offering a rapid and cheap means of garnering revenue for the economy and the government. There are, however, a number of costs which must be borne. These will depend upon both the character of the business which the center attracts and the characteristics of the local economy.

A brass-plate center may not incur any real costs, but the benefits will be correspondingly low. A center which aspires to become an important functional center may need to incur direct costs, such as expenditures on telecommunications, education, supervision, and regulation, while success may also entail several indirect costs, the most important of which are the diminution of autonomy of domestic monetary policy and, perhaps, increased tax evasion by businesses and individuals

If a center is to attract offshore banks, the most important precondition is good communications; for remote areas, the cost of upgrading telecommunications may be high. Expenditures on education and training of local personnel may also be necessary in order to derive any concrete benefit from the presence of offshore banks. Last, the supervision and regulation of offshore banks could entail substantial costs. If the domestic financial system is relatively large and developed, a comprehensive regulatory and supervisory operation will be required anyway, and the extension of these activities to offshore banks will entail little in the way of extra cost. But for a small and unsophisticated local system, the extra cost may be quite large.

To some extent, the direct cost of regulation, in terms of salaries and other expenditures, can be covered by charges against the banks. Any such charges would, however, represent a levy on the banks and, if other centers do not impose them, the banks may move elsewhere. More important, the promised absence of regulation has sometimes been one of the attractions of offshore centers.

The major indirect cost attached to hosting offshore banks is a diminution in autonomy where domestic monetary policy is concerned, together with an increased potential for tax evasion and, possibly, deleterious competitive effects upon local banks. However, diminution of autonomy may not occur, since there may be little to lose.

If offshore banking is rigorously limited to accepting foreign currency funds from, and lending them to, nonresidents, then *ex definitio* there should be no impact upon onshore financial flows. However, in most of the offshore centers, there has been some blurring of the lines between offshore and onshore activity; in particular, several centers have encouraged lending by offshore banks to specific projects—generally, although not always, to those involving the

host country's government. In addition, it may not always be possible to regulate effectively the activities of the offshore institutions. If confidentiality of operations is guaranteed, it may be difficult, even for the regulators, to identify resident and nonresident transactions clearly, particularly in the absence of exchange controls.

Offshore business can also create fiscal problems. Hong Kong, for instance, has reportedly been reluctant to encourage this business because of the increased potential for Hong Kong residents to deposit funds with offshore institutions and then take dummy loans of the same amount. The interest from the loan would then be deductible for tax purposes, while the interest paid on the deposits would not be taxed.

Another possible cost of offshore banking could be the impact of increased competition on the domestic financial system. It is difficult for a broad-based financial system to develop in head-to-head competition with international banks. In particular, if the local monetary authority lacks the willingness or ability to act as a lender of last resort to the domestic banking system, the competitive advantage of the foreign banks, which are able to draw upon their head offices to augment their liquidity, may be so strong as to inhibit further development of indigenous banks. This problem could be avoided by forbidding offshore banks to operate domestically; but, if there are no onshore operations, indirect benefits may not accrue to the host country.

Offshore banks may also increase demand for office space, housing, and professional services; this may cause problems for local residents as the supply of such resources may not be flexible in the short run.

While the benefit-cost equation appears favorable for existing centers, it seems possible, indeed probable, that there is little unsatisfied demand for new offshore centers. There are even some signs at present of an excess supply. If one looks at the existing geographical coverage provided by offshore centers, virtually every area of the world has a selection of offshore centers readily accessible. In addition, improved telecommunications render it easier than before to route paper business through a limited number of centers rather than setting up operations in several widely dispersed centers. In general, therefore, new paper centers are not likely to succeed. In addition, even existing centers might become less important and less profitable if moves to impose controls on the Eurocurrency markets are successful, and/or if New York establishes an International Banking Zone. 🔲

[23]

International Banking Facilities

K. Alec Chrystal

INTERNATIONAL Banking Facilities (IBFs) started operation in the United States in early December 1981. Since then, they have grown to the point where they now represent a significant part of the international banking business worldwide. The purpose of this article is to examine IBFs and to discuss their significance for international banking.

OFFSHORE BANKING

A substantial "offshore" international banking sector, often called the "eurocurrency" market, grew up in the 1960s and 1970s. Its key characteristic is that banking business is transacted in a location outside the country in whose currency the business is denominated. Thus, eurodollar transactions are conducted outside the United States, eurosterling transactions are conducted outside Britain, and so on. Much of this offshore business occurs in major financial centers like London, though some business is literally in islands offshore from the United States, such as the Bahamas or Cayman Islands.

Offshore banking business is somewhat different from that conducted onshore. Though, in both cases, banks take deposits and make loans, offshore banks have virtually no checking deposit liabilities. Instead, their deposits are typically made for specific periods of time, yield interest, and are generally in large denominations.

Offshore banking arose as a means to avoid a variety of banking regulations. For example, offshore banks that deal in eurodollars avoid reserve requirements on

deposits, FDIC assessments and U.S.-imposed interest rate ceilings. The first two of these regulations increase the margin between deposit and loan rates. Avoiding these costs enables offshore banks to operate on much smaller margins. Interest ceilings, where binding, reduce the ability of banks subject to such ceilings to compete internationally for deposits.

Many "shell" bank branches in offshore centers, such as the Caymans and Bahamas, exist almost solely to avoid U.S. banking regulations. Shell branches are offices that have little more than a name plate and a telephone. They are used simply as addresses for booking transactions set up by U.S. banks, which thereby avoid domestic monetary regulations.

IBFs: ONSHORE OFFSHORE BANKS

IBFs do not represent new *physical* banking facilities; instead, they are separate sets of books within existing banking institutions — a U.S.-chartered depository institution, a U.S. branch or agency of a foreign bank, or a U.S. office of an Edge Act corporation.[1] They can only take deposits from and make loans to nonresidents of the United States, other IBFs and their establishing entities. Moreover, IBFs are not subject to the regulations that apply to domestic banking activity; they avoid reserve requirements, interest rate ceilings and deposit insurance assessment. In effect, they are accorded the advantages of many offshore banking centers without the need to be physically offshore.

K. Alec Chrystal, professor of economics-elect, University of Sheffield, England, is a visiting scholar at the Federal Reserve Bank of St. Louis. Leslie Bailis Koppel provided research assistance.

[1] As a result of a 1919 amendment to the Federal Reserve Act initiated by Sen. Walter Edge, U.S. banks are able to establish branches outside their home state. These branches must be involved only in business abroad or the finance of foreign trade. The 1978 International Banking Act allowed foreign banks to open Edge Act corporations which accept deposits and make loans directly related to international transactions.

FEDERAL RESERVE BANK OF ST. LOUIS   APRIL 1984

The Establishment of IBFs

Three regulatory or legislative changes have permitted or encouraged the establishment and growth of IBFs. First, the Federal Reserve Board changed its regulations in 1981 to permit the establishment of IBFs. Second, federal legislation enacted in late 1981 exempted IBFs from the insurance coverage and assessments imposed by the FDIC. Third, several states have granted special tax status to the operating profits from IBFs or altered other restrictions to encourage their establishment. In at least one case, Florida, IBFs are entirely exempt from local taxes.

Restrictions on IBF Activities

While IBFs may transact banking business with U.S. nonresidents on more or less the same terms as banks located offshore, they may not deal with U.S. residents at all, apart from their parent institution or other IBFs. Funds borrowed by a parent from its own IBF are subject to eurocurrency reserve requirements just as funds borrowed from an offshore branch would be.

Four other restrictions on IBFs are designed to ensure their separation from domestic money markets. First, the initial maturity of deposits taken from nonbank foreign customers must be at least two working days. Overnight deposits, however, may be offered to overseas banks, other IBFs and the parent bank. This restriction ensures that IBFs do not create a close substitute for checking accounts.

Second, the minimum transaction with an IBF by a nonbank customer is $100,000, except to withdraw interest or close an account. This effectively limits the activity of IBFs to the "wholesale" money market, in which the customers are likely to be governments, major corporations or other international banks.[2] There is no restriction on the size of interbank transactions.

Third, IBFs are not permitted to issue negotiable instruments, such as certificates of deposit (CDs), because such instruments would be easily marketable in U.S. money markets, thereby breaking down the intended separation between IBFs and the domestic money market.

Finally, deposits and loans of IBFs must not be related to a nonresident customer's activities in the

United States.[3] This regulation prevents IBFs from competing directly with domestic credit sources for finance related to domestic economic activity.

Where Are IBFs Located?

IBFs are chiefly located in the major financial centers (see table 1). Almost half of the nearly 500 IBFs are in New York; California, Florida and Illinois have the bulk of the rest. In terms of value of liabilities, however, the distribution is even more skewed. Of IBFs reporting monthly to the Federal Reserve (those with assets or liabilities in excess of $300 million), 77 percent of total liabilities were in New York, with California (12 percent) and Illinois (7.5 percent) a long way behind. It is notable that Florida, which has 16.5 percent of the IBFs, has only 2 percent of the liabilities of reporting banks.

While the distribution of IBFs primarily reflects the preexisting locations of international banking business, differences in tax treatment between states may have influenced the location of IBFs marginally. For example, the fact that Florida exempts IBFs from state taxes may well explain why it has the largest number of Edge Act corporation IBFs and ranks second to New York in terms of numbers of IBFs set up by U.S.-chartered banks.

Although Florida has the most advantageous tax laws possible for IBFs, it is not alone in granting them favorable tax status. Nine other states (New York, California, Illinois, Connecticut, Delaware, Maryland, Georgia, North Carolina and Washington) and the District of Columbia have enacted special tax laws that encourage the establishment of IBFs.[4]

The reason for the favorable tax treatment for IBFs in states like Florida is not clear. There is no doubt that Florida has tried to encourage its development as an international financial center.[5] The benefits from encouragement of IBFs per se, however, are hard to see. For example, the employment gains are probably trivial. Since IBFs are merely new accounts in existing institutions, each IBF will involve at most the employment of a handful of people. In many cases, there may be no extra employment.

---

[3]"The Board expects that, with respect to nonbank customers located outside the United States, IBFs will accept only deposits that support the customer's operations outside the United States and will extend credit only to finance the customer's non-U.S. operations." See "Announcements" (1981), p. 562.

[4]These provisions vary from case to case. For a summary of the position in New York and California, see Key (1982).

[5]See "Florida's Baffling Unitary Tax" (1983).

---

[2]Foreign governments are treated like overseas banks for purposes of maturity and transaction size regulations.

Table 1
Location of International Banking Facilities

	Total IBFs	U.S.-chartered banks[1]	Agencies and branches of foreign banks	Edge Act corporations	Liabilities of Monthly Reporting IBFs, Other than to Parent Entity		
					Amount (billions of dollars)	Percent of total reported	Number of banks reporting
TOTAL	477	144	264	69	$173.43		
New York	208	38	154	16	133.8	77%	90
California	84	16	57	11	20.1	12	27
Florida	79	27	29	27	3.3	2	8
Illinois	30	6	17	7	13.1	7.5	11
Texas	20	14	0	6			
District of Columbia	11	8	3	0			
Pennsylvania	9	7	2	0			
Washington	7	3	4	0			
Georgia	6	4	1	1			
Massachusetts	5	3	1	1	3.1	1.8	10
New Jersey	4	4	0	0	(There are too few reporting banks in other states for a data breakdown to be made available.)		
Ohio	4	4	0	0			
Connecticut	2	2	0	0			
Kentucky	2	2	0	0			
Michigan	2	2	0	0			
N. Carolina	2	2	0	0			
Rhode Island	1	1	0	0			
Virginia	1	1	0	0			

NOTE: Figures for numbers of IBFs are as of September 28, 1983. Figures for liabilities are as of October 26, 1983. Monthly reporting banks are those with assets or liabilities of at least $300 million. SOURCE: Federal Reserve Board Release G.14(518)A and Federal Reserve Board unpublished data.

[1]One savings and loan association has an IBF that is in the Florida figure.

What Do IBFs Do?

The assets and liabilities of IBFs on December 30, 1981, December 29, 1982, and October 20, 1983, are recorded in table 2; as of October 20, 1983, over 98 percent of their liabilities were dollar-denominated.

The December 30, 1981, figures largely reflect business switched from other accounts either in the parent bank or an offshore branch. Operations of the IBFs themselves are reflected more clearly in the later figures. Consider the latest available figures in the third column of table 2. The most important aspects of these figures is the proportion of business with other banks vs. the proportion with nonbank customers. On the asset side, about one-sixth of total assets are "commercial and industrial loans" (Item 5a) and one-ninth are loans to "foreign governments and official institutions" (Item 5c). The remainder, over 70 percent, are claims on

either other IBFs, overseas banks or an overseas branch of the parent bank. Claims on overseas banks (Items 3a and 5b) are largest, while claims on other IBFs (Item 2) and overseas offices of the parent bank (Item 1) are of broadly similar magnitude.

The liability structure is even more heavily weighted toward banks. Only about 16 percent of the liabilities of IBFs (as of October 26, 1983) were due to nonbanks. Of these, one-third was due to "foreign government and official institutions" (Item 10c) and two-thirds were due to "other non-U.S. addressees" (Item 10d). The latter are mainly industrial and commercial firms.

The high proportion of both assets and liabilities of IBFs due to other banking institutions reinforces the conclusion that they are an integral part of the eurodollar market. A high proportion of interbank business is characteristic of eurocurrency business in which

Table 2

Assets and Liabilities of International Banking Facilities (millions of dollars)

	December 30, 1981	December 29, 1982	October 26, 1983
ASSETS			
1. Gross Claims on Non-U.S. Offices of Establishing Entity	$7,188	$20,125	$30,322
(1) Denominated in U.S. Dollars	6,785	19,150	29,204
(2) Denominated in Other Currencies	403	975	1,118
2. Loans and Balances Due From Other IBFs	903	16.577	26,256
3. Gross Due From:			
A. Banks in Foreign Countries	8,470	26,666	29,093
B. Foreign Governments and Official Institutions	12	276	482
4. Securities of Non-U.S. Addressees	438	1,130	1.875
5. Loans To Non-U.S. Addressees			
A. Commercial and Industrial Loans	17,081	32,808	36,753
B. Banks in Foreign Countries	11,705	30,300	32,237
C. Foreign Governments and Omcial Institutions	7,791	16,960	22,348
D. Other Loans	1,164	1,070	958
6. All Other Assets in IBF Accounts	880	3.839	3.262
7. Total Assets Other Than Claims on U.S. and Non-U.S. Office of Establishing Entity	49,409	132,569	156,484
(1) Denominated in U.S. Dollars (Sum of Items 2 through 6)	48,445	129,626	153,264
(2) Denominated in Other Currencies	965	2,943	3.219
8. Total Assets Other Than Claims on U.S. Offices of Establishing Entity (Sum of Items 1 and 7)	56,597	152,694	186,806
(1) Denominated in U.S. Dollars	55,229	168,776	182,469
(2) Denominated in Other Currencies	1,368	3,917	4,337
LIABILITIES			
9. Gross Liabilities Due To Non-U.S. Offices of Establishing Entity	$29,091	$56,372	$69,756
(1) Denominated in U.S. Dollars	28,779	55,114	68,535
(2) Denominated in Other Currencies	313	1,258	1,221
10. Liabilities Due To:			
A. Other IBFs	1,009	17,382	28,803
B. Banks In Foreign Countries	10,127	37,045	42,446
C. Foreign Government and Official Institutions	2,834	7,439	9,115
D. Other Non-U.S. Addressees	952	13,816	19,073
E. All Other Liabilities in IBF Accounts	336	2.756	2,170
F. Total Liabilities Other Than Due To U.S. and Non-U.S. Offices of Establishing Entity	15,686	80,080	103,674
(1) Denominated in U.S. Dollars (Sum of Items 10.A Through 10.E)	15,258	78,439	101,608
(2) Denominated in Other Currencies	428	1,641	2,066
11. Total Liabilities Other Than Due to U.S. Offices of Establishing Entity (Sum of Items 9 and 10.F)	44,777	136,452	173,430
(1) Denominated in U.S. Dollars	44,037	133,552	170,143
(2) Denominated in Other Currencies	741	2,899	3,257
RESIDUAL			
12. Net Due From (+) / Net Due To (−) U.S. Offices of Establishing Entity (Item 11 Minus Item 8)	$−11,820	$−16,242	$−13,376
(1) Denominated in U.S. Dollars	−11,193	−15,224	−12,325
(2) Denominated in Other Currencies	−627	−1,018	−1,051
Number of Reporters	56	122	146

NOTE: Unless otherwise noted, figures include only amounts denominated in U.S. dollars. This report contains data only for those entities whose IBF assets or liabilities are at least $300 million, that is, for those entities that file a monthly report of IBF accounts on form FR 2072. SOURCE: Federal Reserve Board Release G.14 (518).

FEDERAL RESERVE BANK OF ST. LOUIS   APRIL 1984

there may be several interbank transactions between ultimate borrowers and ultimate lenders.[6]

An important role for interbank transactions is to provide "swaps" that reduce either exchange risk or interest rate risk for the parties involved. Suppose, for example, an IBF has a deposit (liability) of $1 million that will be withdrawn in one month, and it has made a loan (asset) to a customer of $1 million that will be repaid in two months. There is a risk that when the IBF comes to borrow $1 million to cover the second month of the loan, interest rates will have risen, and it will incur a loss on the entire transaction. If, however, this IBF can find a bank that has the opposite timing problem (a deposit of $1 million for 2 months and a loan of $1 million outstanding for one month), the two banks could arrange a swap. The second bank would loan the IBF $1 million in one month and get it back in two months (with suitable interest). The interest rate involved will be agreed on *at the beginning,* so that neither bank would suffer if interest rates should change in the second month.

These swap arrangements enable banks to match the maturity structure of their assets and liabilities. The existence of such swaps explains the high levels of both borrowing and lending between IBFs and overseas branches of their parent bank.[7]

THE GROWTH OF IBFs

Chart 1 shows the growth of total IBF liabilities since the end of 1981. Although the most rapid growth occurred in the first six months of their operation, IBFs have grown considerably over a period in which international banking business in general has been stagnant.[8] Within two years, they have come to be a significant part of the international money market. The liabilities of IBFs as of October 1983 (other than to parent banks) represent about 8½ percent of gross eurocurrency liabilities (as measured by Morgan Guaranty) or about 7½ percent of total international banking liabilities (as measured by the Bank for International Settlements. This includes onshore bank lending).

---

[6]See Niehans and Hewson (1976) for an explanation of the intermediary function of euromarkets. The interbank market is also discussed in Dufey and Giddy (1978), chapter 5.

[7]For a discussion of the role of swaps in foreign exchange markets, see Chrystal (1984).

[8]According to B.I.S. figures, international bank assets grew 8.8 percent in 1982 in nominal terms. This compares with figures typically in excess of 20 percent throughout the 1970s. The combined assets of overseas branches of U.S. banks declined by 0.6 percent in 1982 [see Press Release (1983)], though this partly reflects the growth of IBFs.

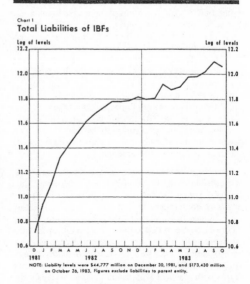

Chart 1
Total Liabilities of IBFs

NOTE: Liability levels were $44,777 million on December 30, 1981, and $173,430 million on October 26, 1983. Figures exclude liabilities to parent entity.

Where did this growth come from? Has the creation of IBFs generated a large volume of new business or has business been shifted from elsewhere? The evidence is that IBF business has almost entirely been shifted from elsewhere. Terrell and Mills use regression analysis to test the hypothesis that the creation of IBFs has led to greater growth of external bank assets.[9] This hypothesis is decisively rejected.

Some evidence concerning the origins of business shifted to IBFs is available in Key.[10] It is convenient to consider separately shifts from existing institutions in the U.S. and shifts from overseas banking centers.

Shifts from Banks in the United States

Up until January 27, 1982, about $34 billion of claims on overseas residents were shifted to IBF books from other U.S. banking institutions. The bulk of this (85 percent) came from U.S. branches of foreign banks — especially Japanese and Italian. Foreign banks typically would have had a higher proportion of assets eligible for shifting to IBFs, while Japanese and Italian banks generally had not established shell branches in Caribbean offshore centers.

---

[9]See Terrell and Mills (1983).

[10]See Key (1982).

9

In the same period, shifts of liabilities (due to parties other than overseas branches of the parent bank) from books of parent entities were much smaller. These amounted to about $6 billion, of which 90 percent came from branches of foreign banks. The small shift of liabilities relative to assets was affected by several factors: the negotiable nature of some deposits (CDs); the existence of penalties for renegotiations before maturity; the delay in passing New York tax relief for IBFs until March 1981; the small proportions of short-term deposits unrelated to trade with the United States; and the availability of accounts with similar returns yet fewer restrictions as to maturity and denomination (such as repurchase agreements).

If only the domestic books of U.S.-chartered banks are considered, the shift to IBFs is extremely small. Key reports a shift of $4.3 billion (through January 27, 1982) of claims on unrelated foreigners and only $0.1 billion of liabilities to unrelated foreigners. An alternative figure for claims shifted to IBFs is obtainable by looking at the change in commercial and industrial loans to non-U.S. addressees plus loans to foreign banks (*Federal Reserve Bulletin*, table A18, for large weekly reporting banks with assets of $750 million or more). This indicates a decline of $3.3 billion in the same period.

Shifts from Other Offshore Centers

Whereas foreign banks were mainly responsible for shifts to IBFs from banks located in the United States, banks chartered in the United States were mainly responsible for shifts of business from offshore centers and other overseas banking locations. Key estimates that U.S.-chartered banks shifted about $25 billion in claims on unrelated foreigners and about $6 billion in liabilities due to unrelated foreigners (through January 27, 1982) to IBFs from overseas branches. The comparable figures for foreign banks were $5½ billion and $9 billion, respectively.

This difference in the propensity to shift assets to IBFs is probably explained by the differential tax incentives of U.S. and foreign banks. U.S. banks pay taxes on worldwide income and may benefit from tax advantages of IBFs. Foreign banks may increase their tax liability to the United States by establishing an IBF instead of operating in an offshore center.

The bulk of business shifted by U.S. banks from their overseas branches has come from the Bahamas and Cayman Islands (collectively called Caribbean). In the first two months of operation of IBFs (11/30/81–1/29/82), liabilities to unrelated foreigners of branches of U.S. banks located there fell by $6.8 billion, while claims on unrelated foreigners fell by $23.3 billion. Much of this

shift reflected the redundancy of shell branches, at least for business with non-U.S. residents, once IBFs were permitted.

While much of the *raison d'être* of Caribbean branches for business with foreigners has been removed by the establishment of IBFs, these branches continue to be important for business with U.S. residents. Terrell and Mills report that the proportion of the liabilities of Caribbean branches due to U.S. residents rose from less than half in mid-1981 to about 70 percent by the end of 1982. However, the attraction of offshore deposits to U.S. residents is likely to decrease as interest regulations on domestic U.S. banks are relaxed, thereby narrowing the gap between domestic and offshore deposit rates.

Based on the figures of the Bank for International Settlements, Terrell and Mills estimate that the proportion of total international banking assets and liabilities due to U.S. banks' offshore branches declined by 4 percent in the first year of IBF operation. Another 3½ percent was lost by other overseas banking centers to IBFs.

THE SIGNIFICANCE OF IBFs FOR INTERNATIONAL BANKING

The primary significance of the experience with IBFs is that it enables us to better understand the forces that led to the growth of eurocurrency markets. In particular, the significant decline in business in Caribbean branches following the creation of IBFs suggests that the growth of business in this area was almost entirely intended to bypass U.S. monetary regulations. Deregulation of domestic banking in the United States will presumably have further effects, since much of the remaining business in Caribbean branches of U.S. banks is with U.S. residents.

The regulatory changes that permitted the establishment of IBFs were intended to ease the burden of domestic monetary restrictions on U.S. banks in the conduct of international banking business.[11] The extent to which this aim has been achieved is probably very limited. This is because IBFs play no role in financing either activities of U.S. residents or the U.S. activities of nonresidents.

Major U.S. banks that were involved in international finance to a significant degree had already found ways around U.S. banking regulations and were not restricted in their ability to compete internationally. The

---

[11]Ibid., p. 566.

fact that major U.S. banks have shifted business to IBFs from offshore centers means, of course, that there must be some benefit from having an IBF. This may result from lower transaction costs, some tax advantages or the greater attraction, from a risk perspective, of deposits located in the United States. However, the biggest gainers among U.S. banks may be medium-sized banks that were big enough to have some international business but not big enough to have an offshore branch.[12]

Other major beneficiaries from IBFs have been the U.S. branches and agencies of foreign banks. It is no accident that well over half of all IBFs have been established by these banks. The benefit to them arises from the high proportion of their existing business that is IBF-eligible, that is, the portion with nonresidents. Not the least of this would be transactions with their parent banks overseas.

CONCLUSIONS

The establishment of IBFs in the United States represents a change in the geographical pattern of international banking. It facilitates the conduct in the United States of some business that was previously conducted offshore. It also increases the ease with which foreign banks can operate branches in the United States. The creation of IBFs, however, does not seem to have in-

creased the total volume of international banking business. Indeed, IBFs have grown at a time when international banking growth has been at its slowest for over two decades. This growth has been largely at the expense of banking offices in other locations.

For the U.S. and world economies, however, IBFs are not of great significance. There may be efficiency gains resulting from the relaxation of U.S. regulations that led to the establishment of IBFs. But such gains are small. Interest rates in world capital markets are unlikely to have been affected. Benefits that accrue to banks located in the United States from their IBF facilities are largely offset by losses in offshore banks, though in many cases the gainers and losers are both branches of the same parent bank.

REFERENCES

"Announcements." *Federal Reserve Bulletin* (July 1981), pp. 561–63.

Chrystal, K. Alec. "A Guide to Foreign Exchange Markets," this *Review* (March 1984), pp. 5–18.

Dufey, G., and Ian H. Giddy. *The International Money Market* (Prentice-Hall, 1978).

"Florida's Baffling Unitary Tax: What Is It, Whom Does It Hurt?" *American Banker*, December 28, 1983.

Key, Sydney J. "International Banking Facilities," *Federal Reserve Bulletin* (October 1982), pp. 565–77.

Niehans, Jürg, and John Hewson. "The Euro-dollar Market and Monetary Theory," *Journal of Money, Credit and Banking* (February 1976), pp. 1–27.

Press Release. Federal Reserve Board of Governors, August 22, 1983.

Terrell, Henry S., and Rodney H. Mills. *International Banking Facilities and the Eurodollar Market*, Staff Studies No. 126 (Board of Governors of the Federal Reserve System, August 1983).

---

[12]It is true that the largest banks have the largest IBFs. However, the cost saving at the margin from IBFs for a bank that had, say, a Caribbean shell operation is much smaller than for a bank that had no offshore booking location.

[24]

Panama as a Regional Financial Center: A Preliminary Analysis of Development Contribution*

Harry G. Johnson
University of Chicago

I. Introduction

A "financial center" of any kind is a city in which are concentrated financial activities—banking, insurance, and ancillary types of financial business— which cater to a region outside the city itself, which may include other cities as well. An "international financial center," like London or New York, and in a lesser way Paris, Hamburg, and Zurich, caters to the financial requirements of a region extending beyond the boundaries of the nation within which the city is located to embrace the whole world or a substantial part of it. In the case of London and New York, at least, the center developed from being a national financial center through the demand for financial services to cater to the needs of its government, citizens, and enterprises as they engaged in economic activities throughout the outside world or a significant part of it. In other words, the major international financial center developed from a strong base as a national financial center in a large and powerful country with the natural market support of citizens of that country who automatically turned to its financial center for financial services they needed in other countries and the advantage of knowing intimately the nature of the customers involved.

"Regional financial centers," on the other hand, such as Hong Kong, Singapore, and Panama, derive their role primarily from a combination of geographical proximity to the countries in which the customers operate and the safety and ease of operation of subsidiaries, branches, and agencies of foreign banks whose head offices lie in the international financial centers, rather than in generating customers in other parts of the region through their own national size and international power and the competence of their own national banks in international financial business. In other words, they are largely hosts to foreign financial institutions that find it convenient to locate offices there rather than magnets of financial

* Based on the research done for a report to the Agency for International Development, Washington, D.C., prepared in 1972. The opinions expressed are the author's and are not attributable to the Agency.

261

Economic Development and Cultural Change

power in their own right, attracting foreign financial enterprises to establish subsidiaries in order to obtain a piece of the action.

This difference—between attracting foreign financial institutions by
virtue of what may be loosely termed "national financial power" and
attracting them by locational and legal advantages for the conduct of
business throughout the neighboring region—is an important one for a
country like Panama, which has been developing as a regional financial
center (located in Panama City). For it means that Panama does not have
the power to enforce conditions on foreign would-be members of its
financial center; instead, it must attract them by making the conditions
of establishment in Panama attractive enough to outweigh both the possibility of conducting business from an international financial center at
larger distance and the possibility of locating somewhere else in the region.

Panama has two major advantages in developing itself as a financial
center. The first is its geographical location; but this may not be all that
valuable an asset in competition with the international financial centers
or with other potential centers in the region, especially as Panama is
obviously deficient in many of the business and personal living amenities
that are taken for granted by people engaged in international financial
business. The second, and more important, advantage that Panama has
consists of two aspects of Panamanian policy. One is that the Panamanian
currency has an absolutely fixed exchange rate on the United States dollar,
and that fixity is maintained automatically by Panamanian monetary
arrangements and not artificially by exchange controls and other devices
for intervention in international trade and payments, such as other larger
countries have resorted to. Doing financial business from Panama is the
same as doing it from the United States, or perhaps even better since the
United States began to intervene in international payments for balance-
of-payments reasons. This arrangement gives Panama a strong comparative
advantage over other countries in the region that can and do manipulate
the international values of their currencies for domestic reasons—and little
comparative disadvantage in relation to the United States, due to the
virtual identity of the balboa with the U.S. dollar. The other is that
Panama has welcomed foreign financial enterprises with liberal banking
laws and a generally laissez-faire attitude and has not (so far) attempted
to coerce them into accepting some governmentally determined concept
of obligations to the state that seriously impede their pursuit of profitable
business. Both of these advantages could readily be destroyed if economic
nationalism in Panama were to lead to the establishment of a national
currency of uncertain management and uncertain future value in terms
of the world's major currencies, or to a misguided effort to regulate the
operations of foreign financial enterprises according to Panamanian ideas
of how such successful multinational enterprises should be run for the
benefit of Panama.

On the other hand, the fact that Panama is in the position of the

Harry G. Johnson

hotel host trying to attract guests raises the question of what the benefits of running a hotel to the proprietor and his dependents and friends really are—concretely, of what the benefits to Panama may be in terms of Panamanian objectives of promoting economic development, reducing unemployment, alleviating poverty, achieving a more equitable distribution of income, and so on. This question is an important one for economic policy, because the promotion of the development of Panama City as a regional financial center will require (1) deliberate abstention from certain types of policy toward foreign, particularly American, enterprises and residents that appeal to the Panamanian popular mind as a way of demonstrating Panamanian sovereignty, independence, and nationhood; and (2) substantial investments of the scarce public resources available for domestic development and social programs.

The purpose of this study is to investigate some of these questions in a preliminary way. Part II discusses in a general fashion the possibilities of gain for a country from being a regional financial center. Part III assembles and analyzes the readily available statistics bearing on the quantitative importance of the theoretical possibilities. Part IV offers some observations on Panama's possible future as a regional financial center in the light of recent international developments.

II. Potential Benefits from a Regional Financial Center

The financial sector of an economy (e.g., the City of London, Wall Street) typically provides relatively good incomes to those employed in it and the prospects of profitable growth of activity and employment and accumulation of assets. The question for Panama is how far the development of a regional financial center largely financed by foreign capital and staffed or at least directed by foreigners has a spillover effect in promoting economic development and increasing the welfare of the citizens of the host country. These are several different avenues by which such spillover effects can occur.

First, an obvious point, but one frequently neglected, are the taxes collectable by central and local governments on the profits of the corporations involved and on the incomes of the foreign employees of those corporations. To the extent that the capital and the skilled people would not be in the country otherwise and therefore would not be subject to local taxes—and to the extent that their presence does not simply replace domestic capital and skills that would otherwise exist—the ability of governments to tax them represents a net gain in taxable capacity. The extra taxable capacity represents a net gain of resources available for expenditure on education of the local population, improved health services, and agricultural or industrial development projects. This point is an important one: even if no citizen seems to be participating directly in the activities in question in any of the ways listed below, the government is participating as a tax collector on behalf of the citizens generally. Of

Economic Development and Cultural Change

course, the government may be forgoing this privilege by giving tax concessions or even subsidies to the enterprises concerned, in which case the advantages have to be looked for in more direct participation by citizens in their activities. Further, if the government attracts foreign capital and foreign skilled workers by giving their activities protection in catering to the domestic market, the gain on the tax side may be more than offset by the loss to consumers from having to pay prices above world market levels for the products supplied. This last possibility, however, applies more to import substitution in manufacturing supported by tariffs, quotas, and exchange controls than to the development of a foreign-financed and foreign-staffed financial center, especially if that center derives most of its income from international rather than local business. The fact that it does so means that it is internationally competitive so that no loss accrues to domestic consumers of its services.

Second, there is the provision of employment to the local population. This has two aspects. One, which is related to the rate of growth of the financial sector, is the employment provided to construction workers building new office buildings or reconditioning and extending old ones. This also includes work in the construction of new apartment buildings and other housing for the incoming foreign staff. The other is employment in the financial section itself. This includes such unskilled jobs as janitor, driver, cleaning and maintenance staff, and low-grade clerical work; more skilled jobs involving such skills as stenography or bookkeeping; and still higher-level jobs at the executive and managerial grades.

From the standpoint of promoting economic development, in the sense of not merely providing employment opportunities at existing wage levels for relatively unskilled workers and a professional/managerial class of citizens, the provision of unskilled-employment opportunities is a useful stopgap in a less developed country with an oversupply of unskilled labor and disguised unemployment in the rural sector. It may also, in the long run, contribute to economic development by urbanizing people who would otherwise be mere peasants scratching a living from the land in remote areas and by exposing them to opportunities for self-advancement of which some will be able to avail themselves. However, the main long-run problems are the development of entrepreneurial ability—an objective which has in the past frequently been promoted by an urban construction boom—and the development of professional and managerial skills capable of earning high incomes for those who possess such skills. In this connection, a financial sector—especially one that is catering to a regional or international and not merely a local market—can perform a very important developmental role both by offering a market for the services of skilled people and by investing resources in improving the professional knowledge and ability of the people recruited. To take advantage of this possibility, however, requires at least one condition and probably two. The first is a strengthening of the local education system to the level of capacity to

264

Harry G. Johnson

turn out graduates (presumably high school graduates, for a country like Panama) who are qualified to assume responsible jobs in financial institutions. This in turn may require a reorientation of teachers and students toward preparation for this type of career instead of the more traditional ones, particularly traditional agriculture. The second may be the exercise of a certain amount of social and political pressure on the foreign financial institutions to experiment with the employment and further training of educated local citizens.

This is a delicate problem on both sides, as shown by long experience with the international or multinational corporation, especially since the Second World War. The corporation has no economic reason to employ expensive imported executives if local people of the same talents and characteristics are available, but it may be ignorant, or biased, about local talent. On the other hand, the political government tends to want prestigious high-paid jobs for nationals without always making sure that the nationals are competent and hard-working enough to deserve them. If they are not and they must be employed anyway, the country, not the corporation, pays—in terms of either functionless high-income recipients or poor decision making.

The third major way in which a country may derive benefits from a financial center is through possible effects on the welfare of its citizens as capitalists or potential capitalists. First, there is the capital gain that landowners, specifically urban landowners, receive from selling land for office and apartment construction at prices substantially above what they paid for it. These capital gains could be reinvested in other forms of enterprise providing employment and economic growth. However, typically they seem to be not so invested but instead are reinvested in rent-earning property; the capital gains provide private wealth but do not contribute to an ongoing development process shared by the population in general.[1] Second, the financial center, through its efficiency in financial intermediation, may provide the citizens with both safer and higher-yielding outlets for their savings than would otherwise be available, thus encouraging them to save and accumulate capital.[2] Third, the financial center may, by its financial-intermediary activities, make finance available to local entrepreneurs on cheaper and more attractive terms than would be otherwise available.[3] One special aspect of this consideration relevant to Panama

[1] It may, however, contribute to the development of the financial center by providing housing appropriate to the incomes and tastes of financial-center employees and executives.

[2] Note that this point differs from the possibility that some local capitalists may acquire an equity share in some foreign enterprises; and it may be an important point, because one of the reasons why economic development does not, at least in the not too short run, lead to a general rise in incomes but instead to much higher incomes for the relatively few and hence to greater and more visible inequality is that the mass of the people have only very low yielding investments available to them.

[3] Again, one of the characteristics of less developed countries is that many citizens may have good investment opportunities but cannot find finance for them except on

is the complementary relationship between the development of the regional financial center and the development of Panama's entrepôt and export trades. In this connection, a financial center not only provides financial services but is an important source of information of various kinds about market conditions in the rest of the world.

The empirical question regarding Panama is how important quantitatively these possible gains from the development of a regional financial center may be. Here there are two conflicting a priori considerations. One is that Panama has a very small population. Hence, taking multiplier effects into account, it would not require a very large absolute amount of direct investment and employment in the financial sector to have a substantial influence on the Panamanian economy and its growth. The other is that the financial sector typically provides little employment per dollar of gross turnover, so that a large financial center measured in financial terms may be contributing little in real terms to the rest of the economy.

There is one special characteristic of financial centers, both international and regional, that deserves special mention. All foreign direct investment in a country generates some multiplier effect on the production of goods and services by local enterprises. However, because financial business involves a great deal of short-term traveling by financial executives from one financial center to another (most notably inspection visits from head-office executives of local subsidiaries) and by actual and potential customers of the financial center to the center, the multiplier effect is concentrated on the tourist trade. This involves a demand for what may be called "business tourism," as distinct from "sight-seeing tourism" and "vacation tourism," the trend being toward the latter and against the former as people become more affluent and less willing to undergo risks and personal discomforts in order to go somewhere and see something unique.[4] Both business tourism and vacation tourism demand a high standard of facilities, including both hotels and restaurants, and convenience and security in moving around the city. This means that the financial center and the tourist industry are to a large extent part of the same development package. And since provision of hotel accommodation of the requisite standard usually requires investment and management by an international hotel-chain company, tourism raises problems of local benefits and developmental effects similar to those of the regional financial center. The central point, however, is that there is a complementary relationship between the financial center and the tourist industry.

The foregoing brief analysis of possible benefits to the host country from the development of a regional financial center runs in terms of real

---

exorbitant terms; others have finance but no attractive opportunities for employing it; and only a fortunate few have both opportunities and ready finance—and thus become the small rich island of elite in a sea of general poverty.

[4] In any case, Panama has little to offer in the sight-seeing line except the canal; its comparative advantage lies in its climate and its beaches and oceans.

Harry G. Johnson

economic effects: employment of people who might otherwise be un-
employed and upgrading of skills, both of which are relevant to Panama's
pressing political problems of poverty and inequality of income distribution; direct training of potential local entrepreneurs or advisers to local
entrepreneurs; and improvement of local capital markets serving local
savers and entrepreneurs and hence stimulating domestic saving and investment. There is an alternative approach, the standard approach both of
governments concerned with short-run policy problems and of the World
Bank, which evaluates every economic phenomenon from the standpoint
of its impact on the balance of payments. This is thoroughly bad economics: it leads to the naive view that capital imports are a good thing and
interest payments on that capital a bad thing, whereas the proper economic question is whether capital imports generate an addition to income
in excess of the obligation to pay interest that they entail. Nevertheless,
the approach is so deeply ingrained in current thinking on development
problems that some attention to it has to be paid—and will be paid in the
next part of this article.[5] Unfortunately, this requires considerable detailed
statistical recalculation, which general readers may fairly safely skim.

III. The Growth of the Financial Center in Panama and the Benefits to Panama

*The World Bank Memorandum on Panama (July 1972) and Some Re-
calculations*
A convenient starting point for the quantitative appreciation of the importance of the Panama City financial center to the Panamanian economy
is the International Bank for Reconstruction and Development and International Development Association (draft) "Memorandum on Current
Economic Position and Prospects of Panama" (July 3, 1972). The basic
data preceding the main text show that finance and real estate together
accounted for 2.5 percent of GNP at 1960 market prices in 1960 and 4.1

---

[5] The difference between the two approaches is so fundamental, but so frequently
ignored even by professional economists, that it is worth illustrating by a homely
example. Suppose I decide to buy a house appropriate to my income and prospects and
secure a mortgage from my bank for $25,000 with interest and amortization spread
over 20 years. On the World Bank standard development view, in the year I get the
mortgage my economic development has been "assisted" by the $25,000; every year
afterward it is "burdened" by the annual interest and amortization payments. On a
commonsense economic view, the bank has helped me only by endorsing my personal
credit worthiness and converting it into a standard mortgage; my "development" is
fostered because otherwise I would either have to wait until I had saved the cost of the
house or pay much higher interest for purely personal borrowing from my neighbors.
One suspects that the official procedure reflects the fact that developing countries believe
that they should get aid as gifts rather than loans, while developed countries like to
maintain a pretense of commercial soundness in aid giving. For the World Bank, the
accounting technique is merely an aspect of a vested interest in enshrouding aid giving
in a morass of financial complexity requiring its own financial expertise to unravel. (It
would have a substantially diminished role if governments insisted on giving inter-
governmental transfers as straight gifts and applying *caveat emptor* to developing countries financing development imports with short-term commercial credit.)

Economic Development and Cultural Change

percent in 1971 (in absolute terms, about 10.6 million balboas in 1960 and 39.8 million balboas in 1971 at 1960 prices), the share increasing at 0.1 percentage points per year in 1960–65 and 0.2 percentage points per year in 1965–71. The banking system made a net contribution to the balance of payments of 6.5 million balboas in 1960, 4.5 in 1965, 10.7 in 1969, 60.3 in 1970, and 40 in 1971. Employment in banks and commerce, as a percentage of the urban labor force, fell, however, from 13.7 percent in 1960 to 10.0 percent in 1970. The text of the Memorandum (p. 3), shows that banking, insurance, and real estate grew at real rates of 10.3 percent in 1960–68, 24.0 percent in 1968–70, and 13.2 percent in 1970–71, as compared with rates of growth of GNP in millions of 1960 balboas of 8.0, 7.7, and 8.6, respectively, for the same periods. Though the figures are only a rough approximation of the growth rate of the "financial center" per se, they suggest that on the average the financial sector has been the fastest-growing sector of the economy in recent years.

The Memorandum makes the following statement about Panama as a financial center (p. 4, par. 6):

> Panama is rapidly becoming an important Latin American financial center with several European, American, Colombian and Ecuadorian banks maintaining branches or regional headquarters in Panama City. During the past year deposits in the banking system by nonresidents rose by a third to $600 million; two-thirds of it from foreign banks and institutions, [Reference to table 6.1 in statistical appendix, reproduced as table 1 below.] Although most of this money was re-lent abroad, the foreign funds lent in Panama rose 43 percent to $225 million, about half the domestic credit extended by the banking system. While the value added from the financial system is only 4 percent of GNP, it has increased about 50 percent in real terms from 1968 to 1970, and its impact on other sectors such as construction, tourism, and other services has become an important factor in the growth of the private sector.

As has been argued in the previous section in general principle, and as will be argued below in more detail, net lending of funds secured from abroad to domestic residents is a fallacious measure of the contribution of the regional financial center to the Panamanian economy. Moreover, the Memorandum compounds the error by assuming that the difference between deposits from nonresidents and credit to nonresidents must consist of credit to residents, whereas it may be (and, as will be shown, is in fact to a significant extent) invested in other forms of foreign assets than credit to nonresidents.

The Memorandum statement is supported by two tables, one for the consolidated banking system and one for the private banks, reproduced here as tables 1 and 2. The row "Overseas operations (net)" and subrows in table 1 are the source of the statement quoted concerning the contribution of foreign deposits to domestic lending. The presentation of the data in this way is confused in the extreme: a balance sheet is a balance sheet,

268

Harry G. Johnson

TABLE 1

SUMMARY ACCOUNTS OF THE CONSOLIDATED BANKING SYSTEM, 1967–71
(MILLIONS OF BALBOAS)

	1967	1968	1969	1970	1971
Net foreign reserves	28.9	31.4	45.4	50.7	74.3
Assets	43.7	48.1	85.4	73.0	118.0
Foreign currencies	14.0	17.7	16.7	22.7	22.9
IMF gold subscription	2.8	2.8	7.0	9.0	9.0
SDR holdings	...	...	...	3.2	3.0
Deposits abroad	23.8	27.3	60.3	30.6	69.5
Demand deposits	(19.9)	(17.3)	(32.7)	(10.0)	(25.8)
Time deposits	(4.0)	(10.0)	(27.6)	(20.6)	(43.7)
Other unclassified	3.1	0.3	1.4	7.5	13.6
Medium- and short-term foreign liabilities	−14.8	−16.7	−40.0	−22.3	−43.7
IMF drawings (net)	−2.7	−5.1	−9.7	−8.8	−13.9
Other liabilities	−12.1	−11.6	−30.3	−13.5	−29.8
Overseas operations (net)	−66.1	−71.1	−112.9	−158.0	−225.5
Credit to nonresidents	30.0	43.4	104.9	246.3	376.2
Deposits from nonresidents	−96.1	−114.5	−217.8	−404.3	−601.7
Deposits of foreign banks and institutions	−57.0	−75.6	−143.2	−272.2	−414.2
Demand deposits	(−30.3)	(−26.2)	(−55.9)	(−186.8)	(−25.9)
Time deposits	(−23.1)	(−47.0)	(−86.2)	(−85.4)	(−388.3)
Restricted deposits	(−3.6)	(−2.4)	(−1.1)	(...)	(...)
Deposits of private nonresidents	−39.1	−38.9	−74.6	−132.1	−187.5
Demand deposits	(−17.0)	(−14.3)	(−13.5)	(−23.5)	(−27.2)
Time deposits	(−21.8)	(−22.9)	(−60.7)	(−105.0)	(−156.6)
Restricted deposits	(−0.3)	(−1.7)	(−0.4)	(−3.6)	(−3.7)
Net domestic reserves	13.7	14.8	12.8	16.6	17.5
Domestic currency	3.0	1.9	3.2	4.7	5.5
Interbank deposits (net)	2.1	0.8	...	−3.3	−1.7
Demand deposits (net)	(2.4)	(7.9)	(4.4)	(1.2)	(1.3)
Time deposits (net)	(−0.3)	(−7.1)	(−4.4)	(−4.5)	(−3.0)
Checks in clearing	9.0	12.5	13.1	18.3	15.5
Cashier's checks in circulation	−0.4	−0.4	−3.5	...	−1.6
Domestic credit	211.5	241.5	295.0	404.4	543.6
Central government (net)	−8.0	−2.1	11.5	16.6	25.7
Credit	(4.2)	(7.3)	(19.8)	(28.4)	(40.8)
Deposits (−)	(−12.2)	(−9.4)	(−8.3)	(−11.8)	(−12.1)
Other government sector (net)	−1.5	−3.3	−9.0	−12.2	−10.6
Credit	(4.9)	(3.4)	(2.3)	(2.8)	(4.9)
Deposits (−)	(−6.4)	(−6.7)	(−11.3)	(−15.0)	(−15.5)
Private sector	229.2	255.0	306.1	407.9	525.2
Unclassified assets (net)	4.8	6.4	6.6	12.9	21.8
Official capital and reserves	−13.1	−13.1	−18.4	−18.4	−19.7
Interbank loans	...	−1.4	−1.8	−2.4	−1.8
Long-term foreign liabilities	5.7	8.1	9.0	9.2	12.5
Domestic private sector claims on banks	182.3	208.5	231.3	304.5	390.1
Demand deposits	65.0	75.0	83.1	99.1	103.8
Time and savings deposits	108.0	122.6	134.3	185.6	236.2
Restricted deposits	2.2	2.8	2.8	4.0	4.6
Private capital and reserves	7.1	8.1	11.1	15.8	45.5

SOURCE.—Controlaria General, IMF, and Banking Commission (table 6.1 in IBRD Memorandum).

NOTE.—Figures in parentheses are excluded from total tabulations.

269

Economic Development and Cultural Change

not a record of operations on the economy, and one should consider the overall operations and not merely deposit taking and lending.

Tables 3 and 4 reconstruct the Memorandum tables to separate the foreign accounts (balance) from the domestic accounts (balance) of the consolidated (private) banking system of Panama. If we take 1970 as the last year for which the source figures are fully consistent from the accounting point of view, the involvement of Panama in international banking

TABLE 2

CONSOLIDATED BALANCES OF THE PRIVATE BANKS, 1967–71
(MILLIONS OF BALBOAS)

	1967	1968	1969	1970	1971
Net foreign reserves...............	27.9	27.8	57.5	41.1	80.0
Assets.........................	34.3	34.2	63.3	48.4	92.3
Foreign currencies............	8.2	10.3	9.6	12.2	12.3
Deposits abroad..............	23.0	23.6	52.3	28.7	66.0
Demand deposits...........	(19.0)	(13.6)	(30.8)	(8.1)	(22.3)
Time deposits..............	(4.0)	(10.0)	(21.5)	(20.6)	(43.7)
Other unclassified.............	3.1	0.3	1.4	7.5	14.0
Liabilities.....................	−6.4	−6.4	−5.8	−7.3	−12.3
Overseas operations (net)..........	−65.9	−71.0	−112.8	−157.9	−212.8
Credit to nonresidents...........	30.0	43.4	104.9	246.3	375.3
Deposits from nonresidents.......	−95.9	−114.4	−217.7	−404.2	−588.1
Deposits of foreign banks and					
institutions...............	−57.0	−75.6	−143.2	−272.2	−400.7
Demand deposits...........	(−30.3)	(−26.2)	(−55.9)	(−186.8)	(−23.1)
Time deposits..............	(−23.1)	(−47.0)	(−86.2)	(−85.4)	(−377.1)
Restricted deposits..........	(−3.6)	(−2.4)	(−1.1)	(—)	(−0.5)
Deposits of private nonresidents.	−38.9	−38.8	−74.5	−132.0	−187.4
Demand deposits...........	(−16.8)	(−14.2)	(−13.4)	(−23.4)	(−27.1)
Time deposits..............	(−21.8)	(−22.9)	(−60.7)	(−105.0)	(−156.6)
Restricted deposits..........	(−0.3)	(−1.7)	(−0.4)	(−3.6)	(−3.7)
Net domestic reserves.............	8.3	19.5	17.0	24.5	26.3
Domestic currency..............	1.3	0.9	1.2	2.2	2.8
Interbank deposits (net).........	2.9	9.5	4.7	9.2	8.1
Demand deposits (net).........	(3.7)	(7.8)	(4.7)	(7.0)	(7.4)
Time deposits (net)...........	(−0.8)	(1.7)	( )	(2.2)	(0.7)
Checks in clearing..............	4.1	9.1	11.1	13.1	15.4
Domestic credit...................	159.6	188.8	224.7	340.0	43.0
Central government (net).........	2.6	1.7	0.9	6.1	23.2
Credit......................	(2.6)	(1.7)	(0.9)	(6.1)	(23.2)
Deposits (−)................	(...)	(...)	(...)	(...)	(...)
Other government sector (net).....	2.9	1.8	0.9	0.2	0.1
Credit......................	(2.9)	(1.8)	(0.9)	(0.2)	(0.1)
Deposits (−)................	(...)	(...)	(...)	(...)	(...)
Private sector..................	154.7	185.7	232.2	320.9	415.4
Unclassified assets (net)..........	−0.6	−0.4	−9.3	12.8	0.3
Long-term liabilities...............	1.9	4.0	5.4	6.2	21.1
To local banks...............	...	...	0.8	1.6	1.5
To foreign banks...............	1.9	4.0	4.6	4.6	19.6
Domestic private sector claims on					
banks.......................	128.0	161.1	181.0	241.5	313.2
Demand deposits...............	51.4	63.1	70.3	85.1	88.3
Time and savings deposits........	68.4	88.0	98.0	138.0	176.6
Restricted deposits..............	1.1	1.9	1.6	2.6	2.8
Private capital and reserves.......	7.1	8.1	11.1	15.8	45.5

SOURCE.—IMF, 1967–70, and Banking Commission, 1971 (table 6.2 in IBRD Memorandum).

NOTE.—The change in reserve definition is partially responsible for the jump in capital and reserves in 1971. Figures in parentheses are excluded from total tabulations.

Harry G. Johnson

represented a net foreign investment of 116.5 million balboas in Panama. (For 1971, if net foreign assets are used as the true figure there was net foreign investment of 163.7 million balboas.) If we take first differences between the balance-sheet figures, the net capital inflow associated with the financial-center function (in millions of balboas) was 4.9 in 1968, 28.7 in 1969, 40.0 in 1970, and 47.2 in 1971 (again using net foreign liabilities as the true figure). For the period 1967–71 (again trusting net foreign liabilities), the total inflow was 120.8 million balboas. Of this total, 112.5 million balboas came in through the private banks.

The net balance-of-payments or capital inflow contribution of the foreign accounts of the banking system, however, is no measure of the economic benefits to the country of the banking system component of the financial center. The potential contribution of the banking sector to the Panamanian economy, in terms of employment, output, multiplier effects

TABLE 3

RECONSTRUCTION OF THE ACCOUNTS OF THE CONSOLIDATED BANKING SYSTEM, 1967–71, FROM TABLE 1 (MILLIONS OF BALBOAS)

	1967	1968	1969	1970	1971*
Foreign accounts:					
Assets:					
Foreign reserve assets	43.7	46.1	85.4	73.0	118.0
Credit to nonresidents	30.0	43.4	104.9	246.3	376.2
Total assets	73.7	89.5	190.3	319.3	494.2
Liabilities:					
Medium and short-term foreign liabilities	14.8	16.7	40.0	22.3	43.7
Deposits from nonresidents	96.1	114.5	217.8	404.3	601.7
Deposits from banks and institutions	(57.0)	(75.6)	(143.2)	(272.2)	(414.2)
Deposits from private non-residents	(39.1)	(38.9)	(74.6)	(132.1)	(187.5)
Long-term foreign liabilities	5.7	6.1	9.0	9.2	12.5
Total liabilities	116.6	137.3	266.8	435.8	657.9
Net foreign liabilities	42.9	47.8	76.5	116.5	163.7
Domestic Accounts:					
Assets:					
Net domestic reserves	13.7	14.8	12.8	16.6	17.5
Domestic credit	211.5	241.5	295.0	404.4	543.6
Total assets	225.2	256.3	307.8	421.0	561.1
Liabilities:					
Domestic private sector claims on banks	182.3	208.5	231.3	304.5	319.1
Net domestic assets	42.9	47.8	76.5	116.5	171.0
Total assets	298.9	345.8	498.1	740.3	1055.3
Total liabilities	298.9	345.8	498.1	740.3	1048.0

* There is a small error (or errors) in the World Bank Memorandum source of this column, since assets and liabilities are not equal. Part of the explanation is a 2.0 over-statement of the total of domestic credit.

Economic Development and Cultural Change

on other sectors, and stimulus to growth—also, possibly, its capacity to reap economies of scale and increase its productivity—depends on its absolute size in terms of assets/liabilities. This size is increased by the attraction of liabilities in the form of deposits and other types of investment from foreigners, whether or not the bank chooses to invest the resources so acquired, as well as its own resources, in domestic or foreign assets yielding an income. The net foreign liabilities remaining after the banking sector has decided how to distribute its total portfolio between domestic and foreign assets are an inadequate measure of the contribution of the banks' foreign banking sector to the economy of Panama.

As can be seen from tables 3 and 4 (and ignoring the errors in the 1971 column), foreign liabilities accounted for a little over one-third of

TABLE 4

RECONSTRUCTION OF THE CONSOLIDATED BALANCES OF THE PRIVATE BANKS, 1967–71, FROM TABLE 2 (MILLIONS OF BALBOAS)

	1967	1968	1969	1970	1971*
Foreign balance:					
Assets:					
Foreign reserve assets.........	34.3	34.2	63.3	48.4	92.3
Credit to nonresidents.........	30.0	43.4	104.9	246.3	375.3
Total assets...............	64.3	77.6	168.2	294.7	467.6
Liabilities:					
Foreign reserves..............	6.4	6.4	5.8	7.3	12.3
Deposits from nonresidents.....	95.9	114.4	217.7	404.2	588.1
Deposits from banks and institutions..................	(57.0)	(75.6)	(143.2)	(272.2)	(400.7)
Deposits from private nonresidents...................	(38.9)	(38.8)	(74.5)	(132.0)	(187.4)
Long-term liabilities to foreign banks....................	1.9	4.0	4.6	4.6	19.6
Total liabilities.............	104.2	124.8	228.1	416.1	620.0
Domestic balance:					
Assets:					
Net domestic reserves.........	8.3	19.5	17.0	24.5	26.3
Domestic credit..............	159.6	188.8	224.7	340.0	439.0
Total assets...............	167.9	208.3	241.7	364.5	465.3
Liabilities:					
Long-term liabilities to local banks....................	...	...	0.8	1.6	1.5
Domestic private sector claims on banks..................	128.0	161.1	181.0	241.5	313.2
Total liabilities.............	128.0	161.1	181.8	243.1	314.7
Net domestic assets.............	39.9	47.2	59.9	121.4	151.6
Total assets.....................	232.2	285.9	409.9	659.2	932.9
Total liabilities.................	232.2	285.9	409.9	659.2	934.7

* There is a small error (or errors) somewhere in the World Bank Memorandum source for this column, since the assets and liabilities are unequal.

Harry G. Johnson

total liabilities of the consolidated banking system in 1967 and a little under two-thirds in 1971. Thus the growth of the banking system over the period has been predominantly due to the growth of the system's international business. Domestic liabilities, whose growth rate may be taken to represent the growth rate of the domestic economy's demand for banking services, slightly more than doubled over the period. Foreign liabilities increased over the same period to six times their original level. For the private banks, domestic liabilities increased to slightly under two and one-half times their original level, while foreign liabilities increased to only a shade under six times their original level.

For insurance, the monetary magnitudes involved are considerably smaller (note that in the tables they are measured in thousands and not millions of balboas) and the figures available less up to date. Table 5 shows, however, that over the period 1963–69 the share of direct premium earnings accounted for by insurance sold outside Panama rose from under one-fifth to about one-quarter, the increases taking place in foreign sales of life insurance (which rose by a factor of seven) and accident insurance (which somewhat more than doubled, but from a much larger initial base). Table 6 incorporates receipts from and payments for reinsurance and shows the net cash flows between Panama and abroad on insurance premium accounts over the same period. The growth of foreign insurance business has meant a net change from a cash outflow of about a million balboas a year to a net inflow of about three-quarters of a million balboas a year.

The foreign insurance business, however, constitutes the mirror image of inward capital investment: such investment involves a capital inflow now in return for a stream of outflows (interest, dividends) in future, whereas insurance involves a stream of inflows in return for a capital payment later on when the event insured against occurs. In either case it is wrong economically to take the net of current flow payments and current capital payments as a measure of net national gain or loss, because the exchange of a capital sum for a flow of current payments in either direction is a voluntary exchange presumably beneficial to both parties; also, the current statistics on one or the other side reflect the magnitudes and time profile of past and/or future transactions. (Specifically, the amount of settlements an insurance company has to make this year reflects the amount of insurance it has sold, and received premiums for, in past years; and the premiums it receives this year reflect commitments to pay out capital sums in future years.) Nevertheless, since the practice is common, table 7 presents the figures on the balance-of-payments impacts of premium and reinsurance earnings or payments by insurance companies in Panama, cash settlements of policies, and the net of the two.

The figures are broken down into the categories of national and foreign companies. The former have a negative and the latter a positive balance-of-payments impact on premium account, since the national com-

273

Economic Development and Cultural Change

TABLE 5

Premiums Earned by Direct Negotiation by Panama Insurance Companies, 1963–69
(Thousands of Balboas)

Year	Life Insurance			Fire Insurance			Accident Insurance			All Insurance			
	Total	Domestic	Foreign	Total	Domestic	Foreign	Total	Domestic	Foreign	Total	Domestic	Foreign	% Foreign
1963	3,171	2,848	323	2,045	1,867	178	7,297	5,606	1,695	12,515	10,317	2,196	17.6
1964	3,622	3,697	525	2,206	2,193	13	7,991	6,153	1,838	13,318	11,442	2,376	17.2
1965	...	3,170	645	1,930	1,903	27	8,957	6,725	2,232	14,701	11,798	2,903	19.7
1966	6,097	3,808	2,290	2,299	2,280	19	10,043	7,529	2,514	18,440	13,616	4,824	26.2
1967	6,895	4,208	2,687	2,053	2,038	16	10,628	8,501	2,127	19,577	14,747	4,830	24.6
1968	6,461	4,438	2,023	2,306	2,286	20	12,329	9,039	3,290	21,096	15,763	5,333	25.3
1969	7,955	5,698	2,257	2,726	2,715	11	14,499	10,503	3,996	25,180	18,917	6,263	24.9

SOURCE.—Hacienda Publica y Finanzas. *Estadistica Panameña*, 1970 and previous years. table 53.

TABLE 6

Direct Premiums Earned and Reinsurance Earnings and Payments by Panama Insurance Companies, 1963–69
(Thousands of Balboas)

Year	Premiums Earned Directly			Receipts from Insurance			Payments for Reinsurance			Net Foreign Payments (−) or Receipts (+)
	Total	Panama	Foreign	Total	Panama	Foreign	Total	Panama	Foreign	
1963	12,513	10,317	2,196	454	304	150	3,733	378	3,355	−1,009
1964	13,818	11,442	2,376	534	335	199	2,400	519	2,881	− 306
1965	14,701	11,798	2,903	397	239	158	3,729	302	4,427	− 366
1966	18,440	13,616	4,824	672	445	227	4,317	299	4,018	+1,033
1967	19,577	14,747	4,830	447	256	191	4,578	301	4,277	++ 744
1968	21,096	15,763	5,333	537	324	213	5,181	376	4,805	++ 741
1969	25,180	18,917	6,263	575	403	172	6,097	408	5,689	++ 746

Harry G. Johnson

panies sell little insurance abroad and reinsure heavily, whereas the reverse is true for the foreign companies. As a corollary, however, the cash settlement transactions of the foreign companies have a negative impact on the balance of payments, whereas those of the national companies have a positive impact (via the reinsurance abroad of insurance issued to domestic policyholders). On net, the national companies have a negative impact on the balance of payments and the foreign companies a positive effect in the period to which the statistics refer, except for the first year. In both cases, the overall picture is a logical and natural consequence of the rapid rate of growth of the business of both types of company. In a long-run static situation, and if we ignore the companies' costs of selling and administering policies, the cash inflow from abroad for the settlement of reinsured policies would be equal to the premiums paid abroad for reinsurance of existing policies, and the premium income on existing policies issued abroad would be equal to the cash outlay on settlement of previously issued policies. But if business is growing, the cash value of maturing policies issued in the past will be less than the cash value of, and therefore of the premium income received from, the policies now outstanding; this principle applies to both the reinsurance of domestic policies and the sale of policies to foreigners.

The difference in the statistical performance, in terms of the balance of payments, should not be given any significance from the policy point of view. It is natural that national companies that can find more business than they can handle with their own financial resources and ability to assume risks should reinsure with foreign companies, and equally natural that foreign companies with superior resources and risk-taking ability should establish regional branches to find direct-insurance business in place of reinsurance business. The important point, as in the case of the banking sector, is that the effects of the insurance sector of a financial center on the domestic economy depend on the overall size of that sector. This can be identified broadly with the total amount of insurance sold, whether sold domestically or in foreign countries, and whether reinsured or not. From this point of view, the statistics of table 5, while showing a more modest expansion of foreign insurance business conducted from Panama than was shown for foreign operations of the banking sector by previous tables, still show that foreign business has made a quantitatively significant contribution to the growth of the insurance sector of the Panamanian financial system and therefore presumably of the Panamanian economy.

Economic Analysis: The Available Statistics
To turn back from the balance-of-payments framework of analysis, the theoretical basis for which has already been sufficiently criticized, to the question of real benefits to Panama from the development of its financial center, most of the readily available statistics unfortunately refer to bank-

Economic Development and Cultural Change

TABLE 7

SOME BALANCE-OF-PAYMENTS IMPACTS OF INSURANCE COMPANIES IN PANAMA
(THOUSANDS OF BALBOAS)

A. FOREIGN DIRECT INSURANCE AND REINSURANCE INCOME AND PAYMENTS*

YEAR	DIRECT PREMIUM		REINSURANCE EARNINGS		REINSURANCE PAYMENTS		NET FOREIGN EARNINGS (+) OR PAYMENTS (−)		
	National Companies	Foreign Companies	National Companies	Foreign Companies	National Companies	Foreign Companies	National Companies	Foreign Companies	Total
1963	313	1,882	145	4	1,684	1,671	−1,226	+215	−1,009
1964	182	2,194	153	46	1,729	1,152	−1,394	+1,088	−306
1965	252	2,651	113	45	2,168	1,259	−1,803	+1,437	−366
1966	222	4,602	135	92	2,570	1,449	−2,213	+3,244	+1,033
1967	197	4,633	122	69	2,958	1,319	−2,639	+3,383	+744
1968	361	4,972	119	94	3,399	1,406	−2,919	+3,660	+741
1969	336	5,927	109	63	4,103	1,586	−3,663	+4,404	+741

B. FOREIGN DIRECT INSURANCE AND REINSURANCE CAPITAL SUM PAYMENTS†

YEAR	DIRECT INSURANCE PAYMENTS		REINSURANCE PAYMENTS		REINSURANCE RECEIPTS		NET FOREIGN RECEIPTS (−) OR PAYMENTS		
	National Companies	Foreign Companies	National Companies	Foreign Companies	National Companies	Foreign Companies	National Companies	Foreign Companies	Net
1963	86	1,074	85	..	407	580	+236	−494	−258
1964	70	1,733	105	..	856	746	+681	−987	−306
1965	216	1,893	63	0	1,002	709	+723	−1,184	−461
1966	131	1,835	56	25	731	380	+544	−1,480	−936
1967	64	2,827	46	26	880	363	+770	−2,490	−1,720
1968	168	2,734	31	41	1,745	348	+1,546	−2,427	−881
1969	198	1,339	32	2,196	1,941	299	+1,711	−3,236	−1,525

Continued overleaf

Harry G. Johnson

TABLE 7—*Continued*

C. NET BALANCE ON FOREIGN PREMIUMS AND CAPITAL PAYMENTS

YEAR	NATIONAL COMPANIES			FOREIGN COMPANIES			TOTAL		
	Premiums	Capital Sums	Net	Premiums	Capital Sums	Net	Premiums	Capital Sums	Net
1963	−1,226	+ +236	− 990	+ 215	− 494	− 279	−1,009	− 258	−1,267
1964	−1,394	+ +681	− 713	+1,088	− 987	+ 101	− 306	− 306	− 612
1965	−1,803	+ +723	−1,080	+1,437	−1,184	+ 253	− 366	− 461	− 827
1966	−2,213	+ +544	−1,669	+3,244	−1,480	+1,764	+1,033	− 936	+ 97
1967	−2,639	+ +770	−1,869	+3,383	−2,490	+ 893	+ 744	−1,720	− 976
1968	−2,919	+ +1,546	−1,373	+3,660	−2,427	+1,233	+ 741	− 881	− 140
1969	−3,663	+ +1,711	−1,952	+4,404	−3,236	+1,168	+ 741	−1,525	− 784

* From Hacienda Publica y Finanzas, *Estadistica Panameña*, 1970 and previous years, table 53.

† Ibid., table 54.

277

ing and not to insurance. This is partly due to the establishment of the National Banking Commission, which naturally collects more directly relevant and up-to-date useful statistics and publishes them more quickly than the official statisticians can do for an economy in which banking is still a relatively small sector.[6] However, the misfortune is not too great, since the banking sector is over three times as large as the insurance sector and has been growing far more rapidly in recent years.

Table 8 shows the growth of the banking system of Panama in terms of the establishment of new banks (regional head offices and/or branches) in Panama City and in other cities from 1964 to the latest year for which data were available. (Two other banks were established up to April 1972: Republic National Bank and Deutsche Südamerikanische Bank, A.G.) Table 9 shows the cumulative totals. A significant feature of the tables is that, while with only one exception the banks have their headquarters in Panama City, they have established roughly as many branches in other cities as they have in Panama City. This may be taken as a reflection of an assumption on their part that other cities also offer the opportunity for profitable business, which in turn implies that they are providing benefits to Panamanians as savers and as entrepreneurs by improving the local capital markets in those cities. On the other hand, it must be remarked that the private banks, on the statistical evidence, show little inclination (and by implication have little incentive) to extend their services of financial intermediation into the interior of the country.

A second possible contribution of the regional financial center to economic welfare and development, as noted in part II, is to provide both employment opportunities and opportunities for employment at higher wages to citizens of the local economy. Unfortunately, data on the breakdown of employment and wages in the regional financial center as between Panamanians and foreign employees are not available. It is assumed, however, that the official statistics refer to Panamanians or that any foreigners included may be deemed to belong to the Panamanian economy.

Table 10 compares the distribution of wages and salaries by range in various components of the private financial sector with the distribution for the private sector as a whole. The evidence shows quite clearly that the financial sector pays its workers wages and salaries above the average for the economy. This in turn suggests that Panamanians would benefit in terms of real income from an expansion of the financial sector relative to the rest of the economy. However, the matter is not so simple: the higher wages and salaries presumably reflect higher skill and educational qualifications, which would have to be acquired by the appropriate training. But the existence of these differentials does indicate that an expansion of the financial sector would provide opportunities for increased employment of Panamanians at substantially increased wages and salaries if they

---

[6] The Commission's activities in the regulatory sphere, however, are a very high price to pay for the availability of good statistics.

278

Harry G. Johnson

TABLE 8

BANKS, BANK BRANCHES, AND AGENCIES ESTABLISHED SINCE 1964 IN PANAMA CITY (PC) AND ELSEWHERE (O)

BANK AND YEAR ESTABLISHED	1965 PC	1965 O	1966 PC	1966 O	1967 PC	1967 O	1968 PC	1968 O	1969 PC	1969 O	1970 PC	1970 O	1971 PC	1971 O	1972 PC	1972 O
Banco Nacional de Panama 1904:																
Branches				2		1				2		1				
Agencies				1	1	1				1						
Caja de Ahorros 1934:																
Branches				1		1		1		2	1	2				
Agencies											3					
Chase Manhattan 1915	1															
First National City 1904	1		1		1	2	1	1		4		2				
Banco Fiducario de Panama 1948			2			1					1					
Banco General 1955																
Companida Nacional de Ahorros 1963									2							
Banco de Colombia 1964			1	1		1	1			1						
Bank of America 1964			1	1		1										
Bank of London and Montreal 1966					1											
Mercantile Bank of Panama* 1966											1					
Banco Cafetero† 1966					1	1		2								
Banco Enterior 1967						1										

279

Economic Development and Cultural Change

TABLE 8—Continued

BANK AND YEAR ESTABLISHED	1965		1966		1967		1968		1969		1970		1971		1972	
	PC	O	PC	O	PC	O	PC	O	PC	O	PC	O	PC	O	PC	O
Banco de Santander y Panama 1967	…	…	…	…	1	…	…	…	…	…	1	1	…	…	…	…
Banco de America 1967	…	…	…	…	…	…	1	…	1	…	1	…	…	…	…	…
Banco de Bogota 1967	…	…	…	…	…	…	1	…	…	1	…	1	…	…	…	…
Banco de Filantropia 1969	…	…	…	…	…	…	…	…	…	…	…	1	…	…	…	…
U.S. Investment Bank, Inc.* 1969	…	…	…	…	…	…	…	…	1	…	2	…	…	…	…	…
First National Bank of Chicago 1970	…	…	…	…	…	…	…	…	1	…	1	…	…	…	…	…
Total Banco Nacional de Ahorros branches	…	…	…	3	…	2	…	1	…	4	1	1	…	…	…	…
Total Caja de Ahorros agencies	…	…	…	1	1	1	…	…	…	1	3	2	…	…	…	…
Total	…	…	…	4	1	3	…	1	…	5	4	3	…	…	…	…
Others: head offices	…	…	1	1	4	…	…	…	1	…	7	4	…	…	…	…
Others: branches	2	…	5	2	4	8	3	3	5	5	1	4	…	…	…	…
Total	2	…	6	3	8	8	3	3	6	5	8	4	…	…	…	…
Grand total	2	…	6	7	9	11	3	4	6	10	12	7	…	…	…	…

Source.—Hacienda Publica y Finanzas, *Estadística Panameña*, 1970, pp. 64 ff.
* No casa principal.
† Casa principal: Colon.

Harry G. Johnson

had previously acquired the requisite qualifications. This is an important point, because efforts to educate the population of less developed countries up to higher skill levels are frequently frustrated and produce political tensions if the expected higher incomes associated with higher training do not in fact materialize.

Table 11 shows the growth from 889 overall in 1960 to an estimated 3,028 in 1971 representing a growth rate of 240 percent over the 11 years, or approximately 20 percent per year compounded. This is to be compared with an annual population growth rate of about 3 percent per annum and a fairly constant proportion of economically active to total population (about 31 percent). However, a more relevant question, given

TABLE 9

CUMULATIVE TOTALS OF ESTABLISHMENT OF BANK HEAD
OFFICES, BRANCHES, AND AGENCIES, 1964–70

	Panama City	Other
Banco Nacional and Caja de Ahorros:		
Branches............................	1	11
Agencies............................	4	5
Total............................	5	16
Private banks:		
Head offices........................	7	1
Branches............................	26	22
Total............................	33	23
Grand total.....................	38	39

the high rate of growth of the monetary size of the banking sector, is how far that growth has led to increases in employment on a commensurate scale. Table 12 relates growth of bank employment to growth of total bank assets. It turns out that the number of employees per million balboas of bank assets has fallen fairly steeply, from 4.7 in 1967 and 1968 to 2.0 in 1971. One factor in this has been inflation, which has increased the price level in Panama and therefore reduced the real value of nominal bank assets and thus the number of employees required to service them. But this factor is trivial, since the Panamanian consumer price index rose only from 105.0 in 1967 to 113.9 in 1971 (base 1962 = 100.0); corresponding figures for wholesale prices (base 1961 = 100) were 105.2 and 118.7. The most probable reason is that the handling of foreign deposits requires fewer employees (though probably employees of higher skills) per million balboas of assets than the handling of domestic deposits; a special consideration is that most of the foreign deposits have come into one or two banks, which may not have increased their staffs because they had excess capacity in the relevant departments. The figures, whatever the explana-

281

Economic Development and Cultural Change

TABLE 10

DISTRIBUTION OF WAGES AND SALARIES BY RANGE, BANKS AND OTHER FINANCIAL ESTABLISHMENTS, AND INSURANCE COMPANIES COMPARED WITH TOTAL PRIVATE SECTOR

SALARY RANGE (BALBOAS)	TOTAL PRIVATE SECTOR		BANKS AND OTHER FINANCIAL ESTABLISHMENTS		BANKS ONLY		INSURANCE		INSURANCE COMPANIES ONLY		BANKS AND INSURANCE COMPANIES ONLY		BANKS, OTHER FINANCIAL ESTABLISHMENTS, AND INSURANCE	
	N	%	N	%	N	%	N	%	N	%	N	%	N	%
Less than 25.00	548	0.7	0	..	0	..	1	0.2	1	0.2	1	0.1	1	..
25– 49.99	2,670	3.4	4	0.2	4	0.3	3	0.5	2	0.4	6	0.3	7	0.3
50– 74.99	8,200	10.4	48	2.4	9	0.6	15	2.4	11	2.0	20	0.9	63	2.4
75– 99.99	9,835	12.7	79	3.9	37	2.4	23	3.7	22	4.1	59	2.8	102	3.8
100–124.99	13,686	17.6	160	7.8	81	5.2	57	9.2	46	8.5	127	6.0	217	8.1
125–149.99	11,935	15.4	240	11.7	164	10.4	59	9.5	54	10.0	218	10.3	299	11.2
150–174.99	8,333	10.7	258	12.6	198	12.6	80	12.9	68	12.6	266	12.6	338	12.7
175–199.99	4,776	6.2	225	11.0	202	12.9	53	8.6	48	8.9	250	11.9	278	10.4
200–249.99	6,058	7.8	328	16.0	288	18.3	108	17.4	93	17.3	381	18.1	436	16.4
250–299.99	3,233	4.2	179	8.8	153	9.7	38	6.1	34	6.3	187	8.9	217	8.2
300–499.99	4,976	6.4	292	14.3	251	16.0	100	16.2	86	16.0	337	16.0	392	14.7
500 up	3,359	4.3	231	11.3	182	11.6	82	13.3	74	13.7	256	12.1	313	11.8
Total	77,609	100.0	2,044	100.0	1,569	100.0	619	100.0	539	100.0	2,108	100.0	2,663	100.0

SOURCE.—Hacienda Publica y Finanzas, *Estadística Panameña* no. 30, table 18, pp. 50 ff. Data are for August 1969.

Harry G. Johnson

tion for them, tend rather to discourage the hope or expectation that the growth of the regional financial center will provide a strong stimulus to the growth of the Panamanian economy as a whole or provide much opportunity for additional employment. (It may be, however, that employment will respond eventually but with a long lag to the expansion of foreign business.)

By contrast, the last row of table 12 attempts a crude estimate of the amount of employment that would be provided by banking in Panama if there were no foreign banking activity and in particular if the banks had to rely on domestic liabilities only as the basis for their business. The estimate is crude and in conflict with the evidence just discussed, because it assumes that employment in banking is proportional to bank liabilities as a measure of banking sector size, regardless of whether the business is

TABLE 11

NUMBER OF EMPLOYEES AND BANKING
ESTABLISHMENTS, 1960-71

Year	Total	Private Banks	Official Banks
1960	889	469	420
1961	1,045	575	470
1962	1,093	597	496
1963	1,416	890	526
1964	1,352	773	579
1965	1,525	797	728
1966	1,731	883	848
1967	2,011	1,098	913
1968	2,331	1,330	1,001
1969	2,518	1,569	949
1970	2,730*	1,664*	1,066
1971	3,028*	1,869*	1,159

SOURCE.—Comision Bancaria Nacional (original source: Direccion de Estadistica y Censo, Contraloria General de la Republica).
* Estimated by the Section for Banking and Monetary Statistics.

TABLE 12

GROWTH OF PRIVATE BANK EMPLOYMENT AND ASSETS

	1967	1968	1969	1970	1971
(1) Private bank employees	1,098	1,330	1,569	1,664	1,869
(2) Total assets (BMN)	232.2	285.9	409.9	659.2	933.8
(3) Employees per BMN	4.7	4.7	3.8	2.5	2.0
(4) Domestic liabilities	128.0	161.1	181.0	243.1	314.7
(5) Total liabilities	232.2	285.9	409.9	659.2	934.7
(6) Ratio of (4) to (5)	0.55	0.56	0.44	0.37	0.34
(7) Domestic assets	167.9	208.3	241.7	364.5	465.3
(8) Total assets	232.2	285.9	409.9	659.2	932.9
(9) Ratio of (7) to (8)	0.72	0.73	0.59	0.55	0.50
(10) Multiply (1) × (6)	60.4	74.5	69.0	61.6	63.5

domestic or foreign. But, if we accept its assumptions, it indicates that, if either the banks had no foreign deposits or if their foreign liabilities had maintained a constant ratio to their domestic liabilities, total employment in the banking sector would have fallen between 1968 and 1971 (though it would have risen, but by far less, between 1967 and 1971). Put another way, only the very rapid expansion of foreign banking business has kept employment in the banking business expanding (of course, a far more sophisticated analysis is required to analyze the combined effects on employment in banking of expansion of domestic liabilities, expansion of foreign liabilities, increasing productivity, and inflation on nominal monetary magnitudes).

Finally, there is the question of the tax revenue collected from the financial sector. Table 13 presents figures on profit taxes collected from private banks and insurance companies for 1965–71. Allowing for the increase in profit taxes that occurred in 1970 and random annual swings, it does not appear either that the rapid growth of the Panamanian financial sector in recent years has contributed significantly to a growth in Panamanian government revenues, or that the financial sector is a very significant source of governmental revenue.[7]

Further, the increase in revenue from this source in 1970–71 was more than accounted for by increased profit tax receipts from insurance companies. However, a fairer comparison perhaps is to take the percentage increases in tax receipts from the two types of institutions between the average for 1965–69, before the tax increase, and for 1970–71 after it. For banks, the increase in profit tax receipts on this basis was approximately 100 percent and for insurance companies approximately 150 percent. But these figures are biased by the abnormally low tax collection from the insurance companies in 1968. If the 1969 figures alone are taken as representative, the increase in tax collections was approximately 115 percent for banks and 119 percent for insurance companies. These figures do not contradict the preceding conclusion that the relatively rapid growth of the banking component of the financial sector has not resulted in a commensurate growth of Panamanian profit tax revenues.

The third row of table 13 gives a more favorable impression of the effects of the expansion of the financial center on Panamanian employment than do the figures for banks only presented in table 11.

All things considered, the evidence collected in this part does not lend much impressive quantitative support to the view that the growth of the financial sector is a powerful lever for promoting Panamanian economic development. This is not to say, however, that positive external effects on the rest of the economy of the kinds discussed in the preceding part may not nevertheless be important. The evidence assembled here is fragmentary

[7] Total current governmental revenue for 1971 was 181.2 million balboas, while revenue from income taxes was 60.0 million balboas; the profit taxes in question accounted for 0.6 percent of total current revenue and 2.0 percent of income tax revenue.

Harry G. Johnson

TABLE 13

PROFITS. TAXES COLLECTED, BANKS AND INSURANCE COMPANIES, 1965–71

	1965	1966	1967	1968	1969	1970	1971
Private banks' profit taxes*......	475,393	576,565	570,913	482,954	485,669	1,141,518	947,026
Insurance profit taxes............	73,184	96,422	82,287	28,797	82,260	125,798	234,377
Total employment (Panamanians) in banks, insurance, etc........	n.a.	3,800	5,700	5,735	6,080	6,745	n.a.

SOURCE.—Government figures, confidential.
* Varying numbers of banks. as shown in table 8: 18 insurance companies. Note that there was a substantial increase in profit taxes in 1970.

Economic Development and Cultural Change

and cannot be taken as far as it needs to be for a thorough cost-benefit analysis even of those aspects of Panamanian financial development that lend themselves most readily to such treatment.

IV. Concluding Comments

Since the preliminary explorations reported in this article were performed in the summer of 1972, the international monetary system has been severely disrupted by the general adoption of "dirty floating" of exchange rates in February 1973 and by the "oil crisis" since autumn 1973. The uncertainties raised for the Panamanian economy far transcend the implications for Panama as a regional financial center. Only a few relevant points may be worth noting, given the speed with which the world environment has been changing recently. First, the rapid inflation that has recently hit Panama, a consequence first of the ability to avoid part of the American inflation by switching to suppliers in countries with undervalued currencies and then of the sudden post–February 1973 increase in the dollar cost of those supplies, raises the question whether Panama will continue to be well served by tight attachment of the balboa to the dollar; if the decision is in the negative, much of Panama's comparative advantage in finance will disappear. Second—a countervailing point—the Asian basin continues to grow in economic importance; in addition, various recent tax and other changes in Britain may partially strangle London as a financial center, make European financial operations more narrowly "European," and widen the scope for regional centers such as Panama. Third, in the long run the "oil crisis," by stimulating Asian and Latin American supplies, may give a more important role to Panama; against this, however, is the possibility that the need to replace the obsolescent canal with vastly improved facilities may give the advantage to some other Central American country.

[25]

The Asian Currency Market: Singapore as a Regional Financial Center

ZORAN HODJERA *

THE CREATION OF THE Asian currency market in Singapore occurred in the period when a number of offshore financial centers, such as those in the Caribbean area, were set up as intermediaries between several national capital markets and the rapidly growing Eurocurrency market. The authorities in these centers provided inducements to banks and other financial institutions, through various fiscal incentives that reduced costs of operations and through abolishing restrictions on non-residents' transactions in foreign currencies. In most cases, the activity of offshore markets is limited to a straightforward intermediation between a major neighboring industrial country that restricts international movements of capital and the Eurocurrency market.

The Asian currency market provides an intermediation function between several Asian countries and the Eurocurrency market. However, soon after its creation in 1968, the Asian market went beyond this function and has now developed a substantial regional network of financial transactions. It provides an arbitrage function between markets in Asia, the Middle East, and Europe; it serves as a major avenue for channeling funds into development projects in many Asian countries; and it also serves as an efficient channel for mobilizing these countries' surplus funds and for placing them elsewhere in the region.

* Mr. Hodjera, Senior Economist in the Research Department, has degrees from the Graduate Institute of International Studies in Geneva and from Columbia University and also has studied at Oxford University. He has been lecturer at the City College of New York, Assistant Professor at Yale University, and Visiting Associate Professor at the University of Virginia. He has contributed a number of articles to economic journals.

Comments on an earlier version of the paper by colleagues in the Fund, by Alan E. Moore of the Bahrain Monetary Agency, and by Sarra Chernick are gratefully acknowledged. The author is also grateful to the Economic Group of the Chase Manhattan Bank and to Robert F. Emery of the Board of Governors of the Federal Reserve System for very useful statistical data. None of these institutions and individuals are, however, responsible for the final product.

The Asian currency market was developed when the economy of Singapore was going through an important period of transition that was caused by the independence of the island in the mid-1960s and by a rapid phasing out of large British military installations. In addition to an important effort of economic development at home, this period of transition has involved expanding financial and trade relations to countries other than the British Commonwealth and the immediate neighbors. The creation of the Asian currency market can be seen as a part of this transition. Since the market's inception, the long-run strategy of the authorities has been to stimulate the development in Singapore of a large financial sector, based on very highly skilled services to be provided to the whole south and east Asian region. Besides contributing to the real income of the island, this growing sector was expected to help to increase the financial resources of Singapore and to attract a host of related economic activities.

This article examines the role of the Asian currency market as a regional financial center. Section I discusses the development of the market and its operations, while Section II discusses the relationship of the Asian market to other international markets and its contribution to Singapore's real income. Section III presents the conclusion.

I.   Development of the Market

Several factors contributed to the establishment of the Asian currency market in Singapore. In the 1960s the rapid economic growth of a number of Asian countries, an increased flow of direct investment, and a greater participation of multinational corporations in the economy of Asia generated a growing pool of foreign currencies in the hands of the private sector. Widening of the Indo-Chinese war in the second half of the 1960s increased foreign exchange expenditures in the region, mostly in U. S. dollars. Thus, when a tightening of credit conditions in the United States in 1967–68 contributed to a rising trend in interest rates in the Eurodollar market, tapping the existing dollar balances in the Asia-Pacific region became attractive for major international banks, particularly for those from the United States. Furthermore, many banks were looking for a site for regional offices from which they would service the increasing number of their branches in the region.

The willingness of the Singapore Government to provide the incentives necessary for attracting international banking business was the key to the development of an international financial center on the island. Although Tokyo and Hong Kong already had highly developed banking systems, Tokyo's financial market was not open to international transactions of the type practiced in the Eurocurrency market, because such transactions were severely constrained by Japan's exchange control regulations of capital flows. Hong Kong had no restrictions on international capital movements, but a 15 per cent withholding tax on interest income from transactions by nonresidents discouraged its use as an international banking center.

REGULATIONS AND INCENTIVES

The Asian currency market was instituted in 1968 when Singapore authorities licensed a branch of the Bank of America to set up a special international department to handle transactions of nonresidents. [1] Regulations governing such transactions [2] that were issued by the authorities were intended to stimulate further entries in the offshore banking. To separate transactions with nonresidents from local and foreign business conducted for residents of Singapore, all banks that were granted licenses were required to set up a special accounting unit for nonresident transactions, named the Asian currency unit (ACU). [3]

The authorities exempted ACU transactions from exchange controls [4] and provided a number of fiscal and banking incentives. The most important of these incentives was the abolition in 1968 of the 10 per cent withholding tax on interest income from nonresident foreign currency [5] deposits. In the following years, several stamp and estate duties

---

[1] Lee (1971), pp. 46-47.

[2] These regulations were codified in the Banking Act and the Foreign Exchange Act, both of 1970.

[3] The Asian Currency Unit (ACU) is a separate set of accounts in which are recorded all transactions with nonresidents. Although ACU operations are not subject to exchange controls, the banks are required to submit to the exchange control authority detailed monthly reports of their transactions, classified by each convertible foreign currency and by each major transaction group.

[4] Singapore's exchange controls on capital movements are rather complex. After World War II, for exchange control purposes, Singapore was part of the U. K. Scheduled Territories (hitherto called sterling area), which included the whole sterling area of that time. Transactions within the area of Scheduled Territories were free of controls. Although Singapore ceased to be a U. K. Scheduled Territory in the 1950s, it made no changes in the list of countries with which transactions were not subject to exchange controls. In February 1976 non-sterling area members of the Association of South East Asian Nations (ASEAN)—Indonesia, the Philippines, and Thailand—were added to the list of postwar sterling area countries as Singapore's Scheduled Territories, not subject to exchange controls. Thus, exchange controls are applicable to all countries that were not members of the sterling area in the 1940s and are not members of the ASEAN.

[5] In operating ACU accounts, the banks were initially authorized to transact with nonresidents in 14 "specified" major convertible currencies and, of course, in sterling area currencies that were not subject to control. (See International Monetary Fund, *Twenty-Seventh Annual Report on Exchange Restrictions*, Washington, 1976.) Since March 1976, ACU banks have been authorized to transact in all convertible foreign currencies.

on negotiable paper in foreign currencies and a tax on income from Asian currency bonds were also abolished. In 1972 the Monetary Authority of Singapore abolished the 20 per cent minimum reserve requirements against deposit liabilities in foreign currencies that the banks operating ACU accounts had hitherto been required to hold. The measure was particularly important, since it permitted an increase in earnings from offshore credit. In 1973 the corporate tax on net income from offshore lending and other offshore activities was reduced from 40 per cent to 10 per cent.

Singapore's offshore operations are regulated by the Monetary Authority of Singapore, which also regulates the country's banking system and administers its exchange controls. The Monetary Authority has been very conscious of the requirement for quality in the operations of this newly developed financial market and has been very selective in granting ACU licenses. The Banking Act of 1970 has permitted foreign commercial banks to set up branches, rather than subsidiaries, so that the risk of insolvency has been passed on to the banks' head offices. Furthermore, in applying for licenses to operate ACU accounts, the head offices have had to provide the Authority with an undertaking to make up for any shortfall in liquidity suffered by their ACU branches in Singapore.

The general aim of the Monetary Authority has been to limit access to the Asian currency market to well-established foreign and domestic banks of medium to large size. [6] A further aim of the Authority has been to protect Singapore from an excessive opening of banks operating in the domestic money market, which could crowd out small purely local banks operating on a modest capital base. Since the creation of the Asian currency market, licenses for an entire range of domestic and foreign banking operations have not been granted to foreign banks. Only 13 foreign commercial banks that were established prior to 1970 were fully licensed. [7] Between 1971 and 1973, only "restricted licenses" were given to new entrants authorizing them to practice a full range of ACU operations, but limiting them in their operation in the local money market. The foreign banks with restricted licenses cannot operate more than one branch in Singapore, cannot offer residents savings account services, and cannot accept from residents deposits of less than S$250,000; but they can grant local currency loans to residents without restrictions. Since 1973 only "offshore banking licenses" have been granted to foreign banks. These banks are permitted

[6] See Wong (1975), pp. 101–102.
[7] However, opening new branches in Singapore by fully licensed foreign banks is subject to the approval of the Monetary Authority, which is rarely given. (See Thorn, 1975, p. 93.)

to receive local funds only through the interbank market, and the deposits they can accept cannot be less than S$250,000. Their local lending is also restricted; they can grant residents only medium-term to long-term loans, the minimum amount being S$1 million. Furthermore, their local lending is subject to the approval of the Monetary Authority. Therefore, the policy of the Monetary Authority has been to progressively limit new foreign banks to those areas of local business in which their operations are complementary to, rather than competitive with, the operations of the local and fully licensed banks.

Another category of foreign banks operating in the Asian currency market are merchant banks. Although they are not regulated by the Banking Act, [8] these banks are subject to the supervision of the Monetary Authority. Merchant banks derive their earnings from financing various commercial and industrial activities, and from operating as underwriters, corporate advisors, and investment managers. Their access to local funds is limited to deposits from commercial banks and finance companies. Those merchant banks that are licensed to operate in the Asian currency market are particularly active in loan syndication, and in the flotation of Asian bonds and other international bonds.

Initially the exchange control regulations did not permit participation of residents in the Asian currency market. However, these restrictions have been substantially relaxed over the years. Residents have been permitted to borrow foreign currencies from the ACU banks for export finance and for other export-related transactions. Individual residents and corporations are permitted to hold limited foreign currency deposits on the ACU account. [9] Insurance companies, pension funds, and provident societies are permitted to hold up to 10 per cent of their assets on that account.

In evaluating the participation of Singapore residents in the Asian currency market, one should take into consideration peculiarities of the exchange control regulations. While payments and capital transfers between Singapore residents and countries other than those belonging to the post-World War II sterling area have been subject to exchange controls, payments and transfers between residents and postwar sterling area countries have not been subject to controls. Under such conditions, a lively triangular arbitrage has been established between Singapore and international capital markets via Hong Kong, which has no exchange controls on payments and capital transfers. This large loop-

[8] Legally, merchant banks in Singapore are governed by the Finance Companies Act of 1970.
[9] The most recent regulation by the authorities, of February 1976, authorizes maximum deposits equivalent to S$250,000 for individuals and S$5 million for corporations. ACU bank lending to residents requires authorization by the Monetary Authority, but loans for exports for up to three months can be made without authorization.

226   INTERNATIONAL MONETARY FUND STAFF PAPERS

hole in Singapore's exchange control system made a natural candidate of Hong Kong for financial intermediation between Singapore and the countries outside the sterling area. However, since Hong Kong has a withholding tax of 15 per cent on interest income from nonresident transactions in foreign currencies, with an elimination of such a tax on transactions by the ACU banks in Singapore, this intermediation has been switched to the Asian currency market, but the ease with which residents can bypass exchange controls on non-sterling area currencies has also increased.

Another difference between Singapore and Hong Kong in the fiscal treatment of foreign banks' offshore transactions involves net income from foreign currency lending abroad, which includes syndication and other similar ventures. While there is no tax on such income in Hong Kong, in Singapore the tax rate was 40 per cent prior to August 1973 and has been 10 per cent since then. It is, therefore, in the interest of foreign banks having branches in both financial centers to maximize earnings from deposits in Singapore and earnings from offshore lending in Hong Kong.

MARKET ACTIVITY

The incentives provided by the Government of Singapore permitted a vigorous expansion of foreign currency transactions in this relatively small capital market (Table 1). The number of banks participating in the market grew from 11 at the end 1969 to 69 by the end of 1976; [10] the size of the market grew from US$123 million to US$17 billion, [11] which amounted to an average annual growth rate of 75 per cent, two and a half times the average growth rate of the Eurocurrency market. However, following the difficulties of some Eurocurrency banks in 1974 and the recession in 1975, the increased caution in granting credit has caused a significant deceleration of the Asian currency market growth.

In the period 1968 to 1970, when credit conditions in the United States were quite tight and U. S. banks were borrowing Eurodollars heavily, the activity of banks operating in the Asian currency market consisted of gathering dollar deposits and placing them in London and Tokyo. As a result of these operations, deposits of the nonbank sector exceeded two thirds of ACU banks' total liabilities (Table 1), while

[10] "Economic Survey of Singapore" (1976), p. 47. Of the 69 ACU banks, which also include local banks, 19 are fully licensed, 12 have restricted licenses, 25 have offshore licenses, and 13 are merchant banks.

[11] The major proportion of the sum total of US$17 billion of assets and liabilities includes interbank transactions; hence, there is considerable double counting. Informal estimates of the *net* size of the Asian currency market would reduce the figures shown in Table 1 as interbank transactions by about 20–30 per cent.

TABLE 1. ASIAN CURRENCY MARKET: NUMBER OF ACU BANKS AND THEIR ASSETS AND LIABILITIES, DECEMBER 1968–DECEMBER 1976

(In millions of U. S. dollars)

Date	No. of ACU banks	Assets			Total Assets/ Liabilities [1]	Liabilities		
		Loans to nonbanks	Interbank funds	Other		Deposits of nonbanks	Interbank deposits	Other
1968 Dec.	1	1	29	—	30	18	13	—
1969 Dec.	11	1	120	2	123	98	24	1
1970 Dec.	16	14	370	6	390	244	141	5
1971 Dec.	21	189	851	23	1,063	238	811	14
1972 Dec.	24	601	2,331	44	2,976	399	2,550	27
1973 June		734	3,034	59	3,827	520	3,274	34
Dec.	46	1,214	4,962	101	6,277	913	5,249	115
1974 June		1,899	6,052	161	8,112	1,324	6,647	141
Dec.	56	2,629	7,528	200	10,357	1,614	8,531	212
1975 June	61	3,246	7,586	184	11,016	1,764	9,036	216
Dec.		3,303	9,098	196	12,597	2,068	10,294	235
1976 June		3,845	10,643	203	14,690	2,109	12,363	218
Dec.	69	4,060	12,939	354	17,354	1,960	15,067	327

Sources: Monetary Authority of Singapore and its *Quarterly Bulletin*, various issues.
[1] Total assets and liabilities include those of Singapore residents; therefore, as accounting identities, they are necessarily equal.

loans to the nonbank sector were less than 5 per cent of total assets. Since the second half of 1970, with an easing of the credit tightness in the United States and in international capital markets, and with new banks entering the Asian currency market, interbank transactions have become by far the most important activity. Although deposits of the nonbanking sector grew substantially in size, their proportion of the ACU banks' total liabilities fell to 15–18 per cent. Loans to the nonbank sector, however, increased faster than the total assets of the banks, reflecting the opening up of business opportunities in the region. Since 1973 the ratio of interbank transactions to total transactions in the Asian currency market has become roughly similar to the ratio in the Euro-currency market. Singapore has become the most important international clearing market for interbank transactions of a large network of banks in south and east Asia and a major source of funds in the region for business investments and government borrowing.

In addition to the commercial banks, suppliers of funds to the Asian currency market are nonbank companies, central banks, some government organizations, and individuals residing outside Singapore. Among the nonbank companies the most important are multinational corporations and major enterprises in the Asian region. Prior to the 1974 liberalization of U. S. constraints on direct investment flows, U. S. multinational corporations with branches in Asia were bypassing controls by using "swap arrangements" with banks in the Asian currency market. [12] Corporations would make short-term deposits with ACU banks; in turn, these deposits would be borrowed by branches in the Asian region. Since 1974, the multinational and regional companies have continued to place their working capital and other liquid assets in the market. Deposits by central banks are not very large; with the accumulation of surplus funds in the Middle East, deposits by government statutory bodies and semigovernmental institutions from that region have become fairly large. Among nonresident individuals, deposits by members of the Chinese community are also significant.

The borrowers other than banks are prime name enterprises in the region, such as large regional and national companies and some smaller enterprises with first-class standing. More recently, governments and government agencies have also appeared as important users of Asian currency funds. Multinational corporations, on the other hand, have a preference for local currency financing of their medium-term needs, which minimizes the exchange rate risk; their borrowing on the Asian

---

[12] See Emery (1975), pp. 13–14 and 27.

currency market has been mostly short term, for working capital needs. [13]

Singapore banks appear to be more selective than the Eurocurrency banks in granting credit. Such caution is in part germane to a higher risk of lending to government and enterprises in less developed countries; in part, this caution reflects the policy of head offices that have provided an explicit guaranty of solvency and liquidity of their ACU branches. Also, this caution reflects at least in part a fairly close supervision of ACU banks by the Monetary Authority. Credit is granted preferably to borrowers in the countries with convertible currencies; for a borrower residing in a country that practices exchange controls, special approval from his authorities is needed to certify that he will be able to obtain the foreign exchange necessary for meeting his repayment obligations.

Geographical breakdown of sources and uses of funds in the Asian currency market distinguish three major regional groupings (Table 2): Asia, including Australia; Europe; and others, including the United States, the Middle East, and Latin America. The Asian region used to supply about 50 per cent of deposits in the market. With an increased flow of funds from the Middle East in recent years, this percentage has fallen somewhat. Lending to the Asian region by ACU banks, however, has always exceeded 80 per cent of total lending, with borrowers situated in Indonesia, Hong Kong, Malaysia, the Philippines, the Republic of China, Korea, and Thailand. Developed countries in the region have also borrowed in the Asian currency market; however, they have preferred to float Eurobonds at fixed interest rates, compared with syndicated loans from the banks at floating interest rates.

Thus, throughout the operation of the Asian currency market, the Asian region has been a net user of funds, while Europe and the rest of the world have been net sources. In June 1976, net claims by ACU banks on the Asian region exceeded US$5 billion. Therefore the market has efficiently fulfilled its role as an intermediary, channeling the funds from major capital markets into a large number of developing countries in Asia.

CURRENCY USED AND TERM STRUCTURE OF LOANS

The U. S. dollar is by far the most important currency used in the market. Since the early years, about 85–90 per cent of ACU banks' assets and liabilities have been denominated in U. S. dollars, which

---

[13] See Bhattacharya (1977), p. 37; also Cushman, *Euromoney*, Supplement (May 1976), p. 12.

TABLE 2. ASIAN CURRENCY MARKET: GEOGRAPHICAL DISTRIBUTION OF EXTERNAL LIABILITIES AND CLAIMS OF ACU BANKS IN FOREIGN CURRENCIES, JUNE 1971–JUNE 1976

(In millions of U.S. dollars)

Date	Liabilities (Sources of Funds)			Total Liabilities/ Claims	Claims (Uses of Funds)			Net Uses of Funds		
	Asia [1]	Europe	All other		Asia [1]	Europe	All other	Asia [1]	Europe	All other
1971 June	448	256	37	741	606	86	49	158	-170	12
Dec.	516	454	93	1,063	916	102	44	400	-352	-49
1972 June	759	613	247	1,619	1,358	118	143	599	-495	-104
Dec.	1,445	1,318	213	2,976	2,411	310	255	966	-1,008	42
1973 June	2,126	1,483	218	3,827	2,963	549	315	837	-934	97
Dec.	3,673	2,083	521	6,277	4,784	1,072	421	1,111	-1,011	-100
1974 June	4,502	2,769	841	8,112	5,976	1,339	797	1,474	-1,430	-44
Dec.	5,460	3,709	1,188	10,357	8,203	1,171	983	2,743	-2,538	-205
1975 June	5,115	4,522	1,379	11,016	8,764	1,168	1,084	3,649	-3,354	-295
Dec.	6,114	4,708	1,775	12,597	10,163	1,439	995	4,049	-3,269	-780
1976 June	6,706	6,021	1,963	14,690	11,910	1,543	1,237	5,204	-4,478	-726

Sources: Monetary Authority of Singapore and its *Quarterly Bulletin*, various issues.
[1] Includes Australia.

ASIAN CURRENCY MARKET   231

reflects the importance of the dollar in the Asian region as a vehicle currency for trade and financial transactions. The dependence on the U. S. dollar also reflects the competitive edge that U. S. banks have in the region, because of their extensive network of branches in Asia. According to tentative estimates provided by a bank in Singapore, 46 per cent of total syndicated credit in 1975 was arranged and taken up by U. S. banks. [14] The dependence on the dollar has increased with the generalized floating of major currencies. Since 1972, 92–95 per cent of assets and liabilities has been denominated in U. S. dollars. [15]

Deposit and loan facilities offered in the Asian currency market are similar to those offered in the Eurocurrency market. [16] Deposits accepted are (a) sight; (b) two-day to seven-day notice, generally limited to US$100,000 or higher; and (c) deposits with fixed-term maturities of up to five years. Contrary to the practice of the Eurocurrency banks, the banks in Singapore accept small fixed-term and time deposits, the amounts sometimes being as low as US$5,000.

Loan facilities offered are (a) short-term, including overnight; (b) fixed-interest rate loans for various maturities that in recent years have often exceeded one year; (c) lines of credit for commercial transactions, for a fixed term but subject to a rollover; and (d) floating interest rate credits for some loans exceeding three years on which the interest rate, based on the interbank offer rate *plus* a margin, is adjusted every 3 to 6 months.

As in the Eurocurrency market, the increase in oil prices in 1974 has resulted in a radical modification of the maturity structure of ACU banks' deposits and loans. It can be seen from Table 3 that ACU banks carefully matched the maturities of their claims and liabilities prior to 1974. This was largely so because unlike in a domestic monetary system credit creation is slight and leakages are substantial in international capital transactions in which ACU banks are operating. Furthermore, the large majority of ACU banks' sight and short-term deposits is drawn from other banks. Prior to 1974, the largest amount of claims and liabilities was concentrated in the range between 3 and 12 months. Small net liabilities in the range of eight days to one year were used to finance net claims in the range exceeding one year. However, transactions with terms exceeding one year were an exception rather than a rule.

[14] See Cushman (cited in footnote 13), p. 13.
[15] This increased dependence on the U. S. dollar in the period of flexible exchange rates is caused by: (a) the dominant role of the U. S. dollar in Asia as a vehicle currency in trade and in most other financial transactions; (b) the importance of multinational corporations with head offices in the United States as participants in the Asian currency market; and (c) the dominance of U. S. banks in financial transactions in the region.
[16] Emery (1975), pp. 13–14 and 27.

TABLE 3. ACU BANKS: MATURITIES OF CLAIMS AND LIABILITIES AND THE NET POSITION, DECEMBER 1970–DECEMBER 1976[1]

(In millions of U.S. dollars)

	Sight to 7 days (1)	Per cent of total	8 days to 3 months (2)	Per cent of total	Total, sight to 3 months (3) (1+2)	Per cent of total	Over 3 months to 12 months (4)	Per cent of total	More than 1 year (5)	Per cent of total	Sum total (6) (3+4+5)
1970 December											
Net position	168		-161		7		-8		2		
Claims	198	51	77	20	275	71	106	28	4	1	385
Liabilities	30	8	238	62	268	70	114	29	2	1	384
1971 December											
Net position	112		-13		99		-180		72		
Claims	165	16	361	20	526	36	416	40	98	9	1,040
Liabilities	53	5	374	36	427	41	596	57	26	2	1,049
1972 December											
Net position	78		-185		-107		-43		132		
Claims	374	13	1,072	35	1,446	48	1,234	42	251	9	2,931
Liabilities	296	10	1,257	43	1,553	53	1,277	43	119	4	2,949
1973 June											
Net position	18		-139		-121		-3		100		
Claims	445	12	1,254	33	1,699	45	1,850	49	221	6	3,770
Liabilities	427	11	1,393	37	1,820	47	1,853	49	121	3	3,794
1973 December											
Net position	66		-268		-202		112		75		
Claims	663	11	2,120	34	2,783	45	3,096	50	298	5	6,177
Liabilities	597	10	2,388	39	2,985	49	2,984	48	223	4	6,192
1974 June											
Net position	-170		-254		-424		219		173		
Claims	586	7	2,685	34	3,271	41	4,237	53	461	6	7,969
Liabilities	756	10	2,939	37	3,695	47	4,018	50	288	4	8,001

Continued overleaf

TABLE 3 continued

Item											Total
1974 December											
Net position	−571	10	−70	37	−641	47	61	45	566	7	
Claims	1,032	16	3,795	38	4,827	54	4,546	44	784	2	10,157
Liabilities	1,603		3,865		5,468		4,485		218		10,171
1975 June											
Net position	−566	7	−502	34	−1,068	42	−48	45	1,144	13	
Claims	787	12	3,722	39	4,509	52	4,924	46	1,400	2	10,833
Liabilities	1,353		4,224		5,577		4,972		256		10,805
1975 December											
Net position	−914	8	−425	38	−1,339	46	−214	39	1,568	15	
Claims	942	15	4,736	42	5,678	57	4,873	41	1,850	2	12,401
Liabilities	1,856		5,161		7,017		5,087		282		12,386
1976 June											
Net position	−1,468	12	−621	48	−2,089	60	12	24	2,068 [2]	16	
Claims	1,799	22	7,029	52	8,828	74	3,462	23	2,391 [2]	2	14,681
Liabilities	3,267		7,650		10,917		3,450		323 [2]		14,690
1976 September											
Net position	−1,207	15	−1,397	46	−2,604	61	267	22	2,338 [2]	17	
Claims	2,369	22	7,381	55	9,750	78	3,430	20	2,694 [2]	2	15,874
Liabilities	3,576		8,778		12,354		3,163		356 [2]		15,873
1976 December											
Net position	—		—		−2,562	62	260	21	2,302 [2]	17	
Claims	—		—		10,829	77	3,624	19	2,901 [2]	3	17,354
Liabilities	—		—		13,391		3,364		599 [2]		17,354

Sources: Monetary Authority of Singapore and its *Quarterly Bulletin*, various issues.

[1] Maturity classification was by original maturity through the first quarter of 1976; thereafter, by outstanding period to maturity. Until the second quarter of 1976, total assets included only balances and fixed deposits with banks, and loans and advances to banks and nonbanks. Foreign notes and coins, Treasury bills, public securities and other securities, fixed assets, and all other assets held by ACUs were excluded. Total liabilities included only balances held for banks, fixed deposits from banks, and amounts borrowed from banks and other creditors. All other liabilities were excluded. From the second quarter of 1976, all assets and liabilities are included.

[2] Outstanding maturities of more than three years are as follows:

	1976 June		1976 September		1976 December	
Net position	1,794		2,018		2,020	
Claims	2,025	14	2,260	14	2,347	14
Liabilities	231	2	242	2	327	2

Since 1974, banks of the Asian currency market have participated in the activity of major financial centers to recycle surplus funds of the oil producing countries. The activity resulted in important modifications of the maturity structure of ACU banks' assets and liabilities. The preference of the OPEC countries for very short-term deposits was reflected in substantial increases in banks' liabilities with maturities of three months or less between 1973 and 1976. [17] On the other hand, a very large increase in demand for medium-term to long-term loans has been reflected in a manifold increase of claims with maturities exceeding one year. ACU banks showed a remarkable flexibility in adjusting to changes in the maturity structure of their assets and liabilities, despite the fact that these changes occurred in a period of unprecedented strains on the international payments system. As in the Eurocurrency market, the techniques used included: (a) loan syndication to spread default risk; (b) rollover clauses on short-term deposits to minimize withdrawal risk; (c) stand-by lines of credit with other banks to buffet the effect of possible liquidity difficulties; and (d) floating interest rates on long-term loans to minimize the probability that deposit rate fluctuation may make them unprofitable. The revival of the Asian bond issues also served to increase the flow of funds for long-term financing.

Nevertheless, banks operating in the Asian currency market have handled the recycling problem with somewhat greater caution than the other financial centers. This caution has been reflected in efforts by the banks to shorten the maturity of loans granted for less than one year, in order to improve the balance with the maturity of their liabilities. This caution was further reflected in a significant deceleration of the growth of the market in 1975 and 1976. Also, the share of loans in excess of one year has been smaller than in the Eurocurrency market. [18] Despite this cautious approach, the Asian currency market has played an important role in contributing to the financing of payments deficits of a number of countries in the region.

[17] At the beginning of 1976, the method of reporting was changed by the Singapore authorities from classification by original maturity to classification by outstanding period to maturity. This has provided better information about the maturity transformation by the ACU banks, but has interrupted the continuity of the series. As is to be expected, the new classification has shortened the maturity of all claims and liabilities. Yet, it has also increased the gap between claims and liabilities with maturities of three months and less, indicating a greater degree of maturity transformation than appeared in the earlier data. This greater degree of maturity transformation is also confirmed by a substantial increase of claims with maturity in excess of one year. The new classification introduced in early 1976 also shows that most longer-term loans are granted on terms exceeding three years.

[18] However, data reported in Table 3 overstate somewhat this difference from the Eurocurrency market. Although most banks report the maturity structure of their credit on the basis of the commitment period, some banks report maturity of credit with floating rate on the basis of a period when interest rates are adjusted, which is three to six months.

SYNDICATION AND ASIAN BOND MARKET

The syndication of banks, for the purpose of handling larger loans on terms exceeding two years, has become more prevalent in Singapore in recent years. Data on flow of syndicated loans are not complete, but it appears that most of these loans were granted to borrowers from the Pacific region, including Brunei, Hong Kong, Indonesia, Korea, and the Philippines. Loans are mostly for development purposes, among which exploration for oil, production of oil and natural gas, and investment in manufacturing are the most prevalent. The maturities of syndicated loans have been three to seven years, with floating interest rates and premia over comparable interbank offer rates varying from $\frac{3}{4}$ to $1\frac{3}{4}$ percentage points. In general, ACU banks have been lead managers, agents, or comanagers of loans floated in Singapore. They have also participated in syndication of loans placed simultaneously on several markets.

From the beginning, one of the main objectives of the Singapore authorities has been to stimulate issues of international bonds, called Asian bonds, as an integral part of the Asian currency market activity. To stimulate the issue of these bonds, the Government of Singapore floated its own international bond issue in 1972 and influenced two domestic banks to do the same. This attempt was not successful on the whole, mainly because it occurred on the eve of a sharp two-year upward trend in interest rates in the Asian currency market (Chart 1), as well as in other international markets, that discouraged flotation of bonds. Furthermore, the secondary market for such assets still did not exist in Singapore. The bond market remained dormant for several years. However, with a substantial decline in interest rates in international markets in 1975, the flurry of new international bond issues in Europe also stimulated the Asian bond market into activity. In the second half of 1975, three new issues were floated in the market, while in 1976, nine new issues totaling US$273 million were floated. A new investment instrument appeared in 1976 in the form of a note issue of US$25 million with a floating interest rate. Borrowers outside the Asian region also appeared in the market. [19] Japanese security companies were very active as lead managers and participants in syndicates underwriting these issues. The maturity of bonds issued ranged between 7 and 10 years; only the 1972 bond issues of the Singapore Government and of the Singapore banks were for 15 years.

Several brokerage houses that came to Singapore in the early 1970s

---

[19] In 1975 and in 1976, the European Investment Bank floated two issues of six-year bonds.

236   INTERNATIONAL MONETARY FUND STAFF PAPERS

CHART 1. SINGAPORE: MATURITY STRUCTURE OF ACU BANKS' BID
RATES ON DEPOSITS, 1971–FEBRUARY 1977

(*In per cent per annum*)

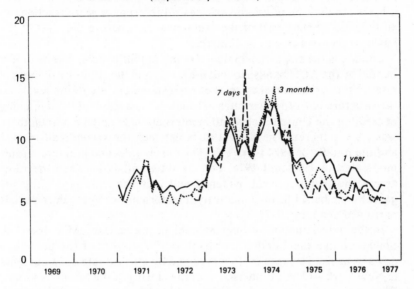

Sources: ACU banks' dollar interest rates: *Straits Times*, and Robert F. Emery; Eurodollar notes: Economic Group of the Chase Manhattan Bank.

contributed substantially to the development of the secondary market for international bonds and for other paper issued by the ACU banks. Improved conditions in the secondary market helped considerably in achieving a wider acceptability for new international bond issues. Nevertheless, bond issues are still limited in Singapore, which suggests that the size of its international market is still modest for efficiently conducting such operations.

II.   Integration with World Markets and Contribution to Singapore

TIME ARBITRAGE AND MARKET INTEGRATION

Singapore has an important time advantage in conducting arbitrage between financial centers in the Pacific region and Europe. The difference in time zones between Sydney, Tokyo, Hong Kong, the Middle East, and Western Europe, on the one hand, and Singapore, on the other hand, is such as to permit banks in the Asian currency market to conduct business with all these financial centers during a normal business day. This also means that Singapore quotations can serve as a basis for determining interest rates on international transactions in all financial centers east of the Mediterranean, before the start of the business day in London or Frankfurt.

London is the single most important market influencing interest rates quoted by the ACU banks, so that the levels and the structure of interest rates in the Asian currency market correspond closely to the level and the structure of Eurodollar rates in London. As a result of the tightening of credit in the United States and in international capital markets, there was a steep increase in interest rates between the second half of 1972 and the middle of 1974 (Chart 1). The ensuing decline in interest rates moderated in 1975 and 1976, but the differentials between the rates across the maturity scale widened and increased the possibility for gains by the banks through maturity transformation. These differentials narrowed again in 1977.

In the determination of interest rates in the market, ACU banks in Singapore use the London interbank rate quotation of the preceding day as a basis. This rate is often modified by interest rate developments in New York and San Francisco after the closing of the London market. With the opening of the Singapore market, the next day, ACU banks proceed gradually with interest arbitrage on dollar transactions with banks from Sydney and Tokyo to Beirut. With the opening of the London market at 3:30 p.m. Singapore time, the two markets merge, and ACU banks adjust their interest rates to correspond to the opening quotation in London. However, since major changes in Eurodollar rates in London occur later in the day when the New York market is also open, but the Singapore market is closed, any major changes in London Eurodollar quotations are reflected in Asian dollar interest rates the next day. [20]

This complex time arbitrage resulted in sizable fluctuations in interest rates on the U. S. dollar between the Asian currency market and Lon-

---

[20] This behavior is confirmed by the regression analysis of the movements in interest rates on seven-day dollar deposits in the Asian and Eurocurrency markets. Matching observation for the last Wednesdays of the months in the Asian dollar market with observation one day earlier in London improves the regression coefficient to 0.98, compared with 0.90 when the regression is estimated with the quotation of the same date. The period of observations was May 1973 to February 1977.

A very close relationship between interest rates on federal funds in New York and on overnight Eurodollars in London (Morgan Guaranty Trust Company, 1977) confirms that interest rate developments in the United States are factors in determining interest rate movements of Eurodollars in London. Therefore, in setting their Asian dollar interest rates at the opening of the business day, most Singapore branches of U. S. banks are heavily influenced by developments in the U. S. money markets. No data on overnight Asian dollar rates are readily available to permit a statistical testing of this hypothesis.

CHART 2. SINGAPORE: DIFFERENCES ON THREE-MONTH BID RATES
BETWEEN SINGAPORE AND LONDON, 1969–FEBRUARY 1977

(*In per cent per annum*)

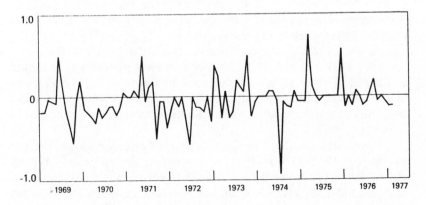

Sources: ACU banks' dollar interest rates: *Straits Times*, and Robert F. Emery; Eurodollar notes: Economic Group of the Chase Manhattan Bank.

don. The variance of the interest differential between these markets can serve as an indicator of a change in financial integration of the ACU banks in Singapore and the Eurocurrency market. Indeed, the variance for the differential on three-month dollar deposits for the period 1969–70 is two and a half times the variance for the period 1975–76. (See also Chart 2.) [21] This indicates that fluctuations in the Singapore-London differential have decreased significantly since the early years. Also, in the early years of operation, deposit rates offered by the ACU banks were fractionally lower than the comparable rates in London, and the loan rates were fractionally higher. The banks could offer lower deposit rates because they were accepting deposits of a much smaller size than that accepted by banks in the major Eurocurrency centers. Furthermore, during the first few years, a wider spread in the Asian currency market permitted the banks to take into account the risk involved in contracting deposit and loan rates prior to the opening of the London market. However, the increase in the size of the market over the years, the learning process in time arbitrage, and competition generated by the increase in international financial integration withered away this differential in charges by the end of 1973.

Another aspect of financial integration between markets and of

[21] The period 1971–74 was dominated by disturbances related to the international monetary crisis and the effects of changes in oil prices. The observations over this period were, therefore, omitted from the comparison.

responses to the risk is shown in the comparative movements of the spread between quotations for offer and bid interbank transactions in the two markets. (See Chart 3, in the Appendix.) Traditionally, such a spread did not exceed ⅛ of 1 per cent in the Eurocurrency market. A doubling of the spread to ¼ of 1 per cent, for a period of time, would reflect a disturbance in the market that had significantly increased the risk to the banks. In the early years, the usual spread in the Asian currency market was ³⁄₁₆ to ⁵⁄₁₆ of 1 per cent on maturities of one month and higher. This wider spread reflected the risk inherent in operations in a new market, and an initial lack of competitive pressures from banks operating in other markets. This difference in spread disappeared in September 1972.

However, the two markets reacted differently to disturbances created by the Middle East war, by the increase in the oil prices, and by difficulties of several banks involved in Eurocurrency transactions. In the Eurodollar market in London, the spread widened on all maturities through the summer of 1974. Despite being much thinner and subject to short-term fluctuation, the Asian currency market reacted with greater calm. The spread for maturities in excess of one month widened only briefly with the increase in oil prices at the end of 1973, and soon after returned to normal. Although this may have reflected less exposure of the ACU banks to the risks generated by the events in 1973 and 1974, it reflected mainly greater confidence by investors as a result of the cautious approach to international lending by the banks. This greater confidence is also shown by the continuous growth of the Asian currency market (Table 1), despite the Herstatt bank failure in 1974. During the same period, the Eurocurrency market experienced a period of retrenchment, with its size decreasing in the third quarter of 1974.

CONTRIBUTION TO SINGAPORE

The Asian currency market has provided substantial benefits to the Asian region by facilitating large inflows of funds that otherwise might not have become available. However, questions have often been raised about the benefits that the market has provided to Singapore, its host country. Recorded flows between the Asian currency market and Singapore [22] (Table 5, in the Appendix) do not provide an adequate picture, because they do not include substantial unrecorded flows coming via Hong Kong. Furthermore, as the balance of payments data indicate (Table 6, in the Appendix), the major contribution of foreign capital to Singapore has come from flows of direct investment that have not

[22] Assets with, and liabilities to, residents in Singapore have seldom exceeded 10 per cent of total assets and liabilities of the ACU banks.

directly involved the activity of the Asian currency market. On the whole, net flows of Singapore's commercial bank capital have reflected cyclical forces at home and abroad; they have experienced inflows in periods of domestic booms and tight money, and outflows in periods of domestic recessions and high liquidity.

The contribution of the Asian currency market to the real income of Singapore can be estimated in terms of: (1) banks' earnings from operating ACU accounts, net of profits remitted to head offices abroad; (2) direct contribution of the Asian currency market to the gross domestic product (GDP); and (3) contribution to the GDP, which would also include external economies generated by the market. While bank earnings from ACU accounts retained by Singapore can be roughly estimated, the remaining two methods can yield only a qualitative evaluation because the relevant data are lacking.

(1) A rough estimate of gross income by banks from operating ACU accounts and of earnings retained by Singapore can be imputed from data on assets and liabilities for various categories of transaction and from quotations of interest rates on these transactions. These estimates are shown in Table 4. Gross income from ACU accounts comes from three main sources: (a) a spread between bid and asked on deposits of $\frac{1}{8}$ of 1 per cent in recent years; (b) a premium on loans to customers other than banks, averaging about 1.5 per cent in recent years; and (c) the earnings from the maturity transformation through borrowing short and lending long. Depending on the maturities involved, the differential between borrowing and lending rates may vary from $\frac{1}{2}$ to $1\frac{3}{4}$ per cent. [23] In addition, one should add (d) earnings from flotations of Asian bonds with an average spread of 1.5 per cent. Total earnings by banks from operating ACU accounts, imputed from these data, amounted to about US$110 million in 1976, which is about 2 per cent of Singapore's 1976 GDP.

Operating costs of ACU banks that are expended in Singapore are imputed in alternative ways. The first takes three U. S.-based international banks that have the lowest ratios of operating costs [24] to income net of interest costs (i.e., total income minus interest payments) on deposits and other borrowed funds. The three banks, whose operating costs in 1976 ranged 50 to 60 per cent of income net of interest pay-

[23] These differentials are affected to an important extent by cyclical movements in the Eurodollar rate. The differentials relate to 1976, a period of declining Eurodollar rates. In that year, the differentials were larger than in 1977, when the interest rates appear to have bottomed out.

[24] Operating costs include (a) salaries and other employees' benefits, (b) rents and other expenses on buildings and equipment, and (c) other transaction costs, such as costs of communications, brokerage fees, and insurance.

TABLE 4. ACU ACCOUNTS: IMPUTED INCOME, 1976

(In millions of U. S. dollars)

Source	Average Interest Rate Differential or Spread	Average Level of Deposits or Assets	Earnings
	Per cent per annum		
1. Imputed gross income			
From spread on deposits	$^1/_8$	11,250.0 [1]	14.1
Premium over SIBOR [2] on loans	*1.5*	3,800.0	57.0
Maturity transformation			
Sight to 3–12 months	*0.5*	150.0	0.8
Sight to over 1 year	*1.75*	1,000.0	17.5
8-day to 3-month to over 1 year	*1.5*	1,000.0	15.0
Flotation of Asian bonds	*1.5*	2,750.0	4.1
Total imputed gross income			108.5
(as a percentage of 1976 GDP) [3]			*1.9*
2. Imputed operating costs in Singapore [50–60 per cent of gross income] [4]			54.5–65.5
(as a percentage of 1976 GDP)			*0.9–1.1*
3. Hypothetical net earnings remitted abroad [5]			
Premium over prime rate	*0.75*		28.5
Maturity transformation over prime rate			16.5
Bond flotations: differential over minimum spread	*0.75*		2.0
Total hypothetical net earnings			47.0
4. Hypothetical operating costs in Singapore [(1)−(3)]			61.5
(as a percentage of 1976 GDP)			*1.1*

[1] Includes 75 per cent of the average deposits in 1976 to US$15 billion. The adjustment is made to take into account double counting in data on interbank transactions. See also footnote 11 in the text.

[2] Singapore interbank offer rate.

[3] US$5.8 billion.

[4] Equal to the range of the lowest ratios of operating cost (net of interest payments) to gross income in three multinational banks based in the United States. See also footnote 25 in the text.

[5] See text, fifth paragraph in section, CONTRIBUTION TO SINGAPORE.

ments, [25] are banks that are heavily involved in worldwide Eurocurrency operations. Although salaries in Singapore are probably below

[25] The three banks are J. P. Morgan (50 per cent), Citicorp (59 per cent), and Bankamerica (60 per cent). These percentages are calculated from income statements in annual reports of the banks and from *Moody's Bank and Financial Manual, 1977*, Moody's Investors Service (New York, 1977).

the average of salaries paid by these banks worldwide, more than one half of ACU banks had been in Singapore three years or less at the end of 1976 and therefore have a much higher ratio of operating costs to gross income than do the banks that were already established. On this basis, the expenditures of ACU banks in Singapore range between US$55 million and US$65 million.

The alternative method is based on a hypothesis of highly competitive conditions in international financial markets. Under such conditions, profits that are repatriated to head offices relate to business risk assumed by the banks. On this basis, earnings in excess of the prime rate, which was 0.75 per cent over the Singapore interbank offer rate (SIBOR) in 1976, were remitted as profits abroad. Imputed in such a way, profits in 1976 amounted to US$47 million, and the amount expended in Singapore was $62 million.

Both methods lead to estimates of earnings from ACU operations that are retained in Singapore amounting to 1 per cent of Singapore's GDP in 1976. It is clear that these calculations are only approximate but despite possible overstating of the extent of the maturity transformation, [26] they should be taken as conservative. The earnings shown in Table 4 do not include income from transactions, such as letters of credit, foreign exchange trading, [27] commitment fees on undrawn loans, and management fees of syndicate leaders and comanagers, [28] as well as income from other services performed for customers whose funds are managed. [29] However, the customary premiums over SIBOR are often shaved when very large funds are involved, although in a small international financial market, such as Singapore's, these large transactions are relatively rare.

Altogether these calculations suggest that operations of the Asian currency market have generated a small, but not negligible, benefit for Singapore.

(2) The second method of estimating the direct effect of the Asian currency market on Singapore's real income is to trace from national income data the contribution of the ACU bank activity to GDP. Direct estimation is, however, not possible, because Singapore's GDP statis-

---

[26] An increasing tendency toward loans with floating interest rates, which are adjusted every six months, tends to decrease the scope for maturity transformation.

[27] Although most transactions in the Asian currency market are in U. S. dollars, they involve considerable amounts of conversion from national currencies into dollars and vice versa, which is an important source of revenue for ACU banks.

[28] See Bee in Mathis (1975), pp. 154–58.

[29] Also, banks can increase their earnings by modifying maturity transformation in the course of cyclical fluctuations of interest rates. When interest rates are declining, they try to minimize the length of maturities of their deposits and to maximize the length of maturities of their loans; when interest rates are rising, they are pursuing the opposite strategy.

tics do not have sufficiently disaggregated breakdown by sectors to show the contributions of the banking sector. There are data on the financial sector that include banking as a major component but also include insurance, real estate, and business services. [30]

Between 1965 and 1975, the growth of the financial sector was substantially higher than the growth of GDP and second only to the growth of the manufacturing sector, the mainspring of Singapore's development during that period. (See Table 7, in the Appendix.) Furthermore, the highest growth rate of the financial sector occurred between 1969 and 1973, which was the period of the fastest expansion of the Asian currency market. Between 1968, the year of the creation of the Asian currency market, and 1975, the ratio of the financial sector's output to the rapidly growing GDP increased from 8.5 to 10.5 per cent. This indicates the increasing importance of financial activity in general, and of banking in particular, in the economy of Singapore.

Between 1970 and 1976, [31] employment in the financial sector (also shown in Table 8, in the Appendix) increased much faster than total employment and even faster than employment in the manufacturing sector. [32] The percentage of highly skilled employees [33] in the financial sector is almost twice as high as the average for the economy as a whole; furthermore, it has been increasing in recent years at a much faster rate. However, the ratio of employment in the financial sector to assets in the banking sector has decreased over the years. On the assumption that the financial and banking sectors experienced a similar growth of employment, this decreasing ratio suggests that important economies of scale in banking are still not realized at the present time.

(3) The third method would be to evaluate both the direct and indirect contributions of the Asian currency market to Singapore's income. The fast growth of international banking transactions has stimulated the location in Singapore of a host of related activities that are essential for the efficient working of the Asian market. These activities include forward and spot arbitrage operations, financial and trade brokerage facilities, business-related travel and travel agencies, international insurance, new hotels, and real estate operations. Favorable access to

---

[30] These data are shown in Table 8, in the Appendix, together with data on total GNP and on the other two major sectors—manufacturing and commerce.

[31] The period for which data are available. There was a change in the sampling procedure in 1974, so that 1974 data may have been understated.

[32] This was caused mainly by the recession in 1974–75, which has affected employment in manufacturing but has not significantly affected the trend of employment in the financial sector.

[33] Highly skilled employees are defined as professional, technical, administrative, and managerial workers, while those less highly skilled include production, clerical, sales, service, and agricultural workers. (See Singapore, *Yearbook of Statistics, 1975/76*, Tables 3.5 and 3.7.)

international finance in Singapore and an excellent communications network have stimulated the location of many enterprises specializing in trade. The same reasons have motivated a number of multinational and large regional corporations and investment companies to locate their Asian headquarters in Singapore. Furthermore, since foreign direct investment plays an important role in the industrial development of Singapore, the existence of a well-developed international financial market on its soil has provided an additional stimulus to foreign firms and foreign capital to locate their operations there. A dynamic international financial market also provides a secure haven for funds from abroad that are not directly tied to the productive process, but, above all, the market serves as an excellent indicator of the political and economic stability of the country. Therefore, the Asian currency market has been a major stimulus to the rapidly growing financial sector of Singapore and to some other related activities. [34]

Despite controls on the participation by residents, the Asian currency market has also had a growing influence on the monetary and financial policies of Singapore. The arbitrage between the Asian market and the Singapore money market, initially via Hong Kong and later also directly, has increased the international mobility of financial capital. This arbitrage has played a major role in progressively relaxing controls over the domestic interest rates, and this in turn resulted in the introduction of a system of competitive interest rate quotations in July 1975. The freeing of interest rates has increased the efficiency of allocating funds among various investment projects, although it may have increased the cost of capital to some sectors that previously could have borrowed at lower controlled rates.

In addition to benefits of the Asian currency market, costs that its development has imposed on Singapore should also be considered. These are mostly direct opportunity costs in terms of real product forgone and some "external" costs related to the effect of market development on other sectors of the economy.

(4) Direct opportunity costs involve the value added forgone by

---

[34] Another method of evaluating the contribution by the international financial market to the real income of the host country was suggested by Johnson (1976, pp. 263–75) in his study of the offshore market of Panama. Johnson singled out the following five ways in which the growth of the financial market can increase income at home: (1) by increasing employment and improving skills of the population; (2) by encouraging saving and capital accumulation through the increase in efficiency of financial intermediation and by lowering the cost of capital in the process; (3) by increasing revenue from taxes on profit of the banks and on income of their foreign employees; (4) by increasing earnings from tourism because international finance involves a great deal of short-term international travel; and (5) by increased rent from land and buildings caused by the market-induced rise in demand for these facilities. Because of the lack of relevant data, Johnson was able to provide only an illustrative analysis of the effect of some of these adjustments on real income in Panama. Quantitative analysis of the contribution of the Asian currency market to real income in Singapore along these lines is not possible for the same reason.

employees who are drawn from other sectors of the economy into the faster growing financial sector. These costs should be examined, however, in the light of Singapore's historical dependence on immigrant labor. [35] Thus, when a shortage of labor developed at the beginning of the 1970s, the authorities liberalized the existing restrictions on immigration and increased the elasticity of supply. [36] In the long run, the opportunity costs of increased employment in financial and related sectors consist of the costs involved in the upward mobility of labor. In its general development program, the Government has instituted a number of skill improvement projects that are supported largely by the industries concerned. In banking, a large proportion of training in foreign banking operations has been financed mostly by the banks but partly by foreign students. Therefore, in a rapidly developing economy, such as Singapore, it is difficult to disentangle specific opportunity costs of expansion of the financial sector from costs of ambitious programs in the overall improvement of skills of the labor force.

(5) Another direct cost with potentially important implications would occur if foreign banks that are remitting profits abroad were to expand local business at the expense of Singapore's domestic banks. This process is, however, minimized by the strict restrictions through licensing procedures of the local activities of new entrants. Furthermore, the phenomenal growth of transactions in the Asian currency market has also increased non-ACU banking activities in which domestic banks are involved.

(6) The major indirect cost of the Asian currency market involves a high level of international reserve holdings that are motivated partly by the Government's desire to support the role of Singapore as an international financial center. Between 1968 and 1976, Singapore's gross reserves increased from US$712 million to US$3,364 million. In the 1960s, the reserve buildup reflected the desire of the authorities to achieve a better ratio between gross reserves and rapidly growing imports. The very comfortable reserve/import ratio in the early 1970s was among the highest for developing countries; in 1976, it was similar to the reserve/import ratio of several other developing countries that had a balance of payments surplus. [37] In view of the complexity of

---

[35] See Buchanan (1972), pp. 65 ff.

[36] The immigration was restricted in the 1950s and particularly in the 1960s because of the authorities' concern about the effect of the closing of British military installations on local employment. However, fast economic development rapidly absorbed labor that was released from these installations. In the 1970s the authorities proceeded to liberalize immigration permits, with efforts being made to obtain labor with skills that have been in short supply locally.

[37] For 1976, reserves amounted to 4.1 months of imports of goods and services in Singapore, 4.3 in the Philippines, 4.6 in Brazil, 5.6 in Thailand, and 5.8 in Colombia. (See *IFS*, August 1977.) However, when entrepôt imports are excluded, Singapore's ratio increases and becomes similar to those of Thailand and Colombia.

criteria that are used by countries in determining the desired level of their reserves, it is not possible to estimate the cost of reserves used to support the Asian currency market.

(7) Before 1973, capital mobility that was increased with the existence of the Asian currency market imposed additional costs in terms of limiting the independence of Singapore's monetary policy. Particularly during the periods of international currency disturbances between 1971 and 1973, ACU banks were instrumental in large-scale arbitrage operations. [38] Since domestic interest rates in 1972–73 were higher than those in the Eurocurrency market and the U. S. dollar was depreciating, the inflow of funds through the banks created an excess of liquidity at home that could not be neutralized by the authorities. Floating of the Singapore dollar in May 1973 permitted the authorities to regain a large degree of independence in their domestic monetary policy. [39]

In summary, it appears that the Asian currency market has provided a modest contribution to real income in Singapore. Rough calculations suggest that a direct contribution in terms of gross earnings from international banks that remain in Singapore is in the order of 1 per cent of GDP. As evidenced by a very rapid expansion of the financial sector, the indirect contribution of additional employment in related activities and of substantial improvement of skills is probably larger. An estimate by the Singapore authorities that the Asian currency market contributed about 3 per cent of its GDP in 1976 appears reasonable.

III. Conclusion

The creation of the Asian currency market in 1968 responded to a need in Asia for an international financial center that would transcend the limitations of its national capital markets and facilitate the flow of capital needed for economic development. However, the market was a direct result of stimuli by the Government, which wished to develop in Singapore regional financial operations contributing to domestic real income and to the economic and political standing of the country. The first nine years of operations of the market have been quite successful. Although still small by international standards, the market has become

---

[38] Monetary Authority of Singapore (1973), p. 30. Such practices were allowed under the regulations on ACU, as specified in the Banking Act of 1970. In 1972–73 these practices consisted in converting the funds into Singapore dollars and placing them with local banks, which in their turn invested them in the booming real estate market. (See also Bhattacharya, 1977, pp. 68–69.)

[39] Monetary Authority of Singapore (1974), p. 84.

an important link in international financial arbitrage around the globe. Banks operating in the market have established an extensive network of transactions in the Pacific region and have developed a host of related activities in Singapore, making it an important financial center for the Asian region.

Although the banks operating in the Asian currency market have drawn a large proportion of their financial resources from Asia and the Western Pacific, one of the important functions of the market has been to channel the funds from the major capital markets and the Middle East into the Asian region. In recent years, a number of international bond issues have been floated in the market and the banks have participated in medium-term and long-term syndicated loan ventures. The banks also have participated in recycling surplus funds of the members of the Organization of the Petroleum Exporting Countries. However, the cautious approach by the banks and the supervision of the Monetary Authority of Singapore have helped the banks to minimize disturbances created by the recent unprecedented strain on the international payments system and by the difficulties experienced in the Eurocurrency market.

All indications show that the market has provided a contribution to the employment and income of Singapore. The direct contribution of the banks operating in the Asian currency market is estimated to be roughly of the order of 1 per cent of GDP. The indirect contribution, in terms of a host of related activities stimulated by the market, appears to be significantly larger. The major costs consist in sizable international reserves, a proportion of which are held as a support during the initial stages of the market's development. A rapid growth and the stability of the market suggest, however, that although net benefits may not be large at the present time, their potential for the future may be sizable.

APPENDIX

CHART 3. SINGAPORE AND LONDON: BID-OFFER SPREAD ON SEVEN-DAY TO ONE-YEAR DEPOSIT RATES OF EUROBANKS AND ACU BANKS, 1971–MID-1977

(In U. S. dollars)

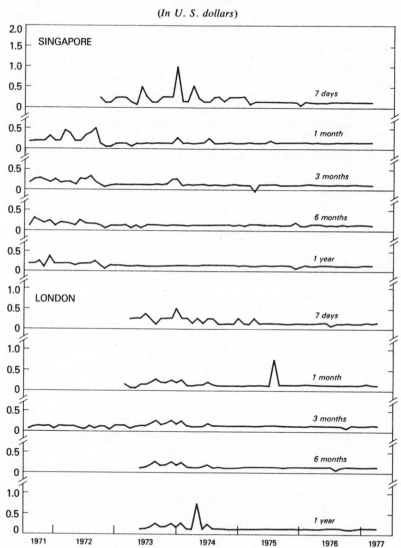

Sources: ACU banks' dollar interest rates: *Straits Times*, and Robert F. Emery; Eurodollar notes: Economic Group of the Chase Manhattan Bank.

ASIAN CURRENCY MARKET   249

TABLE 5. ASIAN CURRENCY MARKET: ACU BANKS' CLAIMS ON AND LIABILITIES TO RESIDENTS OF SINGAPORE, DECEMBER 1973–SEPTEMBER 1976

(In millions of U. S. dollars)

		Claims on			Liabilities to			Net Position (net liabilities)
		Nonbanking sector [1]	Banking sector	Total	Nonbanking sector [1]	Banking sector	Total	
1973	Dec.	185	262	447	296	406	702	255
1974	Dec.	350	223	573	489	676	1,165	592
1975	June	388	251	639	520	754	1,274	635
	Dec.	376	270	646	584	584	1,168	522
1976	June	443	286	729	638	809	1,447	718
	Sept.	466	302	768	527	898	1,425	657

Source: Monetary Authority of Singapore.
[1] Includes statutory authorities of Singapore.

TABLE 6. SINGAPORE: BALANCE OF PAYMENTS, 1969–75

(In millions of SDRs)

	1969	1970	1971	1972	1973	1974	1975
A. Goods and services (net)	-178	-564	-710	-491	-505	-899	-582
Of which,							
Merchandise exports (f.o.b.)	1,461	1,447	1,660	1,882	2,890	4,581	4,131
Merchandise imports (f.o.b.)	1,916	2,300	2,647	2,898	4,013	6,472	6,179
Trade balance	-455	-853	-987	-1,016	-1,123	-1,891	-2,048
Balance on services	277	289	277	525	618	992	1,466
B. Transfers (net)	-13	-8	-12	2	-3	-32	-34
C. Current account (A + B)	-191	-572	-722	-489	-508	-932	-617
D. Capital (net)	16	160	288	363	504	396	481
Direct investment	} 64	} 114	116	172	222	476	496
Other private long-term			17	10	69	63	39
Government	9	13	25	61	9	—	1
Commercial banks	-57	33	130	119	203	-144	-55
E. Errors and omissions (net)	271	583	753	436	350	781	474
F. Overall balance (C + D + E)	96	184	319	310	345	245	338
G. Reserves and related items (increase −)	-96	-184	-319	-310	-345	-245	-338
Reserve position in the Fund	—	—	-2	—	—	—	—
Monetary authorities	-62	-48	-252	-261	-254	-323	-544
Government	-34	-136	-65	-49	-91	78	207

Sources: International Monetary Fund, *Balance of Payments Yearbook*, and Singapore, Department of Statistics.

TABLE 7. SINGAPORE: OUTPUT IN SELECTED SECTORS OF INDUSTRY, 1965–75

(In millions of Singapore dollars)

	1965	1966	1967	1968	1969	1970	1971	1972	1973	1974	1975	Average Growth Rate in Real Terms
Total gross domestic product												
In current prices	2.956	3.331	3.746	4.315	5.020	5.805	6.823	8.156	10.241	12.575	13.681	
In 1968 prices	3.049	3.388	3.789	4.315	4.906	5.579	6.277	7.120	7.941	8.445	8.784	11.3
Per cent of change in 1968 prices		*11.1*	*11.8*	*13.9*	*13.7*	*13.7*	*12.5*	*13.4*	*11.5*	*6.3*	*4.0*	
Manufacturing												
In current prices	447	522	632	770	956	1.186	1.461	1.854	2.429	3.004	3.267	
In 1968 prices	465	531	638	770	942	1.143	1.357	1.584	1.841	1.911	1.885	15.6
Per cent of change in 1968 prices		*14.2*	*20.2*	*20.7*	*22.3*	*21.3*	*18.7*	*16.7*	*16.2*	*3.8*	*–1.4*	
Commerce												
In current prices	814	962	1.134	1.286	1.511	1.639	1.850	2.067	2.772	3.636	3.738	
In 1968 prices	834	962	1.141	1.286	1.437	1.569	1.723	1.896	2.118	2.351	2.392	10.6
Per cent of change in 1968 prices		*15.3*	*18.6*	*12.7*	*11.7*	*9.2*	*9.8*	*10.0*	*11.7*	*11.0*	*1.7*	
Finance [1]												
In current prices	261	276	310	366	446	524	644	794	1.049	1.301	1.442	
In 1968 prices	269	281	314	366	438	502	594	682	804	887	941	13.8
Per cent of change in 1968 prices		*4.5*	*11.7*	*16.7*	*19.7*	*14.6*	*18.3*	*14.8*	*17.9*	*10.3*	*6.1*	

Sources: Department of Statistics, Yearbook of Statistics, Singapore, 1971–76; Ministry of Finance, Economic Survey of Singapore, 1976.
[1] Includes banking, other financing, insurance, real estate, and business services.

TABLE 8. SINGAPORE: EMPLOYMENT AND SKILLS IN SELECTED SECTORS OF INDUSTRY, 1970–76

| | Employment (*thousands*) | | | | Percentage of Highly Skilled [1] | | | |
	1970	1974	1975	1976	1972	1974	1975	1976
Industry total	650.9	824.4	833.5	870.4	12.3	13.0	13.5	13.2
Manufacturing	143.1	234.2	218.1	234.0	5.0	10.3	15.0	10.4
Per cent of total	*22.0*	*28.4*	*26.2*	*26.9*				
Commerce	152.9	172.6	191.7	201.0	4.9	4.3	4.5	4.1
Per cent of total	*23.5*	*20.9*	*23.0*	*23.1*				
Finance [2]	23.1	46.6	50.6	56.5	19.3	21.0	22.5	24.4
Per cent of total	*3.5*	*5.6*	*6.1*	*6.5*				

Sources: Department of Statistics, *Yearbook of Statistics, Singapore*, 1971–76; Ministry of Finance, *Economic Survey of Singapore, 1976*.
[1] Ratio of professional, technical, administrative, and managerial workers to total labor force in each sector.
[2] Includes banking, other financing, insurance, real estate, and business services.

SELECTED BIBLIOGRAPHY

Bhattacharya, Anindya K., *The Asian Dollar Market: International Offshore Financing* (New York, 1977).

Borsuk, Mark, "The Future Development of Offshore Capital Markets in Asia," *Columbia Journal of World Business*, Vol. 9 (Spring 1974), pp. 48–59.

Buchanan, Iain, *Singapore in Southeast Asia: An Economic and Political Appraisal* (London, 1972).

Emery, Robert F., "The Asian Dollar Market," International Finance Discussion Paper, No. 71 (Washington, November 21, 1975).

Euromoney, Supplement (May 1976), pp. 1–60.

First National City Bank, *The Asian Dollar Market* (Singapore, January 1975).

Hewson, John, and Eisuke Sakakibara, *The Eurocurrency Markets and Their Implications* (Lexington, Massachusetts, 1975).

Hughes, Helen, and You Poh Seng (eds.), *Foreign Investment and Industrialisation in Singapore* (Australian National University Press, 1969).

International Monetary Fund, *International Financial Statistics* (August 1977).

———, *Twenty-Seventh Annual Report on Exchange Restrictions* (Washington, 1976).

Ishihara, Michio, "Asian Currency Market Shows Potential for Continued Rapid Growth," *IMF Survey*, Vol. 4 (January 6, 1975), pp. 12–13.

Johnson, Harry G., "Panama as a Regional Financial Center: A Preliminary Analysis of Development Contribution," *Economic Development and Cultural Change*, Vol. 24 (January 1976), pp. 261–86.

Lee, S. Y., "The Asian Dollar Market in Singapore," *Malayan Economic Review*, Vol. 16 (April 1971), pp. 46–56.

Mathis, F. John (ed.), *Offshore Lending by U. S. Commercial Banks*, Bankers' Association for Foreign Trade and Robert Morris Associates (Washington, 1975).

Monetary Authority of Singapore, *Annual Report*, 1973 and 1974.

———, *Exchange Control Manual* (February 1976).

———, *Quarterly Bulletin*, various issues.

Moody's Bank and Financial Manual, 1977, Moody's Investors Service (New York, 1977).

Morgan Guaranty Trust Company, *World Financial Markets*, various issues (1973–77).

Pandit, S. A., "The Asian Dollar and Free Gold Markets in Singapore," *Finance and Development*, Vol. 8 (June 1971), pp. 32–36.

Singapore, "The Banking Act, 1970," *Government Gazette, Acts Supplement* (Singapore), October 30, 1970.

———, "Finance Companies Act, 1970," *Government Gazette*, October 1970.

———, "Monetary Authority Act," *Government Gazette*, 1970, and "Amendment," *Government Gazette*, 1972.

———, "Economic Survey of Singapore," Ministry of Finance, 1975 and 1976.

———, *Yearbook of Statistics, 1975/76*, Department of Statistics (Singapore, 1975).

Thorn, Philip (ed.), *Banking Structures and Sources of Finance in the Far East*, Banker Research Unit (London, 1975), pp. 2–4.

Wilson, Dick (1969), "Singapore: Asian Dollar Center," *Singapore Trade and Industry* (December 1969).

——— (1972), *The Future Role of Singapore* (Oxford University Press, 1972).

——— (1975), "South East Asia's Banking Boom," *The Banker*, Vol. 125 (March 1975), pp. 253–57.

Wong, Pakshong Michael (1972), "The Future for International Banking," *Euromoney*, Supplement (September 1972), pp. 2–3.

——— (1974), "Singapore—Latest Trends in International Business," *Euromoney* (April 1974), pp. 67–69.

——— (1975), "The Asian Dollar Market Now," *Euromoney* (June 1975), pp. 100–102.

[26]

Towards a Theory of Free Economic Zones

By

Herbert G. Grubel

Contents: I. Analytical Description of Free Economic Zones. — II. The Political Economy of the Free Economic Zones. — III. Welfare Effects of Free Economic Zones. — IV. Free Economic Zones for Other Industries? — V. Summary and Conclusions.

In this paper I present a theory capable of analysing the welfare effects of a wide variety of institutional innovations which have in common that they involve the deregulation of, or the lowering of tariffs and taxes on, a range of economic activities that can be effectively separated from the regulated, taxed and protected industries of which they are a part. The partial deregulation of economic activities in this manner will be shown to lead to the expansion of trade, but also to involve potential costs of locational diversion of trade and negative externalities. In the context of the debate over deregulation the development of free economic zones can be seen as a practical compromise that generates powerful local interest groups pushing partial deregulation against the well-known interest groups opposing general deregulation.

In this study I could draw on a limited stock of published research, none of which deals directly with the problems considered to be central in this study, but which provides some useful instutitional information[1].

In the first part I provide a descriptive analysis of free economic zones. Part II presents the political economy and Part III the welfare effects of free economic zones. In Part IV I speculate about the possibility

Remark: Many people have helped me to refine the arguments and find empirical illustrations presented in this paper. I would like especially to thank Walter Block, John Chant, Max Corden, Steve Easton, Sid Fancy, John Helliwell and Lars Svensson. I also benefited from discussions during seminars at the Universities of Mannheim, Zürich, St. Gallen and Pennsylvania; at the German Military Academy in Hamburg, UNIDO in Vienna, the Institut für Weltwirtschaft in Kiel, the HWWA-Institut für Wirtschaftsforschung in Hamburg and the Institute for International Economic Studies in Stockholm.

[1] The economics literature dealing with the free trade zone phenomenon is limited to three theoretical papers, Hamada [1974], Rodriguez [1976] and Hamilton and Svensson [1980], and the more instutitionally oriented papers by Wall [1976], Fernstrom [1976], Ping [1979] and Diamond [1979]. This literature has failed to create a comprehensive theory of free trade zones capable of assessing their welfare effects and suggesting tests for empirical study.

of using the free zone concept for the partial deregulation of other heavily regulated industries. The paper closes with a summary and conclusions.

I. Analytical Description of Free Economic Zones

Free Trade Zones

Free trade zones are areas separated from the surrounding host country's territory by fences or other barriers into which goods from abroad can be brought without quota restrictions or the payment of tariffs and excise taxes, and without being subjected to exchange controls, and to the majority of statistical reporting requirements and regulations aimed at the protection of consumers. Goods can be stored, used in manufacture, exhibited, assembled, sorted and sold in such zones in processes that are subject to the host country's normal laws governing environmental protection, workers' safety and employment conditions. Profits and wages earned in the zones are taxed at regular rates. Goods can be exported as freely as they are imported. However, when goods are brought into the zone's host country, they are subject to the normal import quotas, duties and excise taxes.

In practice free trade zones may be as small as a retail store in an airport or as large as the territory of Hong Kong and they may serve the simple function of warehousing or may contain a broad spectrum of industries. The essential feature of free trade zones for economic analysis is that they lower the host country's level of protection through the reduction of tariffs, quantitative barriers and administrative hindrances to trade[1].

For example, a firm imports goods into the free trade zone, processes or assembles and then exports them. The firm saves the duty on these imports and for these goods the host country's tariff revenues and there-

---

[1] When a free trade zone consists of only a warehouse, it is often called simply a "bonded warehouse". In the United States in recent years factories, such as the one assembling Volkswagen automobiles in Pennsylvania, have been declared free trade zones. In some instances, as in Panama, the free trade zones consist of a large area containing industries of many types. There are also free trade zones devoted to retail stores only, as at many international airports and harbors. According to our definition, Hong Kong represents one very large free trade zone. The Hanseatic cities of Northern Europe and the Free Cities of Germany, similarly used to be large free trade zones.

In developing countries we find also so-called "industrial estates" and "export processing zones". They have all of the characteristics of free trade zones as described in the text but in addition, they often provide subsidized services and facilities to occupants. One such service of great value often provided is an agent that deals with the host country's bureaucracy in the name of the zone's occupants [UNIDO, 1980].

fore average tariff rates are lowered[1]. Many countries have rules under which certain goods imported are assessed at a certain rate, but if these same goods are embodied in a product that has a certain domestic value-added percentage, then they enter at a lower tariff rate. Activities in free trade zones often contribute this required percentage of domestic value added and therefore indirectly lead to the lowering of tariff rates[2]. When imports are subject to quota restrictions, then they can be stored in free trade zones and imported whenever quotas become available. As a result, the effective import restrictions implicit in a given quota are lowered.

Importers value highly other effective duty reducing benefits provided by free trade zone operations. For example, defective goods can be destroyed in the zone before a shipment is imported into the host country and duty is assessed. Free trade zones serve as show-rooms for customers[3]. In addition there are savings in costs of dealing with customs and tax authorities which for small firms often are relatively large.

At the end of 1979 there existed 344 tax-free trade zones, free ports and similar designated areas on 72 countries of the world. In the United States there were about 50 such zones and plans existed for the creation of many more. It was estimated that in 1979 about $ 100 billion of total world trade of $ 1,300 billion went through free trade zones. Forecasts are that by 1985 about $ 300 billion or 20 per cent of world trade would pass through such free trade zones [Diamond, 1979].

Free Banking Zones

Euro-Currency Banking. — It is now widely accepted that one of the primary causes of the rapid growth of Euro-, Asia- and Latin-American currency banking since the 1960s is the exemption which this type of

---

[1] The savings for the exporter and therefore the practical reduction in duty burden from operating in the free trade zone usually is only equal to the opportunity cost of the duty paid since in most countries a system of duty drawbacks returns customs paid on all exported intermediate inputs. However, it should be noted that the economic effect of these savings for exporters may be quite significant since they are relevant to the export activity's value-added base. Therefore it is important to evaluate all of the reductions in protection in terms of the concept of effective protection as developed by Corden [1971].

[2] This characteristic of U.S. tax laws explains why several foreign automobile assembly plants in the United States have been made into free trade zones.

[3] In Hamburg oriental carpet dealers regularly take customers to their large warehouses in the duty free zone. In New York a free trade zone on a dock serves as an exhibition ground for sellers of machinery, to where customers can bring samples of goods for a demonstration of the processing capabilities of the equipment. Diamond [1979] provides an extensive list of benefits for exporters and importers located in free trade zones in a form useful for agents promoting a free trade zone. The sources of reduced operating costs noted here are merely samples designed to make the general point.

42   Herbert G. Grubel

banking enjoys from the taxes implicit in minimum reserve requirements. That this is so can readily be seen by consideration of the following simplified example.

Consider a bank located in Montreal which pays interest on deposits at the annual rate of 8 per cent and therefore pays $ 8 on a $ 100 deposit. Faced by an assumed 15 per cent reserve requirement, this bank can lend out only $ 85 of the deposit and if the loan rate is 10 per cent, it earns $ 8.50. Under these conditions, the $ 100 intermediation business brings the bank net operating revenue of $ 8.50 — $ 8 = $ .50. Assuming that operating costs for labor, etc. constitute $ .45, the before income tax net profit is $ .05 per $ 100 deposit.

Now assume that this bank opens a branch in London, England, and persuades its customers to do business there in return for a marginally higher deposit and marginally lower loan rate. For the sake of simplicity we assume that this margin is so small that in the present calculation it can be disregarded. Under these assumptions and remembering that there are no legally required reserves on foreign currency deposits for banks located in London, the net operating margin of the Montreal bank branch on a $ 100 deposit is $ 10 — $ 8 = $ 2, which is four times that the parent bank could earn in Montreal. If labor and other costs are the same $ .45 per $ 100 of intermediation in London as in Montreal, the London branch shows a before income tax net profit of $ 1.55. Shifting business from the taxed and regulated home base to the free banking zone in London therefore implies an increase in the bank's net profit margin of over 3,000 per cent[1]. Analogous increases in net profit margins are available to banks in most countries on deposits and loans made in foreign currencies.

The preceding example illustrates the strenght of the incentives facing banks to enter the Euro- and other regional currency business and explains why this type of banking has grown from practically nothing in the 1960s to over $ 1,500 billion in 1980. For our purposes of analysis it is important to note that it involves a partial deregulation through the lowering of an implicit tax on a type of business that can be kept separate from the regular and regulated other business in two ways. First, the deregulation applies to business transacted in a geographically defined area, just like

---

[1] In fact, the spread between lending and borrowing rates in Euro-currency markets in individual currencies is narrower than that found in the currencies' home countries by an amount equal approximately to the implicit cost of the respective countries' reserve requirements. In effect, customers are reaping a large share of the benefits of the taxes saved. Portfolio balance considerations of banks, lenders and borrowers prevent perfect arbitrage between the rates in domestic and Euro-currency markets. However, the illustrative calculations are indicative of the strength of the incentives facing banks to escape domestic regulation, which persist as long as lending and borrowing spreads are determined in the domestic markets.

in the case of free trade zones discussed above, but with the important difference that in practice all of the rest of the world is the free economic zone[1]. Second, the deregulation applies to a certain type of business, namely foreign currency deposits, even though it may take place within a geographic territory where the banks' other business is fully regulated.

Free Banking Zone in New York. — In the year 1981, after many years of negotiation, a free banking zone was opened up in New York [Cheng, 1981] and if it is successful, more such zones will be created in other U.S. centers of finance. The basic idea behind the establishment of these zones is the removal of reserve requirements on banks in order to induce the return to the United States of some of the business that has been lost to the rest of the world through Euro-currency banking. The problem faced in the establishment of these zones is how to prevent massive shifts of domestic business into them, which would produce serious inequities between ordinary banks and those operating in the zones. In addition, such shifts would raise the reserve-deposit multiplier and create problems for U.S. monetary policy. The solution to these problems adopted is that banks are freed from U.S. reserve requirements only on deposits in large denominations owned by others than U.S. residents. This particular method for the separation of deregulated from regulated business is likely to limit severely the growth of business in the U.S. free banking zones, though in the end their chances for success involve an empirical question which only actual operation of the zone can provide[2].

Free Insurance Zone

Lloyds of London. — During the great wave of regulatory fervor in the postwar years all industrial countries have imposed increasingly more severe restrictions on the operation of insurance companies. During this period Lloyds of London grew rapidly because it constituted a haven free from regulation.

Lloyds has attracted mainly two types of business from other countries. First, there are the special risks for which there are few or no ex-

---

[1] Germany is the exception since that country's banking laws require the maintenance of reserves on deposits in all currency denominations. As a result, Germany harbors practically no Euro-currency banking business.

[2] It should be interesting to discover how enforceable is the foreign residence requirement in preventing shifts of domestic business into the zone, given the well-known ease with which funds can be funnelled through foreign branches and subsidiaries. Also, given the low cost of information transmission it is likely that new institutions can be developed which permit effective circumvention of the legislation restricting U.S. residents from use of the zone.

perience ratings, such as the cancellation of Olympic Games broadcast opportunities and the cancellation of computer leasing contracts. Second, there are the very large risks of insuring super-tankers and large-scale industrial projects. Lloyds has not attracted from other countries the standard fire, accident and life insurance business for which the local availability of agents is of paramount importance.

It is clear from the preceding description that an effective separation of regulated and deregulated insurance business has taken place in the world. Routine business involving large numbers of relatively small accounts has remained under the control of national regulatory authorities largely because transactions costs of dealing with Lloyds are too large. Special and very big risks, on the other hand, have been shifted to Lloyds either because in the case of special risks the advantages of deregulation are great or in the case of very large routine risks the transactions costs for the insured multinational enterprises are small.

The New York Free Insurance Zone. --- In 1980 New York opened a free insurance zone [Decaminada, 1979; The Economist, 1979]. Similar zones may well be established in other U.S. cities. In the New York zone resident insurance companies can underwrite risks that require a minimum annual premium of $ 100,000 without obtaining the permission of regulatory authorities of the State of New York. In addition they can underwrite many special risks which have been identified by the authorities and whose common characteristic is that regulators in the past have been unable to ascertain promptly and reliably that premiums charged and other conditions of the contract protect the consumer and assure viability of the underwriters. Because of the regulatory delays and costs such risks in the past have been insured by Lloyds.

The intent of the New York free insurance zone is clearly to return some of the business that has been lost to the deregulated environment abroad by offering similar deregulation to New York firms. But through the specification of the nature of deregulated business, an effective separation between regulated and deregulated sectors is assured. Some doubts have been raised about the likely success of the New York insurance deregulation experiment [The Economist, 1979] on the grounds that the success of Lloyds has been due not only to a favorable regulatory environment but also to the special expertise and financial structure of the firm[1]. It remains to be seen how successful will be the New York free insurance zone in exploiting the benefits of deregulation and accumulating the required expertise.

---

[1] Partners in Lloyds face unlimited personal liabilities.

Free Gambling Zones

The State of Nevada constitutes a free gambling zone. It was created in 1931 when the sparse population of the state and its distance from centers of population amounted to the effective separation of markets. Only well-to-do people who could afford to travel to Nevada would be exposed to the risk of deregulation while the masses of ordinary citizens continued to be protected by the regulatory umbrella.

The establishment of gambling casinos in Atlantic City was approved and undertaken in the same spirit as Nevada's, though the strength of the possible discrimination between regulated and deregulated customers is much weaker. Still, in contrast with totally free gambling in New Jersey, limited free gambling in Atlantic City significantly reduces the exposure of ordinary citizens to the temptation of the activity. Already existing proposals for the establishment of other gambling centers in the United States suggest that if Atlantic City is successful, they will be established not in large urban centers but in relatively small resort centers where access by ordinary citizens is limited.

In Europe, where for a long time there has been less regulation of gambling than in the United States, big-time organized gambling through roulette and card games has been permitted only in casinos located in famous 19th century spas such as Baden-Baden and Monte Carlo frequented by royalty and gentry and where access is rather difficult for ordinary citizens. British gambling clubs require membership fees that represent a barrier to use by local residents of moderate means.

Free Enterprise Zones

It is widely accepted that the decay of city cores in Britain and the United States is due to a very significant degree to regulation of business, which affected especially small business and the employment it provided traditionally [Butler, 1980]. In Britain legislation has been passed that led to the designation of some depressed urban areas as Free Enterprise Zones. In these zones a number of burdensome types of regulation and taxation have been eliminated. The U.S. Congress is debating legislation that would permit the establishment of such zones in depressed U.S. cities.

The need to create effective separation between regulated and deregulated business has given rise to as yet unresolved problems in the formulation of the U.S. legislation and has led to problems with the British zones since discrimination in essence is based on geographic location. As a result, the borders of the zones create strong discontinuities. They have induced some business to move from outside the zone into it. In the process they have created a belt of depressed activity and real estate values around the zones. In addition, the zones can develop into tax-havens for large firms. It remains to be seen whether it will be possible to create legislative mechanisms that allow the effective discriminatory deregulation and tax reductions to be channeled properly for the achievement of the stated objective of stimulating the establishment of *new* small enterprises without generating costly additional regulation.

II. The Political Economy of the Free Economic Zones

The preceding description of the types, characteristics and growth of free economic zones raises the question why they have been permitted to develop in the past when there was generally strong faith in the need for and ability of regulation to improve free market institutions. Furthermore, the question arises why they are growing so rapidly in number in recent years when, after widespread realization of the high cost of regulation, efforts to achieve general deregulation have been stalled? In this section I will provide provisional answers to these questions arguing first that free economic zones are an instrument for selective deregulation and second, that they generate powerful interest groups which assure political success.

Selectively Targeted Deregulation

Regulation is basically a blunt instrument. For example, foreign trade restrictions bring costs to all regions of a country while often benefiting only a few. This proposition holds in the case of tariffs on automobile components, which benefit an industry that is often concentrated regionally, but the tariffs raise the cost of automobiles and automobile assembly, harming the interests of other regions, including some which under free trade might have a comparative advantage in automobile assembly. Similarly, regulation often provides paternalistic protection for consumers whether they need it or not. For example, in the insurance underwriting business for large tankers, it is reasonable to assume that the buyer does not need the state's protection concerning rates charged and the fiscal soundness of the insurer, while there is a much stronger case for protecting the public from the sellers of life-insurance policies that use unethical selling techniques and invest customers' funds fraudulently or unwisely. Also, the case for protecting the uneducated and poor from the temptations of gambling is certainly greater than that for protecting the wealthy[1].

---

[1] None of the above examples are to be interpreted as making an absolute case for regulation. I think that the argument about the need to protect the poor but not the rich from the temptations of gambling is paternalism of the worst sort since it is combined with elitism.

The preceding examples suffice to make the case that regulation is basically a blunt instrument that cannot readily be applied to meet the special requirements of regions and groups of people. Seen in the light of this characteristic of regulation it is clear that free economic zones represent an instrument for the selective application of deregulation, permitting in principle the development of an optimum pattern by regions and classes of customers.

However, free economic zones are a useful instrument for selective deregulation only if two conditions are met. First, there must be a need for it and second, it must be technically feasible to achieve a separation of the regulated and deregulated market. In the case of the examples cited above, these two criteria appear to be met, except in the case of free enterprise zones where it is not clear that it is technically feasible to limit deregulation to the economically relevant firms.

Interest Group Backing

It is well known that the deregulation of some U.S. industries has been stalled because the deregulation lowers the welfare of some firms and workers clearly and by a substantial amount so that it is worthwhile for them to form well-financed interest groups lobbying with politicians and presenting them with a credible threat of the loss of blocks of votes in case their industries are deregulated. The beneficiaries of the deregulation, on the other hand, usually are large in number and would gain very little each from deregulation. As a result, they have no incentives to form interest groups and lobby with politicians for deregulation. Consequently, even in cases where it is widely accepted that the sum of small benefits exceeds the large costs to a few, the political process of deregulation is often stalled.

The preceding model of the political economy of regulation, however, can be used to explain why in the case of industries where complete deregulation is stalled, partial deregulation through the creation of free economic zones has been accomplished successfully. The reason is simply that the free economic zones generate benefits sufficiently large and concentrated for some firms, workers and local governments that it is profitable for them to form interest groups for lobbying with politicians in favor of the zones. The costs created by the zones, on the other hand, tend to be small and diffuse and therefore do not generate strong interest groups and political opposition.

The preceding considerations can be illustrated by reference to a free trade zone. When the Volkswagen company considered establishing an assembly plant in Pennsylvania, local workers, small businesses and governments stood to benefit a great deal and they formed a powerful lobby that succeeded in obtaining legislation which granted free trade zone status to the VW assembly plant. The producers of automobile parts in Michigan whose level of protection was lowered through the free trade zone suffered only marginally and in ways which were difficult to establish quantitatively. If they tried to lobby against the Pennsylvania zone, they obviously did not succeed because they were unable to generate a credible voting threat.

In the case of the free banking and insurance zones the pattern of interest group pressures was even more in favor of their establishment because most of the firms in the zones are branches of existing U.S. firms, which expect no reduction in business done in the regulated sector in the United States and instead expect to gain at the expense of foreign firms and by bringing home business that had been lost to partial deregulation abroad. As foreigners have no votes in U.S. elections, opposition from these interests was ineffective and the main battle was in persuading domestic firms unable to open branches in the zone that the planned techniques of discrimination would be successful in preventing loss of business from the regulated sector[1].

III. Welfare Effects of Free Economic Zones

The creation of free economic zones raises welfare through the more selective application of regulation according to the requirements of different regions and groups of customers. In real terms, the deregulation lowers costs of protection and of transactions, permitting welfare gains through the expansion of trade and specialization. Free economic zones are likely to have dynamic effects on the supply of work, technology and entrepreneurship.

However, free economic zones also may reduce welfare through the locational diversion of trade and investment and through the generation of negative externalities. In addition, there are welfare effects of an indeterminate sign due to the redistribution of tax revenue between governmental jurisdictions.

Theoretically, the overall, net welfare effects of free economic zones are indeterminate. Only empirical studies can lead to estimates of net benefits and it is doubtful that some of the effects can ever be measured[2].

---

[1] The New York free banking zone was long delayed by opposition from U.S. banks which were prevented by federal law from opening branches in the zone and which feared that the zone would divert business away from them.

[2] Perhaps it will be possible to employ the methodology used in the empirical study of the effects of trade diversion and creation in connection with economic integration. In these

Real Economic Effects

As was shown above, the creation of a free trade zone amounts to the lowering of the level of protection of the host country. It is well known from the theory of international trade that such a lowering of protection leads to increased levels of trade and specialization, which in turn results in higher community welfare. This proposition is illustrated with the help of the standard Heckscher-Ohlin model in the figure, where the small home-country's import good X and export good Y are measured along the horizontal and vertical axes, respectively. In initial equilibrium production is at point P_0 on the production possibility locus XY, where the protection-distorted domestic relative price line TT' is tangent and the relative price of the traded good is equal to the marginal rate of transformation in production. Trade takes place along the world price line WW' and permits attainment of welfare level C_0, where the domestic price level is equal to the marginal rate of substitution for consumers.

Trade Creation and Locational Trade Diversion

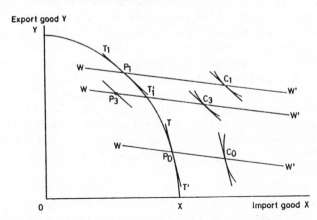

The lowering of protection due to the creation of the free trade zone is assumed to result in the new domestic price ratio T_1T_1' with the new equilibrium output at P_1 and consumption at C_1 after trade at the unchanged world price WW'. The core of standard international trade theory consists of establishing rigorously that consumption point C_1 must imply a higher level of welfare than C_0. It follows therefore that if the creation of

studies externalities and tax effects have also been ignored or treated as residuals. Hodjera [1978], Johnson [1976] and Grubel [1980] have attempted cost benefit studies of regional free Euro-banking centers.

a free trade zone leads only to the lowering of protection and has no other effects, a small country must gain welfare through the increased specialization in production which exploits its comparative advantage. However, the lowering of protection through the creation of a free trade zone does have another effect which requires amendment of the standard model and results.

Locational Trade Diversion

The elimination of protection in the free trade zone may induce production to take place in an inefficient location, resulting in extra costs of production that lower the level of welfare below that which the country could attain if the same reduction in protection had been available uniformly to all firms regardless of location. Two examples may serve to illustrate this important point. First, when bank intermediation business is induced to shift from Montreal to London through the absence of the reserve requirement tax, several extra real costs of doing business are incurred because the London branch of the Montreal bank has to be staffed and supervised over great distances from the parent's headquarters. Lenders and borrowers incur extra costs of communication or travel or perhaps just legal complications by dealing in London rather than in Montreal, where by assumption in the absence of free banking in London they would have done their business at least cost. These added social costs of Euro-currency banking must be offset against the social gains which accrue because the smaller spread between lending and borrowing rates in London induces some extra lending and borrowing and makes capital markets more perfect. It should also be noted that the private incentives for doing business in London rather than Montreal remain in spite of these extra social costs, for otherwise the shift of the business would not take place.

As a second example consider the Swiss village of Nandans, which is located in a high valley between Switzerland and Austria. Because of difficult access from Switzerland in the 19th century this village was granted exemption from Swiss excise taxes and tariffs. In essence, it is a free trade zone which attracts much business through offering low prices especially in heavily taxed and protected gasoline and cosmetics. The economic waste created by this free trade zone is readily apparent as one envisages heavy gasoline trucks slowly lumbering up the steep mountain road to the village. These trucks are followed by long lines of private passenger cars. Once in the village the gasoline is transferred into the tanks of the passenger cars via the pumps of tax-exempt gas stations. After this transfer the cars and trucks return to the lowlands for regular, productive work. It is clear, that the free trade zone induced business in

Nandans is privately profitable, but that it involves a relatively substantial waste of real resources.

In terms of the model in the figure, the inefficiencies caused by the locational diversion of business are shown by production taking place at point P_3, which is inside the efficient frontier. While trade still takes place at the world price line WW', the point of consumption C_3 must necessarily be below C_1 because the only difference between the two situations is that C_1 is reached without the inefficiency cost of the locational diversion of business. Whether or not C_3 is on a higher indifference curve than C_0 is an empirical question that depends on the relative magnitude of the gains from trade creation and the losses due to the locational diversion of trade. However, it cannot be ruled out on logical grounds that because of locational diversions of trade free trade zones result in a net loss of welfare by the criteria of the standard trade model[1].

Defensive Deregulation

At this point of the analysis it is important to introduce a distinction between what might be called offensive and defensive free economic zone creation. When a free trade zone is created in a country we have the offensive case for which all of the preceding conclusions about trade creation and diversion are relevant. However, the creation of the free banking and insurance zones in New York involve a defensive act in the sense that they are a response to prior deregulation abroad in the form of Euro-currency banking and Lloyds of London, as described above. Therefore, these U.S. free zones reverse some of the locational diversion of trading that the prior deregulation had produced and they are more likely to be raising welfare than are the offensive zones.

Generally, the preceding analysis suggests that the costs of trade diversion are likely to be the smaller the more free economic zones there are. In the limit, the number of zones will be so large as to include all of the country's territory and in effect universal free trade is achieved with zero costs of trade diversion.

---

[1] The results of the analysis focusing on the concepts of trade creation and locational trade diversion are strongly reminiscent of results obtained in the analysis of the effects of economic integration [Lipsey, 1960]. In fact, we have here simply another case of the second-best and reconfirmation of the basic principle that partial movement towards free competition does not necessarily result in greater welfare. However, the results of second-best policies are ultimately an empirical matter and in this context it may be useful to note that most studies of the effects of European integration concluded that trade expansion dominated by far trade diversion effects. However, only actual studies of free trade zones from this point of view can establish whether the beneficial effects of integration also prevail in the case of free trade zones. No such studies have been brought to my attention.

In this context it is worth noting that the "underground economy", which recently has become the object of much study [Feige, 1979; Mirus and Smith, 1981] is a form of free economic zone, which involves welfare gains and losses that are analogous to those of free economic zones just discussed. Deregulation that causes economic agents to leave the underground economy are defensive and can lead to a lowering of existing costs of locational diversion costs. Free gambling zones may well have this result if they induce gamblers and the suppliers of gambling services to give up their illegal activities, creating social savings in the form of less crime and corruption.

Capital Flows

Free economic zones generally, but free trade zones in developing countries especially, can give rise to capital flows which have potentially important welfare implications. As is well known, regulation and protection in many developing countries represent serious barriers to the inflow of capital, even if local labor productivity would otherwise make such investment profitable. The establishment of a free trade zone which removes these barriers can induce the inflow of capital which raises the productivity of local labor, may generate dynamic linkage effects and gives rise to income tax revenue from the profits of foreign firms, all of which translates into gains in welfare for the host country. At the same time, the owners of capital in the rest of the world gain since their private yields are increased.

The growth in world welfare caused by the more efficient global allocation of capital is in addition to that of the gains due to the more efficient allocation of given resources in each country discussed in the preceding section. However, as in the case of the effects involving given resources, the flow of capital can result in costs of locational diversion. For example, foreign capital which has located in the Philippines' Bataan free trade zone might have located elsewhere in Philippines if deregulation had been uniform for the whole country. If this is the case, the productivity of the capital is lower than it would have been if it had located in the most efficient place. In the extreme, if the foreign capital comes from a regulated environment, the true social productivity in that zone may be lower than what it was in its country of origin. Again, as in the case of the analysis of the effects with given resources, the net welfare effects of capital flows induced by free economic zones on the host and home country are a function of the empirically determined relative effects of creation and diversion.

Dynamic Effects

All of the preceding arguments about the welfare effects of free economic zones are essentially static in the sense that they considered the results of induced changes within the analytical framework of given resource endowments, technology and the efforts of workers and entrepreneurs. This approach misses what in the longer run may be the most important source of benefits of free economic zones, the dynamic effects. While they are notoriously difficult to predict or even to identify, their importance was stressed in empirical studies of the effects of integration and they underlie the widespread interest in supply side economics in the 1980s. The dynamism generated by selective deregulation has already manifested itself in the more rapid and frequent innovations in banking and insurance services offered, in Euro-currency banking and by Lloyds of London, respectively. It has been due to the fact that only commercial and technical feasibility determined their introduction and regulatory processes could not prevent or even delay them. The well-known past innovations in the free banking and insurance zones are likely to be followed by more and free zones in other industries should result in similar acceleration of innovation.

External Diseconomies

There exist two competing theories of the reasons for regulation. The first suggests that it is the outcome of democratic political processes which enable special interest groups to enrich themselves at the expense of the general public and overall total welfare [Wolf, 1979; Cairns, 1980]. To the extent that free economic zones lower trade barriers under this model they injure only special interest groups and increase overall welfare. Therefore, the estimates of welfare gains due to free trade zones must be revised upward in a way that can never be rigorous.

Under the second model, protection is imposed to eliminate some market failure. Lowering of trade barriers through free economic zones thus leads to the reappearance of external diseconomies and a social cost that has to be included in the welfare analysis presented above.

The impact of the external diseconomies can logically consist of the following extremes. First, the external diseconomies are confined to the host country, as for example might happen if through lowered protection of an import-competing industry the country loses the security benefits of domestic agriculture or of a defense industry. Under these conditions the welfare calculus for the host country has to be adjusted downward. The calculus for the rest of the world requires no adjustment. Second, the external diseconomies accrue mainly to the world as a whole and only

54   Herbert G. Grubel

minimally to the host country. For example, Euro-currency banking is
feared to have raised the probability of a major global financial crisis
because in the absence of national regulatory controls these banks have
invested imprudently large amounts relative to their capital base to individual borrowers of doubtful ability to repay [Grubel, 1979]. Whatever
may be the merit of this argument in practice, it serves to illustrate how
deregulation of banking in Euro-currency markets can result in negative
externalities for the world while most of the benefits from the deregulation accrue to the few financial centers hosting the Euro-currency banks.
In such cases the welfare calculus of the effect of free economic zones must
be amended in obvious ways that are not pursued here.

Finally, it should be noted that if the methods used for discriminating
between regulated and unregulated sectors are working imperfectly, business which should be regulated escapes into the deregulated sector. For
example, it may not be possible to exclude people from free gambling
zones who through excessive losses become public burdens, or firms with
imperfect knowledge may be induced to do business with deregulated
banks and insurance companies that is not in their long-run interest and
leads to social losses. The negative external effects of such imperfect
separation of regulated and unregulated markets must be entered into
the social welfare calculus of free economic zones.

Tax Revenue Effects

Free economic zones cause a redistribution of tax revenue between
governmental jurisdictions that permit some to lower taxes and require
another to raise them (or change expenditures without corresponding
changes in taxation). The resultant welfare effects are well known from
the public finance literature and will not be pursued here. Instead, the
following is limited to a brief taxonomy of the major tax revenue effects.

The local government jurisdiction hosting the free economic zone
gains income directly if it is the landlord of the zone and raises charges
to land users upon establishment of the economic zone[1]. If the local
government has an income tax, revenue is raised by the growth in factor
incomes accompanying the free economic zone trade expansion and as the
tax base is broadened through the migration of capital into the zone from

---

[1] If the owner of the land wishes to maximize his income, he will charge for the use of
the land an amount that is analytically equivalent to the economic rent which accrues to
the occupant. A duty-free camera retail store at an airport, for example, faces a downward
sloping demand curve and sets the price at an output level and accompanying price where
marginal revenue equals marginal costs, with all inputs available at constant prices from the
regulated sector and the rent being determined as a residual. In this extreme case, all of the
benefits from deregulation accrue to the airport authority and the local government owning

the host country and abroad. Overall increased activity and wealth raise excise and property tax revenues of the local jurisdiction.

The senior government of the country hosting the zone suffers a loss of tariff and other revenue generated by regulation equal to that avoided by firms locating in the free economic zone. In addition, there is a shrinking in the income tax base as factor incomes are lowered in industries which contract because of lower protection. Offsetting these losses are higher factor incomes and therefore income tax revenue from export industries and the broader tax base created by the flow of foreign capital into the zone. The rest of the world loses tax base through the outflow of capital.

The most important conclusion emerging from this brief overview is that the local government hosting the zone always gains tax revenue and it should therefore not be surprising that local governments typically are prime promoters of free economic zones. Senior governments, on the other hand, are likely to lose revenue unless the trade expansion and foreign capital inflows are large enough to offset the losses. This may well be one important reason why some senior governments, such as that of Canada, oppose the creation of free trade and economic zones.

IV. Free Economic Zones for Other Industries?

Free Investment Zones

After the analysis of the nature and welfare effects of free economic zones, it may be useful to consider application of the principles developed to other industries which are well known to suffer from heavy regulation. I will do so here for the investment and drug-medical industries.

Paternalism in the regulation of capital markets of the world is very strong, having moved from an initial concern with the accuracy of information disclosed about investment projects to where some governments

---

it. Capital, managers and labor of the store are paid only their opportunity cost in the regulated sector.

If landlords charge rent above the monopolistic optimum, the level of business done in the tax free store will also be less than optimum. I have noted that in some countries duty free airport stores charge prices that appear to be above the optimum and therefore appear to transact very little business. The question arises whether in these cases the stores exploit a very inelastic demand curve, the determinants of which may not be obvious to the casual visitor or whether landlords have set rents too high in ignorance of the elasticity of demand.

On the other hand, it is also possible for landlords to charge less than the optimum amount. In this case the entrepreneur leasing the store enjoys economic rents, which may imply non-desirable income distribution effects. To avoid non-optimal outcomes, the owners of land on which free economic zones are established should set charges through competitive bidding.

have taken it upon themselves to evaluate the economic merit and risk of projects. Inevitably, the legislative requirement to have all capital issues approved by the bureaucracy has resulted in additional costs and delays and in effect requires government officials to do things for which they are not particularly well qualified. Doubts have been expressed that these costs are worth the benfits to investors [Kalymon, 1978].

As in the case of insurance and banking, there is room for disagreement over the net social benefits of regulating capital markets and there exist powerful interest groups benefiting from the regulation. Complete deregulation is therefore unlikely and it may be worth considering partial deregulation through the establishment of free investment zones. In such zones borrowers would not be required to obtain government approval of prospectuses accompanying the issue of new securities. Investors' protection would consist of the remaining applicability of laws which make it a criminal offense to misrepresent facts in prospectuses. Basically, however, investors would be required to have their decisions guided by the principle of "caveat emptor", which would induce them to study prospectuses carefully, use the services of private firms specializing in such evaluations, or both. And, of course, they always have the option of not buying securities in the zone at all.

It may well be that in equilibrium there would be dual capital markets. Risk averse and untrained investors would purchase securities in regulated markets and would be willing to pay the premium and accept delays involved. Firms in relatively stable industries, such as utilities, might find the costs and delays in getting approval acceptable and would be the main suppliers of securities in these regulated markets. In the unregulated zones, on the other hand, securities would be sold to investors with a preference for risky but potentially high return securities and with special skills in evaluating investments. Small and newly created firms in industries where new investment opportunities tend to develop quickly, such as high-technology and resource development, would supply securities and gain greatly in their ability to exploit new opportunities quickly and cheaply.

Free Medical Zones

It is well known that the regulation of drugs, hospitals and medical doctors has resulted in excess costs because the political and bureaucratic incentive structure puts too much weight on the prevention of problems with new products and treatments relative to the cost incurred by delays or cancellations in the introduction of new products and treatments[1].

---

[1] See Grabowski [1976] and Wardell [1979] for studies which indicate that the U.S. cost of obtaining permission to market a new drug was $ 50 million on average in the middle 1970s

There exist in fact free drug and hospital zones in Mexico, some Eastern European countries and in the Swiss Canton of Appenzell[1]. Patients from many countries take advantage of these facilities, often after treatments in their home-countries were unsatisfactory. Because public health-insurance programs in most countries do not cover treatment in such zones abroad, access has been limited to wealthy persons.

The creation of free medical zones in industrial countries would be defensive in the sense defined above and could be achieved simply by setting aside areas within which most of the existing regulation of drugs, treatments and doctors are inapplicable. Patients who consider use of the facilities in the zones would have to rely on their own judgement and that of their doctors and relatives as to the merit of the risks and potential benefits offered. They would have also as protection the desire of firms in the zone to continue in business, which would prevent them from offering drugs and treatments that are ineffective or carry excessive risk in use. Perhaps it would be useful to require that all consultations between firms in the zone and patients be recorded on video tape as evidence that patients had been given full explanations of risks, benefits and costs and had consented to treatment under free will and in possession of their facilities.

It is clear from the preceding considerations that free investment and medical zones do not offer an opportunity for the separation of markets in the same way as do the free banking and insurance zones. In these latter types of zones use is restricted easily to customers who through their size and other characteristics clearly have very little need for the paternalism of the state. In the case of free investment and medical zones it is not possible to use objective criteria to limit access to those who obviously do not need protection. In the case of the medical zone, in fact, arguments can be made that potential users are in special need of state paternalism. For these reasons perhaps the suggested creation of free investment and medical zones has little chance of being implemented in the near future.

---

and involved testing over several years. As a result, life-saving drugs that had been proven effective and safe in Europe have become available in North America only after several years and after much unnecessary suffering and deaths. Some so-called "orphan drugs" are never marketed because expected sales levels would not permit the recovery of the required $ 50 million investment in obtaining government approval, even though, by all medical standards such drugs are effective and safe.

[1] Appenzell is the home of many clinics using "natural" treatment methods for many ailments. Medical doctors can practice and use their titles obtained abroad without having to pass examination required in other Swiss cantons. According to casual observations by Swiss economists, the Canton of Appenzell has attracted many patients from abroad for a long time and business has not been impeded by expensive law-suits or scandals.

However, in principle, the case for free investment and medical zones is much like that for free gambling zones and there may well come a time when like in the case of gambling the costs of regulation become so great that relatively small and politically independent areas will encourage the creation of such free investment and medical zones because of the large local benefits they promise.

V. Summary and Conclusions

In this paper I have described several recent and diverse institutional innovations which have in common that they permit the selective deregulation of economic activity by location or type of customer or both. It was shown that such selective deregulation, referred to conveniently as the creation of free economic zones, generates powerful interest groups which can succeed politically where attempts at complete deregulation are stalled because of some doubts about the merit of the action and because vested interests oppose it politically.

The welfare effects of the free economic zones are theoretically indeterminate. There are gains from the expansion of trade, encouragement of innovation and increased freedom of choice for producers and consumers. Welfare losses may arise from the locational diversion of trade and externalities, including some due to the imperfect separation of regulated and deregulated sectors. Some free economic zones created in New York are defensive in the sense that they are in response to zones created abroad and the accompanying diversion of trade. Such zones are likely to reduce rather than increase the cost of locational diversion of trade.

If the already existing free economic zones are successful commercially and costs in terms of locational diversion and externalities are small, further free economic zones are certain to be created and new industries included. The selective deregulation of the investment and medical industries may be primary candidates for such new initiatives.

References

Butler, Stuart M., *Enterprise Zones.* Washington 1980.

Cairns, Robert D., *Rationales for Regulation.* Economic Council of Canada, Technical Report Series, No. 2, Ottawa 1980.

Cheng, H.-S., "From the Caymans". Federal Reserve Bank of San Francisco, *Weekly Letter*, February 13, 1981.

Corden, W. M., *The Theory of Protection.* Oxford 1971.

Decaminada, Joseph P., *An Analysis of the New York Insurance Exchange and "Free Zone".* Memo of The Atlantic Companies, New York, May 31, 1979.

Diamond, Walter H., *Free Trade Zones Offer Worldwide Opportunities*. Area Development Series, University of Miami, December 1979, pp. 33—47.

The Economist, "New York's Insurance Industry". London, November 17, 1979, pp. 114—115.

Feige, Edgar L., "How Big is the Irregular Economy ?". *Challenge*, Vol. 22, December 1979, pp. 5—13.

Fernstrom, John R., *The Establishment of Free Trade Zones in Promoting Industrial Development*. Thesis for the Industrial Development Institute, University of Oklahoma, 1976.

Grabowski, Henry G., *Drug Regulation and Innovation: Empirical Evidence and Policy Options*. American Enterprise Institute for Public Policy Research, Evaluative Studies, 28, Washington 1976.

Grubel, Herbert G., *A Proposal for the Establishment of an International Deposit Insurance Corporation*. Essays in International Finance, No. 133, Princeton 1979.

—, "A Proposal to Establish an Afro-Currency Market in Nairobi". In: John S. Chipman and Charles P. Kindleberger (Eds.), *Flexible Exchange Rates and the Balance of Payments: Essays in Memory of Egon Sohmen*. Studies in International Economics, Vol. 7, Amsterdam 1980, pp. 297—309.

Hamada, Koichi, "An Economic Analysis of the Duty-Free Zone". *Journal of International Economics*, Vol. 4, 1974, pp. 225—241.

Hamilton, Carl, and **Lars E. O. Svensson,** *On Welfare Effects of a "Duty-Free Zone"*. Institute for International Economic Studies, University of Stockholm, August 1980, processed.

Hodjera, Zoran, "The Asian Currency Market: Singapore as a Regional Financial Center". *IMF, Staff Papers*, Vol. 25, 1978, pp. 221—253.

Johnson, Harry G., "Panama as Regional Financial Center: A Preliminary Analysis of Development Contribution". *Economic Development and Cultural Change*, Vol. 24, 1976, pp. 261—286.

Kalymon, B. C., *Financing of the Junior Mining Company in Ontario*. Ontario Ministry of Natural Resources, February 1978.

Lipsey, R. G., "The Theory of Customs Unions: A General Survey". *The Economic Journal*, Vol. 70, 1960, pp. 496—513.

Manhattan Report Special Edition, *A Forum on Urban Enterprise Zones — Reversing the Decline of Our Inner Cities*. International Center for Economic Policy Studies, April 1981.

Meade, J. E., *The Theory of Customs Unions*. Amsterdam 1955.

Mirus, Rolf, and **Roger S. Smith**, "Canada's Irregular Economy". *Canadian Public Policy*, Vol. 7, 1981, pp. 444—453.

Ping, H. K., "Birth of the Second Generation of Free Trade Zones". *Far Eastern Economic Review*, May 18, 1979.

Rodriguez, Carlos A., "A Note on the Economics of the Duty Free Zone". *Journal of International Economics*, Vol. 6, 1976, pp. 385—388.

Time, "Free Enterprise Oases". New York, July 14, 1980, p. 43.

United Nations Industrial Development Organization (UNIDO), *Export Processing Zones in Developing Countries.* UNIDO Working Papers on Structural Changes, No. 19, UNIDO/ICIS. 176, [New York], August 18, 1980.

Viner, Jacob, *The Customs Union Issue.* Carnegie Endowment for International Peace, Studies in the Administration of International Law and Organization, No. 10, New York 1950.

Wall, David, "Export Processing Zones". *Journal of World Trade Law,* Vol. 10, 1976, pp. 478—498.

Wardell, W., "More Regulation or Better Therapies?". *Regulation,* Vol. 3, 1979, pp. 25—33.

Wolf, Jr., Charles, "A Theory of Non-Market Failure". *Journal of Law and Economics,* Vol. 22, 1979, pp. 107—139.

*   *   *

[27]

Crime, Law & Social Change 24: 293–317, 1996.

Exploring the offshore interface *

The relationship between tax havens, tax evasion, corruption and economic development

MARK P. HAMPTON
Department of Economics, University of Portsmouth, Southsea, Hampshire PO4 8JF, UK

Abstract. The connections between economic development, corruption, and the increasingly globalised financial system are not yet fully understood. This article examines the offshore interface – tax havens and offshore finance centres – that lies between the developed countries and Less Developed Countries (LDCs), part of the international financial system where legitimacy meets corruption. The central argument is that the existence of the offshore interface facilitates and can even encourage onshore corruption. New technology, in combination with strict bank secrecy in the "private banking" offshore networks of major banks, allows rapid international flows of funds, illustrating an increasing synergy between the offshore interface, globalisation and onshore corruption.

Introduction

Tax Havens and Offshore Finance Centres (OFCs) play an important role in the circulation of international financial capital, acting as satellites orbiting the global financial centres of London, New York and Tokyo. OFCs, with their high levels of bank secrecy, attract flight capital from Less Developed Countries (LDCs) that are commonly facing international debt. Ironically, deposits often flow back to the offshore branches of the same international banks that were lenders (Lessard and Williamson 1987). These connections between development, corruption, tax evasion and the increasingly globalised financial system are not yet fully understood. This article explores what could be called the offshore interface – tax havens and OFCs – that lies between the developed countries and LDCs, the international financial system, and the geopolitics that characterises the late twentieth century.

In comparison with other areas of development studies, offshore finance is a somewhat problematic area to research given the nature of offshore

---

* An earlier version of this paper was read at the Development Studies Annual Conference in Dublin, 7–9 September 1995.

294   MARK P. HAMPTON

financial activities based upon secrecy and confidentiality. Customers using OFCs demand secrecy from revenue authorities, governments and sometimes their own next of kin. This criterion applies even for legitimate business customers, transnational corporations (TNCs) and wealthy individuals who seek confidentiality. Additionally, there are two further aspects that can hinder the collection of comparative data: first, the various OFC host governments' attempts to continually portray themselves in the best possible light, and second, the fact that financial services, especially banking, are fundamentally based on the fragile notion of "confidence". This leads to all players wanting to promote the probity and respectability of their OFCs. In combination with the host government's stance, this can lead to a reluctance to reveal much information about offshore activities. This results in a lack of good, international comparative data both for offshore finance in general, and specifically for different OFCs. The problems of measurement of offshore finance are similar to researching the so called "black" or hidden economy, and so estimates of size are often no more than "best guess" activities.[1]

Given this lack of data and secrecy, "snowballing" interviews were used in two OFCs – Jersey and The Bahamas. This "snowballing" technique enabled access to the OFC networks, as initial personal and family contacts led to other interview respondents. The author was then able to conduct a series of semi-structured interviews in the two OFCs.[2] This mass of primary (albeit qualitative) data was then augmented with extensive use of existing secondary sources.

Recent literature includes studies by the Economist Intelligence Unit (Doggart 1993) and the writings of various tax lawyers and other practitioners (Langer 1988; Spitz 1990; Diamond and Diamond 1990; Grundy 1994; Yule 1994). However, most are technical works, written for international tax specialists and generally lacking conceptual depth. In general offshore finance and OFCs seem to be an under-researched area, possibly because of the lack of data and the problem noted above. The few academic studies of offshore finance are R.A. Johns' monographs (1983; and Johns and Le Marchant, 1993), Walter 1985; Naylor 1987 and Ehrenfeld 1992. Johns approaches offshore finance from a broadly neoclassical viewpoint, arguing that onshore frictions – such as fiscal, banking and commercial regulations – push funds offshore to "zero friction" OFCs. However, his neoclassical assumptions have been criticised by Hampton (1993) who argues that an analysis of the political economy of the relationship between onshore state and offshore jurisdiction is fundamental, as this relationship underpins the possibility of an offshore jurisdiction enacting fiscal or bank secrecy legislation to attract international financial capital.

Walter, Naylor and Ehrenfeld focus specifically on the criminal abuses of offshore finance. Theirs could be dubbed the "secret-hot-evil money" approach, perhaps a reflection of the marketability of popular works on the sleazier aspect of international financial flows. Despite some useful comments on the development histories of particular OFCs, all three authors lack any conceptual model or real framework to explain why offshore finance emerged in the post-war period. Elsewhere (Hampton 1993, 1996a), a political economy framework was developed to analyse offshore finance, and, in particular, island OFCs using the Marxist fractions of capital model. However, in this article, the concept of the offshore interface will be introduced and some preliminary suggestions will be made as to its role and significance.

The article will first examine what offshore centres are and how they operate. Private banking, capital flight and the offshore interface are then discussed, including some of the other abuses of OFCs. Next, the article examines some illustrative case material from the Jersey OFC of actual abuses of the offshore interface. Finally, it considers various impacts on economic development, both for the source LDC and the host country of the OFC.

The use of offshore centres

Tax havens and OFCs have gained prominence since the 1960s although some centres existed before this such as Switzerland, Monaco and the Lebanon. The amount of bank deposits in tax havens increased from an estimated $11 billion in 1968, to $385 billion in 1978 (OECD 1987). Difficulties of estimation notwithstanding,[3] by 1991 estimates of the total size of the global offshore business had risen to over one trillion US Dollars (Kochan 1991).

Before looking at how OFCs operate, it is helpful to start with a working definition of an OFC as

> a centre that hosts financial activities that are separated from major reg-
> ulating units (states) by geography and or by legislation. This may be a
> physical separation, as in an island territory, or within a city such as Lon-
> don or the New York International Banking Facilities (IBFs). (Hampton
> 1994: 237)

As Table 1 illustrates, OFCs are often located in small places: inland or mountain enclaves (Liechtenstein, Andorra); coastal enclaves (Monaco), or most commonly, in small islands.[4] Although there is some confusion with tax havens, OFCs can be defined as sites of a range of economic activities (private and wholesale banking, offshore trusts and funds, holding companies, captive insurance and shipping registers) whereas tax havens are based upon pure tax differentials with other countries.[5]

296   MARK P. HAMPTON

Table 1. Main offshore financial centres.

Caribbean & South Atlantic	Europe, Middle East, Africa
Anguilla	Andorra
Antigua	Bahrain
Bahamas	Channel Islands (CI)
Barbados	Cyprus
Belize	Gibraltar
Bermuda	Isle of Man
British Virgin Islands	Liberia
Cayman Islands	Liechtenstein
Costa Rica	Luxembourg
Dominica	Malta
Grenada	Mauritius
Montserrat	Monaco
Netherlands Antilles	Netherlands
Nevis & St. Kitts	Switzerland
Panama	United Arab Emirates
St. Lucia	
St. Vincent	**Asia – Pacific**
Turks & Caicos Islands	
	Cook Islands
	Hong Kong
	Labuan
	Marshall Islands
	Nauru
	Philippines
	Singapore
	Vanuatu
	Western Samoa

Sources: adapted from Gordon Report 1981; International Currency Review 1984: 15–16; and Europa World Year Book 1994.

The central role of secrecy as the basis of most offshore activities results in a lack of data. However, given this constraint it is possible to produce some partial tabulations that hint at the quantitative impact of OFCs. The following three tables use the three categories of OFC introduced in earlier research (Hampton 1993): functional, compound, and notional OFCs. A functional OFC can be defined as the place where actual financial activities take place, the location of full branches of banks, plus other financial services such as fund managers, trust companies et cetera. From the partial data a pattern starts

Table 2. Tier one: functional OFCs, 1994.

	Licenced banks	Banks (real presence)	Number employed in OFC	Percentage of labour force	Assets (A) or liabilities (L) US $ millions	OFC est. contrib to GDP	Offshore companies	Captive insurance companies[a]
Bermuda	3	3	2,600 (1992)	15% (1992)	8,832 L	30% (1992)	7,297 (1993)	1,357
Isle of Man	61	na	5,800	18%	19,650 L	35%	4,180 (1992)	141
Guernsey	73	54	5,000	16%	63,300 L	56%	14,000	280
Jersey	76	67	8,000	20%	97,437 L	54%	29,259	0

Source: Hampton, 1996b. *Note:* [a] Captive insurance is where a wholly owned subsidiary company is used to insure particular risks of its parent company, eg oil tanker fleets.

Table 3. Tier two: compound OFCs.

	Licenced banks	Banks (real presence)	Number employed in OFC	Percentage of labour force	Assets (A) or liabilities (L) US $ millions	OFC est. contrib to GDP	Offshore companies	Captive insurance companies
The Bahamas	396	177	3,330	3%	200,000 L (1993)	16% (1994)	12,600 (1993)	30 (1993)
Bahrain	47 (1993)	na	na	na	65,000 A (1994)	na	na	na
Barbados	16	na	na	na	2,500 L	na	794	236
British Virgin Islands	8 (1993)	na	na	4%	255,000 A	23%	100,000 (1993)	35
Cayman Islands	534	78	1,600	10%	427,000 L	na	29,298	378
Cyprus	19	19	1,500 (1992)	na	920 L	17% (1992)	13,000	9
Gibraltar	29	na	na	na	3,750 L	na	4,000	na
Netherlands Antilles	37 (1993)	na	na	8%	6,000 A	12.8%	30,000	na
Vanuatu	100	na	386 (1994)	na	5,000 A (1988)	10% (1993)	900 (1993)	25 (1993)

Source: Hampton, 1996b.
Note: Data for Netherlands Antilles and BVI 1988; Barbados, the Cayman Islands and The Bahamas 1992; Cyprus, Gibraltar & Vanuatu 1993; unless otherwise indicated.

Table 4. Tier three: notional OFCs.

	Licenced banks	Banks (real presence)	Number employed in OFC	Percentage of labour force	Assets (A) or liabilities (L) US $ millions	OFC est. contrib to GDP	Offshore companies	Captive insurance companies
Anguilla[a]	15 (1990)	4 (1990)	na	na	na	14% (1990)	na	na
Antigua	11	na	na	na	339 L	na	1,400	15
Cook Islands	na	na	na	na	na	na	2,000 (1987)	na
Labuan[a]	21	na	na	na	996 L (1992)	na	197	2
Malta	4	4	na	na	na	na	900 (1992)	na
Mauritius	7 (1994)	7 (1994)	500 (1994)	na	na	12% (1988)	3000 (1994)	0
Turks & Caicos	8	na	na	na	200 L	na	10,000	43

Source: Hampton 1996b.
Note: [a] Until 1996 (or when the infrastructure is finished) banks are physically located in Kuala Lumpur. All OFC data is for 1993, unless otherwise indicated.

300   MARK P. HAMPTON

to emerge – functional OFCs appear to have significant financial sector local employment (over 12% of the labour force). In addition, available data for four functional island OFCs (Bermuda, the Isle of Man, Jersey and Guernsey) suggests that OFC activities contribute over 25% of GDP.

A compound OFC hosts a mixture of functional and notional activities. This category includes centres that have an increasing number of shell offices that eventually become fully operational branches including The Bahamas and the Cayman Islands. Such places have a smaller proportion of the island's labour force employed by the OFC than functional OFCs, broadly employing 3–10% of the economically active, and contributing an estimated 10–24% of GDP.

A notional OFC is where "shell", brass-plate or "cubicle" offices of banks make book entries of financial transactions. In terms of employment and contribution to GDP, as the data are very fragmented and incomplete, all that can be noted is a nominal contribution to both (under 3% and under 10% respectively). However, for lower-income small economies any petty income such as company registration fees may be welcomed (Baldacchino 1993). In the following three tables, the general lack of data on OFCs is indicated by the number of cells showing "na" (not available) in each table.

The problems of lack of data on OFCs mean that the three tables are necessarily indicative rather than authoritative. However, they give a sense of the scale of operation in the main island OFCs. When this partial information is combined with the estimated size of the offshore business (over one trillion US Dollars) this begins to hint at the significance of offshore finance in the global economy.

At present there seems to be movement towards the regional grouping of three economic blocs: the EU, North America and Asia-Pacific. Each bloc has what could be called a Global Finance Centre (GFC) within it; the cities of London, New York and Tokyo, what Hamilton (1986: 111) dubs the "three legged stool" of world finance. Each GFC has a group of satellite OFCs around it servicing the catchment areas. When deposits are attracted to an OFC they are then passed through to the deeper capital markets in the GFCs. Johns (1983: 225) describes the role of OFCs as being a "turntable" for funds. The model of the relationship of OFC to GFC is somewhat different in the Asia-Pacific area, where Tokyo has a different activity base compared with New York and London. In Asia, Hong Kong and Singapore act more like regional centres than normal OFCs.

In addition, hosting offshore finance has been seen as a development option by many LDCs, specifically two main groups: first certain middle-to higher income LDCs, particularly the NICs and near-NICs of Asia (Hong Kong, Singapore and South Korea, the cities of Bangkok and Taipei, and Malaysia's

Labuan island OFC); and secondly small island economies[6] (SIEs) and small territories located in the Caribbean (The Bahamas, the Netherlands Antilles), the Pacific (Vanuatu), the Indian Ocean (Mauritius) or around the edge of Europe (the Channel Islands, Gibraltar, Malta).

Private banking, capital flight and the offshore interface

Arguably, the most significant OFC activity in the 1990s is now offshore banking, specifically the rapid growth area of "international private banking" encompassing bank accounts, trusts and offshore companies. Broadly, this can be attributed to two connected areas: the changing international financial environment; and rising demand for private banking. First, in relation to the supply side, major changes in the international financial environment have had a significant effect on the type of international banking activity. In the late 1980s, the syndicated loans business (Eurocurrency markets) and wholesale banking in general slowed down, reflecting rising real interest rates and the so-called Third World Debt Crisis. Therefore, many international banks rediscovered the concept of private banking for high net wealth individuals (HNWIs) and pursued them aggressively to replace declining wholesale loan activities with free-based private banking.[7]

On the demand side this coincided with increasing global demand for private banking facilities. In 1990 the number of wealthy individuals worldwide (with investible private wealth of over $1 million each) was estimated by Citicorp at around eight million, and this figure appears to be growing (OFM 1990: 10). Broadly, the increasing demand for offshore private bank accounts could be identified as stemming from two sources: regions undergoing rapid industrialisation with concomitant wealth creation; and increasing political instability in many areas, the so-called "new world disorder" of the 1990s with the shift from a bi-polar world to a fragmented, multi-polar world.

An interesting example of the former is the demand for private banking from the Overseas Chinese in the Pacific Rim, especially in Indonesia, Malaysia, Thailand and the Philippines, plus Hong Kong and Taiwan: "for the Chinese community, it is important to get money offshore for safety's sake. They share a common denominator of a lot of money, a lot of family and a lot of fear" (A Swiss banker in Hong Kong, quoted in Friedland, 1992: 29). In terms of demand generated by instability, the break-up of the former Soviet Union and its satellites led to spectacular movements of capital flight which in 1994 were haemorrhaging at a rate of an estimated $1 billion per month (Burns 1994). Elsewhere, elites in many LDCs had long placed assets offshore, but there appears to have been a recent acceleration of such capital flight. Examples include the offshore fortunes of Haiti's "Baby Doc" Duvalier, estimated at

302   MARK P. HAMPTON

$200–900 million, the Philippines' President Marcos with an alleged $2–10 billion (Naylor 1987; Robinson 1994), African examples including Zaire and Nigeria (Watts 1994), and many Latin American examples where funds flowed to Caribbean OFCs and then onwards to Florida real estate (Sampson 1982; Naylor 1987).

More recently, Russian assets held externally in Western banks totalled around $18 billion in 1993 (approximately doubling from 1992), of which around $4.4 billion is held in London[8] (Tett 1994). Interestingly, the Russian use of the Cyprus OFC for "brass plate" offshore companies and bank accounts[9] appears to be increasing. Reportedly, the assets are then transferred to other OFCs such as Switzerland. In all of this, the problem for Western banks is how much of this flow of flight capital is criminal cash from the increasing "Mafia-isation" of the former Soviet economy being laundered through OFCs? (Theodoulou 1994; BBC 1994).

Capital flight appears to be widespread and has a large technical literature (Dooley 1986; Lessard and Williamson 1987; Vos 1992; Boyce 1992; Nyatepe-Coo 1993) but in essence it is based upon a fundamental need for secrecy in the recipient centre, the OFC. Users of international private banking often blatantly disregard the law in their own country concerning offshore bank accounts. This then results in devious (ingenious) methods employed by OFC firms to retain their customers in sensitive locations such as Israel, South Africa (before the mid-1990s) or the Russian Federation from the mid-1990s. An illuminating example of this is a technique employed to disguise the correspondence from the OFC bank to the private customer using plain, handwritten envelopes with a normal postage stamp rather than a normal business style envelope and machine-franked postmark. The disguised letter or account statement is then sent by private bag to the OFC bank's head office in a large capital city for mailing so that the correspondence appears to be a private letter and does not bear the postmark of a known OFC! (source: interview respondents).

Capital flight has attracted academic debate particularly over the connection between capital flight, international private banking and the large external debt of certain LDCs (Gulati 1988; Roberts 1992; Boyce 1992). In general there are two main worldviews on this: what Boyce, 1992 dubs the "Baker-banker" orthodoxy of the Western banks and the IMF; and alternatively, the critical view. In the first view, significant external debt is broadly due to LDC governments' economic mismanagement (including exchange rate overvaluation and inflationary policies); there is no direct causal relationship between capital flight and international private banking except that flight is a symptom of the LDC's crisis as money flees to more economically "rational" locations.

In contrast, Diaz-Alejandro (1984) takes a critical view and argues that Western banks set out to attract international private banking (that is, capital flight), and that capital flight is partly the result of the increasingly globalised financial system. Boyce (1992) uses the metaphor of the "revolving door" to analyse capital flight from the Philippines, arguing that capital flight and external debt are explicitly and intimately interconnected.

However, in the analysis it is possible to go further than Boyce's "revolving door" to consider the operations of offshore finance and international capital flows in relation to the emerging global system. This developing role may be termed the "offshore interface" and is wider than just the location of flight capital, but is the meeting point, the place of convergence, as it were, of many currents. This offshore interface is where what Roberts (1994) calls "fictitious capital" (Eurocurrencies, that is wholesale banking) meets "furtive capital" (private banking and capital flight/retail banking). In addition, it is also a global-local interface; the interface between "developed" countries and LDCs; where corruption connects with legitimacy; and finally a geopolitical interface for global power projections. This last category will be considered later.

Roberts (1994: 111) expands the earlier work of Harvey (1989) arguing that, in essence, global capitalism (as a result of its uneven development) broadly displaces crises both temporally and spatially resulting in "a new geography of finance". She clearly identifies the paradox of offshore finance being both at the margin and at the centre of global capitalism. Given that most OFCs are not independent nation states (and are usually islands or other small jurisdictions) this paradox is also borne out by the somewhat peculiar relationship that they have with the nearby large power. As dependencies, they are both "within and without" the mainland, having some local autonomy but linked to the large onshore state. This peculiar relationship partly creates the offshore interface, but is itself open to penetration by internationally mobile financial capital – that is, international banks (Hampton 1993).

In effect, there has been the confluence of the economic development requirements of certain small economies and the uneven global financial topography (especially regulatory and fiscal) that has been exploited by international financial capital. The phenomenal growth in the 1960s of the "offshore" Eurocurrency markets initially centred in London saw the creation of a massive pool of unregulated, highly mobile private capital. OPEC funds, swollen by the early 1970s oil price rises, in combination with low real interest rates created excess systemic liquidity which the international banks attempted to sop up by extensive loans to LDCs. These developments were facilitated by significant technical advances in telecommunications and computer power that enabled the rapid transfer of funds from centre to centre across the globe.

304   MARK P. HAMPTON

Arguably, a significant proportion of these international loans to LDCs were creamed off as rent-seeking activities by local elites, that is, corruption in the form of over-payments, bribes etc. The funds thus obtained were then transferred into banks located in the offshore interface – ironically, often to "private banking" branches of the very same international banks that had issued the international loan to the LDC country in the first place.

The offshore interface permits an extremely fine distinction between various activities in OFCs, particularly between legal and illegal use as both types require the low levels of taxation and the high levels of secrecy that are provided. Thus the offshore interface provides the continuing potential for abuse by individuals, corporations and the state, although what may be perceived as abuse in one country may be a legitimate business activity elsewhere. This legal relativism can be illustrated in the problematic concepts of tax avoidance and tax evasion.

Tax avoidance can be defined as the legitimate right of an individual to arrange their business affairs so as to minimise tax liability, whereas tax evasion is often a similar activity but is deemed illegal. Interestingly, tax evasion is not universally recognised as a criminal offence in all countries. Switzerland was one of the better known examples of this non-recognition. The distinction between legal tax avoidance and illegal tax evasion is sometimes extremely hard to see clearly. This can be "a very arbitrary matter for many international business activities. This distinction being a question of how the different tax laws are interpreted" (Fleck and Mahfouz 1974: 145). Kindleberger (1970: 181) somewhat fudges the issue by using the term "escape from the jurisdiction" to avoid the problem of this distinction. The effects of tax evasion on the state will be considered later.

It now appears relatively common for criminals to use the offshore interface for money laundering, although the older (often Tier One functional) centres are now arguably more selective in their clientele (Ehrenfeld 1992; Johns and Le Marchant 1993). As centres "gentrify", funds of questionable origin move to less selective, newer OFCs such as Tier Three notional centres. Alternatively, there may be a layering of shell companies to hide the real nature of certain funds, acting as the interface between legality and illegality. Corporate abuse of the offshore interface includes disguising the origins of illegal payments such as bribes, hiding contributions to political parties and sanction busting. The 1986 Guinness Affair is an example where the £ 5.2 million payment was routed through offshore banks in Jersey and London and ended up in certain Swiss banks (Kochan and Pym 1987).

Economic sanctions imposed by certain states on others can be avoided by going offshore. For example, the ban on trade with South Africa in the 1980s was successfully breached by US firms using re-invoicing via offshore companies in the CI and Panama (Naylor 1987; JWP 1989, 2 February); and reportedly, by firms using the Cyprus OFC to avoid sanctions against Bosnia in 1993 (The Guardian 1993, 24 April; Theodoulou 1994). Other corporate abuses include toxic waste disposal sites in LDCs where the holding company is located in an OFC; and the increase in flags of convenience for international shipping that is registered in an OFC (such as Panama or The Bahamas).

Governments in "developed" countries (DCs) have also used the offshore interface (offshore bank accounts and offshore companies) as money boxes for their security services' covert operations in LDCs and elsewhere to supply funds to foreign governments, opposition parties or terrorist groups (Clarke and Tigue 1976; Bloch and Fitzgerald 1983; Naylor 1987; OFC interview sources). The CIA's dirty wars in Central and Latin America are well documented. Although "national security" is a sensitive area for governments, this continuing use of OFCs for nefarious purposes may suggest one reason for many governments' apparent willingness to ignore nearby OFCs, or more generally to tolerate the existence of the offshore interface. Other military uses include using offshore "brass plate" companies to facilitate semi-official mercenaries (such as the security firm KMS Ltd) that can be at arms length and thus safely distanced from the DC government (Bloch and Fitzgerald 1983), and various links to the international arms trade. An example of the latter was the alleged use of offshore companies nominally located in Jersey to disguise equipment purchases for Iraq's Condor missile project (BBC 1989).

The Jersey OFC: an outline case study

Jersey is a good example of the offshore interface in action. As an OFC with a high level of bank secrecy, clearly the island is open to various abuses including tax evasion, money laundering and capital flight. Within the OFC sector some interview respondents seriously questioned the efficacy of its bank regulation:

- "Jersey could be tighter in lots of areas"
- "Jersey is a prostitute. . . (and) welcomes money with open arms"
- "Jersey over-states that it is a clean OFC"
- "it is extremely naive to think that Jersey is not targeted by international financial criminals"
- "it is a potential back door for hot money"

Not surprisingly, respondents who were government employees talked in terms of Jersey being "responsible", "sensible" or taking the "the quality road". Since the 1980s known cases of criminal abuse of the OFC have included a variety of activities as Table 5 shows.

306   MARK P. HAMPTON

Table 5. Publicised abuses involving the Jersey OFC.

Activity	Example	Date	Use of Jersey OFC	Size of total transaction
Money laundering proceeds of crime	Brink's-Mat gold bullion robbery	1983–84	Jersey offshore companies	£ 7.5 million
Tax evasion of income	Ken Dodd, entertainer	1989	bank accounts	£ 700,000[a]
Divesting assets using a trust	Chief Nzeribe	1989	Admin of Bahamas Trust	£ 125 million[b]
Government covert operations overseas	KMS Ltd, operations in Nicaragua ("Irangate")	c1986	Jersey offshore company	$110,000[c]
Capital flight	"Baby Doc" Duvalier	1988	bank accounts	$120 million

Sources: The Guardian 19 November 1987; JWP 21 April 1988; JWP 7 July 1988; JWP 4 August 1988; JEP 14 July 1987; JEP 15 July 1987; JEP 21 December 1989; Daily Telegraph 8 July 1988; The Times 8 July 1988; Bloch and Fitzgerald 1983; Robinson 1994.
Notes:
a This sum was alleged to have been deposited in banks both in Jersey and the Isle of Man, so Jersey's share is unclear.
b In the UK High Court Chief Nzeribe of Nigeria argued that he was bankrupt with liquid assets of a mere £ 2,892 whilst it was alleged that he enjoyed use of assets worth over £ 125 million in the UK alone including a 5,000 acre farm and three Rolls Royce cars. See JEP 21 December 1989.
c Reported in the US Senate's Select Committee findings that the founder of KMS received this sum from the Colonel North's "Enterprise", a slush fund of $48 million set up to aid the Nicaraguan Contras. KMS are also reported to have been employed by UK governments for sensitive missions including guarding embassies et cetera (Guardian 19 November 1987; Bloch and Fitzgerald 1983: 46–49).

Table 5 illustrates some abuses that have emerged into the public domain of Jersey bank accounts, offshore companies and trust administration. As already noted, secrecy, low tax and political stability attract legitimate business, but they are also the conditions sought by illegal business. This raises the fundamental question whether such abuses can be effectively stopped given this overlap of attraction. The proportion of the OFC business that originates from illegal sources is totally unknown, so it is difficult to say if the above examples are representative or anomalies. One common argument often put forward by the offshore industry is that abuses happen, even in "reputable" finance centres like London and New York, since once money is in the international payments system it is incredibly hard to track. Thus money from an illegal source, once paid into a bank in a less regulated jurisdiction such as the Turks and Caicos islands, can then be ultimately transferred to a "reputable" OFC such as Jersey.

Clearly, this is a simplification, as the route taken would be via a whole chain of OFCs and onshore finance centres, possibly using several trusts and offshore companies. This argument places the onus onto the international regulatory system and can be used to justify relative inaction both in the OFC and by the international banks themselves. Nevertheless, the potential cost of one serious scandal could be enormous to a particular centre, resulting in a flight of deposits to rival OFCs.

Effects on economic development: impacts on the source LDC

It is useful to separate the LDC as the source of capital flight from the LDC host of the OFC. The main development impacts appear to be: the effect on legitimacy of the state; a reduction of development possibilities; changing economic activities to rentier; and the loss of savings. However, these impacts have some links and do overlap.

First, the possibilities of corruption becoming seen as a normal activity can undermine local laws in the LDC (Nyatepe-Coo 1993; Watts 1994). But we need to be careful here, as much depends on what is "corruption"; for example is it just a different way to conduct business? In fairness, it can be argued that so-called developed countries are themselves no strangers to corruption as evidenced in the 1990s by the fall of the Italian Berlusconi government, the Belgian arms scandal, or the stream of minor "sleaze" cases in the UK's Conservative government under John Major. Certainly in the UK there is a long history of this, for example the bitingly sarcastic label for the UK state as "Old Corruption" in the eighteenth century (Rule 1992).

However, it can be suggested that there is significant difference both for the global financial system and its effects on a large number of people. Clearly, corruption has always existed in every human society, hence the old adage that money equals power, but it is argued that the post-war emergence of the offshore interface and the increasing global economy facilitates rapid movements of capital. Hutton (1995) sums this up:

> The burgeoning international marketplace – destabilising currency flows, using offshore havens to avoid tax – is hostile to expressions of common and public interest. Private interests have too easily slipped the national leash and have used the ungoverned world beyond national frontiers

308   MARK P. HAMPTON

to undermine what they regard as tiresome, inefficient and bureaucratic efforts to assert the moral and social dimension in human affairs. (Hutton 1995: 26)

The examples of three rapidly industrialising Asian LDCs – Malaysia, Taiwan and Vietnam – appear to indicate a commonly held view of the inextricable link between business and politics. For instance this has been called "Money Politics" in Malaysia where Dr Mahathir's ruling UMNO party owns a number of holding companies with services, construction and media interests (Katz and Cumming-Bruce 1994). In Taiwan the dominant Koumintang party (KMT) are seen as one of island's largest industrial conglomerates with around seven holding companies controlling various activities from cement and petrochemicals to telecommunications. Official figures of the KMT's registered assets totalled around £ 23 billion at the end of 1992 (Tyson 1994), reportedly with large offshore investments into South East Asia (particularly Vietnam and Indonesia) and China.[10] In the case of Vietnam, despite economic growth of around 9% p.a. in 1994, "corruption has become a serious hindrance to economic development" (Hung Tran of Deutsche Bank research, Frankfurt cited by Montagnon 1995). For example international pledges of aid totalled $1.8 billion in 1994, yet estimated actual disbursements were only $200 million arguably because of Vietnamese government red tape and increasing corruption (Gauntlett 1994; Montagnon 1995). Clearly, given the wall of secrecy, the Vietnamese elites' deposits cannot be tracked offshore to particular OFCs, but it is reasonable to suggest that the sweeteners, various "fees" and commissions end up offshore, in the interface with the international financial system.

Bennett (1995) argues that the growth of the informal sector and capital flight in Guyana and Jamaica was

> the rejection of the moral and legal authority of the government on the part of a broad cross-section of society in both countries. . . a major breakdown in state authority. Many of those whose activities would normally have fallen within the context of the formal sector simply chose to ignore the formal state apparatus and its rules and regulations. (Bennett 1995: 240–241)

Thus for Bennett, the breakdown of the legitimacy of the state, especially regarding its regulation of the economy is also connected to the IMF and World Bank pressure to allow the free play of market forces. This, he argues, in combination with other factors, leads to an increasing parallel or informal economy continuing to thrive. Significantly, he cites evidence of how relatively privileged groups in the LDC are enabled to maintain their income levels and patterns of consumption. In other words, the rolling back of the state – that is, massive deregulation – is clearly not sufficient.

A different angle on this problem is taken by Doggart (1993), who argues that there is an increasing impatience with the state and particularly the imposition of increasing levels of tax which drives money offshore. Her argument is similar to that of Johns and Le Marchant, 1993. However, the state (more precisely, part of it, that is the government and administration in many LDCs) is itself pushing both party and individual assets offshore both in "democratic" countries and in more authoritarian regimes.

Secondly, continuing corruption and consequent capital flight in the LDC can reduce the number of development options as there is a continuous transfer of resources away from the poorest in LDC society and an increasingly widening gap between wealthy elite and the urban (and rural) poor. An example of this is the increasing numbers of urban street children or vendors at traffic lights in Nigeria (Watts 1994). The connection between public (sovereign) debt and private capital flight to the offshore interface has been detailed by Vos (1992) and Boyce (1992) for the Philippines.

This net transfer of resources can also be seen in the DCs as evidenced by the tax avoidance by TNCs and HNWIs. This lost revenue could be used to finance public health services, education or environmental programmes (Hutton 1993, 1995). The tax revenue losses to onshore governments are massive: for example the UK government lost an estimated £ 1 billion p.a. in the late 1980s through a loophole in the Capital Gains Tax which allowed assets to be placed in offshore trusts (Sunday Times 1990, 21 October).

Thirdly, increasing corruption and capital flight are connected to a sea change in basic economic activity, from productive uses of capital such as manufacturing, to more of a rentier economy, both for the state and the individual (Murphy et al. 1993). Nyatepe-Coo (1993) and Watts (1994) argue this for Nigeria, noting the explicit link between its oil revenues, increasing corruption and massive capital flight. In addition both authors note the oil producers' increasing connection to the international financial system from the 1970s. Indeed, it is possible to go further and argue that this reinforces the concept of the offshore interface as the actual connection.

Finally, the model of the economy suggested by Vos (1992) is that capital flight can reduce the savings available in the LDC's domestic economy for investment as public debt is transformed into private capital offshore. However, Boyce (1992) argues that rather than this "crowding out", it is more complex. His "revolving door" concept allows for a two-way flow, so that rather than capital flight causing a vacuum into which external debts are pulled, or external debts leading to capital flight, capital flows both ways.

310   MARK P. HAMPTON

Effects on economic development: impacts on the OFC host country

For the host LDC where the OFC is located, there are three main areas of concern: its reliance on highly mobile international financial capital; becoming a rentier economy with limited real economic development; and vulnerability to corruption and tax evasion by its own residents.

First, becoming an OFC can create a reliance on highly mobile international financial capital. In particular, the attraction of flight capital to the OFC's banks from nearby LDCs can be problematic. Naylor (1987) gives the Caribbean example where funds flowed into OFC bank accounts from Latin American LDCs, often syphoned off from aid flows by the local elites. The OFC host gains at the other country's expense; in a sense it is a zero-sum game between LDCs. Also, the process could operate in reverse as the high mobility of flight capital (by definition) could make an OFC vulnerable to the rapid loss of its bank deposits if conditions changed significantly in the home country and the flight capital was attracted back.

Secondly, by hosting an OFC, the LDC could arguably become a rentier economy rather than having direct production as its main economic activity. In a small economy, such a shift has been criticised by Bertram and Watters (1985). In addition, hosting an OFC – even a functional Tier One centre with significant direct local employment et cetera – may still only have a limited development impact. At present, arguments for the economic "success" of Tier One, high income OFCs like Jersey are based upon aggregate indicators such as government revenue surpluses or rising GDP per capita figures (McCarthy 1979; States of Jersey 1994). However such partial indicators are problematic as they mask income distribution within the territory. Despite the lack of data, provisional work in Jersey indicates that there may in fact be a widening income disparity between OFC employees (often immigrants) and the indigenous islanders, with possibly even an increase in absolute poverty.[11] Thus hosting an OFC may not be a cost-free option (Hampton 1994).

Thirdly, there can be a vulnerability to corruption and tax evasion by its own residents. The opening up of a small territory to the influence of powerful external agents such as international banks and TNCs may bring many opportunities for corruption and fraud. As part of the offshore interface with the global financial system, the OFC may become involved with questionable international financial activities. In particular, new OFCs may be less selective in the business accepted compared with older OFCs. The shake-out of dubious and illegal activities from the more "reputable" centres may pressurise operators to use new OFCs that may not be tainted with known connections to money laundering, for example.

In many small territories with a relatively small number of government officials and politicians, the checks and balances are perhaps less developed and there is greater possibility of serious damage. Unfortunately, this has been illustrated in many Caribbean OFCs including Anguilla, The Bahamas, the Cayman Islands, and Montserrat (Walter 1985: 198–202). In the case of Montserrat there were serious problems in the 1980s resulting in the deregistration of many dubious offshore banks and strengthened legislation (Europa World Year Book 1994). Such an association with international crime may permanently alter the island's future development options.

If the OFC government sets low direct tax rates and offers other tax minimising possibilities like offshore companies or trusts, then its own residents may also be tempted to copy the outside users of the OFC and evade their taxes.[12] The cost could be a substantial amount of lost revenue. The jurisdiction may then need to enact laws to attempt to prevent this, following the examples of Switzerland and Jersey where it is difficult for local residents to use the OFC for tax evasion. However, this may merely lead to local residents transferring their funds to rival OFCs, losing both their tax revenue and the business for the host OFC. This links to the earlier section concerning the legitimacy of the state.

Finally, at a more theoretical level, for the LDC host of OFCs: most OFCs are microstates (islands) and so are relatively weak in relation to large DCs, raising the question – do they have any real choice? This would depend upon the theoretical stance taken. Within the orthodox (generally neoclassical) paradigm exemplified by the World Bank and IMF, development economists tend to see hosting an OFC as within the framework of the small economy needing to be an "open door" to the world. The development of an OFC would fit their policy prescription of economies' specialising following their comparative advantage. In this case the comparative advantages would be perceived as including political stability, a well educated labour force and proximity to major industrialised economies. Overall, the Orthodox viewpoint would see an OFC as a positive development strategy for small LDCs.

More radical theorists from the "Managed Dependency" approach such as Baldacchino (1993), while perceiving the situation from a very different angle to the Orthodox School, would also see hosting an OFC in a positive light. They would see setting up an OFC as part of managing the relationship with a large "big brother" economy, a way to increase control of the LDC's economic destiny. In this world view, developing an OFC is seen as useful, a pragmatic choice.

Conclusions

Clearly, the offshore interface, that is the connections between tax havens, tax evasion, corruption, capital flight and economic development are complex,

312   MARK P. HAMPTON

and in this preliminary study have only been sketched in. However, a number of points can be made.

First, the rapid pace of change, especially that of increasing globalisation, the effect of the deregulation of international finance since the late 1970s, and new technologies have resulted in rapid capital flows though the offshore interface. Private banking in OFCs, underwritten by strict bank secrecy legislation, facilitates the easy movement of the gains from corrupt transactions, so that there appears to be an increasing synergy between the offshore interface, the internationalisation of finance and the emergence of a globalised "free market".

This leads to the second point. Given the central role of the international banks as both wholesale lenders to LDCs and private bankers for the world's wealthy (arguably linked by massive flows of capital flight), this has created problems in the implementation of significant change. Clearly, the international banks are powerful players indeed and their international private banking for HNWIs is extremely lucrative. Thus for the banks, the offshore interface is perceived as being basically unproblematic, except they might endorse some nominal offshore regulation.

From the DC governments' point of view, in 1995 the OECD Task Force on Bribery in cooperation with the Financial Action Task Force[13] placed a new emphasis on what it calls "inadequate governance" (or, more transparently, corruption) in LDCs and has called for openness and democracy. However, this occupation of the moral high ground by the OECD can be seen as somewhat hypocritical by many LDCs. Moral outrage at the "cancer of corruption" (Oscar Arias Sanchez, quoted in Adonis and Jack, 1995) needs to be considered alongside the double standards of Western companies that routinely pay bribes to win contracts in LDCs, thus prolonging rent-seeking behaviour.

Finally, an element of irony can be seen as exemplified by the changing nature of the relationship of some OECD countries to LDCs, especially the NICs and near-NICs. In the case of the UK and Malaysia in the mid 1990s, economic stagnation in the former and booming infrastructural projects in the latter resulted in effectively a buyer's market. UK construction firms desperately needed the large Malaysian contracts, whilst the Malaysian government was in a relatively powerful position to choose international contractors. As such this illustrates ". . a powerful subtext shaped by the rapidly shifting balance of power between an ex-colony and its former imperial masters" (Katz and Cumming-Bruce, 1994). In this case, the offshore interface – specifically the role of corruption and economic development – is tacitly ignored. All of this suggests an urgent need for further research on the offshore interface and its role that appears, from this study, to be of increasing importance.

Acknowledgment

The author is grateful to John Christensen, Peter Scott, Shujie Yao and to the journal referees for their helpful criticisms of earlier drafts of this paper. However, the usual disclaimers apply.

Notes

1. For example, 1983 US government estimates of the volume of illegal funds going offshore ranged from $9 billion to over $50 billion (Picciotto 1992: 127).
2. The main series of 23 interviews in Jersey with 19 different respondents took place over Summer 1991. The Bahamas interviews were, in a sense, opportunist as the author was in Nassau attending a conference. This is a good example of the difference between the Positivist paradigm of how to present the order in which the research was done, as opposed to the more muddy reality of the actual research process (Phillips and Pugh 1987). The interviews were augmented by later contact with individuals from other OFCs including Malta, the Isle of Man and Guernsey.
3. For example, like the Eurocurrency markets, there is the serious problem of double counting, thus if the published bank deposits are added up in all the major offshore centres, the total would be misleading given the amount of inter-bank lending so that the same initial deposit could easily appear on the books of several banks across the world. In addition, the amount of money held in offshore trusts is even harder to estimate as trust managers do not have to publish any figures. In Jersey for example, the official size of the total bank deposits was around £ 59 billion by end June 1994 (States of Jersey 1994), however, OFC industry respondents suggest that the size of the Jersey trust business is approximately two to three times this amount, giving an estimated size of £ 120–180 billion.
4. The term "jurisdiction" is used as many OFCs are not independent sovereign states but may be dependent or semi-dependent territories as defined by international law.
5. There is also the political aspect as many territories' governments intensely dislike the tax haven label and even with lack of functional offshore activity claim to be offshore centres or even "international financial centres" (see Hampton 1993; Atkinson 1995).
6. Although there is some discussion over definitions (for example see Doumenge 1983; versus Dolman 1985), broadly the term SIE is used here to refer to islands with populations of under one million.
7. However, historically wealthy individuals have always been the main customer base of the merchant banks.
8. London has some characteristics of a classical tax haven for some types of business especially for non-UK residents and is therefore classified as an OFC by some authors such as Park and Zwick, 1985. However, its role is wider than most OFCs, thus the term Global Finance Centre is preferred.
9. Russian banks are also setting up in Cyprus: by mid 1994 there were 10 Russian offshore banks in the island (Theodoulou 1994).
10. The investment into mainland China probably took place using different layers of offshore holding companies given that direct investment from Taiwan is politically somewhat difficult.
11. This is suggested from local data being collected by John Christensen, Assistant Economic Adviser to the States of Jersey. Private communication to the author, 22 May 1995.
12. As already noted this is somewhat ironic as tax avoidance or evasion are differently defined depending on where you are in the world. In this case, the OFC host whilst condoning "tax planning" for non-residents, makes the same activity illegal for its own residents!

314   MARK P. HAMPTON

13. This was set up in 1989 to combat the increasing international problem of money laundering.

References

Adonis, A. and Jack A. OECD to press for anti-corruption laws. *Financial Times*, 21 March, 1995.

Atkinson, D. Never-never land lives, *The Guardian*, 18 February, 1995.

Baldacchino, G. Bursting the Bubble: the Pseudo-Development Strategies of Microstates. *Development and Change*, vol. 24, 1993, no. 1, 29–51.

The Banker. Mediterranean Banking: Place in the Sun, vol. 142, October, 1992: 48–50.

The Banker. Labuan promises that little extra, "Asia Notes", vol. 143, March, 1993: 21.

(BBC) British Broadcasting Corporation. *Panorama*, current affairs programme broadcast on BBC-1, 1989, 10 April.

BBC. *Dirty Money 2: The Wild East*, documentary programme broadcast on BBC-1, 1994, 13 September.

Bennett, K. Economic decline and the growth of the informal sector: the Guyana and Jamaica experience *Journal of International Development*, vol. 7, 1995, no. 2, 229–242.

Bertram, I. and Watters, R. The MIRAB economy in South Pacific Micro-states *Pacific Viewpoint*, no. 26, part. 3, 1985: 497–519.

Bloch, J. and Fitzgerald, P. *British Intelligence and Covert Action*. London: Junction Books, 1983.

Boyce, J. The revolving door? External debt and capital flight: a Philippine case study *World Development* vol. 20, 1992, no. 3, 335–349.

Browne, C. *Economic Development in Seven Pacific Island Countries*. Washington DC: IMF, 1989.

Burns, J. Prevention and Detection: Mafia gangs target the West. Survey of Fraud, *Financial Times*, 18 October, 1994.

Clarke, T. and Tigue, J. *Dirty Money*. USA: Millington Books, 1976.

Coulbeck, N. *The Multinational Banking Industry*. London: Croom Helm, 1984.

The Daily Telegraph. 12 years for lawyer who helped launder Brink's-Mat raid £ 7 million. 8 July, 1988.

Diamond, W. and Diamond, D. *Tax Havens of the World*, vol. 3, 1990.

Diaz-Alejandro, C. Latin American debt: I don't think we are in Kansas anymore *Brookings Papers on Economic Activity*, no. 2, 1984: 335–403.

Doggart, C. *Tax Havens and their uses* (Revised edition) London: Economist Intelligence Unit, 1993.

Dolman, A. *Paradise Lost? The Past Performance and Future Prospects of Small Island Developing Countries*. In: Dommen P, Hein E (Eds) States, Microstates and Islands. London: Croom Helm, 1985.

Dooley, M., Heikie, W., Tyron, R. and Underwood, J. An analysis of external debt positions of eight developing countries through 1990 *Journal of Development Economics*, vol. 21, 1986, no. 3: 283–318.

Doumenge, F. *Viability of Small Island States*. UNCTAD Document TD/B/950, 1983.

Ehrenfeld, R. *Evil Money: Encounters along the Money Trail* New York: Harper Collins, 1992.

Europa World Year Book. 35th Edition, London: Europa Publications, 1994.

Fleck, F.H. and Mahfouz, R. The Multinational Corporation: Tax Avoidance and Profit Manipulation via Subsidiaries and Tax Havens. *Revue Suisse d'Economie politique et de Statistique*, vol. 110, 1974, no. 2, June: 145–160.

Fowder, N. *Industrialisation and Agricultural Diversification in an Island Economy: Mauritius, the African Success Story?* paper at the Development Studies Association Annual Conference, Glasgow, September, 1990.

Friedland, J. How to be inscrutable. Offshore financial institutions scramble to manage Asia's private wealth. Focus: Investing Offshore, *Far Eastern Economic Review*, 5 March: 1992: 29–30.

Gauntlett, P. Doing business is a costly affair. Survey of Vietnam, *Financial Times*, 8 December, 1994.

Germidis, D. and Michalet, C. *International Banks and Financial Markets in Developing Countries*. Paris: Development Centre for OECD, 1984.

Giddy, I. *The theory and industrial organisation of international banking* in The Internationalisation of Financial Markets and National Economic Policy, (Eds) Hawkins, R. et al., Research in International Business and Finance, vol. 3, London: JAI Press, 1983.

Gordon, R.A. (The Gordon Report). *Tax Havens and their Use by US Taxpayers – An Overview*. Washington DC: IRS, 1981.

Grubel, H. Towards a Theory of Free Economic Zones, *Weltwirtschaftliches Archiv*, vol. 118, 1982: 39–61.

Grundy, M. (Ed) *The OFC Report 1994/95* London: Campden Publishing, 1994.

The Guardian. Panel indicts Mr Reagan's "cabal of liars". 19 November, 1987.

The Guardian. Update, 24 April, 1993.

Guernsey Financial Services Commission. *Annual Report*. Guernsey, 1991.

Gulati, S. Capital flight: causes, consequences, and cures *Journal of International Affairs*, vol. 24, 1988, no. 1: 165–185.

Hamilton, A. *The Financial Revolution* Harmondsworth: Penguin, 1986.

Hampton, M.P. *Offshore Finance Centres and Small Island Economies. Can and Should Jersey be Copied?* unpublished Ph.D. thesis, Norwich: University of East Anglia, 1993.

Hampton, M.P. Treasure Islands or Fool's Gold: Can and Should Small Island Economies copy Jersey: *World Development*, vol. 22, 1994, no. 2: 237–250.

Hampton, M.P. Sixties Child? The emergence of Jersey as an Offshore Finance Centre 1955–71. *Accounting, Business and Financial History*, vol. 6, 1996a, no. 1, March: 49–68.

Hampton, M.P. Forthcoming *The Offshore Interface: Tax Havens in the Global Economy* Basingstoke: Macmillan, 1996b.

Harvey, D. *The Condition of Postmodernity* Oxford: Blackwell, 1989.

Hutton, W. Reconstruction the key to PSBR problem *The Guardian* 24 May, 1993.

Hutton, W. *The state we're in* London: Jonathan Cape, 1995.

Hymer, S. *The International Operations of National Firms* unpublished Ph.D. thesis, Cambridge: Massachusetts Institute of Technology, 1960.

International Currency Review. Tax Havens and Funk Money. vol. 15, 1984, no. 2: 15–26.

Isle of Man Financial Supervision Commission. *Annual Report*. Isle of Man, 1992.

Jardine Matheson Trust Corporation. *Worldwide Asset Protection*. Jersey, 1991.

Jersey Evening Post (JEP). Commons demand over company's "Irangate" link. 14 July, 1987.

JEP. Commercial Relations satisfied with local end of KMS operation. 15 July, 1987.

JEP. African chief: Court orders directors to disclose information. 21 December, 1989.

JEP. Offshore Roundup, 10 March, 1990.

Jersey Weekly Post (JWP). Brinks-Mat gold laundered through Jersey. 21 April, 1988.

JWP. Baby Doc Court case involves 120 m dollars. 7 July, 1988.

JWP. World wide love of Jersey. 2 February, 1989.

Johns, R. *Tax Havens and Offshore Finance: A Study in Transnational Economic Development*, London: Frances Pinter, 1983.

Johns, R. and Le Marchant, C. *Finance Centres: British Isle Offshore Development since 1979*. London: Pinter, 1993.

Katz, I. and Cumming-Bruce, N. Torrents of abuse. *The Guardian*, 2 March, 1994.

Kindleberger, C. *Power and Money-the Economics of International Politics and the Politics of International Economics*. London: Macmillan, 1970.

Kochan, N. and Pym, H. *The Guinness Affair*. London: Christopher Helm, 1987.

Kochan, N. Cleaning up by cleaning up *Euromoney* April, 1991: 73–77.

316   MARK P. HAMPTON

Langer, M. *Practical International Tax Planning* (3rd edition) New York: Practising Law Institute, 1988.

Lessard, D. and Williamson, J. *Capital Flight, the problem and policy responses* Washington DC: Institute for International Economics, 1987.

McCarthy, I. Offshore Banking Centers: Benefits and Costs. *Finance and Development*, vol. 16, 1979, no. 4, December: 45–48.

Mendelsohn, M. *Money on the Move* New York: McGraw-Hill, 1980.

Montagnon, P. Weak claws of a tiger cub: Vietnam needs more reform, not money, *Financial Times*, 7 February, 1995.

Murphy, K., Shleifer, A. and Vishny, R. Why is rent-seeking so costly to growth? *The American Economic Review*, vol. 83, 1993, no. 2: 409–414.

Naylor, R. *Hot Money and the Politics of Debt* London: Unwin-Hyman, 1987.

Nyatepe-Coo, A. External disturbance, domestic policy responses and debt accumulation in Nigeria *World Development*, vol. 21, 1993, no. 10: 1621–1631.

OECD. *International Tax Avoidance and Evasion – Four Related Studies*. Paris, 1987.

Offshore Finance Magazine, (OFM) Jersey: A Special Report, December: 27–37, 1991.

Park, Y. and Zwick, J. *International Banking in Theory and Practice* Reading, (Mass.): Addison-Wesley, 1985.

Peagam, N. Treasure Islands. May, *Euromoney Supplement*, 1989.

Phillips, E. and Pugh, D. *How to get a Ph.D.* Milton Keynes: Open University Press, 1987.

Picciotto, S. *International Business Taxation* London: Weidenfeld and Nicolson, 1992.

Powell, G.C. *Economic Survey of Jersey*, Jersey: Bigwoods, 1971.

Roberts, S. *The Local and the Global: the Cayman Islands and the International Financial System*, unpublished Ph.D. thesis, USA: Syracuse University, 1992.

Roberts, S. *Fictitious Capital, Fictitious Spaces: the Geography of Offshore Financial Flows* in Corbridge, S. Martin, R. and Thrift, N. (eds) Money, Power and Space. London: Basil Blackwell, 1994.

Robinson, J. *The Laundrymen* London: Simon and Schuster, 1994.

Rule, J. *Albion's People. English society, 1714–1815* London: Longman, 1992.

Sampson, A. *The Money Lenders*. Sevenoaks: Coronet Books, 1982.

Sarver, E. *The Eurocurrency Handbook* (2nd edition) New York: New York Institute of Finance, 1990.

Skully, M. *Financial Institutions and Markets in the South Pacific: a Study of New Caledonia, Solomon Islands, Tonga, Vanuatu and Western Samoa*. London: Macmillan, 1987.

Spitz, B. *Tax Havens Encyclopedia* London: Butterworths, 1990.

States of Guernsey. *Guernsey Statistics*. Guernsey, 1992.

States of Jersey. *Annual Report to the States of Jersey by the Economic Adviser.* Jersey: States Printers, 1991.

States of Jersey. *Statistical Digest*. States Printers, Jersey, 1993.

States of Jersey. *Statistical Review* Jersey: States Printers, 1994.

The Sunday Times. The Artful Dodgers. 21 October, 1990.

Tett, G. Russian money aids a bear market: two years after the collapse of the Soviet Union a new breed of spender is coming to London. *Financial Times*, 7 February, 1994.

Theobald, T. Offshore Branches and Global Banking – one bank's view *Columbia Journal of World Business*, vol. 16, part 4, Winter, 1981: 19–20.

Theodoulou, M. Cyprus surrenders to Russian invasion – nobody hurt. *The Observer*, 8 May, 1994.

Thrift, N. *On the Social and Cultural Determinants of International Financial Centres: the case of the City of London* in Corbridge, S., R. Martin and N. Thrift (eds) Money, Power and Space. London: Basil Blackwell, 1994.

The Times. Brinks-Mat: the bullion trail. July 8, 1988.

Tyson, L. KMT makes sure the party is not over: Taiwan's Nationalists seek to continue enjoying the fruits of power, *Financial Times*, 29 November, 1994.

Vos, R. Private foreign asset accumulation, not just capital flight: evidence from the Philippines *Journal of Development Studies*, vol. 28, 1992, no. 3: 500–537.

Walter, I. *Secret Money – the world of international financial secrecy* London: Allen and Unwin, 1985.

Watts, M. *Oil as money: the Devil's excrement and the spectacle of black gold* in Corbridge, S., R. Martin and N. Thrift (eds) Money, Power and Space. London: Basil Blackwell, 1994.

World Bank. *Country Study: Cyprus.* Washington DC, 1987.

Yule, I. (Ed.) *Offshore 94. The Yearbook and Directory of the Offshore Finance Industry.* London: Charterhouse Communications, 1994.

Part V
Exchange and Securities

[28]

FOREIGN EXCHANGE MARKET: STRUCTURE, INTERVENTION AND LIQUIDITY

Gavin BINGHAM*, B.I.S., Basle.

One of the more intriguing paradoxes in international monetary economics is that the scale of official intervention in the exchange market has expanded substantially in recent years despite virtual unanimity among policy makers and academic observers alike that it is bound to be of little avail if not entirely futile (1). Another puzzling, but much more salutary feature of the exchange market is its apparent robustness in the face of serious and repeated financial and real shocks. In the past few years equity markets have been buffeted to a degree without precedent since the 1930s, but foreign exchange markets have been unusually stable despite large swings in real and nominal exchange rates.

The following paper examines the structure and operation of the foreign exchange market to shed some light on the twin issues of the appropriate role of intervention and the impact of market structure on efficiency and stability. It attempts to assess what role intervention can legitimately be expected to play as an instrument of central bank policy. A second aim is to consider what consequences some proposed new practices such as the extensive netting of exchange rate contracts may have on the operation of the market.

The strategy is to look behind the broad macro-economic determinants of exchange rates into the anatomy of the market. In other words the paper is based on the presumption that understanding the micro-structure of the market is essential both for assessing the appropriate role for intervention and for analysing the robustness of the market.

---

* *The views expresses in this paper are purely personal and do not necessarily reflect those of the BIS or any other institution.*
(1) *»...intervention solely on its own can at best only stabilise short term situations and does not have a permanent impact on exchange rates.» Alan Greenspan, Humphrey Hawkins testimony before the US House of Representatives, July 1990.*

G. BINGHAM

The paper is organised in the following manner. The first section describes the structure and functioning of the market, focusing in particular on how its organisation affects price formation, transactions costs and liquidity. The second section briefly and selectively reviews the vast literature on exchange rates and the exchange market. The relationship between turnover, volatility and bid-ask spreads is examined in the third section, and the fourth and final one draws a few conclusions about the role of intervention and the effects of increasing turnover which might follow upon changes in market practices.

1. THE FOREIGN EXCHANGE MARKET

The foreign exchange market can justifiably be considered the deepest and most active international financial market in the world (2). In April 1989 total turnover amounted to $650 billion per day, having grown by over 100% in the three years since the volume of transactions in this market was previously gauged (see Tables 1 and 2). Impelled by the continuing liberalisation of exchange control, by the increasing sophistication of other market participants in managing their risks and by major advances in telecommunications and data processing technology, total foreign exchange market turnover expanded at a much faster pace than either world trade or international banking activity. Transactions presumably have continued to grow since the 1989 survey, but anecdotal evidence suggests that the pace has slackened.

The market in foreign exchange is predominantly a wholesale market, with transactions between banks and other market makers accounting for a good four-fifths of total turnover. Partly for this reason most exchange market transactions are financially rather than commercially driven. Decisions on how to fund particular activities and how to deploy financial wealth often generate exchange market deals. Other foreign exchange transactions are the result of various hedging, arbitrage and position-taking activities. Moreover, since liquidity is ensured by the continuous quotation

(2) See BIS (1989) for information on the size and nature of transactions in the foreign exchange market in April 1989 and a comparison with turnover in March 1986.

FOREIGN EXCHANGE MARKETS

of two-way prices by dealers, some transactions occur when individual traders attempt to square their positions after executing orders they receive in their capacity as market makers. The substantial volume of transactions of financial character suggests that there are a large number of traders with heterogeneous expectations.

Given the significance of financially related transactions, it should not be surprising that foreign trade can account for only a small fraction of total exchange market business. In April 1989 exchange market turnover exceeded foreign trade by a factor of about ten to one in countries with inactive exchange markets and by a factor of well over a hundred to one in some of the offshore financial centres. In countries with the largest foreign currency markets, turnover exceeds foreign trade by a factor of 25 to 85.

The US dollar is by far the most important currency in the market. It figures in about 90% of all transactions, leaving only 10% for deals not involving the dollar on either side of the transaction (see Table 3). One of the reasons why the dollar bulks so large in the market is that it serves as the vehicle currency. Since those who wish to buy or sell third currencies, particularly minor ones, must first buy or sell dollars, its share in total transactions is far greater than would be warranted by its role as an invoicing currency or as a currency of denomination in international banking and capital market transactions.

At first sight the use of a vehicle currency seems rather wasteful since at least two deals are needed for any «final transaction», irrespective or whether it is undertaken for commercial, financial or risk management purposes. However, a vehicle currency is used for essentially the same reasons that money is employed as a medium of exchange in national economies. It eliminates the necessity for the «double coincidence of wants» required for barter. It greatly reduces search costs and waiting time and makes for greater depth in the market for the vehicle currency, thus lowering transactions costs and facilitating decentralised transactions between

G. BINGHAM

pairs of individuals (3).

The dollar became the vehicle currency in the post-World War II years because it was the only major currency not hampered by extensive exchange controls. It could be freely used in exchange market transactions even though foreign trade was often denominated in other currencies. The dollar's replacement of sterling as the principal vehicle currency has started in the post-World War I period and can be attributed to the geopolitical ascendency of the United States. The persistent balance-of-payments deficits of the United States after World War II, first on combined current and long-term capital account and then on current account alone, ensured that there was a continuous net increase in the supply of dollar assets available to foreigners. However, the unrestricted ability to make adjustments in stocks of dollar assets and liabilities was more important than the change in the net external position of the country.

There is one further reason why the dollar dominates exchange market trading. It is the only currency in which there are deep and active markets in a full range of low-risk financial instruments. Here again a chronic deficit, this time of the central government, has played an important role. In other countries the range of government debt is much narrower and secondary markets in public sector paper are much thinner. Those who wish to use non-dollar currencies may have to hold bank claims. This exposes them to greater credit risk, risk that has been growing because of the deterioration in the quality of assets held by banks and pressure on their profits.

The operation of payments systems may also have some bearing on the attractiveness of a currency as a transactions medium in the interbank market. One of the reasons the dollar has remained com-

---

(3) *See Jones (1976) for a discussion of why the unconcerted action of separate individuals may lead to the emergence of a medium of exchange. His reasoning applies equally well to the use of a vehicle currency. Krugman (1980) considers the relationship between transactions costs and the deviation of cross rates from direct exchange rates. See also Chrystal (1984).*
(4) *See BIS (1990b).*

FOREIGN EXCHANGE MARKETS

petitive as a vehicle currency is that the interbank clearing and settlement systems in the United States were rationalised earlier than those in other countries. For example, CHIPS, the multilateral net settlement system for the members of the New York Clearing House Association, was established in 1971, thirteen years before CHAPS, its London counterpart. Subject to bilateral credit limits and net debit limits on each participant's position vis-à-vis the clearing house, intraday credit is available and same day settlement for deals between members has been provided since 1981 (4).

Although the Deutsche Mark and the yen still account for only a small proportion of total transactions, their relative importance has been increasing in recent years. This is in part because direct cross-currency dealing in these two currencies has become feasible. Not only have the markets in assets denominated in these two currencies expanded in the wake of the relaxation of various restrictions and the gradual reduction of collusion among the dominant institutions in the markets, but the threshold for establishing a dealing infrastructure has been exceeded. The volume of transactions in these two currencies has grown so large that it now pays major banks to maintain desks quoting direct cross rates.

It is noteworthy that the increased use of the Deutsche Mark and the yen in the exchange market has not been accompanied by current-account deficits in the countries of issue. Indeed, both Germany and Japan have tended to run fairly large surpluses in recent years. Although the extensive use of a currency in the exchange market may, by augmenting demand for the currency as a transactions or settlement medium, make it easier (or cheaper) to finance a balance-of-payments deficit, a current-account deficit is by no means a necessary condition for the expanded use of the currency. As was indicated above, the ability to make adjustments in the stock of claims denominated in the currency in question is far more important. In fact, in the case of Germany,the country of issue of the second most important currency, (5) even capital-account flows

(5) *The Deutsche Mark and the Japanese yen were shown to be of equal importance in the April 1989 survey of the exchange market, but Germany did not have data on exchange market turnover in that month, and the figures understate the importance of the Deutsche Mark.*

G. BINGHAM

have been perverse. In recent years this country has experienced a net outflow of the short-term banking funds commonly involved in exchange market transactions. However, the stock of banking assets and liabilities underlying the net balance-of-payments flow is so large that there have been sufficient Deutsche Mark assets of a suitable nature to permit the expansion of exchange market trading.

Market structure, price formation and transactions costs

The foreign exchange market is a market without a specific locus operating on the basis of a number of conventions and practices which have evolved over the years. It is also a truly international market in that deals always involve at least one foreign currency. Moreover, counterparties are often located in another country and may be of the nationality of a third country. Because of its international character it is largely an unregulated or, more precisely, a self-regulated market, with codes of conduct sometimes being issued by the authorities in individual centres.

Nonetheless, the exchange market is highly dependent on national institutions regulated or even administered by the authorities. For example, the delivery of the individual currencies involved in a foreign exchange transaction typically takes place through the payments systems of the two countries whose currencies are exchanged, no matter the location or nationality of the counterparties to the deal. For example, a transaction involving the US dollar generally involves transferring dollars through CHIPS and FEDWIRE from the bank account of the seller of dollars to the bank account of the buyer. The other leg of the transaction will involve a reverse transfer in, say, Germany of Deutsche Mark from the account of the buyer of dollars to that of the seller. The reliance on the payments systems of individual countries means that the stability and integrity of the global foreign exchange market depend not only on the soundness of the individual counterparties but also on the robustness of national payments systems and the maintenance of full convertibility.

FOREIGN EXCHANGE MARKETS

The interbank foreign exchange market is what is sometimes termed a dealer's market. In other words prices are not determined by auction or open outcry. Instead bilateral deals are concluded directly between different counterparties. Brokers, who in general do not deal on their own account but quote prices only when a dealer has indicated his willingness to buy or sell a certain amount of foreign exchange at a given price, provide anonymity in the interbank market. In this way they contribute to the depth and breadth of the market. Traditionally there has been no central counterparty standing between the two principals, but the growing popularity of exchange traded currency options and futures and the recently mooted establishment of multilateral netting arrangements could alter this situation. If this were to occur, ensuring the soundness of such a central counterparty would become critical for maintaining systemic stability (6).

By being willing to buy and sell at pre-announced prices, dealers or market makers provide liquidity, or what is sometimes called «immediacy», to the market. In other words they make it possible for the ultimate agent (and also other dealers) to buy and sell without an ultimate counterparty being present at the exact moment the deal is concluded. Market makers, of course, seek compensation for providing this service and earn profits through the bid-ask spread. Although this spread is quite low, the prices at which market makers undertake to buy and sell foreign exchange are not quite as good as those that, at least in theory, could be obtained by an agent willing to search for an «ultimate agent» with which to do the deal.

The nature of the good traded, the number of traders, their location and motivations for dealing and the information at their disposal all have a major bearing on the structure of a market. Dealer markets tend to emerge when the asset in question is freely negotiable, the terms are standardised and credit risk is low or can easily be ascertained (7).

(6) See BIS (1990c).
(7) See Bingham (1990).

G. BINGHAM

If there are a large number of reputable buyers and sellers actively trading in widely disparate locations, intermediaries are more likely to make markets since there is then greater likelihood that an unwanted position will be eliminated through a «spontaneous» offsetting order and it is less likely that two «ultimate agents» can find each other without the aid of an intermediary.

The propensity to make markets will be greatest in markets where the scope for insider dealing is limited and «uninformed» trading for liquidity, hedging or speculative purposes is extensive. When insider dealing is rampant, market makers will be compelled to set wide spreads to compensate themselves for the losses that may arise when they deal with those who have privileged information. In extreme conditions, they may even cease to make markets. On the other hand, market making will be feasible if there are many agents who wish to trade but have only publicly available information at their disposal. Not only will the likelihood of «crossed orders» grow, but market makers will have more information on order flow and potential supply and demand, which will enable them to set finer bid-ask spreads. This in turn may stimulate further trading.

Simply setting out these requirements makes it understandable why the interbank foreign exchange market is a «dealer market». The good is standardised and credit risk is negligible. Counterparty risk in the interbank market is both small and predictable.

There are a large number of agents located throughout the world wishing to conclude deals rapidly, and the scope for insider dealing is limited. Indeed, perhaps the only significant form of such dealing in the foreign exchange market is intervention purchases and sales of central banks which can be presumed to have privileged information about the future course of short-term interest rates.

The cost of transacting in the wholesale market is the bid-ask spread (8). For small deals in the retail market, commissions and

(8) *See Demsetz (1968) for a discussion of the cost of transacting.*

FOREIGN EXCHANGE MARKETS

fees may be important; in addition there is the opportunity cost of forgone interest in the period running up to the value date and, if the account which is credited pays less than a market rate, the lost interest income from using a current account.

To be precise, the ex post cost of purchasing and then selling foreign exchange - or any other asset - is not the bid-ask spread, but the difference between the price aid and the price received. Since both bid and ask rates as well as the difference between them are constantly changing, the spread prevailing in the market at any one time will not necessarily reflect the transactions costs confronting a market participant. Indeed it will do so only under quite strict and unrealistic conditions, namely that the holding period is infinitely short or that there is no trend in the exchange rate over the holding period and the bid-ask spread remains constant.

Measuring the bid-ask spread is not as easy as might first be thought in such a deep and active market. Firstly, as was mentioned above, posted bid-ask prices are not necessarily the ones at which deals are struck. Secondly, there are many dealers quoting prices, and by the very nature of the process of competition, their prices will differ slightly form one another. The economically relevant bid-ask spread - the difference between the highest bid and the lowest ask price available within the decision period of an agent - is not necessarily reflected in the quotations of an individual bank nor on the screens of the major quotation services. Thirdly, the bid-ask spread is not constant. Individual dealers change it depending upon whether they are aggressively trying to alter a position or simply maintaining their presence in the market. The release of a major economic indicator or an unexpected political event augmenting uncertainty can lead to quite considerable changes in bid-ask spreads over the course of a single day.

Table 4 shows interbank bid-ask spreads vis-à-vis the US dollar for a variety of currencies in April 1989, a month largely free of major macro-economic or political shocks. The data were taken from two separate sources, but relate to quotations of individual dealers, not to the prices at which trades were actually consum-

G. BINGHAM

mated nor to the market spread. Both are monthly averages of daily observations, and are snapshots of the market taken at different times of the day. To facilitate comparison across currencies, the spreads are expressed in terms of basis points rather than in the points used by foreign exchange dealers.

Several striking features of the market are evident. Firstly, spreads vary quite considerably from hour to hour even when measured as daily averages over the month. It would also appear that for most currencies the spread is lower at the close of trading in London than at 3 p.m. However, this may simply be a statistical artefact. The data for 3 p.m. are the quotations of a single London clearing bank which may not be aggressively dealing in all currencies at that hour. On the other hand, the close of business data reflect the most recent quotations of a number of different banks. Because the end-of-day quotations are drawn from a larger pool of market makers, it is more likely that they reflect the best prices available. However, it is also possible that rates quoted at the end of the day after dealers have squared their positions and passed their books on to New York are less representative than those quoted at other times of the day.

The differences across currencies in the size of the bid-ask spread are substantial. By and large, spreads tend to be smaller for the most actively traded currencies, but the relationship is not strict. They range between 3 and 6 basis points for the major currencies and extend to 8 basis points for some of the smaller ones. The spread for the yen seems fairly large in April 1989, but this may be attributed to uncertainty about the return on yen-denominated assets. There were widespread expectations that the Japanese discount rate would be raised. Although this did not occur until May, it affected exchange market trading in the preceding month.

The two outlying observations are for the Hong Kong dollar with an exceptionally small spread and the Australian dollar with an unusually large one. In both cases exchange rate variability may have been a factor. The Hong Kong dollar is pegged to the US dollar so there is virtually no risk associated with US dollar/Hong

FOREIGN EXCHANGE MARKETS

Kong dollar deals. On the other hand, the Australian dollar is considered by exchange dealers to display exceptional volatility vis-à-vis the US dollar (9). The Asian market was also closed at the time the spreads were measured. For minor currencies not actively traded in the three major centres, spreads widen when the local market is closed.

2. EXCHANGE RATE DETERMINATION: THEORY AND EVIDENCE (10).

Explanations of exchange rate behaviour need to account for a number of different phenomena: why the price of one currency is what it is in terms of another, why there are long-standing departures from purchasing power parity, why exchange rates show a pronounced tendency to overshoot in the medium term and sometimes display considerable short-term volatility, and what role exchange market intervention can legitimately be expected to play.

Most theories of exchange rate determination can be placed in one of two categories. Theories making use of the national income and flow of funds accounting framework are macro-economic in orientation. Examples include the early theories seeking to explain exchange rates in terms of trade flows and aggregate demand and supply conditions as well as what might be termed the current consensus model based on asset market conditions. The second class of model consists of theories that view the exchange market as any other market, where prices are determined by demand and supply but where restrictions implied by aggregation into national income accounting aggregates play no role. Work on exchange rate determination in the efficient markets tradition falls into the second category. It would of course be unjust to accuse either tradition of failing to recognise the insights of the other. Macro-economic

(9) *However, when volatility is measured using the standard deviation of logarithmic differences in daily exchange rate quotations, the Australian dollar/US dollar exchange rate is no more unstable than that of the major European currencies. See Chart 2.*
(10) *This section attempts to bring together in a brief and synoptic fashion the vast and sometimes contradictory literature on exchange rate determination. It makes no pretence at being exhaustive but does strive to give a fair and accurate account of the evolution of current consensus views on exchange rate determination and the effectiveness of intervention.*

G. BINGHAM

models often exploit demand and supply relationships just as micro-economic theories do, though ones that are highly aggregate, and the monetary and portfolio balance approaches are derived from theories with solid micro-economic foundations.

Macro-economic theories: the genealogy of the current consensus view

Models that seek to relate the exchange rate to macro-economic «fundamentals» such as trade flows or relative asset supplies have evolved as international economic relations have developed. The early theories which saw exchange rates as being determined essentially by trade flows and macro-economic conditions («domestic absorption») were conceived of at a time when current-account transactions dominated international economic relations. They were eventually supplanted by views of exchange rate determination stressing the importance of capital flows as capital movements became more important. The theories formulated at that time, such as the ones associated with Mundell and Fleming which built upon the fact that the flow recorded in both the current and the capital account affect the balance of payments, were in turn supplemented by monetary models that took into account the fact that exchange rates are the relative prices of stocks of national monies and that flow equilibria of the national income accounting framework should not be viewed in isolation from stock equilibria. As international transactions in bonds and other securities increased, it was recognised that it was useful to look beyond national monies and to incorporate non-monetary assets into the analysis, particularly if agents were risk averse and not inclined to hold assets denominated in foreign currency unless they received adequate compensation for the risk of exchange rate changes.

The portfolio balance models with their long and august lineage may be viewed as the mainlaine, «consensus» macro-economic theory of exchange rate determination. The monetary approach, either with or without the sticky goods prices used to account for overshooting, can be seen as a special case of the portfolio balance model in which foreign and domestic bonds are perfect substi-

FOREIGN EXCHANGE MARKETS

tutes. Even the now defunct theories stressing imports and exports of goods can be seen as special cases of this model, as the flows of goods produced from physical capital controlled or financed by financial assets generate the exports and imports that are recorded in the current account.

As useful as they are, the macro-economic models suffer from several shortcomings. Firstly, econometric evidence suggest that their ability to explain the historical pattern and future course of exchange rates is limited (11). Any one model works well for some historical periods but not for others. In particular the ability of these theories to explain exchange rate determination in conditions of generalised floating appears to be deficient. More damagingly, these models are substantially less successful than naive random walk models in generating accurate out-of-sample forecasts. Secondly, although some of the macro-economically inspired theories provide a plausible explanation of the more striking phenomena in the exchange market such as persistent departures from purchasing power parity and the medium-term overshooting of exchange rates, they often have to rely heavily on various dei ex machina such as sticky prices in the goods market.

Micro-economic approaches: efficiency, price formation and the micro-structure of the market

Partly because of the shortcomings of the macro-economic models, attention has been given to micro-economic explanations of exchange rate determination. Unfortunately many of these models have not been much more successful. The first studies spawned by the efficient markets literature found that the exchange market was not «efficient» on the joint assumption of risk neutrality and rationality. Efforts to flesh out the analysis by examining the intuitively appealing proposition that their failure could be attributed to risk premia demanded in a climate of considerable uncertainty about the future course of exchange rates in the post-1973 world of floating, showed that risk premia, if they existed, were small or

(11) *See e.g. MacDonald and Taylor (1989) for a review of some of the empirical evidence.*

G. BINGHAM

insignificant. For this reason attention has been shifted to the other leg of the argument: trying to find some plausible explanation for presumed «irrationality», i.e. of the fact that agents appear not to make use of all available information.

One such explanation points to speculative bubbles. It may in fact be reasonable to ignore fundamentals in the short term if prices in the market are determined by the hour-to-hour or day-to-day trading strategies of speculators or dealers. In such a market there will be multiple equilibria, each depending upon beliefs about the actions of others. Moreover, exchange rates affect consumption, investment and other real economic decisions. Exchange rates that are out of line with today's «fundamentals» may shape the course of economic events so that they are in keeping with the «fundamentals» of tomorrow. In other words, what seems initially to be an unsustainable exchange rate configuration may become sustainable if the world adjusts to it.

Such a view of the exchange market has much to recommend it. Firstly, if there are two classes of traders' «ultimate agents» who base their decisions on the fundamental economic developments and «dealers» or «noise traders» who take a very short-term view and are highly attuned to what other dealers are doing, it is possible to account for both the blatant short and even medium-term departures of exchange rates from levels that would seem justified by the fundamentals and also for the tendency for the fundamentals eventually to re-assert themselves, subject of course to the proviso that prolonged departures of exchange rates from their «economically justified» levels do not affect the underlying equilibrium (12).

Secondly, it helps to explain the curious ambivalence that prevails with respect to exchange market intervention mentioned at the outset. Even though it may be of little avail in the long run, intervention may help to reduce some of the short-term volatility associated with exchange rate bubbles (13). Thirdly, this view pro-

---

(12) *Although this view is the current consensus conception, it was foreshadowed in Keynes' 1936 analysis of speculative markets in the General Theory.*
(13) *See Huang (1981), Meese (1986) and Wadhwani (1984) for empirical evidence on exchange rate volatility and bubbles.*

FOREIGN EXCHANGE MARKETS

vides an alternative to the explanation of medium-term overshooting which stresses differential speeds of price adjustment in the exchange rate and the goods market.

3. OFFICIAL INTERVENTION IN THE EXCHANGE MARKET

Exchange market intervention involves the exchange by the official sector (central bank or Treasury) of domestic currency assets for assets denominated in foreign currency. Such transactions can, and frequently do, entail a change in the balance sheet of the central bank. If the exchange market transaction is not accompanied by any change in domestic monetary conditions, because for example authorities engage in offsetting open market operations, the transaction is said to be sterilised, whereas if it is accompanied by a change in monetary conditions, it is said to be unsterilised. Just what constitutes a «change in domestic monetary conditions» is, however, open to interpretation. It depends on the authorities'operating procedures and intermediate targets as well as on economic agents'expectations. In what follows we will assume for purposes of exposition that the authorities use money market interest rates as their operating target.

Moreover, even when the conceptual issues are sorted out, determining whether a given official exchange market operation is sterilised or not is not at all straightforward. In any given accounting period central banks may engage in numerous and sometimes offsetting transactions in both the foreign exchange and domestic money market, and it may not be possible to determine precisely which operation in the domestic money market «sterilises» a sale or purchase of foreign exchange. Moreover central banks may decide to alter monetary conditions for reasons of their own totally unrelated to events in the foreign exchange market so that, even if there is an ex post change in monetary conditions following official intervention, it may not mean that the exchange market operation was undertaken in order to influence domestic monetary conditions. In fact most monetary authorities make decisions about monetary conditions independently from their decisions to intervene in the foreign exchange market. The former decisions are in

G. BINGHAM

general strategic whereas the latter are tactical. Even in small countries according exchange rates a pivotal role, decisions about the market segment (foreign exchange or domestic money market) in which a transaction is carried out are secondary. For this reason, it is reasonable to treat exchange market intervention as sterilised, which will be the presumption in the following discussion. Such an approach provides a strong test for the effectiveness of intervention. If «sterilised» intervention is effective, a fortiori intervention that is not - intervention which affects domestic monetary conditions - is likely to be still more so.

Mention has been made of the somewhat curious ambivalence that prevails with respect to intervention. Despite the widely held view that it is devoid of any real significance, intervention has not been abandoned and is in fact one of the principal focuses of day-to-day international policy co-ordination. A flippant and somewhat cynical interpretation would be that this is very much a consequence of intervention's impotence. Countries may be willing to «co-ordinate» their policies - abdicate some of their sovereignty - for the sake of international goodwill if their concrete actions undertaken in the name of co-ordination have no real impact.

A second and more substantive explanation relates to differences in time horizons. Intervention may lack significance in the long run but may still be a serviceable tactical device for influencing the tenor of the market in the short run. Moreover, it may not be meant to alter exchange rates so much as to enable the authorities to take the pulse of the market, to maintain orderly market conditions and to provide information to major market participants about official attitudes and policies.

Channels of influence : portfolio adjustment, expectations and uncertainty

There are several ways in which intervention may affect market participants. In the portfolio balance model, domestic and foreign bonds are imperfect substitutes and will be held as long as yields adequately reflect risk. By altering relative asset supplies, sales

FOREIGN EXCHANGE MARKETS

and purchases of foreign currency by the official sector affect private sector portfolios. Private wealth-holders will cease making adjustments in their portfolios when the expected risk-adjusted returns on different assets are equal. The rate of return on domestic bonds is the domestic rate of interest while the rate of return on foreign assets consists of the interest earnings plus any foreign exchange rate gains arising from the depreciation of the home currency.

Sterilised intervention leaves interest rates unchanged but tends to alter the relative supply of domestic and foreign bonds available to the private sector when the authorities automatically offset their operations in the foreign exchange market through open market operations involving public sector debt. Assuming that there is no exogenous change in demand for bonds and that the Ricardian equivalence proposition does not hold, some change in yields will have to occur to re-establish portfolio balance in holdings of foreign and domestic bonds when the central bank engages in sterilised intervention. Since by assumption interest rates do not change, it is only the exchange rate that can adjust to clear the market.

A second way in which intervention may work is by influencing agents'expectations. In conditions where traders dominate the market in the short run and there are multiple equilibria, any action by the authorities which affects expectations can affect exchange rates. If for example traders alter their expectations about the future interest rates as a result of intervention, spot exchange rates will have to adjust because sterilised intervention by definition has no impact on (current) interest rates and because equilibrium will be maintained only if domestic interest rates equal the expected yield of assets denominated in foreign currency.

A considerable amount of empirical work has been done to determine whether and in what way intervention affects exchange rates (14). Just as most of the tests of portfolio balance models suggest that risk premia are insignificant, so too do most of the studies of the transmission of sterilised intervention through asset

---

(14) *See Edison (1990) for a survey of this evidence.*

G. BINGHAM

substitution imply that intervention is not effective, or, if it is, not of any quantitative significance as a result of portfolio re-adjustment. Studies of the expectations or signalling channel have been fewer in number and more tentative in nature, but their results have been less disappointing. Their main implication is that intervention, even when sterilised, may affect market participants' expectations and thus also exchange rates.

It is useful to give some thought to just how these signalling or expectational effects are transmitted. The conventional explanation is that intervention provides information to market participants on the future course of monetary policy or on the likely impact of future policy actions on the exchange rate. Future monetary conditions, or at least expectations of future monetary conditions, are altered. Because a change in expected future interest rates will often lead to a change in current interest rates as a result of term structure relations, the distinction between sterilised intervention working through the expectations channel and unsterilised exchange market operations affecting domestic monetary conditions is not all that sharp.

There is a third way in which the authorities' exchange market intervention may be used for policy purposes, or at least to influence the scope for monetary policy. If markets work effectively, the ability to conduct monetary policy may be limited by asset substitution and covered interest rate arbitrage (15). The extent to which arbitrage is feasible depends in turn on transactions costs. In the foreign exchange market the principal component of transactions costs is the bid-ask spread, which, as will be shown below, depends on exchange rate volatility. This is because, if exchange rate volatility increases, it is more probable that the market maker will be compelled to assume an unwanted open position. He will therefore tend to seek compensation for this increased risk by widening his bid-ask spread.

By intervening in the market the authorities can attempt either to make swings in exchange rates greater or smaller. In the first

(15) *Allen (1977).*

FOREIGN EXCHANGE MARKETS

instance this will tend to widen the bid-ask spread and therefore give the authorities more scope for conducting their own monetary policy. In the second case, where their actions impart stability to the market and reduce bid-ask spreads, the authorities reduce their ability to conduct monetary autonomous policy but increase the efficiency of the market. In effect they «socialise» some of the risk associated with the operation of the exchange market and thereby provide a service to the community that previously was being performed by the banks.

The decision to adopt one or the other of these two strategies - intervening to increase or to reduce exchange rate volatility - depends on views about the working of the market and the appropriate role of the authorities. If arbitrage between domestic and foreign markets reduces the ability of the authorities to conduct an autonomous monetary policy, and if such policy is felt to add to welfare, intervention which reduces exchange rate volatility will be costly. On the other hand, by decreasing the need for private agents to manage particular types of risk, intervention aimed at reducing very short-term exchange rate fluctuations may augment private sector welfare. And, if the public sector has a comparative advantage in smoothing the market, this may add to aggregate welfare.

In order to be able to assess whether intervention in the market can in fact increase or reduce exchange rate stability, it is useful to look at the actual functioning of the market. If it is already so deep and efficient that such activities are superfluous, exchange market intervention, even when undertaken merely to influence the short-term stability to exchange rates, may be futile. The following section examines the relationship between transactions costs, volatility and the volume of business.

4. MARKET STRUCTURE, VOLATILITY AND LIQUIDITY

While considerable work has recently been done on understanding the relationship between market structure and price formation in the securities markets, less attention has been given to this rela-

G. BINGHAM

tionship in the foreign exchange market, no doubt because it has
not displayed unusual instability whereas large and recurrent disruptions have occurred in equity markets since 1987. The following
sections aim at redressing that imbalance by examining the relationship between volatility, turnover and market liquidity in the
exchange market.

Volatility

There are a wide variety of ways in which to measure volatility,
and the choice of the measure has considerable bearing on the
conclusions that are drawn (16). This paper relies on two simple
and easily understood measures: the coefficient of variation of exchange rates and the standard deviation of logarithmic changes in
exchange rates. The first measure is an indicator of the volatility of
exchange rate levels, while the second one shows the volatility of
relative changes in exchange rates. A currency with a clear underlying trend will display greater volatility when the first measure is
used. If that trend arises because the country has a chronically
higher rate of inflation and if inflation generates uncertainty, using
a measure which reflects this may be appropriate. On the other
hand, if the effect of inflation on exchange rate level is correctly
anticipated, a measure which is neutral with respect to trends is
more suitable.

Charts 1 and 2 show the volatility of daily exchange rates of
various currencies vis-à-vis the US dollar using the two different
measures. Three main features stand out. Firstly, irrespective of
what measure is used, volatility is affected by regime shifts. The
most dramatic illustration of this was the shift in 1973 from the
Bretton Woods system of fixed exchange rates to a floating exchange
rate regime. There was a pronounced, steplike increase in exchange
rate volatility at this time. A similar, although much less marked,
increase in volatility occurred in the mid-1980s, when concern about
the overshooting of the US dollar led the authorities of the principal
countries to foresake their previous policy of benign neglect and to

*(16) See Glassman (1987) and Kupiec (1990) for a discussion of variability measures in
the exchange market and in asset markets more generally.*

FOREIGN EXCHANGE MARKETS

take a public stand, first at the Plaza and then two years later at the Louvre, on exchange rate levels. Although the greater willingness to intervene in exchange markets in evidence at various stages from the mid-1980s onwards might have been expected to impart greater stability to exchange rates, this did not occur. Indeed both indicators of volatility suggest it increased at this time. Uncertainty about the precise policy actions to be taken as well as the widespread doubts about the sustainability of the exchange rate configuration then prevailing appear to have led to greater short-term volatility.

The instability in this period may also be explained in terms of the second feature shown in these tables. Instability seems to be associated with overshooting. Short-term volatility increases when an exchange rate reaches a level that is, at least with the benefit of hindsight, not sustainable. For example the Swiss franc was unusually volatile on both measures at the end of the 1970s, when it first climbed to unprecedented levels in real effective terms and then subsequently fell back.

Finally, there does not seem to be much difference in the degree of stability across currencies. Both major and minor currencies display the same degree of volatility. This suggests that increasing market depth does not dampen exchange rate fluctuations. Such a finding is somewhat surprising in that the accumulation of experience with managing exchange rate risk and the very substantial increase in turnover during this period might both have been expected to reduce volatility. The next section looks more closely at this question, examining the relationship between the turnover and the bid-ask spread.

Turnover and transactions costs

An increased volume of transactions can be expected to reduce the bid-ask spread in the foreign exchange market for several reasons. Firstly, the likelihood that a market maker will be able to cross orders - to match various buy and sell orders - grows as the volume of transactions increases. Since the bid-ask spread is set to

G. BINGHAM

provide compensation both for executing the transaction as well as for the risk associated with having to assume an unwanted open position, crossed trades will be particularly profitable. Eventually, however, competition among market makers for these supernormal profits should drive spreads lower (17). Secondly, the fixed costs associated with dealing will be spread over a larger volume of transactions.

Thirdly, increased dealing augments the information on order flow, reservation prices and latent demand at the disposal of the market maker and may give him an opportunity to earn greater profits on his open position. This could in turn give rise to rein-forcing pressures to lower the spread further to attract additional orders and obtain more information. Fourthly, an increased volume of dealing may reduce the market spread or «touch» (the gap between the best bid price and best ask price) even if the bid-ask spread of each individual market maker remains constant. Individual dealers adjust their bid and ask prices more or less continuously as they consciously attempt to eliminate excessively large (or excessively small) open positions assumed as a consequence of accepting orders from any and all entities. The constant readjustment of open positions will tend to make the market «touch» smaller than any individual market maker's bid-ask spread, even when all dealers have the same forecast of the mid rate. An in-

---

(17) *Black (1989) uses this fact together with the proposition that increased exchange rate volatility will be associated with wider spreads to derive the following relationship between the bid-ask spread (Pa-Pb) and the volume of orders from ultimate agents who are price sensitive (Q):*

$$Pa\text{-}Pb = (a+b)o2p/Q$$

where a and b denote the exogenous supply and demand propensities of market professionals or speculators who alter the amount of currency they offer or demand in response to differences between the price at which the trader in question is willing to deal and market expectations of mean exchange rates, and where O2p is the variance of the price at which the dealer can close out his position around the mid rate.

In other words the spread is postulated to vary directly with the volatility of the exchange rate and inversely with the volume of transactions on the additional assumption that markets are competitive and market makters are risk neutral. See Allen (1977) and Booth (1984) for an analysis of the determination of bid-ask in a world where market makers are risk averse and where the market maker has a monopoly in dealing in foreign exchange.

FOREIGN EXCHANGE MARKETS

creased volume of transactions, when accompanied by more frequent readjustment by market makers, will therefore tend to compress the market spread.

A final factor affecting transactions costs is the size of the market and strength of competition. The turnover in some of the minor currencies or in cross trading between second tier currencies may be so meagre that only a few dealers can justify committing resources to market making. Various barriers to entry such as exchange controls and licensing may also influence the amount of competition. Given the importance of the foreign exchange market, it is striking just how difficult it is to determine empirically the exact relationship between transactions costs, volatility and the volume of transactions. Data on the bid-ask prices quoted by individual banks are available and can be used to measure spreads, but they suffer from the deficiencies mentioned in part 1. Information on exchange rate volatility is somewhat less problematic if one is willing to calculate volatility from mid rate quotations (18). Consistent data on the volume of transactions are available only for representative months every three years, and prior to 1989 only for a restricted number of countries.

Although there is good reason to expect market liquidity to increase as the volume of transaction expands and as exchange rate volatility declines, it is useful to examine the available evidence to see whether this in fact occurs. The most promising approach is to use cross sectional data on the volume of transactions in April 1989 together with information on spreads and volatility. This is far preferable to using data on currency futures turnover to measure volume, which has been done in earlier studies (19). Currency futures account for less than 1% of total exchange market turnover and, being comparatively new, have probably grown more rapidly than other types of foreign exchange market transactions. Table 5 shows the results of regressing spreads, as fairly reasonable proxy

---

(18) *The volatilities of the bid and ask rates for individual currencies are virtually identical, which implies that the use of the mid-rate to measure volatility does not have a material impact on the results.*
(19) *Frankel and Foote (1990).*

G. BINGHAM

for transactions costs, on the volume of transactions and volatility in exchange rates.

Two conclusions are suggested by this exercise, which is robust to the choice of the measure of exchange rate volatility. Firstly there appears to be little relationship between the depth of the market and liquidity as reflected in the width of the bid-ask spread, at least in the industrial countries with comparatively unfettered and active exchange markets. Although all the coefficients for turnover have the expected sign, none is significant. One explanation for this somewhat surprising finding is that in these countries the foreign exchange market is already so deep and that further increases in trading do not lead to falling transactions costs.

The second conclusion is that exchange rate volatility is an important determinant of transactions costs. Spreads tend to increase when exchange rate volatility grows. These two findings have some implications both for the role that intervention can play and for the consequences of the mooted introduction of netting in exchange market transactions.

5. CONCLUSIONS

The analysis of the preceding sections may provide some insights into the appropriate role of exchange market intervention in a world of highly efficient and closely integrated financial markets and the implications for market liquidity of a further growth in exchange market turnover which could follow the widespread adoption of netting in foreign exchange clearing and settlement. To be sure, information on the structure and functioning of the exchange market does not in itself explain the persistent tendency for exchange rates to overshoot in the medium term, but it does suggest that explanations which point to the importance of professional dealers who pay little heed to the fundamentals and pit their skills against other «noise» traders are not contradicted by the facts. The great majority of all financial transactions are interdealer trades and the average maturity of forward deals is very short. Of course this does not imply that intervention, unless used in concert with a wide range

FOREIGN EXCHANGE MARKETS

of other policy instruments, can be of any help in counteracting medium-term overshooting. However, it does suggest that intervention can play a useful role as a minor tactical weapon.

One of the principal findings of this paper is that transactions costs in the foreign exchange market depend positively on short-term (day-to-day) volatility in the market but appear to be unaffected by further increases in market depth. Although official intervention on its own cannot reasonably be expected to produce a sea change in exchange rate trends, astutely timed deals with the appropriate counterparty in the right market segment may easily affect short-term exchange rate volatility. Moreover the authorities are the only true insiders in the foreign exchange market. If their operations generate cumulative expectations on the part of others active in the market, the effects may be far larger than the size of the initial transactions would suggest. Accordingly, it would appear that intervention can be useful either as one part of the overall economic policy strategy or if used on its own as a tactical instrument to influence short-term exchange rate stability.

Having said this, it is important to note that this paper has raised, but not answered, the question of how intervention should be used within the tactical armoury. While it can reasonably be expected to affect transactions costs by altering short-term exchange rate volatility, it is not clear whether it is in the greater public good for the authorities to attempt to impart stability to rates, reduce transactions costs and foster market efficiency, or, in the diametrically opposite vein, to augment exchange rate volatility, reduce the scope for the effortless subtitution of assets and thereby win slightly more room for conducting autonomous monetary policy.

The findings of this paper also offer some insights into the benefits which may accrue from the introduction of multilateral clearing arrangements or the expansion of existing bilateral procedures. By allowing dealers to reduce their intra-day exposures, these changes could lead to further expansion of short-term trading. But by placing a clearing house or a clearing mechanism between various

G. BINGHAM

counterparties, multilateral netting arrangements would mean that the soundness of the system no longer depends principally on the timely performance of contractual obligations by the two counterparties of an exchange market deal, but equally well on the integrity of the clearing and settlement procedures. This in turn requires the appropriate regulatory oversight. The costs of such oversight and of the establishment of a new system should be set against its benefits.

It is striking that, quite in contradiction to expectations, transactions costs do not appear to decline as turnover increases. This may well be because the markets are now so large and deep that a further expansion brings few benefits in the form of economies of scale, increased competition or improved market information. If this is the case, new structures such as multilateral netting arrangements which allow the further expansion of the trading may not generate much additional benefit in the form of greater liquidity or lower transactions costs in the exchange market itself. However, since the participants in the exchange market conduct a wide range of banking and financial business, savings in this area may ultimately have benefits outside the exchange market itself.

REFERENCES

ALLEN, WILLIAM A. (1977): «A Note on Uncertainty, Transactions Costs and Interest Parity», Journal of Monetary Economics, Vol.3, pp.367-369.

BANK FOR INTERNATIONAL SETTLEMENTS (1990a): Survey of Foreign Exchange Market Activity, Basle.

BANK FOR INTERNATIONAL SETTLEMENTS (1990b) : Large-value Funds Transfer System in the Group of Ten Countries, May, Basle.

FOREIGN EXCHANGE MARKETS

BANK FOR INTERNATIONAL SETTLEMENTS (1990c): Report of the Committee on Interbank Netting Schemes of the Central Banks of the Group of Ten Countries, November, Basle.

BINGHAM, T.R.G. (1990): «Securities Markets Systems Stability and Regulation: the Macro-economic Dimension», Journal of International Securities Markets, Vol.4, Summer, pp.121-132.

BLACK, STANLEY W. (1989): «Transactions Costs and Vehicle Currencies», IMF Working Paper 89/96, International Monetary Fund, Washington.

BOOTH, LAURENCE D. (1984): «Bid-Ask Spreads in the Market for Foreign Exchange», Journal of International Money and Finance, Vol.3, pp.209-222.

CHRYSTAL, K. ALEC (1984): «On the Theory of International Money», in John Black and Graeme S. Dorrance eds., Problems of International Finance, New York : St. Martin's Press.

DEMSETZ, HAROLD (1968): «The Cost of Transacting», Quarterly Journal of Economics, Vol.83, pp.143-73.

EDISON, HALI J. (1990): «Foreign Currency Operations: An Annotated Bibliography», International Finance Discussion Paper, N⁻380, Board of Governors of the Federal Reserve System.

FRANKEL, JEFFREY A. AND FOOTE, KENNETH A. (1990): «Chartists, Fundamentalists and Trading in the Foreign Exchange Market», American Economic Review, papers and proceedings, Vol.80, N⁻2, pp.181-185.

GLASSMAN, DEBRA (1987): «Exchange Rate Risk and Transactions Costs: Evidence from Bid-Ask Spreads», Journal of International Money and Finance, Vol.6, pp.479-490.

HUANG, R.D. (1981): «The Monetary Approach to Exchange Rate in an Efficient Foreign Exchange Market: Tests Based on Volatility», Journal of Finance, Vol.36, pp.31-41.

G. BINGHAM

JONES, R.A. (1976): «The Origin and Development of Media of Exchange», Journal of Political Economy, Vol.84, n°4, part 1, pp.757-775.

KRUGMAN, PAUL (1980): «Vehicle Currencies and the Structure of International Exchange», Journal of Money, Credit and Banking, Vol.12, N°3, pp.513-526.

KUPIEC, PAUL H. (1990): «Financial Liberalisation and International Trends in Stock, Corporate Bond and Foreign Exchange Volatilities», Finance and Economics Discussion Series, N°131, Federal Reserve Board, Washington.

MACDONALD, RONALD AND TAYLOR, MARK P. (1989): «Economic Analysis of Foreign Exchange Markets: An Expository Survey» in: MacDonald, Ronald and Taylor, Mark P.: Exchange Rates and Open Economy Macro-economics, Basil Blackwell, Oxford.

MEESE, R.A. (1986): «Testing for Bubbles in Exchange Markets: a Case of Sparkling Rates?», Journal of Political Economy, Vol.94, pp.345-373.

WADHWANI, S.B. (1984): «Are Exchange Rates "excessively" Volatile?», Discussion Paper N‾198, Centre for Labour Economics, London School of Economics.

FOREIGN EXCHANGE MARKETS

Table 1
FOREIGN EXCHANGE MARKET ACTIVITY IN APRIL 1989

Countries and items	Net turnover[1]	Of which:[2]			Net spot turnover[1]	Ratio of exchange market turnover to:	
		Business with customers	Net domestic interbank operations	Cross-border interbank operations		foreign trade	international banking assets
	average daily turnover in billions of US dollars						
United Kingdom	187[3]	26	54[3]	107[3]	(119)	69	3.2
United States	129[3]	10	45[3]	71[3]	81	25	4.5
Japan	115	34	31	47	46	37	1.8
Switzerland[4] [85%] ..	57	9.0	11	36	30	83	9.0
Singapore	55	(6.0)	8.0	(41)	(31)	138	4.8
Hong Kong	49	5.4	11	33	(30)	78	3.0
Australia	30	6.0	7.0	15.0	18	59	·
France[4] [95%]	26[3]	5.0	6.0[3]	15[3]	(15)	12	1.4
Canada	15	4.0	2.7	7.8	6.1	12	4.0
Netherlands	13[3]	1.5	3.1[3]	8.5[3]	7.2	11	1.8
Denmark[4] [90%]	13	1.3	1.8	10	(6.4)	36	12.4
Sweden	13	1.6	1.4	8.7	9.5	23	4.9
Belgium[4] [90%]	10	1.3	1.6	7.6	5.2	9	1.1
Italy[4] [75%]	10	1.4	0.8	8.0	7.6	6	2.0
Other countries[5]	22	1.6	4.4	15	16	13	2.8
Total	744	114	189	431	428	32	3.0
Adjustment for cross-border double-counting	-204				-123		
Total reported net turnover	540				305		
Estimated gaps in reporting	100				55		
Estimated global turnover	640				360		

Note: Figures in parentheses are rough estimates. Totals may not tally owing to rounding.
1 The figures for individual countries indicate turnover net of double-counting arising from local interbank business. The totals at the foot of the table are estimates of turnover net of double-counting arising from both local and cross-border interbank business. 2 The items do not always sum to total net turnover because the classification is not exhaustive. 3 Based on estimates of domestic and cross-border interbank business arranged through brokers. 4 No adjustment for less than full coverage; estimated market coverage is given in square brackets. 5 Bahrain, Finland, Greece, Ireland, Norway, Portugal and Spain.

Source: BIS (1990a).

G. BINGHAM

Table 2
GROWTH OF FOREIGN EXCHANGE MARKET TRANSACTIONS, FOREIGN TRADE AND INTERNATIONAL BANKING ACTIVITY

Countries	Exchange market turnover: percentage changes between March 1986 and April 1989			Exports and imports of goods and services: percentage changes between first quarter 1986 and first quarter 1989	International claims of BIS reporting banks: percentage changes between end-March 1986 and end-March 1989
	Net turnover	Transactions with customers	Spot transactions		
United Kingdom ...	108	221	81	62	40
United States	120	134	134	39	39
Japan	140	111	142	82	203
Canada	58	38	53	44	4
Total	116	136	104	54	76

FOREIGN EXCHANGE MARKETS

Table 3
CURRENCY COMPOSITION OF FOREIGN EXCHANGE MARKET ACTIVITY IN APRIL 1989

Currency	Percentage share in total gross reported turnover
US dollar	90
Deutsche Mark	25
Yen	26
Pound sterling	15
Swiss franc	12
Australian dollar	4
French franc	3
Canadian dollar	2
Ecu	1
Other	22
Memorandum item:	billions of US dollars
Gross average daily turnover in all currencies	932.0

Note: Because each exchange market transaction involves two currencies, the sum of all percentage shares amounts to 200%. The figures understate the share of the Deutsche Mark and other European currencies because comparable data for Germany are not available.

Source: BIS (1990a) and national surveys.

G. BINGHAM

Table 4
AVERAGE DAILY BID-ASK SPREADS FOR SELECTED CURRENCIES VIS-À-VIS THE US DOLLAR IN APRIL 1989

Basis points

Currency	at 3 p.m. [1]	at London close [2]	Average [3]
Deutsche Mark	4.47	3.82	4.14
Pound sterling	5.87	3.97	4.92
Japanese yen	7.57	4.16	5.87
Swiss franc	6.08	4.40	5.24
Singapore dollar	5.13	7.95	6.54
Hong Kong dollar	1.28	2.02	1.65
Australian dollar	12.43	12.00	12.21
French franc	7.91	4.63	6.27
Canadian dollar	8.41	7.99	8.20
Dutch guilder	4.86	3.20	4.03
Danish krone	6.87	3.71	5.29
Swedish krona	7.86	3.81	5.83
Belgian franc	10.48	4.11	7.30
Italian lira	7.29	6.16	6.73
Spanish peseta	8.61	8.18	8.40
Irish pound	10.85	4.94	7.90
Norwegian krone	-	4.63	-
Finnish markka	-	4.77	-
Portuguese escudo	6.26	-	-
Greek drachma	3.95	-	-

1 Quotations by Barclays Bank International at 3 p.m. London time. 2 Quotations listed by Reuters Information Service at the close of the London market. 3 Mean of average daily quotations at 3 p.m. and at the close of the London market.

Source: Data Resources International.

FOREIGN EXCHANGE MARKETS

Table 5
CROSS-SECTION REGRESSION OF EXCHANGE MARKET
BID-ASK SPREADS
ON EXCHANGE RATE VOLATILITY
AND TURNOVER USING DATA APRIL 1989

Constant	Volatility		Turnover	$\bar{R}^2$	Notes
	Changes	Levels			
1.95 (1.44)	8.13 (2.89)		- 0.01 (1.25)	0.31	Volatility measured using log differences in quotations.
5.53 (8.54)			- 0.01 (0.91)	0.01	
1.70 (1.25)	7.94 (2.78)			0.28	
1.94 (1.41)	13.99 (1.69)	- 4.78 (0.76)	- 0.01 (1.30)	0.29	
2.69 (1.95)		5.28 (2.27)	- 0.01 (1.06)	0.20	Volatility measured using coefficient of variation of rates.
1.95 (1.46)	0.08 (2.92)		- 0.01 (1.26)	0.31	Volatility measured using standard deviation of percentage changes in quotations.
2.10 (1.46)	8.34 (2.87)		-0.24 (0.92)	0.28	Log transformation of volumes.

G. BINGHAM

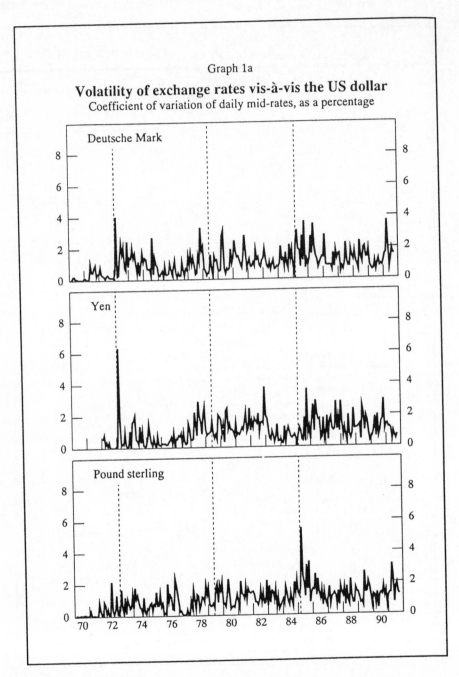

Graph 1a

Volatility of exchange rates vis-à-vis the US dollar
Coefficient of variation of daily mid-rates, as a percentage

FOREIGN EXCHANGE MARKETS

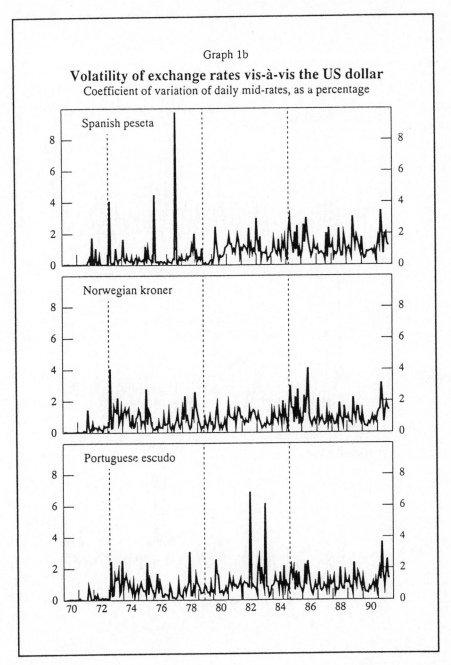

Graph 1b

Volatility of exchange rates vis-à-vis the US dollar
Coefficient of variation of daily mid-rates, as a percentage

G. BINGHAM

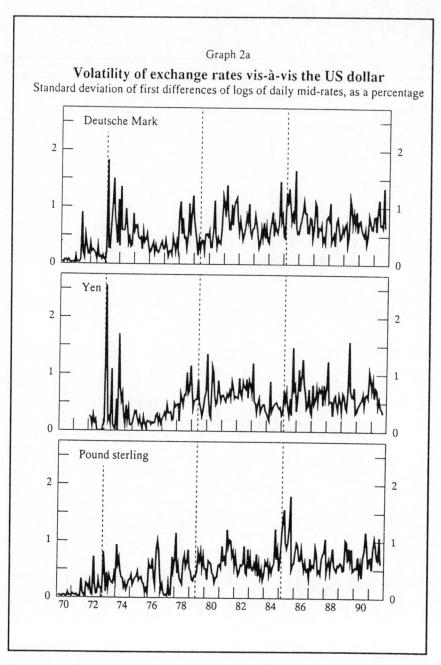

Graph 2a

Volatility of exchange rates vis-à-vis the US dollar
Standard deviation of first differences of logs of daily mid-rates, as a percentage

FOREIGN EXCHANGE MARKETS

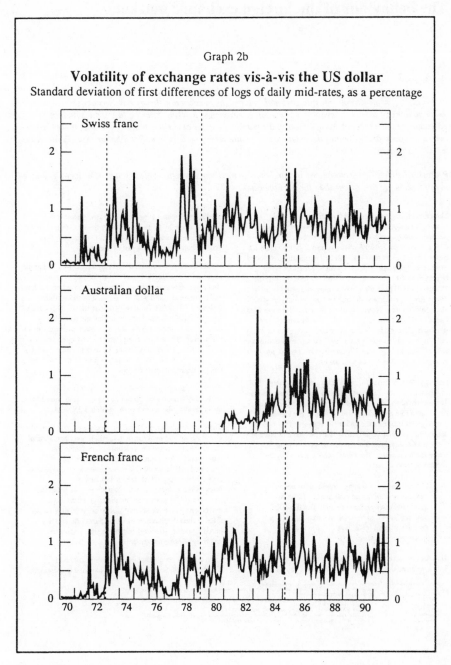

Graph 2b

Volatility of exchange rates vis-à-vis the US dollar

Standard deviation of first differences of logs of daily mid-rates, as a percentage

[29]

The behaviour of the foreign exchange market

By Professor Alan Kirman.[1]

In this article, Alan Kirman considers what developments in economic theory have to contribute to an understanding of the recent evolution of the foreign exchange market. After outlining the standard, efficient-markets *model of the workings of the market, he looks at various reasons why that model has been questioned and examines the extent to which alternative models can offer a better explanation of the market's actual behaviour.*

Professor Kirman was a Houblon-Norman fellow at the Bank in August of last year.[2] The views expressed in this article are his, rather than those of the Bank.

The global foreign exchange (FX) market had a daily turnover of about $1.3 trillion in 1992, corresponding to a net daily turnover of $880 billion; this represents growth of 40% in three years.[3] 60% of this turnover is accounted for by the three main centres—the United Kingdom, the United States and Japan—of which the United Kingdom is the largest, with 60% more turnover than the next market, the United States. The market is becoming increasingly active; on the Reuters electronic dealing system, as many as 40,000 electronic 'conversations' occur per hour and there are 4,000 banks worldwide linked to this system with some 18,000 terminals. The market is also more and more global, with 60% of the daily transactions in 1992 being cross-border and with 80% of the aggregate FX turnover in London, for example, being done by foreign banks.[4]

Globally, 50% of gross foreign exchange transactions involved non-local currencies on both sides of transactions. The growth of the FX market has been much more rapid than that of foreign trade, giving weight to the idea that a growing percentage of the volume is accounted for by dealing for speculative purposes. This has led a number of commentators to argue that the market is becoming intrinsically unstable. The view is characterised by one economist, who says:[5]

> 'These [foreign] exchange transactions began as a means to smooth and facilitate the flows of traditional trade and investment. But this FX 'tail' has grown to be some hundred times larger than the original trade 'dog' . . . FX is a speculators' paradise.'

This does not take account of an alternative view, that the broadening and deepening of the FX market has allowed

market participants to protect themselves against over-exposure by trading with other dealers. In this view, the increased volumes in the FX market simply reflect prudent behaviour on the part of dealers.

Whatever view is correct, the question remains whether the expansion of the market has been stabilising or destabilising. As movements in foreign exchange rates have become larger and more rapid—and with events such as those which followed 'Black Wednesday' (16 September 1992)—there have been calls from some authorities and a number of economists to impose some sort of control or restriction on the market. These have been reinforced by events such as the Swedish government's inability to maintain the level of the krona, even by raising overnight interest rates to 500%, and the depreciation of the lira.

Before considering such calls, however, it is worth examining what recent economic theory has to contribute to understanding these developments in the FX market.

There are a number of questions to be answered. Have the globalisation and increase in volumes in the FX market *of themselves* increased the volatility of exchange rate movements? Are exchange rates less linked to 'fundamentals' than they were, or have the fundamentals themselves changed? If there is less of a link to fundamentals, does that mean that dealers are behaving *irrationally*? In particular, are the large exchange rate movements evidence of irrationality or could they in fact reflect rational behaviour by participants? Would the introduction of 'frictions' into the market reduce the volatility of price movements?

I argue in this article that the increasing size and connectivity of the FX market may have led to increased

(1) Alan Kirman is Professor of Economics at the European University Institute in Florence.
(2) The Houblon-Norman Fund, established by the Bank in 1944, finances academic research into subjects relevant to central banking. More details of the Fund were given in an article in the August 1993 *Quarterly Bulletin.*
(3) The figures here are taken from 'Central bank survey of foreign exchange market activity', a document from the Bank for International Settlements' Monetary and Economic Department, Basle, February 1993, pages 1–42.
(4) Source: 'The foreign exchange market in London', *Quarterly Bulletin,* November 1992, pages 408–17.
(5) From Ohmae, K. *The borderless world,* Harper Business, New York 1990, quoted in Zaher, S. 'Market-makers: A study of the effects of global market integration in the currency trading industry', monograph, School of Management, University of Minnesota, 1994.

volatility. In addition, however, the structure and organisation of the market have to be understood as playing an important role. Recent economic theory, which takes account of the fact that individuals draw information from the actions of others in the market and may imitate the successful, suggests that 'herding' or 'informational cascades' may occur. Nevertheless, this sort of behaviour is by no means necessarily irrational and should not be attributed to some inexplicable market psychology.

Thus both those who argue that the foreign exchange market is now more efficient at revealing underlying imbalances in fundamentals and those who maintain that the intrinsic dynamics of the freer and more open markets have led to greater instability can find comfort from theory and empirical evidence.

One associated argument is as to whether the volatility of markets could be reduced by the introduction of frictions, such as a tax on FX transactions. On this, I suggest that in the light of the evidence we would do better to use our improved understanding of the dynamics of foreign exchange markets, and of the role of their microstructure, to increase the efficiency of interventions to help maintain a certain orderliness, rather than impose restrictions on transactions.

In order to answer the questions posed above, it is necessary to outline the standard, 'efficient markets' model of the foreign exchange market, which suggests that prices should be linked rather strictly to fundamentals and therefore that the globalisation of financial markets should not radically affect prices. I then mention some empirical paradoxes and look at various reasons why this basic model has been questioned, and at whether alternative models offer better explanations of the facts.

The standard efficient-markets model

The behaviour of asset prices in general—and foreign exchange rates in particular—is typically explained by economists by *efficient-market* theories. This term, although used in different ways, basically reflects the following ideas.

The price of an asset should reflect underlying 'fundamentals'. Thus in the case of a stock or share, its price is supposed to reflect the discounted value of all dividends expected in the future and the value of the firm at the end of the life of the claim, if it is for a fixed term.

Secondly, the link between fundamentals and prices is such that all information available about fundamentals—both public and private—should be incorporated into prices. If this is the case, then the only reason for prices to change must be the arrival of completely new information which was not predictable. (If it had been predictable, it would

have been predicted.) Hence asset prices must appear to fluctuate randomly; whether they do has been the subject of extensive debate.

In the case of exchange rates, the efficient-market hypothesis has to be rephrased. Suppose that assets are priced efficiently—in the above sense—in two different countries. Then changes in the exchange rate should effectively equalise the rates of return in both countries: this is so-called 'uncovered interest parity'. It can be objected to on the grounds that it does not take account of the risk involved in such transactions. However, using the forward market allows us to make a risk-free transaction and the forward exchange rate should equalise the rate of return. This is the 'covered interest parity' condition.

In either case, we are back to the original idea: fundamentals determine the rates of return in each country and exchange rates adapt to these. Thus modifications in exchange rates reflect changes in fundamentals. And changes in fundamentals will lead to compensating changes in exchange rates.

One important feature of this approach is that asset values or exchange rates reflect what is *expected* to happen to fundamentals. Since expectations are not measurable, it is clearly not possible to falsify the efficient-market hypothesis directly.

Problems for the efficient-markets model

Yet many of the facts about financial markets seem to be at odds with this kind of theory. Perhaps the most striking is the volatility of asset prices, compared with that of the underlying fundamentals. Despite numerous efforts by economists to explain it, the 'excess volatility' puzzle remains. Why should it be in the case of stocks, for example, that prices are so much more volatile than the associated dividend streams?[1] Once again, it can be argued that the relationship between fundamentals over time is highly 'non-linear' and that small changes in today's values may lead to large changes in the future, thus significantly changing the current price. It is difficult to believe, however, that there could be a sudden change in the fundamentals which would lead agents simultaneously within half a day to the view that returns in the future had gone down by over 20%. Yet this is what would have to be argued for the October 1987 episode on the New York Stock Exchange.[2]

The same is true for sudden and substantial changes in exchange rates. Do they really simply reflect modifications in expectations about future fundamentals? Why does the volatility of exchange rate changes vary over time? How does one reconcile the two ideas frequently expressed by traders, that on the one hand 'fundamentals matter in the long run' but on the other they do not drive exchange rates in the short run?[3]

(1) See Shiller, R J. *Market volatility*. Cambridge Mass: MIT Press, 1989.
(2) Indeed Miller has suggested that substantial changes in the future can result from very small changes in the present, and that such an explanation is not inconsistent with the Crash: see Miller, M H. *Financial innovation and market volatility*. Blackwell, 1991.
(3) See Goodhart, C A E and Figliuoli, L. 'Every minute counts in financial markets'. *Journal of International Money and Finance*, 10, pages 23–52. 1991.

Bank of England Quarterly Bulletin: August 1995

Two things have to be observed before these questions can be addressed. Firstly, changes in prices or exchange rates reflect changes in economic agents' *perceptions* of the future, and not necessarily what will actually occur. Secondly, a clear corollary of the efficient-markets view is that if asset prices change without any obvious change in the fundamentals, some agents must be acting irrationally.

For this reason the sort of empirical puzzles mentioned are frequently explained in terms of market psychology. The implication is that the movements involve some degree of irrationality on the part of those participating in the markets. Sudden changes or departures from fundamentals are taken not as evidence of the inapplicability of efficient-market theories but rather as evidence of a failure of investors or traders to act as rationally as those theories require.

To take an example, in his classic book on market volatility Shiller refers to alternative explanations of price movements as being associated with 'capricious' behaviour or as being 'for no good reason'.[1] His argument to explain 'excess volatility' is that investors may take actions as a result of a movement in asset prices which result in a further change in prices; a sequence of such events may lead to a 'price bubble' which detaches prices from fundamentals. Despite his insistence on the importance of this behaviour, Shiller seems to emphasise the irrationality of such self-induced price movements.

Before considering the argument about irrationality, however, a basic point has to be made. There is no clear consensus concerning the nature of the relationship between fundamentals and prices in many financial markets. In the foreign exchange market, most participants believe in the existence of a relationship between exchange rates and certain macroeconomic fundamentals. But such a relationship is difficult to estimate and may well not be invariant over time, even if one knew which macro variables were important. Thus even without any shock, it is easy to see that there is a potential source of instability. If traders or participants in the market change their view about the nature of the relationship—or about the particular macroeconomic variables which are important—they may, by their very actions, modify the relationship and make it self-fulfilling.

The well known literature on *sunspots* makes this point in an even more striking way.[2] If market agents believe that prices are correlated with sunspots, they will buy and sell accordingly and, as a result, prices will indeed become coordinated with sunspots. Yet one could ask how would this come about, and it can be shown that sensible agents using sensible learning rules may come to believe in the importance of sunspots and that their beliefs will be self-confirming.[3] Thus movements of exchange rates which are not directly correlated to movements in fundamentals are not necessarily the result of irrationality.

An alternative kind of model

What Shiller does show, despite his comments on the irrationality of such behaviour, is the importance of agents' reactions to one another's behaviour. The important point to make is that in financial markets agents do indeed interact directly with one another and not only indirectly through market prices. This apparently innocent remark has significant consequences for the aggregate behaviour of markets. Instead of thinking of a single 'typical' economic agent's response to events, one should consider individuals in a market as not necessarily being homogeneous, and as observing and anticipating the behaviour of other participants. Once one does this, it is much easier to see how a common view can take over a market temporarily and then be replaced by another view.

Once we consider the market as a complex interactive system in which heterogeneous agents with different horizons and different attitudes to risk participate, the price dynamics can be very different from those of more conventional models. Although this sort of idea is familiar to mathematicians and physicists—a number of whom are now employed by major financial institutions—it has only recently influenced the development of economic models of financial markets.

Such ideas are, on an informal level, far from new. In economics, Keynes' beauty contest example has been frequently discussed. Keynes' point was that in deciding which contestant would win a beauty contest one should not take into account one's own judgment, but rather should try to assess which of the candidates was likely to be most pleasing to the judges. The argument can be extended to a situation in which there is a popular vote to decide the winner. And the reasoning can be used in the case of financial markets. Keynes made the point that trying to act with the majority was important for a manager of funds: he or she is less likely to be criticised for making an investment which turns out to be unprofitable if many other market participants made similar investments than if it was purely the result of his or her own judgment.

Arguments such as those of Keynes, while frequently evoked and suggesting that it is not necessarily irrational to 'follow the herd', have until recently been largely anecdotal. However, the particular argument underlying the beauty contest example has now been developed formally,[4] and in the context of a principal-agent relationship it can be shown that agents who invest on the part of others may have strong incentives to imitate the actions of the market participants that they observe. The idea is a simple formalisation of Keynes' notion that sanctions are asymmetric and in this case the agent will have every interest to conform. Yet this may well result in conformity of a sort which is not efficient from a welfare point of view.[5] However, conformism as a

(1) See Shiller (op. cit.).
(2) See Cass, D. and Shell, K. 'Do sunspots matter?', *Journal of Political Economy*, 91, pages 193–227, 1983.
(3) See Woodford, M. 'Learning to believe in sunspots', *Econometrica*, 58, pages 277–307, 1990.
(4) See Sharfstein, D S. and Stein, J C. 'Herd behaviour and investment', *American Economic Review*, 80, 3, pages 465–79, 1990.
(5) The same sort of thing can occur when firms who adopt a technology provide a positive effect for other users of the same technology; a whole industry can get locked into an inferior technology. See Arthur, W B. 'Competing technologies, increasing returns and lock-in by historical events', *Economic Journal*, IC, pages 116–31, 1989.

form of risk aversion is but one of several explanations of why individuals may be influenced by the actions or opinions of others.

It is important to take account not only of the interaction between agents but also of *how* that interaction takes place, and which individuals interact with—or react to—which others. That will depend on the way in which the market is organised; and there is a growing interest in how market microstructure affects the evolution of prices.[1]

Of course, those who maintain the market-efficiency point of view could argue that if different structures give rise to different prices, some of these structures must be unsatisfactory from the point of view of economic efficiency. Empirically though, it may be very difficult to establish this.

All of these arguments suggest that a satisfactory model of financial markets should include the following features:

- Agents should react directly to one another's behaviour.

- The heterogeneity of agents—in terms both of expectations and horizons—should be included.

- The market microstructure, in particular the network of communications within which agents operate, should be considered.

The remainder of this section looks at each of these points and presents a simple example of an economic model which incorporates such features to see how its behaviour compares with the empirical data.

Inferences from the behaviour of others

One of the most important features of markets is that the actions of individuals reveal something about the information that they possess. This feature is poorly incorporated in most economic models and difficult to include in the efficient-markets framework.

To take a few examples that economists have considered, let me look first at the case in which agents receive private signals but also observe the choices made by others. So in the foreign exchange market, in addition to any information acquired from a private source, a trader observes what other participants are doing—or at least proposing to do. If the agent changes his action in the light of this information, a so-called 'information cascade' arises.[2] As more and more individuals act in this way, a trader would have to have almost unbounded confidence in his own information not to conform, particularly if such cascades lead to self-fulfilling outcomes.

In the FX market, a trader's goal is to anticipate the direction of movements in market prices, so he or she gains a great deal of information by listening to the brokers, watching the bid and ask prices on the screens, and telephoning other traders to ask for a quote. Each piece of information modifies the individual information set, but since there is no central equilibrium price this information cannot be incorporated and become public through that price, but only through the observable actions of the individual. The problem with information cascades is that as the number of people involved increases, the cascade reinforces itself. Although quite fragile to start with, cascades later become almost immune to relevant information.

There is a significant loss of efficiency here. The information acquired by early agents would be of use to their later counterparts, but if they choose to follow what others do this information is not made available. In this way, possibly relevant information about fundamentals, for example, might never be used and prices could get detached from these fundamentals. A conclusion that can be drawn from work by a number of economists is that the information obtained by observing the actions of others can outweigh the information obtained by the individuals themselves. It is also clear that as the behaviour of market participants becomes more and more instantly observable—with the development of modern communication technology—the probability of cascades is increased.

Imitation

A second source of herd behaviour is the tendency to imitate those who are successful. This can occur in two ways. Either individuals may be converted to the beliefs held by their successful counterparts, or they may simply imitate directly the choices of the successful. This, in itself, might merely imply a learning process which would lead less successful participants to improve their performance. However two things can happen. An individual may become successful as a result of some chance event, or series of chance events. The fact that he is then imitated may lead to the market moving in the direction he predicts, or it may end in a collapse of what will become apparent was a bubble. It is possible indeed that imitation of success will lead to perpetually changing patterns of behaviour in the market.[3]

Market microstructure: network effects

The way in which a market is organised can have important consequences for the way in which prices evolve. In a market in which there is no centralised price determination, agents will trade with and observe other traders. But traders do not pay equal attention to all the other traders operating in their currencies. Typically, they operate with a limited subset of partners and there are clear reasons for this, in terms of the time cost of monitoring and communicating with others. So the market may be viewed as a complex

(1) See O'Hara, M. *Market microstructure theory*, Cambridge Mass: Blackwell, 1995.
(2) See Hirschleifer, D. 'The blind leading the blind: social influence, fads and informational cascades', *Finance Working Paper No 24–93*, School of Management, UCLA, 1993; Bikhchandani, S, Hirschleifer, D. and Welch, I. 'A theory of fads, fashion, custom and cultural change as informational cascades', *Journal of Political Economy*, 100, pages 992–1,026, 1992; Banerjee A. 'A simple model of herd behaviour', *Quarterly Journal of Economics*, 108, pages 797–817, 1992; Welch, I. 'Sequential sales, learning and cascades', *The Journal of Finance*, 47, 1992; and Kirman, A P. 'Communication in markets: a suggested approach', *Economics Letters*, 12, No 1, pages 101–8, 1983.
(3) See Ellison, G, and Fudenberg, D. 'Rules of thumb for social learning', *Journal of Political Economy*, 101, No 41, pages 612–43, 1993.

Bank of England Quarterly Bulletin: August 1995

A simple example

This example illustrates how some of the features discussed can be incorporated into a model of a financial market. Consider a simple situation in which opinions in the foreign exchange market are divided between those who are *chartists*—ie who extrapolate prices in a more or less sophisticated way—and those who are *fundamentalists*, who believe that prices are essentially determined by underlying fundamental values.[1] As people meet each other in the market (where 'meet' may mean observing an action, making a telephone call or receiving a signal), they will be influenced by the expectations of those they meet, and will be recruited to another's opinion—if different from their own—with a certain probability. Clearly if they keep meeting or observing individuals who share their own opinions, these can only be reinforced. Thus the proportion of people in the market holding a certain opinion will fluctuate as a result of the sequence of meetings that take place.

Individuals then try to assess what the majority expectation is and make their bids accordingly. And the exchange rate is then set to clear the market.

What can be shown in such a simple model is:[2]

- that the proportion of opinions will never settle down, but will continually change;

- at any time, the individuals will be nearly all chartists or nearly all fundamentalists, but periodically the market will switch from being dominated by one to being dominated by the other; and

- that although a market currently dominated by chartists will always return to fundamentals, the time at which it will do so is indeterminate.

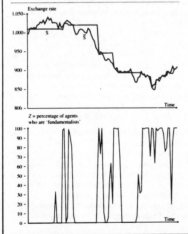

A simulation of such a model is shown in the chart. Z is the percentage of agents who act as fundamentalists, S is the exchange rate and $\bar{S}$ is the exchange rate were it to be completely determined by fundamentals. What can clearly be seen is that the exchange rate S moves away from $\bar{S}$ for a while and then returns sharply. The example has been constructed so that periods of chartist domination maintain the exchange rate constant. This has been done in order to make the figure more readily interpretable, but is just an artefact of the parameters.

Three things are worth noting:

(i) The equilibrium of such a market should be thought of in terms of the so-called 'limit' distribution—the proportion of time the system spends in each state.

(ii) In the model, 'herd behaviour' is rational—in that it is more profitable to act with the majority, particularly if it is known that others do so.

(iii) Individuals do not systematically make mistakes but switch opinions and are justified in doing so, since most of the time their expectations are self-fulfilling.

These features are clearly heavily dependent on the assumption that decisions take place—and expectations modified—in a sequential way. This, however, seems to be an appropriate assumption, given the way in which the FX market works. The rapidity with which meetings, conversations and observations occur in the modern FX market would, of course, have a significant impact on the time it takes to switch from one extreme to the other. *Ceteris paribus*, the more frequent these meetings, the more frequent the change of 'regime'.

Such a model enables one to formalise the idea that in the short run a movement may persist, even though it seems to run counter to what the fundamentals would indicate. Since no information is to be gathered from how long one has been in one state as to when opinions in the market might shift, there is little to be gained from taking a position on the basis of a return to fundamentals at some indeterminate time in the future. This is particularly important since 90% of FX volume is accounted for by intra-day, ie short-term trading.

It is also worth noting that econometric standard tests as to whether the movement of the exchange rate is a random walk—which is what it would have been had it always followed fundamentals and thus satisfied the 'efficient-market' criterion—failed to detect the presence of strong deviations from the fundamentals. So these tests do not seem capable of detecting the presence of bubbles in a series which for part of the time follows a random walk. Furthermore well-known tests for time-dependency in the volatility of the series (ARCH, GARCH, etc) did not reject the presence of such an effect, despite the fact that—by construction—the sort of time structure these tests are supposed to detect was not present in this model.

(1) For a similar model, see Frankel, J A, and Froot, K A, 'The dollar as an irrational speculative bubble: the tale of fundamentalists and chartists', *Marcus Wallenberg Papers on International Finance, 1*, pages 27–55, 1986.
(2) For details, see Kirman, A P, 'Ants, rationality and recruitment', *The Quarterly Journal of Economics, 108*, pages 137–56, February 1993; and 'Testing for bubbles', mimeo, European University Institute, Florence, 1994.

network, with each participant being linked to a subset of others. Not all of these links will be in use at any one time and indeed they will be used with a certain probability, depending on the terms offered and the positions held by the various partners. Thus the market can be viewed as a 'stochastic or random graph'—*graph*, since traders are linked with certain other traders; and *random*, since these links are only used with a certain probability.[1]

The connectivity of this network will be of considerable importance for the transmission of information and for the speed with which a particular view takes over in the market. One thing that is known is that if the probability that any two agents in the market are in contact with each other is not too small, the larger the market the faster information will disseminate. Why is this true?

Suppose that there are N individuals in the market. These individuals trade with or observe only a limited number of others. Thus the reaction by other agents to an action of one will not be instantaneous, but will take place only when one of the agents with whom they are in contact reacts. The reaction will 'percolate' through the system. Assume, for example, that each of the agents observes $\sqrt{N}$ others, ie in a market with 900 participants each individual observes 30 of his counterparts, which does not seem unreasonable. One can show that, if agents do this and N is large, it will take only two steps before every agent is alerted to the fact that an action has taken place.[2]

So, perhaps counterintuitively, epidemics or herd behaviour are more likely to develop rapidly when there are many agents in the market. Two things offset this, however. Traders are not all linked with equal probability to others. The global market is, in fact, still quite strongly segregated into three regions: Asia, Europe and North America. There are troughs of activity at around 4.00 am GMT and between 7.00 pm and 11.00 pm GMT as regional markets open, close or diminish activity. This, together with the second observation—that currencies tend to be traded more specifically in their own markets—probably slows down the transmission of reactions, and may diminish the effect of any particular local movement. (Globalisation may, in this sense, be destabilising if it leads to more integrated markets.)

Although it is clear that the network of communications that traders use is important, what is more difficult to analyse is how the structure of the network develops in the first place. How do traders choose their partners? Why do the probabilities of trading with others evolve away from the uniform situation? Although economists are now paying some attention to this sort of question,[3] little formal analysis has been done. A typical feature that has to be explained is the advent of traders or clients who become the focus of attention of many members of the networks. Their actions are closely monitored and often imitated for a period, and

then the links to them become less important as attention switches elsewhere.

Market microstructure: organisation and prices

In the standard efficient-markets view, little attention is paid to precisely how the market is organised. Thus the particular microstructure of a market is assumed not to have an impact on the evolution of prices. Yet a number of empirical observations bely this. Markets which are organised on an auction basis do not, in general, exhibit the same price behaviour as those for the same product organised on a posted-price basis, or with bilateral deals. Indeed considerable attention is paid by governments, for example, as to which mechanism to use when selling government bonds and privatising public enterprises.[4] This is precisely because the mechanism chosen will affect the prices obtained. So the prices obtained do not simply reflect the underlying 'fundamental' value of the assets or goods being sold, but also the choice of mechanism used to sell them.

In the FX market, there are dozens of market-makers all simultaneously announcing bid and offer prices at which they are prepared to trade in particular pairs of currencies. Even though these prices are posted on screens, at any point in time there will be a dispersion of prices available and transactions will often take place at the same moment in the same currencies at different prices. The explanations for this are clear. It is not possible for traders to keep track of all prices simultaneously, the prices announced are indicative, actual transactions will often take place within and not necessarily at the announced spread, and the prices offered by market-makers, announced by brokers and revealed by electronic broking systems are constantly shifting.

The way in which prices evolve is not the same as it would if there were a central auctioneer who periodically set prices to clear existing bids and offers.[5] Each market-maker's action will depend crucially on his time horizon. If he is 'hit' too often on one side, he will start to acquire a short or long position; this has two consequences. Firstly there is now a substantial element of risk involved and secondly he is acquiring a position which—for most market-makers—has to be closed by the end of the day. Both features will cause the market-maker to modify his prices and possibly his spread. If all trades were between market-makers, for every such movement there would be a countermovement. Even this would not necessarily eliminate any change, since the reaction of the two agents to the trades they had just effected might not be symmetric. In fact, of course, a number of the trades are motivated by outside orders.

The standard argument is that all this is irrelevant to the economist or actor such as a central bank, who is interested in observing and predicting the way in which prices move.

(1) For a simple example of the application of this tool to economics, see Kirman (*op. cit.*).
(2) This rather simplified explanation is based on a mathematical result of Bollobas.
(3) See, for example, Stanley, E A, Ashlock, D, and Tesfatsion, L, 'Iterated prisoner's dilemma with choice and refusal of partners' in *Artificial Life III*. Ed Langton, C G. Santa Fe Institute Studies in the Sciences of Complexity, proc. vol. XVII. Addison-Wesley, 1994.
(4) In general, the simple aim is to maximise revenue subject to certain distributional or 'fairness' constraints.
(5) In fact in some countries there are daily 'fixings' but these only involve a small volume of trade.

Bank of England Quarterly Bulletin: August 1995

The process is analogous, it is argued, to that of a Walrasian auctioneer. If one currency is being sold then those with the highest bids will be hit first, their bids will fall and other participants with lower bids will be hit until the market is back in equilibrium.

But the essential point is that the dynamics of price movements are more complicated than this, for two simple reasons. Firstly if a transaction is observed to take place, it provides information to other market-makers, and this fact alone may cause them to modify their own bids and offers. Furthermore it also provides information to those who place orders with market-makers and their demand may be affected by this information. The identity of the person making the transaction (or on behalf of whom the transaction is being made) may also convey information.

So depending on the way in which a transaction is carried out, the information revealed will be different. Central banks are, of course, well aware of this and can choose, in consequence, whether to intervene openly or to do so in a less detectable way. The significance of this is that their impact on prices will be different depending on their behaviour and not on the fundamentals.

Lastly, as has been mentioned previously, the particular structure of the network of communications within the market and its connectivity will have a significant impact on the way information is transmitted and thus on the evolution of prices.

For all these reasons, the microstructure of the market cannot be ignored when trying to understand the nature of price formation in the FX market. Two aspects of the microstructure must be emphasised. Firstly it will determine how the heterogeneity of opinions or positions of agents are translated into prices and transactions, and secondly it will determine how—and how quickly—information will be transmitted.

Implications of interaction for price dynamics

Before considering the impact of the sort of phenomena discussed above, it is perhaps worth mentioning what is meant by price here. A lot of interest has been focused on high-frequency, or 'tick by tick', data. Each observation is the average of the bid and ask of the indicative quote in question. If the market is adjusting in one direction, the level of the prices will be misleading but the direction of the change will not.

If the market were operating as efficient-market theory says it should and each quote corresponded to the equilibrium price, then there should be no *auto-correlation* between price changes, ie no correlation between successive changes.

However if—as seems more likely—the market adjusts through a series of transactions in response to quotes, then one would expect positive auto-correlation, that is the change in one period is likely to be in the same direction as that in the next. Such a pattern would also be consistent with the sort of herd behaviour I have mentioned.

At the highest frequency, however, auto-correlation is actually negative.[1] This may be a result of looking in *too* great detail at the price series. In fact agents have heterogeneous horizons and may have different expectations. For example, some traders may not be allowed to hold open positions overnight while others will be taking positions on a much longer-term basis. When the market is unsettled, opinions may vary as to the direction of price changes even in the short run. As a result, successive trades will not necessarily be in the same direction. It has also been observed[2] that since different banks offer different spreads, prices may bounce back and forth, for example at the start of a movement from one expectations regime to another.

If we couple together two features of the sort of models discussed above—the different horizons of the agents and the emergence of speculative bubbles—we would have a situation in which volatility would be time-varying, but shorter-term and longer-term volatility would be linked. An initial switch would be transmitted to those with different horizons and would trigger off actions by a large number of market participants. In fact this is precisely what happens in the foreign exchange market: there is correlation between longer-term and shorter-term volatility, but not, for example, between successive observations of short-term volatility.[3]

There is by now a substantial literature on the detection of the time structure of the volatility of foreign exchange rates. Some success has been reported using ARCH, GARCH and more sophisticated versions of these tests.[4] The evidence is far from conclusive and indeed in the simple example discussed in the box on page 290 these tests failed. Nevertheless the total absence of structure in the time series of exchange rates—which the efficient-markets model would suggest—is not borne out by the evidence, and the effort being put into developing and testing trading rules based on the structure of the stochastic process generating exchange rate movements suggests that many market participants realise this.

Although trading rules based on the extrapolation (however sophisticated) of past prices have not been accorded much interest by academics with the exception of two centres,[5] the same is not true for major financial institutions who, according to a recent survey, almost all use 'technical analysis' in their forecasting. Indeed Brock *et al* have shown that even relatively simple 'technical' rules based on the

(1) See Guillaume, D M, Dacorogna, A M, Davé, R R, Müller, U A, Olsen, R B, and Pictet, O V, 'From the bird's eye to the microscope: a survey of new stylized facts of the intra-daily foreign exchange markets', *O&A Research Group Discussion Paper*, 1994.
(2) See Bollerslev, T, and Domowitz, I, 'Trading patterns and prices in the interbank foreign exchange market', *The Journal of Finance*, 48, pages 1,421–43, 1993.
(3) See Guillaume *et al* (op. cit.).
(4) See for example Chiandotto, B, and Gallo, G, Eds, *In Quest of the Philosopher's Stone*, Società Italiana di Statistica, Florence, 1994.
(5) The University of Wisconsin and the Santa Fe Institute.

differences between short-term and long-term moving averages do have some predictive power and therefore are profitable.[1]

Such evidence would seem to be consistent with the sort of stochastic model I have mentioned; the rules would be picking up the changes in prevailing expectations. All of this suggests that the data from the FX market share some of the features of a stochastic model of changing expectations regimes—periods of calm interspersed with periods of higher volatility, and periodic switches from one type of expectation to another.

Would the introduction of friction stabilise the market?

A number of economists have called for the imposition of some sort of globally applied tax on trading. Apart from the difficulty of implementing such a measure, two recent arguments related to the alternative models discussed above suggest that such a measure might be counterproductive.

The first is that since individuals convey information when they act, the introduction of a tax would mean that the signal given by an action might, when individuals act less frequently, be regarded by others as more important and more informative. This is simply because, since the cost of taking any action has been increased, the profit that an agent expects to make before taking an action must be higher. As a result, those observing will interpret an action as having more predictive value than previously.[2] So although the market may be quieter for longer, it will be more susceptible to large and sudden movements.

A rather different argument is that when the market is quiet and exchange rates are less volatile simple predictive rules are quite effective and will start to take over from more sophisticated and time-consuming predictive methods. But it may be the case that the simple rules are unstable, in the sense that, once perturbed, the exchange rate will not return quickly to some stable value. Suppose for the sake of argument that in equilibrium both methods would predict the same rate, then when sophisticated prediction methods are being used the rate will be robust to perturbations. However, precisely because of the market's stability the simple prediction method will reappear and will, sooner or later, lead to a period of high volatility. With more costly transactions the quiet period may be prolonged, but at the possible expense of experiencing greater volatility when a shock occurs.[3]

Conclusion

What I have suggested is a view of the FX market rather different in nature to that underlying the standard efficient-markets model.

Interaction between agents, in terms of the information that is passed and inferred, plays an important role in determining the dynamics of exchange rates. If the view is correct, the greater flow of information as communication technology develops will lead to more frequent changes in 'market opinion', and the increasing number of participants in the market will speed up the transmission of information between them. This in turn will increase the speed with which different price expectations can come to prevail. These tendencies have led—and will no doubt in future lead—to demands for the introduction of some sort of friction into the market, such as a tax on trading to diminish the volatility of exchange rate movements. In statistical terms, the market characteristics could be modified by the introduction of such frictions into the system. It is true that they would change the distribution of price changes and reduce average volatility. But this would be at the expense of a much larger probability of extreme events.[4]

A particularly interesting feature of the sort of model described is that it allows us to explain two important features of the FX market. Firstly, if there is a view on the part of some market participants that fundamentals are important, eventually this view will come to prevail—at least for a period. But the time at which this will occur is unpredictable. This makes the view that fundamentals are of little importance in the short term but matter in the long run perfectly consistent with the facts.

Secondly, the stochastic element in the communication between agents weakens any direct deterministic link between exchange rates and fundamentals in the short run, and explains why in two apparently similar situations there can be very different exchange rate movements.

The relationship between fundamentals and exchange rates is not well understood and seems to vary considerably over time. Furthermore, exchange rate movements depend on what market participants believe that relationship to be, and this also adds weight to the importance of the role of communication between agents in the market. The tendency of commentators to attribute a particular change to a particular piece of news about fundamentals is not justified by the behaviour of the system. Such explanations may give a plausible account of what happened, but do not enable us to make good predictions about future changes: one can make reasonable 'in-sample fits' but can not make good 'out-of-sample predictions'.

Finally, the view of the foreign exchange market as a complex interactive system with many heterogeneous agents, which undergoes periodic shifts in its state, seems not only to be able to explain some of the characteristics of the actual price dynamics of the market, but also to cohere with some of the stylised facts about the way in which the market actually works.

(1) See Brock, W A, Lakonishok, J, and Le Baron, B. 'Simple technical trading rules and the stochastic properties of stock returns', *Discussion Paper, University of Wisconsin*, Madison, 1991.
(2) This argument has been put in Caplin, A, and Leahy, J. 'Business as usual, market crashes and wisdom after the fact', *Harvard University Economics Department, Discussion Paper No 602*, 1992.
(3) This argument is developed in Brock, W A and Hommes, C. 'Rational paths to randomness', *mimeo*, University of Wisconsin, 1994.
(4) See Guillaume *et al (op. cit.)*, who observed that this characterised the EMS record when bands were narrow.

[30]

by Richard Roll

The International Crash of October 1987

All major world markets declined substantially in October 1987—an exceptional occurrence, given the usual modest correlations of returns across countries. Of 23 markets, 19 declined more than 20 per cent. The U. S. market had the fifth smallest decline in local-currency units, but came in only 11th out of 23 when returns are restated in a common currency.

The U.S. market was not the first to decline sharply. Non-Japanese Asian markets began a severe decline on October 19 (their time). This decline was echoed first by a number of European markets, then by North America and, finally, by Japan. Most of these same markets, however, had experienced significant but less severe declines in the latter part of the previous week. With the exception of the U.S. and Canada, markets continued downward through the end of October, and some of the declines were as large as the great crash on October 19.

Various institutional characteristics have been blamed as contributors to the crash. Univariate regressions indicate that the presence of an official specialist, computer-directed trading, price limits and margin requirements were associated with less severe stock market declines in October 1987, while continuous auctions and automated quotations were associated with larger declines. In multiple regressions, however, several of these variables, including price limits and margin requirements, were found to be insignificant.

October's crash could be ascribed to the normal response of each country's stock market to a worldwide market movement. A world market index was found to be statistically related to monthly returns in every country during the period from the beginning of 1981 up until the month before the crash. The magnitude of market response differed materially across countries. The response coefficient, or beta, was by far the most statistically significant explanatory variable in the October crash, swamping the influences of the institutional market characteristics. Only one institutional variable—continuous auctions—had even a marginally significant influence on the estimated beta.

Richard Roll is Allstate Professor of Finance at the Anderson Graduate School of Management of the University of California, Los Angeles.

The author thanks Jim Brandon for his assistance and advice and Robert Barro, Michael Brennan, Eugene Fama, Robert Kamphuis, Roger Kormendi and Alan Meltzer for their helpful comments.

This article will appear in Black Monday and the Future of Financial Markets, by The Mid-America Institute for Public Policy Research, published by Dow Jones-Irwin. It is printed here with the permission of Dow Jones-Irwin.

THE SHARP DROP in U.S. stock prices in October 1987 gave birth to at least one industry—the production of explanations for the crash. Among the most popular are those related to the U.S. market's institutional structure and practices—computer-assisted trading, portfolio insurance, the organized exchange specialists, concurrent trading in stock index futures, margin rules, and the absence of

Footnotes appear at end of article.

Table I Stock Price Index Percentage Changes in Major Markets (calendar year 1987 and October 1987)[a]

	Local Currency Units		U.S. Dollars	
	1987	October	1987	October
Australia[b]	−3.6	−41.8	4.7	−44.9
Austria	−17.6	−11.4	0.7	−5.8
Belgium	−15.5	−23.2	3.1	−18.9
Canada[b]	4.0	−22.5	10.4	−22.9
Denmark	−4.5	−12.5	15.5	−7.3
France	−27.8	−22.9	−13.9	−19.5
Germany	−36.8	−22.3	−22.7	−17.1
Hong Kong	−11.3	−45.8	−11.0	−45.8
Ireland	−12.3	−29.1	4.7	−25.4
Italy	−32.4	−16.3	−22.3	−12.9
Japan	8.5	−12.8	41.4	−7.7
Malaysia	6.9	−39.8	11.7	−39.3
Mexico[b,c]	158.9	−35.0	5.5	−37.6
Netherlands	−18.9	−23.3	0.3	−18.1
New Zealand[b]	−38.7	−29.3	−23.8	−36.0
Norway	−14.0	−30.5	1.7	−28.8
Singapore	−10.6	−42.2	−2.7	−41.6
South Africa[b]	−8.8	−23.9	33.5	−29.0
Spain	8.2	−27.7	32.6	−23.1
Sweden	−15.1	−21.8	−0.9	−18.6
Switzerland	−34.0	−26.1	−16.5	−20.8
United Kingdom	4.6	−26.4	32.5	−22.1
United States	0.5	−21.6	0.5	−21.6

a. Annual average dividend yields are generally in the 2 to 5 per cent range except for Japan and Mexico, which have average dividend yields less than 1 per cent.
b. The currencies of these countries depreciated against the dollar during October 1987.
c. Mexico is the only country whose currency did *not* appreciate against the dollar during 1987.

"circuit breakers" such as trading suspensions and limitations on price movements. Several commission reports about the crash focus on these institutional arrangements.

As regulatory agencies and potential regulatees debate the most appropriate means for preventing another crash, the focus again is on institutional form. The debaters seem to accept without question that the arrangements in place during October were somehow related to the event. Yet there is virtually no evidence to support such a view. If institutional structure of the U.S. market had been the sole culprit, the market would have crashed even earlier. There must have been an underlying "trigger." Some have pointed to the U.S. trade deficit, to anticipations about the 1988 elections, to fears of a recession. But no one has been able to substantiate the underlying cause of the October market decline.

The likely impact of both market structure and macroeconomic conditions can perhaps be deduced by comparing circumstances in the United States with circumstances prevailing in other markets around the world. Indeed, we are blessed with a natural laboratory experiment, for conditions varied widely across countries. To the extent that institutions and economics influence the stock market, we should be able to detect those influences by comparing behaviors in various markets during October 1987.

Table II Correlation Coefficients of Monthly Percentage Changes in Major Stock Market Indexes (local currencies, June 1981–September 1987)

	Australia	Austria	Belgium	Canada	Denmark	France	Germany	Hong Kong	Ireland	Italy
Austria	0.219									
Belgium	0.190	0.222								
Canada	0.568	0.250	0.215							
Denmark	0.217	−0.062	0.219	0.301						
France	0.180	0.263	0.355	0.351	0.241					
Germany	0.145	0.406	0.315	0.194	0.215	0.327				
Hong Kong	0.321	0.174	0.129	0.236	0.120	0.201	0.304			
Ireland	0.349	0.202	0.361	0.490	0.387	0.374	0.067	0.320		
Italy	0.209	0.224	0.307	0.321	0.150	0.459	0.257	0.216	0.275	
Japan	0.182	−0.025	0.223	0.294	0.186	0.361	0.147	0.137	0.183	0.241
Malaysia	0.329	−0.013	0.096	0.274	0.151	−0.134	−0.020	0.159	0.082	−0.119
Mexico	0.220	0.018	0.104	0.114	−0.174	−0.009	0.002	0.149	0.113	0.114
Netherlands	0.294	0.232	0.344	0.545	0.341	0.344	0.511	0.395	0.373	0.344
New Zealand	0.389	0.290	0.275	0.230	0.148	0.247	0.318	0.352	0.314	0.142
Norway	0.355	0.009	0.233	0.381	0.324	0.231	0.173	0.356	0.306	0.042
Singapore	0.374	0.030	0.133	0.320	0.133	−0.085	0.037	0.219	0.102	−0.038
South Africa	0.279	0.159	0.143	0.385	−0.113	0.267	0.007	−0.095	0.024	0.093
Spain	0.147	0.018	0.050	0.190	0.019	0.255	0.147	0.193	0.175	0.290
Sweden	0.327	0.161	0.158	0.376	0.131	0.159	0.227	0.196	0.122	0.330
Switzerland	0.334	0.401	0.276	0.551	0.283	0.307	0.675	0.379	0.290	0.287
United Kingdom	0.377	0.073	0.381	0.590	0.218	0.332	0.263	0.431	0.467	0.328
United States	0.328	0.138	0.250	0.720	0.351	0.390	0.209	0.114	0.380	0.224

The Comparative Performance of Major Stock Markets in 1987

During the entire calendar year 1987, stock market performance varied widely across major countries. Table I gives the total percentage change in the major stock price index for each of 23 countries, in both local-currency and U.S.-dollar terms.[1] The best performer in dollar terms was Japan (+41.4 per cent), the worst performer New Zealand (−23.8 per cent). The local-currency results, however, are quite different from the dollar-denominated results. For example, Mexico had a 5.5 per cent dollar-denominated return in 1987, but was up 158.9 per cent in local currency!

The wide disparity in 1987 returns is typical. Table II shows the simple correlation coefficients of monthly percentage changes in the (local currency) indexes over the pre-crash period for which simultaneous data were available for all countries (mid-1981 through September 1987). The intercountry correlations are mostly positive, but moderate in size. Correlations above 0.5 are relatively rare, and there are only two above 0.7.[2] These modest correlations are in marked contrast to the usual correlation found between any two well-diversified portfolios within the same country. Randomly selected portfolios of U.S. stocks, for example, generally have correlations above 0.9 when there are 50 or more issues included in each portfolio.

Table I also reports total percentage market movements for each country during the month of October 1987. They are all negative! This alone is a cause of wonder. During the whole period of data availability (calendar years 1981 through 1987, inclusive), October 1987 is the *only* month when all markets moved in the same direction, but in that month every stock market fell, and most fell by more than 20 per cent. When just the last three months of 1987 are added to data from the previous 76 months used in Table II, the average correlation coefficient increases from 0.222 to 0.415.[3]

In October Austria, the world's best-performing country, experienced an 11.4 per cent local-currency decline, and Japan declined 12.8 per cent, but the currencies of both countries appreciated significantly against the dollar. The worst performer, Hong Kong, had the same result in both local currency and in U.S. dollars, −45.8 per cent. The rank of the U.S. improves considerably (from 11th to fifth) when the results are expressed in local currency, because the dollar depreciated against most countries during October.

Given the generally low correlations between countries, the uniformity during October 1987, even in local-currency units, is all the more striking. There seems to have been an international trigger that swamped the usual influences of country-specific events.

Table II   continued

Japan	Malaysia	Mexico	Netherlands	New Zealand	Norway	Singapore	South Africa	Spain	Sweden	Switzerland	UK
0.109											
−0.021	0.231										
0.333	0.151	0.038									
−0.111	0.136	0.231	0.230								
0.156	0.262	0.050	0.405	0.201							
0.066	0.891	0.202	0.196	0.212	0.280						
0.225	−0.013	0.260	0.058	0.038	0.156	−0.056					
0.248	−0.071	0.059	0.170	0.095	0.075	0.056	−0.088				
0.115	0.103	0.000	0.324	0.136	0.237	0.180	0.070	0.181			
0.130	0.099	0.026	0.570	0.397	0.331	0.157	0.112	0.192	0.334		
0.354	0.193	0.068	0.534	0.014	0.313	0.250	0.168	0.209	0.339	0.435	
0.326	0.347	0.063	0.473	0.083	0.356	0.377	0.218	0.214	0.279	0.500	0.513

Movements Around the Crash

During the month of October, the declines experienced in all markets were concentrated in the second half of the month. Figures A through F present the day-to-day closing index numbers for each market over the entire month of October, restated to 1.0 currency units on October 1. Figure G plots equal-weighted regional indexes over a shorter period around the crash, beginning on October 14 and ending on October 26. Figure H gives a similar portrait of the six largest individual markets. All eight graphs are plotted in actual world time; the tick marks reflect each index's value at the daily New York market close—4:00 p.m. U.S. Eastern Standard Time.[4] The graphs are on the same vertical scale and plotted for the same world time, so they can easily be compared.

The earliest significant declines occurred on October 14 (in the North American markets and in France, The Netherlands and Spain). Most world markets experienced at least some decline for the week ending October 16. In the U.S. market, by far the largest daily decline occurred on October 19. However, many European markets split their declines between their 19th (preceding the U.S. decline) and their 20th. In the cases of Belgium, France, Germany, The Netherlands, Sweden and Switzerland, the biggest down day was their 19th.

In the Asian markets, Hong Kong, Malaysia and Singapore had major declines on both their 19th and 20th, the movement on their 19th preceding the U.S. decline by more than 12 hours. (These markets close before the North American markets open.) Japan fell only slightly on its 19th, but it joined Australia and New Zealand for a major drop on the 20th (i.e., late in the day on October 19 in the U.S.), lagging the major U.S. decline by several hours.

On a given calendar day, the North American markets are the last to trade. Most of the other markets around the world displayed dramatic declines on their October 19—foreshadowing the crash in North America. With just a few exceptions, the most important being Japan, other countries experienced most of their declines either prior to the opening of the U.S. market on the 19th or approximately straddling the U.S. market's October 19 session (i.e., on October 19 and 20, local time).

This seems to be some evidence against the widely expressed view that the U.S. market pulled down all the other world markets on October 19. However, it is true that the U.S. experienced one of the largest declines in the previous week (see Figure H). So there remains the possibility that other market crashes, though generally occurring before the major U.S. crash, were in fact precipitated by the relatively modest U.S. decline from October 14 through 16.[5]

Following the crash, there was a one-day advance in most markets (including the U.S.) on the 21st. Figure G shows that this advance began first in the Asian and Pacific markets, then spread to Europe and finally to North America. Many markets resumed a substantial decline after October 21, however. From the 22nd through the end of October, every market except the U.S. fell, and every decline except that of Canada was substantial (in local-currency units).[6] Some of these cases were at least partial holdovers from market closures on the 19th (e.g., Hong Kong) or drawn out by successive encounters of exchange price limits. In Europe and Asia, however, the weekend from the 23rd to the 25th was just as bad, and in a few cases worse, than the great crash weekend of October 16 to 19. (See Figures C, D and E or Figure G.)

The overall pattern of intertemporal price movements in the various markets suggests the presence of some underlying fundamental factor, but it debunks the notion that an institutional defect in the U.S. market was the cause. It also seems inconsistent with a U.S.-specific macroeconomic event. If anything, the U.S. market lagged the initial price movements that began in earnest on October 14, and it also did not participate in further declines that occurred during the last weekend in October. This would not be the observed empirical pattern if, for instance, portfolio insurance and program trading in New York and Chicago were the basic triggers of the worldwide crash.

October 1987—Before and After

The strong market decline during October 1987 followed what for many countries had been an unprecedented market increase during the first nine months of the year. In the U.S. market, for instance, stock prices advanced 31.4 per cent over those nine months. Some commentators have suggested that the real cause of October's decline was overinflated prices generated by a speculative bubble during the earlier period. Of the 23 countries in our sample, 20 experienced

Figure A   October 1987 Stock Prices—North America

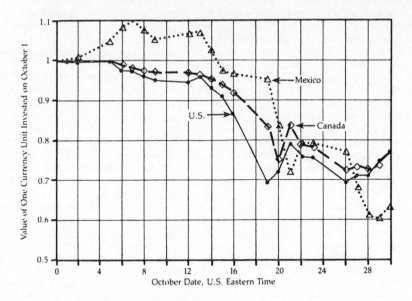

Figure B   October 1987 Stock Prices—Ireland, South Africa, U.K.

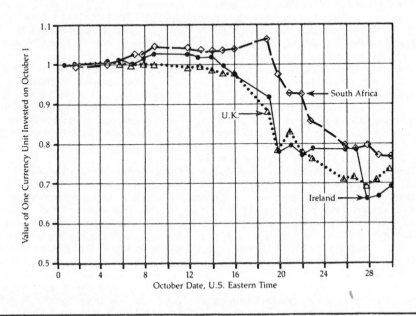

Figure C October 1987 Stock Prices—Larger European Countries

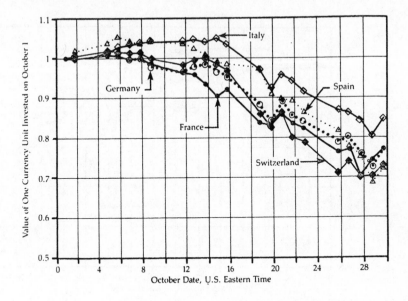

Figure D October 1987 Stock Prices—Smaller European Countries

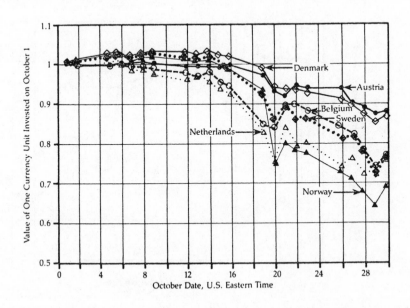

Figure E   October 1987 Stock Prices—Asian Markets

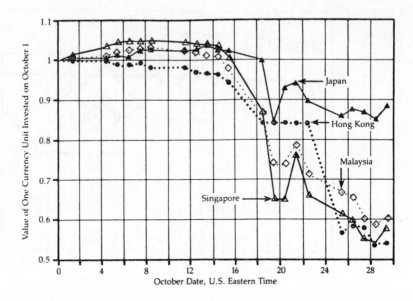

Figure F   October 1987 Stock Prices—Australia and New Zealand

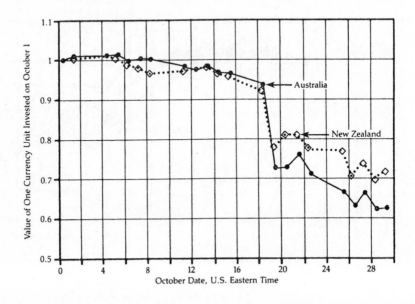

Figure G   Regional Indexes—October 14–October 26

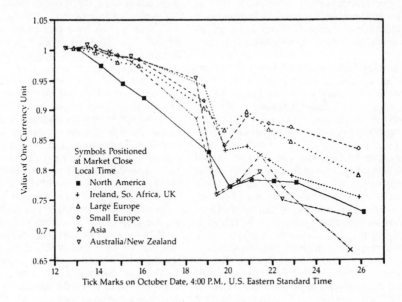

Figure H   The Six Largest Markets—October 14–October 26

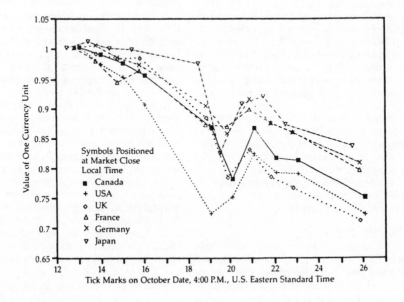

stock price increases over the January to September period. There was, however, wide disparity in the extent of the advance.

One symptom of a speculative bubble might be an inverse relation between the price increase and the extent of the subsequent crash. Figure I presents a cross-country comparison of the January-September 1987 return versus the October decline.[7] There is in fact a significant negative cross-country relation. The regression line shown on the figure indicates a statistically significant association, with an R^2 of 0.543.

There is, however, a conceptual difficulty in ascribing these results to the existence of a speculative bubble: The same pattern would arise if there were underlying common factors driving stock price changes in all countries. Suppose, for instance, that there is a fundamental macroeconomic factor related to world industrial activity, that it influences the market in every country, but that each country's amplitude of response is different. If that factor happened to be positive from January through September of 1987, while other country-specific influences happened to be relatively stable, we would have observed price advances in most countries (although advances of widely-varying amounts). If the same factor happened to decline dramatically in October, those countries with the greatest amplitude of reaction would have displayed the largest stock price declines. The overall result would be a cross-country negative relation such as that indicated in Figure I. In other words, high "beta" countries do better in worldwide bull markets and worse in bear markets, thus inducing a cross-country negative relation when a bull market period is compared cross-sectionally with a bear market period.

To ascertain whether 1987 was really a speculative bubble followed by a crash, as opposed to a simple manifestation of the usual world market behavior, one would be obliged to identify and estimate a factor model over an entirely different period and use the prefitted response coefficients with fundamental macroeconomic factors measured during 1987.

Since the Crash

In the aftermath of the crash, some have alleged that it was actually an overreaction and that it will soon be reversed; i.e., that it represented just the opposite of a corrected speculative bubble (but was still irrational). If this is true, strong and sharp price increases should occur sometime. However, as Figure J shows, there has been no evidence of a rebound during the successive four calendar months.

Certain regions have performed better than others. Asia, North America and the smaller European countries have experienced moderate price increases, particularly after the first of December 1987. Conversely, other regions (Australia, New Zealand) have performed rather poorly, or have shown little movement in either direction from the level established at the end of October. The interocular test in Figure J reveals an ordinary pattern, one that could be expected over just about any four-month interval—some differences across markets, but certainly no dramatic and worldwide reversal anywhere close to the size of October's decline.

A world index constructed by equally weighting the local currency indexes and normalized to 100 on September 30, 1987 fell to 73.6 by October 30. By February 29, 1988, the index stood at 72.7. Thus the price level established in the October crash seems to have been a virtually unbiased estimate of the average price level over the subsequent four months. If a sizable correction is going to occur, it is apparently going to take a while.

Institutional Arrangements and Market Behavior

Our world laboratory experiment provides insights into the possible influence of each major element of a market's institutional structure. The stock markets around the world are amazingly diverse in their organization. Table III provides a list of some of the particular features in place during October 1987.[8]

Among the features that have figured prominently in post-crash discussions are the extent of computerized trading, the auction system itself, the presence or absence of limits on price movements, regulated margin requirements, and off-market or off-hours trading. Additional features that could be of significance include the presence or absence of floor brokers who conduct trades but are not permitted to invest on their own accounts, the extent of trading in the cash market versus the forward market, the identity of traders (i.e., institutions such as banks or specialized trading firms), and the significance of transaction taxes.

Some markets have trading for both immediate and forward settlement. When forward set-

Figure I   1987 Returns, October vs. January–September

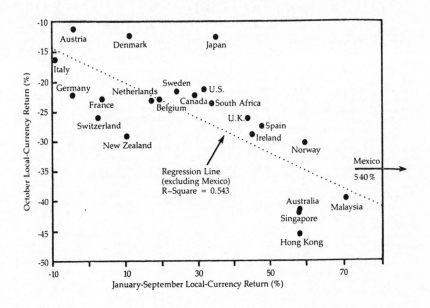

Figure J   Regional Indexes—October 14, 1987–February 29, 1988

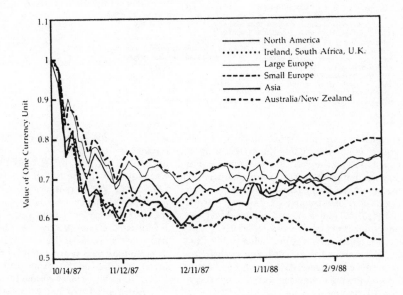

Table III　Institutional Arrangements in World Markets

Country	Auction	Official Special-ists	Forward Trading on Ex-change	Auto-mated Quota-tions	Computer-Directed Trading	Options/Futures Trading	Price Limits	Transac-tion Tax (Round-Trip)	Margin Require-ments	Trading Off Exchange
Australia	Continuous	No	No	Yes	No	Yes	None	0.6%	None	Infrequent
Austria	Single	Yes	No	No	No	No	5%	0.3%	100%	Frequent
Belgium	Mixed	No	Yes	No	No	No^a	10%/None^b	0.375%/ 0.195%	100%/25%^b	Occasional
Canada	Continuous	Yes	No	Yes	Yes	Yes	None^c	0	50%^d	Prohibited
Denmark	Mixed	No	No	No	No	No	None	1%	None	Frequent
France	Mixed	Yes	Yes	Yes	Yes	Yes	4%/7%^e	0.3%	100%/20%^f	Prohibited
Germany	Continuous	Yes	No	No	No	Options	None	0.5%	None	Frequent
Hong Kong	Continuous	No	No	Yes	No	Futures	None^g	0.6% +	None	Infrequent
Ireland	Continuous	No	No	Yes	No	No	None	1%	100%	Frequent
Italy	Mixed	No	Yes	No	No	No	10–20%^h	0.3%	100%	Frequent
Japan	Continuous	Yes	No	Yes	Yes	No^i	–10%	0.55%	70%^j	Prohibited
Malaysia	Continuous	No	No	Yes	No	No	None	0.03%	None	Occasional
Mexico	Continuous	No	Yes	No	No	No	10%^k	0	None	Occasional
Netherlands	Continuous	Yes	No	No	No	Options	Variable^l	2.4%^m	None	Prohibited
New Zealand	Continuous	No	No	No	No	Futures	None	0	None	Occasional
Norway	Single	No	No	No	No	No	None	1%	100%	Frequent
Singapore	Continuous	No	No	Yes	No	No^n	None	0.5%	71%	Occasional
South Africa	Continuous	No	No	Yes	No	Options	None	1.5%	100%	Prohibited
Spain	Mixed^o	No	No	No	No	No	10%^p	0.11%	50%^p	Frequent
Sweden	Mixed	No	No	Yes	No	Yes	None	2%	40%	Frequent
Switzerland	Mixed	No	Yes	Yes	No	Yes	5%^q	0.9%	None	Infrequent
United Kingdom	Continuous	No	No	Yes	Yes	Yes	None	0.5%	None	Occasional
United States	Continuous	Yes	No	Yes	Yes	Yes	None	0	Yes	Occasional

a. Calls only on just five stocks.
b. Cash/forward.
c. None on stocks; 3-5% on index futures.
d. 10% (5%) for uncovered (covered) futures.
e. Cash/forward, but not always enforced.
f. Cash/forward; 40% if forward collateral is stock rather than cash.
g. "Four Spread Rule": offers not permitted more than four ticks from current bids and asks.
h. Hitting limit suspends auction; auction then tried a second time at end of day.
i. Futures on the Nikkei Index are traded in Singapore.
j. Decreased to 50% on October 21, 1987 "to encourage buyers."
k. Trading suspended for successive periods, 15 and then 30 minutes; effective limit: 30–40%.
l. Authorities have discretion. in October, 2% limits every 15 minutes used frequently.
m. For non-dealer transactions only.
n. Only for Nikkei Index (Japan).
o. Groups of stocks are traded continuously for 10 minutes each.
p. Limits raised to 20% and margin to 50% on October 27.
q. Hitting limit causes 15-minute trading suspension. Limits raised to 10–15% in October.

tlement exists, the forward contracts often have a greater volume of trading than cash contracts. For instance, on the Paris *Bourse*, there is a once-a-day auction in the cash market conducted by designated brokerage houses, but there is continuous forward trading in the larger stocks from 9:30 to 11:00 a.m. and repeated call auctions thereafter in forward contracts for all stocks. The limit moves are different too; they are 7 per cent in the forward market and 4 per cent in the cash market.[9] However, there are no limits on the price movements of foreign securities. All trading is done by registered stock brokers, a requirement of French law. Block trading is conducted between the previous day's high and low prices, and block volume constitutes about one-half of all equity trading.

To judge the importance of any particular institutional characteristic, one could compare the market behavior in Table I or in Figures A to F with the presence or absence of the characteristic given in Table III. For example, computer-directed trading is prevalent in Canada, France, Japan, the United Kingdom and the United States. In local-currency terms, these five countries experienced an average decline of 21.25 per

Table IV Local-Currency Returns in October 1987 and Market Characteristics

	Auction	Official Special.	Forward Trading	Auto. Quot.	Comp. Trading	Options/ Futures	Price Limits	Trans. Tax	Margin Reqs.	Off-Ex. Trading
	Cont. = 1 Else = 0	Yes = 1 Else = 0	Yes = 1 Else = 0	Yes = 1 Else = 0	Yes = 1 Else = 0	Yes = 1 Else = 0	None = 0 Else = 1	Non-0 = 1 Else = 0	None = 0 Else = 1	None & Infr. = 0 Else = 1
	Average October Local-Currency Return for Countries in Zero/One Variable Group (%)									
Group 1	−29.69	−19.53	−24.70	−28.99	−21.25	−27.31	−22.08	−26.31	−23.54	−25.94
Group 0	−21.39	−29.47	−26.93	−23.14	−27.89	−25.50	−29.25	−27.08	−30.22	−27.38
Diff.	−8.31	9.94	2.23	−5.85	6.63	−1.80	7.17	0.78	6.68	1.44
T-Value	−2.66	3.53	0.51	−2.05	2.31	−0.57	2.25	0.22	2.20	0.41
	Multiple Regression of October Local Currency Return on Zero/One Variables									
Coeff.	−7.324	6.528	−2.867	−6.065	7.518	1.194	1.638	1.845	2.111	1.452
T-Value	−1.304	1.068	−0.417	−0.954	1.110	0.222	0.232	0.298	0.449	0.258
TS T-Val	−1.762	1.628	−0.592	−1.287	1.631	0.267	0.335	0.343	0.594	0.406

intercept = −26.5; adjusted R-squared = 0.254

cent during October; the 18 countries without widespread computer-directed trading experienced an average decline of 27.89 per cent. Taken as a characteristic in isolation, computer-directed trading (e.g., portfolio insurance and index arbitrage), if it had any impact at all, actually helped mitigate the market decline.

The Quantitative Impact of Market Arrangements on the Extent of the Crash

To obtain a quantitative estimate of the impact of each qualitative institutional characteristic, we converted the entries in Table III into zero/one values and computed both univariate and multivariate results based on the converted numbers. Table IV defines the zero/one variables and presents the basic results.

The top panel of the table shows simple cross-country means for the countries in each univariate zero/one category. For example, if the auction in a particular country is conducted on a continuous basis, that country is assigned to group 1; if there is a single daily auction, or a mixed auction, the country is in group 0. Table IV shows that continuous-auction countries had October declines of 29.69 per cent on average, while the non-continuous-auction countries had October declines that averaged 21.39 per cent.

The t-value of the difference provides a statistical measure of significance. If the t-value is above 1.65 (in absolute terms), the odds are roughly 10 to one that the variable is significant,

when judged on a univariate basis (i.e., in isolation).[10] Six of the 10 variables were related to the magnitude of the crash. Continuous auctions and automated quotation systems were associated with larger declines, while the presence of an official specialist, computer-directed trading, price limits and margin requirements were associated with smaller declines. Forward trading, options and futures trading, transaction taxes and trading off the exchanges were not significantly associated with the size of the crash.

Univariate results may be misleading, however. A characteristic that appears to be significant may merely be a proxy for some other characteristic that is the true cause of the observed difference. This is certainly possible here, not only because the different institutional characteristics are correlated across countries, but also because other relevant influences may have been omitted.

The bottom panel of Table IV presents a multivariate comparison in the form of a cross-country regression of October returns (in local-currency units) on all the zero/one variables. The explained variance (adjusted R^2) was 25.4 per cent, but none of the ordinary t-values from the cross-sectional regression indicates statistical reliability. This reveals the presence of multicollinearity in the explanatory variables, which makes it difficult to assess the relative importance of each one.

Moreover, the observations in this cross-sectional regression may not be cross-sectionally independent, in which case the ordinary t-values will be biased, although the direction of bias is impossible to determine without knowledge of the covariance structure of the residuals. In an attempt to repair both multicollinearity and cross-sectional dependence, we constructed another t-value by using the time series of cross-sectional returns for the period prior to October. The method is explained in the appendix.

With the time-series-derived TS t-values, several characteristics have at least marginal statistical reliability. The presence of an official monopolistic specialist and computer-directed trading were associated with less severe market declines in October. Continuous auctions were marginally significant and associated with greater market declines. Note that these three variables have coefficients with roughly the same magnitude in both the univariate and the multivariate computations, while variables such as price limits and margin requirements have much larger coefficients in the univariate calculations.[11]

Although the regression in Table IV indicates some statistically significant associations between certain market characteristics and the October decline, one should hesitate to conclude that even a strongly associated variable actually contributed to the decline. Markets differ in their amplitudes of response to the same underlying trigger, and certain institutional features may have been adopted because of a high amplitude. For example, it is conceivable, though perhaps improbable, that price limits are abandoned in markets with great volatility. This could have given rise to an association between the absence of price limits and the severity of price decline in October 1987, without there actually having been a mitigating influence of limits.

The Typical Market Response to World Movements and the Crash

In addition to institutional arrangements, another potential explanation for the variety of declines in different markets is that a fundamental, worldwide triggering variable caused the crash, and that the relative movement of each market was simply the usual relation between that particular market and the underlying factor. In order to assess this possibility, we used data from February 1981 through September 1987 to construct a world market index.[12] The

index was equally weighted across countries using local-currency-denominated returns.[13] The following simple market model was fitted to the available time series of monthly returns for each country:

$$R_{j,t} = a_j + b_j R_{M,t} + e_{j,t},$$

where

$R_{j,t}$ = the monthly percentage change in the index of country j for month t,

$R_{M,t}$ = the world market index percentage change,

$e_{j,t}$ = an unexplained residual, and

a_j and b_j = fitted coefficients.

The slope coefficient b_j is the so-called beta, which measures the relative magnitude of response of a given country to changes in the world market index. The appendix gives details of these regressions for each country. Every country exhibited a statistically significant relation with the world market index, with the average R-square being 0.243.

The market model fitted for each country up through September 1987 was used to predict the country's return in October 1987, conditional on the world market index movement in October. The prediction errors (or out-of-sample residuals) were then related cross-sectionally to market characteristics (i.e., to the zero/one variables used previously). The top panel of Table V gives the results.

No coefficient is statistically different from zero. Thus none of the institutional market characteristics was associated with an unusually large or small October return after the worldwide market movement was taken into account. In other words, the magnitude of each market's decline was explained by that market's ordinary relation with world market events. Nothing was left to be explained by the particular institutional arrangements in place.[14]

The second panel of Table V gives some additional evidence about the overwhelming influence of the world market "factor." In the cross-sectional regression reported there, the October index return (not the residual) was related to the institutional zero/one characteristics plus the market-model slope coefficient (or beta) from the time-series regression for each country calculated up through September. This panel differs from the cross-sectional multiple

Table V Local Currency Market Model and Market Characteristics

	Auction	Off. Special.	Forward Trading	Auto. Quot.	Comp. Trading	Options/ Futures	Price Limits	Trans. Tax	Margin Reqs.	Off-Ex. Trading	Beta
	Cont =1 Else = 0	Yes = 1 Else = 0	Yes = 1 Else = 0	Yes = 1 Else = 0	Yes = 1 Else = 0	Yes = 1 Else = 0	None = 0 Else = 0	Non-0 = 1 Else = 0	None = 0 Else = 0	None & Infr. = 0 Else = 1	

Market Model Prediction Errors in October 1987 vs. Market Characteristics

	Auction	Off. Special.	Forward Trading	Auto. Quot.	Comp. Trading	Options/ Futures	Price Limits	Trans. Tax	Margin Reqs.	Off-Ex. Trading	Beta
Coeff.	1.688	3.540	8.529	−4.381	1.670	−3.614	−2.201	−5.669	0.551	−0.951	
T-Value	0.361	0.697	1.491	−0.828	0.297	−0.809	−0.376	−1.103	0.141	−0.203	

intercept = 5.89; adjusted R-squared = 0.088

Multiple Regression of October Local-Currency Return on Zero/One Variables and on Typical Response

	Auction	Off. Special.	Forward Trading	Auto. Quot.	Comp. Trading	Options/ Futures	Price Limits	Trans. Tax	Margin Reqs.	Off-Ex. Trading	Beta
Coeff.	−1.443	4.010	4.080	−5.460	4.218	−1.476	0.020	−3.088	1.338	0.179	−16.642
T-Value	−0.281	0.786	0.654	−1.046	0.741	−0.326	0.003	−0.571	0.346	0.039	−2.615
TS T-Val	−0.351	1.046	0.779	−1.169	0.945	−0.339	0.004	−0.638	0.387	0.049	−2.251

intercept = 6.42; adjusted R-squared = 0.498

Market Model Betas, January 1981–September 1987 vs. Market Characteristics

	Auction	Off. Special.	Forward Trading	Auto. Quot.	Comp. Trading	Options/ Futures	Price Limits	Trans. Tax	Margin Reqs.	Off-Ex. Trading	Beta
Coeff.	0.353	−0.151	0.417	0.036	−0.198	−0.160	−0.097	−0.296	−0.046	−0.077	
T-Value	1.691	−0.665	1.631	0.154	−0.787	−0.803	−0.371	−1.288	−0.266	−0.366	

intercept = 1.21; adjusted R-squared = 0.255

regression in Table IV only by the inclusion of the beta. Comparing the two regressions, we observe that none of the market characteristics remains even marginally significant. In contrast, the beta is highly significant, and its coefficient (−16.6 per cent) is a large fraction of the average world market portfolio return.[15] It is more than four times the magnitude of any other estimated coefficient in the regression.

Because this regression uses total percentage changes during October, it may be subject to cross-sectional dependence. A time-series t-value was computed, using the methods described in the appendix. The results are qualitatively the same: Only the market-model beta is statistically significant in explaining October 1987 returns.

There is one remaining problem: It seems at least conceivable that the typical magnitude of response of a given country to a world market movement is itself a function of the institutional arrangements in that country's stock market. For example, perhaps margin requirements or limits on price movements reduce the market-model beta relative to the level it would otherwise achieve in their absence. If so, the dominance of the beta in the October-return cross-sectional re-

gression in Table V and the absence of a statistically significant market characteristic in the cross-sectional regression for market-model residuals during October may still not entirely remove the suspicion that some of the institutional arrangements had an influence on the crash. Instead of showing up directly, their influence could have been exerted by reducing or increasing the estimated magnitude of response.

To check out this possibility, we computed another cross-sectional regression, this time with the dependent variable being the estimated beta itself and the explanatory variables the zero/one market characteristics. The bottom panel of Table V reports the results.

Two characteristics are marginally significant—continuous auctions and forward trading. Forward trading, however, did not show up as an influence on either the total returns in October or on the October market–model residuals. Although it may be an influence on the typical response of a market to world movements, it does not seem to have played a role in the crash. Continuous trading, however, may be a culprit. Countries whose stock markets conduct continuous auctions did worse during the crash. These markets are also associated with larger betas, hence tend to swing more widely in response to worldwide market influences.

If we were willing to accept this result as evidence of causation, we might go on to speculate on why continuous auctions might be prone to larger price swings. A continuous auction conducts trading throughout the day, as orders are received, while a non-continuous auction collects orders over a 24-hour interval and clears all of them at a given time. The continuous auction is more dynamic, and it certainly offers a larger inducement for a trader to act quickly. Quick decisions are less important in a non-continuous regime, because others may reach similar conclusions before the appointed time for the auction. Acting quickly, in an attempt to beat others to the next trade, could lead to more frequent errors and even to panic. Perhaps haste made waste in October 1987.

Market Liquidity

"Liquidity" may have influenced country responses during the crash. Liquidity is not a well-defined term, but most market observers seem to regard smaller markets as less liquid, hence prone to greater price volatility, susceptible to psychological influences, and probably less "efficient." To examine this idea, we used the aggregate dollar value of stocks traded on each stock exchange as a proxy for liquidity.

On September 30, 1987, the 23 national markets in our database differed widely in aggregate capitalization. The smallest was Norway ($2.65 billion) the largest Japan ($2.03 trillion). The United States market capitalization was $1.85 trillion.

Because market capitalization differs across countries by a factor of almost 100, we used its logarithm in the statistical estimation. Log (Market Cap) was included along with the zero/one institutional characteristics and the estimated market-model beta to explain the cross-sectional differences in return during October 1987. It was completely insignificant, having a t-value of only 0.348, and left all the other coefficients virtually unchanged.[16]

Given the previous information about returns around the crash, the lack of a liquidity effect is probably not all that surprising. Some of the smallest markets (Austria and Denmark) performed relatively well in October, while others (Malaysia and Mexico) did poorly. Similarly, some larger countries (Japan) had small de-

clines, while others (the U.K.) were more severely affected. The relative extent of the October crash was related to characteristics other than sheer size. ∎

Footnotes

1. The data source was Goldman, Sachs & Co., "FT-Actuaries World Indices," various monthly editions. The indexes are the most widely followed in each country. A complete list of each country is contained in Goldman, Sachs & Co., "Anatomy of the World's Equity Markets."
2. Between Canada and the U.S. and between Malaysia and Singapore.
3. The previous 76 months go from June 1981 through September 1987.
4. For example, Tokyo is 14 hours ahead of New York, so its observation for October 1, Tokyo time, is plotted as October 0.41666 (i.e., 10/24) New York time. The non-Japanese Asian markets are plotted according to Japanese time, although they are one hour later. Similarly, Mexico is plotted New York time, South Africa is plotted British time, and New Zealand is plotted Australian time. Mexico is one hour behind New York; South Africa and New Zealand are two hours ahead of Britain and Australia, respectively.
5. As Figures G and H show, most other markets did decline even earlier than the U.S. on each day from the 14th through the 16th.
6. Canada's decline from October 22 through October 30 was only 1.62 per cent. Thirteen countries had at least 10 per cent declines in this period.
7. Mexico was excluded from the figure and the regression line because its return during January–September 1987 was 540 per cent in local currency units (although only 271 per cent in dollars); it seems to be an outlier.
8. The data presented in Table III are not easily available. Jim Brandon telephoned every country on the list and interviewed a person knowledgeable about each market. The author thanks Neville Thomas and Michael Crowley, Australia; Robert Schwind, Austria; Mme. Moeremhout, Belgium; Jim Darcel, Canada; Jorgan Brisson, Denmark; M. Douzy, France; Michael Hanke, Germany; Patrick Leong, Hong Kong; Tom Healy, Ireland; Alessandro Wagner, Italy; Moriyuki Iwanaga, Japan; Mr. Izlen, Malaysia; Armando Denegas, Mexico; Paul Koster, The Netherlands; Cathy Gruschow, New Zealand; Melvin Tagen, Norway; Gillian Tam, Singapore; Mrs. De Kock, South Africa; David Jimenez, Spain; Les Vindeyaag, Sweden; Brigette Borsch, Switzerland; and Matthew Hall, United Kingdom.
9. The French market exhibits a unique concept of price limits. They are not enforced if the entire

market seems to be moving in the same direction. According to our informant, enforcement applies only when an individual stock "appears to be manipulated."

10. An explanation of the statistical methods used to obtain the t-value is contained in the appendix.

11. The univariate difference in means across zero/one groups is identical to the slope coefficient in a cross-sectional regression of the October return on a single zero/one variable (for a proof, see the appendix). Thus the effect of multicollinearity can be directly gauged by comparing the slope coefficient in the second panel of Table IV with the corresponding group mean differences in the first.

12. Goldman, Sachs & Co. provided monthly market index levels beginning in January 1981. However, their database does not include Mexico until May 1981. The first month is lost by calculating the monthly percentage change in the index. Thus the index includes 22 countries from February 1981 and 23 countries from June 1981. Dividend yields are available for the latter part of the data period, but dividends have little variability and were thus omitted from the calculations without harm. Because of this omission, the index percentage change for a given month differs slightly from the monthly total return.

13. Indexes were actually constructed both on a common-currency basis and a local-currency basis, and both equally weighted and value-weighted (by the dollar value of total country capitalization). Time-series regressions between individual country returns and the various indexes yielded surprisingly similar slope coefficients (betas). There were differences in R-squares, of course, because the exchange rate adjustment essentially adds a noisy but relatively uncorrelated random variable to the local-currency return. The intercepts also differed, by roughly the difference in mean returns in local currency and in dollars.

14. Note that cross-sectional dependence is probably not material in this regression, simply because the principal source of that dependence, general worldwide market movements, has already been removed.

15. Even this coefficient is probably understated in absolute magnitude because the beta is only an estimated coefficient and is thus an error-contaminated regressor.

16. In particular, the coefficient of beta was about the same (-15.6) and still highly significant (t-value of -2.16). Cross-sectionally, the beta estimated from February 1981 through September 1987 is moderately correlated with the log of market capitalization at the end of September 1987. A cross-sectional regression of beta on log size gives a slope coefficient of -0.147 with a t-value of 1.68. But when both variables compete in a cross-

sectional regression predicting the October decline, the beta wins in the sense of being uniquely significant.

Appendix

T-Values for the Univariate Differences

For each institutional characteristic, two portfolios were formed corresponding to whether the group variable was zero or one. As an example, when the institutional characteristic was computer-directed trading, the first portfolio consisted of an equal-weighted combination of the countries with computer-directed trading (Canada, France, Japan, the United Kingdom and the United States, from Table III), and the second portfolio consisted of an equal-weighted combination of the other countries (the 18 without computer-directed trading). There is a total of 20 such portfolios, two for each of 10 institutional characteristics.

The return for each of the 20 portfolios was calculated for all available data periods before October 1987. Except for Mexico, this was February 1981 through September 1987. For Mexico, it was June 1981 through September 1987. Thus, during the first four of 80 months, Mexico was missing from the 10 portfolios to which it later belonged.

For each month and each institutional characteristic, a return difference was formed by subtracting the portfolio return for group 0 from the portfolio return for group 1. This is tantamount to buying long those countries with a "1" and shorting those countries with a "0" *for a particular characteristic*. There were thus 10 time series of return differences, one for each institutional characteristic.

The standard deviation of the return difference was calculated from the 10 time series. Finally, the t-value was calculated as the return difference in October 1987 divided by the calculated time-series standard deviation.

Univariate Regression

The slope coefficient from the regression of y on a zero/one variable x is simply the difference in group means of y. For proof of this, consider the following definitions:

$$N = \text{total sample size,}$$
$$n = \text{number of observations, with } x = 1,$$
$$p = n/N \text{ and}$$
$$Y, Y_1, Y_0 = \text{respectively, the sample mean of } y, y$$
$$\text{with } x = 1, \text{ and } y \text{ with } x = 0.$$

Then it is straightforward to show that the ordinary-least-squares bivariate regression slope coefficient of y on x is:

$$b = [p(Y_1 - Y)]/[p(1 - p)],$$
$$= \{Y_1 - [pY_1 + (1 - p)Y_0]\}/(1 - p)$$
$$= Y_1 - Y_0.$$

Time-Series T-Values

The second panels of Tables IV and V present t-values obtained from a time series not including the cross-section month (October 1987). For every month when all countries had available data (June 1981 through September 1987), a cross-sectional multiple regression was calculated between the actual monthly index percentage changes and the explanatory variables, the zero/one variables (corresponding to Table IV), and the zero/one variables plus the country's market model beta (corresponding to Table V). The vector of 10 (11) cross-sectional coefficients corresponding to panel 2 of Table IV (Table V) for month t formed a single time-series observation.

The standard deviation of each element in the vector of coefficients was then computed across all time-series observations. The TS t-value was the estimated cross-sectional coefficient in October 1987 divided by its corresponding standard deviation as computed in steps 1 and 2.

Market–Model Results

Table AI gives means, standard deviations and market–model regression results for local-currency returns, using an equal-weighted, local-currency world market index.

Table AI Local-Currency Index Percentage Changes and Equal-Weighted World Portfolio (Feb.1981–Sept. 1987)

Country	Sample Size (months)	Average % Change (per month)	Standard Deviation (%/month)	Market Model Regression		
				Slope (t-values)	Intercept (t-values)	Adjusted R-Squared
Australia	80	1.634	5.896	1.218 (7.208)	−0.563 (−0.938)	0.3921
Austria	80	0.985	5.128	0.563 (3.152)	−0.031 (−0.048)	0.1016
Belgium	80	1.899	5.191	0.808 (4.785)	0.442 (0.736)	0.2170
Canada	80	0.855	4.931	1.116 (8.492)	−1.159 (−2.481)	0.4738
Denmark	80	1.463	5.306	0.579 (3.127)	0.419 (0.637)	0.1000
France	80	1.748	5.602	0.901 (4.995)	0.123 (0.191)	0.2326
Germany	80	1.503	4.923	0.739 (4.567)	0.171 (0.297)	0.2009
Hong Kong	80	1.439	9.248	1.533 (5.201)	−1.326 (−1.266)	0.2480
Ireland	80	1.926	6.445	1.193 (6.074)	−0.226 (−0.324)	0.3124
Italy	80	1.911	7.783	1.192 (4.688)	−0.240 (−0.266)	0.2098
Japan	80	1.989	4.651	0.557 (3.483)	0.983 (1.729)	0.1235
Malaysia	80	0.433	8.108	1.137 (4.197)	−1.618 (−1.681)	0.1738
Mexico	76	6.555	16.110	2.135 (3.914)	2.655 (1.345)	0.1603
Netherlands	80	1.529	4.988	1.050 (7.440)	−0.365 (−0.728)	0.4076
New Zealand	80	2.190	6.609	1.019 (4.726)	0.352 (0.460)	0.2127
Norway	80	1.656	6.381	1.110 (5.553)	−0.346 (−0.487)	0.2742
Singapore	80	0.874	7.858	1.251 (4.930)	−1.383 (−1.534)	0.2278
South Africa	80	2.181	7.247	0.713 (2.790)	0.895 (0.985)	0.0791
Spain	80	2.352	6.443	0.716 (3.196)	1.060 (1.331)	0.1045
Sweden	80	2.513	6.109	0.872 (4.290)	0.940 (1.302)	0.1805
Switzerland	80	1.010	3.876	0.795 (7.117)	−0.424 (−1.068)	0.3860
United Kingdom	80	1.888	4.567	0.950 (7.288)	0.176 (0.379)	0.3975
United States	80	1.221	4.243	0.856 (6.933)	−0.324 (−0.738)	0.3734

[31]

US investment banks as multinationals[1]

Brian Scott-Quinn

Introduction

Studies of financial services firms as multinationals[2] have tradition-ally concentrated on commercial banking with little attention being paid to investment banks. One possible reason for this relative lack of academic interest is that this industry sector has traditionally been organized through private partnerships, which are secretive about their operations compared with manufacturing companies or commercial banks. In contrast with commercial banks, which started to become joint stock companies around 1860, it was not until 1960 that investment banks started to become public companies. A second reason is that the size of the whole industry in the United States in terms of capital employed has until recently been less than that of any one of the largest US commercial banks. This is because commercial banks employ their own equity, debt and deposits to enable them to act as principals in their transactions with lenders and borrowers, while investment banks have tradi-tionally acted as brokers. A third reason is that only in the 1980s has the securities industry come to the attention of the world outside Wall Street and the City of London, mainly as a result of the extent to which securities market transactions during this period have substituted for the deposit and loan transactions of commercial banks.

The previous chapter in this book, by Huertas, while a study of one particular commercial bank, also explores the reasons for US commercial banks entering securities markets and for securities firms becoming multinational. While these chapters were prepared independently, there are many parallels in them. The framework of analysis – the internalization model – is the same. Citibank's move from correspondent relationships to its own overseas subsidiaries and branches parallels investment banks' move from commission-splitting arrangements with overseas brokers to own offices and

268

US investment banks as multinationals

branches overseas. Huertas notes that very few US banks (or overseas banks) were multinational until after 1960 and the reasons for the change he relates to macroeconomic, regulatory and microeconomic factors. This chapter also dates the start of the multinationalization of investment banks to 1960 and for similar reasons, but also sees 1980 as the start of a new period of 'globalization and integration' in investment banking, something not paralleled in the Huertas paper. Finally, the emphasis he places on the need for high throughput of product relative to inventory in a financial engineering operation is exactly parallel to the need for high throughput in a securities market making operation. In both cases this is an important factor generating the need to maximize customer volume by tapping business globally. When allied with the increasing demand for cross-border services in banking and securities, it becomes clear that there are many types of financial service that can only be provided economically by a multinational.

The focus of this chapter is on firms that are classified by the SEC as investment banks.[3] In addition, however, we will be looking at the overseas investment banking subsidiaries of US commercial banks principally to see if their motivations for FDI differ from those of the investment banks. These subsidiaries are able to undertake overseas corporate securities market transactions that would be illegal for them in the United States under the Securities Acts (in particular the Glass Steagall Act). We will concentrate on activities in London, which was the overseas centre to which US investment banks were first attracted.

Concepts and definitions

Investment banks are concerned principally with effecting securities transactions for their corporate and investor clients, thereby contributing towards the creation of public securities markets. In examining the structure of firms in the industry therefore, a principal focus of our attention will be on the nature of the costs involved in making markets and the means by which firms can minimize these in order to be more competitive.

Internalization is one of the principal means by which firms in manufacturing industry minimize transactions costs.[4] Internalization means co-ordinating related activities within a single firm rather than through market transactions. In the case of international activities, internalization means co-ordinating activities in different countries within one firm through a management structure rather than through arm's-length transactions between

269

Brian Scott-Quinn

independent firms.[5] Multinational enterprises are simply collections of firms in different countries under common ownership. Transactions between them thus become internal rather than market transactions. In the case of investment banks, our objective is to demonstrate that the extension of the scope and geographical spread of their activities has been a response to the need to compete in terms of price, speed and quality of service. Internalization has been the means by which they have improved their competitiveness in all three areas.

What investment banks do

The range of activities of the twenty-one large investment banks in the SEC study differ widely. However, there are core activities that all are involved in and which clearly distinguish them from commercial banks. Investment banking involves assessing market risk, finding investors and minimizing the time for which assets are held on a balance sheet as distinct from traded. Deposit or commercial banking on the other hand involves seeking deposits, assessing credit risk and using deposits to make loans to build up a balance sheet. In investment banking, the objective is to maximize asset turnover and control *market* risk, while in commercial banking the objective is to maximize balance sheet size subject to controlling the level of *credit* risk. Given the difference in asset turnover rates, it is not surprising that commercial banks have for many decades been highly capitalized public companies while securities firms have historically been private partnerships with limited capital. One of the questions we shall examine is why, in the 1960s and 1970s, securities houses have experienced the need to raise additional capital either by dissolving their partnership status or by accepting an investment from an outside firm.

The major activity of investment banks is their involvement in either primary or secondary securities markets or in both.[6] These remain roles distinct from those of commercial banks (*qua* commercial banks) and are the ones that we shall be examining in this paper. *Primary market* activity involves arranging the flotation of new securities issues in the primary market for corporate, sovereign and public sector customers (henceforth called simply corporates). Two types of new securities issue are arranged. The Initial Public Offering (IPO) and the secondary offering, i.e. one which is simply adding to the existing stock of securities. *Secondary market* activity involves the provision of liquidity to investors by participation in secondary markets either as broker (agent) or as dealer (principal) or both (broker/dealer).

270

US investment banks as multinationals

The processes involved

There are three principal processes involved in providing primary and secondary market services, as shown in Figure 14.1.

Origination involves developing contact with corporate clients, the arrangement of the terms of the contract between the corporate and the final investors, and the formation of a syndicate which will provide for the distribution of the issue. An origination house need only have one office in the major financial centre of a country.

Distribution involves continuous contact with potential investors in securities and the sale of securities to them when new issue merchandise is made available through a syndicate or, in the case of an integrated house, from the origination department. In order to maintain continuous contact and knowledge of investor requirements a distribution house also provides secondary market services to investors. Since investors are widely scattered, distribution houses have a chain of offices. The distribution side will normally also provide research, which is intended to indicate when the 'true' value of securities differs from their current market price.

Market making involves providing the liquidity that is central to the operation of a secondary market. Given that there is frequently no double co-incidence of wants in time or deal size between buyers and sellers of securities, the trading house bridges the time and size gap between them by taking principal positions (long and

Figure 14.1   The Investment Bank. Internal relationships and external interfaces

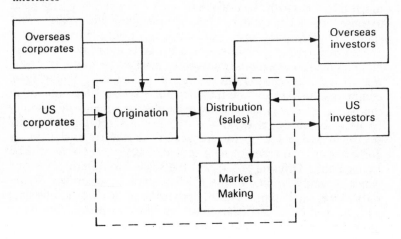

Brian Scott-Quinn

short inventory positions) on its own account. For the provision of this *immediacy* service, the trader is rewarded by a margin between the price at which he buys and the price at which he sells (the bid/offer spread).

Specialization or integration in the industry

Historically each of these activities was undertaken by a specialized intermediary. Origination was provided by what has always been called 'investment banks'. Distribution was handled by so called 'wire houses', i.e. nationwide offices linked together by telegraph. Professional trading was handled by trading houses in New York, whose skill was in making markets, and by 'specialists' on the floor of the NYSE. Overseas distribution was undertaken by foreign houses with whom US firms had relationships similar to 'correspondent banking' relationships in the commercial bank environment.

Primary and secondary market activities are closely related, and they are thus frequently considered to be joint products. This arises from the fact that the client base for the distribution side of the primary market is likely to be the same client base as for the sales team on the secondary market side, since most investors participate in both primary and secondary markets. Also, as we have noted, prices for secondary offerings in the primary market are based on prices at which existing securities are trading in the secondary market. Thus there is a *prima facie* reason to believe that there may be benefits from integration of primary and secondary market activities.

Closer examination suggests, however, that the links between the two activities are only at the distribution and sales level. Origination is not a joint product with a sales and trading operation except for the pricing input that trading can provide. In practice we find that since origination and distribution are two such different activities, with different personnel and a different client base, integrated investment banks are split into two sections – the buy side and the sell side. The buy (or origination) side transacts with corporates, while the sell (or distribution) side transacts with institutional investors.

The trading (market making) function differs from origination or distribution in that it is one which can be provided either within each separate firm, i.e. fragmented trading in an over-the-country (OTC) telephone market or consolidated in a central market place (floor trading). In the UK, the Stock Market prior to Big Bang was a central market place to which brokers brought their orders. Post

272

US investment banks as multinationals

Big Bang, the market has become fragmented, i.e. all but a few brokers now have in-house market making, though each house is linked to the others through screens and telephones.

Breadth, depth and efficiency in market making

Efficiency in a market is measured as total trading cost. Trading costs are classified either as explicit transaction costs or as implicit execution costs. Explicit transaction costs are visible and easily measured; they include commissions and taxes. Implicit execution costs are not easily measured; they exist because orders may, as a result of their size and/or sparsity of counterpart orders on the market, execute at relatively high prices (if they are buy orders) or at relatively low prices (if they are sell orders).[7]

The function of the market making department in an integrated firm is to balance risk and reward on the trading book in order to provide immediacy to clients with low implicit execution cost and minimum risk to the firm. Two factors that give rise to low transactions cost, immediacy and minimum risk to the market marker are the depth and breadth of the in-house market that the firm can create from its own client base. Depth is measured as the number of buy and sell orders that the firm has available to it at prices around the last transactions price, i.e. the supply and demand schedules of traders (investors) immediately available to the market maker. Market depth should lead to low execution costs. Breadth is the availability to a market maker of traders with different expectations and different motives for wanting to hold a particular security. Market breadth should further reduce execution costs and also reduce volatility.

Depth and breadth in a market making department mean that the firm will generally be able to match orders coming in on one side very quickly with clients who are willing to take the other side of the deal. Thus if the house (investment bank) sells merchandise to one client at the offer price, it can buy it in from another at the bid price or only slightly more within a very short time.

The ability to do this is a function of the size of the sales team, the depth and breadth of their client base and their ability to know which clients might be interested in acquiring particular positions. This in turn is in part a function of having been involved in the primary distribution and hence knowing who currently owns the securities.

If the firm cannot complete the deal quickly in-house it can either hold the position in inventory until another client comes along with the opposite side of the transaction, or it can close the

273

Brian Scott-Quinn

position in the professional (inter-dealer) marketplace. If it does the latter, however, it is likely to have to pay the offer price to buy the security, and thus will not make any 'turn' on the transaction. Alternatively, if it waits until one of its own customers is able to unwind the deal, it has a carrying cost of holding inventory (the difference between the running yield and the cost of funds) and also a considerable price risk. Thus not only do the high fixed financial costs of a market making operation mean that a high throughput is necessary to keep down average running cost, but also the production process itself needs a very high throughput of transactions to minimize implicit trading costs and risk for the market maker.

Investors' supply and demand schedules are thus an input to the immediacy creation and transactions cost minimizing process. The availability of potential client bids and offers to the dealing desk of an OTC market maker of itself makes the process more efficient because of better matching opportunities and hence risk reduction, quite apart from any consideration of fixed costs. Thus the availability of clients with heterogenous expectations with whom the market maker has strong relationships is likely to be critical to achieving competitiveness both in terms of minimum transactions cost and also immediacy. Thus to be a low cost provider of immediacy the private in-house market has to try to reproduce some of the features of the public market.

The argument for centralized public floor markets (order consolidation) has always been that such centralization overcomes this problem of insufficient depth and breadth available to any particular private market making house. Centralizing turns marketability services into a public good since the benefits in terms of lowered transactions cost and immediacy that result from a consolidated order flow are available to all comers. Thus there is a private benefit to each participant from the existence of every other trader's transactions, i.e. from the broadest and deepest possible market.

Despite this clear benefit, markets have increasingly become fragmented since the 1960s. The eurobond market, since it began in 1963, has always operated as an OTC market since the firms involved in it are geographically distributed around the world. The NYSE is de-centralized for 'block' transactions which take place 'upstairs' in the trading houses away from the specialist. As institutional investors have come to dominate NYSE trading at the expense of individuals, block trades have become the major part of the market and thus the specialist's role has diminished. In London, what was once a centralized market became fragmented

274

US investment banks as multinationals

at the time of Big Bang. It was further fragmented in February 1989 with the introduction of a rule which eliminated the need to disclose large orders to the market on the day of the transaction.

There has been a worldwide trend away from centralized public markets towards private in-house markets. There are two forces driving this trend. The first is the decline in profitability from offering immediacy in competitive central markets where price information is freely available to traders (investors) electronically. The second is the increasing proportion of 'block trades' in many markets which are difficult to transact on public exchanges with minimum impact on price. These factors have forced firms to take steps to expand the depth and breadth of their client base in whatever countries may offer them potential business, and to try to develop a private in-house market.

The globalization of financial markets and intermediaries

Traditionally, financial markets in different countries have been segmented as a result of the high costs of international transactions, due to regulatory constraints and cartels and information assymetries between dealers in different countries which limited the extent of investor arbitrage. There were consequently considerable inefficiencies across markets. The 1960s and 1970s saw increasing cross-border financial activity as investors began to explore the possibilities of overseas investment. But it was not until the 1980s that markets became increasingly global and integrated as transactions costs fell and transactions volumes increased. Transactions cost has been falling sharply partly as a result of deregulation and partly from improving communications and computer technology which has facilitated international arbitrage.

The fact that markets have become global and integrated does not of itself imply that the intermediaries which offer services to investors and borrowers in these markets need operate in more than one country. Every type of service which is available from these markets can be supplied by a financial firm in the same country as the investor or borrower and can be accessed through *trade* in financial services. Indeed, financial services are, *par excellence*, the type of value-adding activity that can, with modern technology, be transported at virtually no cost across national boundaries and would therefore seem to be highly suited in terms of cost minimization to be supplied by export rather than by local production. It is somewhat surprising therefore that from the 1960s to the present day, a period which saw the introduction of low cost communications technologies, US investment banks and

275

Brian Scott-Quinn

the investment banking subsidiaries of US commercial banks also moved from being exporters to setting up or expanding their own facilities overseas.

We will look at this development in three historical stages:

1   *Up to 1960*, investment banks relied principally on agency relationships similar in nature to correspondent banking relationships. As the period up to 1960 was prior to the development of the multinational investment bank, we only refer to it briefly.

2   *In the 1960s and 1970s* these firms set up sales branches or subsidiaries in London (or in a few instances, Paris or Geneva) to service existing foreign clients with US (domestic) investment products, i.e. US equities. They were thus simply replacing sales through overseas agents with sales through direct investment facilities. They then moved to producing low cost debt origination services for their existing US corporate clients when the eurobond market came into existence in London in the mid to late 1960s. At the same time, commercial banks which already had corporate banking activities in London set up eurobond origination subsidiaries to allow them to offer dollar bond origination services to their US corporate clients. While in the United States they could not offer bond origination, in London they could. They thus immediately came into competition with the investment banks for the first time.

3   *In the 1980s* the whole scale of foreign direct investment by investment banking institutions not only in London but also in Tokyo increased quite dramatically. In eurobonds, there was a large upstream investment in global distribution to replace the large syndicates that had been used before. In Treasury bonds, there was downstream investment in market making in London and Tokyo, which involved large outlays not only on people, equipment and software and buildings, but also on inventory. But most dramatic of all was the decision by many US investment and commercial banks to enter completely new territory by commencing market making and distribution in foreign domestic equity and bond markets. Finally, during this period, these various operations which had in many cases been relatively autonomous, were increasingly integrated with each other worldwide and with the parent company.

Given the central importance of transactions cost in determining the competitiveness of transactions-oriented investment banks, we

276

US investment banks as multinationals

will be looking at the phenomenon of overseas direct investment as the means by which these firms have been able to reduce transactions costs and increase immediacy for both domestic and overseas clients and thus increase their competitiveness.

We will examine the progression of the representative firm in the industry from being single capacity (broker, market maker or originator), to being integrated across all three, then to being multinational and finally global. We will look also at the successive types of firm organization involved – the private partnership and the public company.

US securities houses up to 1960

Many US investment banks that are dominant today, can trace their origins back to the originating firms which dominated the great railroad financings in the nineteenth century. Some of these were partnerships of Jewish financiers who, unlike the Yankee houses, often enjoyed the business advantages of extensive family ties around the world.[8] There were also numerous joint ventures between European and US firms. In the early nineteenth century the need to fund public debt resulted in US bankers going to London, which proved a good source of capital for US needs.[9] However, only a few US houses had an office in London itself, the best known of which was J.S. Morgan.

Just as primary distributions were generally undertaken by co-operative arrangements between firms in different countries, until the beginning of the 1960s so also were secondary market transactions. The traditional way of doing this was through an arm's-length relationship between a US investment bank (*qua* broker) and a broker in the country of the investor. Thus, for example, an investor in London would ask his own broker to obtain certain shares for him and his broker in turn would approach a US broker with whom he had a relationship and arrange to buy the securities. The brokers would normally have a commission-splitting arrangement. The London broker might also give his client access to the US broker's research.

The process was quite effective but relatively slow in terms of information flow. There was also no certainty as to the price at which the securities would be acquired given the problems of communication until the 1960s. Thus in terms of transactions cost and immediacy, the procedure did not score highly.

Brian Scott-Quinn

The incorporation and integration of US investment banks in the 1960s and 1970s

The US domestic securities market

The 1960s and 1970s were an era when the structure of the investment banking industry in the United States changed dramatically. This change is well documented by Hayes[10] who notes that this period saw integration by brokers back to trading and origination, which coincided with those firms going public in order to replace 'nervous insider funds' with permanent public investors' money.

Securities markets overseas

(a) Investor services

The first question to be answered is why US investment banks did not continue to use agents overseas. The second question is why, when they did set up offices overseas, they did not undertake market making, which it might be thought would allow them to offer a much better service to their foreign clients in terms of immediacy.

In terms of explicit transactions cost (i.e. commissions and taxes), there is little reason to believe that any great reduction in cost would result simply from setting up an overseas office. The commission level would be the same and the taxes, etc. would be unchanged. In terms of implicit transactions cost, this would be unchanged too since the actual trading would still be carried on in New York. Thus we rule out a reduction in explicit or implicit transactions cost as being primary motivating factors.

Why then did they set up overseas offices? Given that an investor has already made the decision to acquire foreign equities, the principal feature distinguishing the 'product' of different suppliers is the quality of service (principally advice) on which equities to buy and speed of information flow. It was never possible to achieve speedy information flow through agents. Furthermore, the quality of advice and general service is encapsulated in the purchaser's eyes in the brand name of the company which supplies the service to him.[11] If the agent provided a very high quality of service under his own name, the goodwill from providing the service would accrue to the agent. He would thus become the stronger partner in the arrangement with the US investment bank and could set the terms of trade between them in this intermediate product market. Conversely, if the US investment bank's trade name was used, he would be unlikely to want to push

278

US investment banks as multinationals

this name from a brand point of view since it would reduce his bilateral negotiating power with the US partner. The only solution to this bilateral negotiating problem is for the US partner to set up his own facility in order to capture all the economic rent that accrues from the creation of a brand identity. Thus by internalizing the international market link, he can achieve a higher rate of profitability on his overseas sales. While this problem existed well before the 1960s, the volume of such transactions before then was limited. In addition, the capital constraints that existed before the majority of investment banks became public companies in the 1960s and 1970s encouraged them to limit capital expenditure overseas.

Why did US investment banks not set up overseas market making, which is the analogue to production in a manufacturing firm? It is useful at this point to compare manufacturing and securities markets products. The principal difference is that in the case of the latter, production and purchase need to be simultaneous while in the former case they need not be. The time zone problem makes the servicing of overseas clients with the same quality of service as domestic clients impossible unless a market making operation is set up. This is because immediacy can only be provided by having a market making operation in the time zone where the securities are being sold. Otherwise immediacy can only be offered when European (or Japanese) trading hours overlap with those in the US. However, a market making operation cannot function efficiently at providing immediacy at relatively low volumes of activity. In the case of US stocks, although there was considerable demand across all securities, for any individual stock there was insufficient demand to make market making economic. If all US investment banks had co-operated it is possible that a market could have been set up in a small number of securities such as GM, IBM and GE. But without such a central marketplace to aggregate orders as there is on the New York Stock Exchange no single equity could generate adequate volume. There was thus insufficient market depth in Europe or Japan outside New York opening hours in the absence of a centralized exchange to allow efficient market making. Until certain other changes took place in the 1980s, therefore, US equity operations outside the US remained as sales offices rather than also becoming market making centres.

(b) Corporate issuer services – the eurodollar bond market

The commencement of business in the eurobond market by US investment banks and the investment banking subsidiaries of

279

Brian Scott-Quinn

commercial banks was driven initially neither by the idea of servicing US corporate clients nor investors. The eurobond market came into existence in London in 1963 started by UK merchant banks, brokers and US investment banks in the wake of the closure of the foreign dollar bond market in New York. This happened when the US government imposed a punitive tax – interest equalization tax – designed to stop foreigners using the New York capital markets.

As a result, the market in dollar bond issues for non-US borrowers moved to London and it was logical for US investment banks which already had offices there (US equity sales) to start trading dollar bonds and also to originate bond issues for (non-US) borrowers who previously used their services to access the New York bond market. US investment banks had no obvious competitive advantage operating in London and at this time did not dominate the market.

But in 1968 the US authorities issued new rules on fund raising by US multinationals wishing to make investments overseas. From then on such investment had to be financed by raising funds outside the US. These rules, the Foreign Direct Investment Rules (FDIR), resulted in an immediate and very sharp increase in demand for *origination* services by US corporations outside the United States. Note, however, that the reason for US investment banks setting up London eurobond subsidiaries post-FDIR was not to service the subsidiaries of multinationals operating overseas. It was to service the head offices of US multinationals in the United States. In this respect it was quite different from the branches and subsidiaries set up by commercial banks abroad to service the local subsidiaries of US multinationals. Initially it was simply that because of the Interest Equalization Tax (IET), intermediating offshore was cheaper than intermediating onshore. However, it was quickly apparent that there were other reasons why intermediating offshore was cheaper. The principal one was that while coupon income on US domestic bonds suffered withholding tax, coupon income on eurobonds was free of withholding tax. Thus even a lower before tax yield on a eurobond compared with a domestic bond could still give a higher after tax yield to an investor who, for whatever reason, did not pay tax on his coupon income. In addition the securities were bearer rather than registered which was attractive to certain types of investor who wished to avoid drawing official attention to their wealth.

The market was thus driven principally by the lower funding cost that could be offered to US corporate treasurers if they raised their funds offshore, a situation analogous to that in the eurodollar market where offshore intermediation could provide a lower cost

280

US investment banks as multinationals

of funds as an input to eurodollar corporate banking than could domestic intermediation. It was not possible to use agents in the United Kingdom to provide origination services on behalf of US investment banks. The transactions cost would have made such deals uneconomic. The clients were principally from the US and all the documentation and historical knowledge of the client was in files and working knowledge of personnel in New York. As a result, much of the work on origination continued to be conducted in the US with a team flying over to Europe if necessary at the time of the actual issue.

Although something of the order of 50 per cent of US corporate fixed-rate funding since 1968 has been carried out in the eurobond market rather than the domestic market, the eurobond market did not replace the domestic market any more than the eurodollar market replaced the domestic deposit market. The reason is that while arbitrage between the two markets by both investors and issuers results in yields remaining relatively close, the yield differential moves continually over time, being sometimes positive and sometimes negative. It varies because of the tendency for interest rates and the exchange rate to be correlated, which means that foreign (but not domestic) investors believe that the currency gain from rising interest rates is likely to offset the fall in the bond price as a result of rising interest rates (and vice versa). Also, companies of different credit rating may have comparative advantage in either the domestic or the eurobond market.

While US banks undertook origination in London and many also engaged in professional market making, they did not invest in the facilities necessary for international distribution of securities. This important element in the chain of activities in primary market issues was effected through syndicates which were dominated by the distribution capability (placing power) of the Swiss and German universal banks. In this era it was clear that it was not economic to internalize distribution within a single US investment bank or even a syndicate of them.

Global integration of investment banks in the 1980s

Up to 1979/80, the US multinational investment bank had little more than a large office in London and perhaps some much smaller ones in other European countries, perhaps an Arab country and possibly (though less likely) Japan.

From 1980 onward, the development of the US investment bank as a multinational changed qualitatively. 1979/80 was a watershed time in the political world. Two political leaders,

281

Brian Scott-Quinn

Margaret Thatcher and President Reagan, both committed to the doctrine of monetarism as the means to cure inflation, and to greater use of markets to achieve their political objectives, acceded to power. The Federal Reserve was also committed to an activist interest rate policy. The outcome was a number of macroeconomic and regulatory changes which have greatly impacted the financial sector.

Macroeconomic changes

Both leaders instituted monetarist policies. The outcome was much higher interest rates in both countries and an inversion of dollar and sterling yield curves. The interest rate rise caused sharp falls in stock markets. The new activist policy, using interest rates to attempt to control money supply combined with rapidly changing inflation expectations resulted in highly volatile financial asset prices – interest rates, exchange rates, bond prices and stock prices.

The so called 'supply side' economics which was being followed in the US held that cutting taxes would increase the growth rate of the economy. An unintended outcome was a large increase in the size of the external deficit. At this time also, the authorities in both the US and the UK foreswore the use of active intervention in the foreign exchange markets. Thus the financing of payments imbalances was left principally to the private sector.

Deregulation

The generation of a current account surplus in the UK in 1979 led to the abolition of exchange controls. Switzerland also abolished its exchange controls in 1979/80. In Japan, the Foreign Exchange Control Act, designed to concentrate foreign exchange in official hands, was amended in 1980. In 1981, Germany abolished restrictions on non-resident purchases of domestic bonds. In 1984, the US abolished withholding tax on interest paid to non-resident investors in government and corporate bonds, making them much more attractive to foreign investors.

In the financial markets the UK took the lead in 1982 by starting the process of allowing foreigners to buy into Stock Exchange firms and started a process of deregulation which culminated in Big Bang in 1986. The increased competitiveness of the UK financial markets led to competitive pressure on other financial markets to deregulate. In a number of countries,

US investment banks as multinationals

regulations restricting the proportion of assets held by pension funds that could be invested in foreign securities were also eased.

Outcome of changes in the 1980s

The result of these macroeconomic and regulatory changes was to alter the type of product that was required by investors. The first important change was that as a result of financial asset price volatility, immediacy became ever more important both for borrowers and for investors. The secular fall in profits, however, suggests that investors were unwilling to pay for the additional immediacy in an environment where the industry was already starting to suffer from excess capacity.

The second change was that institutional investors worldwide started to diversify their portfolios more substantially than in the past through purchases of foreign securities. This resulted first from the increasing freedom to take investment funds out of a number of countries, the freedom to invest in a number of countries and a growing belief in the benefits of international rather than simply domestic diversification. An increasing porporportion of bond funds became multicurrency, while equity portfolios began to be structured around 'international equities'. Quite apart from the increasing proportion of investment funds worldwide, which were diversifying internationally, there was also an increasing realization that foreign portfolio investment had become both easier as a result of telecommunications improvements and cheaper because of the deregulation of financial markets.

Response to changes in the economic and regulatory environment

In *eurobonds*, there has been forward integration from origination into global distribution. In US *Treasury bonds*, there has been backward integration in London and Tokyo from sales into trading. At the same time, there has been global integration of the operations in New York, Tokyo and London. In US equities, there has, at least for a few actively traded 'international' US issues, been integration back to trading. A quite different response to the changing environment has been the move by some firms to enter the domestic securities markets of other countries and to try to build up a new client base.

In our view, this increasing integration of US firms in the 1980s can been seen principally as a competitive response to the declining margins brought on by deregulation (the converse of lower

283

Brian Scott-Quinn

transactions costs for investors) and increasing volatility in financial asset prices.

Investment banks compete on price, immediacy and 'quality'. It was necessary therefore for them to take steps that would lead to improvements in these three areas. We will now look at each type of integration in detail.

Eurobonds

Traditionally in New York, the origination and distribution of bond and stock issues had been carried out by separate types of institution. The integration between the various functions in the vertical chain from origination, through distribution to wholesale market making was through syndicates and arm's-length relationships. The investment banks were the originators. They restricted their activity to relationships with corporate clients (buy side). They structured and priced deals and arranged the syndicates. The selling was undertaken by the wire houses, which were the brokers with a nationwide selling organization with hundreds of local offices. Finally there were the trading houses in New York who provided professional market making services to brokers across the nation and to institutional investors.

The strength of the US investment banks in London was that they had a strong corporate client base in their US clients and, in addition, generally had bond trading skills. What none of them had was much distribution capability in bonds outside the United States. But prior to 1980, this was not a great disadvantage. Investment funds for eurobonds came principally from Europe and oil producing countries. Distribution in Europe was undertaken mainly by the European universal banks – German, and particularly Swiss. The Swiss banks had a captive non-resident client base whose money was mainly managed on a discretionary basis. This allowed the Swiss banks to place securities of their own choice at full issue price into client portfolios. US investment banks had reasonably good distribution in OPEC countries based on salesmen in London, and in this market were at no particular disadvantage *vis-à-vis* European banks. From 1982 onwards, however, OPEC surpluses were declining and in some OPEC countries, reserves started to fall. Thus this source of demand effectively dried up.

At the same time, Japan was becoming an ever-growing source of funds. This resulted in most major US investment banks believing that they would need to enter the Tokyo market in order to tap the funds available in this centre.

From 1980 onwards US investment banks were forced to increase greatly their investment in their London subsidiaries.

284

US investment banks as multinationals

Prior to this, the use of the large syndicate for distribution had allowed the level of investment in London to be minimized. But in the 1980s, it became clear that integrated houses were more competitive than non-integrated.

The reason for this lies in the increasing importance during this period of price in the awarding of mandates by treasurers. If we take a group of originators, all of whom have an equally good reputation and all of whom are tendering for a mandate, then the award of a mandate may become simply a question of price and immediacy. Deals were frequently being arranged by lead managers at a price such that the $2^1/2$ per cent spread (transactions cost) which is supposed to reward the lead manager, co-managers, underwriters and selling group had to be given away to price-sensitive investors (i.e. the issue sold at a price close to 97.5 per cent of par) in order to provide an attractive and competitive yield. For co-managers and underwriters participating in the deal, unless they had access to investors who were price insensitive, they would generate little revenue from the deal and indeed frequently suffered losses.

The firms which were able to continue to generate revenue from such issues were of two types – those which lead managed the issue (originators) and therefore received the *precipium* on the issue (i.e. a payment out of the spread before any other member of the syndicate is paid) and those who had access to price-insensitive clients. These include the Swiss banks with non-resident discretionary clients and the Japanese securities houses with their domestic client base. These two groups are price insensitive because of an asymmetry of price information available to them relative to their securities house. The lack of information in the case of Swiss clients arises from the fact that they are often not institutional investors but rich private individuals often living far from Switzerland and unable to access (and frequently uninterested in accessing) price information services. In the case of Japanese clients, social relationships between investors and securities houses count for more than in the west and seem to allow a reward for service given rather than a pure free competitive market return. In addition, price information services are not yet widely available. US investment banks have attempted to build such a price-insensitive client base by integrating into distribution, but their relative lack of success can be judged by the decline in their position in the origination league tables. This lack of success is because the type of clients US investment banks generally have access to in turn have access to exactly the same information on 'true' price that they do.

285

Brian Scott-Quinn

The eurobond new issue market is thus highly competitive at two interfaces – with the majority of corporates and with many professional institutional investors – but less competitive at certain other parts of the investor interface. It is competitive for issuers as a result of the high degree of sophistication that they have gained over the years and more importantly their access to 'up to second' prices from information providers such as Reuters on comparable secondary market trading prices. They are also able to force potential lead managers from all the major securities houses to bid competitively for a mandate to lead the issue (bought deal).

In order to fully distribute an issue, US originators without in-house distribution in Japan, Switzerland and Germany, must distribute through Japanese, Swiss and German investment banks who will not purchase an issue unless they can be assured a reasonable margin for themselves. The consequent low profitability has caused many US houses to cease offering origination services in this market.

Internalization theory predicts that as transactions costs in markets fall, market transactions between specialist firms become more attractive relative to internal transactions in integrated houses. It is surprising therefore that it was during a period when transactions costs *were* falling that US investment banks were integrating forward into distribution. The reason for this is explained by this interface being one where in certain countries, costs were not falling. If, however, the market interface between investment banks and investor clients in Switzerland and Japan becomes more competitive, we would expect to see, on the basis of this theory, that more firms would specialize once again and more originators would simply rent distribution when they had arranged an issue. This has already happened in the UK equity market as a result of the lowered transactions costs (and broker profits) resulting from Big Bang. One major originator that integrated into distribution in 1986 (Morgan Grenfell) closed its distribution arm in 1989 and now once again rents distribution capability through the market in the form of a syndicate.

Final Product Market Interfaces   Links between intermediaries and final clients can be of two clearly distinct types – transactional and relationship based. In a transactional link, the investor selects afresh which firm to conduct business with each time he wishes to transact, simply on the basis of cost and immediacy. Such sell side clients tend to be those who transact frequently in either the primary or secondary markets and for whom search costs are low. These tend to be the institutional fund managers who use the

286

US investment banks as multinationals

securities they buy and sell as inputs to their final retail financial product market. These final product markets are highly competitive in many countries as a result of the ease with which the performance of fund managers can be compared. On the buy side, the clients who are most price sensitive are those who access the bond markets perhaps a dozen times per year and have access to price information from screens.

Those clients with whom investment banks have close relationships are those for whom it is likely that search costs are higher and where a relationship based on trust and knowledge by the investment bank of the client's business needs and objectives reduces the implicit transactions cost for the client. This would apply particularly to corporates and investors who have not transacted at all or only infrequently in a particular market. In seeking a firm with which to form a relationship (a partnership) they will choose to rely in large part on 'general reputation' of the firm.[12]

It is for this reason that we emphasize the importance of brand name identification and franchise. We view clients who have a relationship with an investment bank as being in a partnership with them in a not dissimilar way to partnerships between integrated parts of the same firm. This can thus be viewed as a type of 'internalization' of what would otherwise be a market (transactional) relationship. The outcome of the internalization of the client interface is that the client will accept a trade-off between the transactions costs that he incurs and the benefits he derives from the partnership that is more in favour of the firm. This seems to be the type of relationship which Japanese securities houses have with many of their clients. Thus a benefit that the multinational firm can develop is the value that is capitalized in its reputation and the ability this gives it to obtain a better price from clients who are 'quasi integrated' with them. Consideration of this type of internalization is critical in understanding vertical and horizontal (geographic) integration in the securities industry.

Geographical dispersion of a client base (breadth) also makes it more likely that heterogeneity of expectations about the prospects for a particular security will allow a greater depth of internal (and hence more profitable) market for any investment bank. It will also allow more international arbitrage transactions to be set up by the investment bank on which the potential benefits for particular clients outweigh any higher trading cost, i.e. the client is willing to pay for the idea (information) and for the ability to execute the whole cross-border transaction with a high degree of immediacy and price certainty.

Brian Scott-Quinn

Treasury bonds

Trading in London and Tokyo In the 1980s, the ever-growing balance of payments deficit of the United States, in particular its bilateral deficits with Japan and Germany, have been financed in considerable part by the export of US Treasury bonds. In the case of London, which services European investors in Treasury bonds, secondary market transactions in the 1970s and early 1980s were batched during the London morning and then executed at Wall Street opening at 2 p.m. However, during the 1980s volume built up to such levels that it became economic to run a trading book in London. The same argument applies to Tokyo.

Global integration of trading in New York, London and Tokyo Any US investment bank which did not trade US treasuries in other time zones would be at a competitive disadvantage to those who did. We have noted already that the best risk/return trade-off in running a market making book arises from maximizing the rate at which the positions on the book are turned over. By running a book which moves around the world from New York to Tokyo to London and back to New York, a trading house can maximize the revenue on the book while minimizing the risk. Thus running the 'immediacy creating plant' 24 hours a day almost as a continuous flow process has given rise to gains in efficiency and hence the ability to offer more competitive pricing. Given the large volume of activity in these securities undertaken by foreigners, any house which did not do this would generate less trading revenue relative to position losses arising between New York close and re-opening the next morning than those houses which had 24 hour operations. They would thus be unlikely to be competitive in pricing. 'Passing the book' from country to country requires a high degree of trust between the individuals involved. It is also impossible to allocate profit generated on the book to different individuals in different time zones since there will be many deals in which the two sides of the transaction (the buy and the sell) will be generated in different countries. Integration of the various trading operations within a multinational is thus the only feasible way of operating.

Foreign equity markets

The driving force in foreign equity markets appears to be different from that in the debt markets. It has become clear from market research undertaken by securities firms that the increasing degree of globalization of equity portfolios resulting from the economic

288

US investment banks as multinationals

and regulatory changes we have already noted will lead investors to seek the lowest 'search cost' solution to their global investment needs compatible with low transactions cost and immediacy. Potential investor clients, including the existing clients of US investment banks, will be seeking investment bank partners which are able to service them with global equities without the need to use a range of foreign brokers. Not only do clients want a global dealing capability, they also want research to be global, i.e. they want comparisons of stocks and sectors across countries.

Such a service can be provided in four ways – through arm's-length relationships with overseas stockbrokers, or strategic relationships with overseas firms, or by acquisition of existing overseas equity operations, or by setting up a greenfield operation from scratch.

Until the 1980s the first method was the only one that was used. The clear change in the 1980s has been to foreign direct investment in production, sales and research facilities initially in the UK and subsequently in Tokyo and in other major financial centres. In trying to explain this, we will look at the economics of the London market as this was the first market to deregulate and allow foreign firms to enter.

Broker/dealer integration Prior to Big Bang, when market making (jobber acting as principal) and stock broking (agent dealing with investors) were legally separate, brokers were remunerated by a fixed commission while market makers generated revenue from the bid/offer spread associated with the provision of immediacy. Most US investment banks used a commission-splitting arrangement with a UK broker to service their own clients with UK equities. Since Big Bang, in the absence of a commission (i.e. net trading) on a high proportion of large deals, this arrangement was no longer possible.

Global franchise integration A further reason why US firms were forced to integrate into local production is that ultimately, as all major firms try to become global providers of financial services, the host country firms who would be able to offer them the most competitive service in international equities would be the very firms who would also be trying to build an international equity clientele themselves. Thus the problem described previously of building a global brand-name would arise.

Brian Scott-Quinn

Divergent market entry motives – investment banks v. commercial banks

Investment banks

US investment banks nearly all made a greenfield entry into UK securities markets while the commercial banks all made acquisitions. The strategy being followed by the investment banks has been different from that of the commercial banks and from the major UK firms which came into UK equities in 1986. Their entry strategy is to compete only in 'international equities', i.e. those high market capitalization stocks which interest international as well as domestic investors. It is clear that the investment banks which have eschewed acquisition have only a limited objective from their participation in foreign equity markets. It is to enable them to offer a service in 'international' equities to an international investment clientele in the US and abroad which they already service with US equities.

Such investors' views on the desirability of holding or selling a financial asset may vary according to their location. For example, currency factors may be decisive for overseas investors whereas they may not be for domestic. The global firms can tap this non-homogeneous investor base whereas a purely domestic firm cannot. The more stocks are held internationally, the more valuable it should be to have an international clientele. This clientele should give valuable information on changes in the supply/demand pattern between countries in particular securities, and hence on potential price movements. In addition, if investors view the provision of a service in global equities from all the major markets as a value-added service compared with a separate service from domestic firms for each market of the world, then there may be sufficient spread realized in the transaction for profitability, i.e. investors may be willing to pay more to reduce search and co-ordination costs. Thus this theory would predict that ultimately only international houses will be able to trade international equities profitably.

Commercial banks

While most investment banks chose to set up greenfield operations, most investment banking subsidiaries of US commercial banks chose to enter the market through acquisition. Corporate acquisitions in general are made at a price such that the return on investment in the acquisition at the time of takeover is less than the

290

US investment banks as multinationals

cost of capital of the acquirer.[13]

The only logical reason for such an acquisition at a price above the 'true' market price is the belief by the acquirer that through the gains from integration into the new parent company, the return on assets and equity will be increased to a satisfactory level. This implies that the new parent will bring some benefit to the new subsidiary from internalizing it and integrating it with its existing operations. In the case of US commercial banks, however, given that they have no US or international equity client base and that they cannot deal in equities in the US, there are no obvious synergies to be achieved through the acquisition of a UK equity operation.

If there were synergies to be achieved, now or in the future (for example, if the Glass Steagal Act were to be repealed), the one area in which they might be achieved would be in terms of a global franchise for the name of either the commercial bank or the equity market subsidiary. In practice, what has happened is that the UK stockbroking subsidiaries have in general resisted integration. Where this has been undertaken forcibly, the major revenue earners have left the firm and with them has gone much of the ability to generate rent from the brand name.

In contrast, for investment banks, setting up as domestic producers and distributors of a local equity market product has always been seen as part of a strategy for building a global franchise for the parent company's name based on their existing equity market expertise in the United States and their domestic and international equity client base. For them, therefore, it would have been illogical to have purchased the goodwill of a UK broking house which was principally in the acquired name, only to immediately change it to the parent company name.

We have not so far considered another one of the options, which is to form partnerships with firms overseas. Such relationships are unlikely to be successful for the same reason as we adduced for the failure of arm's-length relationships, i.e. the problem of the allocation of the rent that accrues from the global franchise inherent in the trading name of the provider of the service. Nonetheless, we would expect that as the problems of entry into foreign equity markets become more apparent, new types of relationship falling short of full ownership will come to be considered.

Summary and conclusions

Competition in investment banking takes place in three arenas –

Brian Scott-Quinn

the transactions price, the provision of immediacy and the 'guarantee of quality'. Most of the changes in the structure of the US investment banking industry since the Second World War, both domestic and overseas, can be explained by actions taken by individual firms to improve their service in these three areas.

Internalization of functions which were previously organized by separate companies has reduced the costs of providing final services. The change in corporate structure in the 1960s and 1970s from partnership to public company status has provided the capital that is necessary to increase the supply of immediacy. Effecting quasi-integration with certain non-price-sensitive clients overseas has allowed firms to extract the economic rent that results from clients having different trade-offs between price and immediacy of service on the one hand, and implicit quality guarantee provided by the brand name on the other. The capitalized value of this brand name and its implicit guarantee of quality has become the most valuable asset that a firm has from the point of view of attracting both clients and skilled staff. The reason for this is that there are no long-term unique or patentable technologies in the industry nor any firm specific advantages apart from the ability to internalize itself and the capitalized value of this which is inherent in the global use of the brand name.

Given that the profitability of market making is in large part a function of the volume of order flow and the non-homogeneity of customer expectations, capturing the potential overseas order flow has been necessary to improve the breadth and depth of internal market making in each investment bank. Extending on from this has been the need for each investment bank to be able to offer as full a geographical range of equity market products as is economic to provide in order to allow clients to arbitrage between geographical markets. Given the value of brand name in building a business and the problems and costs of sharing the use of it with partners overseas, it has been necessary to internalize its use and thus make direct investments overseas in both sales and production to service clients rather than continuing to use arm's-length relationships. This in turn has only become possible since the 1960s as a result of the move to incorporation and the additional capital this provided.

Notes

1   I am grateful to my colleagues Mark Casson and Geoffrey Jones for their help and advice on this chapter, and also to former colleagues at Security Pacific and Hoare Govett.

292

US investment banks as multinationals

2   See for example list of references in Mira Wilkins' chapter in this volume.
3   See *The Securities Industry in 1981*, Securities and Exchange Commission, Washington, DC, 1982.
4   P.J. Buckley, and M.C. Casson, *The Future of the Multinational Enterprise*, London, Macmillan, 1976.
5   See for example, O.E. Williamson, *Markets and Hierarchies: Analysis and Anti-trust Implications*, New York, Free Press, 1976.
6   E. Bloch, *Inside Investment Banking IInd. ed.*, Homewood Ill., Dow Jones Irwin, 1989.
7   Robert A. Schwarz, *Equity markets – Structure, Trading and Performance*, New York, Harper and Row, 1988.
8   S.L. Hayes, *Evolving Competition in Investment Banking, Working Paper*, Graduate School of Business Administration, Harvard University. See also John McKay's chapter in this volume, on the Rothschilds.
9   S.L. Hayes, A.M. Spence and D.V.P. Marks, 'Investment banking competition: an historical sketch' in J. Peter Williamson (ed.), *Investment Banking Handbook*, New York, John Wiley, 1988.
10 Hayes, op. cit.
11 See M.C. Casson, *The Firm and the Market: Studies in the Multinational Enterprise and the Scope of the Firm*, Oxford, Blackwell and Cambridge, Mass., MIT Press, 1987, Chapter 4.
12 *International Investment Banks, a survey*, New York, Wall Street Journal, 1988.
13 See for example B.S. Black and J.A. Grundfest, 'Shareholder gains from takeovers and restructurings', *Journal of Applied Corporate Finance*, 1988, volume 1, number 1, Spring.

[32]

Financial Innovation

CHARLES LUCAS

The provision of financial services has steadily undergone a process of change driven by innovation. Still, close observers of the marketplace agree that financial innovation accelerated greatly in the 1980s in three essential areas: (1) markets, (2) products and services, and (3) the technology to produce them. In discussing the causes of this burst of innovation, we will see that it was propelled by essentially macroeconomic forces, all having to do with the increased volatility of exchange rates, the acceleration of inflation, and the current account imbalance that appeared in the 1970s. These forces shifted in pattern and were sustained throughout the 1980s. The nature and degree of change in the last decade has transformed the functioning of the financial structure so greatly that a number of fundamental public policy issues, such as the functioning of monetary policy and construction of safety nets, now need to be rethought. Because this process is of great importance to central bankers, it is useful to consider its concrete manifestations. This paper will discuss these manifestations first in the area of capital market instruments, then in the area of derivative instruments, and finally in the effect of technology on market players. My conclusion will consider regulation and market discipline.

Capital Market Instruments

The first and most important category is new capital market instruments. These are financial instruments that perform the same function that financial instruments have historically performed—they execute a transfer of a principal amount of cash in the borrowing-lending arrangement. In this first category of capital market instruments (borrowing and lending instruments), we have seen a proliferation of innovative products that are in some ways similar to and in some significant respects different from the bank loans, corporate bonds, and equity transactions traditionally offered by the financial sector for this purpose.

Debt Product Innovation

The parade of innovation was led off by the syndicated credit, developed in the mid-1970s in connection with the aftereffects of the first oil crisis.[1]

The oil crisis had led to massive energy-related current account imbalances; a small group of energy-producing countries had accumulated large surpluses, while a large group of users of energy products had accumulated deficits. A borrowing-lending transaction was needed, but there was a collective judgment in the community of policymakers that they did not want to, or could not in the short term, dramatically alter entities to accommodate the necessary scale of financing.

The world presented the financial structure with a problem that could not be solved with its existing mechanisms, mainly the conventional bond markets. The borrowers were nations with particular sovereign risk characteristics, and the scale of lending that was needed far exceeded the capacities of single institutions. A mechanism was required that would allow a number of institutions with access to liquidity to combine in a single transaction. The result was a new instrument, the syndicated credit, designed to meet the specific risk characteristics required.

This was a period of accelerating inflation, in which bond holders—holders of fixed-rate assets—were suffering serious losses in the value of their portfolios and withdrawing from the market rather than placing new money. In fact, they were trying to get themselves out of fixed-rate assets. Banks in particular avoided fixed-rate lending. Everyone was concerned that inflation would continue to accelerate, making fixed-rate lending even more disastrous. For that reason, this new instrument contained an interest rate structure different from that of the conventional instrument of the time, which had a medium-term maturity (seven years or longer). The instruments were developed with floating-rate interest arrangements because the intermediaries that admitted the instruments to the banks had access only to floating-rate liabilities and could not afford to take the risk of borrowing at a floating rate and lending at a fixed rate in a period of rising rates. These factors necessitated a new instrument, and the market produced it.

The essential elements of the process are visible in that first episode. By the early to the mid-1980s, it had become clear that these types of innovations were proliferating. A whole string of borrowing and lending transactions with new attributes appeared. Assets became securitized, which means that the conventional bank loan, ordinarily not a negotiable instrument, was executed with a change in the associated legal indenture that made it a negotiable asset. Thus, it began to look more like a bond underwriting in its economic function but nevertheless remained an asset of a depository institution. Banks sought to securitize their assets because of the liquidity pressures that were a consequence of the events of the 1970s and early 1980s. The banks wanted the ability to sell their assets and redeploy their resources. Liquidity of the instrument was more important than ever before in the history of banking. In response, a means developed of taking an instrument that was not liquid and making it liquid: assets that had traditionally been held in commercial and savings bank portfolios were packaged into securities for resale in the secondary market.

On the liability side, many instruments appeared with essentially the same characteristic—for example, medium-term notes, perpetual floating rate notes, Eurocommercial paper—specifically, instruments designed to be used by borrowers looking for certain aspects of short-term risk characteristics but with a lengthened maturity.

"Non-Straight Debt"

In the latter half of the 1980s, we began to see yet more complex borrowing and lending instruments that may be called "non-straight debt." This term plays off the market term "straight debt," which basically refers to the straight bond, the traditional fixed-rate, medium-term corporate borrowing. "Non-straight" is everything else that has been invented: callable bonds, indexed bonds, warrant bonds, junk bonds.

Let me give you an example: the bull-bear bond, which is a type of indexed bond. Suppose that $200 million of these bonds is issued at a floating or fixed rate; it does not matter which. The principal amount at maturity is indexed to the price of something else, most commonly gold. Half of the $200 million is set up so that the amount returned on maturity is a direct function of the price of gold. A 10 percent rise in the price of gold produces a 10 percent higher return at maturity; a 10 percent fall means a 10 percent lower return. The return on the other $100 million is inversely related to the price of gold. If the price goes up, the principal is reduced by 10 percent, and vice versa. In other words, there is a bull portion and a bear portion. By selling equal amounts of both portions, there is no risk with respect to the principal, because however much one tranche goes up, the other goes down.

The rationale for this instrument is that buyers are willing to pay a slightly higher price for the non-straight issue than for a straight issue because the bull-bear feature allows them to speculate or to hedge another exposure. For example, a gold producer or an industrial enterprise that uses gold in production may want to hedge its price over a medium-term exposure and can do so with a bull-bear bond. The investor can select the tranche of such an asset and achieve a price hedge against another commodity. There are many such instruments, of different maturities and indexed against all sorts of things. All a market maker has to worry about is whether there are two sides to the market and whether someone needs the particular implied futures contract on the other commodity that is embedded in the instrument.

Equity Product Innovation

If we turn from the debt side to the equity side, we discover hardly any innovations. One temporary attempt was made to develop an international equities market. An international equities market is different from the entry of foreign investors into national equities markets. I define an international equities market as one in which the original underwriting is conducted internationally and assets are traded, either in the context of an exchange or not, in a true international sense. We have seen some equity linkages in conventional debt borrowings, in particular in the Euromarkets. For example, London underwriters of equity-linked bond transactions coming out of Japan—that is, dollar-denominated bond transactions with detachable or nondetachable equity warrants embedded in them—were quite successful. That was really a regulatory arbitrage and a product of the fact that it is expensive to raise new equity in Tokyo.

The closest thing to innovation with respect to equity is still in the category of debt borrowing. In fact, during the 1980s, in the United States, something on the order of $350 billion of outstanding net equity was retired, that is, was essentially replaced by debt, giving rise to what Paul Volcker, then chairman of the Federal Reserve System, called the "leveraging of America." Not only was there a massive emission of new debt instruments, but there was actually a reduction in the amount of equity outstanding. From a central banker's point of view, this is not the function of a financial market, and certainly not in a period of sustained economic growth. Rather, it is a historical anomaly, and nobody really understands its significance.

Derivative Instruments

The second category of innovation comprises what the market calls derivative instruments, or transactions that do not contain an exchange of principal amount. They are defined and priced in relationship to some other financial or real asset. Futures, forwards, swaps, and options are the four main forms. While forwards, notably foreign exchange forwards, and futures have been in the U.S. financial marketplace for some time, the 1980s saw a geographical proliferation of exchanges willing to trade such contracts. In addition, huge numbers of such contracts were invented, many of which failed. However, I will concentrate on swaps and options. The swap in particular has characteristics that differ radically from existing financial instruments.

Swaps

Swaps are a huge market—the total outstanding amount of the swaps market, what is called notional principal amount, is in the range of half a trillion dollars globally.[2] Yet surprisingly few people are familiar with it. Each swap individually is a simple and subtle transaction, one in which two counterparties agree to exchange streams of payments over time. This is because each party has lower-cost access to funds in a particular market than does his counterparty. Accordingly, each party can issue the original debt more cheaply than his counterparty can and then they swap their obligations.

The first major swap transaction took place between the World Bank and IBM in 1983, in connection with the simultaneous borrowings of those two institutions in dollars and Swiss francs.[3] At the time the World Bank was lending in Swiss francs and wanted to borrow in Swiss francs, but it had basically exhausted its borrowing ability in that market and so faced rising costs. IBM was a dollar borrower that had never borrowed in Swiss francs, and did not anticipate a need for them because it had only very limited operations in Switzerland. Nevertheless, Salomon Brothers, the investment bank, called IBM and said, "We have a way to make your cost of funds cheaper. Do your next $100 million borrowing in Swiss francs." Basically, IBM could borrow Swiss francs more cheaply than the World Bank could. In fact both institutions borrowed in currencies they did not want—the World Bank in dollars, IBM in Swiss francs. Each then converted the proceeds into currencies they did want. The World Bank converted dollars into Swiss francs, and IBM its Swiss francs into dollars. They did this simultaneously, underwritten by Salomon Brothers with no other legal or business connection. The two institutions then swapped their debt liabilities: IBM agreed to service the World Bank's dollar debt, that is, to make the interest payments and supply an amount at maturity, in exchange for a commitment by the World Bank to pay IBM's Swiss franc debt. Thus, each ended up with the currency it needed and with a debt obligation, but the debt obligation was at a lower interest rate than each could have obtained directly in the currency it actually needed.

Streams exchanged in this way can be anything against anything. All that must be agreed is the notional principal amount (the common amount against which the streams will be calculated) and the maturity. All other rates are market-determined, for example, the market rates on Swiss franc and dollar denominated bonds. The swap opens up the possibility that any institution may borrow in any geographic arena, in any instrument, and for any maturity, provided that there is a counterparty. Anything can be swapped against anything as long as there is a market for the underlying assets, because if there is a market, someone can hedge it. If someone can hedge it, someone can deal in it. Gold can be swapped against oil because there are futures markets in these commodities. Fixed rates can be swapped against floating rates in the same or different currencies.

The swap has immense implications for the financial world. It is probably the most powerful instrument yet invented, because of its ability to increase the speed and volume of transactions. It can bridge all kinds of market segmentations—legal, regulatory, and geographic. That kind of price arbitrage mechanism is a far more powerful tool in globalizing markets than, say, the portfolio manager's technique of diversifying currencies.

Options

Options are troublesome for central bankers, for lawyers, and for certain other financial players. They are most troublesome for people who do not know anything about them, including many of those who trade them. An option is a contract conveying the right, but not the obligation, to buy or sell a specified financial instrument at a fixed price before or at a specified future date. The distinguishing characteristic of an option relative to all other financial instruments is that it is asymmetrical with respect to benefits and risks. The buyer of an option gains the right, but is not obligated, to purchase an asset at a fixed price. For example, Ms. Smith has a three-month option on a stock priced at $30 a share today. If the market price rises to $35, she can choose to exercise the option, buy shares at $30, sell them for $35, and pocket $5 a share less the cost of the option itself. If, on the other hand, the market price falls to $25, she can choose not to exercise her $30 per share option. She has lost only the cost of the option. Thus the asymmetry: the buyer has the option to benefit from a movement in the asset price favorable to her and to avoid the consequence of a loss if it moves against her.

That asymmetry of benefit is matched by an asymmetry of risk. The seller, or "writer," of the option faces the mirror image of that risk, which cannot be hedged by anything other than an exactly matching option. The way to hedge these things is by constantly adjusting a cash hedge in the actual market, and therein lies the rub. If the volatility of the market price for the underlying asset increases, the seller is whipped back and forth. The seller prices the option on some assumed volatility of the underlying price; if the volatility increases, loss is inevitable. If prices are more stable, however, the seller makes a lot of money. The buyer of this instrument is betting on the price of the underlying asset, while the seller is betting not on price but on volatility of price. In that sense the option is a different kind of financial asset: a volatility asset.

Options have been around for a long time. The first options that were traded were in the Japanese rice market in the 11th century. What was new in the 1980s was their proliferation, both geographically and across the range of instruments. Now there are options that are still unrecognized. In the United States, for example, a home mortgage that contains a legal provision entitling borrowers to repay the instrument at their discretion before maturity is a type of option. The problem in the U.S. thrift industry crisis was that a very large number of managers of thrift institutions did not understand that they were in the options business. And in today's world, the options business is almost the only one they are in. It is the options risk in their portfolios that makes or breaks them, much more than the credit risk.

Consider what happened in the 1970s. U.S. thrift institutions sat with fixed-rate mortgages while their floating-rate liabilities and interest rates went through the roof. They went broke because the value of their assets fell through the floor. In the early 1980s, these institutions began issuing high-rate 15 percent mortgages. They believed that they could avoid making the same mistakes again. They borrowed funds at fixed rates that were a half point lower than the mortgage interest rates they were charging. Had they locked in profits for the next 30 years? No, because as interest rates fell, the mortgage payers exercised their options, repaying 15 percent mortgages and replacing them with 9 percent mortgages. The thrift institutions, however, still had their 14.5 percent liabilities, so they went broke again.

In fact, each time these institutions went broke, it was for a different reason. In large part, the problems of the 1980s were the result of a failure to recognize that prepayment risk had to be managed using the discipline of options portfolio management—the only way to manage such risk. If it is not managed in this way, an institution can lose money hand over fist. If it is managed properly—and many institutions did manage it correctly—the institutions survive.

This process is what economists call "unbundling."[4] Historically, the various forms of risk that appear in any financial transaction—credit risk, maturity risk, liquidity risk, price risk—have been permanently combined. The new process destroyed that bundle and replaced it with new and active transactors, including households. Now, at the corporate and portfolio manager level, each component of financial risk is treated separately. Not only did unbundling become possible in the 1980s; it became pervasive.

This change is an irreversible one that central bankers must think about. The essential force behind it is a macroeconomic story: the stresses that were imposed on everybody by accelerating inflation, inflation rate differentials between countries, and exchange rate volatility. Without the dramatically increased capacity of every kind of economic actor—corporate finance vice president and portfolio manager alike—to alter exposures far more radically and flexibly than in earlier decades, the level of bankruptcies and the risk of a downward economic spiral like that of the 1930s would have been far greater. For, while a substantial amount of risk was only transferred and still exists, without the new processes we would have been in much worse shape at the end of the 1980s than we actually were.

Effect of Technology on Market Players

Technology is an important factor. A swaps market could not exist without PCs and spread sheet software to provide cheap, flexible, generic processing power. Creating a swaps market requires the capacity to perform net present value calculations rapidly and flexibly. The options market requires slightly more expensive software, but there are now options packages for $500. Moreover, because the same few firms sell those packages to everybody, there are common reference points for pricing financial products.

The process of innovation, as mentioned above, accelerated in the 1980s for fundamental economic reasons, producing what Sam Cross called "the search for the quark," that is, the search for the unbundled components of financial risk essential to creating markets and to pricing and trading those risks separately.[5] It is going to be a permanent activity. The cost of developing the needed analytic and management tools has been paid, it is sunk; on the margin it is possible to produce more tools very cheaply. People today are not searching for the quark. They are what I call "alchemists"; they have available to them competitively priced, infinite supplies of whatever risk they want.

Everybody is a corporate finance specialist today. As recently as 15 years ago, an analyst who took in tradable assets produced for a client, either borrower or lender, a customized transaction that fit the client's needs. The analyst earned his or her fees by figuring out the risks and hedging those exposures. Such transactions made up a relatively small, specialized part of the financial services industry. Now, because everyone has access to the same markets, anyone can do specialized transactions cheaply.

Thus, for instance, my Visa card says "National Wildlife Federation," since my child wants to save the whales. Accordingly, a certain percentage of the earnings of my card are given to the National Wildlife Federation. Even in a retail service like credit cards, the process of innovation is taking place, with the result that the credit card business, like the swaps business and the options business, has become commodity-like. The servicing companies can process Visa cards for any organization. All that is needed is an additional tag on an account that says, "Take a piece of the profit out of that and give it to the National Wildlife Federation." In terms of production technology, it is just another field in a relational data base. In this context what is produced in a very generic way is something that, from a marketing point of view, is highly specialized and differentiated. One can describe that process as alchemy. It is increasingly common throughout the financial structure.

Regulation and Market Discipline

From the point of view of financial structure and regulation, the bottom line of this process of innovation is that the world we created in the 1930s is obsolete in far more profound ways than most of us recognize. That world, built for safety and soundness but not for efficiency, was one in which financial markets were intentionally segmented, competition intentionally limited, profit margins more or less guaranteed, and a safety net created in almost all countries to protect depositors and also the buyers of assets from financial intermediaries.

The new process has destroyed that segmentation. It is difficult to know in today's world what a bank is or does. Banks trade swaps as market makers in order to manage their maturity profile. The chairman of Bankers Trust may not care what his balance sheet looks like because the balance sheet is matched, or hedged. If his loan is fixed, his borrowing is fixed; if his loan is floating, his borrowing is floating; if he has loaned for seven years, he has borrowed for seven years; if he loans in dollars, he will borrow in dollars. There is no risk in his balance sheet. Even if he accurately predicts that interest rates are going to go down, by the time he shifts his portfolio to become a long lender and short borrower, the market movement has long since happened. So he does not even try. He simply goes into the swaps market and becomes a fixed receiver and a floating payer.

Today, bankers rarely hold a nonnegotiable asset. Everything on their balance sheets is negotiable. Are their organizations still banks? They look like "traditional" banks, but should they be supported by the safety net? What are the real risk profiles that they run? If they are subject to bank regulation, what kind of regulation should that be? Should their enterprises have access to lender of last resort support? If bankers have these advantages, what about the mutual fund managers across the street, who have similar balance sheet profiles and risk exposure?

The other counterparty in a swap transaction is just as likely to be an insurance company as another bank. Insurance companies today are big traders in the swaps market because they have massive portfolios to manage. So the maturity gap risk that traditionally was a banking intermediation function is now done by both regulated and unregulated entities. For bank regulation, this means, at the least, that the scope for regulation is far narrower than it was in the more segmented world, in which regulatory costs could be imposed without destroying the industry. In today's world, imposing regulatory costs can drive business to competing institutions that perform the same economic function but within a different institutional, regulatory, and legal structure. At the same time, competitive pressures are so intense that underregulation is likely to destroy the banking industry as financial institutions become increasingly competitive. Remember what Adam Smith predicted: if there are enough competitors in a market, they can drive profits down to zero.

Everyone agrees that market discipline is desirable, but the question is, how much discipline can be absorbed before the system of insuring that risk starts to break down. The potential exists for thrift industry disasters to occur in other countries, in other industries, or in other segments of the financial service industry. How we will deal with that potential remains to be seen.

With few exceptions, the industrial countries decided to alter their financial structures dramatically and move to something close to a universal banking system model. They plan to stop trying to segment these markets and to allow a blurring of the distinctions between institutions to a much greater degree. A wave of legislation mandating changes in the financial structures of the developed world has been implemented in the last several years—changes which the United States and Japan alone resisted with the result that they developed the most segmented financial structures of the industrial countries. It is easy for me as a market economist to conclude that this is an unsustainable phenomenon. Financial structure and regulatory convergence are driven by market forces, and resisting that trend will cost a great deal. Here we see the dilemma. The thrift industry in the United States went bankrupt in part because it failed to understand the technologies that the world imposed on it. Ironically, the regulatory safety net may destroy part of the financial sector by making its institutions uncompetitive with other institutions that can perform similar economic functions without the cost burden that the safety net adds.

Notes

1. See, for example, Jerome Levinson, "A Perspective on the Debt Crisis," 4 *American University Journal of International Law and Policy* 489 (Summer 1989).

2. For information on the size of the swap market, see the quarterly publication of the Bank for International Settlements, *International Banking and Financial Market Development*.

3. For more on the rise of the swap market, see Henry C. Hu, "Swaps, the Modern Process of Financial Innovation and the Vulnerability of a Regulatory Paradigm," 138 *University of Pennsylvania Law Review* 333 (1989).

4. See, generally, the definition of "unbundling" offered by Douglas Blair and Devra Golbe in the *New Palgrave Dictionary of Money and Finance* (1992).

5. Sam Y. Cross, Chairman, Study Group Established by the Central Banks of the Group of Ten Countries, which prepared *Recent Innovations in International Banking* (Basle: Bank for International Settlements, 1986).

Financial Markets in 2020

By Charles S. Sanford, Jr.

At Bankers Trust, we spend a lot of time anticipating trends in the financial markets, not only those affecting short-term price movements but also those that are responsible for the long-term evolution of the system itself.

Anticipating the longer term is especially compelling today considering the speed at which the financial system is changing. Even our inherent romanticism doesn't let us forget that we are straddling the 20th and 21st centuries, a period when more than ever the future seems just around the corner.

But there's the future and the future. For the purpose of this paper, let's impose a stop-loss on our observations. I like the year 2020. For one thing, it is the year when the Jet Propulsion Laboratory predicts that Voyager will stop transmitting data back to Earth—a forecast that for some reason I find exciting. Twenty-seven years also is far enough away to allow trends to develop, yet near enough to be useful for long-range planning. And it doesn't hurt to know that 20/20 stands for perfect vision. Maybe that alone will improve the odds of my being correct.

Thus this paper will focus on the period between now and the year 2ust 1993.u020, contemplating how the financial functions will

evolve over that period and how quickly change will come.

Anyone who deals in the financial markets knows that anticipating trends is difficult at best. But he or she also realizes that not to try is tantamount to accepting the most unlikely scenario of all: no change. So I will plunge ahead.

CONSTANTS AND CHANGE

Heraclitus said it best: "All is flux, nothing stays still. Nothing endures but change." That is true. Nonetheless, between now and 2020 two phenomena will remain constant. First, human nature will not change. Second, the basic financial functions, as I will define them, will not change, although how we perform these functions will change.

First for human nature. A very basic element of that nature is a hunger for security—law and order, job security, retirement security, decent and affordable health care, and financial security. For a variety of reasons, people have begun to feel that organizations, especially governments, designed to provide their basic security no longer can be relied on.

This societal change is having a profound impact on financial institutions' relationships with their clients and employees, who once automatically accepted an institution's promise that "We know what is best for you."

Charles S. Sanford, Chairman, Bankers Trust, delivered this paper at the Federal Reserve Bank of Kansas City's Symposium on "Changing Capital Markets: Implications for Monetary Policy," Jackson Hole, Wyoming, August 1993.

By necessity, not by preference, people are becoming more involved in creating their own security by doing their own homework and making their own decisions. "One-way broadcasting" and "command and control" styles are no longer acceptable. This pervasive sense of vulnerability is putting risk management at the top of the agenda for many people and organizations. To the degree that financial institutions can better help their clients deal with risk, the clients are very ready for change. In any event, gaining their trust will be an essential challenge for financial institutions.

In addition to the sense of individual vulnerability, two other facets of human nature will affect the pace of change: people's inherent thirst for knowledge and their frequent aversion to change. The first is the motivator behind financial innovation and the second is the greatest barrier to it.

That barrier is deeply entrenched, as evidenced by a report from an observer at the Digital World Conference, which was held in Los Angeles in July 1993: "Given that this was a conference on digital technology for industry insiders, I saw very few laptop computer note takers; 99 percent used paper and pen. Very few had mobile telephones with them, and consequently the lines at the pay phones were lengthy."

We see that even technologists have trouble adjusting to the new environment. I have no doubts, though, that their children, steeped in today's technology, will be far less likely to be lining up for pay phones by the time they dominate the work force—well before 2020. It won't be long before the impact of the "computer games" generation is strongly felt at the policy-making level.

Countering any inertia that works against change is the human drive for knowledge. And this thirst has been whetted by rapid advances in financial theory, as exciting and as portentous as the 20th century's major developments in physics and biology. A substantial portion of this paper will deal with those developments.

Let me emphasize, however, that this paper looks *only* at the future impact of *currently* available technology. It does not delve into Buck Rogers speculation about new inventions (or Star Trek, depending on your age and frame of reference). And it does not talk about couch potatoes with virtual reality helmets operating out of hermit huts. It recognizes that an ocean of new technologies is available to today's markets, but that the process toward implementation of these technologies has hardly begun.

Some may believe that the predictions in this paper are too bold, but I believe that if anything, change will be faster and more far-reaching.

THE BASIC FINANCIAL FUNCTIONS

As the existing technologies come onstream, they will affect how the basic financial functions will be performed. These functions are (1) financing, (2) risk management, (3) trading and positioning, (4) advising, and (5) transaction processing. This paper will avoid many standard financial terms of 20th century thought. Although financial functions will be the same, they will be looked at differently in the 21st century. Thus we will not refer to "loans," "borrowings," or "securities," but to "claims on wealth" or "financial claims." We will avoid the term "banks" because banks, certainly as we know them, will not exist.

Financing

Financing facilitates the movement of funds from suppliers to users. Usually it starts with the identification of users and suppliers by a financial institution and ends with the creation of products to satisfy both.

Successful products created by a financial intermediary enable each party to meet its needs for timing and location of cash flows and for the amounts of money to be supplied or used. The intermediary also helps clients assess the merits of alternative products, seeking to find the least costly source of money for users and getting the best possible return for suppliers, taking into consideration their appetites for risk.

Risk management

Risk management is the process of moving clients closer to their desired risk profiles by helping them shed unwanted risks or acquire new risks that suit their portfolios. At times, this can be done simply by matching a client who wants to shed a risk with one who wants to acquire that risk. More often, it involves unbundling, transforming, and repackaging risks into bundles tailored to fit the particular needs of various clients.

Trading and positioning

Trading and positioning is the buying and selling of claims on wealth. It provides liquidity to clients so they can more easily alter their portfolios or raise cash. It also moves market prices of financial claims closer to their fair values and makes market prices more visible and reliable.

Advising

Advising is making decisions on behalf of clients or giving them information and advice that help them make better decisions for themselves.

Transaction processing

Transaction processing is the storing, safeguarding, verifying, reporting, and transferring of claims on wealth.

As noted, some of these functions are taking on new forms and are becoming more sophisticated, but they will be needed as much in 2020 as they are today.

TECHNICAL AND MARKET ENVIRONMENT IN 2020

Again, technology is driving these changes. Information technology already is helping us execute these financial functions better and faster by providing improved data collection, calculation, communications, and risk control. By 2020, those tools will be much cheaper and far more powerful. As indications of this trend: A transistor, once costing $5, costs less than a staple today; entire reference libraries are now stored on one 5-inch compact disc, and computer users have become accustomed to increasing their processing power by a factor of 10 every five to seven years at no additional cost. And the progress is geometric because each element—computation, availability of data, communications, and algorithms—feeds on the others.

This revolution in information technology is enabling the financial world to operate on a much more complex level than before.

At times the speed and power at which computation and communications tasks can be accomplished is so much greater than in the past that it brings qualitative change, not just quantitative change. For example, the options business could not operate as it does today without high-speed computers to track its intricacies, including the monitoring of risk profiles and valuations. Computer technology has made it possible to disaggregate risk on a broad scale and redistribute it efficiently, enabling management to maintain greater risk control while giving employees more freedom to use their own judgment. In other words, information technology allows a financial organization to decentralize while improving control.

The ability to program computers to digest ever-larger amounts of information more and more quickly enables us to apply sophisticated automated logic—what we call "automated analytics"—to many problems, such as performing elemental arbitrage tasks. Eventually these programs will be embedded on computer chips, which will be able to solve progressively more complex problems—and on a global basis.

Indeed, by 2020, a true global marketplace will be established, with everyone—individuals, companies, investors, organizations, and governments—linked through telephone lines, cables, and radio-wave technology. With the touch of a button, people will have access to other individuals and vast databases around the world. Such access will be readily available through phones, interactive television, workstations, or hand-held "personal digital assistants" that combine all these functions.

Organizations will be "fully wired" so that their computers will capture incoming and internally generated data, analyze the information, and make it instantly available to any authorized person, wherever he or she may be. Armies of clerks and administrators no longer will be needed to serve as messengers, translators, reconcilers, or summarizers of information. As discussed below, this will change how firms are managed.

To further increase the system's efficiency, all financial claims (including claims on volatility) will be in book entry form, and ownership of all these claims will be transferable instantly anywhere around the globe via 24-hour multicurrency payment systems. Settlement risk will be eliminated and with it a major bottleneck to transaction flows. This has enormous implications for releasing capital and lowering transaction costs.

WEALTH ACCOUNTS

A key to the system will be "wealth accounts," in which companies and individuals will hold their assets and liabilities. These accounts will contain today's relatively illiquid assets such as buildings and vehicles as well as what we know today as stocks, bonds, other securities, and new types of financial claims. These accounts would also contain all forms of liabilities.

Computers will continuously keep track of these items in the wealth accounts and will constantly mark both assets and liabilities to market, making these items effectively liquid. Within an individual wealth account, the arithmetic sum of the items will be the net worth. Yesterday's income and today's wealth will always be known with a high degree of confidence.

The wealth accounts will be the focal point for financial processing and reporting. The integrity of these accounts will be validated by institutions, much the same as checking accounts or mutual funds are today. Wealth accounts will be instantly tapped via "wealth cards." For example, this will allow you to pay for your sports car by instantly drawing on part of the wealth inherent in your vacation house.

Wealth accounts will simplify the provision of credit. In the ultimate extension of today's home-equity lines, instant credit will be available to companies and individuals secured with the current value of their wealth accounts. Leverage constraints will be established by investors and perhaps central banks. Some investors will continue to extend unsecured credit on the basis of an individual's expected income stream, but this would violate this writer's strongly held view that one should never extend unsecured credit to anything that eats.

Owners of wealth accounts will use automated analytics to help them determine their risk/reward appetites and suggest appropriate actions to achieve those targets. If the owner approves, the wealth account would proceed to automatically implement the program. Of course, some people will prefer the advice of a human on more complex or large transactions, for both expert judgment and psychological comfort.

Automated analytics will also provide customized investment management, making the wealth accounts far superior to today's mutual funds. In effect, individuals will have the option to manage their own mutual fund.

All seekers of financial claims will understand that to get full access to the financial markets they will be legally responsible for keeping their wealth accounts up to date. These accounts will be electronically accessible to any authorized user, directly or through computerized analytics programs. Privacy will be maintained as with today's checking accounts.

Global electronic bulletin boards will be the principal medium through which buyers and sellers will post their needs and execute transactions. Many financial claims (including what are known today as loans and securities) will bypass middlemen (commercial and investment banks) and will be bought and sold by electronic auction through these global bulletin boards, with minimal transaction costs.

Today we have only a few recognized rating agencies. In 2020 we will have hundreds—perhaps thousands—of specialized providers of news, data, and analysis that will provide interactive electronic bulletins, on demand, real-time, and tailored to each subscriber's particular notion of risk.

There will be no special need for retail financial branches because everyone will have direct access to his or her financial suppliers through interactive TV and personal digital assistants. True interstate banking will have arrived at last! Or more accurately, true "global banking" will have arrived, as every household will be a "branch."

A key feature of 2020 is that nearly everything could be tailored to a client's needs or wishes at a reasonable price, including highly personalized service from financial companies. Firms will be selling to market segments of one.

In addition to the bulletin boards that will be open to anyone who pays a nominal fee, users and suppliers of financial claims will be networked to each other to exchange real-time data and documents (computer-to-computer), to automatically execute most day-to-day transactions, and maybe to confer via virtual reality electronic meetings. On any given deal, firms may compete not only with their natural competitors but with their nominal clients as well. In effect, supplying financial assistance will be a free-for-all. It will not be limited to those calling themselves "financial institutions" because any organization or individual will be able to reply to needs posted on the bulletin boards. That means an organization that specializes in financial matters may, at times, find itself competing directly with its clients.

Other elements of the financial world of 2020 are especially hard to predict. What form will robbery and fraud take? As we said, human nature will not change and dishonesty will be around in 2020 as it is today. Voice recognition, DNA fingerprinting, and secure data encryption will instantly verify transactions, preventing today's scams. But new forms of "information crime" will appear.

Geography will be less of a constraint. Many employees could be geographically dispersed, such as those engaged in processing (for cost advantages), in sales and marketing (to be close to the customer), and in handling local problems that require local solutions. But the people responsible for creating products and overall strategy will still have to be in major cities. These people need the creative stimulation that is found primarily in cities, where they will thrive on face-to-face contact with people from different backgrounds and cultures and from different disciplines—artists, scientists, businesspeople, and lawyers.

PARTICLE FINANCE

In fact, a convergence is taking place among these disciplines as finance becomes more like science and the arts. Financial theory is becoming increasingly important and tremendously useful as theoretical advances have emerged in the last few years. These include portfolio theories, asset pricing theories, option pricing theories, and market efficiency theories.

Many of the financial world's most creative people are devoting their time to these theories and are radically improving our comprehension and management of risk. They deal with variables as straightforward as interest rates and as complex as the weather—all of which have an enormous impact on the markets.

This path-breaking work is providing a solid platform for innovation in practice as well as in theory. The rapidly growing acceptance of derivative-based financial solutions is one very important example of this.

At this point, however, the science of markets is at an extraordinarily early stage of development. We are still in a "Newtonian" era of "classical finance," in which we tend to look at financial instruments—such as stocks, bonds, and loans—in static, highly aggregated terms.

Models based on classical finance analyze risk at the level of "securities" (or options on these securities) and usually assume that the volatilities of the securities are constant over time and can be estimated with statistical averages of past price data—a stationary world where there is no progress, no structural change, no evolution. But in reality, a security's volatility is based on a highly aggregated bundle of many complex underlying risks that are unlikely to be stationary and that usually interact with one another. Classical finance also assumes that human beings are rational economic decisionmakers—an assumption that frequently appears to be violated.

Most classical finance models looking at Bankers Trust would concentrate on the "beta" of its stock—the stock's volatility relative to the market. These models would have great difficulty dealing with the multitude of underlying critical risk factors that produce beta, such as changes in financial market volatility, changes in

global product, the volumes of our transaction processing, an earthquake in Japan, changes in consumer confidence in the United Kingdom, or a change in our corporate strategy. We describe these critical factors as "financial attributes." Beta ignores them or grossly summarizes them as homogeneous packets of white noise.

Theoreticians, however, are not ignoring them. Researchers have begun to look for a theory—what we call "The Theory of Particle Finance"—that will help us better understand an asset's financial attributes.

Finding such a theory is not just around the corner, but we are seeing interesting signs of progress, and by 2020 a much more powerful financial discipline will be in place. We are beginning from a Newtonian view, which operates at the level of tangible objects (summarized by dimension and mass), to a perspective more in line with the nonlinear and chaotic world of quantum physics and molecular biology.

Quantum physics, which operates at the level of subatomic particles, and which may eventually bridge subatomic and astronomical events, goes much deeper than Newtonian physics—beyond objects to molecules, to atoms and to subatomic particles.

Similarly, classical biology operated at the level of the organism and was preoccupied with taxonomy and anatomy. Biology advanced by probing deeper into the cells and genes, which are much closer to the fundamental building blocks of life. This made it possible to explain some of the critical interactions among cells, organisms, and the environment.

Like quantum physics and modern biology, particle finance is beginning to look beneath beta to identify an asset's financial attributes, including the attributes' individual and collective volatility. Efforts also are being made to integrate these attributes into the desired financial claims.

This work is creating order from apparent disorder, providing building blocks that will allow the more effective packaging and management of risk in an economy whose structure is constantly changing.

The purpose of this research is to reach the most efficient balance of risk and return—getting a higher expected return on the same risk or getting the same return with lower risk.

As noted earlier, the theory of particle finance is still in its infancy—but by 2020, it will be much further advanced, aided by an explosion in computing power and financial data. We can't say which of today's early attempts to advance the theory of particle finance will work, but already the developments are intriguing.

For example:

(1) Chaos theorists are attempting to find the underlying structure and pattern—if they exist—of the apparent randomness of changes in asset values. (The "Random Walk" may not be completely random after all.)

(2) Researchers are building neural networks that mimic certain complex properties of the human brain. When harnessed to massive computing power, it is hoped that these neural networks will find meaningful patterns in the "noise" of financial attributes and, learning from experience, will strip away some of the apparent randomness of financial events.

(3) "Fuzzy logic" is a mathematical way of drawing definite conclusions from approximate, vague, or subjective inputs. Because it attempts to embody certain kinds of human perception and decisionmaking skills, it may help us understand complex interactive systems that involve human intervention (like financial markets).

(4) Combinations of these and/or other new methods may produce the answer. For example, information gleaned from the neural networks might be used to define "fuzzy" relationships in the system and then to write "fuzzy" rules to control the processes or to predict the system's behavior in new situations.

The 2020 technology environment promises much greater market efficiency through better information and lower transaction costs. How-ever, as particle finance uncovers myriad risk variables, now existing but "invisible," it also uncovers the inefficiencies associated with these variables. Also, the constants of human nature will still produce financial fads and bouts of irrational market euphoria and gloom (although we can hope that better information will dampen their intensity). The ideal of a perfectly efficient market will not be achieved by 2020, if ever.

Particle finance and more powerful technology will substantially reduce the amount of unwanted risk borne by individuals, institutions, and the system as a whole. We will find better ways to quantify, price, and manage today's familiar risks. We will also uncover, quantify, price, and manage risks that exist today but are hidden from view. The net benefits will be great—even granting that new and unforeseen risks could be created by this environment.

APPLYING PARTICLE FINANCE

Meanwhile, progress is being made at the front lines as well as in the labs. Pioneers in the derivatives business are successfully identifying, extracting, and pricing some of the more fundamental risks that drive asset values, such as interest rates, currency values, and commodity prices. Even though today these early applications look crude and primitive, they have already created a new and powerful process for solving important and practical financial problems. These range from limiting an airline's exposure to fuel price increases to helping a company hedge the value of a pending acquisition.

And important new applications are already on the runway: credit derivatives and insurance derivatives, for example.

Long before 2020, credit risks will be disaggregated into discrete attributes that will be readily traded, unbundled, and rebundled. Intermediaries will manage a large book of diversified long and short positions in credit attributes.

They will make markets in credit risk attributes and in bundles of attributes customized to suit the particular needs of their clients.

Such tailored products will permit each business to price and manage credit risk arising from its activities in a way that is best for that business. Perhaps even residual credit risks left after this process will be covered by a third-party insurance policy.

As the discipline of particle finance evolves, the primary job of financial institutions will be to help clients put theory to practical use. Just as today's man on the street does not practice particle physics, he will not practice particle finance in 2020.

It may often be done for him or her through automated analytics. For example, particle finance and automated analytics would provide much better asset allocation advice than is available today—allocating positions across many financial attributes rather than just picking the stock-bond mix.

The more advanced automated analytics programs will be like today's sophisticated computer chess programs, which can beat most players, but not all. As a result of competition from automated analytics, experts will be challenged to move on to higher and higher levels of wisdom and creativity.

However, the financial professional who prices the risk attributes will continue to use a combination of automated analytics and judgment. He or she will be responsible for the validation of the logic and historical data used in the automated analytics. In addition, forecasts of prospective market conditions will continue to play a critical role in pricing risk attributes, especially where prospective events are influenced by nonlinear relationships or structural changes that are not evident in past data or experience. We would expect a combination of chaos theory, fuzzy logic, and other tools to assist with predictive problems.

While advances in financial theory and technology will give talented people more powerful tools to apply their human creativity, they will not be replaced with robots. The CAT scan did not replace skilled neurologists—it gave them a tool that allowed them to apply their judgment with more precision and power.

In addition, highly skilled and creative specialists will continue to be needed to define and solve problems that are particularly complex and unique. These financial specialists will be the highest practitioners of particle finance, combining a creative grasp of financial possibilities with a psychoanalyst-like ability to help clients understand the true nature of their preferences for risk and return.

THE ROLE OF CENTRAL BANKS

The role of central banks will change as financial markets change. Two basic functions of central banks will be to protect us from systemic risk and to keep inflation in check.

The mechanisms by which central banks will deal with inflation in the world of 2020 are not clear. One method might be the use of margin requirements to control the amount of credit extended against wealth accounts. Clearly, capital controls and fixed exchange rates will be relics of an earlier age.

Another mission will be to avoid systemic collapse. We emphasize that this is *not* the same as dampening market volatility. Nor will regulators have to concern themselves with the fate of individual institutions, ending government-sponsored bailouts. Examiners will monitor the risk attributes of individual institutions to judge whether and how they contribute to the risk attributes of the system as a whole. (Everything else is random noise that cancels out at the portfolio level.)

Central bankers will focus on the prospective behavior of the system as well as current values of key targets. They will operate in the alphabet of financial risk as many advanced professionals do today—"delta" risk, the change in the values of instruments that are derived from the values of other instruments; "gamma" risk, the impact of highly nonlinear price changes on the behavior of the portfolio; "vega" risk, the change in the behavior of the portfolio arising from changes in the implied volatilities of the underlying instruments; and "theta" risk, the change in the behavior of the portfolio arising from the passage of time.

To effectively operate in this environment, central bankers will have to thoroughly understand and use the new computer and communications technology. Human nature being constant, they will also need to understand the psychology of crowd behavior and its prospective impact on financial market stability.

Thus central banks will have tools to prevent systemic collapse in the world portfolio similar to the tools that financial institutions will use to manage the corporate systemic risk in their portfolios. These tools will include real-time data and automated analytics.

Insuring against systemic risk will require a globally coordinated effort, which could well be the biggest challenge to the central banks. Will governments be able to put aside their parochial nationalistic agendas?

A FEW IMPLICATIONS FOR FINANCIAL INSTITUTIONS ARISING FROM PARTICLE FINANCE IN 2020

Particle finance presents a cornucopia of new business opportunities for financial institutions. Myriad risks, perhaps inexhaustible risks, are yet to be uncovered, described in "probability of occurrence" terms and then rebundled to satisfy client needs. There will always be a need for new disciplines and technologies to measure and deal with these risk attributes. In addition, all of these attributes and bundled products must be stored, safeguarded, verified, reported, and transferred.

Financial professionals will constantly be reeducating themselves. We, for example, are creating a "Bankers Trust University," where our people will be encouraged to spend many of their working hours.

Obviously, in the era of the theory of particle finance, financial organizations will look very different from the way they do today and will require a new type of manager.

With virtually no layers of management, financial organizations will attract an array of highly skilled and creative experts, including a wide array of people from science and mathematics.

Senior management will be like conductors of orchestras guiding their "artists" and "scientists" through example and influence rather than by "command and control." One of the important jobs of top managers will be to get their technical experts and managers to play in the same key. They are temperamentally different from one another, but as finance, science, and the arts continue to gradually merge, the scientist, artist, and manager will become more alike. The leaders' most important functions will be to inspire by articulating a clear vision of the organization's values, strategies, and objectives and to know enough about the business to be the risk manager of risk managers.

Superior judgment will always be essential and will continue to be valued highly since it will not be embedded on silicon. Depth of talent will be critical to success, so recruiting and retaining people will remain management's most important job. Technology will never replace the subtlety of the human mind. People will be the most important factor in 2020, just as they are now. We must learn how to grow wise leaders from the ranks of specialists, a difficult task.

CONCLUSION

These concepts will not flourish unless society blesses them. A social critic may say they are nothing more than a financial engineering exercise designed to enrich a few at the expense of many—a zero-sum game.

Not true. For as risk management becomes ever more precise and customized, the amount of risk that we all have to bear will be greatly reduced, lowering the need for financial capital. This will have a tremendous social value because financial capital that had been required to cushion these risks will be available elsewhere in society to produce more wealth to address soci-

ety's needs. In addition, this will liberate human capital by the greater leveraging of talent.

And these concepts will not flourish unless our clients bless them. As valuable as macro capital generation may be, it is not enough. On a micro basis, individuals and organizations must see value for themselves; clients must buy the service. Their trust must be earned by delivery of objective diagnostic help and solutions of value to them. We shall earn it.

Part VI
Regulatory Issues

[34]

GLOBALIZATION OF PAYMENT NETWORK AND RISKS

Yoshiharu Oritani

The recent development of information telecommunications technology has created global networks for instantaneous transmission of information. The technology in turn has made possible immediate financial transactions and payment settlement around the world. At the same time, however, it has intensified competition among international financial centers and heightened risks. In order to respond to these issues, close cooperation among central banks of the major industrial countries and the development and installation of a highly cost-efficient and fail-safe network for settlement of payments are indispensable.

Development of the Globalized Payment Network

Factors Contributing to Development

The basic factor contributing to the ongoing globalization of the payment network is the high-tech progress being made in information telecommunications technology. This technology has recorded quantum growth

Solomon, E.H., (ed.), *Electronic Money Flows*.
© 1991 Kluwer Academic Publishers. ISBN 0–7923–9134–9. All rights reserved.

The Globalization of Financial Services

with such advances as launching of communications satellites and installation of the optical fiber cables in the trans-Pacific submarine cable (completed in 1989).

The accelerated deregulation of the value-added network (VAN) has also served to promote the rapid increase in the establishment of global communications networks. Since financial transactions and payment settlements are basically performed by means of telecommunication, the impact of electronic telecommunications on payment procedures is greater, the wider the area is that is covered by technology.

Consequently, globalization of the telecommunications network has served to promote globalization of the payment network through two separate routes. One is indirectly through development of a global network required for collecting information on financial markets and contract matchings by means of the telecommunications network. This in turn has increased the volume of global financial transactions and, as a result, demand for global settlement of financial transactions has grown. The second route is directly through the establishment of the global network for instantaneous payment made feasible by advances in the telecommunications technology. With increasing convenience and cost efficiency of the payment system, the volume of global transactions has increased and spurred the development of the network.

The extensive development of the global payment network has become inevitable because globalization of the payment network has been promoted by the continuing advancements of the telecommunications technology.

Developing Forms of Global Payment Networks

When the networks of payment systems become globalized, they fall into the following two general forms.[1]

The first is depicted in figure 5–1. Here, a country's dedicated payment network becomes globalized by being linked with the international in-house network of a financial institution. This type is based on a financial institution's in-house on-line network connecting its overseas branches, and is made feasible by the development of technology for interconnecting networks.

The other form is depicted in figure 5–2. In this second case a global network is not based on any in-house network. It is, rather, a global payments network, utilizing the services of a commercially operated global telecommunications network.

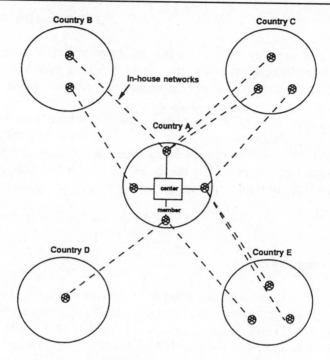

Figure 5–1. Global Network Based on In-House Networks

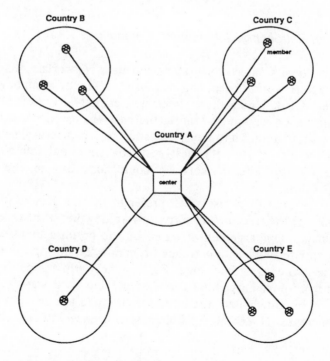

Figure 5–2. Global Network Directly Linked with Members

In one such type the center for settling payments is an entity independent from the one operating the network. The network could be a public utility that offers global telecommunication services (such as Euroclear, based on utilizing the GE Mark III as a host computer). Another network of this type is SWIFT, the global network without a center for settling payments, whose main purpose is to transmit payment information among financial institutions. The second form of network system for global settlement of payments has its centers in the United States and Europe. Presently there is no center for global payments with an operational base in Japan.

Globalization of Risk

Concomitantly with globalization of the payment system network, the risks inherent in the system have been globalized. The major risks include the following: (1) loss of status by a country either as a center of a payment network or as an international financial center, or (2) the globalization of a payment network's so-called systemic risk.

Risks of Retreat from International Competition

International Competition Among Payment Networks. As each nation's payment network is becoming globalized, competition among the networks is intensifying. Under these circumstances, network users in each country will find it easier—more than in the past—to use the services of foreign networks, in addition to their domestic one. The user will prefer to employ the network offering the best cost efficiency and reliability; and consequently the inferior network could lose out in the international competition.

Some argue that "users will prefer to use the service of the payment network of the creditor's country, just as they prefer the creditor country's currency." This argument is based on the premise that does not clearly differentiate between a currency's function for storing value and its function as a means of exchange. For instance, when Japan's surplus in its balance of payments grows cumulatively and an upward valuation of the yen can be anticipated, the trend for choosing the yen as a store of value will increase. Nonetheless, if the cost efficiency and reliability of Japan's network is inferior to those of other countries' networks, the yen will be little used as a means of payment.

Competition Among International Financial Centers. Currently most of the world's financial transactions are concentrated in the three major financial centers—New York, London, and Tokyo. With the expanding globalization of the payment network, competition among these financial centers could intensify. This is because globalization of the payment network, together with that of the information network on financial transactions, will have the effect of reducing the significance of financial transactions conducted separately in regional financial centers. It could also reduce the necessity for the existence of financial centers in many countries of the world.

Which country's international financial center will win out in the competition will depend on whether its payment network can survive the competition. In this instance, the decisive factor favoring survival will not necessarily be how large a country's cumulative surplus of balance of payments is but rather how adequate is its infrastructural support for international financial transactions—such as the payment network, as well as the country's political stability, legal framework, and accounting systems.

Globalization of Systemic Risk

The globalized payment network entails various risks, which could instantaneously spread worldwide through the network. Major issues are not only the relative risk affecting the actual users of the network but also the so-called systemic risk which affects third parties in a chain reaction because they happen to subscribe to the service to the network.

Participants in the payment network—banks and others—are directly exposed in general to two types of risks: credit risks and liquidity risks. Credit risk occurs when the payment network accepts remittances of funds that the remitter does not possess. Credit risk is inevitable, especially when the payment system finally settles the net credit and debit position of participating banks after a lapse of time following completion of the transactions. Liquidity risk occurs when the account of a participant in the transactions turns to deficit in the short term—and when the participant's plan for remaining liquid fails and it cannot raise the needed funds to remain liquid at short notice.

Both types of risks entail systemic risk. Systemic risk occurs when the relative risk involving only the two parties in a transaction "spills over" so as to affect multiple participants (banks, etc.) in a chain reaction. This occurs when a bank participating in a network becomes insolvent and its creditor banks become insolvent as a result. Or, the chain reaction effect of liquidity risk may occur without necessarily any of the participants falling into the worst case of insolvency; it may occur as a result of a simple mistake, such as a numerical error occurring in a remittance transaction.

These systemic risks may arise originally in the payment network confined to a single country; however, as the network expands globally, there is the danger that the trouble originating from one participant on one side of the globe may produce a chain reaction among participants on the other side of the world.

How To Cope with Globalization of Risks

The basic requirement for forestalling retreat from international competition is the establishment of a payment network that is both cost-efficient and fail-safe. To ensure this, the network must be designed to cope with any systemic risks. The following sections describe the three ways by which this can be accomplished.

Establishment of an Efficient Payment Network

It is essential to establish a fail-safe and efficient payment network in order to forestall any declines in international competition. The actual designing and development of an efficient system should start with the conversion of a system based on paperwork to that based on electronics. The new system must include payment systems transferring funds and securities.

Various kinds of obstacles confront the creation of an electronics payment system, of which the major ones are: (1) the technical cost of developing the system, and (2) inconvenient regulations and tax treatments. The technical cost of establishing an electronic system has been reduced by the recent cost reductions achieved in computer hardware and the development of software (for instance, Computer Aided Software Engineering). On the other hand, the second type of obstacle cannot necessarily be eliminated by the development of technology. In order to forestall the risk of retreat from international competition, any obstacles in a nation's regulations and tax structure that hinder conversion of the paperwork type to the electronics kind should be reformed beforehand.

Assuring Fail-Safe Operation of the Payment Network

In order to cope with these risks of credit and liquidity, it is imperative that parties directly involved in transactions take the necessary precautions. In the case where relative risks could develop into a chain reaction-like systemic risk, this can be prevented by cutting off the direct interdependence among the banks.

The central bank of a nation is in the position effectively to implement this requirement because settlement by transfer of funds among the participants' deposits held in the central bank would constitute "finality" to the transaction. Finality is defined by President Corrigan of the Federal Reserve Bank of New York (Corrigan, 1990) as follows: "Finality means that at the very instant an institution receives an advice of payment of confirmation of delivery through a system for a particular transaction, the money in question is 'good money,' even if at the next instant the sending institution goes bust."

The central bank is authorized to create "good" money in the form of bank notes and deposits held at the central bank. Therefore, when both the remitting bank and the bank receiving the remittance are participants in the payment network overseen by the central bank, the insolvency of the remitting bank will be prevented from affecting the bank receiving the remittance.

If any bank other than the central bank is responsible for operating the payment network, however, it may be impossible to prevent the insolvency of the transmitting bank from affecting other banks. In such a network where a payment netting scheme is employed, when a bank's debit position cannot be settled, the position of all banks participating in the system will be recalculated—after eliminating the amount of funds that cannot be settled; this is referred to as "unwinding." In most such instances, the remittance of funds from the insolvent bank is regarded as being void. In this case, in addition to the liquidity risk, caused by the fact that the anticipated funds had not been remitted at the anticipated time, a credit risk may arise from the insolvency. The latter could chain-react to cause insolvency among the participating banks.

Hence, in order to enhance the fail-safe functions of the payment network of each country and cope with globalization of system risks, participating banks should opt for joining the payment network with each country's central bank as the core. This will ensure finality to settlement of accounts.

Maintenance and Reinforcement of the "Club" Rules

The services provided by the payment system are not, by nature, strictly private goods, nor are they strictly public goods. According to Buchanan's definition (Buchanan, 1965), they could best be described as "club goods." This is because the services provided by the payment system—such as the transmittal and receiving of remittances—jointly benefit all members in the network. In other words, the services fulfill the necessary and sufficient condition of club goods "collectively consumed" by all participants. This aspect of the club goods differentiates them from private goods. On the other hand, membership in the payment system can be limited because of the application of "exclusion of nonmembers from club goods." In this sense, club goods differ from public goods.

Consequently, the payment system cannot be permitted to operate without rules and regulations. The payment system works in a manner unlike the market for clearly private goods, whose transactions are based on the principle of laissez-faire. Nonetheless, since the payment system's services are not purely public goods, it should not be operated under the government's rules and regulations, either. For this reason, the payment system traditionally has been operated as an interbank club sponsored by the central bank—an entity intermediate between the government and the private sector—under rules and regulations subscribed to by the member banks.

This tradition has been respected by all governments of industrially advanced countries, where no government holds supervisory power over the payment operations of the central bank. The reason for this is as follows. In addition to the club goods characteristics of the payment network operated by the central bank, the bank's monetary policy comprises measures designed to ensure liquidity for the member banks and cope with the aforementioned liquidity risk. Consequently, should the government hold supervisory power over the central bank's payment operations, there could exist the danger of the government's intervening in the central bank's monetary policy. This threat would imperil its independence from the government.

Be that as it may, any payment network based on rules and regulations that contravene the above requirements of nonintervention from the

GLOBALIZATION OF PAYMENT NETWORK 123

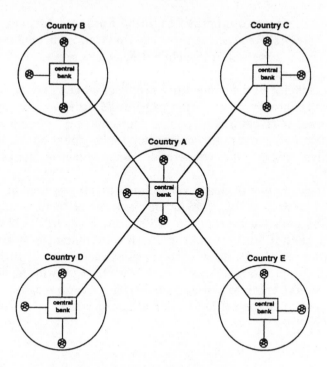

Figure 5–3. Global Network Linking Central Banks

government will lose credibility and, consequently, it will be exposed to the risk of its international competitiveness declining. Hence, it becomes imperative that the rules on club goods be maintained and reinforced.

Cooperation of Central Banks

As for desirability of the international competition among payment networks mentioned earlier, the discussion of the desirability is deeply related to the discussion on international competition among national currencies. This is because the payment network of the central bank can be regarded as a flow aspect of money. On the desirability of competitive money supply, there is no consensus among monetary economists. While economists such as Friedman (1959) supports the monopolistic supply of money, other economists such as Hayek (1976) argues for a competitively determined supply of money. The separation of opinions on the supply of money reflects the differences of approaches to the European Monetary Union. While the Delors Report supports the unification of money in the European Community (EC), the United Kingdom argues the competing currency approach.

Since the scheme of the competitive supply of money has not yet proved to work in the history, the scheme can not be acceptable in the global market. Then, it is natural to pursue the unification of money in the globally integrated market. As the first step to the global central bank that issues unified money, the cooperation among central banks is very important.[2]

One of the examples of such cooperation is to link payment networks of the national central banks. This linked payment network would be the third type of global network, and is depicted in figure 5–3. A global network of central banks would contribute to minimize systemic risk resulting from the globalization of the payment networks. This is because the network can facilitate a cross-border funds transfer with finality and a quick extension of credit to a troubled bank when a central bank, or central banks, want to play the role of lender of last resort.

Notes

1. Frankel and Marquardt (1987) described the postwar structure for making international large-value payments and analyzed changes affecting the global payment system structure.

2. The international competition of national currencies and national payment networks has some possibility to increase the risk of worldwide depression or inflation. Because the competitive supply of money scheme is argued to have the risk of inflation, and because the lack of the lender of last resort in the competitive currencies scheme could increase the risk of bank failures and subsequent depression, the central bank has an important role to play here. The central bank can issue money without a limit and stand neutral, not as a competitor. This fact makes it possible for the central bank to play the role of the lender of last resort. (This point is clearly stated by Goodhart, 1988.)

References

Buchanan, James M. 1965. "An Economic Theory of Clubs." *Economica* (February).

Corrigan, E. Gerald. 1990. "Perspectives on Payment System Risk Reduction." In David B. Humphrey, ed., *The U.S. Payment System: Efficiency, Risk and the Role of the Federal Reserve.* Boston: Kluwer Academic Publishers.

Frankel, Allen B, and Jeffrey C. Marquardt, 1987. "International Payments and

EFT Links." In Elinor Harris Solomon, ed., *Electronic Funds Transfers and Payments: The Public Policy Issues*. Boston: Kluwer Academic Publishers.

Friedman, Milton. 1959. *A Program for Monetary Stability*. New York: Fordham University Press.

Goodhart, Charles A.E. 1988. *The Evolution of Central Banks*. Cambridge: The MIT Press.

Hayek, F.A. 1976. *Denationalisation of Money*. The Institute of Economic Affairs.

REGULATING BANKS' SECURITIES ACTIVITIES: A GLOBAL ASSESSMENT

The author identifies the key differences in national regulatory policies regarding combined banking/securities businesses and assesses the potential dangers and competitive disparities associated with such regulatory diversity. One key issue is whether troubled securities firms are going to be backed by their affiliated banks; the answer may depend on the nationality of the firms.

Richard Dale

There is widespread agreement among policy-makers, regulators, academics and members of the financial community that banks should be free to engage in securities activities. Indeed, the EC has adopted the universal banking model in its second Banking Co-ordination Directive, the UK and Canada have recently removed barriers between the banking and securities industries, and the US and Japan are considering proposals for ending the statutory separation of commercial and investment banking.

However, there is no international consensus on the new regulatory framework that should govern combined banking/securities businesses. National authorities have adopted divergent approaches which reflect fundamental differences of view as to how financial markets behave, how different institutional structures respond to financial shocks and what kinds of regulatory safeguard best serve the twin objectives of stability and efficiency. The result is that banks will soon be conducting their international securities business on the basis of incompatible national regulatory arrangements, implying significant competitive distortions as well as uneven lender of last resort coverage for financial institutions operating in different jurisdictions.

The purpose of the present article is to identify the key differences in national regulatory policies with respect to combined banking/securities businesses and to assess potential dangers and competitive disparities associated with regulatory diversity in this area. The first section examines the policy alternatives, the second section focuses on the divergent regulatory approaches adopted in Europe, North America and Japan, and the final section assesses the broader policy implications.

Policy choices

Essentially, there are three alternative regulatory regimes for banking and securities businesses. The first, very simply, is to prohibit the combination of these two businesses within a single organisation. At the opposite extreme, regulatory authorities may allow banking and securities business to be freely intermingled, as in the case of universal banks. Finally, by way of compromise, an attempt may be made to construct a financial market regime in which banks undertake securities business on terms which segregate the risks incurred by the bank and its related securities entity.

Statutory separation

Separation of the banking and securities industries through the imposition of statutory barriers involves heavy but unquantifiable costs in the form of economies of scope foregone and the apparatus of enforcement. Among other disadvantages of this approach is the difficulty of defining banks' permissible activities in a situation where the distinction between traditional bank lending and securities operations is becoming increasingly blurred. Furthermore, even statutory barriers cannot prevent banks being exposed to securities markets through, for instance, lending to securities firms. Indeed, such exposure was a major concern during the stock market crash of 1987[1]. Nevertheless, a complete prohibition of the riskier types of securities activities, including dealing in and underwriting equities, does limit the scope for risk-taking by banks while confining the lender of last resort function to deposit-taking institutions undertaking conventional banking business. Under this regime regulation is strictly functional, with bank and securities market regulators having separate, non-overlapping responsibilities.

Universal banking

The universal banking model lies at the opposite end of the spectrum[2]. Here economies of scope can be maximised and it is left to the bank to decide whether it can conduct its securities business more efficiently through separately capitalised subsidiaries, through a holding company structure or through the bank entity itself. Whatever the corporate structure, there are no regulatory constraints on intra-group financial transactions (though "Chinese walls" may inhibit transfers of information) and risks are permitted to flow freely from one part of the conglomerate to any other part. In other words, the bank is exposed to all risks incurred within the group.

Under a universal banking regime it is important that the regulatory/supervisory function be organised along institutional lines. Since major problems arising in a bank's securities arm would expose the bank itself to the risk of insolvency, it makes no sense from a prudential standpoint to regulate the two functions separately. Therefore, a single agency should be given regulatory responsibility for the activities of the whole group.

An argument could be made for requiring such mixed banking-securities businesses to adhere to more stringent capital adequacy standards than specialist stand-alone banks and securities firms. The capital "penalty" would reflect the additional social costs associated with the higher risk of bank failure and the fact that, in the case of banking conglomerates, the lender of last resort function would have to be extended to securities activities, since these would be inseparable from the banking function. Indeed, the strongest argument against universal banking, to be set against its undoubted merits in terms of operational efficiency, is that it widens the official safety net to non-bank activities.

Risk segregation through firewalls

Policy-makers are therefore faced with a dilemma. On the one hand, formal separation of banking and securities business may involve costly inefficiencies; on the other hand, a permissive regime in which the two businesses can be freely mixed creates risks for the financial system, for the deposit insurance fund and for the lender of last resort. And because neither approach meets the twin policy objectives of efficiency and safety, much attention has been given to devising a third option which might enable banking groups to diversify into securities business while containing securities market risks within the bank's securities unit. Any such scheme which claims to resolve the apparent conflict between efficiency and safety deserves particularly careful consideration.

The first step in seeking to insulate a bank from the risk incurred by its securities operations is to separately incorporate

those operations. Whether this should be done through a holding company structure, in which the bank and the securities firm become subsidiaries of the holding company and affiliates of each other, or whether the securities firm should be a subsidiary of the bank, is a matter for debate[3]. The preferred view appears to be that there is less risk of legal separation being overturned by the courts and the bank found liable for the obligations of its related securities firm if a holding company structure is used. In other words, such a structure makes it less likely that the courts will "pierce the corporate veil". As one US commentator has put it:

"piercing cross-wide [through the holding company] *would be less likely than piercing upward* [through the bank]. *That is, if a non-bank subsidiary failed, the likelihood that a banking subsidiary would be held liable for its debts is considerably smaller than the (already small) likelihood that the parent holding company would be held liable."* [4]

Whatever form of corporate structure is chosen, the next step is to construct firewalls between the bank and its related securities firm to ensure, so far as possible, full legal, economic and market separation. Broadly, these firewalls are of three kinds: they may place restrictions on intra-group financial transactions, they may seek to separate the identity of the bank and securities firm, and they may require separate management.[5] In addition, Chinese walls may be introduced which aim to prevent conflict of interest abuses by restricting information flows within the group.

Restrictions on financial transactions, or "funding firewalls", are intended to prevent a bank from becoming directly exposed to its securities affiliate/subsidiary through extensions of credit or the acquisition of bad assets.[6] Funding firewalls do, however, have several shortcomings as an insulating device. In the first place a bank, under the pressure of events, may well breach the walls, in contravention of the law. Secondly, situations may arise where a securities firm may need the support of its banking affiliate/parent, and where denial of that support could trigger a collapse. The president of the Federal Reserve Bank of New York, Mr Gerald Corrigan, has suggested that in such circumstances funding firewalls could become

Exhibit 1: Formal separation

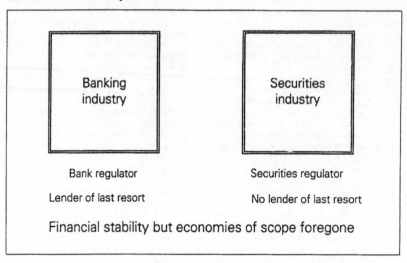

Banking industry

Securities industry

Bank regulator

Lender of last resort

Securities regulator

No lender of last resort

Financial stability but economies of scope foregone

Exhibit 2: Universal banking

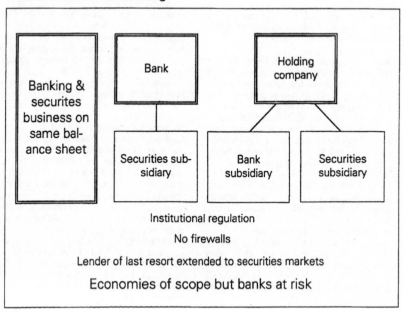

Banking & securites business on same balance sheet

Bank

Securities subsidiary

Holding company

Bank subsidiary

Securities subsidiary

Institutional regulation

No firewalls

Lender of last resort extended to securities markets

Economies of scope but banks at risk

SECURITIES ACTIVITIES

Exhibit 3: Risk segregation with firewalls

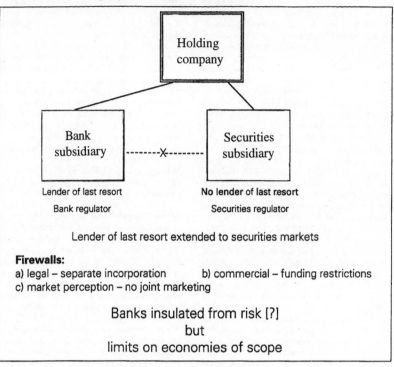

Lender of last resort   **No lender** of last resort

Bank regulator   Securities regulator

Lender of last resort extended to securities markets

Firewalls:
a) legal – separate incorporation   b) commercial – funding restrictions
c) market perception – no joint marketing

Banks insulated from risk [?]
but
limits on economies of scope

Exhibit 4: Risk segregation through 'narrow banks'

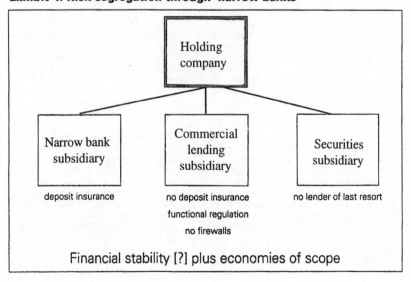

deposit insurance   no deposit insurance   no lender of last resort

functional regulation

no firewalls

Financial stability [?] plus economies of scope

Thirdly, while funding firewalls seek to prevent contagion through the assets side of a bank's balance sheet, the more serious problems are likely to arise on the liabilities side — that is, through confidence-induced deposit withdrawals. Even if effective asset insulation were achieved, this would not ensure protection on the liabilities side. Finally, funding firewalls involve important costs. They are difficult to enforce and they deny to diversified financial groups the benefit of a group funding role for the in-house bank.

Firewalls may also be used to separate in the public mind the identity of a bank and its related securities firm. Such separation is intended to prevent contagion *via* confidence effects in the event that the securities firm should experience publicised financial difficulties. Restrictions under this heading may include (in the extreme) prohibition on joint marketing of bank and securities firm products, separate premises for the two businesses and a ban on the use of similar names. Where joint marketing is permitted, a minimum safeguard would be contractual documentation making it clear that the bank is not liable for the obligations of securities firm products. The major disadvantage of this class of restriction is that it limits economies of scope on the marketing side and, in the case of a separate premises requirement, adds very significantly to operating costs.

Finally, firewalls may require separate management of a bank and its related securities firm, by prohibiting common directors, officers or employees and mandating separate accounts and record-keeping. Such restrictions are aimed primarily at reinforcing legal separation of the two businesses. However, once again the costs may be heavy, since a fragmented management structure is hardly conducive to successful exploitation of economies of scope. Furthermore, in times of crisis — the very contingency for which firewalls are built — it may be too much to expect that management will remain separate.[8]

In addition to these prudential safeguards, it is likely that regulators of banking conglomerates will wish to establish Chinese walls designed to prevent conflict of interest abuses and unfair competition. In particular, a bank may be prevented from disclosing to its related securities firm any non-public customer information relating to the creditworthiness of an issuer or other customer of the securities firm. From the point of view of securing competitive equal-ity such a restriction may be desirable, but it also erodes the potential benefits to be derived from financial diversification.[9]

In summary, the separate incorporation of securities activities, buttressed by firewalls that seek to insulate the related bank legally and managerially as well as in terms of corporate identity, may go some way toward protecting the bank from non-bank risks. In such a regime the hope would be that the lender of last resort function could be confined to the bank. And to the extent that risks were segregated in this way, regulation could be organised along functional lines — although any doubts about the effectiveness of the insulating mechanism would call for some form of institutional supervision.

Other forms of risk segregation

From this brief review it is obvious that the effectiveness of firewalls in insulating a bank from the risks incurred by a related securities firm will depend on the height of the walls and the rigour with which they are enforced. At the extreme, firewalls may impose such severe constraints on intra-group financial, marketing and managerial relationships as to negate the benefits of diversification — in effect, internalising Glass-Steagall-type barriers within the diversified group and thereby eliminating all economies of scope. Even so, there can be no assurance that a bank will not be adversely affected by any problems experienced within its securities subsidiary/affiliate. Indeed, recent episodes involving, *inter alia*, Drexel Burnham Lambert (see below) and British Commonwealth Merchant Bank, not to mention numerous earlier US cases, suggest that cross-infection on the liabilities side may defeat all efforts to insulate the banking entity. Certainly, this is the view of several leading regulators, as typified by the following comments of Mr Gerald Corrigan, president of the Federal Reserve Bank of New York:

> *"What the marketplace tells us with almost unfailing regularity is that in times of stress, some parts of a financial entity cannot safely be insulated from the problems of affiliated entities. Investors, creditors and even managers and directors simply do not generally behave in that fashion and the larger the problem the less likely they are to do so. Because this pattern of behaviour seems so dominant and because the authorities throughout the world generally frame*

SECURITIES ACTIVITIES

extreme, absolute firewalls can aggravate problems and instabilities rather than contain or limit them." [10]

It would seem, then, that attempts to reconcile the conflicting objectives of efficiency and safety through the use of firewalls are unlikely to succeed, and may even be counter-productive. In recognition of this fact, a number of ingenious proposals have bee put forward in an attempt to square the circle.

One such proposal is based on the idea of the "narrow bank". [11] Under this scheme financial holding companies (FHCs) would be free to engage, through separate subsidiaries, in any business activity (including non-financial activities). However, a bank entity within the FHC structure would be required to operate as an *insured* money market mutual fund, accepting insured deposits and investing in highly liquid, safe securities in the form of government obligations. In effect the deposit-taking function would be separated from the lending function, the latter being conducted by separately incorporated FHC lending subsidiaries wholly funded by uninsured liabilities such as commercial paper. Since the bank could not, legally, bail out a non-bank affiliate (as its assets would have to consist entirely of government securities), the possibility of contagion would be minimised if not altogether eliminated and deposit insurance, although retained for confidence reasons, would not be strictly necessary.

A variant of the narrow bank proposal is the idea of a "secure depository". [12] Here banks would be able to hold only marketable assets traded on well-organised exchanges. Regulatory capital would be calculated daily and subject to immediate corrective action in the event of any shortfall — an approach similar to that currently adopted by securities market regulators. All liabilities of the bank would be insured although, as with the narrow bank, prompt corrective action would make deposit insurance very much a second line of defence. The secure depository could be part of a financial conglomerate whose non-bank activities would not need to be circumscribed in any way. The commercial lending function would have to be undertaken by a separate non-bank affiliate whose obligations would be uninsured. Transactions between a secure depository and an affiliate could not threaten the solvency of the depository since the latter's assets would be marked to market daily. Therefore there would be no need for firewalls.

The authors of the secure depository proposal have also suggested as an alternative the "secured deposit" approach. [13] Under this scheme banks would be able to conduct any activity they wished, but their deposit liabilities would have to be collateralised with marketable assets which would be placed in the legal custody of a third party. Loans that could not be securitised would be funded by uninsured liabilities. Rather than ensuring the safety of the corporate entity that accepts deposits, the purpose here would be to ensure the safety of deposits within a larger corporate entity. The secured deposit scheme would therefore do away with the need for separate incorporation of risky activities and allow financial institutions to function as German-style universal banks, with no activity constraints or firewalls.

The great difficulty with each of these proposals, apart from the fact that they involve a major restructuring of banking as we know it, is their failure to ensure broad-based financial stability. [14] A newly defined core banking system, embracing marketable assets funded by insured deposits, would be protected. But the key problem for bank regulators has always been the funding of non-marketable commercial loans. Under each of these schemes, commercial lending would be conducted outside the core banking system but would presumably be funded, as at present, by short-term liabilities. These would be uninsured deposits in all but name. The familiar problems of deposit runs, forced asset disposals and contagious crises of confidence would therefore be merely shifted to other areas of the financial marketplace.

For instance, under the secure depository proposal commercial lending could be undertaken by a finance affiliate whose obligations would not be insured. Such finance companies would be far more vulnerable to funding crises than are present-day banks enjoying the protection of deposit insurance. Furthermore, it is far from clear that a multiple collapse of finance companies would be any less devastating for the financial system and the economy as a whole than would be the multiple failure of conventional banks. Finally, in times of stress it is reasonable to expect that there would be a massive transfer of funds from the uninsured to the insured financial sectors, as lenders sought to safeguard their assets. The potential for such large-scale destabilising movements of funds would, arguably, increase the fragility of the financial system and defeat the whole purpose of the proposed reforms.

It is difficult to avoid the conclusion that there is a problem here without a solution. Policy-makers may give precedence to the safety and soundness of the financial system by separating the banking industry from securities markets — with whatever loss of efficiency and competitiveness that such a division may entail. Alternatively, they can give priority to efficiency and the exploitation of economies of scope by allowing banks to engage freely in securities activities — while accepting a much greater potential for contagious financial disorders and a correspondingly larger role for the lender of last resort. However, attempts to achieve both safety and efficiency by using the apparatus of firewalls, separate legal entities and other risk insulation techniques promise neither safety nor efficiency — and quite possibly achieve the worst of all worlds by combining costly restrictions with hard-to-detect risk "seepage".

National practice

Having analysed the various policy alternatives for regulating banks' securities activities, it is necessary to review national practice in this area. One clear trend to emerge from the discussion that follows is the increasing determination of national authorities to permit banks to participate in securities markets. However, there is no common approach to managing the risks associated with financial diversification; within individual countries policy has tended to shift erratically, and the latest moves towards liberalisation generally lack a firm analytical base.

Germany and Switzerland

Germany and Switzerland are traditional universal banking countries where securities business is typically, but not always, conducted off the banks' own balance sheet. Regulation is institutional rather than functional, with the Federal Banking Supervisory Office, in the case of Germany, and the Federal Banking Commission, in the case of Switzerland, responsible for supervising a bank's securities as well as its banking business.

Swiss and German banks have been forced to separately incorporate their US securities activities in order to conform to the Glass-Steagall Act, but even here risks

are free to flow between the securities entity and its related bank. This key point was underlined recently when Crédit Suisse sought to reduce its regulatory capital requirements by creating a holding company structure in which Crédit Suisse and its US investment banking arm, Crédit Suisse First Boston (CFSB), became affiliate companies owned by CS Holding (CSH) (previously CFSB had been an indirectly-held subsidiary of Crédit Suisse). However, in October 1989 the Federal Banking Commission ruled that the new holding company structure did not exempt Crédit Suisse from providing full capital cover for group subsidiaries and that the bank would have to consolidate itself with CSH as if it, and not CSH, were the group holding company. The reasoning behind the commission's decision was that the bank would be obliged as a matter of commercial self-interest to support CSFB if the latter should get into difficulties, even though there was no legal obligation to do so. The Commission's decision, and its reasoning, were upheld on appeal by a ruling of the Swiss Federal Supreme Court in December 1990.[15]

It is clear, therefore, that universal banks cannot escape from the risks incurred by their securities operations, and it follows that capital adequacy rules apply to the group rather than to the bank. A further, though less explicit, consequence of this denial of risk segregation is that the lender of last resort function extends to banks' securities activities.

United Kingdom

In broad terms, the UK has adopted the universal banking model as a consequence of the Big Bang restructuring of securities markets. That is to say, banks are free to undertake securities business off their own balance sheet or through a separately incorporated securities subsidiary. Furthermore, if they choose the latter there are no formal restrictions preventing UK banks from funding their securities subsidiaries — ie, there are no firewalls, and risks may flow through from the securities subsidiary to the bank.[16]

However, the universality principle is subject in the UK to two major qualifications. In the first place, gilt-edged market makers are "ring-fenced" within the banking groups to which they belong. Such marketmakers must be separately capitalised, they can generally have no subsidiaries operating

SECURITIES ACTIVITIES

Exhibit 5: Crédit Suisse Holding Company Structure (end 1990)

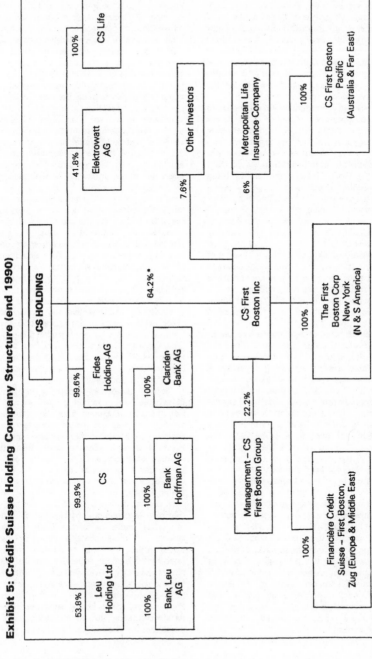

* CS Holding owns 73.5% of the voting
N.B. Percentages shown are capital stakes, not voting rights.

in financial markets (downstream protection), and they are supported by comfort letters from their major shareholders (upstream protection). These mechanisms of risk insulation are justified, *inter alia*, on the grounds that gilt-edge market-makers have direct access to the Bank of England as lender of last resort, although it seems somewhat incongruous that firms operating in the gilt-edged market are protected in a way that the banks which own them are not.

A second important qualification arises from the statutory distribution of regulatory responsibilities in the UK. Parliament chose to divide responsibility for regulating combined banking/securities businesses between the Securities and Investment Board (SIB) and the Bank of England, the SIB being responsible for regulating businesses authorised to conduct securities/investment activities under Section 25 of the Financial Services Act of 1986, while the Bank is responsible for supervising the banking activities of those firms authorised to undertake such business under the Banking Act of 1987. In other words, combined banking/securities businesses are subject to functional rather than institutional regulation, with different parts of the same financial group being treated separately for regulatory purposes.

This division of regulatory responsibilities presents serious difficulties given the integrated nature of risks incurred within combined securities/banking businesses, and the consequent need for an overall assessment of such businesses' financial condition. In other words, functional regulation cuts right across the universal banking model. In order to alleviate this difficulty the Bank of England and the SIB have between them developed the concept of "lead regulator" whereby each UK supervisor retains statutory responsibility for the institution it authorises, while the lead regulator for the group promotes exchanges of information between supervisor and co-ordinates any necessary remedial action. While the lead regulator innovation does introduce an institutional element into the functional statutory framework, it cannot hope to deliver the same quality of prudential supervision as would a regime in which all parts of a financial group are subject to consolidated supervision by one overall group supervisor (assuming, of course, that the group supervisor commands the necessary expertise).

Europe

In launching its single European market programme, the EC commission at the outset adopted a financial regime based on the Swiss/German universal banking model. That is to say, banking is defined broadly to include the securities business, questions of corporate financial structure are left to individual banking organisations to decide as a purely commercial matter, and no attempt is made to segregate banking from non-banking risks within financial conglomerates.

Having prescribed a universal banking regime, the EC Commission ran into difficulties when it sought to formulate a capital adequacy directive for mixed securities/banking businesses.[17] On the one hand it was recognised that banks, unlike securities firms, are vulnerable to contagious funding crises and should therefore be subject to a stricter definition of regulatory capital than that applied to securities houses. On the other hand, in the interests of competitive equality, the Commission proposed that supervisors should be able to apply a more permissive definition of regulatory capital to a bank's own securities trading book. The effect of this hybrid capital adequacy test, which allows more liberal use of subordinated debt as capital backing for securities activities, is that the burden of absorbing losses on a bank's trading book may have to be borne by the equity capital that supports the rest of the bank's business. Therefore under the EC regime banks that engage in securities business may carry a higher risk of insolvency than specialist banks.

To put it another way, under the proposed EC scheme, banks and their securities activities are fully integrated from the point of view of exposure but treated separately for the purposes of capital adequacy assessment. An important — and incongruous — element of functional regulation is thereby introduced into a pooled risk regime that surely calls for an institutional approach to prudential regulation.

A further difficulty arises from the multifarious arrangements within the EC for regulating banks' securities business. In general, securities activities carried out by banks on their own balance sheets are regulated by the banking supervisor, but this is not necessarily so — for instance, UK banking and securities supervisors have overlapping responsibilities in such cases. Furthermore, where banks' securities business is conducted through separately incorporated subsidiaries, the securities subsidiary may be the primary responsibility of the securities supervisor (as in the UK and Spain).[18]

United States

The Glass-Steagall Act represented an unequivocal decision by the US congress to separate the risks associated with commercial and investment banking. However, the statute left an important loophole in overseas markets which US regulatory authorities were happy to tolerate in order to strengthen US banks' competitive position abroad. Furthermore, the strict segregation of domestic banking and securities business was relaxed during the 1980s as a result of a number of decisions by the Federal Reserve Board, exercising its discretionary authority under the Bank Holding Company Act.[19]

These moves culminated in the decision of September 1990 to allow a bank holding company's "Section 20 subsidiary"[20] to underwrite corporate debt and equity securities on a limited scale and subject to detailed firewall requirements. On the face of it the Federal Reserve Board appeared to be giving its support to a new regulatory regime, in which risk segregation techniques such as separate incorporation and extensive firewalls were to be used as a means of allowing banks expanded securities powers without widening the official safety net.

However, the reality was somewhat different. The quantitative limits imposed on securities business undertaken by Section 20 subsidiaries are designed both to meet the statutory wording of the Glass-Steagall Act and to minimise the overall risks incurred by the securities subsidiary. In other words, bank holding companies are being allowed to engage in potentially risky securities activities but on a scale that would be highly unlikely to jeopardise the solvency of the securities subsidiary, still less the bank. In this situation firewalls are being employed only as a back-stop, rather than as a central mechanism for segregating risks. The Section 20 subsidiaries therefore represent a hybrid solution to regulating banks' securities activities — involving both costly firewalls and a severe limitation on the extent of banks' participation in securities markets.

The Bush Administration's proposals for repealing Glass-Steagall, introduced in February 1991, rely much more heavily on risk segregation.[21] This is to be achieved through a financial services holding company (FSHC) structure in which the bank and its securities affiliate would be separated by

firewalls and the official safety net would be explicitly confined to the bank. In the Treasury's words, "creditors of the FSCH or (non-bank) financial affiliate should receive no federal protection in the event of FSHC insolvency".[22] In contrast to the limits currently placed on bank holding companies' Section 20 subsidiaries, a bank's securities affiliate could, under the Administration's scheme, undertake securities business on whatever scale it chose — subject, of course, to the SEC's regulatory capital requirements for securities firms. Consistent with this risk segregation regime, regulatory responsibilities would be allocated on a functional basis.

The authors of the Administration's proposal evidently harbour some doubts about the effectiveness of their attempts to segregate risks. Thus in order to allow for the possibility of cross-infection, banks which choose to have securities affiliates will have to maintain especially high capital ratios.[23] Furthermore, the bank regulator is to be given "umbrella oversight" of the holding company, thereby providing an element of institutional regulation designed to detect and correct problems within non-bank affiliates that could pose a threat to the bank. In short, the apparatus of risk segregation is in this case being combined with other safeguards more properly associated with the universal banking model — with adverse competitive implications for US banks (see below).

However, the main criticism of the Administration's proposal is that the holding company structure and firewalls which lie at the heart of the scheme are likely to prove redundant. There is already ample evidence to suggest that a bank will be quickly infected by a non-bank affiliate's problems, firewalls or no firewalls, the most recent and spectacular example being provided by the collapse of Drexel Burnham Lambert.

On 13 February 1990 Drexel Burnham Lambert Group, Inc. ("Drexel"), the holding company parent of Drexel Burnham Lambert Inc., a major securities firm, and Drexel Burnham Lambert Government Securities Inc., a registered government securities dealer, filed for Chapter 11 bankruptcy.[24] Drexel had become increasingly dependent on short-term credit markets, borrowing as much as $1bn on an unsecured basis, largely through the issuance of commercial paper. In December 1989 Standard and Poor's had reduced its rating on Drexel's commercial paper, with the result that Drexel's borrowing from this

Exhibit 6: Proposed Financial Structure in the US

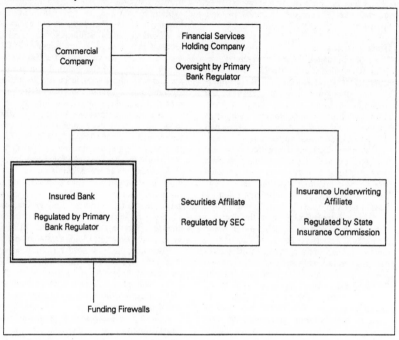

Funding Firewalls

SECURITIES ACTIVITIES

source dried up. But because a large proportion of Drexel's assets were not readily marketable (in particular it had a large portfolio of "junk" bonds), its balance sheet could not be contracted in line with its reduced funding capacity. The result was an acute liquidity crisis, described by the Chairman of the Federal Reserve Board, Mr Alan Greenspan, in the following terms:

> *"As doubts emerged about the ability of Drexel to meet its obligations in a timely and predictable way, it suffered what in banking terms would be called a 'run'. The run extended across the various units that make up Drexel — including both regulated and unregulated affiliates, and including affiliates that seemed to be solvent, as those whose status was in doubt."* [25]

Of particular significance was the fact that Drexel's government securities subsidiary, which was adequately capitalised, stringently

regulated and soundly run, found its access to funds cut off when questions were raised about the health of the parent company. The unmistakable implication is that all parts of a financial conglomerate that rely on short-term borrowing become vulnerable when confidence in *any* part of the organisation is shaken.

This unwelcome message from the markets appears to have had a major impact on the thinking of some regulators. In July 1990 Mr Greenspan delivered the follow congresssional testimony, revealing his own deep misgivings on the whole risk segregation issue:

> *"The Board has for some time held the view that strong insulating firewalls would both protect banks (and taxpayers) from the risk of new activities and limit the extension of the safety net subsidy that would place independent competitors at a disadvantage. However, recent events, including the rapid spread of market pressures to separately regulated and well-capitalised units of*

Drexel when their holding company was unable to meet its maturing commercial paper obligations, have raised serious questions about the ability of firewalls to insulate the unit of a holding company from funding problems of another. Partially as a result, the Board is in the process of re-evaluating both the efficacy and desirability of substantial firewalls between a bank and some of its affiliates. It is clear that high and thick firewalls reduce synergies and raise costs for financial institutions, a significant problem in increasingly competitive financial markets. If they raise costs and may not be effective, we must question why we are imposing these kinds of firewalls at all." [26]

Despite the lessons of the Drexel affair and growing official scepticism about the effectiveness of firewalls, the US Administration has proposed a new financial structure in which the stability of the US banking system may depend on the ability of firewalls to insulate banks from securities market risks. At the same time the requirement that banks with securities affiliates must have additional capital will undermine US banks' competitiveness *vis-à-vis* their European counterparts without doing anything to neutralise the most potent source of cross-infection — namely, confidence-induced withdrawals of funding.

Canada
Historically, Canada's banking and securities industries were separated under the "four pillars" policy which established formal legal barriers between banking, insurance, securities and trust business. [27] These domestic restrictions did not, however, prevent Canadian banks, like their US counterparts, from conducting investment banking operations through their subsidiaries in London and elsewhere. Banks have been permitted to acquire domestic securities subsidiaries since 1987, but regulatory policy governing the relationship between a bank and its related securities entity has undergone important changes during the course of this liberalisation process.

The Government's 1985 Green Paper setting out its proposals for financial reform followed a risk segregation approach, using a holding company structure and strict firewalls between a bank and its non-bank affiliates. This was similar to the scheme now adopted by the US Administration. However, in a

major policy switch the Government, in its subsequent 1986 Blue Paper, abandoned the risk segregation model in favour of a more permissive regime in which banks would be able to diversify through securities subsidiaries with relatively few restrictions on intra-group financial transactions (in effect low firewalls). The legislation submitted to Parliament in 1990, by lifting these residual restrictions, marked a further shift towards the universal banking model — although the outer shell of risk segregation was retained in the form of a separate incorporation requirement for banks' securities (and other non-bank) business.

Consistent with this approach, the Government has attempted to introduce an institutional element into its supervisory arrangements, in particular by reaching accords with the various provincial authorities that regulate banks' securities subsidiaries. In effect these agreements give the federal bank regulator the right to be consulted on regulatory matters affecting the solvency of a securities subsidiary. Nevertheless, the federal/provincial division of regulatory responsibilities for banks and securities firms makes it very difficult to achieve a satisfactory institutional oversight of banks' securities activities.

Japan
After the Second World War the US, as occupying power, imported the main restrictions of the Glass-Steagall Act into Japan. Nevertheless, the separation of banking and securities business has been less complete in Japan, where banks, unlike their US counterparts, are empowered to invest in equity securities and Japanese banking groups have been able to acquire major interests in securities firms through a complex web of cross-shareholdings. [28] These differences apart, the Japanese authorities have in effect extended the official safety net to major securities houses which typically have direct access to the Bank of Japan's discount window. Paradoxically, therefore, statutory risk segregation has failed to confine the lender of last resort function to the banking sector.

Since the mid-1980s, the Japanese authorities have been considering proposals for dismantling the present constraints on banks' securities activities. In June 1991 the Ministry of Finance appeared to be favouring a proposal under which banks would be able to establish separate securities subsidiaries, but the question of what, if any firewalls might be required remained undecided — as did the more fundamental issue of whether the new structure would continue to segregate bank from non-bank risks. Indeed, in the Japanese context the whole debate about banks' securities powers is linked to concepts of fairness rather than to the more familiar Western policy goals of safety, soundness and efficiency. Thus the Ministry of Finance is evidently inclined to limit the pace at which city banks can expand their securities activities because of the marketing advantages they enjoy in the form of extensive branch networks — an approach that turns on its head the traditional case for expanded securities powers based on economies of scope. More paradoxically, the Ministry has proposed that banks' securities subsidiaries should be allowed to engage in underwriting (a high-risk activity) but should be excluded from brokerage business (a lesser risk activity).[29]

Conclusion

From the above survey it should be apparent that in addressing the issue of financial diversification, national policy-makers and regulators have only one thing in common — a desire to extend the boundaries of banks' permissible securities activities. How this should be done, whether risks should be segregated and what the role of the lender of last resort should be — all these matters are the subject of divergent and often confusing national initiatives.

The policy disarray surrounding the key issue of financial market structure has disturbing implications for the stability of the international banking system. In particular, it is clearly unsatisfactory that the EC and the US should be moving in opposite directions on the key issue of risk segregation. Within Europe it must be assumed — as in the Crédit Suisse case — that a bank will always stand behind a related securities firm. In the US, the administration's proposed holding company and firewall structure is explicitly designed to ensure that a troubled securities firm is *not* supported by its bank affiliate. There is a further implication that within Europe the lender of last resort function may have to be extended (directly or indirectly) to bank-related securities firms. In contrast, the US Administration's scheme is intended to confine the official safety net strictly to the banking sector.

The coexistence of these diametrically opposed regulatory structures is fraught with difficulties. In times of global financial stress

there may be a temptation, within Europe, for lenders to shift their exposure from stand-alone to bank-related securities firms, on the grounds that the latter are more likely to receive official support. More importantly, in such circumstances there will be a strong inducement for lenders to withdraw funding from US securities firms (whether or not bank-related) in favour of securities firms affiliated to European banks. In the meantime, US banks which are part of diversified financial groups will face a competitive disadvantage *vis-à-vis* their European counterparts because of their mandatory holding company structure, higher capital requirements and restrictive firewalls.

Notes

(1) An SEC report noted that some broker-dealers experienced problems obtaining credit during the week of 19 October 1987 — to the point where the Federal Reserve Bank of New York felt obliged to encourage certain city banks to support the securities industry. See *Market Break*, October 1987, US Securities and Exchange Commission, February 1988, pp 5–24 to 5–30.

(2) For recent discussions of universal banking, see George Benston, *The Separation of Commercial and Investment Banking*, op cit pp.179–214; Richard Herring and Anthony Santomero, "The Corporate Structure of Financial Conglomerates", *Journal of Financial Services Research*, Vol 4, No 4, December 1990, pp.471–497; and Alfred Steinherr and Christian Huveneers, "Universal Banks: the Prototype of Successful Banks in the Integrated European Market", Centre for European Policy Studies, 1989.

(3) See, for instance, "Bank Powers: Insulating Banks from the Potential Risks of Expanded Activities", US General Accounting Office, April 1987, pp 26–41; and "Mandate for Change: Restructuring the Banking Industry", Federal Deposit Insurance Corporation, August 1987, pp 105–125.

(4) Samuel Chase, "The Bank Holding Company — A Superior Device for Expanding Activities?", in *Policies for a More Competitive Financial System*, Federal Reserve Bank of Boston, June 1972, p 82.

(5) For an assessment of firewalls see "Using Firewalls in a post-Glass-Steagall Banking Environment", Statement of Richard Fogel, Assistant Comptroller General, before the subcommittee on Telecommunications and Finance, Committee on Energy and Commerce, US House of Representatives, 13 April 1988.

(6) In addition, funding firewalls may be advocated as a means of preventing banks using cheap insured deposits to fund their securities affiliates, thereby allegedly conferring a competitive advantage on bank-related securities firms. However, to the extent that independent securities firms also have access to bank finance, this argument for firewalls is unpersuasive.

(7) Statement before the Senate Committee on Banking, Housing and Urban Affairs, May 3 1990, p 38.

(8) See the example of the *Amoco Cadiz* cited by the Chairman of the Federal Reserve Board, Mr Paul Volcker, in evidence to the Subcommittee on

Commerce, Consumer and Monetary Affairs of the Committee on Government Operations, US House of Representatives, 11 June 1986.

(9) An assessment of the information advantages enjoyed by universal banks is provided by Alfred Steinherr and Christian Huveneers, op cit pp.6–7.

(10) Statement before the Senate Committee on Banking Housing and Urban Affairs, 3 May 1990, op cit p.39.

(11) See Robert Litan, "What Should Banks Do?", The Brookings Institution, 1987, pp.144–189.

(12) See George Benston, Dan Brumbaugh, Jack Guttentag, Richard Herring, George Kaufman, Robert Litan and Kenneth Scott, "Blueprint for Restructuring America's Depository Institutions", The Brookings Institution, Washington D.C., 1989, pp.19–23.

(13) Ibid pp 23–25.

(14) A proposal advanced by Gerald Corrigan is vulnerable to the same criticism. He would distinguish between banks authorised to accept insured transaction deposits and financial holding companies authorised to offer uninsured transaction accounts. Under the proposal, commercial activities could be combined with non-bank financial activities and non-bank financial activities could be combined with banking. Commercial-financial conglomerates would not have access to the lender of last resort, but since the financial activities of these groups would be integrated with the non-commercial financial-banking sector, there would be every possibility of cross-infection spreading within the financial system whenever the financial unit of a commercial concern failed. See Gerald Corrigan, "Financial Market Structure: A Longer View", Federal Reserve Bank of New York *Annual Report* 1986, pp 3–54.

(15) For a summary of the Court's decision see "Crédit Suisse loses its Supreme Court appeal", IBCA, London, January 1991. It should be noted that because Swiss law gives the Banking Commission regulatory authority only over banks, and not their holding companies, the Commission had to deal with CSH at one remove via Crédit Suisse. Hence the requirement that Crédit Suisse consolidate itself with CSH for regulatory purposes.

(16) For a detailed description of the UK's financial regulatory structure see Richard Dale, "UK Regulation of Financial Conglomerates After Big Bang", Discussion Paper No 91–11, Department of Accounting and Management Science, University of Southampton, May 1991.

(17) See Richard Dale, "The EEC's approach to capital adequacy for investment firms", this *Journal*, Vol 4, September 1990, pp.1–9.

(18) See "Systemic Risks in Securities Markets", OECD, 1991, pp 37–38.

(19) See Richard Dale, "US Banking Reforms: Repealing Glass-Steagall", Vol. 5, Summer 1991, pp 105–111.

(20) Under Section 20 of the Glass-Steagall Act, a bank may not be affiliated with any company "principally engaged" in securities business. However, bank holding companies may establish "Section 20 Subsidiaries" which undertake securities underwriting and distribution on a limited scale that does not amount to being principally engaged in securities business.

(21) See "Modernising the Financial Services System: Recommendations for Safer, More Competitive Banks", US Treasury Department, February 1991.

(22) Ibid. p.58.

(23) The Statutory basis for this premium capital requirement is set out in draft legislation ("The Financial Institutions Safety and Consumer Choice Act of 1991") placed before Congress by the US Administration.

(24) For a full account of Drexel's collapse see Statement of Richard Breeden, Chairman US Securities and Exchange Commission, before the Committee on Banking, Housing and Urban Affairs, US Senate, concerning the Bankruptcy of Drexel Burnham Lambert Group Inc, 1 March 1990.

(25) See Testimony before the Subcommittee on Economic and Commercial Law, Committee on the Judiciary, US House of Representatives, 1 March 1990, p.14.

(26) See Testimony before the Committee on Banking, Housing and Urban Affairs, US Senate, 12 July 1990, p 14.

(27) For a review of Canada's changing regulatory structure see Richard Dale, "The New Financial Regulatory Framework in Canada", *Journal of International Banking Law*, Vol. 3, Issue 3, 1988, pp 117–126.

(28) See, generally, Richard Dale, "Japan 'Glass-Steagall' Act", *Journal of International Banking Law*, Vol 3, 1987, pp 138–146.

(29) See Naoyuki Isono, "Recommendations point to liberalising financial system", *Japan Economic Journal*, 15 June 1991, p 1.

Prof. Richard S Dale is Coopers Deloitte professor of international banking and financial institutions, Department of Accounting and Management Science, University of Southampton, UK.

This paper was presented at a London School of Economics Financial Markets Group conference on The Internationalisation of Capital Markets and the Regulatory Response on 8 November, 1991, the proceedings of which will be published in book form some time in 1992.

The author wishes to acknowledge the support of the Economic and Social Research Council, which funded this research.

SECURITIES ACTIVITIES

[36]

International Banking Regulation

RICHARD DALE

Until the early 1970s banking regulation was considered to be the exclusive preserve of national policymakers. However, the growth of international lending and the emergence of multinational banks servicing this business from offices spread across the globe made regulators aware of the need to coordinate their activities. First, the interpenetration of national banking markets by foreign banking establishments called for a clear understanding as to which authority was responsible for regulating which banks. Second, the close linkages between national banking systems through the interbank market meant that financial stability in one jurisdiction could be adversely affected by problems originating in another jurisdiction. And, finally, the fact that banks from different countries were competing for business within a global market raised the possibility of competitive distortions arising from uneven national regulatory arrangements. It was against this background that regulators from the leading industrial countries felt it necessary to establish a forum to coordinate their policies.

Today, the trend towards globalization of financial markets is proceeding apace, given further impetus by the dismantling of exchange controls, a dramatic rise in cross-border investment flows, and increased access to domestic banking markets by foreign institutions. A number of other developments are also posing a challenge to regulators. First, banking is no longer a distinct financial service, but has become intermingled with other financial activities, including securities business. The process of securitization,

International Financial Market Regulation. Edited by B. Steil
© 1994 John Wiley & Sons Ltd

by which banks repackage and sell loans to nonbank investors, has further blurred the boundaries between bank lending and securities market financing. Second, banks' heavy involvement in the explosive growth of over-the-counter derivatives markets has provoked a major controversy over the systemic risks associated with derivatives trading and the appropriate regulatory response.

Finally, and perhaps most importantly, the banking industry is facing intensified competition on a number of fronts. Within the domestic markets price cartels, administered interest rates, and other restrictive practices are being dismantled; cross-border competition is increasing due to enhanced reciprocal rights of access (notably within the single European market); and there is now a growing competitive threat from nonbank financial institutions (securities firms and insurance companies) which are eroding banks' share both of aggregate lending and of short-term savings.

The ever changing financial environment in which banks operate ensures that the regulatory problem can never be finally resolved: new issues emerge and old issues reappear in a different form. This chapter assesses the current international regulatory agenda in the light of the trends noted above. It first reviews the evolution of the Basle regulatory regime, then considers a number of issues in preventive regulation (i.e., regulation designed to prevent bank failures). Next it examines the question of supervisory standards, before dealing with some major issues in protective regulation (the role of deposit insurance and the lender of last resort). Finally it draws some general conclusions on the future direction of regulatory cooperation.

EVOLUTION OF REGULATORY COOPERATION

Until the mid-1970s there was no formal machinery for coordinating national regulation of international banks. However, the disturbances that followed in the wake of Herstatt Bank's collapse in the summer of 1974 focused attention on the interdependence of national banking systems and led, in the following year, to the creation of a standing committee of bank supervisors, under the auspices of the Bank for International Settlements (BIS), comprising the Group of Ten (G-10) countries plus Luxembourg. This Committee on Banking Regulation and Supervisory Practices (CBRSP) (called the Cooke Committee, after its first chairman) sought not to harmonize national laws and practices, but rather to interlink disparate regulatory regimes with a view to ensuring that all banks are supervised according to certain broad principles (Cooke 1981).

One of the earliest and most far-reaching initiatives of the Cooke Committee was to develop broad guidelines for the division of responsibilities among national supervisory authorities. These guidelines, which were approved by the G-10 central bank governors in December 1975, became known as the Basle Concordat (CBRSP 1975).

The Concordat embodied the key principle that the supervision of solvency is essentially a matter for the parent authority in the case of foreign branches and primarily the responsibility of the host authority in the case of foreign subsidiaries.

Although the Concordat represented a significant step towards greater international supervisory cooperation, it suffered from a number of defects which began to become apparent from 1978 onwards. In the first place, the primary supervisory responsibility accorded to host authorities for the solvency of foreign subsidiaries ran counter to another important initiative of the Cooke Committee. This was the recommendation, endorsed by the G-10 central bank governors in 1978, that supervision of banks' international business should be conducted on a consolidated basis, the object being to limit the opportunities for regulatory evasion. There was a clear danger here that host countries would look to parent authorities to supervise locally incorporated subsidiaries of foreign banks under the principle of consolidated supervision, while home authorities would rely on host countries to exercise their responsibilities under the Concordat.

The controversy surrounding the handling of Banco Ambrosiano's collapse in 1982 was one factor prompting a reappraisal of the original Concordat and the emergence of a revised version, which was approved by the central bank governors in June 1983 (CBRSP 1983). The authors of the revised Concordat clearly had the Ambrosiano case in mind when they introduced more precise guidelines for the supervision of holding companies. Apart from closing such supervisory gaps, the revised Concordat sought to address directly the question of adequacy of supervision.

The authors of the 1983 Concordat attempted to deal with the problem of supervisory standards by introducing what might be described as a *dual key* approach to the operation of foreign banking establishments. Under the revised guidelines, if a host authority considered the supervision of parent institutions of foreign banks operating on its territory to be inadequate, it should prohibit or discourage the continued operation of such offices, or alternatively impose specific conditions on the conduct of their business. In addition, where the parent authority considered the host authority's supervision to be inadequate, it should "either extend its supervision, to the degree that it is practicable, or it should be prepared to discourage the parent bank from continuing to operate the establishment in question." Each national supervisory authority therefore had to satisfy itself that its banks' foreign operations were being conducted in jurisdictions with sound supervisory practices and that foreign banks to which it was host were subject to adequate supervision within their home jurisdiction.

In April 1990 an addendum to the Basle Concordat (the Supplement) was

170 _____ International Financial Market Regulation

approved (CBRSP 1990). This was designed "to supplement the principles of the Concordat by encouraging more regular and structured collaboration between supervisors." The Supplement addressed the information needs of both parent and host authorities, included recommendations on the role of external audit and urged countries whose secrecy laws inhibited the transmission of supervisory information to review these requirements.

In July 1988 the Basle Committee launched a major new regulatory initiative when it announced that the G-10 countries had approved the guidelines establishing minimum capital adequacy standards for international banks (CBRSP 1988). The purpose of this agreement is twofold: firstly, to strengthen the soundness and stability of the international banking system; secondly, to ensure competitive equality among international banks — the competitive concern being that banks operating on a low capital/assets ratio can support a higher level of banking business for any given level of capital than can more highly capitalized institutions.

The Basle Accord on capital adequacy standards should be viewed as an important landmark in international supervisory cooperation. It represents the first move towards global regulatory harmonization, as distinct from the regional harmonization initiatives introduced within the European Community. It also signifies a departure from the original purpose of the Basle Committee which was to coordinate national regulatory regimes but not to seek to impose a common regulatory framework. Common capital adequacy rules, considered in more detail below, may turn out to be only the first stage in a more comprehensive program of international regulatory harmonization.

The supervisory weaknesses revealed by the collapse of BCCI in the Summer of 1991 prompted a reassessment of the Basle approach to banking regulation. Accordingly, in July 1992 the Basle Committee, with the endorsement of the central bank governors of the G-10 countries, issued a new set of "minimum standards" for the supervision of international banks which are intended to have greater force than earlier guidelines (CBRSP 1992). These standards have been summarized by the Committee as follows:

1. All international banking groups and international banks should be supervised by a home-country authority that capably performs consolidated supervision.
2. The creation of a cross-border banking establishment should receive the prior consent of both the host-country supervisory authority and the bank's, and if different, the banking group's home-country supervisory authority.
3. Supervisory authorities should possess the right to gather information from the cross-border banking establishments of the banks or banking groups for which they are the home-country supervisor.

4. If a host-country authority determines that any one of the foregoing minimum standards is not met to its satisfaction, that authority could impose restrictive measures necessary to satisfy its prudential concerns consistent with these minimum standards, including the prohibition of the creation of banking establishments.

The key requirement is that all international banks should be supervised by a home-country authority "that capably performs consolidated supervision." This is further spelt out as meaning that the authority concerned should (1) monitor banks' global operations on the basis of verifiable consolidated data; (2) be able to prohibit the creation of corporate structures that impede consolidated supervision; and (3) be in a position to prevent banks from establishing a presence in suspect jurisdictions.

If the minimum standards are not met, the host authority is called on to exclude banks from the jurisdiction concerned or alternatively to accept responsibility for supervising these banks' local operations, subject to appropriate restrictions (which may, by implication, include mandatory incorporation of such operations).

Finally, in April 1993 the Basle Committee issued a package of proposals intended to extend the scope of the Capital Adequacy Accord by incorporating market risk and interest rate risk and clarifying permissible netting arrangements (CBRSP 1993). Under these proposals (discussed below) specific capital charges would be applied to banks' trading positions, including derivative positions, in debt and equity securities, and a measurement system would be introduced in order to identify banks that might be incurring exceptionally large interest rate risk. This latest initiative again underlines the emphasis now being given to the establishment of a common global regulatory framework for international banks, in marked contrast to the original Basle approach which specifically rejected harmonization in favor of the much looser concept of regulatory coordination based on an agreed allocation of regulatory responsibilities.

Looking back at the evolution of the Basle regulatory regime over the past twenty years it is clear that the pressures behind regulatory convergence have shifted. Initially the predominant concern was the safety and soundness of the financial system. More recently competitive equality, or "the level playing field," has become the main driving force. This helps to explain the new emphasis on harmonization initiatives designed, above all, to remove competitive disparities between rival banking systems.

However, several key issues remain unsolved. What factors should determine the boundaries between regulatory harmonization on the one hand and regulatory competition on the other? Should the Basle regime, like its EC counterpart, be based on legally binding obligations rather than, as at present, on voluntary compliance with broadly drawn guidelines? Given the new concern with ensuring minimum supervisory standards, how are such standards to be assessed, monitored and enforced? And, perhaps most important of all, has the Basle machinery itself been outdated by the globalization of financial markets, bearing in mind that the BIS has no formal supervisory authority over banks which own it or over banking supervisory authorities? Should the IMF or some other supranational agency now become involved with establishing a truly global regulatory framework for international banking? These and other more specific issues are considered in the discussion that follows.

ISSUES IN PREVENTIVE REGULATION

The distinction is made here between *preventive* regulation, intended to prevent banks from getting into difficulties, and *protective* regulation, designed to safeguard depositors and the financial system in the event of bank failures. This section is concerned with preventive regulation, a later section deals with protective regulation.

1988 Basle Accord

The central pillar of preventive regulation is capital adequacy.[1] At the international level this is embodied in the minimum risk-weighted capital ratio laid down by the 1988 Basle Accord that came fully into effect at the beginning of 1993. The Basle ratio has been widely accepted by the international financial community as an indicator of banks' financial strength. Indeed, it appears that financial markets have been rewarding banks for achieving capital ratios in excess of the regulatory minimum, thereby encouraging institutions to target ratios well above the Basle norm. For instance, one recent study suggests that US banks' capital raising since 1990, which has taken industry well beyond the Basle requirements, has been partly prompted by business strategy rather than regulatory considerations, a strategy that has been rewarded by the stock market.[2] The implication is that the Basle capital ratio may be better viewed as a form of disclosure, valued by the marketplace, rather than as a binding regulatory requirement.

Despite it ready adoption by financial markets, the Basle concept of capital adequacy is open to criticism. The risk weightings encourage banks to substitute government debt for business loans to an extent that gives public sector borrowers privileged access to credit markets at the expense of private borrowers. The fact that residential mortgage loans are given a minimum risk weighting only half that of other commercial loans may similarly give undue preference to the housing sector. More generally, the simple aggregation of risk-weighted assets under the accord gives no recognition to the potential benefits of portfolio diversification, in marked contrast to the approach of some securities regulators who make allowance for noncovariant risk exposures (although it should also be said that risk covariance is more easily measured in relation to traded securities than it is for nontraded bank loans). Furthermore the Basle distinction between Tier I (essentially equity) capital and Tier II capital, which includes eligible subordinated debt, has encouraged the growth of complex debt instruments whose contribution to the capital strength of the issuing bank may be difficult to assess.

Some critics have alleged that the phased introduction of the Basle capital adequacy regime, coinciding as it did with recession in much of the industrialized world, held back economic recovery by impeding credit growth through a capital-constrained banking sector. On the other hand, it is difficult in practice to distinguish between the role of the capital requirements and other influences (e.g., changing risk perceptions) that could have adversely affected bank credit expansion.

Perhaps the most serious concern about the Basle Accord relates to the uniform 100 percent risk weighting applicable to commercial loans to the private sector. That is to say, the capital requirement for a loan to a triple-A multinational company is precisely the same as it is for a loan of similar size to a small unquoted property developer. In this key area of loan quality there are no differential risk weightings. The result is that aggressively managed banks may be tempted to shift their loan portfolios towards high risk borrowers, while cautiously managed institutions are unrewarded for their prudence.

This problem is further exacerbated by the Basle Accord's failure to formulate specific guidelines on provisioning — deductions from profit to reflect anticipated loan losses. The approach to provisioning adopted by the Basle Committee is based on the idea of recognizable asset impairment. Provisions set aside against impaired assets are "specific" and are not eligible for inclusion in regulatory capital. On the other hand, "where ... general loan loss reserves or provisions are not allocated in any way ... to an identified deterioration in any asset or group or subset of assets, and are therefore genuinely available to meet losses which are subsequently identified wherever they may occur, ... it would be reasonable to include them in capital" (CBRSP 1991). General provisions defined in this way may therefore be included in Tier II capital.

One major drawback of this Basle approach to provisioning is that the concept of identifiable asset deterioration is essentially subjective and can therefore result in considerable latitude in banks' provisioning decisions. Indeed, disparities in national regulation, accounting practices, and fiscal incentives are reflected in significant variations in provisioning policies as between different jurisdictions (Table 7.1). From a supervisory standpoint the most worrying consequence of variable provisioning practices is that the

Table 7.1 Percent Net Provisions of Commercial Banks

		1986	1987	1988	1989	1990	1991
Australia*	bs	0.25	0.35	0.38	0.51	0.86	1.20
	gi	5.26	7.40	7.77	10.96	19.13	24.24
Austria	bs	–	–	–	0.39	0.50	0.52
	gi	–	–	–	16.35	19.49	19.62
Belgium	bs	0.31	0.28	0.40	0.43	0.20	0.31
	gi	14.18	13.93	20.46	23.61	11.54	17.13
Canada	bs	0.75	0.68	0.60	1.16	0.36	0.54
	gi	20.57	17.49	13.68	25.56	8.28	11.93
Denmark†	bs	0.39	0.70	1.09	0.87	1.21	–
	gi	18.27	20.82	24.87	26.64	40.51	37.66‡
Finland	bs	0.21	0.48	0.40‡	0.24	0.19	−0.01
	gi	6.14	13.65	10.51‡	7.43	5.86	−0.42
France	bs	0.61	0.53	0.52	0.53	0.50	0.52
	gi	21.25	19.03	19.31	21.57	21.05	22.16
Germany	bs	0.55	0.44	0.25	0.42	0.53	0.47
	gi	15.05	13.26	7.77	13.07	16.51	15.03
Greece§	bs	0.32	0.25	0.24	0.36	0.50	0.82
	gi	10.61	8.91	8.06	11.54	13.68	16.70
Italy	bs	0.58	0.49	0.56	0.51	0.54	0.50‡
	gi	12.18	11.12	12.41	11.49	11.69	10.51‡
Japan	bs	0.04	0.03	0.05‡	0.04	0.03	0.07
	gi	2.42	2.16	3.34‡	3.36	2.37	5.72
Luxembourg	bs	0.66	0.51	0.37	0.37	0.52	0.42
	gi	46.05	39.66	29.54	32.37	44.06	36.87
Netherlands*	bs	0.34	0.19	0.42‡	0.36‡	0.30‡	0.29
	gi	10.68	6.13	13.26‡	12.19‡	11.72‡	11.48
Norway	bs	0.92	0.85	1.58	1.58	1.96	4.50‡
	gi	20.69	24.12	40.16	36.04	55.14	146.01‡
Portugal	bs	0.84	1.35	1.43	1.59	–	1.79
	gi	24.90	32.35	32.07	32.36	34.43‡	29.35
Spain	bs	0.79	0.91	0.80	0.61	0.59	0.72
	gi	17.20	18.38	15.13	11.88	11.55	13.80
Sweden	bs	0.84	0.81	0.93	0.86	0.40	−3.42‡
	gi	20.94	23.45	27.20	28.64	14.10	−122.09‡
Switzerland	bs	0.51	0.51	0.47	0.54	0.55	0.96
	gi	19.00	19.06	17.82	18.90	20.70	30.26
Turkey	bs	0.67	1.62	1.69	1.20‡	1.08	1.15
	gi	12.02	22.14	20.58	16.23‡	11.76	12.55
UK	bs	0.54	1.53‡	0.31	1.60	0.95	1.32
	gi	10.95	29.98‡	6.03	31.48	19.55	26.32
US	bs	0.78	1.27	0.56	0.97	0.95	1.01
	gi	16.34	26.30	11.14	18.90	18.57	18.50

bs: as percent of average balance sheet total.
gi: as percent of gross income.
* All banks.
† Commercial banks and savings banks.
‡ Break in series.
§ Large commercial banks.
Source: OECD, *Financial Market Trends*, June 1993, 63.

concept of capital adequacy, which lies at the heart of the Basle regulatory regime, is seriously undermined. For instance, if Bank A has made cumulative general provisions of 3½ percent on its commercial loan portfolio whereas the provisioning level for Bank B, on a loan portfolio of similar quality, is only 2 percent, then Bank B's risk-weighted Tier 1 capital ratio may appear to be 1½ percentage points higher than Bank A's. If the difference in provisioning coverage relates to specific rather than general provisions then the distortion would be reflected in the total risk-weighted capital asset ratio.

In either case, the Basle capital adequacy regime will give a false reading of the relative financial strength of individual banks. This point is borne out by US research, which demonstrates that by using examiner asset classifications to identify banks that are underprovisioning it is possible to greatly enhance the ability of risk-based capital ratios to separate high- and low-risk banks (Jones and King 1992).

Market Risk Proposals

The primary objective of the 1988 Basle Accord was to establish minimum capital standards designed to reflect credit risk. In April 1993 the Basle Committee issued supplementary proposals for the supervisory treatment of market risks incurred by banks, covering open positions in debt securities, equities and foreign exchange. For this purpose a distinction is made between a bank's longer-term investment and its trading book, the idea being that the original Basle credit risk-weightings should be applied to the former, and the new capital requirements for market risk to the latter.

These proposals on market risk raise a number of controversial issues. Most fundamental of these is the extent to which bank supervisors should adjust their capital adequacy standards in an attempt to achieve competitive equality between banks and nonbank securities firms. According to its authors, the Basle proposals "contain features which bank supervisors acting on their own would not necessarily favour but are prepared to adopt in the hope that further convergence with securities regulators will be achieved at some future date" (CBRSP 1993, p.2). In other words, the perceived need for a common regulatory framework for banks and securities firms has induced bank supervisors to lower the standards they would ideally wish to apply to banks. Implicitly, therefore, the prudential goal of safety and soundness is being subordinated to the broader objective of establishing a level playing field for all financial institutions undertaking securities business.

The difficulty of reconciling conflicting objectives is most clearly evident in the proposed definition of regulatory capital. The Basle Committee states that "were the Basle proposals to be designed for banks alone, [the Committee] would favour the retention of the present definition of capital"

(CBRSP, p.10). However, in the interests of establishing common capital adequacy rules for banks and securities firms the Committee proposes that banks should be permitted to employ an additional form of short-term subordinated debt for the sole purpose of meeting part of the capital requirement for market risks. In order to ensure that such short-term subordinated debt is available to absorb losses it is proposed that it should be subject to a lock-in clause, which stipulates that neither interest nor principal may be paid (even at maturity) if such payments means that the capital allocated to the trading book would fall below a specified threshold level. The difficulty here is that if the lock-in clause were triggered, and it became known that a bank had failed to repay maturing debt obligations, confidence in the bank could be severely damaged and a deposit run could develop. It is presumably for this reason that several members of the Basle Committee do not favor the use of this newly proposed Tier III capital for banks.

There are some further potential difficulties associated with the Basle proposals. The distinction between a bank's trading book and its longer-term investments is not clear-cut, raising the possibility of regulatory circumvention. Furthermore, the need for such a distinction is open to question; a persuasive case could be made for marking to market *all* banks' securities holdings and then applying an appropriate capital requirement based on market risk. This would avoid the considerable problems that are likely to arise in defining a bank's trading book.

The proposed minimum capital standard for equity positions held in the trading account is problematical. The approach used is the so-called building-block technique, based on separately calculated charges for specific and general market risk. Specific risk refers to possible adverse movements in the price of an individual security, whereas general market risk is the risk of a broad market movement unrelated to any specific securities. It is suggested that the capital charge for specific risk should be between 4 and 8 percent (see below) and for general market risk a standard 8 percent. The Basle Committee acknowledges that the choice of this building block method may conflict with the objective of securing wider convergence with securities regulators, the point here being that the US Securities and Exchange Commission applies a single risk charge or "haircut" to securities firms' equity positions. In order to meet this difficulty it is proposed that national authorities should have discretion to continue to apply a comprehensive approach, combining specific and general market risks, so long as it can be demonstrated that the alternative method, "by its very nature," requires capital charges equal to or greater than the building-block methodology. This issue of equivalence is likely to prove contentious.[3]

Finally, the Basle proposal on market risk for equities is likely to encounter serious difficulties when it comes to the treatment of specific risk. The Committee suggests that the capital charge for specific risk should be between 4 and 8 percent, depending on the diversification of the portfolio and the extent to which it contains liquid and marketable stocks. However, the Committee has been unable to formulate a clear definition of liquidity or diversification and is therefore proposing to allow national authorities to develop their own criteria. Clearly, the delegation of such a key area of risk assessment to national regulators is in direct conflict with the aim of establishing common capital adequacy standards and must inevitably lead to competitive distortions within securities markets.

Interest Rate Risk Proposals

In addition to applying capital requirements to market risk, the Basle Committee, in its April 1993 package of supervisory proposals, seeks to establish a methodology for measuring interest rate risk. It should be noted that the Basle approach adopted here is quite different to that followed in relation to other types of risk, notably market risk and credit risk. For every type of risk there is a two-stage policy problem: first how to measure the risk and second how to discourage excessive risk-taking through, for example, appropriate capital charges. In the case of market risk and credit risk the Basle Committee has formulated both a measurement system and detailed capital requirements. In the case of interest rate risk the Committee's stated purpose is quite different, namely to develop a measurement system which supervisors can use for observation purposes as a means of identifying "outliers", leaving each authority free to decide how to respond to institutions identified as high risk.

This approach immediately raises two issues. First, is it advisable on the one hand to develop a highly complex methodology for measuring interest rate risk which is to be applied internationally, and on the other hand, to leave national authorities with total discretion as to how this information should be used for supervisory purposes? In other words, may not any benefits associated with a uniform system of measurement be entirely offset by variable national treatment of the risks so measured?

A second, and related, point is that it may be dangerous to adopt different supervisory regimes for different kinds of risk. That is to say, if credit risk is subject to specific capital adequacy requirements, while interest rate risk is penalized only when a bank's exceptional exposure makes it an outlier, there could well be a tendency for banks as a whole to substitute interest risk for credit risk. And if banks are prompted to increase interest rate exposure, then the benchmark level of risk in relation to which outliers are identified will itself increase — raising questions about the effectiveness of the outlier approach.

In any event, it seems highly likely that once a measurement system for interest rate risk has been agreed, competitive pressures will eventually induce national supervisors to seek further international agreement on common arrangements for discouraging excessive risk-taking in this area.

In addressing the question of how to measure interest rate risk, the Basle Committee has focused on the extent to which the economic value (rather than the current earnings) of a bank is exposed to future changes in interest rates. The proposed measurement system involves the following stages:

1. All interest-rate-sensitive asset, liability and off-balance-sheet positions would be placed into one of thirteen time-bands based on the instrument's maturity or repricing characteristics.
2. The positions within each time-band would be netted and the resulting net position for each time-band would then be weighted by an estimate of its duration.
3. The duration weights would be adjusted to reflect the relative volatility of interest rates across the term structure.
4. The net balance of these individual weighted positions would provide the basis for measuring a bank's interest rate risk.

The Committee itself identified several key problems in this formulation which as yet remain unresolved. First, should an institution's interest rate risk be viewed on a whole-book basis, embracing both the trading book and the banking book, or should these two operations be assessed separately? In a world of universal banking, where there is no risk segregation between different businesses conducted within a single banking group, economic logic would point to a consolidated approach to risk measurement.[4] However, since a bank's trading book is to be isolated for separate treatment under the proposed capital adequacy rules relating to market risk (which in the case of debt securities incorporates interest rate risk), it might seem inconsistent to combine the trading and banking books for the purposes of calculating interest rate risk exposure.

A second problem identified by the Committee concerns the treatment of items where either the interest repricing date or the maturity is uncertain. The most obvious example is non-interest-bearing transaction deposits which, for some banks, may constitute a relatively stable core deposit base, largely insensitive to changes in market interest rates. The extent to which such liabilities should be treated as long-term for interest rate risk purposes has been left open for debate by the Committee.

Finally, there is a question as to what extent, if at all, short and long positions within and between different time bands, and in different currencies, should be treated as offsetting. Again, the Committee has yet to reach a consensus on the extent to which such offsetting is permissible. Concerning the recognition of hedging between offsetting positions in different currencies, the Committee is seeking outside views on whether there is a practical method of recognizing interest rate correlations between currencies.

International Banking Regulation _____ 179

Derivatives

The Basle proposals on market risk incorporate capital adequacy requirements to cover banks' debt and equity derivatives. These requirements embrace forward rate agreements, futures and options on debt instruments, interest rate and cross-currency swaps, forward foreign exchange positions, futures and options on both individual equities and on equity indices, as well as options on futures and warrants. In principle, all derivatives (except for those held outside the trading book) would be converted into positions in the relevant underlying and become subject to the proposals for applying specific and general market risk under the building-block methodology.

However, regulators' concerns over derivative products go well beyond the need to establish an appropriate capital adequacy framework.[5] In the first place there has been an explosive increase in the trading of financial derivatives (Table 7.2). In particular the outstanding volume of the over-the-counter (OTC) or customized derivatives rose nearly ninefold in the five

Table 7.2 Markets for Selected Derivative Instruments, Notional Principal Amounts Outstanding at Year-end, in Billions of US Dollars Equivalent

	1986	1987	1988	1989	1990	1991
Exchange-traded instruments*	583	725	1,300	1,762	2,284	3,518
Interest rate futures	370	488	895	1,201	1,454	2,159
Interest rate options[†]	146	122	279	387	600	1,072
Currency futures	10	14	12	16	16	18
Currency options[†]	39	60	48	50	56	59
Stock market index futures	15	18	28	42	70	77
Options on stock market indices[†]	3	23	38	66	88	132
Over-the-counter instruments[‡]	500[e]	867	1,330	2,402	3,451	4,449
Interest rate swaps*	400[e]	683	1,010	1,503	2,312	3,065
Currency and cross-currency interest rate swaps[§¶]	100[e]	184	320	449	578	807
Other derivative instruments[§#]	–	–	–	450	561	577
Memorandum item						
Cross-border plus local foreign currency claims of BIS reporting banks	4,031	5,187	5,540	6,498	7,578	7,497

e = estimate
* Excludes options on individual shares and derivatives involving commodity contracts.
† Calls plus puts.
‡ Only data collected by ISDA. Excludes information on contracts such as forward rate agreements, over-the-counter currency options, forward foreign exchange positions, equity swaps and warrants on equity.
§ Contracts between ISDA members reported only once.
¶ Adjusted for reporting of both currencies.
# Caps, collars, floors, and swaptions.
Source: *Recent Development in International Interbank Relations*, Bank for International Settlements, 1992, 49.

years from 1986 to 1991, representing an annual increase of well over 50 percent.

The rapid growth of any new financial market gives pause for thought, but in the case of derivatives there are a number of other concerns. It has been claimed that derivatives increase the volatility of financial markets by promoting speculation; that their intellectual complexity impedes effective risk control by senior management and regulators; that derivatives trading creates large off-balance-sheet exposures that reduce market transparency; and that the market linkages created by derivatives increase the potential for generalized financial contagion.

In June 1993, concerns of this kind prompted the following warning from former BIS General-Manager, Alexandre Lamfalussy:

> ... the phenomenal growth of derivatives and associated trading techniques has reduced the transparency of market participants' balance sheets and has obscured the transmission of disturbances across market segments and institutions. This has severely complicated the assessment of the nature and distribution of risks in financial operations, at the level of both the individual firm and of the system as a whole. The implication is that market participants may not be in a position to impose the necessary discipline on financial institutions to prevent the risk of the buildup of systemic problems (Lamfalussy 1993, p.4).

Since 1992 there have been three major supervisory reviews of derivatives — from the BIS, the US regulatory agencies and the Bank of England — each expressing concerns about potential risks in the derivatives business. The Group of Thirty (G-30), the New York-based consultancy group, has now sought to redress the balance in the derivatives debate by publishing an authoritative study of the OTC derivatives market prepared largely by market participants (Group of Thirty 1993). Among other matters on which the authors are at pains to offer reassurance are

1. *Market size.* According to the G-30 the scale of global derivatives activity is "unimposing compared to that of traditional financial activities." For instance, the value of swaps written in 1991 was less than 1 percent of the annual turnover in the foreign exchange market and swaps outstanding represented less than one-third of domestic and international bonds outstanding. Furthermore, actual risk exposures, measured by replacement cost, typically represent between only 1 and 3 percent of the notional principle value of the derivatives portfolio.
2. *Benefits of Derivatives.* Users of financial services often overlook important benefits from derivative products. In particular, the G-30 study argues

> where financial markets are segmented nationally or internationally, whether due to market or regulatory barriers or to different perceptions of credit qualities in various markets, the use of derivatives has delivered unambiguous cost-savings for borrowers and higher yields for investors.

This assertion is supported by specific examples of the advantageous use of derivatives by corporations, government entities, institutional investors, and financial institutions.

3. *Derivative risk exposures.* While acknowledging that the management of derivative risk exposures is more complex than in the case of traditional banking products, the G-30 study states that these risks (essentially market, credit, operational, and legal) are not different in nature from those encountered in ordinary bank lending and securities business. Furthermore, a survey of industry practice conducted for the study (involving responses from eighty dealers and seventy-two end-users) suggests that most dealers have developed rigorous risk management systems for this purpose.

4. *Overall economic impact.* In examining the impact of derivatives on the overall economy, the study points out that academic research strongly indicates that derivatives trading either has no effect on, or reduces, volatility in underlying markets. On the positive side, it is argued that derivatives have expanded risk management techniques, while reducing transaction costs and increasing the liquidity of markets.

While presenting a positive case for derivatives, the G-30 study also makes twenty best practice recommendations for industry participants, focusing mainly on risk management. And although it does not examine regulatory issues in any detail (the whole question of capital adequacy is ignored) the study does make four additional recommendations aimed specifically at national authorities. In summary, policymakers should (1) recognize the benefits and promote the use of netting arrangements; (2) remove legal uncertainties relating to inter alia, the enforceability of derivative transactions and bilateral close-out netting arrangements; (3) amend tax laws that impede the use of derivatives; and (4) provide guidance on accounting and reporting of derivatives.

In the light of the G-30 study, where does the debate over derivatives now stand? It should be recognized first of all that the G-30 authors have performed a useful service in demonstrating through clear prose and intelligible examples the considerable benefits that derivatives transactions can offer to borrowers, lenders, investors, and intermediaries. Here the balance of the debate needed to be redressed. However, on the key issue of systemic risk the G-30 analysis is much less persuasive.

To begin with, official concerns about the growth, size, and concentration of the derivatives market cannot be easily dismissed. A total exchange-traded and over-the-counter (OTC) derivatives market has come from nowhere ten years ago to a position where its gross value exceeds the volume of banks' international lending (Table 7.2) and cannot reasonably be described as "unimposing compared to that of traditional financial activities" (the words of the G-30 authors).

Even when the market is netted down to reflect its replacement cost or market value, the credit exposures are hardly trivial. The G-30 study states that, measured in this way, the fifty leading US banks have an *average* OTC derivatives exposure equivalent to "only" 11 percent of their total assets or 120 percent of their total capital. However, since the study also reveals that the top eight US banks account for nearly 90 percent of this exposure, it is clear that some large banks have exposures far in excess of 11 percent of assets.

Some of the largest participants in the derivatives markets (for example, affiliates of insurance companies) are unregulated but the G-30 authors express confidence that potential counterparties can evaluate the risks of trading with unregulated entities and believe they should be free to do so. This view is in direct conflict with the Bank of England, which states in its recent derivatives review that "the unsupervised status of, for example, large swap players represents a supervisory hole at the very heart of the derivatives market" (Bank of England 1993, at 76).

The real point about the size and concentration of the derivatives market is surely this. No market can constitute a threat to financial stability merely by virtue of its size (witness the $220 trillion per annum foreign exchange market). However, when a certain category of activity represents (on whatever measurement basis) a major segment of some banks' overall business, that activity is certainly large enough to cause systemic problems if it is not conducted in a safe and proper manner.

This observation leads directly to the second major weakness of the G-30 study. The authors take comfort from the fact that their survey of market practitioners demonstrates high standards of risk control within the industry — "the risks associated with complexity, concentration, liquidity, and linkages between markets are manageable and being managed." The implication is that it is sufficient to rely on market participants themselves to regulate their activities. Yet this is surely too simplistic. For obvious reasons, responses to questionnaires are perhaps not the best way to gauge whether risks are being properly managed. This consideration apart, it only requires some large participants to behave imprudently for the stability of the entire market to be threatened. From this perspective it is insufficient that "most dealers have gone to great lengths to establish sophisticated techniques to manage their exposures" or that there is "nearly universal" (actually 85 percent) reliance on mark-to-market measures for risk management. In short, voluntary compliance with industry-led standards is no substitute for regulatory oversight, a point recently taken up by David Mullins, Vice Chairman of the US Federal Reserve Board (Mullins 1993).

The most serious weakness of the G-30 study, however, is that it does not appear to recognize, let alone address, the fundamental regulatory problem posed by banks' derivatives trading. Banks are subject to comprehensive regulation because if left to themselves *some* institutions will always incur risks that are excessive when judged by the damage which their failure can inflict on the financial system and society generally. If a major slice of the banking industry's business becomes too complex and opaque to regulate effectively, then there is a supervisory blind spot which aggressively managed institutions will undoubtedly exploit in order to escape from the regulatory constraints on risk-taking. Yet in the words of Paul Volcker's foreword to the G-30 study

> the authors believe that the amount of capital needed to support derivatives exposure is a matter of judgement for individual institutions depending on their appetite for risk and their ability to measure and manage it.

This is not a position that can be easily sustained. The stability of the financial system should not be jeopardized by those (perhaps few) institutions whose appetite for risk exceeds an appropriate level, or whose competence to manage risk falls below some appropriate standard. It may be useful to debate what those appropriate limits and standards should be and how they should be enforced; but at the end of the day risk-taking in the derivatives market, like other forms of banking risk, must surely be subject to regulatory constraints.

SUPERVISORY STANDARDS

The supervisory weaknesses revealed by the collapse of BCCI in 1991 prompted a reassessment of the Basle approach to banking regulation.[6] Two issues, in particular, had to be addressed. First, a central principle of the Basle Concordat is that the soundness of a bank cannot be properly assessed unless regulators can examine the totality of each banks' business worldwide through the technique of consolidation. Yet BCCI's complex structure enabled it not only to escape consolidated supervision but to confuse regulators deliberately by shuffling its assets between different jurisdictions.

Secondly, the BCCI collapse demonstrated the ease with which a fraudulent bank could exploit weakly regulated offshore centers in the absence of any machinery for ensuring the adequacy of supervisory standards. On this point the Bingham Report on BCCI concluded that "the need for some independent monitoring of supervisory standards is in my view clear" and that host supervisors "must be reassured by some form of independent verification that the home supervisor is really doing his job" (Bingham 1992, at 3.27).

The Basle Committee has attempted to meet these concerns by introducing the requirement that all banks should be supervised by a home-country authority "that capably performs consolidated supervision." However, the effectiveness of these new guidelines depends on the ability of national authorities to monitor each other's quality of supervision, so they can exercise an informed judgement as to whether banks from a particular jurisdiction should be excluded from their territory or subject to special restrictions imposed by the host authority.

Under the Basle guidelines one country is called upon to assess another country's quality of supervision on the basis of the latter's statutory powers, administrative practices and supervisory record. But there is no new multilateral machinery to assist in the monitoring process and it is difficult to see how bilateral relationships can provide adequate information about supervisory standards in particular jurisdictions. In order to overcome this problem, the Bank of England has proposed a system of peer group review under which each country's supervisory arrangements would be assessed by a panel of supervisory authorities from other countries. However, it is as yet unclear whether this kind of approach would have the broad support among non-G-10 countries that would be needed to make it viable. If the Basle approach proves inadequate to the task then there may eventually be pressure for the International Monetary Fund (IMF) to conduct formal supervisory reviews as part of its country surveillance procedures.[7]

Supervisory Responsibilities

The issue of supervisory standards is often discussed as if the supervisory function were the exclusive concern of regulatory authorities. Yet this is not the case. There is indeed a vigorous debate about the respective supervisory roles of regulators, market participants and bank auditors and there are also varying national practices in this area.[8]

At one extreme there are those who believe that systemic banking instability is typically the consequence of excessive regulation which raises expectations of official intervention and depositor protection in the event of bank failures. That expectation, so it is argued, undermines the disciplinary role of financial markets and removes the normal market penalties for excessive risk-taking. According to this view, bank safety and soundness would be enhanced if primary responsibility for monitoring banking risks were placed firmly with depositors. Under this regime bank regulation would be aimed mainly at enforcing stringent disclosure requirements so as to enable depositors to assess the relative riskiness of individual institutions.

The Reserve Bank of New Zealand's recent proposals on banking supervision come closest to this free-market model. In setting out its proposals the Reserve Bank explains its general approach in the following terms:

> ... we see scope to shift the emphasis towards more market scrutiny and away from direct prudential regulation. We consider that regular scrutiny of registered banks by the marketplace can, and should, play an important role in promoting prudent banking practices. The maintenance of prudent banking practices can also be enhanced by increasing the involvement of private sector monitoring agents, such as external auditors and rating agencies. Prudential regulation and official monitoring have complementary roles to play, but are not the principal mechanism, nor substitutes for market-based private mechanisms. Our general thinking is that a rebalancing of policy which brings market-based mechanisms a little more to the fore, would enhance the overall soundness of the banking system, and at the same time afford banks greater scope to prudently respond to customer needs.[9]

In essence, the Reserve Bank's proposed regulatory regime consists of six key elements.

1. The Basle capital adequacy rules will continue to apply.
2. A US-style scheme of corrective action will be imposed, involving automatic penalties for banks with a capital deficiency.
3. Strengthened disclosure requirements for banks, including public disclosure of mandatory credit ratings.
4. A reduced role for prudential regulation by the central bank, with discontinuation of banks' existing prudential returns and residual monitoring based largely on banks' public disclosure statements.
5. An increase in the ability of the financial system to withstand individual failures by, for example, introducing a more robust payments system.
6. Limiting the role of the lender of last resort and reducing the perception that the government underwrites the prudential soundness of banks.

The underlying assumptions behind the Reserve Bank's new emphasis on market surveillance are that (1) depositors are in a position to make a realistic risk assessment of individual banks and (2) the market response to changed risk perceptions will not be seriously destabilizing. However, there must be serious doubts about both propositions.

First, it is optimistic to expect financial markets to form a realistic view of the financial standing of banks given the difficulties of assessing either the quality of banks' loan portfolios or the adequacy of provisioning policies (see above). The second area of doubt concerns the question of confidence. It is well established that when a bank runs into difficulties financial markets tend to respond by rationing credit. Put another way, the emergence of a large risk premium on a bank's borrowings may deter rather than attract potential lenders. Therefore market discipline may become destabilizing. Furthermore, if markets were heavily dependent on credit rating agencies for their risk assessments, a publicized downgrading could become the trigger for a bank run.

Notwithstanding these potential pitfalls, the New Zealand experiment in market-based supervision could provide important insights into banks' behavior in a deregulated setting. In the meantime there is continuing debate at both national and international levels about the most appropriate balance between official intervention and reliance on market discipline.

The controversy over market self-regulation versus official intervention extends to the role of auditors. There are two questions here: what obligations should bank auditors have towards the supervisory authorities; and should bank auditors owe a duty of care not only to shareholders but also to depositors, general creditors and other stakeholders? On the first point, the UK government has followed the recommendations of the Bingham Report by introducing proposals for imposing a statutory duty on bank auditors to report to the regulators information relevant to a bank's fulfilment of the authorization criteria set out in the Banking Act of 1987.

On the second point, UK case law has established that an auditor's duty of care is confined to shareholders.[10] This may leave depositors, as the predominant suppliers of funds to banks, in an unsatisfactory position since the interests of shareholders and depositors may not be the same. Furthermore, if auditors reported and owed a duty of care directly to depositors, the burden of supervision could be shifted away from the regulatory authorities. On the other hand, such a move would probably have to be accompanied by a ceiling on auditor legal liability in order to prevent the costs of professional indemnity insurance from becoming prohibitive.

To the extent that supervisory responsibility is retained by the regulatory authorities, there remains the issue of whether this responsibility should be discharged by the central bank or by a specialized regulatory agency. A recent analysis of this issue showed that the functions of banking regulation and supervision on the one hand, and monetary policy on the other, were separated in about one half of countries reviewed, but that because of the increasing scale of government support for failing banks there was a tendency for the regulatory/supervisory function to shift away from the central bank to an independent body more directly under political control (Goodhart and Schoenmaker 1993). However, there appears to be no overwhelming argument in favor of one particular approach, and, as the Bank of England has itself pointed out, where the supervisory and monetary functions are separated there still has to be very close cooperation between the two (Quinn 1993).

PROTECTIVE REGULATION

Having considered a number of international supervisory issues arising out of preventive regulation, this section addresses some key problems associated with protective regulation in the form of deposit insurance and lender of last resort arrangements.

Coordination or harmonization of national deposit insurance schemes is not currently on the Basle agenda. Nevertheless, the EC's adoption of a directive on deposit insurance, establishing a minimum level of deposit protection in all member states, raises the question of whether there is a need for a global initiative in this area. Alternatively, is it preferable to permit or even encourage a multiplicity of competing national schemes that widen depositors' choice?

The answer to this question is partly dependent on the policy underlying deposit insurance. If, as in the UK, deposit insurance is viewed mainly as a form of consumer protection then it would seem unnecessary to harmonize territorially based national deposit protection schemes. As the Bank of England recently put it

> So far there has been no international convergence of deposit insurance schemes. This is unsurprising given that they are generally a matter of social policy, which remains a national sovereign prerogative (Bank of England 1991, p.12).

If on the other hand, deposit insurance is intended to act as a safeguard against systemic risk, the case for harmonization is somewhat more persuasive. Because of the close interlinkages between financial markets, there is a common interest in the stabilization of the deposit base within the international banking system.

However, the case for harmonization also depends on whether or not national authorities seek to protect depositors in other ways. In particular, where there is a tradition sustaining banking *institutions* through officially organized support operations, deposit insurance may be largely redundant. Under such circumstances, harmonization achieves little and may indeed only serve to emphasize national differences in the handling of troubled banks.

A recent survey of bank failures demonstrates very clearly that, outside the US, deposit insurance arrangements are seldom invoked; the preference is to recapitalize failing institutions through combined official and private sector support (Goodhart and Schoenmaker 1993). That being the case, the prudential argument for harmonization of deposit insurance schemes would seem to be weak. Nevertheless, some degree of harmonization might be desirable if this were accompanied by arrangements designed to give home-country authorities an incentive to perform adequately their responsibility to undertake consolidated supervision (see below).

Prudential questions apart, it might be considered desirable to harmonize deposit insurance arrangements in order to avoid competitive distortions. But here again the issue is not straightforward. In the first place, the presence and extent of any competitive distortion will depend on precise arrangements for resourcing the insurance fund and on the level of premiums charged. For instance, it is quite possible that banks subject to a scheme offering relatively low insurance coverage for depositors could enjoy a competitive advantage over banks subject to a more protective scheme—if insurance premiums under the two schemes fail to reflect potential claims on the insurance fund. In other words, the *pricing* as well as the *coverage* of deposit insurance is crucial to the question of competitive distortion. Furthermore, even if both schemes were funded on an actuarial basis, depositors might well prefer to place their money with banks offering higher deposit interest rates, albeit with less insurance coverage.

A second complication, as explained above, is that deposit insurance may be largely redundant in those countries where other forms of protective intervention are the preferred method of dealing with bank failures. Under these circumstances, even identical insurance schemes identically priced may disguise serious competitive distortions associated with different levels of de facto protection for depositors. Put another way, competitive distortions arising from alternative protective arrangements can only be eliminated by standardizing national procedures for handling troubled banks, which is hardly a practical proposition at the present time.

In summary, the case for harmonizing deposit insurance schemes internationally, as the EC has done regionally, is not persuasive. Nevertheless it is interesting to note that while both the US and the EC have recently introduced new policy initiatives on deposit insurance, these moves are in opposite directions (Dale 1993b). The US authorities, faced with increasing financial instability, have sought to neutralize the "moral hazard" consequences of what is now seen as excessive protection for depositors. This they have done by introducing automatic penalties for banks with capital deficiencies; exposing depositors to greater risk through a limitation on the Federal Deposit Insurance Corporation's powers to protect uninsured depositors; and imposing a regime of risk-related deposit insurance premiums that seeks to penalize high-risk institutions. By contrast, the EC has adopted a directive that largely ignores the moral hazard issue by extending the scope of deposit protection within the Community without imposing any limit on the coverage offered by individual member states. While recognizing that a move towards common international standards of deposit protection may not be appropriate at this time, it is surely disquieting that different financial regions are following such divergent policies on deposit insurance.

Lender of Last Resort

Historically, central banks have preferred not to articulate their lender of last resort (LLR) policy, except in the broadest terms, on the principle that to do otherwise is tantamount to "showing the cat the way to the dairy." Yet from an international perspective cooperation in this area is important since in the

International Banking Regulation _____ 189

absence of guidelines there is a danger that troubled institutions could be denied liquidity support in circumstances that might lead to systemic instability.

There are three key parameters governing the LLR function: the conditions that must be met before support is provided; the institutions that are eligible for such support; and the allocation of LLR responsibilities between national authorities.

The traditional role of the LLR is to provide short-term, secured credit to solvent banks experiencing temporary liquidity problems. However, there has been a growing tendency in recent years for governments, if not central banks, to provide capital infusions to insolvent institutions; the most notable recent example is the large-scale official support provided to Scandinavian banks (Table 7.3). The Bank of England, on the other hand, has stated that it will "not ordinarily" provide support to a bank facing solvency problems but it concedes that the distinction between solvency and liquidity problems is not always clear, that losses may therefore be incurred in exercising the LLR function and that its capital and reserves are therefore available for this purpose (Quinn 1993). In some other countries, notably the US, attempts are being made to curb the LLR function with a view to instilling greater discipline into financial markets, but no national banking system of any significance has been able to dispense altogether with LLR facilities.

There is also controversy as to which institutions should be eligible to receive LLR support. This issue has come to the fore with the fusion of banking and securities business within conglomerate corporate structures.[11] Where such businesses are combined within the same legal entity the LLR cannot avoid supporting the securities side of the operation as well as the bank. Where a bank's securities business is conducted in a separate subsidiary it may, in theory, be possible to segregate the risks and to confine the LLR role to the banking entity. However, in practice a bank would no doubt be obliged to support a troubled securities subsidiary or affiliate as a matter of commercial self-interest, a view upheld by the Swiss Federal Supreme Court in a recent legal ruling on the question.[12] If a bank is obliged to underwrite its securities unit's risks, then again the LLR is drawn into supporting securities activities.

Where securities and banking business is conducted by unrelated firms, the LLR function is typically confined to the banking sector. For instance, the Bank of England has argued that LLR assistance should not be extended to nonbanks, on the grounds that banks are distinct because their liabilities are uniquely volatile and only they supply the ultimate means of payment — money (Quinn 1993). Against this it could be argued that the liabilities of securities firms are also liquid, that banks are heavy lenders to the securities industry, and that the failure of a major securities firm could have destabilizing consequences for the banking system. It is no doubt partly for these reasons that the Japanese authorities have been reluctant to witness the collapse of large or even middle-ranking securities firms (witness the rescue of Yamaichi Securities in 1965 and Cosmo Securities in 1993).

The third aspect of the LLR function is the allocation of LLR responsibilities between national authorities. In the past this has been a source of contention, particularly in relation to banks' foreign subsidiaries (Dale 1984, p. 178). But now that the principle of consolidated supervision has been firmly endorsed by the Basle Committee, there would appear to be an implication that the foreign offices of multinational banks (whether branches or subsidiaries) should look to home-country authorities, not host-country authorities for LLR support. This division of responsibilities is unhelpful where, as in the case of BCCI, the home country has no LLR capacity and it may therefore be appropriate for host authorities to insist that a branch or subsidiary of a foreign bank should have access to an LLR in its country of origin as a precondition for authorization.

CONCLUSIONS

The initial focus of the Basle Committee was to reach agreement on the division of regulatory responsibilities between national jurisdictions. Subsequently attention shifted to the need to establish minimum supervisory standards. More recently concerns about competitive equality have been the driving force behind regulatory harmonization initiatives. Are we then moving towards a global framework for international bank regulation and supervision, or is there still scope for national autonomy in these matters?

In examining this question it is perhaps helpful to review alternative regimes aimed at safeguarding stability within the international banking system. Essentially, there are three possible approaches.

Firstly, countries hosting foreign banks (whether branches or subsidiaries) could rely on an incentive system designed to encourage home-country authorities to "capably perform consolidated supervision" (the key Basle requirement). The necessary incentive could be provided by making the home country responsible for insuring the worldwide deposits of both branches and subsidiaries of banks headquartered on its territory. This approach, which has been followed by the EC in respect of branches only (Commission of the European Communities 1992) would however involve international agreement on minimum standards of deposit protection in order to ensure that the incentive scheme operated effectively. Under this regime the cost of supervisory and regulatory failures would be at least partly borne by the authorities responsible for carrying out consolidated supervision.

A second approach would be to subsidiarize banks' foreign operations so

Table 7.3 Bank Support Operations in Selected Countries

Countries	Recipients				Total support*		Government support†	
	Number		Assets as Percent of Industry	As Percent of Recipients' Assets	As Percent of GDP	In billions of Local Currency Units	As Percent of Total Support	As Percent of Government deficit‡
	Absolute	As Percent of Industry						
Norway§								
1988	2	1.0	2.5	5.4	0.1	0.8	25.0	1.3¶
1989	7	3.8	3.9	16.5	0.6	3.9	14.6	6.5¶
1990	9	5.3	4.5	6.8	0.3	1.9	–	–
1991	17	10.5	59.4	4.1	2.0	14.0#	59.8#	298.9#
1992	11	7.4	69.8	2.8	1.7	12.0#	100.0	50.6#
Finland**								
1991 (individual)	28	6.3	15.7	3.7	0.9	4.6	84.5	13.2
1992 (individual)††	22	6.0	23.8	15.1	5.7	28.2	86.2	58.9
1992 (general)‡‡	135	33.0	92.4	1.1	1.6	7.9	100.0	19.2
Sweden§§								
1991	1	0.8	18.2	1.5	0.3	4.2	100.0	19.8
1992	3	2.7	26.9	7.1	2.0	29.3	100.0	26.0
1993¶¶	1	0.9	4.4	50.7	2.4	34.0	100.0	24.1
Japan								
1991–92##	2	0.3	0.1	3.3	0.0	28.0	–	–

*Total support provided to institutions in distress by private guarantee/insurance funds or by governments. It includes guarantees but excludes the acquisition of bad assets.
†Including the central bank.
‡Scaling factor only: the support granted represents in part the acquisition of assets whose eventual contribution to government revenues is difficult to quantify.
§Around one-eighth of the support in the form of guarantees.
¶Surplus.
#Excluding a concessionary loan programme for which all banks were eligible amounting to some NKr 15 billion.
**No support in the form of guarantees. Authorised support up to end-1993 not utilized by end-1992 amounts to some FM 25 billion, or around 5 percent of 1992 GDP.
††A single joint stock company was formed through a merger of forty-one savings banks, some of which were in distress.
‡‡General capital injection.
§§Around one-third of the support in the form of guarantees.
¶¶Industry assets, total number of banks, GDP and government deficit in 1992.
##Only mergers assisted by the bank deposit insurance fund.
Source: Bank for International Settlements, 63rd Annual Report, June 1993, 172.

that the host authority could satisfy itself as to the financial soundness of foreign banks located within its jurisdiction, while also insulating local depositors from risks originating in the parent institution. This possibility has been examined both by the US and the UK authorities, who have concluded that mandatory incorporation of local offices of foreign banks would impose heavy costs on the international banking system without necessarily insulating local depositors from risks associated with the parent bank (Bank of England 1992).

The third approach is to harmonize both regulatory and supervisory standards in all major banking jurisdictions. This is the route currently being followed by the Basle Committee, which has sought to achieve regulatory harmonization through the Basle Accord and recent supplementary proposals. But there remain important areas of national discretion (notably on provisioning against loan losses) which create the potential for regulatory anomalies. Furthermore, harmonization of supervision remains a long way off. The BCCI collapse, which reflected supervisory rather than regulatory failures, has demonstrated very clearly that harmonization of regulation without harmonization of supervisory standards is of limited value, since capital adequacy requirements become meaningless when capital cannot be reliably measured or monitored. The logic of the present Basle approach therefore points to continuing harmonization initiatives aimed at a more complete alignment of both regulatory and supervisory arrangements.

These alternative regulatory regimes have been discussed from a prudential standpoint. However, as pointed out above, in recent years the objective of competitive equality has tended to displace prudential concerns as the main driving force behind international regulatory cooperation.

Within the international banking system the problem of competitive equality has three distinct dimensions. First, competitive equality may be applied to the relationship between rival financial centers. Here, there has been little attempt to establish a level playing field through harmonization initiatives. Instead, market pressures have brought about a gradual liberalization of monetary reserve requirements, stamp duties, withholding taxes, and other key regulatory determinants of the location of international financial activity. In this area we have seen global convergence through regulatory competition rather than regulatory coordination.

Second, the concept of competitive equality may refer to the relationship between national banking industries. The elimination of competitive distortions in this sense has been a major concern of the Basle Committee and a prime objective of the Basle Accord on capital adequacy. Yet it is worth noting that the potential for competitive distortions between banks of different nationality arises partly because of the official safety net (deposit insurance and LLR support) that underlies all banking systems. If the risks incurred by highly leveraged banks were reflected in higher default rates, correspondingly poor credit ratings, and higher risk premiums on deposit rates, then poorly capitalized institutions would enjoy no obvious competitive advantage over their more heavily capitalized counterparts. Viewed in this way, it is the official protection afforded to banks and their creditors, rather than differential capital requirements per se, that is responsible for competitive distortions.

Recent history suggests that most, though not all, national authorities are inclined to strengthen rather than weaken the official safety net (see above). Against this background it seems likely that the Basle Committee will come under pressure to extend the boundaries of regulatory harmonization in an attempt to remove any remaining sources of competitive inequality between banks of different nationality.

Competitive equality concerns the relationship between banks and nonbanks undertaking similar business. Here, the main focus is on securities operations, regulators having made it an explicit objective to establish a level playing field between institutions undertaking securities business in the belief that to allow securities firms to compete on more favorable regulatory terms than banks, or vice versa, would be both inequitable and damaging to the efficient operation of financial markets. The reasoning here is open to criticism, since the objectives of bank regulators and securities regulators are quite different. A troubled securities firm is expected to wind down its business, which can generally be accomplished quite rapidly because of the marketability of the firm's assets. By way of contrast, a bank is most emphatically not expected to respond to financial problems by going out of business since if it were to do so its nonmarketable assets could be sold quickly only at a heavy discount, which would leave depositors and other creditors exposed to losses. Therefore the main objective of bank regulators is to sustain banks as going concerns and in the event of capital impairment to allow them time to raise new capital, strengthen management, and conserve financial resources by, for instance, cutting dividend payments.

Partly for the above reasons, threats to bank solvency are more damaging socially than threats to the solvency of securities firms. Therefore there is a case for saying that securities business should be more highly regulated when undertaken by banks. By insisting on a level playing field regulators must *either* relax their preferred regulatory requirements for banks (as the Basle Committee has acknowledged in relation to its market risk proposals) or else impose needlessly stringent controls on nonbank securities firms. Either way, the emphasis on competitive equality gives rise to operational inefficiencies and social costs. If, at the same time, banks and their creditors are given official LLR protection that is denied to nonbank securities firms, there is a further inducement for securities business to be routed through the banking sector.

In summary, because banking is a protected industry national differences in regulatory arrangements and supervisory standards are not reflected in banks' funding costs. Uneven prudential regulation may therefore give rise not only to systemic concerns but to concerns about competitive equality between rival national banking industries. It is against this background that the Basle Committee has shifted its focus from regulatory cooperation to regulatory harmonization. To date these harmonization initiatives have not prevented the emergence of potentially important regulatory anomalies. In the case of the 1988 Basle Accord the unitary risk-weighting for commercial loans and the scope for divergent provisioning practices are hardly consistent with the notion of common capital adequacy standards. The Basle Committee's proposals on market risk fail to address the concepts of diversification and liquidity which have a key bearing on capital adequacy; and the Committee's proposals on interest rate risk develop a methodology for measurement without considering an appropriate regulatory response. The policy of partial harmonization has therefore resulted in important gaps which, over time, may have to be addressed. On the supervisory side the Basle Committee is still feeling its way, the major question here being whether a more formal mechanism for assessing national supervisory standards may have to be introduced in due course. These issues, together with intractable problems associated with the attempt to create a level playing field for banks and nonbanks, are more than enough to fill the regulatory agenda until the end of the millennium.

ENDNOTES

1. Schaefer (1992) examines the case for capital regulation from a finance theory standpoint.
2. See Cantor and Johnson (1992). However the fact that banks issue capital in excess of the Basle requirements is not necessarily inconsistent with the view that they are capital constrained. For one thing, the Basle ratios are minimum standards and individual banks may be subject to national requirements above the minimum. Secondly, banks may themselves wish to maintain a cushion of capital above the regulatory minimum so as to avoid future supervisory constraints.
3. For a critique of the building-block approach see Breeden (1992).
4. On the issue of risk segregation see Dale (1991).
5. The discussion of derivatives in this section draws on Dale (1993c). See also IMF (1993), Deutsche Bundesbank (1993).
6. For an assessment of the national and international supervisory response to BCCI see Dale (1993a).
7. On this point see Office of the Comptroller of the Currency (1991).
8. For a general discussion of these issues see US Treasury (1991).
9. Cited in *Financial Times Financial Regulation Report*, 1993, 3.
10. In *Al Saudi Banque v. Clark Pixley* (1989) it was held that the company's auditors owed no duty of care to lending banks. In *Caparo Industries v. Dickman* (1990)

the House of Lords determined that the auditor's duty of care is confined to the general body of shareholders.
11. For a general discussion of the LLR implications of the mixing of banking and securities business see Dale (1991).
12. For a summary of the court's decision see IBCA (1991).

REFERENCES

Bank of England. (1991) *Response to Treasury and Civil Service Committee, Issues Relating to BCCI*, September.
————. (1992) *Further Response to the Treasury and Civil Service Committee's Fourth Report on Banking Supervision and BCCI*, October.
————. (1993) *Derivatives: Report of an Internal Working Group*, April.
Bingham. (1992) *Inquiry into the Supervision of the Bank of Credit and Commerce International*. London, HMSO, October.
Breeden, R. (1992) 'SEC letter to IOSCO on capital adequacy.' *International Securities Regulation Report*, November 3, 11–12.
Cantor, R. and Johnson, R. (1992) 'Bank capital ratios, asset growth and the stock market.' *Quarterly Review of the Federal Reserve Bank of New York*, **17** (3) 10–24.
CBRSP. (1975) *Report to the Governors on the Supervision of Banks' Foreign Establishments*, September.
————. (1983) *Principles for the Supervision of Banks's Foreign Establishments*, May.
————. (1988) *International Convergence of Capital Measurement and Capital Standards*, July.
————. (1990) *Supplement to the Concordat: the ensuring of adequate information flows between banking supervisory authorities*, April.
————. (1991) *Proposals for the inclusion of general provisions — general loan loss reserves in capital*, February.
————. (1992) *Minimum standards for the supervision of international banking groups and their cross-border establishments*, June.
————. (1993) *The Prudential Supervision of Netting, Market Risks and Interest Rate Risk*, April.
Commission of the European Communities. (1992) 'Proposal for a council directive on deposit guarantee schemes.' *Official Journal of the European Communities*, **(C163)**, June.
Cooke, P. (1981) 'Developments in co-operation among bank supervisory authorities.' *Bank of England Quarterly Bulletin*, **21**(2), June.
Dale, R. (1984) *The Regulation of International Banking*, Cambridge, UK, Woodhead-Faulkner.
————. (1991) 'Regulating banks' securities activities: a global assessment.' *Journal of International Securities Markets*, Winter, 277–290.
————. (1993a) 'Bank regulation after BCCI.' *Journal of International Banking Law*, January, 8–17.
————. (1993b) 'Deposit insurance: US-EC policy clash.' *Journal of International Securities Markets*, Spring/Summer, 5–15.
————. (1993c) 'How risky are derivatives?' *Journal of International Banking Law*, September, 345–348.
Deutsche Bundesbank. (1993) 'Off-balance-sheet activities of German banks.' *Monthly Report*, October, 45–67.

Goodhart, C. and Schoenmaker, D. (1993) 'Institutional separation between supervisory and monetary agencies.' *Special Paper No. 52*, LSE Financial Markets Group, April.

Group of Thirty. (1993) *Derivatives: Practices and Principles*, New York, July.

IBCA. (1991) *Credit Suisse Loses its Supreme Court Appeal*, London, January.

IMF. (1993) *The Growing Involvement of Banks in Derivative Finance — A Challenge for Financial Policy, Systematic Issues and International Finance*, Washington, D.C., August.

Jones, D. and King, K. (1992) 'An analysis of the implementation of prompt corrective action.' *Finance and Economic Discussion Series, No. 204*, Federal Reserve Board, Washington, D.C., July.

Lamfalussy, A. (1993) *Capital Allocation and Risk Management.* Remarks at the International Monetary Conference, Stockholm, June.

Mullins, D. (1993) *Remarks on the Global Derivatives Study Sponsored by the Group of Thirty.* Before the International Swaps and Derivatives Association, New York, July 28.

Office of the Comptroller of the Currency. (1991) Evidence submitted to the House of Commons Treasury and Civil Service Committee.

Quinn, B. (1993) *The Bank of England's Role in Prudential Supervision.* Speech before the conference organized by Westminster and City Programmes, 'Re-examining City Regulation,' London, March 24.

Schaefer, S. (1992) 'Financial regulation: the contribution of the theory of finance,' in J. Fingleton and D. Schoenmaker, (eds.) *The Internationalisation of Capital Markets and the Regulatory Response.* London, Graham and Trotman.

US Treasury. (1991) *Modernizing the Financial System*, Washington, D.C., February.

DERIVATIVES AND RISK MANAGEMENT:
INSIGHT FROM THE BARINGS EXPERIENCE

Brian Quinn*
Bank of England

I want to consider three questions which have been asked in relation to the Barings affair. First, was Barings really a derivatives problem? Secondly, does the episode throw any light on whether derivatives create particular difficulties for central banks in preventing or dealing with systemic risk? And then finally, a question which we have been asked many times, why didn't the Bank of England mount a rescue for Barings? Did this have anything to do with the answers to the preceding two questions?

Properly specified, the first question really is: to what extent and in what respects can Barings' collapse be attributable to problems in trading derivatives? Now there are limits on what I can say, since the Board of Banking Supervision's investigation into this incident is not yet complete. It's fun to speculate, but I'm not sure that it really adds to the sum of human knowledge at this stage. Derivatives clearly played an important and perhaps central role in the Barings collapse. However, the question is were they decisive? I think there are several important aspects to consider in seeking an answer to this question.

The collapse arose directly from losses in trading derivatives. This is not in dispute. Barings' operation in Singapore was designed to act primarily as an arbitrage futures trader between the Singapore, Osaka and Tokyo exchanges and, in particular, on the Nikkei 225 contract and the 10-year Japanese Government Bond (the "JGB"). Although the risk-taking in this sort of operation can be very significant indeed, Barings' operations in Singapore and Osaka were supposed to be strictly offsetting. However, as we all now know, in fact Barings were running very large open positions in these contracts. Nevertheless, couldn't that have happened in the cash markets? What is different about derivatives which might lead you to the view that it was Barings' involvement in this category of financial instrument which explains why they failed?

It is said that derivatives are *intrinsically* much more complex than corresponding cash instruments. However, if you look at what Barings was doing in Singapore, it did not involve sophisticated and complex instruments such as structured notes. Barings was either undertaking straightforward matching arbitrage in two contracts or taking positions in straightforward futures. Neither, in itself, was very complex. So, in this particular case, I don't think that you can say that the complexity of derivatives was an explanation for the problems which Barings faced.

The second thing said of derivatives is that they permit you to build up an open position with great speed. This is undeniably true. However, I think that it's also possible to point to the spot markets in foreign exchange and in the bond cash markets where you can also rapidly develop large open positions, if the

---

*Brian Quinn is Executive Director of the Bank of England.

corresponding controls are not in place. So, to my mind, it is
not open and shut that the speed of position-building at Barings
was solely a function of derivatives trading. The same effect
could possibly have been achieved using a range of cash
instruments.

The third attribute of derivatives which is often mentioned
is the gearing which can be achieved. However, once again, many
cash markets have leveraged features. I do not profess to know
all of the details of the Orange County affair, but it has been
put to me that it was not essentially a derivatives problem but
rather a problem which arose out of excessive gearing on a
particular instrument. This instrument was complex but that is
not what brought the problem. I think it is, therefore, fair to
conclude that leverage is not unique to derivatives and did not
necessarily provoke what happened to Barings. Moreover, the SIMEX
and Osaka exchanges have margining requirements (both for initial
and variation margin) which, depending on the size of those
requirements, can also reduce the size of a position which can be
built for a given up-front cash payment.

It is also argued that derivatives are not transparent and
that this too played a part in the collapse of Barings. I think
there is something to this point, but I think it is limited in its
strength because, in this case, the products were exchange traded.
I accept that there could have been disparities between exchanges
in regard to the publication of data. This is undoubtedly an
important consideration, since one would need to see both sides of
a deal to judge whether it was properly arbitrage trading or
whether it was position building. Nevertheless, in an exchange-
traded system, where there is published data, problems of the
magnitude we saw at Barings were observable. That they were not
observed is, of course, another story.

So as I go through the list of features which are attributed
to derivatives products, I find they are not unique to derivatives
and, in this particular case, it is not easy to argue that, in
themselves, they were the fundamental problem.

As an aside, it is interesting to note that the Bank of
England, in its efforts over the relevant weekend to find a
solution to the problem, explored the possibility of actually
using derivatives to cap the losses on Barings' positions, since
the open and uncontrolled potential size of the loss was the
essential stumbling block which prevented a rescue.

We explored this possibility with several large,
sophisticated international investment banking groups. We wanted
to know whether a put option could be devised so that a limit
could be placed on the loss at the opening of the next day's
trading. Well, we tried but couldn't find a cost effective
answer. What defeated our efforts was a combination of the size
of the overhang, the fact that is was known in the market by all
potential counterparties and the fact that there was no single
effective counterparty on the other side of the trade. In
principle, it might have been possible had there been a single
counterparty for a negotiated agreement to have been reached to
put a limit on the losses and then close out the position. But
that just was not possible in this case.

And then, finally, the size and the cost of the option put
it beyond the reach of those who might have been prepared to
explore this possibility. That was a disappointment to us. In
principle, we would have thought it possible -- and I think it
might have been -- but it was too difficult in the short time
available to us.

So let me summarize the answer to my first question. Was
Barings a derivatives problem? Clearly their difficulties arose

out of derivatives. But I think it can be argued plausibly that the difficulties could also have arisen in the cash markets. Nevertheless, I retain a lingering feeling that the size of the futures contracts, together with the ability to gear up quickly, created the potential for the emergence of large position-building -- not a problem in itself, provided that controls were in place to manage it. That, of course, poses the question as to whether the fundamental cause of Barings' collapse was not so much derivatives as it was a matter of controls. And that, I hope, is a question to which the answer will be found as the Board of Banking Supervision completes their official investigation.

Let me turn now to my second question. The G30 Report on derivatives concludes that it is hard to find justification for the view that derivatives pose greater systemic threat than other financial activity. Does Barings throw any light on this assertion? In particular, did the failure of Barings create any particular problems for the Bank of England -- or indeed, any other central monetary authority -- in their attempt to avoid wider systemic problems?

In seeking to answer this question, I went back to the G30 report and looked at what they saw as the potential sources of systemic risk arising out of derivative operations. It is worthwhile to go through them now and see whether we should revise our opinions in the light of the Barings affair.

The first concern identified by the G30 was the possibility that markets might become illiquid because of the nature of derivative activities. Well, in this case liquidity was forthcoming both for the instruments involved and for the markets. SIMEX and Osaka provided liquidity and the margin held by both of those exchanges which had been placed by Barings' trading operations was important in this regard. There is, of course, no assurance that OTC problems would have been solved in quite as straightforward a manner. However, I have to enter a qualification here because we do not know precisely how the contracts were closed out in Singapore, Tokyo and Osaka. Indeed, in defense of OTC trading, we cannot be sure that collateral would not have been available because the practice of taking collateral to support OTC transactions is growing every day.

The other source of liquidity problems might have been if other institutions of a similar size with a similar business profile had seen their funding withdrawn on a systemic scale. I have to say that we saw this as a real risk in the situation over that weekend. In the light of this, on the Monday morning after our efforts to engineer a rescue for Barings had failed, we issued a statement saying that, should any other institution in the UK find itself facing liquidity pressures, a special facility would be made available at the Bank of England. The reason we were prepared to take such a step was because we had no reason to question the solvency of other institutions in that class. It was a nervous time, as these times can be, but in the event the facility was never drawn upon. So, although we were standing ready to provide liquidity, that readiness was not tested and so, in this particular case, it does not look as though derivatives created a liquidity problem. Of course, one doesn't know what the situation would have been had we not made that statement. But, of course, that was the purpose of issuing a statement.

Another potential source of systemic difficulties identified by the G30 was settlement risk (i.e., the inability of counterparties to close out transactions). Well, again, because they were exchange traded instruments, SIMEX, Osaka and Tokyo ensured settlement of the outstanding contracts and that was done in what I have to say was an admirably calm and measured way.

That didn't solve all the problems, however, because when a company is in administration, the administrator has the job of trying to conduct the business and to complete outstanding obligations. Additionally, there was still the possibility that we could find another institution which might have agreed to buy Barings. In these circumstances, some counterparties were not prepared to pay monies owed into Barings' existing correspondent accounts with other banks because they and the administrators were concerned that the funds might be seized by those banks to cover their own claims on Barings. Moreover, those who held collateral were very reluctant to release it and many who had outstanding foreign exchange transactions were also reluctant to complete for similar reasons.

However, many counterparties were prepared to pay those funds into accounts for the administrators held by ourselves. In these circumstances, the Bank of England stepped in and acted as a matched principal between the administrator on the one side and the market counterparties on the other. This was not a new role for us; together with the Federal Reserve Bank in New York, we had carried out a similar function in the Drexel affair. Of course, at the end of the week, ING took over Barings and problems of settlement were largely solved.

Another kind of potential systemic problem is counterparty risk. In a sense, this risk was largely untested because Barings was bought by another bank. Had ING not come in, I think it is entirely possible that some counterparties would have lost money, but it is not clear that this possibility was made worse by the fact that Barings' problems arose out of derivatives trading. This risk is present in any bank failure. Again, it is not clear to me that derivatives were part of the problem (or would have been part of the problem) if there had been counterparty failures.

Moreover, staying with counterparty risk, Barings was not a large global player in several different futures markets and so there was limited concentration risk, which was another factor which took up the attention of the G30 report. Now SIMEX, in principle, was a concentration risk. To the extent you have an exchange trade, the exchange stands on the other side of every contract. In this instance, of course, the problem was dealt with by the Singapore authorities and the margin paid by Barings (both initial and variation) went a very long way to enable them to close out those contracts. This meant that this particular form of concentration risk, the failure of the exchange, did not arise in this case.

Netting arrangements were also put to the test and performed satisfactorily. That was a source of considerable relief since there have been many questions about the robustness of netting agreements in this kind of situation. However, client funds -- as those of you in Chicago will know only too well -- did pose some difficulties. There was great anxiety in the immediate aftermath of the failure as to whether client funds which had been placed with Barings could be identified and repaid. You may remember that this concern was particularly acute in the case of Japan, since it was not clear whether separation of client funds was assured by law. Once again, there was a problem, but not one that was a problem of derivatives. Any kind of bank failure would have raised these issues. All that the Barings collapse did was to expose the problem of the ambiguity surrounding client funds.

One of our other speakers this afternoon, Professor Marshall, has already mentioned connected markets. The worry here was that problems in the derivatives markets would have knock-on consequences in the cash markets. The place where this was most likely to have occurred would have been the relevant underlying cash markets in Japan. You may remember that there was great speculation over the weekend about the possible effects, given the fact that there was a very large party with very large known open positions. Indeed, there were forecasts from some commentators that the Nikkei would fall by something like 20% on the Monday. The long-heralded meltdown was about to occur. In the event, the Nikkei fell by no more than 4% and, in fact, recovered in the course of the next business day.

What can we conclude from all this? Well, in this case, and I repeat, in this case, the G30 conclusion seems to have been justified; but there are a number of important qualifications. Barings was not a major player in the derivatives markets. Liquidity and settlement facilities were provided quickly by the Bank of England in London and by the Monetary Authority of Singapore. It cannot be ruled out that a failure by a major player in an OTC product could have quite different results. Of course, we can take some comfort from the fact that the wholly unexpected failure in an important derivatives market did not create mayhem, but I think the interesting question it leaves behind is, what did the central banks and the other monetary authorities involved learn from the episode? The report of the Board of Banking Supervision will, I hope, go some way to answering this question.

Now, lastly, Chairman, I would like to say a word about the answer to the last question which I posed, namely why didn't the Bank of England rescue Barings? It may be just worthwhile going over considerations which were in our minds during the weekend of 24 to 26 February.

In 1993 the Governor set out in the Bank of England lecture to the London School of Economics the principles that would determine whether any particular bank in difficulties might expect to be given lender of last resort assistance. Guided by those principles, we went through the list of possible solutions. First, was there a commercial solution? Could the existing shareholders have provided the capital required to plug the hole that had been discovered? The answer to that was clearly "no" in this instance because the holding company was fully owned by a charity, the Baring foundation, which was not financially capable of repairing the damage.

In the absence of possible support from the shareholders, we looked to see whether the wider banking community might be prepared to provide its support. That was a very interesting possibility. If we had been able to quantify and cap the losses arising from the open positions, then I believe there was a fair chance that some institutions could have got together and provided a solution. Indeed, a number of them tried to do just that on the Sunday evening; the problem was that it was not possible to put a number on the likely loss Barings was facing and, in the light of this, there was no way in which those institutions could come forward and recapitalize the bank, since it would effectively amount to them writing a blank check.

As I have already said, we sought to find out whether there was a single counterparty on the other side, in which case we could have sat down and negotiated to see whether there was some kind of commercial transaction that could have been done. In the event, there was no such counterparty but rather a very fragmented population on the other side of those transactions.

Given that we had tried to cap the exposure via a put option and failed, and that a commercial buyer had failed, the question then was whether there should be official support. In weighing up this matter, we again looked to the criteria set out in the

Governor's LSE lecture. The first and most important criterion is whether the direct effects of the failure of the bank (in terms of losses to counterparties) would be likely to cause failures of other firms or even the collapse of markets.

This is the hardest question of all, I think, for a central banker to answer. You have to assess on the weight of the evidence available to you what is the likely balance of probabilities. That is always a difficult judgment to make, and no less on this occasion. At that time, Mexico's financial problems were very much in the minds of the market. There had been a stream of real or imagined derivatives problems, of which Orange County was only the most notable example. There was considerable turbulence in the currency markets and there was just the possibility that the collapse of Barings would have carried right through the financial system with horrific effects.

However, as we looked through the events and the markets, we could not persuade ourselves that there was a real enough risk to justify our seeking to apply public funds in support of the institution. There was, of course, also the important question of whether we would be prepared to write a blank check when the financial community had judged that it should not.

The second aspect to consider when weighing up how to respond to such a crisis is to examine whether the situation is a problem of solvency or liquidity. If it is a solvency problem, in normal circumstances it's very hard for a central bank to persuade itself that it should devote public funds to saving an institution which has suffered terminal losses. Liquidity can be a different matter. Had other parties recapitalized the bank, then I think it likely that the Bank of England would have been ready to provide liquidity to Barings in order to prevent any kind of systemic knock-on effects.

The other questions which arise when assessing whether to undertake a rescue -- such as: Where do the costs fall? Is there an exit for the central bank that relieves it of the finance burden of providing support? -- never arose because, of course, we did not intervene.

I don't think it can be said too often that the risk of serious systemic disturbance was the key consideration for us. A number of people have enquired after the event why we didn't save Barings when in recent years we saved a number of much smaller institutions, some of whom were perceived to be much less worthy than Barings. This question misses the point. You do not save a bank because of its name or its size. You save it because of the effect which the failure of that bank might have on the rest of the system.

Did we make the right decision? Of course, you can never tell. You cannot know what the financial and social costs might have been had you taken the other course. You assess the probabilities, take your courage in both hands and make a decision. Let's hope that we won't be put in that position again very soon.

Thank you very much.

[38]

COUNTERACTING FRAUD: THE CASE OF BCCI REVISITED

Mervyn K Lewis

Introduction

Two financial scandals which unfolded in September 1996 demonstrated once again the central role of offshore centres in many financial deceptions and cover-ups. In one case, Peter Young, a fund manager at Morgan Grenfell Asset Management apparently set up a string of Luxembourg-based holding companies which appear to have been used both to hide losses and to disguise that holdings of unlisted securities in funds exceeded permitted amounts for unquoted stocks. The holding companies were the beneficiary owners of many of the investments, acquired at discounted prices.[1] In the other case, coincidentally involving someone with the same surname, a Nottingham-based foreign exchange trader, with links to a subsidiary of a Swiss bank, operated an offshore currency investment fund out of Jersey from which $27 million disappeared in suspicious circumstances, leaving many investors, half of them US citizens, with extensive losses.[2]

Commenting in the wake of the second scandal, the Assistant District Attorney of New York County, John Moscow, drew attention to some of the wider implications of the legal and regulatory environment in offshore centres such as Jersey. In particular, he questioned whether Jersey's legislators are capable of fighting the huge amounts of money organised crime seeks to conceal in the world's financial centres. Continuing, he noted that:

> My experience with both Jersey and Guernsey has been that it has not been possible for US law enforcement to collect evidence to prosecute crime ... In one

Mervyn K Lewis is National Australia Bank Professor at the School of Economics, Finance & Property, University of South Australia case we tracked money from Bahamas, through Curacao, New York and London, but the paper trail stopped in Jersey.

He added that:

It is unseemly that these British dependencies should be acting as havens for transactions that would not even be protected by Swiss bank secrecy laws. One has to wonder why Swiss banks would set up subsidiaries in these jurisdictions.[3]

Interestingly, Moscow was the prosecutor who began the investigation that eventually led to the closure of the Bank of Credit and Commerce International (BCCI) in 1991 and his present comments about the offshore connection echo many of those which he made following BCCI's demise. In the light of these recent scandals it is perhaps timely to look again at the BCCI saga and see what has been learnt from the episode, and what issues remain unresolved.

The Background

When BCCI was indicted by a New York grand jury on charges of fraud, money laundering, bribery and theft, District Attorney Robert Morgenthau called it "the largest bank fraud in world history".[4] The indictment alleged that BCCI fraudulently solicited deposits by falsely representing itself as a healthy bank when in fact it had been virtually insolvent for years, and there was such a huge hole - nearly $12 billion out of $20 billion assets - in the bank's accounts that the bank's 250,000 creditors (mainly former depositors) faced an initial distribution in 1995 of only 20 per cent.[5] This marks the first time in recent history that a large European-based bank has been allowed to default on ordinary depositors.

Although District Attorney Morgenthau described BCCI as "a sleazy institution with no morals" and "a corrupt criminal organisation", it is not clear whether BCCI began as a fraudulent enterprise. *The Financial Times* special report *Behind Closed Doors* argues that BCCI may not have set out to be a fraudulent bank, but its obsession with secrecy and power soon made it a natural breeding ground for malpractice.[6] However, there are grounds for questioning this sanguine view. When BCCI was first registered as a company in Luxembourg in 1972, its largest shareholder was an obscure London solicitor, seemingly acting as a nominee for other shareholders whose identities have never been established. New York Assistant District Attorney John W. Moscow notes that the answer to the question, "Who owns BCCI, and where did the capital come from, *if indeed it ever came?*" is that in fact the capital of the bank was not there; the books were falsified to a massive degree.[7]

What can be said was that BCCI was founded in 1972 by Pakistani businessman Agha Hasan Abedi, and was uniquely shaped by his ambitions for it. Initially

4

capitalised at just $2.5 million, the bank grew rapidly until it had operations in 69 countries and (recorded) assets of $20 billion. Although born in Lucknow, India, Mr Abedi made his name in Pakistan working first for Habib Bank and then helping to found United Bank. He wanted to create an institution that was committed to social and economic development in the Third World. Abedi's philosophy was that:

> We serve a purpose for society and humanity at large, absolutely without consideration or bias towards caste, creed, colour, religion or race ... [the BCCI] leadership ignites in every member of our family the highest quality of vision and the highest moral quality. Courage and purity will prevail.[8]

These views made it very popular in the Indian sub-continent and also in the Gulf region, where the bank courted wealthy Arab investors and encouraged the Islamic connection. As a result, BCCI was able to attract investments from Islamic banks, which believed (incorrectly) that the funds were being handled and invested according to Islamic banking principles. More importantly, when Bank of America, which had been one of the initial but minor shareholders in BCCI, sold its stake in 1980, prominent Arab financiers, notably the Bin Mahfouz family of Saudi Arabia and the family of Sheikh Zayed Bin-Nahyan, the ruler of Abu Dhabi, were left as the leading shareholders. (As reported in the *New Statesman*, Bank of America became worried about BCCI when auditors from Bank of America were sent to the United Arab Emirates to check on a BCCI branch, only to discover that this local branch did not, in fact, exist.) Later in 1990, Abu Dhabi increased its equity stake in the bank from 39 per cent to 77 per cent by buying out the Saudi investors, while also providing $600 million of new capital.

The Structure of BCCI

By 1990, BCCI was one of the largest private banks in the world. However, despite the largely Arab ownership, BCCI was run by Abedi, his deputy Swaleh Naqvi, and a cabal of insiders, largely Pakistanis, fiercely loyal to Abedi and Naqvi. Moreover, London was the effective head office of the organisation - a fact recognised by the Bingham report - despite the cavalier view of some Bank of England officials that "the mind and management" of BCCI were really in Abedi's briefcase or wherever he happened to be.[9] Lord Justice Bingham acknowledged that BCCI was widely perceived to be a UK bank, even though the Bank of England had refused to grant BCCI a banking licence and had allowed it to operate only as a deposit-taking institution. As Justice Bingham observes, BCCI was accordingly not entitled under Section 36 of the UK Banking Act to use a banking name, but this provision of the Act was not enforced by the British authorities.

5

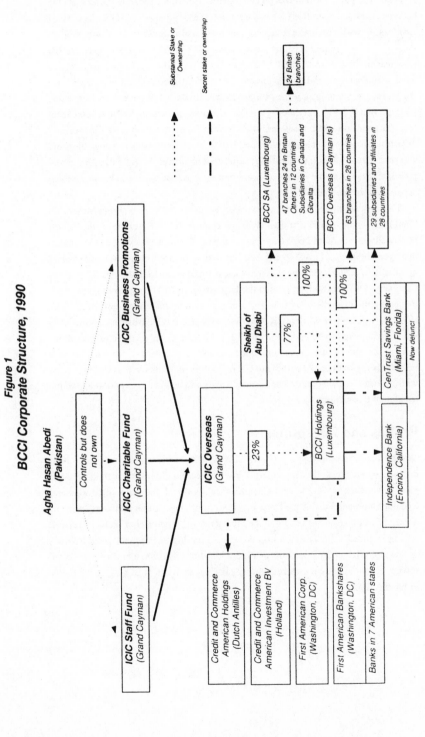

Figure 1
BCCI Corporate Structure, 1990

Agha Hasan Abedi (Pakistan)

Controls but does not own

ICIC Staff Fund *(Grand Cayman)*

ICIC Charitable Fund *(Grand Cayman)*

ICIC Business Promotions *(Grand Cayman)*

ICIC Overseas (Grand Cayman)

Credit and Commerce American Holdings *(Dutch Antilles)*

Credit and Commerce American Investment BV *(Holland)*

First American Corp. *(Washington, DC)*

First American Bankshares *(Washington, DC)*

Banks in 7 American states

Sheikh of Abu Dhabi

23%

77%

100%

100%

BCCI Holdings *(Luxembourg)*

CenTrust Savings Bank *(Miami, Florida)* Now defunct

Independence Bank *(Encino, California)*

BCCI SA *(Luxembourg)*

47 branches 24 in Britain
Others in 12 countries
Subsidiaries in Canada and Gibralta

BCCI Overseas *(Cayman Is)*

63 branches in 28 countries

29 subsidiaries and affiliates in 28 countries

24 British branches

Substantial Stake or Ownership

Secret stake or ownership

Sources: Financial Times, 22 July 1991, p12. The Independent, 10 July 1991, p22. The Economist, 3 August 1991, p20.

Mr Abedi and his management group were able to balance these interests by means of an intricate and virtually impenetrable corporate structure. The structure is set out in Figure 1, which was pieced together from three separate sources. At the heart of the global operations was a parent holding company in Luxembourg (BCCI Holdings), with the main banking business split between two subsidiaries incorporated in different offshore jurisdictions - BCCI SA in Luxembourg and BCCI Overseas in the Cayman Islands. London operations, which provided the effective head office and "mind, management and central direction of the group" (in Bingham's terminology), were sourced from a branch (and not even a full one at that) of BCCI SA (Luxembourg). This complex structure, based around legal incorporation in Luxembourg and the Cayman Islands, was to pose fundamental difficulties for regulatory control. BCCI Holdings, as a non-bank holding company, was not even subject to banking supervision, while by operating in many jurisdictions without having a clear home country base, BCCI avoided close national supervision in any one.[10]

The intricate structure also served to conceal corporate control. From May 1990, Sheikh Zayed of Abu Dhabi owned 77 per cent of BCCI. Before then, the largest bloc of shares was owned by a Cayman company, ICIC (Overseas), used to maintain management interest in BCCI. Mr Abedi and his supporters always said that he had no shares in BCCI. But the Cayman-based International Credit and Investment Company (Overseas) which owned the large stake in BCCI, appears to have been owned by three smaller Cayman-based organisations, rather than companies - the ICIC Staff Benefit Trust, the ICIC Charitable Fund and ICIC Business Promotions. All were believed to be under the control of Mr Abedi, but as these organisations were not companies they were not required to submit accounts, even under Cayman Islands tax regulations. According to UK regulators, ICIC (Overseas) was the "bank within a bank" which diverted depositors' funds and was at the heart of many of the fraudulent transactions.

Frauds and Deceptions

Despite rapid expansion in the 1970s and 1980s, BCCI had a controversial reputation in financial markets. It was widely known in banking circles under three other guises: the Bank of Crooks and Criminals International, the Bank of Crooks and Cocaine International and the Bank of the Columbian Cocaine Industry. None of the credit-rating agencies accorded the bank a rating. It had a poor financial record, having incurred a $150 million loss on options trading in 1985, and overall losses of $48 million and $498 million in 1988 and 1989. In 1988, its officers were the subject of drug money-laundering charges in Florida to which BCCI pleaded guilty in January 1990.

After BCCI executives had been convicted in the United States of money laundering, the Bank of England asked Price Waterhouse, by then BCCI's sole auditor, to carry out an investigation of BCCI's UK activities under the UK Banking Act.[11] Until then, Price Waterhouse's reports had voiced some concerns about high concentrations of lending to a small number of parties, but the auditing firm considered the level of provisioning and capital to be adequate, and had sounded no note of alarm. Indeed, Price Waterhouse had even commented favourably on BCCI's due diligence with respect to money-laundering precautions! In addition, the Bank of England's own Banking Supervision Division took the view that at the date of the indictment in Florida, BCCI's systems and controls had been adequate in the UK, and possibly elsewhere as well.

However, in April 1990, Price Waterhouse reported a number of false or deceitful accounting transactions booked in the Cayman Islands and other offshore centres. In October 1990, the auditors reported that "the previous management may have colluded with major customers to misstate or disguise the underlying purpose of significant transactions." By June 1991, Price Waterhouse's report gave a comprehensive and detailed account of the frauds and deceptions which had been practised in the group over a substantial number of years so far as they were then known. Reference was made to transactions involving:

(i)   falsification of accounting records;

(ii)   use of external vehicles to route fund transfers and "park" transactions;

(iii)   the use of nominee and hold-harmless arrangements;

(iv)   the fraudulent use of the Ruling Family's funds;

(v)   creation of 70 companies to facilitate and disguise lending to the Gulf Shipping Group;

(vi)   collusion with third party banks to make loans to BCCI customers, so as to avoid disclosure of such lending on BCCI's balance sheet;

(vii)   collusion with customers and others to give false confirmations to the auditors of fictitious and non-recourse loans and loans received as nominees;

(viii) Central Treasury losses;

(ix)   ICIC (Overseas).[12]

From the Price Waterhouse report, it would seem that these transactions were directed to a number of major frauds.[13]

8

Trading losses. First, BCCI lost heavily on trading activities in financial markets amounting to $849 million between 1977 and 1985, using clients' names to trade for its own account. These losses continued, and in 1990 amounted to $495 million.

Bad loans. Second, BCCI made bad loans to prominent businessmen in the Middle East. Authorities say that BCCI often failed to require documentation for major loans. As much as $1 billion may have gone to three borrowers: Saudi financier Ghaith Pharaon; former Saudi intelligence chief Kamal Adham; and the Gulf group, a shipping and trading conglomerate. All individuals involved had close ties to BCCI or its executives. As the Washington Post notes: "the bank that allegedly was intended to help the poor was taking deposits from the poor and giving big loans to the rich, without much collateral".[14] In some cases, no payments had been made on the loans for years. Some of the alleged borrowers deny ever receiving the money, and BCCI could well have been using their names as covers for its own misuse of the funds.

Bank ownership. Third, as sketched out in Figure 1, BCCI secretly acquired ownership of several banks in the USA. For a fee, prominent individuals served as fronts for BCCI. The bank lent the nominal investors funds to buy the shares, excused them from repayment, and held the shares as collateral. Many of the investors were BCCI shareholders, who claimed that they planned to rely on BCCI management to provide investment advice, but said that BCCI would have no role in running the banks. The truth was that the banks were run by BCCI.[15]

Share acquisitions. Fourth, BCCI acquired secret control of its own shares. Price Waterhouse showed that $476 million from BCCI (Overseas) and $308 million from ICIC (Overseas) were funnelled to fake shareholders for stock purchases in transactions similar to those which enabled BCCI to gain control over First American Bankshares, the American bank it secretly acquired in Washington. It persuaded several of the Middle East's ruling families, and some businessmen, to pose as owners of BCCI's Luxembourg holding company so as to give the illusion of financial strength.[16]

Cover ups. Fifth, following on from these activities there were the countless frauds and deceptions undertaken to cover the initial problems. BCCI's auditors discovered a "bank within the bank", controlled via ICIC (Overseas), and used by the inner cache of top officials to hide losses on bad loans and trading positions. When holes developed in the balance sheet, the secret bank plugged them by raising deposits without recording them on the balance sheet. These unrecorded deposits were presented on the books and used by BCCI as though the funds were its own capital rather than belonging to depositors, so enabling it to meet capital requirements and maintain balance sheet size. The bank took out fictitious loans, then drew them down to cover losses in various parts of the group.

Eventually, however, these unrecorded deposits had to be repaid and the fictitious loans had to generate income. New inflows of deposits were then needed to keep the balancing trick going. Yet BCCI was largely shut out from the main source of funding used by banks - the interbank markets - as bankers became increasingly wary of BCCI's reputation. When the bank was closed down, it held only $2 billion from other banks;[17] many banks obtain more than half of their funds from interbank sources and professional wholesale markets.[18] Instead, in order to sustain the inflow of funds, BCCI was forced to raise deposits in ever more exotic locations (Nigeria, Communist China, East Africa) and to become less fussy about the origins and uses of the funds. As a result, money was laundered for drug-dealers, and clients were helped to evade taxes and get around exchange controls. BCCI was one of the few banks able to transfer private cash from Panama to Switzerland or from the USA to Pakistan, often via bank secrecy locations such as the Cayman Islands. Currency deposits into BCCI's office in New York would be booked 'as if' made in India, Pakistan or Bangladesh.[19]

Often, in bank frauds relating to senior officers of a bank, illegal payouts and payoffs are involved as members of the management group siphon off cash flows and come to see the bank as an opportunity to use depositors' money for themselves. In this respect, BCCI seems unusual. Admittedly, loans were made to 'related parties' - friends and associates of BCCI's top management - which were never repaid. Nominees received handsome fees for acting on behalf of BCCI in share deals. Deposits of 'related parties' fell as other deposits increased, enabling those 'in the know' to get their money out in time. However, BCCI's executives do not seem to have enriched themselves enormously.[20] Rather, much as seems to have been the case with Nick Leeson and Barings, the motivation may have been the retention of power, prestige and influence. But as management had to resort to ever more complex and frequent deceptions to keep the sinking enterprise afloat, and as more and more unrecorded deposits and fictitious loans had to be repaid and replaced by yet more unrecorded deposits and fictitious loans, the scheme spiralled out of control. Nevertheless, the objective "might have been to keep a bank going when it never made a profit so that its officers could continue to be very important people of great status."[21]

Regulatory Issues

As *The Economist* observes, "when a bank goes wrong, its customers have two guardians: the auditors, to warn them of trouble in the bank's accounts, and the

10

regulator, to steer the bank to safety or shut it down. In the case of the Bank of Credit and Commerce International, the auditors did not warn and the regulators took a long time to steer".[22] BCCI's auditors, Price Waterhouse described the bank as engaging in "probably one of the most complex deceptions in banking history"[23] and it is now accepted by the regulators that the existence of two sets of auditors for BCCI, while in itself neither illegal nor unethical, did help BCCI to conceal its true position.[24] Was the same true of the regulators?

Certainly the BCCI saga raises fundamental questions about the way in which global banks are regulated by national authorities. With financial markets having become so internationalised, the present regulatory regime coordinated through central bankers' meetings in Basle may no longer be appropriate. The system of international bank regulation is based around the Basle Committee, the 1975 Concordat, and the Basle Concordat 1983.[25]

Basle Committee. The Committee on Banking Regulations and Supervisory Practices was established at the end of 1974 by the governors of the central banks of the Group of 10 nations plus Luxembourg. It met at the Bank for International Settlements in Basle and became known as the Basle Committee. Its object was to achieve international agreement on standards of good practice and collaboration in the banking supervisory field.

1975 Concordat. In 1975, the Committee produced a report on the supervision of banks' foreign establishments. This Concordat distinguished between subsidiaries, branches and joint ventures and provided guidelines on the allocation of supervisory responsibility between host and parent authorities in regard to liquidity, solvency and foreign exchange exposure. The 'host authority' is that in the country where the subsidiary or branch or joint venture is actually carrying on business. The 'parent authority' or 'source authority' is that in the country where the parent company of the subsidiary or the head office of the branch or joint venture is incorporated or established. The Concordat was intended to ensure that no foreign banking establishment should escape supervision and that supervision should be adequate.

1983 Concordat. In 1983, the Basle Committee issued a paper revising and updating the 1975 Concordat. This paper acknowledged that gaps in supervision can arise out of structural features of international groups (for example where a group is headed by a non-bank holding company) and recorded agreement on four important matters: first, that supervisors cannot be fully satisfied about the soundness of individual banks unless they can examine the totality of each bank's business worldwide through the technique of consolidation; second, that no foreign banking establishment should escape supervision; third, that supervision should be adequate;

and fourth, that there should be co-operation and an exchange of information between the supervisors in a bank's parent country and those in its host country. If supervision by a host authority is inadequate, the parent authority should either extend its supervision so far as practicable or discourage the parent bank from continuing to operate the establishment in question. If a host authority considers supervision by a parent authority to be inadequate or non-existent, the host authority should discourage or, if it can, forbid the operation of such foreign establishments in its territory; alternatively, it should impose specific conditions governing the conduct of the business of such establishments. The principle of consolidated supervision was said to be that parent banks and parent supervisory authorities monitor the risk exposure of the banks or groups for which they are responsible on the basis of the totality of their business wherever conducted.

In many ways, BCCI provided a test of these principles since it appears to have been structured in a way that was intended to minimise regulatory constraints (see Figure 1). This is an important aspect of the affair because it is precisely those banks which are seeking to avoid regulatory attention that need to be supervised most closely. A number of points emerge.

The holding company. First, BCCI Holdings, the parent entity of BCCI, was a Luxembourg holding company. This company escaped regulation under Luxembourg banking law because as a non-bank holding company it was not classified as a bank. Holding companies which own banks should be subject to supervision, as they are in the USA where the holding company structure is the norm. The 1983 Concordat highlighted the attention which banking supervisors were by that time giving to consolidated supervision (that is, the supervision of banking groups on the basis of all their operations wherever conducted), but the Directive did not extend to non-bank holding companies.

The parent home authorities. Second, BCCI's banking operations were split between two main subsidiaries incorporated in different jurisdictions - Luxembourg and the Cayman Islands. This structure effectively ruled out consolidated supervision. Table 1 sets out the guidelines of the 1983 Concordat. Formally, the Luxembourg Banking Commission (Institut Monetaire Luxembourgeois - IML) was the primary regulator under the Basle rules, especially for the supervision of solvency. However, IML argued that it was too small an organisation to carry out supervision of a world-wide group such as BCCI since only 1-2 per cent of the group's business was in Luxembourg. As for the Cayman Islands, BCCI (Overseas) was in reality "effectively unsupervised" by the Cayman Island authorities, in Lord Justice Bingham's opinion.[26] The risk that substandard loans might be switched around the group to places where they were least likely to be questioned was

12

expressly recognised, and suspected of having been done at a global level. As *The Economist* put it: "bad loans on the bank's books would disappear into offshore accounts when regulators came calling; good assets would conveniently emerge."[27]

Table 1
Areas of Primary Responsibility Recommended by the Basle Committee of Banking Supervisors, 1983

Form of foreign establishment	Supervision of liquidity	Supervision of solvency
Branch	Host + Source authority	Source authority
Subsidiary	Host authority	Host + Source authority
Joint venture	Authority in country of incorporation	Authority in country of incorporation

Source: Lewis and Davis

US host supervision. Third, BCCI's divided home bases created peculiar problems in the United States. BCCI SA (Luxembourg) had operations in the states of New York and California, while BCCI Overseas (Cayman Islands) operated in the state of Florida. Under the system of regulation that was in place in the United States at that time, no single regulatory authority had the power or responsibility to regulate all three branches. As a consequence, the BCCI group was able to shuffle assets from state to state, revealing particular assets to more than one regulator - a minuscule part of what it was able to do globally.[28]

UK host supervision. Fourth, the difficulties faced by US host authorities, abeit magnified by the dual regulatory system, were faced to different degrees by other host supervisors and especially those in the United Kingdom, if only because the UK was host to more of BCCI than other countries. In these circumstances, London could have acted to curtail BCCI's activities in the UK. Under the 1983 Concordat, each national supervisory authority must satisfy itself that banks' foreign operations are being conducted in jurisdictions with sound supervisory practices and that foreign banks to which it is host are subject to adequate supervision in their home jurisdiction. If a host country considers that the supervision of parent institutions of foreign banks on its territory is inadequate, it should prohibit or discourage the continued operation of such offices or alternatively impose specific conditions on the conduct of their business. This did not occur in the case of BCCI, at least in the

UK. As noted earlier, BCCI was not even entitled to call itself a bank in Britain, but still did so. By contrast, some countries such as Australia, Portugal and Saudi Arabia did refuse BCCI entry because of supervisory concerns.[29]

UK consolidated supervision. Fifth, as an alternative, the Bank of England could have taken over BCCI's consolidated supervision. In the words of *The Economist:*

> When a bank with branches in Britain keeps its corporate home elsewhere, the Bank of England generally defers to the "home" regulator. But it can take over if that regulator lacks the capacity for proper supervision, or if the bank's main business is in Britain. On both counts the Bank of England could have claimed leadership from the feeble regulators in BCCI's corporate homes, Luxembourg and the Cayman Islands. Luxembourg has only 15 bank supervisors. And BCCI's top executives actually ran it from London. True, it was a fiendish bank to regulate: it had no single address and committed many of its crimes under the cover of Cayman's banking-secrecy laws. But if the Bank of England had taken control earlier it might have averted the debacle.[30]

The Bingham Report reveals that Bank of England officials came to much the same conclusion, albeit reluctantly, as early as 1982. Mr Brian Gent, a deputy head of Banking Supervision, wrote a long and thoughtful paper in June of that year in which he pointed to continuing prudential concerns about BCCI, the risks inherent in the structure of the group, the crying need for a single overall supervisor, the fiction of the group's Luxembourg location and the arguable anomaly of the Bank's reliance on Luxembourg assurances when the group's principal place of business was in the UK. The thrust of his argument was that no supervisory authority other than the Bank of England could reasonably be expected to take on the supervision of BCCI and that the Bank should do so, rather than let a large international group continue in business on a largely unsupervised basis. That paper took nearly two years to emerge finally as Bank policy. When in 1984 Mr Peter Cooke, Head of Banking Supervision and Chairman of the Basle Committee, sought Mr Abedi's co-operation in moving the incorporation of BCCI to the UK to enable the Bank to supervise it, Abedi refused on the spot.

> Abedi called on Cooke, who intended to broach the Bank's plan with him. Cooke began to do so, describing the Bank's unease at the existing structure and recommending the integration of [BCCI] SA and Overseas. Abedi was resistant. He spoke again of his eventual plans to move [BCCI] Overseas into the US, but he would not contemplate a merger with [BCCI] SA. Cooke's message was couched in oblique terms, but (as he felt) conveyed to Abedi both the Bank's willingness to accept the group into the UK, on appropriate conditions, and also

14

that there could be no recognition without acceptable reorganisation. Abedi, usually compliant (at least overtly) and ingratiating, was on this occasion truculent and angry. The Bank's initiative, under consideration for nearly two years, thus fell at the first fence. (Bingham Report p.40-1).

That ended the matter. Lord Justice Bingham comments (p.41):

> I find it surprising that no effort was made to bring the Bank's traditional authority to bear on Abedi to seek to secure his compliance ... the Bank was, I think, rather easily deterred.

The college of supervisors. Sixth, the solution which emerged, at the suggestion of a Dutch central banker, was that BCCI be supervised by a cooperative group of international supervisors. A scheme was accordingly devised for twice-yearly meetings of national supervisors responsible for BCCI. It was envisaged that BCCI's management and the auditors would attend part of these meetings, and that the auditors would report on the financial conditions of the group. This proposal was accepted by the Governors, the Board of Banking Supervision, the IML, the auditors and the management of BCCI. The college of regulators was established in 1987 and first met in May 1988. Initially, the college consisted of regulators from the UK, Switzerland, Spain and Luxembourg, but the membership was expanded to include Hong Kong and the Cayman Islands in 1989 and France and the United Arab Emirates (UAE) thereafter. From 1987, too, Price Waterhouse became sole auditor of the group, a function previously shared with Ernst and Whinney; this action was taken in response to pressure from regulators who believed that by engaging different auditors for its two principal banking subsidiaries BCCI was obscuring its global operations.

But the College must be seen as a failure, both in terms of its conception and its practical achievements. Bingham's judgement was as follows (p.52):

> The College was a unique response to a unique problem. No one knew quite what to expect from it. The College was seen by the supervisors and PW as an advance on the clearly unsatisfactory supervisory regime then in force. But it was a second-best solution. No one thought it likely to be as effective as a single, efficient consolidated supervisor, and the establishment of the College did not of itself do anything to tackle the root of the problem, which lay in the structure of the group.

The Financial Times notes that:

> The college also did nothing to bring BCCI under tighter control. If anything, it did the opposite by ensuring that each college member felt only one-eighth responsible.[31]

15

According to *The Banker*, in this case:

> In effect shared supervision meant little or no supervision ... BCCI apparently developed ... into a fine art ... play[ing] regulators off against one another and hid[ing] behind the weaker links ...[32]

Weak regulators. Seventh, in BCCI's case, the weaker links were the Luxembourg and Cayman authorities; neither was in a position effectively to regulate BCCI. The Basle Concordat supposes that the home country will regulate its own banks and that the host country will largely restrict its activities to making sure that local laws are followed. As the Bingham Report notes (p.186):

> It makes very good sense that supervision should be primarily conducted by the home supervisor, who is closest to the bank and best placed to monitor but if host supervisors are increasingly to rely on the home supervisor they must be reassured by some form of independent verification that the home supervisor is really doing his job.

However, in this respect, as revealed by BCCI and later financial scandals, not all countries can be treated as equals.

Lessons for the Present Day.

One lesson relates to fraud. While some financial crashes occur on a grand scale - the US savings and loan crisis, the property lending saga, the Mexican and Argentine crises, the Japanese banking losses - fraud remains a common theme in most individual bank crashes and large company losses. We may never know whether BCCI engaged in theft and deception on a large scale from its inception, but in other ways it evidenced what is now a well trodden path. Individuals gamble with depositors' money and incur trading losses. These fraudulent actions rarely begin in a big way but invariably the individuals - and the management supporting their trading strategy - get in deeper to cover their losses. Eventually, the cover up spirals out of control as happened with Barings, Sumitomo and BCCI. Yet, even in this company, BCCI was distinctive because of the amounts involved, and the number of years over which the balancing act was sustained. In order to explain how this could be done, we come to the second lesson.

The second lesson concerns bank secrecy havens. Lord Bingham introduced his recommendations with the following observation (p.181):

> BCCI grew before banking supervision, in the UK or internationally, had come of age. A similar bank established today could scarcely hope to assume the form it did or last so long. Thus the focus of attention in the aftermath of this debacle should not simply be to prevent a second BCCI (although the aim must of course

16

be to achieve that at least). But the aim must also and more importantly be to ensure that supervisory law, principles and practice generally create conditions hostile to the growth of fraud and friendly towards its early detection and eradication.

In the case of BCCI, it was able to avoid detection for so long by hiding transactions in financial centres with stringent secrecy laws. Disguised related party transactions, in which BCCI would appear to be lending depositors' funds to other parties while in fact lending the money to itself, were its lifeblood. But it also used money laundering as a source of funds and bribed public officials to deposit government accounts with the bank. None of the paper trails created to disguise these activities could have been sustained for long without access to bank secrecy jurisdictions. For example in one of the 'simple' cases, payments of bribes to Peruvian officials went from BCCI SA in London, to BCCI Overseas in Grand Cayman, to the office of a Californian bank in New York, to a branch of a Swiss Bank in New York and then to the numbered account in another branch of a Swiss bank in Panama.[33]

As Mr Justice Bingham notes and recommends (p.186):

> ... certain financial centres offer impenetrable secrecy and tend, for that reason to be favoured by those with something to hide. Supervisors appear up to now to have tolerated the use of such centres, perhaps because they felt unable to do anything else. It seems very highly desirable that a much tougher line should be taken in future: I suggest that the involvement of such a centre should itself, in appropriate circumstances, be ground for refusing or revoking authorisation.

Lord Justice Bingham was by no means the first to draw attention to this problem. Noting a number of scandals involving offshore financial havens, Barnes wrote in 1985:

> Financial fraudsters and tricksters can simply move their base to another country. And while there are havens specially designed to attract those with things to hide or avoid, then national legislation cannot really be successful. The British Government should consider its policy towards such havens. It should also consider how it can allow the Channel Isles and the Isle of Man to be the base of so many UK operations needing cover.

> Finally, it must consider whether large UK businesses should be controlled by, or connected with, companies registered in tax havens, thereby concealing their true ownership and distribution of profits. Obviously these are difficult legal problems. However, unless they are resolved, investors (and customers) cannot properly be regarded as 'protected'.[34]

17

This is an important lesson of BCCI. The bank secrecy statutes of the various jurisdictions in which BCCI operated were such that no one - no auditor, no regulator, indeed no one outside the inner circle of managers - knew the true identities of the owners of the bank or of its various borrowers. Yet without such knowledge, it is impossible for a regulator to evaluate whether frauds are being committed.

The third lesson concerns the issue of whether there will be a second BCCI. Was BCCI, as Lord Justice Bingham argued, with Brian Quinn concurring, a "unique case"[35] - by implication, a one-off which is unlikely to be repeated? Robert Morgenthau (1996, p.19) thinks not:

> I have no doubt that we would see another BCCI in the future, and then another after that. The nefarious conditions that created the demand for BCCI's services - drug money laundering and arms smuggling being just two of the more prominent examples - continue to exist and will do so for the foreseeable future. Where there is a demand for services by people with money, those services will be provided, and unless the soil in which BCCI grew and flourished can be rendered less fertile for banks of this kind, other corrupt enterprises are certain to rise in its place. To view BCCI as an anomaly of no lasting concern would be a grave error.

As he also notes (p.18):

> the simple truth is that the wire transfer and the bank book are as much the tools of the drug trade as the scale [of the business] and the gun.

In this respect, law enforcement and banking supervision are not nearly so foreign to each other as they may appear to be; "illegal wire transfers are as ubiquitous as hand guns." (*Ibid.*, p.18). Yet this similarity does not find reflection in actual policy. Governments spend vast amounts on drug detection and prosecuting those dealing in drugs, but little on catching those individuals facilitating money laundering. Perhaps this emphasis evidences the underlying realities in terms of the ease of detection and here we come back to the issue of bank secrecy jurisdictions, and the central role that off-shore financial centres play in global money laundering (OECD 1996). Modern technology makes it possible to move vast sums of money virtually instantaneously into and out of bank secrecy havens, and the combination of ever more efficient high-speed worldwide money transfer systems with bank secrecy statutes perhaps has the potential to make fraud almost untraceable.

18

Notes

1. *The Independent* (7 September 1996) p.20.

2. *Wall Street Journal* (17 September 1996) pp.1, 8.

3. *The Observer* (22 September 1996) Business Section pp.1, 13.

4. *The Washington Post*, National Weekly Edition (5-11 August 1991) p.6.

5. *The Economist* (10 June 1995) p.96.

6. *Financial Times* (1991) p. 5.

7. Comments at an International Monetary Fund Seminar, Washington, 1992.

8. Quoted in *Investors Chronicle* (23 August 1991) p.14.

9. Bingham Report (1992) p.36.

10. Johns (1992) p.66.

11. Testimony given by the Governor of the Bank of England to the House of Commons Treasury and Civil Service Committee on 23 July 1991.

12. These are contained in the Bingham Report (1992) p. 140.

13. *Financial Times* (1991) pp.4-5; *The Economist* (27 July 1991) pp.73-74.

14. *The Washington Post*, National Weekly Edition (5-11 August 1991) pp.6-8.

15. *The Washington Post*, National Weekly Edition (16-22 September 1991) pp.10-11.

16. *The Economist* (3 August 1991) p.21.

17. *The Economist* (13 July 1991) p.94.

18. For example, Continental Illinois Bank - the US bank which collapsed in 1984 - drew nearly 80 per cent of its funds from interbank and wholesale money markets (see Lewis and Davis (1987) chapters 4 and 5).

19. Comments by Moscow at International Monetary Fund Seminar, Washington, 1992.

20. *Financial Times* (1991) p.5.

21. *The Washington Post*, National Weekly Edition (5-11 August 1991) p.6.

22. *The Economist* (13 July 1991) p.14.

19

23. *The Washington Post*, National Weekly Edition (5-11 August 1991) p.6.

24. Comments by Brian Quinn, Executive Director for Banking Supervision and Operations, Bank of England at Financial Markets Group Conference, May 1993.

25. These are examined in Dale (1984) and Lewis and Davis (1987), and outlined in the Bingham Report.

26. Bingham Report (1992) p.35.

27. *The Economist* (13 July 1991) p.93.

28. Morgenthau (1993), p.20.

29. *Financial Times* (1991) p.36.

30. *The Economist* (20 July 1991) p.102.

31. *Financial Times* (1991) p.37.

32. *The Banker* (4 August 1991) p.4

33. Morgenthau (1993) p.26.

34. *Accountancy* (March 1985) p.19

35. The description is that of Quinn (1993).

References

Barnes, P. (1985) 'Investor Protection - a Finger in the Dam?', *Accountancy* (March) p.19.

Bingham Report (1992) *Inquiry into the Supervision of the Bank of Credit and Commerce International.* Chairman: The Right Honourable Lord Justice Bingham (London: HMSO).

Cicutti, N and Treanor, J. (1996) 'Morgan Facing Claims Avalanche from Investors', *The Independent*, Business Section (7 September) p.20.

Dale, R. (1984) *The Regulation of International Banking* (Cambridge and Englewood Cliffs, New Jersey: Woodhead-Faulkner and Prentice Hall).

Fielding, N. (1991) ' Founder Controls Bank Through Cayman Trusts', *The Independent*, (10 July), p.12.

Financial Times (1991) *Behind Closed Doors. BCCI: The Biggest Bank Fraud in History* (London: *Financial Times*).

Hampton, M. P. (1996) 'Exploring the Off-shore Interface. The Relationship
    Between Tax Havens, Tax Evasion, Corruption and Economic Development',
    Crime and Law and Social Change, 24, pp.293-317.

Investors Chronicle (1991a) 'The Bank That No-one Was Watching' (12 July)
    pp.10-11.

Investors Chronicle (1991b) 'BCCI Customers Face Heavy Losses' (12 July) p.25.

Investors Chronicle (1991c) 'The Biggest Bank Fraud in the World' (23 August)
    pp.14-15.

Investors Chronicle (1991d) 'Who Are BCCI's Mysterious Satellites?' (20
    September) pp.16-17.

Johns, R. A. (1992) 'Offshore Banking', *The New Palgrave Dictionary of Money
    and Finance*, Volume 3 (London: Macmillan).

Lewis, M. K. and Davis, K. T. (1987) *Domestic and International Banking*
    (Oxford: Philip Allan).

Mafson, S. and McGee, J. (1991) 'BCCI's Network: A Global Con', *The
    Washington Post,* National Weekly Edition (5-11 August) pp.6-8.

Morgenthau, R. M. (1996) 'International Bank Fraud: A Local Prosecutor's
    Perspective', *Special Paper No. 54, LSE Financial Markets Group* (August).

Moscow, J. W. (1992) 'The Future of Bank Regulation after BCCI', Comments by
    J. W. Moscow at Seminar on Current Legal Issues Affecting Central Banks, June
    17 (Washington, D.C.: International Monetary Fund).

OECD (1996) 'Financial Action Task Force on Money Laundering Annual Report
    1995-1996', *Financial Market Trends, 65* (November) pp.39-97.

Quinn, B. (1993) 'The Bank of England's Role in Prudential Supervision', *Special
    Paper No. 54, LSE Financial Markets Group* (August).

Sesit, M. R. (1996) 'Off-shore Hazard: Isle of Jersey Proves Less Than a Haven to
    Currency Investors', *Wall Street Journal, Europe* (17 September) pp.1, 8.

Shepard, C. E. and Swordson, A. (1991) 'Retracing the BCCI Missteps', *The
    Washington Post*, National Weekly Edition (16-22 September) pp.10-11.

Sweaney, J. (1996) 'Jersey Government Dragged into Bank Scandal After £17
    million Goes Missing', *The Observer* (Business Section), p.1.

The Economist (1991a) 'Behind Closed Doors' (13 July) pp.14-15.

The Economist (1991b) 'The Many Façades of BCCI' (13 July) pp.93-94.

The Economist (1991c) 'Blaming the Bank of England' (20 July) pp.101-107

The Economist (1991d) 'The BCCI Trail' (27 July) pp.13-14.

The Economist (1991e) 'All Things to All Men' (27 July) pp.73-74.

The Economist (1991f) 'The Opening-up of BCCI' (3 August) pp.19-21.

The Washington Post (1991) 'BCCI: Three Questions' (15-21 July).   **[21]**

Acknowledgement

The author wishes to thank L. M. Algaoud of the School of Management and
Finance, University of Nottingham for assistance in collecting the materials. Mrs
Judy Melbourne of the University of South Australia kindly prepared the
manuscript.   **[22]**

Name Index